The

Philosophical

Roots

of

Anthropology

CSLI Lecture Notes Number 86

The Philosophical Roots *of* Anthropology

William Y. Adams

CSLI Publications
Center for the Study of
Language and Information
Stanford, California

CSLI Publications
Center for the Study of Language and Information
Leland Stanford Junior University
02 01 2 3 4 5

Library of Congress Cataloging-in-Publication Data

Adams, William Yewdale, 1927–
The philosophical roots of anthropology / William Y. Adams.
p. cm.–(CSLI lecture notes : no. 86)
Includes bibliographical references and index.
ISBN 1-57586-129-1 (cloth : alk. paper).
ISBN 1-57586-128-3 (pbk. : alk. paper)
1. Anthropology–Philosophy. 2. Anthropology–History. I. Title. II. Series.
GN33.A33 1998
301'.01–dc21 98-26003
CIP

∞ The acid-free paper used in this book meets the minimum requirements of the American National Standard for Information Sciences–Permanence of Paper for Printed Library Materials, ANSI Z39.48-1984.

This book was designed and set in type by Tony Gee in Minion, a typeface designed by Robert Slimbach and issued by Adobe Systems. Paperback cover design by Tony Gee. The book was printed and bound in the United States of America.

CONTENTS

Preface vii

1 Ideology, Philosophy, Anthropology, and the Other 1

2 Progressivism: The Tap Root 9

3 Primitivism 75

4 Natural Law 113

5 "Indianology" 193

6 German Idealism 263

7 Other Roots; Other Trees 335

8 In Search of the Anthropological Self 399

An Annotated Bibliography of Secondary Sources 425

Index 443

To my brother, the philosopher,
Ernest W. Adams

PREFACE

THIS BOOK is the by-product of two things. One was a course titled The History of Anthropological Theory, which I taught regularly for twenty-five years. In the effort to broaden and deepen my understanding of the subject, my reading in time carried me farther and farther beyond the conventional boundaries of anthropology–first into the sister disciplines of sociology and psychology, and then, increasingly, into the philosophic literature of prescientific ages. I became, in the process, more and more dissatisfied with the shallowness and myopia of anthropology's self-understanding. While we anthropologists rightly take credit for making humanity aware of its own prehistory, and the importance of that prehistory to human self-understanding,[1] we seem hardly to have discovered anthropology's own prehistory, or to have realized its importance. We have simply not looked deeply enough below the surface of overt theory to discover the powerful philosophical and ideological undercurrents that run beneath it. Or, to use another metaphor, we have not looked beneath the trunk of the tree to discover its roots.

But studying the history of anthropology has also led me increasingly to reflect on my individual history as an anthropologist and as a person, seeking to uncover the sources of my particular anthropological convictions. I once thought that they had been imparted mostly by my teachers and by my reading; I now realize that most of them rest ultimately on moral convictions that are much older and run much deeper. Some of those convictions are the outcome of my personal experiences growing up among the Navajo Indians and elsewhere, but others are part of the general fabric of Western philosophical thought, and long antedate the origins of anthropology itself. To the extent that my experiences and my convic-

1. Cf. esp. Glyn Daniel, *The Idea of Prehistory* (Harmondsworth, Eng., 1964).

tions are shared by many and perhaps most other anthropologists, I think that what I have discovered about myself is relevant to them also.

I am convinced, after a lifetime of study, that very few anthropological ideas are really new. Indeed I have the feeling that practically all of the great theories in all the social sciences are old philosophies renamed. "The ancients have stolen all our best ideas," as some wag put it. Indeed it could hardly be otherwise, when thinking men and women for several thousand years have been reflecting, and sometimes agonizing, over the human condition. We moderns may be better educated, but we are not endowed with better cerebral equipment than our forebears, and it does not stand to reason that we should think of questions to ask or answers to propose that never occurred to earlier generations.

I am convinced too that the endurance of most ideas depends less on their intellectual and logical content than on their ideological appeal. Practically all our ideas about humankind involve gut-level convictions–stated or unstated–about what is right and wrong in the human condition, and they endure so long as we feel intuitively that they are correct. Again, how could it be otherwise? Our minds seem to be programmed in such a way that it is virtually impossible to make any generalizing statement about the condition of humanity without at least implying, "This is as it should be" or "This is not as it should be." This applies especially to statements of a comparative nature, for, unhappily but inescapably, to compare is to judge.

If we are myopic as regards our debt to earlier thinkers, we are at least equally so in recognizing how much we are influenced by the currents of popular ideology. Reading most of the standard histories of anthropology, one might conclude that the intellectual development of the discipline since the 1860s has been largely autonomous. Nothing could be farther from the truth. The self-confident progressivism of Morgan, Tylor, and other early "evolutionists" was but one reflection of the optimistic faith in progress characteristic of the Victorian age; the anti-progressive historicism of the early twentieth century (mirrored by concurrent developments in history and psychology) reflected the general disillusionment with progress brought on by the arms race that culminated in World War I; the social concern of midcentury anthropology, shifting its attention (belatedly) from the past to the problems of the here-and-now, arose in an era of economic depression which spawned a broad series of ideologies of social concern, including Fascism, Nazism, and the New Deal; the monumentally self-confident Scientism of the post-World War II years reflects an era when faith in science and its accomplishments was boundless, thanks in large part to the achievement of nuclear fission; Postmodernism and other antinomian movements of today are thoroughly in tune with the restless anomie of the present troubled times. Like it or not, most anthropologists are not, and never have been, inner directed; they are blown this way and that by the winds of popular ideology as surely as is the rest of mankind.

Like most anthropologists I accepted for a long time the premise that our intellectual roots go back no farther than the moral philosophy of the Enlightenment,[2] or perhaps at the outside to the Humanism of the Renaissance.[3] I recognized that many of our best ideas were anticipated in antiquity, and I always began my course in the history of anthropology with a week on the Greeks and Romans,[4] but I treated them as accidental foreshadowers rather than as direct progenitors. It was only when I read Anthony Pagden's excellent *The Fall of Natural Man*[5] that I realized that the doctrine of natural law furnishes a connecting link between ancient and modern anthropologies; a link that was not broken even in the darkest of the so-called dark ages. What I had once thought of as interesting recurrences of thought I began to see more and more as long-continuing traditions. It was out of that awareness that I formed the intention of writing this book.

This is not, however, a history of anthropology in any conventional sense. First of all, it is a history only of ideas and not of activities. Moreover, it is a history only of a few very old and very persistent ideas, which in latter days have exerted a powerful but largely unrecognized influence in shaping the discipline of anthropology, particularly in North America. It goes without saying that there have been many other influences, that do not lie within the limited compass of this book.

As the title of the book suggests, I am concerned mainly with the roots rather than with the trunk of anthropology. To put it another way, I am more concerned with the prehistory than with the history of the discipline. Thus, I have devoted much more space to the development of ideas before 1860 than to the "historical era" of the later years. My hope is that this volume may serve as a kind of prolegomena–like Ibn Khaldûn's *Muqaddimah*[6]–to a more general work on the history of anthropology that I may one day write.

2. Cf. esp. Marvin Harris, *The Rise of Anthropological Theory* (New York, 1967), pp. 8–52.
3. See John H. Rowe in *American Anthropologist* 67, no. 1 (1965): 1–6.
4. Cf. Clyde Kluckhohn, *Anthropology and the Classics* (Providence, 1961); Annemarie Malefijt, *Images of Man* (New York, 1974), pp. 3–22; Stanley Casson, *The Discovery of Man* (London, 1940), pp. 21–91.
5. Cambridge, 1982
6. See Chapter 2.

I have to make it clear too that my reference throughout is chiefly to North American anthropology. I have chosen for extended discussion a handful of philosophical or ideological currents whose influence has been and is very widespread, but which occur in North America in a unique combination not found in the anthropologies of other countries. I had originally thought of a more comprehensive work, exploring simultaneously the major philosophical influences in British and in French anthropology, but in the course of writing it became increasingly clear that these are separate trees with separate roots. There never has been, at least in this century, such a thing as unitary anthropology; there is on the contrary a series of national traditions, each with its own individual history and its special ideological commitments. Some of the major non-American anthropologies will be considered briefly in Chapter 7, but my concern there is mainly to consider how and why they differ from the anthropology of America.[7]

I should acknowledge also that I have no academic credentials in philosophy; for better or worse I am wholly self-taught. I was led into the subject, unavoidably, in seeking for the original sources of anthropological thought, but my reading has been neither exhaustive nor entirely systematic. Probably 90 percent of the philosophical works that I have cited in these pages were unfamiliar to me before I began to write the book, and I still have not read most of them; I have relied heavily on secondary sources for the interpretation of works or doctrines that were not accessible to me in the original languages.[8] It may be therefore that some of my interpretations will not meet the approval of better-schooled philosophers, or that my literary sources will be considered inadequate.

In a book about the history of ideas, it is important to recapture as accurately as possible the discourse in which those ideas were developed and expressed. To that end, I have been unable to avoid what are today regarded as sexist and elitist terms such as Primitive Man and Noble Savage. Those words in their time were powerful metaphors for the non-western Other, and they were the universally accepted vocabulary of the sexist and elitist world of their day. To render them in more innocuous language for the sake of present-day political correctness would be to rob them of nearly all their metaphoric power, for those who coined and used them. I can

7. For a more thorough, insider's view of the history of British anthropology see Adam Kuper, *Anthropologists and Anthropology* (London, 1973); for an insider's view of German anthropology see Jürgen Zwernemann in *Culture History and African Anthropology* (*Uppsala Studies in Cultural Anthropology* 6, 1983). There is up to now no satisfactory insider's history of French anthropology, so far as I am aware.

8. These are listed in an annotated bibliography at the end of the work.

only insist they speak for their times, and not necessarily for the present-day predilections of this author. In the use of gender pronouns, the best compromise I can devise between literal correctness and metaphorical correctness is to use "he or she" whenever the reference is to a category of real people that might potentially have included persons of either sex, but just "he" in reference to metaphoric abstractions like Primitive Man, the Noble Savage, and the Other. It is an essential feature of these constructs that they are in some sense unitary, and they must be rendered by a unitary pronoun.

Whether or not there ever really was such a thing as Primitive Man, or whether he is simply a constructed Other of the Western imagination (as Adam Kuper now seems to believe[9]), is a question that this book will not attempt to answer, for it is irrelevant to my purposes. My concern throughout is with what anthropologists and their philosophical predecessors *thought* they perceived, without attempting to decide what they did or did not really perceive.

Throughout these pages I have tried, within reason, to avoid editorializing, although my prejudices undoubtedly show through here and there. But I believe that all the doctrines I have discussed are worthy of a respectful hearing, for they all represent legitimate attempts to understand the Other. As such, they all have their place in the anthropological discourse.[10] I have not, however, written the book just as a historical exercise, and I certainly have not written it to support the postmodernist notion that "anything goes"–a perspective that I specifically disavow. I wrote the book rather from a conviction that the cure for anthropology's current malaise, or part of it, lies in improved self-understanding. This theme will be pursued at some length in the final chapter, where I will indeed editorialize.

Looking back over the text after having completed it, I can see, more clearly than at the beginning, that I have had four main agendas. The first and most straightforward is to enlarge and correct the historical record as regards the development of anthropological ideas. The second agenda, following logically from the first, is to show that North American anthropology is fundamentally and appropriately different from the anthropologies of other countries, and why this is so. The third agenda, following in turn from the second, is to show that American anthropology carries its own special burden of philosophical and ideological legacies from earlier times, which are not always consistent with one another.

9. In *The Invention of Primitive Society* (London, 1988).

10. For a generally parallel view, see Robert F. Murphy, *A Century of Controversy* (Orlando, Fla., 1985), esp. pp. 285–286.

Last and most importantly, however, I have wanted to show that, since the dawn of history, the confrontation between civilized Self and primitive Other has created moral dilemmas that remain unresolved down to the present day. Like it or not, to compare is to judge. Each of my five major chapters, dealing with Progressivism, Primitivism, natural law, German Idealism, and "Indianology," describes one particular way in which Western thought has attempted to deal with this dilemma. American anthropology, in staking out the domain of the Primitive for its own, has fallen heir to all of them, but has been unable fully to resolve the inherent contradictions among them. They remain as a troublesome but also as a stimulating problem within our discipline.

ABOUT THE AUTHOR

Long before it became fashionable, I prefaced each of my major books with a few paragraphs of self-introduction, to let readers know "where I am coming from."[11] In the present work it is perhaps sufficient to say that, in an anthropological career of sixty years, I have been strongly influenced by all five of the doctrines that are the major subjects of this book. By Progressivism because it is, when all is said and done, the mainstream of all Western historical thought.[12] By Primitivism because, like most anthropologists of my generation, I am an unabashed nature lover, attracted to those things and those peoples that seem closest to nature, and I am repelled at times by the complexities of civilization. By natural law because, like most nature lovers, I am an instinctive teleologist. In spite of my efforts to rationalize, I tend to think that whatever is recurrent must be natural, and part of some intended order. By Indianology because I grew up partly on an Indian reservation, and my earliest anthropological interests were wholly in American Indians. By German Idealism because my first formal anthropological training was at the University of California (Berkeley), in the last days of the great Kroeber-Lowie tradition.

I have never succeeded either in fully reconciling the five above named doctrines or in discarding any of them, nor has any other anthropologist to my knowledge. Rightly or wrongly, therefore, I believe that my dilemma is also anthropology's dilemma, and that is my rationale for writing this book.

---

11. See *Shonto: a Study of the Role of the Trader in a Modern Navaho Community* (Washington, D.C.: *Bureau of American Ethnology Bulletin* 188, 1963), pp. 22–26; *Nubia, Corridor to Africa* (London, 1977), pp. 5–8; *Ceramic Industries of Medieval Nubia* (Lexington: *Memoirs of the UNESCO Archaeological Survey of Sudanese Nubia*, vol. 1, 1986), pp. 2–11; *Archaeological Typology and Practical Reality* (Cambridge, 1991), pp. xix–xxi.
12. See esp. Robert A. Nisbet, *Social Change and History* (New York, 1969).

ACKNOWLEDGMENTS

A list of all the people who have contributed to the development of my anthropological ideas would be as long as all the preceding pages of this preface. I must confine myself to acknowledging those individuals who have contributed more specifically to the development of the manuscript, once the project was underway. The work was read in its entirety by my brother, Ernest W. Adams, Professor of Philosophy at the University of California, and by my colleague Tomas Håkansson in the Department of Anthropology at Kentucky. Chapter 4 (Natural Law) was read by Professor Alan Perreiah in the Philosophy Department at Kentucky; Chapter 5 (Indianology) was read by Dr. Wilcomb Washburn at the Smithsonian Institution; Chapter 6 (German Idealism) was read by Professor Daniel Brezeale in the Philosophy Department at Kentucky, and also by Professors Andreas Kronenberg, Klaus Müller, and Christian Feest, all of the Johann Wolfgang Goethe-Institut in Frankfurt-am-Main. To all these I owe a profound debt for comments, suggestions, and references.

CHAPTER 1

IDEOLOGY, PHILOSOPHY, ANTHROPOLOGY, AND THE OTHER

AFTER MORE than a century of existence, anthropology has only just begun to understand its proper role among the social sciences. It is, we now recognize, the systematic study of the Other,[1] whereas all of the other social disciplines are, in one sense or another, studies of the Self. Only anthropology dares to suggest that in studying the Other, we may learn more about ourselves than we do by studying ourselves. As such, anthropology has staked out a unique scientific turf, which was formerly the domain of the philosopher, the literateur, and the moralist.

As a figure of myth and of moralization, the Other is as old as the Self–necessarily, since the two are interdefined. The Other serves always as the yardstick by which we measure our own worth or our unworthiness, our distinctness or our common humanity. The Other figures prominently in some of the earliest literature that has come down to us, as well as in the mythology of countless present-day peoples. The ancient Egyptian despises the Nubian as "miserable,"[2] while the Greek acclaims him the justest of men and beloved of the gods;[3] the Nubian for his part despises the Egyptians as "uncircumcised, and eaters of fish."[4] The Navajo looks down on the Paiute because he is dirty and "lives on the vermin of the desert," and looks up to the Hopi for his possession of superior ritual powers.[5] The

1. For recent, extended discussion of this issue see Jacob Pandian, *Anthropology and the Western Tradition* (Prospect Heights, Ill., 1985), pp. 49–95, and Bernard McGrane, *Beyond Anthropology* (New York, 1989).

2. See William Y. Adams, *Nubia, Corridor to Africa* (London, 1977), p. 1.

3. Cf. Arthur O. Lovejoy and George Boas, *Primitivism and Related Ideas in Antiquity* (Baltimore, 1935), pp. 348–351.

4. Adams, *Nubia*, p. 263.

5. Clyde Kluckhohn and Dorothea Leighton, *The Navaho* (Cambridge, Mass., 1946), p. 77.

Other is better than we or worse, different or similar, but is never morally neutral; comparisons with the Other always reflect, for better or worse, on ourselves.

Like all the other social sciences, anthropology came into existence in the nineteenth century. Indeed, the transformation of what used to be called moral philosophy into what came to be called social science was one of the signal achievements of that century. As late as the 1830s moral philosophy was taught in all universities, while political economy, psychology, sociology, and anthropology were all equally unknown in the halls of academe. A century and a half later moral philosophy has shrunk to a pitiful few courses surviving in departments of philosophy, while political science, economics, psychology, sociology, and anthropology all boast faculties and curricula that are larger, in most cases, than are whole departments of philosophy. The significance of this development was far more than academic; it had powerful repercussions in the fields of public policy, law, and religion as well. Almost from the moment of their founding, the social sciences became arenas for the debate of fundamental issues about the nature and destiny of humanity—questions that formerly had been the exclusive province of the philosopher and theologian.

The special task of anthropology, in this context, has been to invest the Other with scientific rather than with purely historical or moral significance. In the process we have elevated the old truism that "travel broadens the mind" to the level of scientific theory and method. And I think we have succeeded a good deal better than some of today's pessimists would acknowledge. The cross-cultural study of beliefs, behaviors, and—very importantly—languages, not to mention the ethological study of our primate cousins, has brought us much closer to an understanding of what is and is not basic human nature than have the other social sciences, for all their more rigorous methodology and their experimental procedures. But what we have not done, and indeed cannot do as long as we remain human, is divest the Other of his or her older, moral significance.

If the social sciences offered new arenas for the debate of old questions, they also developed new vocabularies. The modern social scientist approaches his or her topic armed with a battery of conceptual tools like solidarity, legitimacy, personality, and even culture, that were unknown in their modern forms two hundred years ago. Indeed, the failure to develop effective conceptual vocabularies was perhaps the most conspicuous failing of earlier moral philosophers. As the source of their ideas was basically intuitive, they were mostly content to express them in intuitive language, assuming that their hearers and readers would share the same intuitions.

The canons of evidence have also changed. Where earlier philosophies had depended for conviction mainly on logic, the social scientist demands the external evidence of observation and experience. Conscious data collection, quantification, and even experimentation have become accepted as the touchstones of truth.

But if the battlefields and the weapons and the rules have all changed, the basic issues of human nature and human behavior have not. Before the nineteenth century, thinking men and women had already been speculating, and sometimes agonizing, over the human condition for at least 2,500 years. It was unlikely that upstart social scientists would think of new questions to ask that had not already occurred to their predecessors. By and large, the social sciences sought new ways to answer old questions.

New ways of answering are not, however, the same as new answers. To a quite extraordinary degree, the supposedly new methods came up with the same old answers; scientific rigor confirmed what logic and intuition and common sense had long since suggested. In one way or another, nearly all of the great social science "theories" are in fact older philosophies renamed—a point to which I will return again and again in later chapters. This is quite simply because, in taking over the territory of the moral philosophers, the social sciences have also and unavoidably taken over their moral commitments. With the most earnest of intentions, it has been no more possible for the anthropologist than for the philosopher to objectify the Other, because it is not possible to objectify the Self.

The five doctrines that are the principal concern of this book all involve conceptions of the Other that began in philosophy and then have passed, consciously or unconsciously, into anthropology. Both their origin and their ideological power are frequently unrecognized in histories of the discipline, but they continue nevertheless to exert a significant influence on anthropological theory and practice down to the present day. They are the ideological undercurrents of anthropological thought, which I have chosen here, using another metaphor, to call the roots of the discipline.

THEORY, PHILOSOPHY, AND IDEOLOGY

If social science theory is usually underlain by philosophy, it is equally apparent that philosophy—at least moral philosophy—is usually underlain at a still deeper level by ideology. Ideologies, as I define the term here, are gut convictions about what is right and wrong, and systems of action based on those beliefs. They are the oldest and most universal of human idea systems, originating far back in time and far below the level of conscious reflection. It is, and apparently always has been, virtually impossible to make any generalizing statement or hold any thought about *Homo sapiens*

—that is, ourselves—without at the same time at least implying moral judgment: "This is as it should be," or "This is not as it should be." We can scarcely avoid such implied judgment even when we discuss the actions of particular individuals, let alone of the whole race.

Theory, Philosophy, and Ideology

Ideologies, as Durkheim recognized, are universal; they are at the heart of every functioning human social system.[6] Unlike theories and philosophies, they are without histories or intellectual pedigrees. They are simply unchanging convictions about what is right and wrong that trace back beyond human memory. In some civilizations, however, they have been developed into philosophies by a class of professional thinkers and teachers. At this point, we may say that gut-level belief has been raised to the level of rational reflection. In a still more restricted number of civilizations they have been further elaborated into social science; rational thought has become scientific theory. Finally, there is a powerful feedback: the purported findings of social science are advanced in support of the same ideologies that were their original wellsprings.

Figuratively speaking, one might suggest that different parts of the human anatomy are involved at the different stages of cognition. Ideologies proceed from the gut and perhaps to some extent from the heart: they are based on unexamined convictions. Philosophies may involve the heart also, but supposedly not the gut. Most prominently, however, they bring the head into play. Finally, theories are supposed to proceed from the head only. In reality, however, the heart and the gut are not fully disengaged when ideology evolves into philosophy and philosophy into theory. The primordial moral commitments that were the wellsprings of ideology and philosophy remain as powerful hidden agendas in social science as well, and certainly above all in anthropology and psychology. Consequently, we can sometimes hear anthropologists enunciating quite different and sometimes contradictory convictions from the head and from the heart, as I will suggest in Chapters 2 and 3.

Because the boundaries between ideology, philosophy, and theory are fuzzy at best, I will talk about various currents of belief in the following pages as "doctrines," usually without labeling them specifically as ideologies or as philosophies or as theories. Originally they were perhaps pure ideologies; later they combined ideology and philosophy; now more often than not they partake of all three. I am convinced, however, that it is the ideological undercurrent, rather than the appeal either to logic or to evidence, that accounts for the centuries-long persistence of supposedly scientific doctrines, no less than of religious doctrines.

---

6. Especially in *The Elementary Forms of the Religious Life* (Glencoe, Ill., 1947), pp. 1–20.

SCIENCE OR NONSCIENCE?

The foregoing is not meant to suggest, as many anthropologists now do, that anthropology is not and cannot be a science. Science is the great, largely unexamined buzzword of our times. There is not, and never has been, any single, orthodox definition of what constitutes science. Just as every Christian sect wants to define Christianity in such a way as to include itself in and, as much as possible, to include all the others out, so every would-be scientific discipline defines science in such a way as to describe itself, but not, if possible, the others. When the physical scientist insists that social science is not "real" science, he or she merely means that it is not physics; when the sociologist condemns anthropology as nonscientific he or she merely means that it is not sociology. Commonly, too, each new generation redefines science to include whatever it is now interested in doing, and if possible to exclude what the previous generation was doing. The issue of science in anthropology, and its relation to philosophy, will be further considered in the last chapter.

I agree with present-day critics that social science cannot divest itself of moral judgment, so long as its practitioners are human beings; I see no reason to argue that it therefore cannot be science. Science to my mind is a particular system of truth involving a few simple, axiomatic propositions: that the universe is governed by impartial laws and not by a superwill; that the laws are at least to a degree discoverable through observation and experimentation, but not by revelation; that every effect proceeds from a cause; and that identical causes will (usually) produce like effects. Nothing in that catalogue precludes the exercise of moral judgment as to whether the causes and the effects are desirable or undesirable. Moral judgment only becomes nonscientific when it defines good and bad on the basis of what is supposedly intended by divine will.

UNIVERSALIST, COMPARATIVE, AND PARTICULARIST APPROACHES

Anthropological theories generally fall into three broad categories, which may be designated universalist, comparative, and particularist. All three have co-existed almost since the beginning of the discipline. Universalist theories, such as Structuralism, seek to discover and explain what is common to all peoples; comparative theories, such as Social Evolutionism, seek to explain the differences between one people and another on the basis of some overarching general principle; particularist theories such as Configurationism seek to understand the different qualities of each culture, and how they came about. These different kinds of theory cast the Other into different roles: the Other as Us (universalist), the Other as previous Us (comparative), and the other as not-Us (particularist). In this book I shall consider in detail one or two doctrines, or approaches, in each of the three categories. Progressivism and Primitivism are comparative approaches; natural law is universalist; German Idealism and "Indianology" are particularist.

Universalist, Comparative, & Particularist Approaches

Although for analytical convenience I have chosen to discuss the five philosophic traditions separately, I do not mean to suggest that they developed in isolation or in opposition to one another. On the contrary, they have been interwoven in complex and periodically shifting patterns since the earliest times. Both Progressivism and Primitivism have in different ways been closely bound up with the doctrine of natural law. Progressivism has at times combined even with Primitivism, its theoretical antithesis. Primitivism for its part has been closely associated both with German Idealism and with Indianology, while in twentieth-century American anthropology German Idealism and Indianology have for all practical purposes merged.

IDEOLOGY, PHILOSOPHY, AND THE NATIVE AMERICAN

The five principal doctrines I have chosen for discussion have more in common than a generalized concern for the Other. In one way or another and at one time or another, all of them took the Native American as their archetypal Other. Herein lies their special relevance to American anthropology; they are part of the ideological baggage that inescapably became ours when we claimed the field of Native American studies as our own. I have long been convinced that the unifying cement of American anthropology, which brings a certain coherence to all its disparate parts, is not any particular body of theory or practice, but simply the "possession" of the American Indian as its main field of study. Among other things it continues to justify the four-field conjunction of ethnology, linguistics, archaeology, and physical anthropology–an unstable confederation that was brought together in the early days of anthropology, but that long ago came apart everywhere outside North America. By the same token I have argued that an American anthropologist–whatever his or her special interests–who does not know the basic American Indian ethnographic data is like a professor of English who has never read Shakespeare. It is not a question of speciality; it is a question of basics. Not to know the Indian data is not to know why we are what we are.

Surely no event in all history has fired the imagination of thinking men and women in quite the same way as did the discovery of the Americas. They were so new, so strange, but above all so utterly unexpected–an entire world unaccounted for not only in the Bible, but in the total store of received human wisdom up to that time. Bacon perceptively observed in the *Novum Organum* (1621) that "by the distant voyages and travels which have become frequent in our times, many things in nature have been laid open and discovered which may let in new light upon philosophy."[7] Most importantly, from the standpoint of moral philosophy, the Americas represented Europe's first encounter with the truly primitive for nearly two thousand years. Here were peoples not only without letters and advanced technology, but even, in the boreal regions, without husbandry. Throughout the Middle Ages Europeans had measured themselves against the yardstick of the infidel Saracen; here now was a vastly different and more ambiguous Other, far more primitive materially than Saracen or European and yet, at the same time, one whose moral inferiority was far more problematical.

Such a discovery could not fail to have ideological repercussions, and in time it influenced all of the major currents in European philosophical thought.[8] The progressivist found in the Native American a kind of ethnographic "missing link:" a living exemplar of that primordial state of society about which he had so long conjectured.[9] The primitivist found in him the quintessential Noble Savage. The believer in natural law found confirmation that all human societies are governed by similar laws, which must therefore be part of nature's order, and the rationalist found that such laws, being part of nature itself, are basically reasonable. At a later date the German idealist found the most satisfying of Others, in terms of his total cultural distinctness, while the American Indianologist found an Other with whom he or she could specially identify as a dweller on the same soil. All these perspectives became, and remain, part of the legacy of American anthropology. Although its fruition was a long time in coming, I think it could be argued that anthropology, or at least American anthropology, became inevitable from the moment when the New World was discovered.

Long before they were absorbed into anthropology, the five doctrines discussed in this book represented different attempts to resolve the moral

7. Quoted from *The Works of Francis Bacon,* ed. J. Spedding, R.L. Ellis, and D.D. Heath (London, 1875), vol. IV, p. 82.

8. For extended discussion see Fredi Chiappelli, ed., *First Images of America: the Impact of the New World on the Old* (Berkeley, Calif., 1976). Particularly illuminating is the contribution of Wilcomb E. Washburn, "The Clash of Morality in the American Forest" (pp. 335–350).

9. Cf. esp. Ronald L. Meek, *Social Science and the Ignoble Savage* (Cambridge, 1976).

dilemma arising from the contact between "civilized" and "primitive" peoples. "For five hundred years," writes Curtis Hinsley, "the New World Indian has served as the object and mirror of Western ambivalence toward the exercise of power and the direction of progress."[10] The recent, often acrimonious debate over how–or whether–to celebrate the Columbus Quincentennial illustrates with dramatic clarity that the dilemma remains unresolved. It has been and remains a source of continuing tension within the discipline of anthropology; a subject to which I will return at the end of the book.

10. In George W. Stocking, Jr., ed., *Romantic Motives*, p. 169. *History of Anthropology* 6 (Madison, Wis., 1989).

CHAPTER 2

PROGRESSIVISM: THE TAP ROOT

A GENERATION AGO Robert Nisbet suggested that all Western scholarship rests ultimately on a theory of inevitable and innate progress: a natural process that is scientifically observable.[1] It will be obvious to readers of this book that I do not fully share Nisbet's perspective, but there can be little doubt that Progressivism has been the single most powerful influence in Western historical thought. If any one doctrine can be identified as the tap root of anthropology, it must be Progressivism. It is one of the deepest roots, in terms of its antiquity, and remains one of the stoutest. Anthropologists know it mainly in its latter-day guise as Social Evolutionism, but this is only a renaming of a much older doctrine, taking advantage of the intellectual popularity of evolutionism in the past century.

THE DOCTRINE AND ITS VARIANTS

Progressivism is simply that doctrine, or ideology, that identifies human cultural history with progress. Hildebrand has characterized it in terms of three essential tenets: "first, the belief that history follows a continuous, necessary, and orderly course; second, the belief that this course is the result of a regularly operating causal law; and, third, the belief that the course of change has brought and will continue to bring improvement in the condition of mankind."[2] As we will see a little later, however, this definition conflates a number of different "ideas of progress."[3] Not all of them

1. Nisbet, *Social Change and History* (New York, 1969).

2. George H. Hildebrand in Frederick Teggart, compiler, *The Idea of Progress*, rev. ed. (Berkeley, Calif., 1949), p. 4.

3. For a minutely particularized analysis of the concept of progress and its many different philosophical and historical meanings, see Charles Van Doren, *The Idea of Progress* (New York, 1967).

necessarily involve a belief in a causal law, and not all of them envision a continuation of the process into the future.

Progressivism in any event is a doctrine that celebrates the triumph of culture over nature. The progressivist speaks approvingly of "taming" the wilderness, "harnessing" the rivers, "reclaiming" the desert, and "civilizing" the savage. It is also a doctrine that celebrates the triumph of mind over matter, insofar as progress is identified with advances in technology and the arts.[4] For the progressivist the Golden Age is in the present, or, just as often, in the future, since Progressivism is often a utopian doctrine.

The doctrine and its variants

Progressivism is necessarily a philosophy of history. It is also, just as importantly, a philosophy of prehistory. Indeed, progressivist theories, at least in anthropology, tend to compare the present with a remote, prehistoric past much more often than with an immediate past. Contrary to the suggestion of Glyn Daniel,[5] the conception of prehistory is not a new idea in Western thought; it is almost as old as philosophy itself. Greek thinkers were well aware that their ancestors had received the art of writing from the Phoenicians in the not very distant past, but that there was a long age—or several ages—of Greek history antedating the oldest written records. They regularly offered imaginary scenarios of the prehistoric past,[6] comparable in many details to the "conjectural histories" of Enlightenment philosophers.

Idealist Progressivism, Historical Progressivism, and Modernism

The discussion thus far might suggest that Progressivism is a unitary doctrine, but this is far from the case. As Charles Van Doren has shown at great length, the "idea of Progress" is not a simple one.[7] Over the centuries it has been subject to a wide variety of interpretations by politicians, historians, and philosophers, and many different doctrines have been labeled progressive or progressivist in one sense or another. For purposes of discussion here, it will be necessary to distinguish two kinds of Progressivism, which I will call Idealist Progressivism and Historical Progressivism. The former is essentially mentalistic, the latter usually though not always materialistic.

Idealist Progressivism is largely a matter of faith: a belief that through-

4. Cf., for example, Arthur O. Lovejoy and George Boas, *Primitivism and Related Ideas in Antiquity* (Baltimore, 1935), pp. 192–196.

5. *The Idea of Prehistory* (Harmondsworth, 1964).

6. Cf. esp. Ludwig Edelstein, *The Idea of Progress in Classical Antiquity* (Baltimore, 1967), p. 21, and W. K. C. Guthrie, *In the Beginning* (London, 1957), pp. 32–38, 95–102.

7. Van Doren, *The Idea of Progress.*

out history the human condition has been steadily improving and will continue to do so into the indefinite future. Progress for the idealist is usually measured in intellectual and artistic rather than in material or social terms.[8] The process is seen as wholly innate, not proceeding from any external cause; it is likened to the maturation of the individual human mind in the course of a lifetime. For this reason the idealist progressivist usually does not seek to buttress his or her theory with specific historical verification.

Historical Progressivism is supposedly a more empirical doctrine, in which historical (including prehistoric) evidence is adduced to show that there has been continual improvement in the human condition. Progress is likely to be measured primarily in material, social, and political terms, rather than in purely intellectual ones, and it is attributed in large measure to advances in science and technology. But while convinced of the reality of progress up to his or her own time, the historical progressivist is often less sanguine that it will continue in the future. It is, of course, mainly Historical Progressivism that is relevant to anthropology, both because of its concern for culture history and prehistory and because of its materialist outlook.

Obviously, it is not necessary to conceive of progress as occurring simultaneously in all the different domains of human life. In Western intellectual history there have been many partial progressivists, who believed in progress in some domains of life but not in others. In fact, it is possible to recognize three rather distinct threads of progressivist thought, which may be called Material Progressivism, Social Progressivism, and Intellectual Progressivism. Over the centuries they have been intertwined at various times and in various ways, but they were not merged into a single, comprehensive doctrine until the Enlightenment, about 250 years ago.

A distinction must finally be made between Progressivism in general, and what I will call Modernism. The latter merely argues the superiority of the present age over some particular moment in the past, without asserting a general principle of Progress. The so-called Quarrel of the Ancients and the Moderns, for example, insisted on the superiority of the seventeenth century in comparison to the time of classical antiquity, but did not insist that there had been continual progress from the one to the other.[9] On the contrary, the intervening Middle Ages were seen as a time of retrogress. In contrast to fully developed Progressivism, which has had

8. See esp. J. B. Bury, *The Idea of Progress* (New York, 1932), pp. 5–7.
9. See ibid., pp. 78–119, and Hippolyte Rigault, *Histoire de la querelle des Anciens et des Modernes* (Paris, 1856).

a rather intermittent intellectual history, the Modernist outlook has been fairly prevalent in many times and places.

HISTORICAL CONTEXTS

Progressivism is a philosophy of optimism, and in some sense a doctrine of self-congratulation. It says of the present age, "This is as it should be." The Other, meaning in this case earlier peoples, becomes a yardstick by which the progressivists measure their own superiority. No people, so far as I know, has ever propounded a progressivist doctrine without placing itself at the top of the ladder of progress. No wonder, then, that the doctrine flourishes in self-confident times: in pre-Socratic Greece, in the Enlightenment, in the Victorian age, and again in the America of the 1950s and 1960s.[10] It is noteworthy that these same eras witnessed a flourishing of scientific discovery and theorizing: Progressivism, it seems, has always been the ideological handmaiden of science. It is a doctrine of and for an expanding world: of knowledge, of understanding, and of conquest.

Progressivist thinking was notably absent in the earliest civilizations, which had no need of it. According to their own understanding Egyptians, Mesopotamians, and Chinese had been superior to other peoples since the moment of creation; they had had no need to climb a ladder to achieve their position of preeminence. Greeks and Romans on the other hand were well aware that theirs was an upstart civilization, the successor and heir to several much earlier ones. Their supremacy could only be attributed to progress, not to creation, and they fashioned a vision of history accordingly. A similar consideration led to the revival of progressivist thinking in the Enlightenment: another age that was confidently certain of its superiority in comparison to earlier times.[11]

PROGRESSIVISM IN ANTIQUITY

As has just been noted, the earliest civilizations had no need of Progressivism. Whether or not the Greeks and Romans had a genuine idea of progress has also been much debated by philosophers and historians.[12] Writers in the nineteenth and early twentieth centuries–themselves enthusiastic believers in progress–were convinced that the ancients had an-

10. Cf. Sidney Pollard, *The Idea of Progress* (New York, 1968), p. viii.

11. As reflected, for example, in the "Quarrel of the Ancients and the Moderns." Cf. Rigault, *Histoire de la querelle des Anciens et des Modernes.*

12. Cf. Edelstein, *Idea of Progress in Classical Antiquity*, pp. xi–xxiii; Guthrie, *In the Beginning*, pp. 80–94.

ticipated them, while latter-day skeptics of the mid-twentieth century have denied that there was any true idea of progress in antiquity.[13] The issue really involves the distinction between Idealist and Historical Progressivism. Pessimists that they mostly were, the majority of Greeks and Romans were doubtful that progress could continue indefinitely into the future, and in that sense they were not idealist progressivists. There were nevertheless plenty of thinkers–especially in the pre-Socratic age–who believed firmly in progress up to their own times, and who offered a coherent and logical theory of progress.[14] Some even formulated detailed scenarios of prehistory, remarkably similar to the "conjectural histories" that became popular in the eighteenth century. These prescient sages were historical progressivists, and incidentally the forefathers of anthropology, in the full sense of the word. As Edelstein puts it, they "formulated most of the thoughts and sentiments that later generations down to the nineteenth century were accustomed to associate with the blessed or cursed word–'progress.'"[15]

The earliest clear suggestion of Progressivism that has survived from classical times is found in a poetical fragment from Xenophanes (late sixth century B.C.): "The gods did not reveal to men all things from the beginning, but men through their own search find in the course of time that which is better."[16] It is clear even in this short fragment–as in so many later writings down to modern times–that progress is conceived of as the product of human ingenuity and invention.

The progressivist viewpoint was much more fully elaborated a century later in the work of three other pre-Socratics: Anaxagoras, Protagoras, and Democritus.[17] Although their theories differed in details, they all spoke unequivocally of the progressive humanization of the animal, Man. Moreover, they regarded the process as adaptive; that is, necessary for the survival of an otherwise helpless animal. The fullest and most articulate surviving example of ancient Progressivism has been attributed to Democritus, though its authorship is not absolutely certain;[18] it survives in the form of a paraphrase by the much later historian Diodorus Siculus.[19] The

13. See, e.g., Bury, *Idea of Progress*, pp. 7–20, and Charles A. Beard in the same volume, p. xi.

14. Edelstein, *Idea of Progress of Classical Antiquity, passim;* Guthrie, *In the Beginning.*

15. Edelstein, *Idea of Progress of Classical Antiquity*, p. xxiii.

16. Ibid., p. 3.

17. Ibid, pp. 22–26.

18. See Benjamin Farrington, *Greek Science* (Baltimore, 1953), p. 82, fn. For extended discussion of the sources of early Greek Progressivism, see Thomas Cole, *Democritus and the Sources of Greek Anthropology. American Philological Association, Philological Monographs,* no. XXV (Cleveland, 1967).

19. First century B.C. For the reference see Farrington, *Greek Science*, p. 82, footnote.

scenario proposed by this thinker envisions the gradual evolution of human beings from earlier and more primitive life forms, and then the successive development of social institutions, of languages, and of fire, clothing, housing, and cultivation. The author concludes with the observation that "it is necessity that teaches man everything."[20]

Progressivism in antiquity

The scenario attributed to Democritus exhibits four recurring features of Graeco-Roman Progressivism. First, it clearly envisions the biological evolution of man from earlier and simpler organisms. Second, it offers a fairly detailed scenario of prehistory, before the beginning of the historic period. Third, it attributes progress mainly to advances in technology.[21] Finally, while there is a clear picture of material and intellectual progress, nothing is said or implied about the state of society. Nevertheless, it was to take philosophy and anthropology over two thousand years to come back to the same level of understanding achieved by Democritus, if indeed he was the original author of the passage.[22]

A century later, Dicaearchus was to add another important dimension to progressivist thinking, when he represented progress in terms of a succession of stages, based on modes of subsistence: from hunting and gathering to pastoralism to agriculture.[23] As we will see later, this three-stage scenario was to remain a basic feature of progressivist theory right down to the end of the nineteenth century.

Greek Progressivism was the ideological handmaiden of Greek science, just as, two thousand years later, Enlightenment Progressivism was the handmaiden of Enlightenment science. In Greece, both science and Progressivism flourished during the optimistic, expansionist years preceding the Persian and Peloponnesian wars. Progressivist thinking was reflected not only in philosophy, but also in poetry and drama, where the earliest state of society was depicted as barbaric and crude in comparison to the enlightened present.[24] This outlook found expression in the celebrated boast of Pericles that "all of the world's culture had culminated in Greece, and all Greece in Athens."[25] But after the decline of the city-states both science and Progressivism languished, and the Greek outlook be-

---

20. Ibid., p. 84

21. Cf. Edelstein, *Idea of Progress of Classical Antiquity*, pp. 33–34.

22. Farrington (*Greek Science*, p. 82, footnote) suggests the possibility of a still earlier source.

23. The passage survives only in later paraphrases by Porphyry and Varro. The version given here is from Porphyry. For the text see Lovejoy and Boas, *Primitivism and Related Ideas in Antiquity*, pp. 368–369.

24. Farrington, *Greek Science*, pp. 40–45.

25. Pericles' Funeral Oration, as quoted by Spencer Harrington in *Archaeology* 45, no. 1 (1991): 34.

came conspicuously more pessimistic.[26] Plato and Aristotle were modernists of a sort, but, like many other Greeks in their time, they were essentially believers in historical cycles rather than true progressivists.

There was, nevertheless, a certain revival of Progressivism in later Hellenistic and in Roman times—associated again with advances in science.[27] Archimedes, Polybius, and Hipparchus (third and second centuries B.C.) not only celebrated the achievements of their own day, but envisioned a continuation of progress into the future. "Archimedes felt sure that his discoveries were only the beginning of further inquiry, and he published his results with a view to the cooperation of his successors as well as of his contemporaries."[28] The late Stoic philosophers of the first century A.D. seem clearly to have believed in a law of endless progress.[29]

It was left to the Roman poet Lucretius, in the first century B.C., to pen what has become the best-known example of ancient Progressivism. His long poem *De Rerum Natura* is much better known than is the work of his Greek predecessors, and he is often cited as a pioneer progressivist, but in fact he was merely retelling in verse what by then was an old and familiar story.[30]

It is interesting to note that the ancient progressivists were, in general, far more overtly materialist, and far less statist, than were their successors in the early modern period, at least until the eighteenth century. Since the Hellenic city-state was a notoriously unstable institution, it is not surprising that thinkers of the time did not view progress mainly in social or political terms. They saw it rather in terms of continual advance in the technical arts—a process of necessary adaptation which led in turn to advances in society and culture.[31]

Ancient Progressivism, like Enlightenment Progressivism, was always philosophical and conjectural rather than strictly historical. As Edelstein observes, "the analysis of prehistory always remained in antiquity a philosophical construction based on analogies, studies of proverbs that were taken to be relics of prior wisdom, and similar data and never became historical in the modern sense."[32] From the standpoint of the anthropologist

26. Cf. Edelstein, *Idea of Progress of Classical Antiquity*, pp. 57–64.
27. Ibid., pp. 141–142.
28. Ibid., p. 143.
29. Ibid., pp. 168–178.
30. Cf. ibid., pp. 161–162. Moreover Lucretius was, properly speaking, a believer in historical cycles rather than an unalloyed progressivist. He believed that civilization would ultimately be destroyed, and the whole story as he had told it would be repeated. See especially Lovejoy and Boas, *Primitivism and Related Ideas in Antiquity*, pp. 222–242.
31. Edelstein, *Idea of Progress in Classical Antiquity*, pp. 33–34.
32. Ibid., p. 84.

it is particularly noteworthy that the Greeks and Romans never conjoined their Progressivism with their fairly extensive ethnography. That is, they never saw the various primitive peoples described by Herodotus, Strabo, Pliny, and a host of others as exemplifying an early stage in their own development. On the contrary, Greek ethnography was usually connected with Primitivism rather than with Progressivism, as we will see in the next chapter. The Progressivism of classical times was, nevertheless, primarily historical rather than idealist, insofar as it did not envision the inevitable continuation of progress into the future.

Progressivism in antiquity

I think it is fair to conclude that Graeco-Roman Progressivism was, in the final analysis, elitist. At least in its later stages, the progress and intellectual enlightenment envisioned by the ancients was something that had been enjoyed only by the governing classes, not by the plebeians or the slaves. It was left to the Enlightenment, two thousand years later, to achieve a more truly universalist Progressivism. And yet, as Kluckhohn put it, "the wonder… is that they went so far, so early."[33] Democritus and Dicaearchus, in particular, came closer to formulating a comprehensive doctrine of cultural evolution, as anthropologists would understand it, than did any subsequent thinker before the eighteenth century.

Augustine's *City of God* (A.D. 426) marks the transition point between ancient and medieval Progressivism, as between so many other aspects of ancient and medieval thought. Augustine felt compelled to challenge the theory of historical cycles then prevalent among Greek and Roman thinkers–a theory that would have allowed for the recurring appearance of a Savior. He argued that human history is like the life of the individual; it travels a single immutable course from a fixed beginning (the Creation) to a fixed end (the Kingdom of God), and can happen only once.[34] This is certainly Progressivism of a sort, drawing considerably on the thought of earlier classical writers, but progress is now seen as divinely ordained rather than as part of the natural order.

THE REBIRTH OF PROGRESSIVISM

Augustine's vision of progress as providential rather than natural became the established canon of Progressivism in the West for the next thousand years. It was only when the authority of the church began to weaken, in the fifteenth and sixteenth centuries, that scholars began once again to think about history in naturalistic terms. However, this did not signal an abrupt

33. Clyde Kluckhohn, *Anthropology and the Classics* (Providence, 1961), p. 42.
34. Hildebrand in Teggart, *Idea of Progress*, pp. 9–10.

return of Progressivism; rather, a general faith in progress revived gradually among European thinkers over a period of two centuries or more. The way was unquestionably led by the humanist philosophers of the Renaissance, who revived (and indeed revered) many of the ideas of classical antiquity. Yet the humanists were far too enamored of all things Greek and Roman to think in terms of true progress. If anything, most of them were degenerationists, comparing their own times unfavorably with the classical past.

Progressivism: The Tap Root

A longer step toward the revival of Progressivism was taken by pragmatic political philosophers such as Machiavelli,[35] Bodin,[36] Bacon,[37] and Hobbes,[38] who, as Bacon put it, "openly and unfeignedly declare or describe what men do and not what they ought to do."[39] Yet the political philosophers too were far from being true progressivists. Machiavelli essentially revived the classical theory of historical cycles,[40] and Bodin was in general agreement, though he believed that the cycles exhibited a general upward spiral.[41] Francis Bacon professed a more general faith in the continual improvement of human knowledge, but at the same time saw it impeded by many political and ideological obstacles. Moreover, he did not suggest any such thing as a law of progress. Nevertheless, as Bury observes, "in laying down the utilitarian view of knowledge he contributed to the creation of a new mental atmosphere in which the theory of progress was afterward to develop."[42]

Contributing to the revival of Progressivism in quite another way was the work of Réne Descartes, whose new philosophical system, based on scientific observation and reason, was to become the foundation for all subsequent development in Western science. "Cartesianism affirmed the two positive axioms of the supremacy of reason, and the invariability of the laws of nature; and its instrument was a new rigorous analytical method, which was applicable to history as well as to physical knowledge."[43] Thus, Providence was finally banished from the interpretation of history. Yet Descartes himself was not really interested in history. As Bury observes, "a theory of progress was to grow out of his philosophy, though he

35. In *The Prince* (1513).

36. *The Six Books of the Republic* (1576).

37. *Novum Organum* (1620).

38. *Leviathan* (1651).

39. Quoted in Margaret Hodgen, *Early Anthropology in the Sixteenth and Seventeenth Centuries* (Philadelphia, 1964), p.111.

40. Cf. Hildebrand in Teggart, *Idea of Progress*, p. 126.

41. Ibid.

42. Bury, *Idea of Progress*, p. 53.

43. Ibid., p. 65.

did not construct it. It was to be developed by men who were imbued with the Cartesian spirit."[44]

The first true progressivists of modern times were Blaise Pascal and Bernard de Fontenelle.[45] Both men revived Augustine's analogy between the steady advance of collective human knowledge and the steady growth and maturation of the human individual. "As with an individual," Fontenelle argued, "the race steadily grows in wisdom with the passage of time, for nature is constant and orderly in her purposes and would not permit decline. But unlike an individual, the race will live and go on growing in wisdom forever. This was a "law" of the necessary progress of human knowledge."[46] Yet Fontenelle did not, and apparently could not, conceive of progress in the realm of human social institutions.

The rebirth of Progressivism

It is noteworthy that almost none of the early modern progressivists before the eighteenth century concerned themselves in any way with prehistory, or even considered that there had been such a primordial time. They were either idealist progressivists pure and simple, or else they measured progress only from the baseline of classical antiquity. Their theories did not require an "idea of prehistory."

Thus by 1680, as Pollard observes, "we discover an absolute confidence among philosophers in the progressiveness of science and technology. By contrast, hopes that society as such might progress also were, at best, weakly expressed minority views...."[47] The formulation of a comprehensive doctrine of social progress was to be the unique achievement of the Enlightenment, mainly in the eighteenth century.

THE ENLIGHTENMENT

To quote once again from Pollard, "The eighteenth century, which saw the first wave of optimism about the destiny of mankind, also saw it reach its highest point. It opened with a fair degree of agreement on progress in only one field: science and technology. Before its close, firm convictions had been expressed about the inevitability of progress in wealth, in civilization, in social organization, in art and literature, even in human nature and biological make-up."[48] Indeed, the Enlightenment saw enormous ad-

---

44. Ibid., p. 69.

45. Harriet Martineau, *The Positive Philosophy of Auguste Comte* (London, 1875), vol. II, pp. 356–357; Pollard, *Idea of Progress*, p. 28; Hildebrand in Teggart, *Idea of Progress*, p. 126; Bury, *Idea of Progress*, p. 110.

46. Hildebrand in Teggart, *Idea of Progress*, p. 126.

47. Pollard, *Idea of Progress*, p. 13.

48. Ibid., p. 18.

vances, or at least changes, in every aspect of Western man's understanding of man–both as Self and as Other. Our concern here, however, will be only with those aspects of Enlightenment thought that are specifically relevant to Progressivism.

Although many philosophers of the seventeenth century were Cartesians in spirit, it was John Locke, at the end of the century, who first overtly declared that history follows determinable laws no less than do physical phenomena.[49] Moreover, in his *Two Treatises on Government* (1690) he laid out a quite specific scenario of prehistoric social development, based on the appropriation of landed property.[50] He was in addition an early pioneer in the use of what came to be called the "comparative method," which will occupy us in more detail later. In all of those respects he laid the foundations for progressivist thought in the century that followed. Yet Locke was not in all respects a progressivist; he believed in a fixed rather than an evolving social order.[51]

Although Locke was English, the flowering of social thought in the century that followed took place mainly in France and in Scotland. We will first briefly consider the main currents of eighteenth century thought in the two countries and will then turn to a more detailed consideration of three specific elements of progressivist theory that were concretely formalized in the Enlightenment, and subsequently became essential to the development of progressivist thinking in anthropology.

Enlightenment in France

The French Enlightenment surely represents the apogee of philosophical optimism in Western thought. Its protagonists believed not only in the triumph of pure reason but in the ultimate perfectibility of man, largely through the reform of social institutions.[52] And these were not ivory tower intellectuals; they were men active in public life. "For them the prospect of implementing their ideas seemed immediate," as Manuel writes. "Saint-Simon on his death-bed exhorted his disciples: 'The pear is ripe–pluck it!'"[53]

It has been suggested that the first social progressivist of the French Enlightenment was the Abbé Saint-Pierre, whose *Observations on the*

49. *An Essay Concerning Human Understanding* (1690).
50. *Two Treatises on Government*, ed. Peter Laslett (New York, 1965), pp. 336–338.
51. Pollard, *Idea of Progress*, p. 27.
52. Cf. esp. Frank E. Manuel, *Shapes of Philosophical History* (Stanford, Calif., 1965), pp. 92–114.
53. Ibid., p. 96.

Continuous Progress of Universal Reason was published in 1737.[54] In spite of his ecclesiastical calling, the abbot was a thoroughgoing Cartesian and a deist. For him, however, social progress was a possibility and an ideal rather than a historical reality.

Far more widely read and more influential than the work of Saint-Pierre was that of Charles Louis, Baron Montesquieu, whose *Spirit of the Laws* (1748) was cited by nearly all later moral philosophers, and greatly influenced the founding fathers of the American republic. However, Montesquieu's position as a progressivist was somewhat ambiguous. He was a firm believer in natural law (and as such will occupy us again in Chapter 4), and one of his main aims was to trace the causal relationship between natural law and systems of man-made law.[55] He at least implied a progression from the laws of hunting society to those of pastoral society to those of agricultural society. Yet elsewhere he proclaimed a kind of doctrine of cultural relativism which is, in fact, his most original contribution to social thought. "The political and civil laws should be in relation to the climate of each country, to the quality of its soil, to its situation and extent, to the principal occupation of the natives, whether husbandmen, huntsmen, or shepherds: they should have relation to the degree of liberty which the constitution will bear; to the religion of the inhabitants, to their inclinations, riches, numbers, commerce, manners, and customs."[56] Montesquieu was generally inclined to attribute differences in "manners and customs" to geographical factors rather than to levels of evolutionary development.[57]

By common acknowledgment, the foremost progressivist of the French Enlightenment was Jacques Turgot (1727–1781). Very little of his thought was published in his own lifetime, but his posthumously published work was to have a profound influence on all subsequent social thinking.[58] His ideas were sketched in a preliminary way in a lecture, "A Philosophical Review of the Successive Advances of the Human Mind," in 1750, and then were somewhat more fully developed in *Plans for Two Discourses on Universal History*,[59] –discourses that in fact were never written.

54. Bury, *Idea of Progress*, p. 128.

55. Cf. ibid., p. 24.

56. Montesquieu, *The Spirit of the Laws*, trans. Thomas Nugent (London, 1748), vol. I, p. 7.

57. Cf. Bury, *Idea of Progress*, pp. 146–147; Marvin Harris, *The Rise of Anthropological Theory* (New York, 1968), p. 42.

58. See Ronald L. Meek, trans. and ed., *Turgot on Progress, Sociology, and Economics* (Cambridge, 1973), p. 10. Turgot was particularly admired by Thomas Jefferson, who had a bust of the French sage in his foyer at Monticello.

59. These were originally delivered as lectures in 1750. Written texts circulated in manuscript for many years, and were apparently thoroughly familiar to many contemporary thinkers

In the first of the plans he characterized material and social progress in terms of a succession of developmental stages, largely determined by modes of subsistence. This will be discussed in more detail later, in connection with the development of evolutionary stage theory. In the second of the plans he dealt with intellectual and artistic progress, which he associated with the evolution and gradual perfection of language. Technological progress followed in turn from intellectual progress. It could be argued therefore that Turgot was something of a materialist in the first of the plans, and something of a mentalist in the second. He was not quite an all-out progressivist, for he stopped short of suggesting that there had been progress in the creative arts.

Turgot did not imagine progress as a smooth and unbroken flow. On the contrary, he anticipated the *Sturm und Drang* historical vision of Fichte and Hegel, which will occupy us in Chapter 6. "It is only through upheavals and ravages that nations have been extended, and that order and government have in the long run been perfected" he wrote.[60] He also recognized that some peoples had made far more progress than others, a fact he attributed to "the chances of education and of events," rather than to inherent differences of ability or to climate (as had Montesquieu).[61]

Contemporaneous in time with the work of Turgot was that of Charles Helvétius, whose *De l'Esprit* was published in 1758. Like Turgot he laid out a scenario of prehistory in terms of developmental stages, and he agreed completely with Turgot in insisting that differences in intellectual development between individuals and between peoples were due purely to circumstance. His most original contribution, however, was to measure progress in terms of increasing human happiness rather than of intellectual maturation. Helvétius might therefore be called the first Utilitarian, and indeed his work was to have a large influence on nineteenth-century English thought.[62]

If Montesquieu was a relativist and Turgot (at least at times) was a materialist, their great contemporary Voltaire was an out-and-out mentalist. To trace the history of "the human spirit" from the "barbarous rusticity" of the age of Charlemagne to the "politeness" of his own age "was really to write the history of opinion, for all the great successive social and political changes which have transformed the world were due to changes of opin-

both in France and in Scotland, but they were not officially published until 1808, in the *Oeuvres de Mr. Turgot, Ministre d'État* ed. Du Pont de Nemours (Paris, 1808–1811), vol. 2, pp. 275–323. For discussion see Meek, *Turgot*, pp. 3–4.

60. Meek, *Turgot*, p. 71.

61. Ibid., pp. 88–90.

62. See especially Pollard, *Idea of Progress*, pp. 33–35; also Bury, *Idea of Progress*, pp. 165–167.

ion. Prejudice succeeded prejudice, error followed error; 'at last, with time men came to correct their ideas and learn to think.'"[63] But Voltaire was an uncertain progressivist; his view of history was tempered with a good deal of skepticism and cynicism.

At the opposite extreme, the most dogmatic materialist of the French Enlightenment was the Baron d'Holbach. His *The System of Nature,* pseudonymously published in 1770, was sometimes called "the Bible of atheism," for it denied the existence both of God and of free will. "Man is the work of nature; he exists within nature and is subject to nature's laws...[64] There is neither accident nor chance in nature; in nature there is no effect without sufficient cause, and all causes act according to fixed laws...[65] Man is therefore not free for a single instant of his life...."[66] The Baron was optimistic about the continuing and conjoint progress of science, material comforts, education, and human happiness, but he also envisioned a long, slow and painful process, led by philosophers who would be "only one step ahead of the pack."[67]

French philosophical optimism increased apace in the course of the eighteenth century, and found its most passionate expression just at the moment when the whole current of Enlightenment Progressivism was about to be extinguished by the French Revolution and its aftermath. It is an extraordinary irony that the Marquis de Condorcet's *Sketch for a Historical Picture of the Progress of the Human Mind* (1795) was written at a time when its author was in public disgrace, and hiding from Robespierre's police. Condorcet's vision of progress was derived almost entirely from Turgot, but he wrote with the passion of a prophet rather than in the calm spirit of an inquirer.[68] His scheme of ten historical stages, which will occupy us later, was the most detailed scenario of history (and prehistory) offered by any Enlightenment thinker.

Enlightenment in Scotland

The outburst of philosophic optimism in eighteenth-century France was paralleled, both in time and in content, by a similar outburst in Scotland. However, the leading thinkers of the Scottish Enlightenment were generally more hard-headed than most of their French counterparts. Their vi-

63. Quoted from Bury, *Idea of Progress*, p. 149.
64. *System of Nature* (London, 1770), vol. I, p. 1.
65. Ibid., p. 75.
66. Ibid., p. 219.
67. Pollard, *Idea of Progress*, p. 36; see also Bury, *Idea of Progress*, pp. 169–171 and Harris, *Rise of Anthropological Theory*, pp. 22–23.
68. See Bury, *Idea of Progress*, pp. 206–207.

sion of progress had neither the idealistic glow of Turgot, Helvétius, and Condorcet nor the dogmatic rigor of d'Holbach. They were also better grounded ethnographically than the French–surprisingly, since the main ethnographic sources on which they drew were French: Lafitau's *Moeurs des Sauvages Ameriquains*[69] and Charlevoix's *Journal Historique d'un Voyage de l'Amerique.*[70] Lehmann observes that "A marked characteristic of this movement of thought was a combination of empiricism, realism and idealism that was peculiarly Scottish... there was a marked tendency, even on high theoretical levels, to keep one's feet on the ground–a tendency to base theory always on the facts of everyday experience and to apply that same theory to the practical conduct of life."[71] According to the same author, the four main currents of Scottish Enlightenment thought were a rising interest in law, a new concern with problems of government and public policy, a distinct historical-mindedness, and what may be termed a sociological perspective.[72]

They were an unusually close-knit group: personal friends as well as, in many cases, teacher and pupil. As Evans-Pritchard observes, "In some ways it may be said that all the Scottish moral philosophers wrote the same books. They started off with the idea that a study of man must be a study of social institutions of men in groups.... Kames' book, like those written by his contemporaries, purports to be a history of man in his progress from savagery to the highest civilization and improvement. This was the aim of all the philosopher-sociologists of the period, and phrased in much the same words."[73]

The two stimulating geniuses of the Scottish Enlightenment were Francis Hutcheson and David Hume. The former was interested mainly in the nature of morality, and only more or less incidentally in history. "His chief concern is not... to inquire into points of history about facts, but to show that wise and just motives enter into the making and maintaining of states."[74] His influence on the subsequent development of moral philosophy in Scotland was mainly as a teacher rather than as a writer.[75]

---

69. Paris, 1724; published in English as *Customs of the American Indians Compared with the Customs of Primitive Times*, ed. and trans. William N. Fenton and Elizabeth L. Moore (Toronto, 1974).

70. Paris, 1743.

71. William C. Lehmann, *John Millar of Glasgow* (Cambridge, 1960), p. 94.

72. Ibid., pp. 96–108. For additional perceptive discussion of the Scottish Enlightenment thinkers in their historical and political context see Daniel Walker Howe in *Comparative Studies in Society and History* 31, no. 3 (1989): esp. 574–580.

73. E. E. Evans-Pritchard, *A History of Anthropological Thought* (New York, 1981), p. 14.

74. Gladys Bryson, *Man and Society* (New York, 1968), p. 85.

75. See ibid., pp. 2, 11.

Hume is best remembered for his skeptical and anti-inductivist theory of knowledge,[76] but he also wrote extensively on history. Like Ibn Khaldûn and Vico before him, he set himself the task of discovering the laws of history; he wanted to be to history what Newton was to physical science.[77] But his historiography was sometimes at odds with his philosophy of knowledge, for he often treated received historical truth as nonproblematical.[78]

The extent of Hume's Progressivism is debatable. On one hand, the theory of indefinite progress, in the abstract, left him cold.[79] On the other hand, he often acknowledged specific progress in such domains as social and political organization, technology, and the arts.[80] However, Hume's primary influence on Scottish Progressivism was as a provocateur; many of the later writings of his progressivist countrymen were intended to refute his skeptical philosophy.[81]

According to Ronald Meek, the immediate progenitor of Scottish Progressivism was Adam Smith. *The Wealth of Nations* was not published until 1776, but Smith was apparently giving progressivist lectures at the University of Glasgow, and indulging in conjectural history, as early as the 1750s. The lectures are presumed to have influenced John Dalrymple, Lord Kames, and Adam Ferguson, all of whom preceded Smith into print.[82] Since this is partly a matter of conjecture, however, I will deal with the major progressivist works of the Scottish Enlightenment in the order of their appearance in print.

The publication of Adam Ferguson's *An Essay on the History of Civil Society* (1767)[83] is a significant milepost in the history not only of Progressivism but of social thought more generally. The author has been cited more than once as a pioneer of sociology,[84] much as his great friend and contemporary Adam Smith has been cited as a pioneer of economics. Like all writers of the period, Ferguson used "civil society" to designate what we

---

76. See Bertrand Russell, *A History of Western Philosophy* (New York, 1945), pp. 659–674.

77. Bryson, *Man and Society*, p. 19.

78. Ibid., pp. 106–107.

79. Bury, *Idea of Progress*, p. 219.

80. Bryson, *Man and Society*, pp. 104–105.

81. Ibid., pp. 2, 11.

82. For extended discussion of the chronology of Scottish progressivist thought, see Ronald Meek, *Social Science and the Ignoble Savage* (Cambridge, 1976), pp. 106–116.

83. Evans-Pritchard (*History of Anthropological Thought*) cites, apparently erroneously, an original publication date of 1766.

84. Ibid., pp. 18–29; Bryson, *Man and Society*, p. 31; Louis Schneider in Adam Ferguson, *An Essay on the History of Civil Society* (New Brunswick, N.J., 1980), pp. v–xxvi; W. C. Lehmann, *Adam Ferguson and the Beginnings of Modern Sociology* (New York, 1930).

would now call civilization, and his work is in the fullest sense an essay on the evolution of civilization.[85]

What is extraordinary in the work of Ferguson is the extent to which he anticipated the later ideas of Comte, of Spencer, and of Durkheim. However much he may have been influenced by the unpublished work of Adam Smith, he was the first since Aristotle to insist clearly and unambiguously that man is by nature and instinct a social animal, and cannot be understood in any other terms. He ridiculed those earlier conjectural prehistorians like Hobbes and Locke, who had imagined a primordial state of humanity without any institutions of government. "Society appears to be as old as the individual, and the use of the tongue as universal as that of the hand and foot." And again, "Men are to be taken in groupes [sic], as they have always subsisted. The history of the individual is but a detail of the sentiments and the thoughts he has entertained in the view of his species: and every experiment [i.e., hypothesis] relative to this subject should be made with entire societies and not with single men."[86] In other words, the proper study of mankind is the human group.

Ferguson's proto-anthropology was as advanced as his proto-sociology. To begin with, his ethnographic grounding was far superior to that of most of his fellow progressivists–not from personal observation but because he had steeped himself in the ethnographic literature, including innumerable travel accounts.[87] Like most of his fellow Scots he was an avowed empiricist; unlike several of them he put this principle into action by insisting that reconstructions of prehistory should be based as much as possible on the actual study of living primitives and not on logic or conjecture.[88] He was very conscious of the ethnocentric fallacy of reasoning backward from the civilized to the primitive; of assuming that whatever was seen to be progressive and desirable in civilized society must, a priori, have been lacking in primitive society.[89]

The result is that Ferguson's "image of the primitive" was much more conformable to that of modern anthropologists than were those of the purely conjectural prehistorians. He recognized the diversity among primitive cultures, and also some of their virtues; indeed, at times he sounded almost like a primitivist: "Who would... suppose, that the naked

85. Bryson, *Man and Society,* p. 42. Before its publication the work was titled by its author *A Treatise on Refinement* (Ibid., p. 41).
86. Ferguson, *Essay on the History of Civil Society,* p. 4.
87. Cf. Harris, *Rise of Anthropological Theory,* p. 29.
88. Ibid.; Evans-Pritchard, *History of Anthropological Thought,* p. 20; Schneider in Ferguson, *Essay on the History of Civil Society,* p. xix.
89. Adam Ferguson, *An Essay on the History of Civil Society* (Philadelphia, 1819), p. 138.

savage would... excell us in talents and virtues; that he would have a penetration, a force of imagination and elocution, an ardour of mind, an affection of courage, which the arts, the discipline, the policy of few nations would be able to improve."[90] Unlike many contemporaries he recognized that the institution of private property was as old as society itself; it was not a latter-day development necessitated by advancing technology. He was definitely a believer in the psychic unity of mankind, preferring whenever possible to attribute cultural parallels to independent invention rather than to diffusion.[91] And he had, at least implicitly, a concept of culture that sounds remarkably like Durkheim, not to say Kroeber: "Throughout he adheres to his general viewpoint, that culture, like society, is a natural growth, collectively produced, and having its existence outside, and apart from individual minds, which it shapes."[92] This perspective may help to explain why Ferguson, though ultimately neglected in the British Isles, was much read and admired in Germany (Cf. Chapter 5).[93]

Ferguson was the first to introduce, in English, the classificatory triad of Savagery, Barbarism, and "Civility," later to be made famous by Lewis Henry Morgan.[94] His fairly detailed scenario of prehistory will occupy us later. Here it is enough to indicate that he was one of the first progressivists to recognize kinship as a significant variable in the human social order, and he was one of the first to put forward the theory of primordial matriliny, which was to become so fashionable in the next century.[95] On this particular topic, however, his work was very shortly surpassed by that of his colleague John Millar, whose *Observations Concerning the Distinction of Ranks in Society* was published in 1771.

Millar's work was broader in scope and deeper in its ethnographic and historical background than anything previously published, either in France or in Scotland. Ronald Meek asserts that

> In Millar's books and lectures... the new social science of the En-

90. Ibid., pp. 138–139.

91. See esp. Lehmann, *Adam Ferguson*, pp. 89–93.

92. Evans-Pritchard, *History of Anthropological Thought*, p. 23. Ferguson's "theory of culture" was more fully developed in his later *Principles of Moral and Political Science* (Edinburgh, 1792) than in the *Essay on the History of Civil Society*. For discussion see especially Lehmann, *Adam Ferguson*, pp. 66–79.

93. Cf. Ferguson, *Essay on the History of Civil Society*, p. 19; Bryson, *Man and Society*, p. 31.

94. Who nowhere acknowledged his debt to Ferguson, though it was almost certainly considerable.

95. Cf. Harris, *Rise of Anthropological Theory*, pp. 30–31. The genesis of this idea can actually be traced back at least as far as the sixteenth century Spanish theologian Juan López de Palacios Rubios; see Anthony Pagden, *The Fall of Natural Man* (Cambridge, 1982), p. 53.

lightenment comes of age. For one thing, the range of topics with which it deals is appreciably increased: although Millar's main emphasis is still on the development of law and government, he is also concerned to explain the changes which occur (for example) in the condition of women, in father-child and master-servant relationships, in manners and morals, and in literature, art, and science, as society develops. No one before Millar had ever used a materialist conception of history—for, in his hands, that is what it in effect became, so ably and consistently to illuminate the development of such a wide range of social phenomena.[96]

Of particular importance for the subsequent development of anthropology was Millar's treatment of the history of marriage and kinship institutions, which was far more detailed than that of any predecessor. He dealt specifically with such matters as matriliny, matrilocal residence, bride price, polygyny, polyandry, and wife lending. As it happened, many of his ideas on these subjects were mistaken, for, despite his broad ethnographic and historical reading, he was still forced to rely more on logic than on sound ethnographic evidence in reconstructing the prehistoric past.[97] He believed that the status of women in the earliest societies was very low but had improved successively through each of the later stages of social progress. It may be noted, however, that Millar's discussion of "the authority of a chief over the members of a tribe or village" anticipates to a quite surprising extent the currently fashionable theory of chiefdoms in anthropology.[98]

Millar might be called the first multilinear evolutionist, for he insisted that societies in different parts of the world followed generally parallel but by no means identical courses of development, because of differences in environment and in cultural tradition.[99] It is clear from the tone of his discussion on this subject that Millar had an implicit concept of culture at least as well developed as that of Ferguson, and like Ferguson he was a believer in psychic unity.

The Progressivism of Adam Smith, at least in its published versions, is much more narrowly economic and less sociological than is that of either Ferguson or Millar. Thus while *An Inquiry into the Nature and Causes of the Wealth of Nations* (1776) is hailed as a landmark in the evolution of

96. Meek, *Social Science and the Ignoble Savage*, p. 161.

97. For discussion see Harris, *Rise of Anthropological Theory*, pp. 31–32, and Evans-Pritchard, *History of Anthropological Thought*, p. 33.

98. See Lehmann, *John Millar of Glasgow*, pp. 244–261.

99. Millar, *Observations Concerning the Distinction of Ranks in Society* (London, 1771), p. 2.

modern-day economics, its direct influence on sociology and on anthropology has been slight. Smith did, however, expound, even more clearly than did Millar, a materialist interpretation of history: "in a certain view of things all the arts, the sciences, law and government, wisdom and even virtue itself tend all to this one thing, the providing [of] meat, drink, rayment, and lodging for men. . . ."[100]

William Robertson stands somewhat apart from the other Scottish progressivists in that he was primarily a historian rather than a philosopher, and the main body of his published work is narrative rather than speculative. But in his *History of America* (1776) he had necessarily, like all his contemporaries, to fall back on a large measure of conjecture, and he offered a schema of American prehistory not dissimilar to that of Ferguson. As a good historian, however, he insisted that reconstructions of the prehistoric past should rely as much as possible on ethnography rather than on speculation–an issue to which we will return a little later. The earlier philosophers, he said, "entered upon this new field of study with great ardor; but... too impatient to inquire, they hastened to decide; and began to erect systems, when they should have been searching for facts on which to establish their foundations. . . ."[101] He even hinted, for the first time, at the possible contribution of archaeology: "It is only by tradition, or by digging up some rude instruments of our forefathers, that we learn that mankind were originally unacquainted with the use of metals, and endeavored to supply the want of them by employing flints, shells, bones, and other hard substances. . . ."[102] Finally and importantly, he warned of the ethnocentric fallacy characteristic of so many contemporary ethnographic accounts: "There is not a more frequent or more fertile source of deception in describing the manners and arts of savage nations, or of such as are imperfectly civilized, than that of applying to them the names and phrases appropriate to the institutions and refinements of polished life."[103]

The last major thinker of the Scottish Enlightenment was Dugald Stewart (1753–1828), who had been a student of Robertson. His interests, however, were more psychological than sociological, and he was not an important contributor to the development of progressivist thought except in his role as biographer of several of his Scottish predecessors.[104] It

100. Quoted from Meek, *Social Science and the Ignoble Savage*, p. 126. The original source of the quotation was apparently a set of unpublished lecture notes.

101. *History of America* (1812), vol. I, p. 268.

102. Ibid., p. 309.

103. Ibid., vol. II, p. 204.

104. He published biographies of Adam Smith, William Robertson, and Thomas Reid. For the full citations see Bryson, *Man and Society*, p. 278.

was he who belatedly gave a name to the practice that had been so diligently followed by most of his Enlightenment predecessors: that of writing "conjectural history." "In this want of direct evidence, we are under a necessity of supplying the place of fact by conjecture; and when we are unable to ascertain how men have actually conducted themselves upon particular occasions, of considering in what manner they are likely to have proceeded, from the principles of their nature, and the circumstances of their external situation." What Stewart had called conjectural history should of course more properly be called conjectural prehistory, since it involved imagined scenarios of the preliterate past.[105] Philosophers of the French Enlightenment, who also indulged in this practice, had sometimes referred to it as *histoire raisonné.*

Three basic features of Enlightenment Progressivism

The century of the Enlightenment saw the flourishing not only of "conjectural prehistory" but of two other, related concepts that were later to be called "evolutionary stage theory" and "the comparative method." All of them were first suggested, or at least hinted at, long before the eighteenth century, but it was only in the Enlightenment that they became standard and indeed essential components of progressivist thinking. A century later, all were to be built into the foundations of anthropology from the moment of its inception. We must therefore look in somewhat more detail at each of the three.

Conjectural prehistory. In his influential book *The Idea of Prehistory,* Glyn Daniel suggested that the idea is a modern one, depending as it does on confirmation by archaeological discoveries that were mostly made in the nineteenth century. It is clear, however, that the author's concern was not really with the idea of prehistory but with the discovery of prehistory, which was indeed a very recent development. But as we have already seen, the idea long antedated its empirical confirmation.

We saw earlier that the Greeks and Romans had a well-developed concept of prehistory, and sometimes offered quite detailed if speculative reconstructions of the course of human cultural development in the primordial ages before writing. But this idea died out almost completely in the Middle Ages. It was obviated in part by the traditional, biblical version of history, and in part by the short, 6,000-year chronologies of human exist-

105. *Collected Works of Dugald Stewart,* ed. William Hamilton (Edinburgh, 1854–60), vol. X, p. 34.

ence which themselves came to have almost the status of holy writ.[106] The best known of these is the oft-ridiculed Ussher-Lightfoot chronology, which fixes the Creation at 4004 B.C.,[107] but in fact it was only one of many similar chronological schemes that passed for accepted history throughout the Middle Ages.[108] The putative 6,000-year time span, half of which was occupied by familiar and civilized European history, obviously did not leave much room for speculative reconstructions of earlier ages. Moreover, the Old Testament provided what for many was a satisfactory account of the course of human development since the moment of the Creation.

The Enlightenment

So long as progressivists were concerned mainly with technical and with intellectual progress, they had no particular need of a concept of prehistory. In the technical and intellectual spheres, progress was obvious enough simply in the span of recorded history—as the protagonists of the "Moderns" were at pains to argue. It was only when the philosophers turned their attention from science and art to society and polity that the issue of progress became more problematical. While arguing for the superiority of seventeenth-century science and art, many thinkers were still sufficiently enamored of Greek and Roman political institutions so that they had difficulty arguing for social progress, and indeed almost none of them did.

Since the Enlightenment social philosophers could not perceive social progress during the 2,500 years of the historic era, they were forced instead to imagine a long and steady progressive development of society during the preceding, precivilized centuries. In this they found Biblical tradition to be of little help, inasmuch as the Old Testament offered a picture of a tribally organized, nomadic pastoral people extending all the way back to the moment of creation. It seemed obvious to the logicians of the eighteenth century that mankind could not have "held dominion over the beasts in the field" from the moment of its first emergence; animal domestication could only have come about after a long period of hunting. In the absence of any reliable documents, and of archaeological evidence, the Enlightenment progressivists simply employed logic and imagination to construct a scenario of prehistoric cultural development. In the process, they arrived at a vision of prehistory strikingly similar to that imagined by Democritus and Lucretius more than 2,000 years earlier—perhaps not surprisingly, since the ancient scenarios were also based entirely on logic.

The idea of prehistory was not wholly lacking before the eighteenth

106. Ibid., p. 18; Thomas R. Trautmann, *Lewis Henry Morgan and the Invention of Kinship* (Berkeley, Calif., 1987), p. 205.

107. Trautmann, *Lewis Henry Morgan.*

108. Ibid., pp. 205–211.

century. Hints of it can be found already in the sixteenth century in the work of the Spanish reformer Juan Luis Vives, whose extraordinary and almost forgotten tract, *On the Relief of the Poor,* was published as early as 1526,[109] and also in several works of the seventeenth century. But it was only in eighteenth century progressivist thought that the idea of prehistory became a logical necessity rather than a mere speculative indulgence. Basic to nearly all the scenarios of prehistory was another notion to which we must now turn: the idea of progress in stages.

Progressivism: The Tap Root

Stage theory. The conception of human history in terms of successive, predictable stages is a very old and recurring theme in Western thought. In ancient and in Renaissance times, however, it was generally associated not with progressivist but with cyclical theories. The stages in the history of any given "nation" were likened to the seven ages of man, from birth through maturation to death, as for example in Shakespeare's *As You Like It.*[110] Our concern here, however, is with progressivist stage theory, and more particularly with that theory which associated the main stages of progress with differing modes of subsistence. As we saw earlier, such a progression was actually proposed by Dicaearchus in the fourth century B.C.[111] Indeed, his idea of a three-stage succession from foraging to pastoralism to agriculture was to become almost a gospel; it was repeated with only minor variations by later scholars for more than 2,000 years.

One of the earliest modern examples of stage theory can be found in the *Historia natural y moral de las Indias,* published by the Spanish ecclesiastic José de Acosta in 1589. The author classified all of the world's "barbarians" into three general categories of advancement, based on their levels of development in government, religion, and language.[112] In the following century, progressive stage theories were also propounded by Hugo Grotius in *The Law of War and Peace* (1625), by Samuel Pufendorf in *The Law of Nature and Nations* (1672), and by John Locke in *Two Treatises on Government* (1690). The stages of prehistoric development envisioned by all of these authors involved mainly evolving institutions of property holding.[113]

A long step forward, from the standpoint of anthropological theorizing, is represented by Montesquieu's *Spirit of the Laws* (1648). The author did not propose in so many words a sequence of developmental stages based on subsistence, but he spoke in several places of natives as divided

109. For the text see J. S. Slotkin, *Readings in Early Anthropology* (Chicago, 1965), pp. 50–52.
110. Jaques, in Act II, Scene vii. For discussion see Hodgen, *Early Anthropology,* pp. 463–466.
111. See n. 23, supra.
112. For extended discussion of Acosta's theory see Pagden, *Fall of Natural Man,* pp. 146–197.
113. Meek, *Social Science and the Ignoble Savage,* pp. 12–16.

between "husbandmen, huntsmen, and shepherds." However, it was not until Turgot's discourses of 1750 that stage theory attained once again the level of specificity proposed by Dicaearchus two millennia earlier.

> In the beginning, when men could devote themselves to nothing but obtaining their subsistence, they were primarily hunters, in much the same situation as the savages of America. But in countries where certain animals like horses, oxen, and sheep were to be found, 'the pastoral way of life' was introduced, resulting in an increase in wealth and a greater understanding of 'the idea of property.' Eventually, in fertile countries, pastoral peoples moved on to the state of agriculture, and as a result of the surplus which agriculture was able to generate there arose 'towns, trade, and all the useful arts and accomplishments,' a leisured class, and so on.[114]

Here, then, we have the first unambiguous theory of a three-stage progression, from hunting to pastoralism to agriculture, since Classical times.

Subsequent thinkers of the French Enlightenment who made use of Turgot's stage theory, in whole or in part, included Rousseau, Helvétius, Goguet, Quesnay, De Pauw, and Condorcet.[115] Rousseau of course was much more a primitivist than a progressivist, and as such will occupy us extensively in the next chapter. Yet he offered an imagined scenario of prehistory more detailed than any of his predecessors; he merely regretted rather than celebrated the process, at least its later stages.

The quintessential stage theorist of the French Enlightenment was the Marquis de Condorcet, whose *Sketch for a Historical Picture of the Progress of the Human Mind* was published in 1795. He improved on Turgot by adding another six stages to the original three-stage evolutionary scheme. However, all but one of the later stages (stages 4–9) were simply chapters in recorded European history, and they were defined almost entirely on the basis of intellectual rather than of material criteria. The tenth stage, as yet unrealized, was to be the rule of pure reason.[116]

The earliest published version of stage theory in Scotland is to be found in John Dalrymple's *Essay towards a General History of Feudal Property in Great Britain* (1757).[117] His scheme of hunting-pastoral-farming

114. Ibid., p. 10.
115. Ibid., pp. 76–98, 145–150.
116. For discussion see especially Bury, *Idea of Progress*, pp. 202–216; Pollard, *Idea of Progress*, pp. 79–84; and Meek, *Social Science and the Ignoble Savage*, pp. 207–209.
117. Since Turgot's work was not officially published until the early 19th century, Dalrymple technically gets credit for the first clear publication of three-stage theory anywhere. See Meek, *Social Science and the Ignoble Savage*, pp. 99–100.

stages is very similar to that of Turgot, but also places considerable emphasis on the evolving institutions of property, in the tradition of Grotius, Pufendorf, and Locke. His work was closely followed by that of Henry Home, Lord Kames, who in 1758 published both *Essays on the Principle of Morality and Natural Religion* (2nd edition)[118] and *Historical Law-Tracts.* Although three-stage theory made an appearance in both these works, it was much more fully developed in the second.

The applications of stage theory by Ferguson, by Millar, and by Adam Smith were so similar in their general outlines that they need not be discussed separately. For all of them, as for Turgot, prehistoric social progress was closely tied to, and triggered by, evolving modes of subsistence, and all of them accepted without question the hunting-pastoralism-agriculture sequence that was coming to have something of the status of dogma. The three Scotsmen concentrated on somewhat different aspects of prehistoric culture and society–Ferguson on the institutions of property and government, Millar on the evolution of kinship and familial relations, Smith on the organization of labor and production–but they were not in any real disagreement as to the "facts" of prehistory.[119]

William Robertson's scenario of American prehistory, in his *History of America,* involved a subtle but potentially significant shift of emphasis. While he repeated the familiar three-stage periodization of Ferguson, and borrowed from him the terms Savagery, Barbarism, and Civilization, he offered an important methodological qualification. Stage theory, he insisted, must not be used to "create" historical facts, but only to organize and interpret what was actually known historically or ethnographically. "Robertson's use of the [stage] theory was by no means dogmatic or mechanical: his intention throughout was to use it, not as a substitute for the facts, but rather as an organisational framework within which the facts could usefully be set."[120] In that sense he was turning away from conjectural prehistory and toward the complementary practice of "ethnographic prehistory," to which we must now give our attention.

It is important to notice that, from the beginning to end of the eighteenth century, all progressivists took for granted the hunting-pastoral-agricultural sequence that had first been proposed by Dicaearchus 2,000 years earlier. It was not until near the end of the nineteenth century that the reality of a separate pastoral stage, preceding agriculture, began to be questioned.

---

118. There is no mention of stage theory in the first edition of this work.
119. For more detailed discussion of their schemes see Meek, *Social Science and the Ignoble Savage,* pp. 107–130, 150–155, 160–177.
120. Ibid., p. 144.

Ethnographic prehistory: the "comparative method". While the progressivists of the Enlightenment based their theories of prehistory mainly on logic, a few were prescient enough to recognize that they had also a certain kind of "empirical" evidence at their disposal: the ethnographic descriptions of living primitives, especially in North America. The idea that living tribal peoples may exemplify the earlier stages of human cultural development in general first appears in European literature in the seventeenth century. In the progressivist writings of the Enlightenment we find ethnographic data on the Native Americans at first cited incidentally, to illustrate what were essentially logical theories of prehistory, and then increasingly cited as basic data for the formulation of theories. Thus, throughout the eighteenth and nineteenth centuries, conjectural prehistory came more and more to be supplemented by what we might call ethnographic prehistory. This was the approach to which Auguste Comte later gave the name "the comparative method."[121]

The Enlightenment

The term comparative method has caused a lot of confusion in anthropology, for it is used in at least four different senses. To linguists it refers to the comparison of a number of different, related languages in order to establish their degree of relationship, and to reconstruct a hypothetical proto-language from which they all descended. To practitioners of holocultural survey it refers to the comparison of a selected sample of world cultures to test the degree of universality or variability in particular cultural traits. To archaeologists it refers to the use of data from the ethnographic present to interpret the remains of the prehistoric past. Finally, to progressivists it refers to the assumption that living primitives can be taken as representative of stages in our own early cultural development–the meaning intended by Comte when he coined the term in 1842.

But the practice if not the name was already an old one by Comte's time. It had been given very succinct expression a century and a half earlier by John Locke, when he wrote that "In the beginning all the World was *America*." [122] Half a century earlier still, Juan de Solórzano had written that "as the Indians now are, so we Spaniards once were."[123] And, if we can believe Adam Ferguson, "Thucydides… understood that it was in the customs of barbarous nations that he was to study the more ancient manners

121. Auguste Comte, *Cours de philosophie positive,* 4th ed. (Paris, 1877), vol. IV, pp. 317–319.

122. *Two Treatises on Government,* ed. Peter Laslett (New York, 1965), p. 343.

123. In *De Indianum Jure,* first published in 1629. See James Muldoon, "As the Indians Now Are, So We Spaniards Once Were: Juan de Solórzano Pereira and Social Evolution" paper read at the 20th Annual Meeting of the International Society for the Comparative Study of Civilization, Santo Domingo, June 1, 1991.

of Greece. . . ."[124] This mode of thought was in time to become the cornerstone of Enlightenment and all subsequent progressivist thinking. It established the basic connection between ethnography and prehistory (and, incidentally, American Indians) out of which anthropology was later to take shape.

Curiously enough there were, long before Comte, a few thinkers who advocated the comparative method without practicing it, and a large number who at least implicitly employed the method without specifically advocating it. Before the nineteenth century only a few thinkers did both.

Progressivism: The Tap Root

Among the early advocates of studying ethnology as the key to prehistory, priority must surely be accorded to the great Islamic social historian Abdel Rahman Ibn Khaldûn (1332–1406). He set out to write a universal history, became convinced of the unreliability of traditional, textual sources, and decided that the only way to understand the patterns of history is to study the ways of living peoples, starting with the most primitive. He therefore prefaced his seven-volume history[125] with a three-volume introduction, the *Muqaddimah*,[126] in which he in effect proposed a comparative natural science of Man. He was decidedly prescient in his observation that "Primitive culture is defined primarily in terms of an economic way of life, which, in turn, colors the other aspects of a community, and distinguishes it from civilization."[127] But Ibn Khaldûn's claim to immortality, like that of a good many other philosophers and theoreticians, lies more in what he proposed than in what he accomplished. The main body of his work, the *Kitab al-ibar*, is a fairly conventional history, reflecting few of the insights that are found in the great introduction.

The programmatic recommendations of Giambattista Vico, in *The New Science* (1724), are so similar to those of Ibn Khaldûn that it is hard to believe that he was unaware of the work of the great Arab historian. Vico like Ibn Khaldûn was a historian dissatisfied with the traditional sources and the traditional methods of historiography; he "set himself the task of formulating the principles of historic method as Bacon had formulated those of scientific. . . ."[128] *The New Science* is, like the *Muqaddimah*, a work

---

124. Ferguson, *Essay on the History of Civil Society*, p. 80.

125. *Kitab al-Ibar wa-diwan al-mubtada wa-l-khabar fi ayyam al-arab wa-l-ajam wa-l-barbar wa-man asarahum min dhawi al-sultan al akbar.* It seems to have been written mainly between about 1375 and 1380, though the author continued to work on it until the end of his life. It was of course originally and for many centuries a work in manuscript. It was first published in printed form, edited by Nasr al-Hurini, at Bulaq in 1867.

126. Translated and published in English by Franz Rosenthal (London, 1958).

127. Muhsin Mahdi, *Ibn Khaldûn's Philosophy of History* (Chicago, 1957), pp. 193–194.

128. R. G. Collingwood, *The Idea of History* (New York, 1956), p. 63.

of historical criticism, and the "science" referred to is, once again, a comparative natural science of Man. "Savages, at all times and in all places, are savages in mind; by studying modern savages we can learn what ancient savages were like…."[129]

But Vico and Ibn Khaldûn were primarily advocates rather than practitioners of the comparative method. Perhaps the first scholar who both advocated and employed the method in any systematic way was Antoine Goguet, whose *On the Origin of Laws, Arts, and Sciences, and Their Progress among Ancient Peoples* was published in 1758. In addition to sketching out the usual, conjectural scenario of prehistory, he wrote: "I have referred to what the writers, both ancient and modern, have to tell us about the manners of savage peoples. My belief is that the behaviour of these nations can provide us with very sure and certain knowledge about the condition in which their first tribes found themselves…."[130]

By the end of the eighteenth century, the conscious use of comparative method had advanced to the point that J.-M. Degérando could write *Considerations on the Various Methods to Follow in the Observation of Savage Peoples* (1800), a practical guide to be employed by members of the *Société des Observateurs de l'Homme,* who were about to embark on an expedition to Australia.[131] It is noteworthy that Degérando's guidebook, which covered such topics as language (and how to learn it), subsistence, clothing, folk psychology and mythology, social organization, the status of women, political organization, military arts, economics, amusements, and religion, anticipated by three quarters of a century the *Notes and Queries in Anthropology* prepared by the Anthropological Institution of Great Britain and Ireland (first edition 1874) and the *Questions on the customs, beliefs, and languages of Savages* of James Frazer (first edition 1887), both of which were prepared for the same purpose. Degérando was clear about the reasons for undertaking the recommended studies: "Here we shall find the material needed to construct an exact scale of the various degrees of civilization, and to assign to each its characteristic properties; we shall come to know what needs, what ideas, what habits are produced in each era of human society."[132] In short, the comparative method was to be employed not merely to reconstruct the first stage in the progress of society,

---

129. Ibid., p. 70.

130. *De L'Origine des Loix, des Arts, et des Sciences; et de leurs Progrès chez les Anciens Peuples* (The Hague, 1758), vol. I, pp. xxx–xxxi.

131. This obscure work apparently survives only in a few copies. An English translation by F. T. C. Moore, with the title *The Observation of Savage Peoples,* was published at Berkeley in 1969.

132. Ibid., p. 63.

but to reconstruct all of the subsequent stages as well. The author was, in that sense, the first to achieve (or at least to recommend) a full merger of the two major themes of Enlightenment Progressivism: stage theory and the comparative method.

The first employment of comparative method in support of a specifically progressivist argument is perhaps to be found in Fontenelle's somewhat neglected essay, *The Origin of Fables* (1687). Alluding to similarities in the mythology of the Incas and of the ancient Greeks, "Fontenelle adduced cultural similarities between the early Greeks and the American Indians, *not* as evidence that the latter were genetically descended from the former, but as evidence that both peoples had the same barbarous and ignorant way of life–out of which, he added, they were eventually drawn 'by the same means' to a higher stage."[133] But it was Locke, three years later, who unequivocally fixed the canon of comparative method for the next two centuries with his dictum that "In the beginning all the World was *America*,"[134] and, a bit later in the same book, "*America*... is still a pattern of the first Ages in *Asia* and *Europe* [italics in the original]".[135]

With the work of Father Joseph Lafitau we reach a milestone in the development of comparative method. His *Customs of American Savages Compared with Those of Earliest Times,* published in 1724, was based on five years of missionary work among Iroquoian Indians in eastern Canada. Comparing what he had learned about the Indians with what he could read about the earliest European peoples, he constructed a generalized model of primeval human society that rested far more on empirical evidence, and less on conjecture, than did the work of any previous author, with the possible exception of Ibn Khaldûn. "I have not limited myself," wrote Lafitau in his introduction, "to learning the characteristics of the Indians and informing myself about their customs and practices, I have sought in these practices and customs, vestiges of the most remote antiquity."[136] Lafitau's comparisons included the Pelasgians, the Hellenians, the later Greeks, the ancient Romans, the Iberians, the Gauls, the Thracians, the Scythians, and a number of other peoples.[137]

In short, Lafitau was the first to employ the comparative method inductively, or in other words as a genuine method rather than as a literary device, as Comte intended when he coined the term. Earlier authors had

133. Meek, *Social Science and the Ignoble Savage,* p. 28.
134. Locke, *Two Treatises on Government,* p. 161.
135. Ibid., p. 383.
136. *Customs of the American Indians Compared with the Customs of Primitive Times,* ed. and trans. William N. Fenton and Elizabeth L. Moore (Toronto, 1974), p. 27.
137. Meek, *Social Science and the Ignoble Savage,* p. 63.

cited examples of Native American custom from time to time to support their conjectures about the earliest human society; Lafitau was the first who allowed his firsthand ethnographic knowledge to shape his conjectures. William Fenton has called his work "the first blaze on the path to scientific anthropology,"[138] and it was to have a profound impact on nearly all later thinking in the eighteenth century. As Meek writes, it was "very widely quoted by the social scientists in the second half of the century–so widely, indeed, as to indicate that it was regarded by them as playing rather a special role. Many of them seem to have believed, rightly or wrongly, that Lafitau's book had provided a convincing demonstration of the fact that contemporary American society could be regarded as a kind of living model–conveniently laid out for study, as if in a laboratory–of human society in the 'first' or 'earliest' stage of its development."[139]

It is unnecessary to trace in any detail the development of comparative method after Lafitau, for nearly all subsequent Enlightenment thinkers employed it routinely. Native America simply became the paradigm for the first stage in three-stage (or four-stage[140]) evolutionary theory; "the zero of human society," as Lewis Henry Morgan would later call it.[141] "No one who reads the work of the French and Scottish pioneers of the 1750s can fail to notice that all of them without exception were very familiar with the contemporary studies of the Americans; that most of them had evidently pondered deeply on their significance; and that some were almost obsessed by them."[142]

Finally, at the end of the eighteenth century, progressivist sentiment passed beyond the bounds of conventional philosophy and found expression in two long works of verse: Henry James Pye's *The Progress of Refinement* (1783) and Richard Knight's *The Progress of Civil Society* (1796). The latter was virtually an updated Lucretius, comprising six "books" various titled Of Hunting, Of Pasturage, Of Agriculture, Of Arts, Manufactures, and Commerce, Of Climate and Soil, and Of Government and Conquest.[143]

---

138. "J.F. Lafitau (1681–1746): Precursor of Scientific Anthropology," p. 173. *Southwestern Journal of Anthropology* 25 (1969).

139. Meek, *Social Science and the Ignoble Savage*, p. 57.

140. In the nineteenth century a number of progressivists added a fourth stage, variously called "Modern" or "Industrial."

141. *League of the Ho-De-No-Sau-Nee, or Iroquois* (Rochester, 1851), p. 348.

142. Ibid., p. 128.

143. See Meek, *Social Science and the Ignoble Savage*, pp. 209–213.

THE NINETEENTH CENTURY

The French Revolution and its Napoleonic aftermath are usually cited by intellectual historians as marking the end of the Enlightenment. However, progressivist thinking was by no means extinguished; it was merely diverted into different channels. Not surprisingly, in view of political developments, the progressivists of the early nineteenth century had considerably less faith in pure reason and in benevolent government than had their Enlightenment predecessors. On the other hand, they accorded an important role to religion not only in history but in the future progress of society, whereas their predecessors had dismissed it as an anachronistic survivor from unenlightened times. Indeed, Saint-Simon considered that "religion is merely science clothed in a form suitable for the emotional needs which it satisfies."[144] As Bury observes, this concession allowed the early nineteenth-century progressivists to overcome one of the unresolved problems in Enlightenment social history: the seeming retrogress of the Middle Ages. From the standpoint purely of religious evolution, the early medieval period could be seen as marking a distinct advance over the somewhat chaotic polytheism of classical times.[145] This line of thinking was later to exert a powerful influence on some early anthropologists, especially in France.

Progressivism: The Tap Root

A good many factors besides Napoleon conspired to produce a disjunction between eighteenth- and nineteenth-century progressivist thinking. For a time, the "dismal" population theory of Malthus dealt a severe blow to believers in technological progress, suggesting as it did that the benefits of technical advances are always and promptly canceled out by increases in population.[146] It was the conflation of social with biological evolutionary theory, around the middle of the century, that eventually offered a way out of the Malthusian dilemma.

The increasing transformation of society through industrialization presented another kind of dilemma. Unlike their Enlightenment predecessors, who were liberal aristocrats or academics, many of the leading nineteenth-century thinkers were scions of the industrial and commercial class. They looked with great favor on the comforts, security, and opportunity provided by the industrial order, but could not ignore its adverse effects in terms of rural impoverishment and a widening gap between haves and have-nots. Thus, progress became more morally problematical

144. Bury, *Idea of Progress*, p. 283.
145. See esp. Ibid., pp. 282–299.
146. *An Essay on the Principle of Population* (London, 1798).

than in earlier times. While eighteenth-century progressivists could take the morality of progress for granted, nineteenth-century progressivists had first of all to demonstrate its morality.

This dilemma had a number of consequences. One of them was that nineteenth-century thinkers reverted to a much more Hobbesian "image of the primitive" than had their immediate predecessors, in the effort to show that industrial civilization, for all its drawbacks, was still a vast improvement over anything that went before. The eighteenth century had pictured a childlike savage, leading a life of discomfort and want; the nineteenth century often pictured a greedy, vicious, and amoral brute. Where eighteenth century thinkers found a survival of the savage in the rural peasant, the nineteenth century often found him in the urban criminal classes.[147] It was, not coincidentally, in the nineteenth century that the word "savage" acquired its present, pejorative connotation, where earlier it had merely been another word for "primitive."

The nineteenth century

Another transforming factor was the emergence and rapid differentiation of the sciences, as we know them today. Moral philosophy gave birth to political economy, sociology, psychology, and, latterly, anthropology; natural history gave birth to geology, paleontology, botany, zoology, and ethnology. Nearly all of the leading progressivists of the nineteenth century were at pains to argue that their enterprise was scientific rather than philosophical, and they strove to fit it into a more general program of scientific endeavor.

But Progressivism did not only become a "scientific" doctrine in the nineteenth century; it also became a political doctrine, or rather several of them. As we saw earlier, many of the thinkers of the French Enlightenment were men active in public life, who confidently expected to see their progressivist ideas realized in the field of policy. They were, of course, forestalled by the intrusion of the Napoleonic Empire. But in the later nineteenth century different aspects of "scientific" Progressivism became serviceable to the ideological interests both of capital and of labor, and the doctrine became overtly politicized. Thereafter it was increasingly difficult to be a progressivist without at the same time staking out a political position. The situation has been nicely summarized by Sidney Pollard:

> The two great streams into which the progressivist philosophy had become divided in the nineteenth century, could each be pressed

147. George Stocking, *Victorian Anthropology* (New York, 1987), pp. 213–223.

into service by the two main emerging social classes, capital and labour. The *dirigiste*, organized, scientific and planned social ideal, could be used [as] the basis of modern socialism as a working-class ideology. The opposite, anarchic, free, private enterprise doctrine had become, in the hands of British political economy, the ideology of the capitalist class.[148]

The apogee of political Progressivism was reached, of course, in the work of Marx and Engels. However, for nearly a century their doctrine stood well apart from the mainstream of theoretical development; it was repudiated by nearly all progressivists except for a small handful of self-confessed disciples. For this and other reasons it seems better to consider Marxism as a separate doctrine, in Chapter 7, rather than to include it here in a general survey of Progressivism.

Finally, in the latter half of the nineteenth century, the political and moral muddle of Progressivism was further confounded by the introduction of race as a significant variable, as we will see later in the chapter.

From moral philosophy to sociology

In France, the chain of intellectual filiation that led from Montesquieu through Turgot to Condorcet was continued in the nineteenth century by Henri Saint-Simon and then by several of his pupils, the most influential of whom was Auguste Comte. These men (possibly inspired by the example of Napoleon) were far more ambitious than their Enlightenment predecessors. More than philosophic speculators, they were comprehensive system-builders in the tradition of Bacon, Newton, and Descartes. Although their work was suffused throughout with a spirit of Progressivism, the study of social progress formed only a small part of their more far-reaching theoretical formulations, which typically encompassed all of the natural sciences as well as the human ones. It was, indeed, these men who first insisted on the inclusion of the study of man among the sciences.

Saint-Simon is important in the history of social thought mainly as a transitional figure–a bridge between the eighteenth and the nineteenth century. Certainly he inherited from Condorcet, and passed on to his students, that boundless faith in progress that was characteristic of the Enlightenment. He was a prodigiously creative but not very disciplined

148. Pollard, *Idea of Progress*, pp. 118–119. For more on the politicization of Progressivism see also Stocking, *Victorian Anthropology*, pp. 31–36.

thinker, whose ideas were scattered widely and unsystematically through a large body of letters and miscellaneous writings. But, as Pollard observes, "In spite of the ill-organized nature of Saint-Simon's works (or perhaps because of it) he managed to originate a staggering number of new thoughts developed out of the heritage of the eighteenth century, and influencing the thought and the history of the nineteenth."[149] He certainly inspired, or actually originated, most of the progressivist ideas of Comte, including the theory of cognitive evolution for which the latter is best remembered.[150] Most important, perhaps, he began the transformation of moral philosophy into social science by insisting that the study of man and of history belongs among the natural sciences.[151] He gave to the study the name "social physiology," which Comte later shortened to "social physics" and then to "sociology."

Auguste Comte, the most distinguished pupil of Saint-Simon,[152] looms as a significant but ambiguous figure in the histories alike of philosophy, of sociology, and of anthropology. By his own reckoning he was not only the founder of a complete new philosophic system, but was one of the four greatest thinkers of all time, after Aristotle, Montesquieu, and Condorcet.[153] Yet the precise import and implications of his philosophy of Positivism have never been clear; it has been taken to mean many different things by different people, including its own author.[154] But while nearly everyone agrees that Comte's philosophical reach exceeded his grasp, he has often been identified as a founder–or *the* founder–of sociology, since it was he who gave the discipline its name.[155] He has not been accorded so important a place in the history of anthropology, but his influence was acknowledged by several pioneer anthropologists in the later nineteenth century, and the historian Frederick Teggart has identified him as a major influence in the development of anthropological theory and method.[156]

The more general aspects of Comte's philosophy of Positivism will occupy us, briefly, in Chapter 7. Our concern here will be more specifically

149. Pollard, *Idea of Progress*, p. 105.

150. On this see especially Keith Taylor, trans. and ed., *Henri Saint-Simon 1760–1825* (New York, 1975), p. 33.

151. For extended discussion of his thought and contributions see ibid.

152. For discussion of some of his other pupils and their theories, see Bury, *Idea of Progress*, pp. 285–289, and Pollard, *Idea of Progress*, pp. 106–109.

153. See Stanislav Andreski, *The Essential Comte*, trans. Margaret Clarke (New York, 1974), p. 10.

154. Ibid., p. 9.

155. See ibid.; also Bury, *Idea of Progress*, p. 290; G. Duncan Mitchell, *A Hundred Years of Sociology* (Chicago, 1968), pp. 3–4.

156. *Theory and Processes of History* (Berkeley, Calif., 1962), pp. 110–127.

with his contribution to progressivist thought. Of his abiding faith in progress there can be no doubt, for the whole of his major opus, *A Course of Positive Philosophy,* [157] is suffused with it. He not only took for granted that there had been major progress in every branch of human endeavor; he took for granted that all other thinking people recognized this as well. Consequently he made little effort to support his assertions with evidence; his work has a much weaker historical and ethnographic foundation than had that of his Enlightenment predecessors. His concern was not so much to demonstrate *that* progress had taken place, or even *how* it had taken place, but rather *why* it had taken place.

The heart and core of Comte's Progressivism is a three-stage theory of cognitive evolution, which represents his most original contribution to the doctrine:

> Studying the total development of the human intelligence..., I believe I have discovered a fundamental law to which it is subjected from an invariable necessity, and which seems to me to be solidly established, either by rational proof drawn from a knowledge of our nature, or by... an attentive examination of the past. This law is that each of our principal conceptions, each branch of our knowledge, passes successively through three different theoretical states: the theological or fictitious, the metaphysical or abstract, and the scientific or positive.[158]

This mode of analysis was subsequently to exert a strong influence on the thinking of Durkheim, Mauss, and Lévy-Bruhl, all of whom propounded theories of cognitive evolution in the early twentieth century.[159]

In the hindsight of today's anthropology, Comte's version of Progressivism represents a step backward—virtually a step back from the eighteenth to the seventeenth century. His theory was wholly mentalistic, with progress seen as innate. It is extraordinary that the purported founder of sociology did not propound a general theory of social progress, nor did he attempt to link his cognitive stages to stages of social or economic or political development. And this most insistent advocate of the comparative method made almost no use of it himself. His knowledge of the ethnographic literature on primitive peoples was virtually nil, and his history was sketchy.

---

157. Paris, 1830–42.
158. Andreski, *Essential Comte,* pp. 19–20.
159. See Evans-Pritchard, *History of Anthropological Thought,* pp. 47–48.

In Progressivism, as in so many other aspects of his thought, Comte's contribution was methodological and terminological rather than genuinely theoretical. In giving a name to the comparative method he was only labeling what progressivist thinkers had been doing for a century. Nonetheless, his insistence on the use of the method was far more articulate and more detailed than that of any previous author. There are many historical "facts," he argued, that cannot be ascertained in any other way, and that are essential for a proper understanding of evolution and of history. (He was, incidentally, the first to introduce the term "evolution," which he used specifically in the social and not in the biological sense.[160]) He believed that the comparative method, properly applied, could yield not only a general but a highly particularized scheme of prehistory. "I must leave to my successors the particularising of this primordial conception through the methodological interconnection of ever-decreasing intervals. The final stage, doubtless never to be achieved, would consist in establishing the line of every kind of progress from one generation to the next...."[161]

Frederick Teggart has summarized the Comtean comparative method far more succinctly than ever did Comte himself:

> In sociology... it is necessary to consider the principal forms of society in order of their increasing importance. To determine this order, we must, in the first instance, compare the different states of human society as they exist throughout the world at the present time. Owing to causes that are not well understood, all groups have not yet attained the same level of development, and as a result of this inequality the early stages of civilized groups may all be observed today among primitive peoples distributed in different parts of the globe. The comparative method, therefore, presents to us, at the present moment, all the possible stages of human development as something to be submitted to direct scrutiny.[162]

Two fundamental implications of the Comtean comparative method are its ahistoricism and its uniformitarianism. It is not necessary to study historical documents, because all the different stages of human cultural evolution are laid out for our inspection in the present world; it is not necessary to make allowances for differences of environment or history, because all peoples pass through the same developmental stages in the same

160. See Ibid., pp. 189–190.
161. Ibid., pp. 201–202.
162. Teggart, *Theory and Processes of History*, pp. 102–103.

order. This position, enthusiastically championed by some pioneer anthropologists and rejected by others, gave rise to debates that profoundly influenced the development of anthropological thought at the end of the nineteenth century, and indeed from then until the present. The historical anthropology, the functionalism, and the multilinear evolutionism of the twentieth century were all, in their different ways, born out of opposition to Comtean uniformitarianism.[163]

Perhaps most important was Comte's insistence that the comparative method must employ a worldwide ethnographic data base.[164] In this respect he made a definite programmatic contribution to the subsequent development of anthropology. The comparative method became, in his philosophical scheme, far more crucial than for any previous scholar. It was one of the three basic ways of determining facts, along with observation and experimentation.[165] (The problem of what, for Comte, constituted a "fact" will be considered in Chapter 7.)

In sum, as Andreski observes, "his value derives from his quality as a commentator on the nature and the results and the methods of the sciences, rather than as a scientific discoverer."[166] His place in the history of Progressivism and of anthropology is alongside Ibn Khaldûn and Vico–not for what he accomplished but for what he recommended.

Comte's work was far from influential in his own lifetime; indeed he lived much of his life in poverty and obscurity.[167] It was not until just about the time of his death (1857) that he was "discovered," and his work began to have a significant influence both in France and in England.[168] One of the first English thinkers to be influenced by him was John Stuart Mill, who did much to popularize the ideas of Comte in England while at the same time pointing out their limitations. In his early work, *A System of Logic* (1843), he offered an essentially Comtean vision of progress in terms of the advancement of rational thought. His later, better-known *Principles of Political Economy* (1848) shows much more influence from the Scottish moral philosophers, and includes a revival of the familiar four-stage theory of progress based on modes of subsistence.

But in addition to these influences, Mill was also, inevitably, influ-

163. For discussion, see esp. ibid., pp. 110–127.

164. However, this did not extend to the comparative study of civilized societies. He specifically dismissed the study of Chinese and Indian civilizations as an irrelevance. See Ibid., p. 200.

165. Ibid., pp. 197–198.

166. Ibid., p. 11.

167. See especially Evans-Pritchard, *History of Anthropological Thought*, p. 41.

168. See Bury, *Idea of Progress*, p. 307.

enced by his father, James Mill, one of the founders of Utilitarianism (see Chapter 7). As a result, he was caught in the middle of an emerging ideological dilemma, which he was never able to resolve. As Pollard observes, "he attempted to bridge in his philosophy the two disparate, almost incompatible streams into which eighteenth-century optimism had been divided: the individualist libertarian defence of the social *status quo*, associated particularly with the economists and the Utilitarians, and the progressive urge to engineer further social change by means of greater central social control."[169] In the later nineteenth century the first of these viewpoints was to become a rallying position for capitalists, and the second for socialists.[170] Mill's work had a significant influence on the young Karl Marx; particularly his observation that "the fundamental problem of the social sciences, is to find the laws according to which any state of society produces the state which succeeds it and takes its place."[171]

The nineteenth century

Another, briefly important progressivist of the mid-nineteenth century was Henry Thomas Buckle, whose *History of Civilization in England*[172] for a time exerted a considerable influence on the study of history. Buckle followed in the footsteps of Ibn Khaldûn and Vico in that he set out to write a comprehensive history but felt compelled to preface it with a lengthy introduction explaining his purportedly new, scientific methodology.[173] As Bury observes, he

> took the fact of progress for granted; his purpose was to investigate its causes. Considering the two general conditions on which all events depend, human nature and external nature, he arrived at two conclusions: (1) In the early stage of history the influence of man's external environment is the more decisive factor; but as time goes on the *rôles* are gradually inverted, and now it is his own nature that is principally responsible for his development. (2) progress is determined, not by the emotional and moral faculties, but by intellect; the emotional and moral faculties are stationary...."[174]

Buckle thus took a materialist position as regards the earlier stages of progress, but a mentalist position as regards the later ones. In his view the superior development of European civilization was due to the fact that it

169. Pollard, *Idea of Progress*, p. 114.
170. Ibid., pp. 118–119.
171. *A System of Logic* (London, 1843), p. 595.
172. London, 1857–1861.
173. Ibid., vol. I, pp. 1–166.
174. Bury, *Idea of Progress*, p. 310.

alone was governed by intellect, whereas all other civilizations were governed by emotional and moral considerations, which he associated specifically with religion.[175]

Far more influential, for a time, than either Mill or Buckle was their contemporary, Herbert Spencer. He stands in relation to nineteenth-century British thought as Comte does to French thought: at the transition point between moral philosophy and social science. He was the founder of sociology in England as Comte was in France, but like Comte he also sought to be much more: a polymath who surveyed and clarified many different branches of learning. And his work, like Comte's, has largely passed into oblivion, because his reach so far exceeded his grasp.

Nevertheless, Marvin Harris is quite right in insisting that Spencer deserves a larger place in the history of anthropology than he is usually accorded,[176] for he was the source of many ideas and influences that are wrongly attributed to Darwin. It was he who first recognized, long before *The Origin of Species,* the analogy between social and biological evolution. Indeed, his vision of social progress ultimately owed far more to biology than it did to ethnology. It was Spencer who, before Darwin, popularized the term "evolution" in England, and it was he who coined the phrase "survival of the fittest," which he applied both to species and to societies.

Spencer's social Progressivism evolved over a long period of time, and through several revisions.[177] The doctrine in its fully developed form appeared in *Principles of Sociology,*[178] and has been thus characterized by Stocking: "the law of all change–'whether it be in the development of the Earth, in the development of Life upon its surface, in the development of Society'–was 'an evolution of the simple into the complex, through successive differentiations.' The cause of this universal transformation of the homogeneous into the heterogeneous lay in the fact that 'every active force produces more than one change–every cause produces more than one effect.'"[179] Spencer was a stage theorist of sorts, but on a much more cosmic scale than any predecessor:

> evolution proceeds through three main stages: (1) The simplest form is the gradual concentration of scattered, moving elements into a coherent aggregate, with a concomitant loss of motion in the elements; (2) The intermediate form arises within the coherent ag-

175. Ibid.
176. Harris, *Rise of Anthropological Theory,* pp. 108–141.
177. Stocking, *Victorian Anthropology,* pp. 132–135.
178. London, 1876.
179. Stocking, *Victorian Anthropology,* p. 135.

> gregate when minor concentrations of matter take place within it. These changes slowly transform the homogeneous mass into a heterogeneous one, with divisions and subdivisions down to the most minute; (3) The highest form of evolution is established when the forces of the differentiated parts balance the forces to which the entire aggregate is exposed. The "equilibrium" can never become static because the forces upon the aggregate are constantly changing, thus giving rise to a countertendency toward dissolution. The result must be a moving equilibrium in which there is a constant internal adjustment to the changing forces. These laws operate in the evolution of every conceivable organization of force and matter: in stellar systems, in plant and animal organisms, and in human societies.[180]

It was within this frame of reference that Spencer formulated the organic model of society, which was to have a significant influence on later social thought both in Britain and in France. "A society... is like an organism; it grows, it becomes differentiated both in structure and function, with an increasing mutual dependence of the parts; and as a unit, it is quite unlike its separate parts. The only significant difference between an organism and a society is that in the former the seat of consciousness is located in a small part of the aggregate and in the latter it is diffused almost equally throughout the individual units."[181]

Obviously, then, Spencer's "theory of evolution" was far less uniformitarian than were the views of his predecessors. For the same reason it was less particularized as to detail. The scheme did not admit of uniform stages of social evolution, and the closest that Spencer came to social stage theory was in envisioning a general progress from what he called "militant" to "industrial" society–his codewords for "primitive" and "civilized." The term "militant" signified the fact that the functioning of primitive society was based on compulsory cooperation, whereas in civilized society (which, like any good Victorian, Spencer equated with industrialism) cooperation was voluntary and based on economic interdependence.

The three-volume *Principles of Sociology* was not a textbook of sociology as we would understand it today, but a massive conjectural prehistory and history–by far the longest and most analytical that had been published up to that time. Spencer dealt in succession with the evolution of re-

---

180. Quoted from Abram Kardiner and Edward Preble, *They Studied Man* (Cleveland, 1961), pp. 45–46.
181. Ibid., p. 50.

ligious ideas, social systems, marriage and family institutions, ceremonial institutions, political institutions, ecclesiastical institutions, professional institutions, and industrial institutions. Yet the work was not really well grounded ethnographically, despite a profusion of ethnographic citations scattered all through its pages. The citations were drawn from a massive, tabulated catalogue of "primitive customs" that had been compiled by an assistant of Spencer's, and they were salted in wherever they were needed to buttress an argument, without any real understanding of cultural contexts.[182] This was to prove fatal in the eyes of the pioneer anthropologists. By the time *Principles of Sociology* appeared in 1876, it had already been preceded by the early works of Tylor, Morgan, and McLennan, who were able to point out that Spencer's evolutionary ideas were not really well supported by ethnographic or archaeological evidence.[183] It is undoubtedly that deficiency that accounts for Spencer's exclusion from the ranks of pioneer anthropologists, in the hindsight of twentieth-century historians.

Spencer's evolutionary vision was both behind and ahead of its time. In its mentalism, its failure to consider the role of subsistence modes, and its cavalier use of decontextualized ethnography it was less well developed than the eighteenth-century schemes of Ferguson and Millar, and certainly far behind Morgan's *Ancient Society*, which appeared a year after *Principles of Sociology*. Yet the view of social evolution as a continual branching process rather than a linear one, and the elevation of this perception to the level of a general law, was well ahead of the view of any other thinker of the nineteenth century, or indeed of the next three generations.

Enter race–and physical anthropology

The conflation of social with biological evolution, first proposed by Spencer, was to have a sinister consequence: it allowed the introduction of race as a significant variable in the evolutionary process. Europeans had believed in the biological reality of races for a long time, and in the taxonomic schemes of Linnaeus and other pioneer systematists they were given a status almost equivalent to that of a species.[184] Yet the eighteenth century progressivists had not attempted to fit them into a general theory of history and progress. They were treated as interesting but not significant human variations, much as they were by the ancient Greeks. But once social progress was coupled with biological evolution, it became

182. See Stocking, *Victorian Anthropology*, p. 136.
183. Ibid.
184. See T. K. Penniman, *A Hundred Years of Anthropology* (London, 1935), p. 44.

possible to explain cultural variations by suggesting that dark-skinned peoples had not progressed at the same rate, biologically or culturally, as had light-skinned peoples, and that this must be due to an inferior genetic endowment.[185]

It was in these circumstances that the well-established discipline of comparative anatomy was transformed into physical anthropology, standing alongside cultural anthropology as one of the two interrelated approaches to the study of evolution. Although in the twentieth century physical anthropology was to find many other agendas, in the nineteenth century it was almost wholly devoted to the comparative study of race, and the effort to relate it to general evolutionary theory.

The nineteenth century

While nineteenth-century Progressivism became increasingly confounded with racism, there was by no means a complete convergence of doctrines. Not all the racists were progressivists–on the contrary many were degenerationists–and not all the progressivists were racists. But the appropriation and misuse of racist evolutionary theory by the proponents of segregation, eugenics, colonization, and other such invidious programs did much to discredit evolutionary theory in the eyes of anthropologists in the early twentieth century. In the end, the injection of racism set back the development of evolutionary theory by something like half a century.

Enter kinship–and cultural anthropology

In the later Victorian era Progressivism was once again flourishing as the dominant popular ideology in Europe and America, and its ascendancy was associated once again with advances in science and technology.[186] In the immediate past, moreover, discoveries in paleontology, geology, and archaeology had greatly lengthened the understood time span of human existence,[187] and the evidence of ethnology was furnishing an increasingly detailed picture of what the earliest human societies must have been like. Out of this conjunction of circumstances arose the new discipline of anthropology: a discipline that promised at last to provide scientific confirmation for the heretofore philosophic doctrine of Progressivism (now renamed Social Evolutionism). Anthropology, in short, succeeded in uniting within a single historical overview the two basic preoccupations of the Victorian intelligentsia: progress and science.

185. See Harris, *Rise of Anthropological Theory*, pp. 80–107.

186. Cf. Bury, *Idea of Progress*, pp. 324–333; Stocking, *Victorian Anthropology*, esp. pp. 1–6.

187. See especially Daniel, *Idea of Prehistory*.

The birth of anthropology has often been connected, in professional histories, with the triumph of Darwinism,[188] but this claim of paternity is largely spurious. The pioneer anthropologists E. B. Tylor and John McLennan specifically disavowed any intellectual debt to Darwin, and Lewis Henry Morgan never mentioned him.[189] As we have seen, the idea of continuous social progress was already a very old one by the time *The Origin of Species* appeared on the scene, and it had already been given the name "evolution" by Comte in 1842.[190] Moreover, the continual, linear upward progress of human society envisioned by most of the Progressivists was (and remains) something very different from the continual, adaptive branching and specialization of biological species envisioned by Darwin.[191] Darwinian evolutionism, as originally proclaimed, was not without an element of Progressivism, but progress was seen as reactive and adaptive rather than as active and innate.[192]

Progressivism: The Tap Root

In fact, the earliest, so-called evolutionary anthropologists, Tylor, Morgan, and McLennan, did not employ the term "evolution" at all; they continued to speak unhesitatingly of progress. It was not until near the end of the nineteenth century that the majority of social progressivists followed the lead of Spencer, and renamed their doctrine Social Evolutionism. They thus availed themselves of the scientific cachet by now enjoyed by Darwinism, and could assert or suggest that social evolution is "the continuation of biological evolution by other means."[193] That claim undoubtedly had a lot to do with the eventual acceptance of anthropology as a legitimate science, and it continues to be asserted down to the present day. Yet Social Progressivism did not really become evolutionary, in any sense that Darwin would have understood, until the middle of the twentieth century.[194] The only role that can legitimately be claimed for Darwin in the birth of anthropology is that of an approving onlooker.

Anthropology as we know it was born, directly and specifically, out of the marriage between ethnography and Historical Progressivism. As we

188. For example J. G. Frazer, "The Scope and Method of Mental Anthropology," *Science Progress* 16 (1922): 581; Franz Boas, *The Mind of Primitive Man* (New York, 1911), p. 175; R. R. Marett, *Psychology and Folk-lore* (New York, 1920), p. 102.
189. Tylor, *Primitive Culture*, 3rd ed. (London, 1891), p. vii; McLennan, *Studies in Ancient History* (London, 1886), p. xv.
190. See Evans-Pritchard, *History of Anthropological Thought*, pp. 189–190.
191. For discussion, see esp. Teggart, *Theory and Processes of History*, p. 111.
192. See Ibid., pp. 136–137.
193. Cf. Marshall D. Sahlins and Elman R. Service, eds., *Evolution and Culture* (Ann Arbor, Mich., 1960), p. 23.
194. See for example Davydd Greenwood, *The Taming of Evolution* (Ithaca, N.Y., 1984); Elman R. Service, *A Century of Controversy* (Orlando, Fla. 1985), pp. 299–301.

have just seen, this union had been in the making for a couple of hundred years, and had been recommended programmatically by Vico and by Comte, not to mention Ibn Khaldûn. But the union was cemented, and the birth of anthropology legitimized, mainly through the work of a small group of Victorian-era jurists: Johan Bachofen, Henry Sumner Maine, John McLennan, and Lewis Henry Morgan, whose interest in the history of law led them to investigate its preliterate origins. These scholars added an essential and heretofore missing dimension to the relationship between ethnography and Historical Progressivism. Quite simply, they discovered (or rediscovered) kinship as the organizing basis of primitive society. Johan Bachofen "discovered" matrilineal descent, in the sense that he gave it a name and a logical, coherent place in the prehistory of human society; it could thenceforth be regarded not as a bizarre aberration of savages but as a logically necessary stage through which all of our ancestors had passed.[195] John McLennan did the same for the principle of exogamy.[196] Henry Sumner Maine did the same for the corporate kin group; he also recognized the gradual transition from kin-based to territorially based institutions in the development of human society.[197] Finally, it was left to Lewis H. Morgan to discover the truly extraordinary variety of kinship systems that prevail among different human groups and to offer a coherent explanation for their variation.[198]

The nineteenth century

All of these authors went on to formulate evolutionary scenarios that envisioned the progression of human society through a succession of stages involving different modes of kinship organization, but also moving increasingly away from kinship and toward territoriality as the basis of social organization. Primitive Man thus emerged for the first time as a type concept defined by specific, positive characteristics, rather than simply as "civilization writ small." The jurists began also to formulate that arcane conceptual vocabulary for describing kinship, and social relations more generally, that was to become part of anthropology's professional stock-in-trade. Finally, toward the end of the nineteenth century, they began to speak overtly of anthropology and to accept for themselves the ascriptive label "anthropologist," though in fact none of them earned a living at it.

---

195. *Das Mutterrecht* (Basel, 1861). Bachofen was anticipated to a limited extent by Ferguson and Millar, neither of whom, however, made matrilineal descent an important feature of their evolutionary schemes.

196. *Primitive Marriage* (Edinburgh, 1865).

197. *Ancient Law* (London, 1861). Maine, a political conservative, was not a true progressivist, but he nevertheless contributed importantly to the development of progressivist thought. See Stocking, *Victorian Anthropology*, pp. 117–128.

198. *Systems of Consanguinity and Affinity in the Human Family* (Washington, D.C., 1870).

First on the scene was Johan Bachofen, whose *Das Mutterrecht* was published in 1861. He did not really "discover" matrilineal kinship;[199] both Ferguson and Millar had postulated that the earliest human societies reckoned descent through the mother. He was, however, the first to make it a subject of central concern. But his general theory of social evolution was a bizarre one, based on a highly romanticized interpretation of classical mythology that in some ways anticipated Freud.[200] *Das Mutterrecht* stands far outside the mainstream of social evolutionary theory, and John McLennan was apparently unaware of it when in 1865 he proclaimed some of the same ideas in *Primitive Marriage.*

As a progressivist, McLennan's original preoccupation was with symbolic bride capture–a feature of marriage ceremonies that recurs with surprising frequency in many parts of the world. Like many thinkers of his time, McLennan was inclined to view all such illogical customs as "fossilized" survivals of what were originally rational behaviors. Thus, he pictured a time at the dawn of prehistory when males really had to capture their mates from neighboring tribes, because, through infanticide, they had killed off most of the females in their own groups. While this scenario was as farfetched in its way as that of Bachofen, it did lead McLennan to a recognition of the general principle of exogamy–perhaps the single most important concept in the vocabulary of social anthropology.

McLennan had been reared in the intellectual tradition of the Scottish Enlightenment,[201] and it is perhaps not surprising that he was the first nineteenth-century progressivist to revive the idea of fixed evolutionary stages, at least as regards the institution of marriage. He pictured a progression from the initial practice of forcible bride capture through subsequent stages of "archaic polyandry," "fraternal polyandry," polygyny (accompanied by the shift to patrilineal descent), and finally monogamy. As a stage theorist, however, McLennan was soon to be upstaged by the far more comprehensive scheme of Lewis Henry Morgan, who put such an indelible stamp on all subsequent progressivist thinking that it has persisted down to the present day.

Morgan's career furnishes a classic example of a man carried away by an idea. Although much influenced by Enlightenment thought, he was not, in the beginning, an unalloyed progressivist. His early work on the

199. As suggested, for example, by David Schneider in *Matrilineal Kinship* (Berkeley, Calif., 1961), pp. vii–viii.

200. See Stephen F. Holtzman in Timothy H. H. Thoresen, ed., *Toward a Science of Man: Essays in the History of Anthropology* (The Hague, 1975), pp. 125–129.

201. On this, see esp. Peter Rivière in John F. McLennan, *Primitive Marriage* (Chicago, 1970), pp. xxvii–xxxvi.

League of the Iroquois[202] betrays no particular theoretical or ideological orientation; it is particularist ethnography in the best tradition of Indianology (see Chapter 6). He began his monumental comparative study of kinship[203] as a hypermigrationist, convinced that the co-occurrence of Iroquoian kinship terminology in America and in India was proof of the Asiatic origin of the Native Americans.[204] It was, of all people, his clergyman friend and mentor, J.F. McIlvaine, who persuaded him that the worldwide distribution of kinship systems was more logically explained by evolutionary than by migrationist theory.[205] By the time he published *Ancient Society* in 1877, this idea had taken hold of him completely. Morgan was now led to discount the enormous cultural and social differences among different American Indian groups, so determined was he to fit them all into a single evolutionary niche.[206] For the same reason he was skeptical of the cultural achievements of the Aztecs, which he thought had been exaggerated by the Conquistadores.[207]

The basic theoretical program of *Ancient Society* hews closely to the three-stage evolutionary model that had been developed by the Enlightenment moral philosophers but then had been set aside for more than half a century. Morgan even borrowed the terms Savagery, Barbarism, and Civilization, which had been coined just a century earlier by William Robertson. But he went substantially beyond the moral philosophers in three important ways: first by subdividing the major evolutionary stages into substages, second by introducing forms of kinship organization as a major variable in the evolutionary progression, and third by buttressing his schema with masses of ethnographic as well as some archaeological evidence. Seemingly, therefore, it was Morgan who removed prehistory from the domain of speculation and placed it firmly within the domain of science.[208]

Each of the stages and substages in Morgan's schema was heralded by a specific advance, usually in the material sphere. The major stages, as in earlier conjectural histories, were marked by new and more productive subsistence strategies, while the substages were marked mostly by techni-

---

202. Morgan, *League of the Ho-De-No-Sau-Nee, or Iroquois.*

203. *Systems of Consanguinity and Affinity in the Human Family.*

204. See Trautmann, *Lewis Henry Morgan*, esp. pp. 84–147.

205. Ibid, pp. 158–160. For discussion of the influence of McIlvaine see also Adam Kuper, *The Invention of Primitive Society* (London, 1988), pp. 43–46.

206. See esp. *Ancient Society* (New York, 1877), pp. 62–185. The same propensity is evident in his *Houses and House-Life of the American Indians* (Washington, D.C., 1881), a work that was originally meant to be the last chapter of *Ancient Society.*

207. See esp. *Ancient Society*, pp. 186–214, and *Houses and House-Life*, ch. X–XI.

208. For the outlines of the scheme, see Morgan, *Ancient Society*, pp. 3–18.

cal innovations. In this respect Morgan combined the Progressivism of the Enlightenment philosophers, with its emphasis on subsistence, and the Progressivism of the Greeks, with its emphasis on advancement in the technical arts.

Morgan's scheme did not quite do away with "pastoralism" as a separate stage in the evolution of subsistence systems–an idea that had been accepted by many progressivists since the time of Dicaearchus. Although he was never totally explicit on the subject, Morgan at least implied that the transition from "Savagery" to "Barbarism" in the New World was heralded by the domestication of plants, but in the Old World by the domestication of animals. The cultivation of cereals, in the Old World, followed later, and was stimulated by the need to produce fodder crops for the animals.[209]

In view of Morgan's enormous influence on later progressivist thinking, we are bound to ask how much he really added to the already existing corpus of progressivist thought–especially in comparison to the thinkers of the Scottish Enlightenment, to whom he owed far more than he ever acknowledged. At a purely theoretical level the answer must be: very little. What *Ancient Society* achieved, however, was a comprehensive and logically coherent synthesis of nearly all the older trends in progressivist thought: materialist, social, and intellectual. This is clearly signaled by the titles of the book's four parts. Part I, Growth of intelligence through inventions and discoveries, harks back clearly to the Greek progressivist tradition, as well as to the thinkers of the seventeenth century. Part II, Growth of the idea of government, builds upon the specifically social Progressivism of both the French Enlightenment and the Scottish Enlightenment. Part III, Growth of the idea of the family, builds upon the foundations laid by Ferguson and Millar, but adds a great deal of new understanding based on Morgan's own work on comparative kinship; it is the most substantively original part of the work. Part IV, Growth of the idea of property, follows in the already well-developed tradition of Grotius, Pufendorf, Locke, and several of the Scottish thinkers–perhaps most conspicuously Adam Smith. To all of these theoretical interests Morgan was able to add a mass of supporting ethnological and archaeological evidence, making the progressivist position seem far more scientific and empirically grounded than any predecessor was able to do. In all those respects *Ancient Society* is a milestone from which nearly all subsequent progressivist theory can be measured.

In histories of anthropology the name of Morgan is often coupled with

209. Ibid., pp. 25–26.

that of E. B. Tylor, the two being identified as the twin pioneers of "social" evolutionism.[210] But this conjunction obscures much more than it clarifies, for the two men represent very different streams of progressivist thought. The fundamental difference in their outlooks is reflected in the titles of their magnum opera: Morgan's *Ancient Society* and Tylor's *Primitive Culture*.[211] Morgan did not employ the term "culture," and clearly did not think of it as conceptually separable from society. Tylor on the other hand gave us our enduring concept of culture, but took very little interest in the development of society. The nature of his interests and his outlook is clearly reflected in the subtitle of *Primitive Culture:* "Researches into the development of mythology, philosophy, religion, language, art and custom." With the exception of "custom," none of these are topics dealt with by Morgan; on the other hand Tylor's list contains no mention of kinship, law, or government–the primary concerns of Morgan.

In short, Tylor was an intellectual progressivist in the tradition of the seventeenth century, while Morgan was a social progressivist (as well as a technological progressivist) in the tradition of the eighteenth century. What the two men had mainly in common was their extensive use of ethnological and archaeological evidence to support their positions. But whereas Morgan was clearly a system-builder and a theoretician, Tylor was always somewhat averse to systematization.[212] Progress (like Morgan he never used the term "evolution" in his earlier works) was something he took for granted and apparently regarded as innate; he never attempted to develop a theory to account for it.

Both Morgan and Tylor were enormously influential in the subsequent history of anthropology, but not in the same way or on the same people. The influence of Morgan can be seen especially in the work of later social evolutionists like McLennan, Powell, and (initially) Rivers, while the influence of Tylor was primarily on students of the history of religion, such as Frazer, Robertson Smith, and Marett. But in my view Tylor belongs as much among the German Idealists as he does among the progressivists, and from that perspective he will be further considered in Chapter 6.

It is an irony of history that the enduring legacies of Morgan and of Tylor are not directly related to their Progressivism, which has been largely superseded. Morgan's continuing influence rests basically on his sociological (and specifically kinship oriented) approach to the understanding of Primitive Man, while Tylor's influence lies in his culturological approach.

---

210. Cf. Harris, *Rise of Anthropological Theory*, pp. 142–216.

211. London, 1871.

212. Robert H. Lowie, *A History of Ethnological Theory* (New York, 1937), pp. 83–84.

It is a further irony that the sociological approach of Morgan, the American, has been much more influential in twentieth-century Britain than it has been in America, while the culturological approach of Tylor, the Englishman, has been more influential in America.

By the end of the nineteenth century, then, there were two rather divergent streams of progressivist thought in anthropology: the social, focusing primarily on the evolution of kinship, and the cultural, focusing primarily on the evolution of religion. The two evoked markedly different images of Primitive Man, who, when all was said and done, was still a product much more of imagination and retrodiction than of ethnography. In the imagination of social evolutionists the earliest savage was brutal, promiscuous, and governed wholly by instinct; in the imagination of cultural evolutionists he was something of a philosopher, seeking in perfectly rational ways to find an explanation for the mysteries of nature and experience.[213] Tylor phrased the contrast neatly in an 1877 review: "it was the 'besetting sin' of all who studied primitive man 'to treat the savage mind according to the needs of our argument, sometimes as extremely ignorant and inconsequent, at other times as extremely observant and logical.'"[214]

This anomaly underscores the major deficiency of early evolutionary anthropology: its persisting ethnographic weakness. If we except the youthful, and limited, field experiences of Tylor and Morgan, we can observe that evolutionary theory continued to be formulated by scholars who had never seen a "savage" in the flesh. Any significant amount of firsthand experience would have made it equally impossible to believe in Primitive Man as brute and in Primitive Man as speculative philosopher. That fundamental weakness left the domain of anthropological theory wide open to attack by the diligent field ethnographers who invaded and took it over at the beginning of the twentieth century.

The role of ethnography

The natural sciences of geology, paleontology, botany, zoology, and ethnology were all born out of the Renaissance collecting mania, and for a long time they were all associated primarily with museums. But until the late eighteenth century they were wholly undifferentiated; the "naturalist" was perforce a collector and cataloguer of stones, fossils, leaves, bones, artifacts–and queer customs. Differentiation took place mainly in the early nineteenth century, and it was then that ethnology emerged as a discrete

213. For discussion see Stocking, *Victorian Anthropology*, pp. 208–228.
214. Quoted from Ibid., p. 187.

scholarly field with its own specialized practitioners, votaries, and theoreticians. François Péron, who accompanied a French exploring expedition in 1802, may have been the first individual specifically appointed to carry out ethnographic researches.[215] Ethnological societies were founded in London, Paris, and New York between 1838 and 1843, and ethnological museums followed a generation later.

The growth of ethnology was to be of enormous importance for the later history of anthropology, but it did not have much immediate impact on progressivist thinking. Although both Degérando and Comte had advocated the collection of ethnographic data for the specific purpose of refining progressivist theory, the armchair thinkers who followed them generally found the existing literature sufficient for their intellectual purposes; they felt no need to undertake field research to provide further support for their ideas. For their part the early field workers were mostly not progressivists, or at least they did not carry out their researches in the hope of supporting progressivist theory. It was not until the 1870s and 1880s, when progressivist theorists like Morgan and Tylor became aware both of the gaps and of the errors in the older literature, that field ethnography was fully wedded to the service of Progressivism.

A leading figure in this enterprise was the dynamic John Wesley Powell, the founder and longtime director of the Bureau of American Ethnology. Powell orchestrated the work of a small army of ethnological, archaeological, and linguistic field workers, whose findings were published in the annual reports of the Bureau. Not all of these authors were progressivists, and Powell allowed them to express their ideas in their own ways and words. However, he regularly prefaced their reports with introductions of his own, which interpreted the findings of the fieldworkers in terms of evolutionary theory.[216] As the organizer and sponsor of a large part of the anthropological field work done in America in the late nineteenth century, Powell did more than any other individual to forge an ongoing alliance between Progressivism and field research. In this respect he was the first to put the Comtean (and Viconian and Ibn Khaldûnian) program into practice in a systematic way. Powell and his Bureau will be further discussed in Chapter 5, for they played a key role also in the systematic development of Indianology.

---

215. Although he was given the title "anthropologist" rather than "ethnologist;" see Gordon Hewes in *Current Anthropology* 9, no 4 (1968): 287–288, and Stocking, *Victorian Anthropology*, pp. 275–276.

216. See Curtis M. Hinsley, Jr., *Savages and Scientists* (Washington, D.C., 1981), pp. 125–143, and Wallace Stegner, *Beyond the Hundredth Meridian* (Boston, 1954), pp. 251–269.

Enter the Australians–exit the Americans

Toward the end of the nineteenth century ethnographic data from Australia began to make its appearance in the literature, through the pioneering researches first of Fison and Howitt,[217] and then of Spencer and Gillen.[218] The result was an immediate and almost an electric transformation of ethnographic prehistory, for the native Australian promptly and permanently displaced the Native American as that "zero of human society" from which all progress supposedly started. Here were peoples with neither agriculture nor animal husbandry, who seemed to have almost nothing in the way of material amenities, and yet whose social institutions and mythology were far more complex than might have been expected. The most elementary "image of the Primitive" had to be redefined to accommodate these revelations.[219]

Progressivism: The Tap Root

The native Australian world, as seen by the pioneer ethnologists, was governed by totemism–a complex body of beliefs and practices that seemed to bridge the gap between social organization and religion. This was of vital importance, for it now became possible for the first time to fit religious evolution into a more general scheme of social evolution–something never achieved by either Morgan or Tylor. So influential was the Australian data that it became the foundation for major studies by Frazer,[220] Durkheim,[221] and Freud,[222] all published within a three-year interval. From that time onward, progressivist histories of religion have always taken Australian totemism as their zero point.

Evolutionary uniformitarianism had the same stultifying effect on Native Australian studies as it had earlier on Native American studies. Once they were consigned to the role of ethnographic zero point, the Aborigines became, so to speak, a single entry in the ethnographic encyclopedias, ignoring the very substantial environmental and cultural diversity on the island continent. The effect on Native American ethnography was just the opposite: liberation from the shackles of uniformitarianism made it possible to recognize and investigate, belatedly, the enormous cultural diver-

---

217. Lorimer Fison and A.W. Howitt, *Kamilaroi and Kurnai* (Melbourne, 1880); A.W. Howitt, *The Native Tribes of South-east Australia* (London, 1904).
218. Baldwin Spencer and F.J. Gillen, *The Native Tribes of Central Australia* (London, 1899); *The Northern Tribes of Central Australia* (London, 1904).
219. For discussion of the impact of Australian ethnography on anthropological thinking, see especially Kenelm Burridge, *Encountering Aborigines* (New York, 1973), and Kuper, *Invention of Primitive Society*, pp. 92–104.
220. James Frazer, *Totemism and Exogamy* (4 vols., London, 1910).
221. Émile Durkheim, *Les Formes Élémentaires de la Vie Religieuse* (Paris, 1912).
222. Sigmund Freud, *Totem and Tabu* (London, 1913).

sity among North American Indians. This was to become one of the primary tasks, and achievements, of American cultural anthropology in the early twentieth century, as we will see in Chapter 5.

Archaeological prehistory–finally

The nineteenth century

As we have seen, the "idea of prehistory" was already an old and well-established one by the beginning of the nineteenth century. All kinds of prehistoric scenarios had been proposed, based on the combination of imagination and ethnography. But none of the erstwhile "prehistorians," with the very partial exception of Robertson, had supposed that prehistory could be subjected, through excavation, to direct empirical investigation.

It was the dramatic discoveries of the early nineteenth century, at Brixham Cave and Kent's Cavern in England and in the Somme Valley in France, that made a place for archaeology in the house of science and in the service of Progressivism.[223] These discoveries forced an enormous lengthening of the estimated time span of human existence on earth, leaving room to conceive of a gradual rather than a rapid process of evolution. During the same years the Danish archaeologists Thomsen and Worsaae had proposed the "three-age theory" of European prehistory, dividing it into Stone, Bronze, and Iron ages.[224]

It was left to the financier John Lubbock–no field archaeologist–to develop the first scenario of prehistory based primarily on archaeological evidence. His basic frame of reference, in *Pre-Historic Times* (1865) was the Danish three-age system, with the further important modification that he divided the Stone Age into earlier and later divisions, which he called Paleolithic and Neolithic. In the main body of the volume he surveyed what was then known of European archaeological prehistory, starting with the latest periods (iron age) and working back to the earliest (Paleolithic). There followed a chapter on North American archaeology, which however he could not very well periodize, due to the extreme scantiness of archaeological evidence. The last three chapters all dealt with "modern savages," and attempted to survey the literature on living primitives in such a way as to throw additional light on the prehistoric periods that had been defined archaeologically. Lubbock was thus the first to combine archaeological and ethnographic evidence in any serious way, to produce a general scheme of prehistory. His four stages, however, were strictly archaeological stages, based on cutting-tool technology; he did

---

223. See Glyn Daniel, *A Hundred Years of Archaeology* (London, 1950), pp. 57–62.
224. Ibid., pp. 38–54.

not attempt to correlate them with the subsistence stages of Enlightenment thinkers or with the stages in cognitive evolution conceived by Saint-Simon and Comte. Moreover, the work was not strictly progressivist, for a great deal of prehistoric cultural development was attributed to diffusion. *Pre-Historic Times* in any case filled such a need in the archaeological literature that it continued to be published up to 1920, with successive revisions to keep abreast of the latest archaeological discoveries.

In the years after 1870, the excavations of Lartet, Christy, and others in central France made it possible to further subdivide Lubbock's Paleolithic phase into Lower and Upper Paleolithic, and eventually to subdivide these in turn into a sequence of highly specific archaeological "cultures," defined mainly by stone tool types: Acheulian, Mousterian, Aurignacian, Solutrean, and Magdalenian.[225] These were fitted into a strictly progressivist scheme, and as late as the middle of the twentieth century were still treated as forming a single evolutionary progression, in the best tradition of eighteenth-century stage theory.[226] Latterly, prehistoric archaeology has largely freed itself from the constraints of unilinear evolutionism, but it is still very much in the grip of stage theory, in the tradition begun by Thomsen, Worsaae, and Lubbock.

Summary of the nineteenth century

Within the newly formulated social sciences, the nineteenth century saw the transformation of Progressivism into what has come to be called Classical Evolutionism. Its tenets and assumptions have been thus summarized by Stocking:

> that sociocultural phenomena, like the rest of the natural world, are governed by laws that science can discover; that these laws operate uniformly in the distant past as well as in the present; that the present grows out of the past by continuous processes without any sharp breaks; that the growth is naturally from simplicity to complexity; that all men share a single psychic nature; that the motive force for sociocultural development is to be found in the interaction of this common human nature and the conditions of external environment; that the cumulative results of this interaction in different environments are manifest in the differential development

225. Ibid., pp. 93–109.
226. They were thus presented to me when I was a student at the University of California in the late 1940s.

> of various human groups; that these results can be measured, using the extent of human control over external nature as the primary criterion; that other sociocultural phenomena tend to develop in correlation with scientific progress; that in these terms human groups can be objectively ordered in a hierarchical fashion; that certain contemporary societies therefore approximate the various earlier stages of human development; that in the absence of historical data these stages may be reconstructed by a comparison of contemporary groups; and that the results of this comparative method can be confirmed by "survivals" in more advanced societies of the forms characteristic of lower stages.[227]

As we have already seen, there is almost nothing in the foregoing catalogue that was not anticipated in the eighteenth century, if not earlier. What the nineteenth century achieved was a coherent synthesis of a great many formerly disparate traditions, and their acceptance as constituting a legitimate science, eventually called anthropology, rather than a field of philosophy.

Evolutionism, thus conceived, was not merely the dominant ideology of early anthropology; in England and America it was the only ideology. The new discipline was so wholly devoted to this one idea that it could just as aptly have been called "progressology" or "evolutionology." It was in the service of that ideology that the four previously disparate enterprises of ethnology, archaeology, linguistics, and physical anthropology were brought and for a time held together, for each of them in its own way provided support for the evolutionary/progressivist doctrine.[228] This rather odd and uncomfortable confederation of older parts lasted as long as Progressivism itself remained dominant in anthropology.[229] Afterward it came unstuck everywhere except in North America, and the four "subdisciplines" once again went their separate ways. The persistence of "four-field anthropology" in North America was due to special circumstances, which will be considered in Chapter 5.

Progressivism remained dominant in anthropology for as long as it remained dominant in popular ideology, which is to say until around the end of the nineteenth century. By that time it was pretty apparent to

227. *Victorian Anthropology*, p. 170.

228. The fact that anthropology is an unstable confederation of older, previously separate parts is one of the most misunderstood features of the discipline. There is a tendency to think of ethnology, archaeology, linguistics, and physical anthropology simply as specializations that have branched away from a previously unified discipline.

229. For confirmation of the existence of "four-field anthropology" in Great Britain, see Alfred C. Haddon, *A History of Anthropology* (London, 1910).

thinking persons that the vaunted industrial productivity of the Victorian era was being diverted more and more into armaments, and World War I was becoming visible just over the horizon.[230] The result was a general loss of faith in the inevitably of progress, and especially in the conjunction of progress and science. This disillusionment was very shortly to be reflected within anthropology.

THE TWENTIETH CENTURY

Progressivism: The Tap Root

The turn of the twentieth century witnessed a genuine revolution in American anthropology, involving not merely a change of paradigms but also a changing of the guard. The early, preprofessional progressivists were dead or in retirement, and their place was taken by a new and very different cohort of academic anthropologists, recruited almost entirely by Franz Boas. Nearly all the newcomers came from the German or German/Jewish intellectual community in and around New York City, and they were thoroughly steeped in the relativistic, nonevolutionary traditions of German Idealism. These individuals developed what has come to be called the American historical school of anthropology, which will be much more fully discussed in Chapter 6.

Progress and the Boasians

It is certainly wrong to suggest, as some historians have done, that the American historical anthropologists disavowed the idea of cultural evolution.[231] By their time the basic outlines of Stone Age prehistory had been much too firmly established by archaeology to be ignored or denied, and none of the Boasians did so. Similarly, none of them could or did ignore the obvious parallels between prehistoric cultural development in the Old World and the New. In fact, Kroeber, Goldenweiser, and Wissler all published introductory anthropology textbooks with strongly progressivist overtones.[232] And Lowie, one of the most frequent critics of misplaced evolutionary theory, also wrote *The Origin of the State*,[233] whose purpose, he said, was "simply [to] prove that the germs of all possible political de-

230. William E. Gladstone, surely one of the apostles of Victorian Progressivism, resigned from the British government in 1894 in protest against the increasing militarism of the times. See Winston Churchill, *The Great Democracies* (New York, 1958), p. 363.

231. For example, Leslie White, *The Science of Culture* (New York, 1949), p. 110; Harris, *Rise of Anthropological Theory*, pp. 336–337; Nisbet, *Social Change and History*, p. 224.

232. A. L. Kroeber, *Anthropology* (New York, 1924); Alexander Goldenweiser, *Early Civilization* (New York, 1922); Clark Wissler, *Man and Culture* (New York, 1923).

233. New York, 1927.

velopment are latent but demonstrable in the ruder cultures."[234] What the Boasians did object to, following the lead of their mentor, was the misuse of evolutionary doctrine to justify such non-egalitarian movements as colonialism, Social Darwinism, and eugenics. It would be correct to say that they disavowed the ideology of Progressivism in its late Victorian form, but not that they abandoned altogether the idea of progress.[235] Indeed, Kroeber even proposed objective criteria for measuring progress: "the atrophy of magic...; the decline of infantile obsession with the outstanding physiological events of human life; and the persistent tendency of technology and science to grow accumulatively."[236]

I think it can be easily demonstrated, from their writings, that most of the historical anthropologists of the early twentieth century were at least closet evolutionists. What they objected to (apart from ideological abuses of the evolutionist doctrine) was the uniformitarianism of their nineteenth-century predecessors. They insisted that particularities of environment and history had as much to do with the shaping of cultures as did any general evolutionary process–a theme that we will pursue further in Chapter 6.

It was really the configurationists and the functionalists of the mid-twentieth century, not their historically oriented predecessors, who finally discarded the evolutionist orientation that had dominated anthropology from the beginning. By turning the primary focus of the discipline from the study of past cultures and culture history to the study of the here-and-now, they made evolution (and indeed all forms of historical doctrine) not so much objectionable as irrelevant. "The present can be understood in terms of the present; we have no need of history," was the basic doctrine of the functionalists.[237] Again, they did not really disavow evolution or progress; they simply turned their backs on them as worthy or interesting subjects of study.

The result of this development was a deep division in the ranks of anthropologists. While the ethnologists turned away from Progressivism and toward Relativism, the archaeologists remained firmly wedded to Progressivism, as for the most part they still are. This split was sufficient, in Europe, to dissolve altogether the marriage of prehistoric archaeology and ethnology, and in America it caused a kind of intellectual alienation that

---

234. Ibid., pp. 112–113.

235. On this, see Julian H. Steward, *Theory of Culture Change* (Urbana, Ill., 1955) p. 21.

236. A. L. Kroeber, *Anthropology* (New York, 1948), p. 304.

237. Cf. Bronislaw Malinowski, *A Scientific Theory of Culture and Other Essays* (Chapel Hill, N.C., 1944), esp. pp. 117–119, 147–176; A. R. Radcliffe-Brown, *Structure and Function in Primitive Society* (Glencoe, Ill, 1952), pp. 1–3, 178–187.

was certainly very conspicuous in my student days, in the 1940s and 1950s. Evidence for this can be found in the severe critiques of archaeology published by Clyde Kluckhohn[238] and his disciple Walter Taylor,[239] who castigated archaeologists for their continuing preoccupation with historical issues.

Evolution rehabilitated

At the end of World War II the prestige of science was colossal. This had been the first great high-tech war, and American public opinion credited the victory over Japan as much to the atomic scientists at Los Alamos as to the soldiers on the beaches. Nuclear fission was supposed to herald the dawn of a new era, in which electricity would be "too cheap to meter," and we would soon dig a canal across Nicaragua using nuclear explosives; rocketry would revolutionize air travel as well as inaugurating space travel. Predictably and inevitably, Progressivism once again flourished in those heady times. Sociologists envisioned the gradual reduction and elimination of crime, Skinnerian psychologists foresaw the "operant conditioning" of minds to produce a consensus around national goals and values, and anthropologists revived once again the doctrine of Social Evolution, albeit in a modified form.

Major credit for the revival of Evolutionism certainly belongs to Julian Steward, although the extent and nature of his contribution has been disputed. He represents in many ways a bridge between the prewar and postwar traditions in American anthropology, and this makes his reputation somewhat equivocal among the more radical of the "neo-evolutionists," who would like to disavow any connection with the Boasian tradition.[240] It was, in any case, his prewar field work among Great Basin Shoshoneans–initially very much in the Boasian tradition–that led him to formulate the doctrine of cultural ecology.[241] Slightly later, the task of editing the monumental *Handbook of South American Indians*[242] caused him to ponder the obvious parallels exhibited by the rise of "civilization" (i.e., complex society) in different parts of the world,

238. "The Place of Theory in Anthropological Studies." *Philosophy of Science* 6 (1939): 328–344. "The Conceptual Structure in Middle American Studies," in Clarence L. Hay et al., eds., *The Maya and their Neighbors* (New York, 1940), pp. 41–51.

239. *A Study of Archaeology, American Anthropological Association Memoir* 69 (1948).

240. For discussion of Steward and some of the controversy surrounding him, see esp. Robert F. Murphy in Sydel Silverman, ed., *Totems and Teachers* (New York, 1981), pp. 171–204.

241. Steward, *Theory of Culture Change*, pp. 30–42.

242. *Bureau of American Ethnology Bulletin* 143 (6 vols., 1946–1950).

and this became a major theoretical preoccupation of his later years. He proposed a revised scheme of evolutionary development which he called Multilinear Evolution.[243]

Steward's original claim for Multilinear Evolution was relatively modest. He simply revised the very ancient idea that cultural evolution in different parts of the world had exhibited broadly parallel trajectories of development, although there were significant regional differences resulting mainly from different ecological circumstances.[244] The preoccupation with cultural differences that had characterized the Boasians was valid and meaningful, but at the same time one should not lose sight of the obvious evolutionary parallels.

In place of previously conceived evolutionary stages, Steward proposed what he called "culture types." "Instead of narrow technological terms like 'Old Stone Age,' 'New Stone Age,' and 'Bronze Age,' such potentially typological terms as 'Formative,' 'Florescent,' or 'Classical,' and 'Empire' or 'Fusion' will be used. . . ."[245] Nevertheless, in most later evolutionary formulations, including those of Steward himself, the so-called culture types can hardly be distinguished from the stages envisioned in earlier progressivist thinking: they represent a predictable and irreversible progression. Thus Steward analyzed the rise of complex societies in various parts of the Old and New worlds in terms of the same succession of "types:" Hunting and Gathering, Incipient Agriculture, Formative, Regional Florescent States, Initial Empire, Dark Ages, Cyclical Imperial Conquests, Iron Age Culture, and Industrialism.[246]

Steward's most lasting contribution to evolutionary theory was undoubtedly the ecological dimension, in terms of which *adaptation* became for the first time a key concept. All cultures tend to evolve in roughly parallel ways, but they must first and foremost adapt themselves to the resources and opportunities of their particular environments, and this is the main explanation (although not the only one) for conspicuous differences between one culture and another, and between one cultural progression and another. Steward's ecological perspective has been accepted by virtually all subsequent evolutionist thinkers, though many have disagreed with other aspects of his theory.

Steward's most important ideas were published in the late 1940s and early 1950s. Not long afterward, Marxism began to make itself felt for the

243. Steward, *Theory of Culture Change*, pp. 11–29.
244. Ibid., pp. 18–19.
245. Ibid., p. 26.
246. Ibid., pp. 178–209.

first time as a significant force in North American anthropology. Steward had been highly critical of the evolutionary theory of Marxism, which he felt was too generalized to have any real descriptive or predictive value,[247] but writers of the 1960s and 1970s were more sympathetic toward the Marxist perspective. The result was a number of attempts to reconcile or to synthesize the Marxist and the Stewardian visions of evolution. One such was the distinction between specific and general evolution proposed by Sahlins and Service, the specific being more or less conformable to Stewardian multilinear evolution and the general to the universalist Marxist tradition.[248] This general line of thought, combining Stewardian, Marxist, and other perspectives, has come to the called Neo-evolutionism.

Space does not permit a discussion of the many variants of neo-evolutionist theory that have appeared since Steward's time; only a few of the more influential can be mentioned. Two such are the generally similar formulations of Morton Fried in *The Evolution of Political Society* (New York, 1967), and of Elman Service, first published in *A Profile of Primitive Culture* (New York, 1957). On the basis mainly of social and political institutions, Fried characterized all human societies as Egalitarian, Ranked, or Stratified, with the State coming in as a late form of stratified society. Service, on the basis of essentially the same criteria, classified all societies as comprising Bands, Tribes, Chiefdoms, or States. For both authors these were not merely taxonomic categories; they were irreversible evolutionary sequences. A more recent and particularized formulation, by Allen Johnson and Timothy Earle, proposes three major stages which are divided into substages, somewhat after the fashion of Morgan.[249] In contrast to Steward, all of these schemes represent a partial reversion to the uniformitarianism of the Enlightenment, including its propensity for three-stage or four-stage partitioning.

Neo-evolutionism since the time of Steward has always self-consciously defined itself in contrast to the Unilinear Evolutionism of Morgan and the Universal Evolutionism of Marx.[250] Viewed from that narrow perspective, it is unquestionably an improvement over both its immediate predecessors, particularly as regards its vastly enhanced ecological per-

247. See Ibid., pp. 16–18.

248. Sahlins and Service, *Evolution and Culture*, pp. 23–44.

249. Allen W. Johnson and Timothy Earle, *The Evolution of Human Societies* (Stanford, Calif., 1987).

250. Steward, *Theory of Culture Change*, pp. 15–18; Stephen K. Sanderson, *Social Evolutionism* (Oxford, 1990), pp. 91–102; Elman Service, *Cultural Evolutionism* (New York, 1971), pp. 6–10; Harris, *Rise of Anthropological Theory*, pp. 634–687; Johnson and Earle, *Evolution of Human Societies*, pp. 2–5.

spective. If we look at it in the broader context of progressivist thinking since the eighteenth century, however, Neo-evolutionism appears somewhat less revolutionary. The theories of Turgot, Ferguson, and Millar, though deficient in ethnographic and archaeological grounding, were clearly ecological, insofar as they related all forms of social and moral progress to advances in the basic mode of subsistence. Montesquieu, Robertson, and especially Millar were all highly conscious of the role of environment in the differential development of cultures in different areas. And the "culture types" of Steward and his successors, though certainly different from the evolutionary stages based on technology that were proposed by Morgan and by Lubbock, are much less different from the stages based on subsistence that were proposed by most of the French and Scottish thinkers a century earlier. It could be suggested that Neo-evolutionism is not so much a revolutionary advance as a corrective to the excessive rigidity of late-nineteenth-century schemes.

In sum, Neo-evolutionism, at least in its philosophical import, is considerably closer to the eighteenth century than it is to the nineteenth. It retains at least three basic features of Enlightenment Progressivism: 1) periodization of evolution in terms of an irreversible succession of stages; 2) differentiation at least of the earlier stages primarily on the basis of subsistence strategies; 3) characterization of the prehistoric stages on the basis mainly of ethnographic studies of living peoples (i.e., the comparative method).

The most obvious advances represented by Neo-evolutionism, in comparison to eighteenth-century theory, are its greatly enhanced ecological understanding, and, resulting therefrom, its more refined periodization of the stages of prehistory. After 2,500 years the neo-evolutionists have finally eliminated that "pastoral stage," intermediate between hunting/gathering and agriculture, that was dear to the hearts of progressivist thinkers from Dicaearchus to Morgan. At least some of the neo-evolutionists have also freed themselves from the limitations of the age-old triadic model, and can speak of five, six, seven, or more stages of evolutionary development. These improvements are due mainly to vastly increased ethnographic knowledge, for archaeology has contributed surprisingly little to the formulation of evolutionary theory even in the recent past. Archaeologists for the most part are consumers rather than producers of evolutionary theory; they take the ethnographically defined stages of the theorists and apply them prescriptively to the interpretation of the material remains they uncover.

Enter the Bushmen–exit the Australians

The enhanced ecological perspective of Neo-evolutionism required a new ethnographic foundation, especially in regard to the most primitive forms of society. Existing literature on the Australians and other hunter/gatherer peoples–mostly now fifty to a hundred years old–was found to be lacking in the kind of detail necessary for a full understanding of how these peoples exploited their environmental resources on a day-to-day and year-to-year basis. However, by the 1960s very few hunting and gathering peoples were still living under anything like aboriginal conditions; their cultures had been heavily transformed through contact with the products and the agents of industrial civilization. A partial exception was, apparently, offered by the San (Bushmen) peoples of southwestern Africa. Accordingly, these peoples became the subject of intensive ethnographic and ethnoarchaeological studies in the 1970s and 1980s, designed to discover, while there was still time, how hunter/gatherers really make a living. Most influential were the studies of the Harvard Kalahari Group, directed originally by Richard Lee.[251]

Results of these studies were surprising to most anthropologists, for they seemed to contradict several centuries of received wisdom about the most primitive human societies. It was found that the San, despite their reputation as hunters, actually relied far more on plant food than on animal food for their daily and yearly diet, exploiting an extraordinarily wide variety of native flora. Their food-procuring activities were nevertheless highly pragmatic and variable, allowing them to take advantage of whatever food resources were most readily available in any given season and in any given area. Most surprisingly, if was found that hunting and gathering was neither a highly insecure nor a labor-intensive mode of subsistence; the San groups could meet their subsistence needs without a tremendous investment of time and effort, leaving abundant time for leisure activities. As Lee wrote, "it is becoming clear that, with a few conspicuous exceptions, the hunter-gatherer subsistence base is at least routine and reliable and at best surprisingly abundant."[252] Marshall Sahlins went so far as to characterize the !Kung Bushmen as "an original affluent society."[253]

These findings seemed to dispel once and for all the Hobbesian vision of primordial human life as "nasty, brutish, and short," and to confirm instead the rather utopian vision popularized by Marx and Engels (see Chapter 7). At all events, the findings of Lee and others became at once the basic paradigm for hunter/gatherer society, displacing the Australian Aborigines just as, three generations earlier, the Australians had displaced

---

251. For a list of references, see Johnson and Earle, *Evolution of Human Societies*, p. 38.
252. Richard Lee and Irven DeVore, eds., *Man the Hunter* (Chicago, 1968), p. 30.
253. Ibid., pp. 85–89. See also Marshall Sahlins, *Stone-Age Economics* (Chicago, 1972), pp. 1–39.

the North American Indians from the position of "zero of human society." The work of Lee and his group has since come in for severe criticism from some quarters,[254] but for the most part the San, and particularly the !Kung subdivision, still remain everybody's favorite model of Primeval Man.[255] Nearly all introductory anthropology textbooks have a section, or at least a sidebar, on the !Kung.

The enduring philosophical dilemma

Perhaps the most problematical feature of Neo-evolutionism is the claim that it has finally freed Evolutionism from any suggestion of progress, thereby making it a wholly scientific doctrine.[256] Evolutionary change, we are told, is strictly adaptive, meaning apparently that it was and is necessary for survival–otherwise Mankind would have died out.[257] If this is true, then of course Neo-evolutionism cannot properly be called a progressivist doctrine, in spite of its huge and obvious debt to three centuries of antecedent progressivist thinking. But the claim raises philosophical as well as moral questions that have not been satisfactorily answered.

First and most fundamental is the question of what is meant by progress. While no progressivist has addressed this question in a rigorous or formalistic way, it is possible to recognize at least four objective measures of progress that have been offered by different thinkers in the past: 1) a quantum increase in the amount of knowledge that can be received, processed, and transmitted by individuals and by societies, as a result partly of accumulating experience and partly of advances in communicative technology; 2) technological advances making it possible to achieve any given end (say, cultivation of an acre of wheat or making a pot) with a lessened expenditure of energy, thereby releasing energy for other activities; 3) technological advances that decrease the physical discomforts of life imposed by weather, etc.; 4) an increase in the average amount of happiness enjoyed by individuals in the course of a lifetime. To these the twentieth century would certainly add a fifth measure: the lengthening of life expectancies and decrease in suffering from disease and injury through advances in medicine.[258]

254. Cf. Edwin M. Wilmsen, *Land Filled with Flies* (Chicago, 1989); Edwin M. Wilmsen and James R. Denbow, "Paradigmatic History of San-Speaking Peoples and Current Attempts at Revision," *Current Anthropology* 31, no. 5. (1990): 489–524.

255. Cf., for example, Johnson and Earle, *Evolution of Human Societies*, pp. 38–54.

256. Cf. Steward, *Theory of Culture Change*, pp. 13–14; Johnson and Earle, *Evolution of Human Societies*, pp. 2–5.

257. Cf. Johnson and Earle, *Evolution of Human Societies*, pp. 4–5.

258. On the issue of progress, see also Sahlins and Service, *Evolution and Culture*, p. 27.

Neo-evolutionists might be disposed to argue the happiness issue; I think they would be hard put to deny that there has been progress according to any of the other four measures on the preceding list. If, then, most neo-evolutionists would admit that there really has been progress as well as evolution, they would seem to be implying that progress and evolution are separate processes, which have to be separately measured. Yet I think most would agree that both evolution and progress are directional, and few would really suggest that they proceed in different directions.[259]

Progressivism: The Tap Root

If evolution is to be decoupled from progress, then it clearly becomes necessary to specify also what is meant by the term evolution, and how much is explained by it. If evolution encompasses only those cultural changes that appear to be adaptive–that is, necessary for survival–then it leaves an enormous amount of cultural history unaccounted for. The concept thus defined has a good deal less explanatory power than has traditionally been claimed for it, as Gertrude Dole noted.[260] Moreover, it is really impossible to demonstrate scientifically that any change was necessary for survival, since the matter cannot be tested experimentally. The concepts of evolution and of adaptation can only be applied deductively and retrodictively: to suggest that such-and-such a change must have been adaptive, or it wouldn't have happened. This perspective reduces the human being from the status of actor to mere reactor: capable of using enormous creative powers in response to external stimuli but not, apparently, capable of using them on his or her own initiative to improve the comforts and the enjoyment of life. But the issue of evolution versus progress is a much more philosophically profound one than has generally been acknowledged, and a fuller discussion of it is beyond the compass of the present book.

SUMMARY

The idea of progress–a gradual but predictable bettering of the human condition from age to age–has been one of the cornerstones of Western historical and philosophical thought since ancient Greek times. Human history (and prehistory) thus perceived is imbued with a basic directionality, from the worse to the better. However, ideas about what constitutes "the better," what causes it, and how it can be measured have changed in accordance with the ideological preoccupations of different eras, and different philosophies. Some have measured it mainly in terms of improved

259. See Gertrude Dole in Raoul and Frada Naroll, eds., *Main Currents in Cultural Anthropology* (New York, 1973), pp. 250–254.
260. Ibid.

material circumstances, some in terms of intellectual maturation, a few in terms of aesthetic achievements. All progressivists agree, however, that their age is superior to those that preceded it.

Summary

Progressivism is thus basically a doctrine of self-congratulation. It has flourished mainly in optimistic times: times of scientific advances and expanding imaginations. It was particularly conspicuous in pre-Socratic Greece, in the Enlightenment, in the Victorian age, and in the generation following World War II. Consistently, Progressivism has been the ideological handmaiden of Science: the doctrine that legitimizes all scientific discoveries, and labels them as "advances."

For most of its history, Progressivism was a purely philosophical or ideological doctrine, resting on faith rather than on any good empirical evidence of improvement in the human condition. In the absence of such evidence, early progressivists devised imaginary, and imaginative, scenarios of history and prehistory in which they pictured the gradual emergence of enlightened present-day institutions out of earlier and ruder institutions. The defining characteristics of primitive society, thus conceived, were wholly negative: they were whatever civilization was not.

Beginning in the Age of Discovery, ethnographic information about living primitives, especially in the Americas, began to provide the progressivists with what they saw as empirical confirmation for their ideas. Here indeed were living peoples whose circumstances conformed in a general way to the imagined early condition of mankind. They must be "fossilized" survivals from ancient times, who had somehow failed to progress. And in the nineteenth century, archaeology began also to provide confirmation, with evidence of early peoples who had indeed lived without metals or agriculture or permanent dwellings, just as the progressivists had always imagined.

Out of the conjunction of progressivist theory with ethnographic and archaeological researches, the discipline of anthropology was born in the latter half of the nineteenth century. The early anthropologists not only added greatly to the store of ethnographic and archaeological evidence; they also arranged that evidence in orderly progressions to provide seemingly irrefutable confirmation for what had long been only a philosophical doctrine. Progressivism was transformed, seemingly, into a science, and its name was anthropology. "Progress" was renamed Social Evolution or Cultural Evolution, terms with unimpeachable scientific credentials.

In the generations since 1860, the fortunes of social evolutionary theory (née Progressivism) within anthropology have closely mirrored the popularity of the doctrine among the public at large. It remained absolutely central to the discipline during the bumptiously optimistic Victorian era, went out of fashion when the world lost faith in progress around the time of World War I, came back strongly, in the guise of Neo-evolutionism, in the heady, science-dominated years following World War II, and is now once again on the wane in a troubled and self-doubting time. Yet it remains deeply embedded in the anthropological fabric, and must still, in view of its historical role, be identified as the tap root of anthropology in America.

CHAPTER 3

PRIMITIVISM

If PROGRESSIVISM is a very ancient and very pervasive doctrine in Western thought, its rhetorical power has nevertheless been challenged from the beginning by the contrary doctrine of Primitivism. As Bell has written, "The nostalgia of civilized man for a return to a primitive or pre-civilized condition is as old it seems as his civilized capacity for self-reflection. It is a familiar characteristic of human nature that almost every step toward what would generally be regarded as an increased sophistication or progress is accompanied by misgivings frequently leading in turn to doubts about the whole enterprise of civilization."[1]

THE DOCTRINE AND ITS VARIANTS

Primitivism as a historical doctrine is simply the other side of the coin from Progressivism. Primitivists and progressivists often share a common view as to the course of human cultural development but view it with very different emotions: the primitivist with regret, the progressivist with approval. For the primitivist, the Golden Age was far in the past, and often at the very beginning of the world. Everything since has been a tale of increasing corruption of the originally pure state of nature, including Natural Man. In its most extreme form, Primitivism may involve a belief in the general superiority of animals over human beings–an ideology that can be recognized in some ancient Greek philosophy[2] and again in the animal-rights movement of today. Thus while Progressivism is commonly (though not always) a statist doctrine, Primitivism is inherently antistat-

1. Michael Bell, *Primitivism* (London, 1972), p. 1.
2. Arthur O. Lovejoy and George Boas, *Primitivism and Related Ideas in Antiquity* (Baltimore, 1935), pp. 389–420.

ist. Primitivism also differs from Progressivism in that it usually lacks the notion of inevitability; the primitivist tends to hope that the original, pure state of human society or human character may somehow and someday be recovered.[3]

Clearly implicit in Primitivism is the superiority of nature over culture, and sometimes also of heart over mind. The suggestion is common, especially among the primitivists of antiquity, that man has been corrupted, and has in turn corrupted his planet, through too much thinking. It was, before all, the grace of blessed ignorance that was vouchsafed to Adam and Eve at the beginning. Primitivism is also avowedly anti-materialist, linking humanity's corruption to the development of the technical arts and to the love of luxury that accompanies them. Though the modern primitivist often misdirects the sharpest condemnation at capitalism, it is clear that what he or she really regrets is not capitalism but industrialism. The environmental abuses and the oppression of tribal peoples that are blamed on capitalism have, after all, occurred just as conspicuously in communist countries.[4]

The doctrine and its variants

Primitivism, like Progressivism, comes in a number of forms. Lovejoy and Boas have distinguished no fewer than eleven variants of primitivist theory, but for our purposes it will be sufficient to notice their two main categories of Historical Primitivism and Cultural Primitivism.[5] On the one hand, Historical Primitivism is the doctrine to which I have already alluded, which accepts the general evolutionary scenario offered by the progressivist but views the whole process as one of decline rather than of advancement. Cultural Primitivism, on the other hand, is an ahistorical doctrine; its adherents simply glorify the simple life and those who lead it without necessarily suggesting that this was the original human condition.[6] This was a perspective embodied in the ancient world by Diogenes,[7] and in the modern world by Thoreau.[8] Historical Primitivism and Cultural Primitivism are closely intertwined doctrines and express a common discontent with the existing human condition, but they had somewhat different origins and have also had different histories, as will be apparent in later discussion.[9]

---

3. For discussion, see esp. Lois Whitney, *Primitivism and the Idea of Progress* (Baltimore, 1934), pp. 137–167.
4. Cf., for example, Oleg Glebov and John Crowfoot, eds., *The Soviet Empire: its Nations Speak Out* (Chur, 1989), pp. 150–152.
5. *Primitivism in Antiquity*, pp. 1–22
6. For extended discussion of the various kinds of Primitivism, see ibid.
7. See ibid., pp. 127–130.
8. Henry D. Thoreau, *Walden* (Boston, 1854).
9. See also Arthur O. Lovejoy in Whitney, *Primitivism and the Idea of Progress*, pp. xii–xv.

To the two major categories distinguished by Lovejoy and Boas we can add a third, which I will call Paternal Primitivism. The admiration of the paternal primitivist is not for the institutions of primitive culture but for the supposedly pure and noble character of Primitive Man himself. This is, in particular, the doctrine that finds expression in the persona of the Noble Savage, to whom we will return in a moment. Unlike the two forms of Primitivism previously discussed, Paternal Primitivism can be and often is blended with Progressivism, for it is quite possible to regret the lost childhood innocence of Mankind while at the same time recognizing that the loss was inevitable. We will find this attitude especially prevalent among New World primitivists.

It is worthwhile to distinguish also between what I will call Idyllic Primitivism and Heroic Primitivism. The idyllic perspective imagines a primitive world of peace and harmony, while the heroic pictures a world torn by the conflict of mighty, opposing forces. In Greek philosophy, for example, Idyllic Primitivism is represented by the image of the blameless Ethiopian, while Heroic Primitivism is represented in the Homeric epics. Idyllic Primitivism has been and is much more influential in anthropological thinking than is Heroic Primitivism, and it will mainly concern us in the present chapter. As we will see in Chapter 6, however, Heroic Primitivism played an important role of the development of German Idealist philosophy.

Thus, while the primitivist generally prefers the Other to ourselves, the moral implications of this can be rather ambiguous. As Lovejoy and Boas observe, "Equalitarians, communists, philosophical anarchists, pacifists, insurgents against existing moral codes, including those of sexual relations, vegetarians, to whom may be added deists, the propagandists of 'natural religion'... all these have sought and, as they believed, found a sanction for their preachments... in the supposed example of primeval man or of living savages."[10] In the present-day world, environmental conservationists, feminists, animal-rights activists, and a good many others could be added to the list.

Primitivism is not precisely the same as Degenerationism, though the two doctrines share a similar philosophic outlook as regards the corrupt state of Mankind. But degenerationists may measure the human decline from any earlier point in time, recent or remote. For most Renaissance scholars, the Golden Age was represented by classical antiquity, whereas genuine primitives were regarded as nothing more than exotic human fauna. However, earlier medieval Degenerationism (like some early Greek Degenerationism) measured man's decline all the way back to a pristine utopia at the beginning of the world.

10. Lovejoy and Boas, *Primitivism in Antiquity*, p. 16.

Primitivism, at least in modern times, has been mainly a commitment of the heart rather than of the head. As such, it has found much fuller expression in poetry and fiction than it has in works of scholarship, where it is apt to be a kind of philosophical undercurrent rather than an overt doctrine. We have no difficulty in identifying poets like Wordsworth, writers like D.H. Lawrence, and philosophers like Rousseau as unabashed primitivists. The most that can be said of most historians and ethnographers, however, is that their work shows primitivistic tendencies or implications, without suggesting that the authors were out-and-out primitivists. For all that, Primitivism has been a powerful philosophical undercurrent, at least in American anthropology, throughout the twentieth century, and remains so today.

The doctrine and its variants

HISTORICAL CONTEXTS

If Progressivism is an optimistic doctrine of self-congratulation, Primitivism is just as conspicuously a pessimistic doctrine, and frequently a form of self-castigation. It says of the present age, "This is not as it should be." Rarely content merely to extol the virtues of the primitive Other, the primitivist takes the opportunity at the same time to condemn the corruption of his/her own time and place. The Primitive becomes the yardstick by which one measures one's own unworthiness; one's fall from grace. Not surprisingly, this is a doctrine that flourishes in times of doubt and uncertainty. In Hellenistic Greece it arose after the fall of the city-states; in eighteenth-century Europe it arose as a backlash against the monumental confidence of Enlightenment rationalism; in present-day America it is conspicuously a reaction against the self-confident hubris of the post-World War II era, and an evidence of the troubled times in which we now live.

Although there are hints of it elsewhere, Primitivism, like Progressivism, is mainly a Western philosophical doctrine. The peculiarly Western form actually combines two more general ideologies, Puritanism and nature-love, which in one guise or another have been present in many civilizations. It is only in the West, however, that the two have consistently been blended, from Greek times onward. In China, to cite a counterexample, we find nature-love expressed in painting and poetry, and Puritanism in the doctrines of Taoism and Buddhism, but the two are quite separate traditions.

Western Primitivism, then, can be seen as a kind of vicarious Puritanism, which allows us to celebrate the simple, virtuous life without having to emulate it. The odd individual who does indeed try to emulate the primitive in his or her personal life, like Diogenes in antiquity or Thoreau in the more recent past, is looked upon even by his fellow primitivists as "odd" indeed. Primitivism, in short, is one of those doctrines of vicarious salvation and vicarious atonement that are distinctive features of Western ideology.

The Noble Savage

Since earliest times, the primitivist ideal has found embodiment in the persona of the Noble Savage: one of the most enduring, and endearing, inventions of the human imagination.[11] As a literary figure he is as old as the Scythians of Herodotus,[12] and as modern as the Lakotas in the film *Dances with Wolves.* Indeed, the two are hardly to be distinguished, so similar are the characters and the virtues attributed to them. Kevin Costner, the producer of *Dances with Wolves,* surely owed far more of his inspiration to Herodotus and Seneca than he did to any ethnographic source.

The Noble Savage is a compendium of all that is best in Man, physically, mentally, and spiritually. Physically he is hardy, brave, and capable of extraordinary feats of self-denial; mentally he has a heightened aesthetic sensitivity and a love of nature and of harmony;[13] morally he is benevolent and generous.[14] He is also, either by reason or by instinct, a conservationist and ecologist, appreciating his place in the grand scheme of nature and taking no more from it than his immediate needs require.[15] Unhappily, however, his qualities of physical hardihood are not matched by a similar toughness of mind. The Noble Savage of imagination is all too easily corrupted by the temptations of the civilized life and its luxuries, when the opportunity is presented, and is noble no longer. His supposed devotion to nature and to conservation is, it would seem, a rather fragile commitment; he is easily lured from the path of righteousness on which nature placed him. He has, in sum, the mind of a child in the body of a warrior.

The Noble Savage is sometimes a dweller in an admittedly mythical land, such as the Isles of the Blest or the Land of the Houyhnhnms.[16] He gains rhetorical power, however, when he can be placed in a terrestrial context and thus identified as a fellow mortal. The Greeks regularly locat-

11. For extended discussion of the concept, see Lovejoy and Boas, *Primitivism in Antiquity,* pp. 287–367, and Hoxie N. Fairchild, *The Noble Savage* (New York, 1928).
12. See Lovejoy and Boas, *Primitivism in Antiquity,* pp. 321–322.
13. On this point see especially Whitney, *Primitivism and the Idea of Progress,* pp. 91–136.
14. Ibid., pp. 82–90
15. See especially Bell, *Primitivism,* pp. 7–31.
16. Lovejoy and Boas, *Primitivism in Antiquity,* pp. 290–303.

ed him at the outermost margins of the known world: an Aethiopian or a Scythian or a Hyperborean.[17] Above all, it was the Scythian who represented the primitive ideal to ancient thinkers: the list of Greek and Roman writers who celebrated his simple, noble virtues reads almost like a roll-call of the great thinkers of antiquity: Homer, Herodotus, Aeschylus, Aristophanes, Strabo, Cicero, Seneca, Horace, and Virgil, to name but a few.[18]

Historical contexts

The Noble Savage pretty much went into hiding during the Middle Ages, when non-Christians were seen either as unconverted pagans or, worse, as infidel heathens, both of whom were condemned to damnation.[19] The Noble Savage made a somewhat hesitant reappearance during the Renaissance,[20] and then rose to his fullest glory after the discovery of America. Within a century of the discovery, the Native American emerged in the European imagination as the quintessential Noble Savage: the hero not only of philosophical musings but of countless plays, novels, poems, and even operas extolling his pure, uncorrupted virtues.[21] His fortunes have waxed and waned in later centuries, according to the general optimism or pessimism of the times; at the moment of this writing he seems to be making a very strong comeback after two generations of neglect. Very occasionally the Red Man has had to share the Noble Savage role with Polynesians and other putative primitives, but he continues to enjoy pride of place as the most perfect exemplar of the type.

PRIMITIVISM IN ANTIQUITY

The earliest clearly recognizable example of Primitivism that has come down to us is the Garden of Eden myth. There are a few other hints of it in the Old Testament, as when the Hebrew prophets extolled the simpler virtues of the nomadic past, before the people settled in Canaan and were corrupted by the luxuries of sedentary life.[22] There are suggestions of Primitivism also in some very early Hindu philosophy.[23] As usual, however, it was the Greeks who gave the doctrine its fullest and most articulate expression in antiquity; indeed, Primitivism is a recurrent theme throughout the

17. Ibid., pp. 304–367.
18. Ibid., pp. 315–344.
19. According to the Athanasian Creed; see *Contra Gentes and De Incarnatione*, trans. and ed. Robert W. Thompson (Oxford, 1971).
20. Cf. Fairchild, *Noble Savage*, p. 3.
21. See Whitney, *Primitivism and the Idea of Progress*; Fairchild, *Noble Savage*; Bell, *Primitivism*, p. 79; and Roy H. Pearce, *Savagism and Civilization* (Berkeley, Calif., 1988), pp. 169–236.
22. W. F. Albright in Lovejoy and Boas, *Primitivism in Antiquity*, pp. 429–431.
23. P.-E. Dumont in Lovejoy and Boas, *Primitivism in Antiquity*, p. 445.

history of Greek philosophy. Pessimists that they mostly were, the Greek thinkers were much more drawn to Primitivism or to cyclical theories of history than they were to Progressivism.

Historical Primitivism and Cultural Primitivism were fairly distinct currents in Greek and Roman thought. Historical Primitivism was mainly a literary and mythological tradition: it was expressed in fables telling of man's degeneration from an earlier Golden Age.[24] It is doubtful if any of the authors, at least after Homer and Hesiod, regarded these as in any sense historical. It may be noted too that while the theme of the fables was strongly degenerationist, it was not always strictly primitivist. The Golden Age was seen as a morally purer time, but not always as a more primitive one in any technical sense.

There are nevertheless a few surviving fragments from antiquity that offer a nonmythological and supposedly naturalistic picture of prehistory as a simpler and happier time. Outstanding among them is the *Life of Greece* of the late fourth century historian Dicaearchus.[25] He "dwelt upon the physical and moral superiority of primitive men and suggested two psychological roots of the evils of civilization, which were to be made much of by later, and especially by modern, writers: (a) a multiplication of desires which led... to the pursuit of goods not needful for happiness, and to mutual conflict; and (b) the craving for distinction."[26] Other ancient writers who reflected a degree of naturalistic as opposed to a mythological Historical Primitivism were Tacitus and Pausanias.[27]

Cultural Primitivism (as well as Paternal Primitivism) found expression mainly in Greek ethnography: in the admiring pictures of the Aethiopians, the Hyperboreans, the Arcadians, the Albanians, the Illyrians, the Germans, the Hebrideans, and especially the Scythians that were painted by a truly extraordinary host of writers.[28] Almost invariably, the virtues of these peoples were contrasted with the sorry state of contemporary Greek or Roman society. For the most part, however, the writers did not suggest that the happy primitives represented the survival of an earlier and happier stage in the prehistory of their own societies.

The quintessential primitivists of the Hellenic period were undoubtedly the Cynics, who not only venerated the primitive life but sought actively to lead it, as exemplified in the well-known case of Diogenes.[29] As Lovejoy

24. See Lovejoy and Boas, *Primitivism in Antiquity*, pp. 23–102.
25. See ibid., pp. 93–96.
26. Ibid., p. 93.
27. Ibid., pp. 97–98.
28. Ibid., pp. 303–367.
29. Ibid., pp. 127–130.

and Boas have observed, "The Cynic ethics may be said to reduce... almost wholly to primitivism. Cynicism was the first and most vigorous revolt of the civilized against civilization in nearly all its essentials...."[30] Later the doctrine passed on to the Stoics, whose numbers included both historical and cultural primitivists. They were less personally committed to the simple life than were the Cynics, but were even more philosophically doctrinaire in their espousal of Primitivism.[31]

Primitivism in antiquity

The outstanding spokesman for Stoic Primitivism was the Roman moralist Seneca (first century A.D.). In his *Moral Epistles*

> Most of the usual elements of the eulogy of the state of nature are present, and receive... their most rhetorical elaboration in ancient literature: the emphasis on the physical superiority of primitive men, on the advantages they gained from having no arts, on their communism. Both the soft and hard aspects of their life are dwelt upon; it was at once easy and austere.[32]

The last significant primitivist in antiquity may have been Plutarch (first to second centuries A.D.), who argued not only for the superiority of primitive over civilized man, but for the superiority of animals over men in general.[33]

MEDIEVAL PRIMITIVISM

The Christian theology of the Middle Ages did not provide a fertile ground for Primitivism, at least in its classical forms. According to church doctrine, unconverted pagans were as surely damned as were heretic Muslims, and therefore could hardly be held up to admiration. Even the Scythians, the quintessential Noble Savages of antiquity, were redefined by medieval thinkers as cruel and evil savages.[34] Nevertheless, a certain kind of Historical Primitivism could still find expression in speculations about the original human condition, focused now exclusively on the Garden of Eden myth.

The Garden of Eden was indeed a source of continual fascination to medieval theologians for more than a thousand years, since the brief and

---

30. Ibid., p. 118.
31. Ibid., pp. 260–286.
32. Ibid., p. 263.
33. Ibid., pp. 403–420.
34. Cf. George Boas, *Essays on Primitivism and Related Ideas in the Middle Ages* (Baltimore, 1948), pp. 134–136.

ambiguous biblical depiction left room for a variety of conflicting interpretations.[35] The original character of Adam, the true symbolic significance of the Tree of Knowledge, and the moral implications of the Fall, were all subject to prolonged and heated debate. Was Adam an ignorant and spoiled child of God, a Noble Savage, or a man fully imbued with divine wisdom that was subsequently lost? Was the knowledge of Good and Evil something that man could and should have lived forever without, or was it a fruit that he was inevitably and necessarily destined to taste sooner or later? Did the Fall represent a loss or a gain in overall human wisdom? One can see in these debates a kind of symbolic deflection of the immemorial issue between progressivists and primitivists: does the Primitive (i.e. Eden) represent a kind of idyllic childhood that mankind must, nevertheless, necessarily outgrow if it is to survive, or does it represent the way we were intended always to live?

Apart from the Garden of Eden myth, Mankind's vicarious yearning for a simpler and purer world found its outlet in utopias and arcadias of the imagination, continuing a tradition that was already well developed in Greek times. "Atlantis, the Hesperides, and Avalon are fundamentally the same place," as Fairchild has written.[36] "Wits might call it the 'land of cookery,' but to most men of the Middle Ages it was the Land of the Blest. Indeed, this locality, originally pagan, became confused with the Earthly Paradise."[37]

Paradoxically, while the Middle Ages provided limited scope for philosophic and speculative Primitivism, they witnessed an unprecedented flourishing of personal and practical Primitivism in the ascetic and monastic movements. Personal asceticism was already a common practice of the Cynics and Stoics of late antiquity, but it found a new legitimation in the Christian doctrine of otherworldliness.[38] There was a fairly clear continuum of development from pagan to Christian asceticism, and the simple woolen gown assumed by the earliest Egyptian ascetics was in fact the traditional philosopher's gown of the Cynics.[39] One popular legend even pictured a friendship between Seneca and St. Paul, thus providing a legitimizing link between pagan and Christian ascetic doctrines.[40]

Another aspect of medieval Primitivism that shows a clear continuity from earlier times is its anti-intellectualism: the disparagement of both art

35. Ibid., esp. pp. 15–86.
36. *Noble Savage*, p. 6.
37. Ibid.
38. Cf. Boas, *Primitivism in the Middle Ages*, pp. 87–128.
39. Ibid., p. 105.
40. Ibid.

and science as being vain and worldly. This was to find perhaps its most articulate expression in the encyclical *De contemptu mundi* of Pope Innocent III (early thirteenth century). "Let scholars scrutinize, let them investigate the heights of heaven, the stretches of the earth, the depths of the sea, and let them dispute over each particular, and explore whole subjects, let them spend their time in learning and teaching. For what shall they discover from this occupation but labor and pain and affliction of spirit?"[41] Like Diogenes a millennium and a half earlier, the Pope argued not so much that the arts and sciences are contrary to God's will but that they are without practical value.[42]

EARLY MODERN PRIMITIVISM

As we have just seen, both Progressivism and Primitivism flourished in classical antiquity, when they were consciously opposed doctrines. In the Middle Ages both were superseded to a considerable extent by Christian salvationism, and both revived in the early modern period. However, their dialectical relationship has rarely again been as clearcut as it was in Greek and Roman times. Modern Primitivism is largely a doctrine of the heart rather than of the head, and it has found expression much more often in literature than in philosophy or, latterly, in social science. This does not mean however that Primitivism has not been a major influence within anthropology, for anthropologists are influenced by literary as well as scholarly currents, and they are apt to speak from the heart just as often as from the head.

Medieval and early modern Arcadianism

In the Middle Ages, arcadias of the imagination flourished precisely because Christian doctrine did not permit the identification of any actual living peoples as Noble Savages. However, the deficiency of an ethnographic Noble Savage was remedied, for many romantics, with the discovery of the New World. "The learned and the popular, the Christian and the pagan, traditions were reconciled by the discovery of America. Did not the newly-discovered island or continent lie both eastward and westward? And did not the bounty and beauty of that land equal all that was ever said or sung of the Blessed Isles? 'I am convinced,' wrote Columbus, 'that there is the terrestrial paradise.'"[43] But early ethnographic accounts of the Indi-

41. Quoted from ibid., p. 127.
42. Ibid., p. 127.
43. Fairchild, *Noble Savage*, p. 6

ans were by no means wholly favorable; indeed they were increasingly less so as detailed information found its way back to Europe.[44] As a result, many romantic idealists continued to prefer imagined arcadias to supposedly real ones, and the tradition of Arcadianism persisted well into the eighteenth century, as for example in Swift's *Voyage to the Country of the Houyhnhnms* (1727).

Even works that purported to depict Native American life were often based much more on the arcadian tradition than they were on ethnographic reality. The authors of romantic fiction merely used America as a setting for arcadian romances in the same way that Mozart used Egypt as a setting for *The Magic Flute*, without bothering about the realities of Egyptian culture. In keeping with the general tradition of arcadian literature, there was a notable preference for sylvan settings: either the woodlands of eastern North American or the forests of Brazil. For their part, the primitivist philosophers merely introduced the American Native as a foil for the criticism of contemporary society; they were therefore obliged to portray him as the quintessential Noble Savage, and were untroubled by ethnographic reality.

In any case the discovery of the New World provided new and vastly enlarged scope for the doctrine of Primitivism, for those who were not too scrupulous of ethnographic detail. From the moment of the discovery we can trace several different strains of primitivistic thought, which tended to wax and wane more or less concurrently. We have, as before, to distinguish between Historical Primitivism, Cultural Primitivism, and Paternal Primitivism, but we have in addition to recognize several different bodies of primitivistic literature: in ethnography, in philosophy, and in fiction. All were relatively muted in the first centuries after the conquest of America, swelled to enormous prominence during the Romantic Era of the late eighteenth and early nineteenth centuries, subsided again during the Victorian era, and are conspicuously reviving in the later twentieth century.

Primitivist ethnography

The discovery of the Americas created, on the part of educated Europeans, a seemingly insatiable demand for information about the new lands and peoples. That demand gave rise, in the following two centuries, to a prodigious body of ethnographic and pseudo-ethnographic literature, which will occupy us at length in Chapter 5. Here we need only notice the thread of Primitivism that, from the beginning, ran through the published de-

44. See esp. Benjamin Bissell, *The American Indian in English Literature of the Eighteenth Century*, pp. 5–7. *Yale Studies in English*, vol. LXVIII (1925).

scriptions of the American Indians. We have already noted the professed admiration of Columbus, and closely similar sentiments can be found in the discovery narratives of Champlain,[45] Hawkins, Drake, Raleigh,[46] and Captain John Smith.[47] All of them spoke in praise of the simple virtues, the goodwill and the generosity of the Indians, even while devising schemes to take every possible advantage of them. These individuals had, of course, a certain vested interest in promoting colonization; moreover, their portrayals of the Indian were not based on anything like profound ethnographic knowledge. During the seventeenth century, as permanent settlements proliferated on the newly discovered shores, ethnographic accounts became increasingly detailed but also much less romanticized. Indeed there was a growing emphasis on Indian barbarity, which was to find lurid expression in the enormously popular captivity tales.[48]

As in many later ages, the primary defenders, and professed admirers, of the Indians were missionaries. First and most outstanding among them was Bartolomé de Las Casas, whose *Breuisima Relación de la Destruyción de las Indias* was first published in 1539, and subsequently was translated into many European languages. In it, the author presented the classic depiction of the Indian as a simple child of nature. Subsequent translations of Las Casas' work into French and English were to have a profound effect on romantic literature in the seventeenth century; this was especially true of the English translation entitled *Tears of the Indians,* published in 1636.[49] Sentiments like those of Las Casas were also expressed by a number of the French Jesuits who served in Canada, and whose annual reports to Paris were published in the *Jesuit Relations* between 1601 and 1791.[50] Outstanding among them were Paul Le Jeune (1634), Jacques Marquette (1673), and Joseph Lafitau (1724).[51]

A measure of ethnographic primitivism can be found also in the work of at least a few early travelers and settlers in the New World. Among them may be mentioned Cadwallader Colden, whose *History of the Five Indian Nations* was published in 1747; James Adair, who published a *History of the American Indians* in 1775, and especially Jonathan Carver, author of the

45. Cf. Margaret Mead and Ruth Bunzel, eds., *The Golden Age of American Anthropology* (New York, 1960), pp. 29–34.

46. Cf. Fairchild, *Noble Savage,* pp. 12–15.

47. *Generall Historie of Virginia, New England, and the Summer Isles* (London, 1624).

48. See Bissell, *American Indian in English Literature,* pp. 5–7.

49. See esp. Fairchild, *Noble Savage,* pp. 120, 148, 156–158, 168, 171–172.

50. Cf., for example, Bissell, *American Indian in English Literature,* pp. 22, 42.

51. For Le Jeune, see R. G. Thwaites, ed., *The Jesuit Relations and Allied Documents 1610–1791* (Cleveland, 1897), vol. 6, pp. 21–23, 163–173; for Marquette, see Ibid., vol. 59, pp. 125–135; for Lafitau, see Joseph Lafitau, *Customs of the American Indians Compared with the Customs of Primitive Times,* trans. and ed. William N. Fenton and Elizabeth L. Moore (Toronto, 1974).

very influential *Travels through the Interior Parts of North America* (1778–1779).[52] But perhaps the most overtly primitivistic work of the colonial era was the *Letters from an American Farmer,* published by J. Hector Crevècoeur in 1782. The author was, as Fairchild observes, "at the same time one of the first real Americans, and a Frenchman steeped in the philosophy of nature."[53] At one time during his American residence he actually contemplated joining an Indian tribe but hesitated for the sake of his children, for "those who experience the savage life in childhood are never willing to return to civilization."[54] In the same romantic vein was William Bartram's *Travels through North and South Carolina, Georgia, East and West Florida, and the Cherokee Country* (1791). Bartram stands out among the early ethnographic primitivists because he was one of the few who idealized not only the character of the Indian but the social and political institutions of Indian society itself.[55] Worth mentioning also is John Davis's *Travels of Four Years and Half in the United States of America* (1803), in which the author stated that "The *Indians* of *America* want only a historian who would measure them by *Roman* ideals, to equal in bravery and magnanimity the proud masters of the world."[56]

Ethnographic Primitivism in the age of exploration was not wholly confined to the Americas. The publication in 1773 of *Hawkesworth's Voyages,* a compilation based on the journals of Captain Cook and two of his associates, did much to establish the Polynesian as a Noble Savage, in competition with the Native American.[57] A little later, George Keate's *Account of the Pelew Islands* (1788) did the same for the Micronesian.[58] The Primitivism and romanticism so evident in both these works is not to be found in the original travel journals on which they were based; it was a romantic touch added in each case by the compiler and editor.[59] Both works immediately became great favorites among popular writers, inspiring a large number of poems and novels.[60]

---

52. See esp. Fairchild, *Noble Savage,* pp. 97–100. For extended discussion of Carver's influence on subsequent European thinking, see also Daniel E. Williams in Christian Feest, ed., *Indians and Europe* (Aachen, 1989), pp. 195–214.
53. Fairchild, *Noble Savage,* p. 100. For discussion of Crevècoeur, see also Bissell, *American Indian in English Literature,* pp. 46–48.
54. Fairchild, *Noble Savage,* p. 101. In a later work, published in 1801, Crevècoeur almost completely repudiated the Primitivism and the admiration for the Indian expressed in the *Letters.* See Ibid., p. 103.
55. See Bissell, *American Indian in English Literature,* pp. 21–22, 46–48.
56. Quoted from Whitney, *Primitivism and the Idea of Progress,* pp. 110–111.
57. See Fairchild, *Noble Savage,* pp. 104–112.
58. Ibid., pp. 112–117.
59. Ibid., pp. 105–112.
60. Cf. Whitney, *Primitivism and the Idea of Progress,* pp. 113–118.

A curious subclass of "ethnographic" literature–a kind of "reverse ethnography"–is represented by those documents that purport to record the impressions of Native American visitors to Europe. They belong to a larger genre, usually called "Letters of a Foreign Visitor," that was popular throughout the eighteenth century. Most examples were supposedly from Oriental visitors, but not a few were attributed to North American Indians, who indeed were brought to Europe for exhibition in considerable numbers from the time of Columbus onward. Some of the letters were wholly fictitious; others were based upon real visits by real Indians. The authorship in all cases is suspect, however, because these documents almost without exception were satirical in tone and intent, contrasting some of the more obvious absurdities of eighteenth-century European civilization with the superior virtues of the primitive world. European law and religion were especially singled out for ridicule. The "letters," in short, belong to the general class of philosophic satire that flourished throughout the eighteenth century. Properly speaking their place is in the domain of primitivist philosophy rather than of ethnography.[61]

It is noteworthy that the early ethnographic primitivists, whether explorers, missionaries, or settlers, were for the most part paternal rather than cultural or historical primitivists. Few of them expressed any admiration for the institutions of native culture; their admiration was for the supposedly childlike simplicity of native character.

Primitivist philosophy

If many early explorers and missionaries were closet primitivists, it was the cloistered schoolmen of Europe who most firmly reestablished Primitivism as a philosophic doctrine. The Spanish reformer Juan Luis Vives was cited in the last chapter as a pioneer social evolutionist of the early modern era, but he was at the same time a pioneer primitivist, for he recognized that at a certain point in the evolutionary process, man had been corrupted by his own success. Vives in effect arrived at the same compromise between Progressivism and Primitivism as had Dicaearchus two millennia earlier: progress up to a certain point, and degeneration thereafter. The same idea was to be echoed by a great many later writers, and above all by Rousseau.

Vives's scenario of primitive society was a purely imagined one, but most of the primitivist philosophers who followed him drew upon ethnographic accounts of native peoples–especially the Native Americans–to

61. For a very full discussion of these, see Bissell, *American Indian in English Literature*, pp. 55–77.

buttress their arguments. The pioneering work in this genre may have been Montaigne's essay "On Cannibals," first published in 1580.[62] Montaigne claimed to derive his information from a "plain, simple fellow" who had dwelled for ten or twelve years in "Antarctic France" (usually identified as Brazil), and who was able to describe in detail the pure customs and the idyllic, not to say utopian government of the natives. Like any good primitivist, Montaigne lost no chance to contrast the pure simplicity of the natives with the corruption and depravity of his own society.[63]

Primitivism

The philosophic Primitivism of seventeenth and eighteenth centuries was closely associated with, or rather implicit in, the search for natural law, which will occupy us in the next chapter. It was widely accepted that primitive men, who lived close to nature, were more likely to be governed by natural law than were civilized men, whose greed and love of pleasure had carried them away from it. This idea may have found its earliest expression in Erasmus's *In Praise of Folly,* first published in 1511. "Erasmus... praised ignorance in words which almost startlingly suggest Rousseau."[64] *In Praise of Folly* was accorded no great importance by its author, but it became the most widely translated and most widely read of all Erasmus' works. Milton found it "in every one's hands" at Cambridge in 1628.[65] In the centuries that followed, its theme was to be repeated again and again both by primitivists and by seekers after natural law.

Thus Pierre Charron, in *Of Wisdom* (1607)[66] argued that the laws of nature may be more often "graciously followed" among peasants and "simple men" than among learned people, who have so far degenerated that they no longer readily recognize or follow what nature intended. Comparable sentiments can be found in the works of many English authors of the seventeenth century. Nathaniel Culverwel, for example, wrote in 1654 that "one only finds the recognition and the practice of the law of nature among men unspoiled by art."[67] Similar ideas were expressed, in one way or another, by Matthew Tindal, Benjamin Whichcote, Henry More, Joseph Glanvil, Samuel Clarke, and Lord Shaftesbury.[68] The work of Shaftesbury, in particular, became widely popular, and exerted a strong influence on a subsequent generation of primitivist and romantic thinkers.[69]

62. Michel de Montaigne, *Essays,* trans J. M. Cohen (Harmondsworth, 1958), pp. 105–119.
63. Ibid., pp. 113–114.
64. Quoted from Fairchild, *Noble Savage,* p. 18.
65. *Encyclopaedia Britannica,* vol. 8 (1958), p. 677.
66. English translation by Samson Lennard, 1615.
67. Quoted in Whitney, *Primitivism and the Idea of Progress,* p. 19.
68. See ibid., pp. 12–40.
69. Cf. ibid., p. 27; Frederick Copleston, *A History of Philosophy* (New York, 1985), Book Two, vol. V, p. 176.

These scholars were quite explicitly historical primitivists rather than paternal primitivists. They believed that the primitive societies of their own time gave evidence of how all human society had originally been organized, and therefore, by implication of what nature intended. It should not be supposed, however, that the worthy philosophers had any real ethnographic knowledge of primitive society, or felt any need of it. Notwithstanding the availability of evidence from the Americas, their primitive societies were pristine utopias of the imagination as surely as were the arcadias of the Middle Ages.[70]

Early Modern Primitivism

In the popular mind, philosophic Primitivism is inseparably linked to the name of Jean Jacques Rousseau. Yet his doctrine has been widely misunderstood, for he seems to have been much more often cited than read.[71] The important point to notice about Rousseau is that he was not a despairing social critic, like so many of the English romantics. He was on the contrary an idealistic reformer, as will be apparent to anyone who reads *The Social Contract* (1750) as well as the *Discourse on the Origin of Inequality* (1755). "Rousseau did not suggest a movement to destroy all the libraries and all the works of art in the world, to put to death or silence all the savants, to pull down the cities, and burn the ships. He was not a mere dreamer, and his Arcadia was no more than a Utopian ideal, by the light of which he conceived that the society of his own day might be corrected and transformed."[72]

Like several of the philosophers we have previously discussed, Rousseau came to his Primitivism from an interest in and a search for natural law. He shared with many predecessors the belief that natural law is most readily discoverable in living primitive societies, where it has not yet been overlaid with art and artifice. Yet his work had no more ethnographic foundation than had those of Charron and Culverwel. The *Discourse on the Origin of Inequality* is liberally sprinkled with references to Brazil, the Orinoco, and Canada, but they do not reflect any real research into the fairly extensive ethnographic literature available at the time.[73] Indeed, Rousseau made it plain at the outset of the *Discourse* that he was writing conjectural prehistory as surely as was his contemporary Turgot. "Let us begin, then, by setting aside all the facts, for they are irrelevant to the

70. In a later work, *An Account of European Settlements in America* (1757), Burke showed a substantial knowledge of American Indian ethnography, but the "natural society" envisioned in his earlier essay was a purely imagined one, not based on ethnographic accounts.

71. Cf. Irving Babbitt, *Rousseau and Romanticism* (New York and Boston, 1919); Fairchild, *Noble Savage*, pp. 120–139.

72. J. B. Bury, *The Idea of Progress* (New York, 1932), p. 182.

73. Cf. Bissell, *American Indian in English Literature*, p. 42.

problem. The investigations that may be made concerning this subject should not be taken as historical truths, but only as hypothetical and conditional reasonings, better suited to casting light on the nature of things than to showing their real origin...."[74]

Rousseau was as much a product of the French Enlightenment as were Turgot and Helvétius, and his philosophic vision was less different from theirs than is commonly supposed. Though certainly a primitivist, he was at the same time a would-be progressivist. The vision of primitive society that he idealized was not the "pure state of nature" but a society that had progressed far enough to develop definite institutions of kinship and territoriality, but without formal laws or government. It was at this juncture that progress had gone wrong, mainly through the introduction of agriculture and metallurgy, which had led to landed property rights and the occupational division of labor.[75] He honestly believed, at least in his earlier writings, that the evil effects of later civilizational developments could be overcome by enlightened education, and human progress could be set back on its proper course.

A decidedly eccentric primitivist philosopher was James Burnett, Lord Monboddo, whose multivolume *Antient Metaphysics* was published between 1779 and 1799.[76] He was a product of the Scottish Enlightenment, as Rousseau was of the French Enlightenment; like Rousseau he was a partial progressivist and at the same time was enamored of the simple virtues of primitive society. But Monboddo's admiration extended even to apes, which he found to be "gentle and affectionate, social by disposition, endowed with a capacity for 'intellect and science;' and to have a sense of justice and honor, of the decent and becoming in behavior. In fact, in the orang-utan, Monboddo finds the last existing specimen of the true primitive man."[77] Monboddo elsewhere discoursed on the virtues of going naked, and of living on a diet exclusively of raw vegetables, in emulation of the apes.[78]

In general, then, the philosophic primitivists shared with the ethnographic primitivists an interest in natural law. However, their Primitivism differed from that of the ethnographers in two important respects. First, they were both historical and cultural primitivists, but for the most part

74. Lowell Bair, trans, *The Essential Rousseau* (New York, 1975), p. 144.

75. Bury, *Idea of Progress*, pp. 180–181.

76. For discussion, see esp. Bissell, *American Indian in English Literature*, pp. 44–46, and Whitney, *Primitivism and the Idea of Progress*, pp. 281–289.

77. Quoted from Whitney, *Primitivism and the Idea of Progress*, p. 282. The author apparently included chimpanzees and gorillas in his category of "Orang Outang."

78. Bissell, *American Indian in English Literature*, p. 45.

they were not paternal primitivists. On one hand they admired the institutions of primitive culture (as they imagined them), and also believed that these represented the modern-day survivals of man's earliest condition; on the other hand they were not particularly admirers of the character of the Noble Savage. Second, their Primitivism was usually a rhetorical, and occasionally a satirical, device, and as such had no real need of a solid ethnographic foundation.

Early Modern Primitivism

Primitivist literature

I am as free as nature first made man,
Ere the base laws of servitude began,
When wild in woods the noble savage ran.

Those lines, from Dryden's *Conquest of Granada* (1669), represent what is believed to be the earliest appearance of the Noble Savage under that name, although he had already been around in other guises since remote antiquity.[79] Dryden's verse signalizes a momentous new development: the appearance of Primitivism as a major theme in poetry, drama, and fiction. Increasingly, in the centuries that followed, Primitivism was to find expression in those media rather than in prose works of philosophy or ethnography. Indeed poetic and fictional Primitivism became mainstays of the Romantic movement, which dominated the late eighteenth century and the first half of the nineteenth. The special and novel quality of Romantic Primitivism, as we will see, was its pervading sense of pathos: a regret for humanity's lost innocence.

THE ROMANTIC MOVEMENT

Popular usage identifies the Romantic era as a time of reaction against Enlightenment rationalism, beginning in the last quarter of the eighteenth century and extending to the middle of the nineteenth.[80] However, such lineal periodization oversimplifies a complex relationship. Romanticism was indeed a reaction against the excessive rationalism of the Enlightenment, but for that very reason it began to find expression concurrently with the Enlightenment itself, and it strongly affected such Enlightenment thinkers as Rousseau and Monboddo. In tracing the history of ideas, therefore, it seems better to speak of a Romantic movement, extending

79. Fairchild, *Noble Savage*, p. 29.
80. See for example R. B. Mowat, *The Romantic Age* (London, 1937).

over the whole of the eighteenth and the earlier nineteenth century, rather than confining discussion narrowly to the so-called Romantic Era.[81]

Primitivist thinking was a significant component of the Romantic movement, as Progressivism was of the Enlightenment, but it was by no means the only one. More broadly, there was a heavy emphasis on natural instincts and aesthetic sensibilities, in preference to dispassionate cerebration. "The romantic movement is characterized, as a whole, by the substitution of aesthetic for utilitarian standards," as Russell observes.[82] Not coincidentally, there was a renewed appreciation for the importance of religion, as we saw already in the discussion of nineteenth-century Progressivism.

Inevitably, Romanticism found its primary outlet not in didactic essays but in the more aesthetically expressive media of verse, fiction, drama, art, and music. To a large extent, Primitivism was carried along on this tide. It was in these circumstances that the Noble Savage of poetry and drama really came into his own as the primary embodiment of primitivist sentiment. In the process, his purported character underwent a subtle transformation, as required by the ethos of the times. While the savage of early modern and Enlightenment literature was commonly portrayed as a primitive rationalist, meeting the challenges of his time and circumstances in logically appropriate ways, the savage of the romanticists was above all a creature of heightened emotional and aesthetic sensibilities: an appreciator and lover of that great natural order of which he saw himself to be a part.[83] As we will see later, both of these visions of the Noble Savage have come down to us in twentieth-century anthropology, as legacies respectively of the Enlightenment and of Romanticism.

It would require several pages to enumerate the poems, novels, plays, and operas with American Indian themes that appeared in the eighteenth and nineteenth centuries. A lesser but still significant number of works were set in the South Seas, and a courageous few were set in Africa. Very occasionally the Laplander, the Scottish Highlander, and assorted European peasantries were also cast in the role of Noble Savage. While these works were, inevitably, somewhat varied in style and content, a very high proportion of them emphasized the contact and the contrast between the savage and the European as their main dramatic focus. The contrast was not invariably to the European's disadvantage; some of the novels, in par-

---

81. For a good discussion of the movement, see Bertrand Russell, *A History of Western Philosophy* (New York, 1945), pp. 675–684.
82. Ibid., p. 678.
83. For discussion, see esp. Whitney, *Primitivism and the Idea of Progress*, pp. 69–136.

ticular, were lurid, fictionalized captivity accounts that dwelt upon the barbarities of the Indians toward their captives. In a far greater number, however, the noble simplicity and aesthetic sensitivity of the native was set off against the greed and insensitivity of the European. It will be possible here only to notice a few of the most outstanding or influential examples of romantic primitivist literature.[84]

Drama and opera

In the late seventeenth and early eighteenth centuries the stage play, with or without music, was still the most popular fictional medium for most Europeans. Only gradually, in the course of the eighteenth century, did it yield supremacy to the novel. It is not surprising, then, that some of the earliest expressions of Romantic Primitivism were to be found in drama. Priority apparently belongs to William Davenant's opera, *The Cruelty of the Spaniards in Peru*, first performed in 1658.[85] It was followed within a decade by two plays attributed to Dryden: *The Indian Queen* (1664) and *The Indian Emperor* (1665), which also dealt with Spanish America.[86] These works, which were stimulated by the English translation of Las Casas's *Breuisima Relación* in 1656, were the precursors of a whole genre of "Peruvian" plays and operas as well as poems produced in the latter part of the eighteenth century. The dramatic theme of all these works was, of course, the contrast between the cruelty and cupidity of the Spaniards and the nobility and generosity of the Indians.[87]

Another play with a legitimate, if romanticized, historical basis was Robert Rogers's *Ponteach,* written in 1766 but never performed. It was based on Pontiac's Rebellion against the English colonists in 1763, of which the author was an actual observer, but the perspective is nevertheless wholly pro-Indian.[88] Other, purely fictional plays were similar in plot and theme to the more numerous novels of the period, which will be discussed later. *The Indians,* attributed to William Richardson (1790), has a

84. The works cited here are all in English; I have not attempted to survey the equally large literature of Romantic Primitivism in French and German. For German literature, see esp. Edith A. Runge, *Primitivism and Related Ideas in Sturm und Drang Literature* (Baltimore, 1946). Runge makes the important point that eighteenth century German Primitivism was almost purely philosophic rather than ethnographic; not an idealization of any early stage of society or of living primitives, but simply a celebration of the irrational in human nature.

85. See Bissell, *American Indian in English Literature*, pp. 118–121.

86. Ibid., pp. 121–127.

87. For additional discussion, see ibid., pp. 154–181, and Whitney, *Primitivism and the Idea of Progress*, pp. 79–82.

88. See Bissell, *American Indian in English Literature*, pp. 133–137.

plot reminiscent of *Romeo and Juliet,* but according to Bissell is "of importance for its many realistic details of Indian life, combined with a sentimental idealization of the characters...."[89]

Primitivist operas did not differ significantly in theme or construction from the nonmusical dramas.[90] During the seventeenth and eighteenth centuries there were at least two operas dealing with the Spanish conquests in Peru and Mexico,[91] and one based on the endlessly popular tale of Inkle and Yarico,[92] to be discussed in a moment. Worthy of special note, however, is John Gay's *Polly,* a sequel to his much better known *Beggar's Opera.*[93] In the sequel, the scandalous Polly Peachum follows her lover Macheath to the West Indies, falls among Indians, and in the end is redeemed to virtue by her admiration for their simple, honest ways and by her love for Cawwawkee, the chief's son, whose nobility throughout the opera is contrasted with the rascality of Macheath.[94] The piece however is, like its predecessor, essentially a spoof; one of the rare instances in which the primitivist motif is treated lightheartedly.

Novels

The archetypical primitivist novel was Aphra Behn's *Orinooko; or, the Royal Slave,* published at the astonishingly early date of 1688. As Bissell observes,

> the publication of this exotic romance in 1688 makes it antedate, by a number of years, not only the writings of Rousseau, but of the various philosophers and poets in whom critics are wont to discern the inception of the whole naturalistic movement... we have here, as has often been stated, a work which anticipates the fundamental doctrines of romanticism, preaches humanity and natural goodness, besides expressing other ideas and sentiments not current at the time, but destined to flourish about a century later....[95]

---

89. Ibid., p. 143. For synopses of the plot, see ibid., pp. 142–146, and Whitney, *Primitivism and the Idea of Progress,* pp. 118–122.
90. For a discussion of Indian depictions in opera, see Götz Corinth in *European Review of Native American Studies* 9, no. 1 (1995): 5–8.
91. See Bissell, *American Indian in English Literature,* pp. 118–121, 140–142.
92. Ibid., pp. 138–140.
93. The work was written in 1728 but, because of suppression by the Lord Chamberlain, was not performed until 1777.
94. For fuller discussion, see Bissell, *American Indian in English Literature,* pp. 127–130.
95. Ibid., p. 78.

Orinooko, the hero of the piece, is actually a native African, enslaved and brought to South America where most of the action is laid. Noble Indians also figure prominently as background characters in the story. Mrs. Behn's novel served as inspiration for a great many later ones–not a few of them by women–as well as for a drama produced by Southerne in 1696.[96]

After *Orinooko* only one or two other primitivist novels were published in English before the middle of the eighteenth century. Thereafter, however, they appeared in a steady stream until well into the following century. As always, the great majority were set wholly or partially in America, and involved the contact and conflict between Indians and Whites. These works exhibited the usual hallmarks of eighteenth century fiction: convoluted plots and subplots, sudden and coincidental appearances and disappearances, fair damsels abducted and rescued (but always, miraculously, spared "a fate worse than death"), a rich cast of major and minor characters, and a great deal of implicit or explicit moralizing on the defects (or occasionally on the virtues) of civilization. A number of the novelists adopted the epistolary format; that is, their works are in the form of letters sent by settlers in America to their kin back in England.[97]

The literary stock-in-trade of a great many of the novels is the captivity or, less commonly, the voluntary residence of a European among the Indians. But while the genuine captivity tales of the period (to be discussed in Chapter 5) are mostly horror stories, in the fictional captivities the reverse is more often true: the prisoner is treated with kindness and respect, and is made to see the superior virtues of Indian character in contrast to that of the Europeans, including (sometimes) himself. An interesting switch on this theme is the "reverse captivity," in which a native is taken to Europe, is disgusted by his adventures and encounters there, and in the end escapes happily back to his pristine wilderness. The captivity and the reverse captivity served equally well to allow the authors to philosophize on the contrast between primitive and civilized man.

The anonymous *Adventures of Emmera; or, The Fair American,* published at Dublin in 1767, may serve to epitomize the eighteenth-century primitivist novel. The plot has been summarized by Fairchild:

> Emmera, the heroine, is reared in the wilderness near Lake Erie. Her father, a man with a past, detests the civilization from which he

96. For more extended discussion, see ibid., pp. 77–84, and Fairchild, *Noble Savage,* pp. 34–41.

97. For extended discussion of the novels, see Bissell, *American Indian in English Literature,* pp. 78–117.

> has fled, and hopes to form a community in which men can live according to the dictates of nature. But the father dies, and is forced to commit his daughter to the care of one Chetwyn, an English rascal of quality. Chetwyn tries to win the girl by a recital of the joys of civilized life, but Emmera... shrinks in horror from his account of European complexities. Colonel Forrester, an enemy of Chetwyn's, kidnaps her, but the redmen rescue her from her white seducer. Eventually, however, the heroine goes with Chetwyn to England, only to be horrified by the greed, cruelty, and injustice which surround her. The upshot of the matter is that Emmera and the reformed Chetwyn return to America, there to dwell happily and innocently in the wilds, with only the good Indians for company.[98]

Poetry

Inevitably, Romantic Primitivism attained its fullest and purest expression in verse. An especially popular poetic form comprised "the imaginary speeches of aged chieftains who dwell upon the simplicity and innocence of their people before the coming of the whites."[99] These works convey precisely the same pathos that a hundred years later was so eloquently captured on canvas in Fraser's celebrated painting, *The End of the Trail*, which shows a totally dejected and demoralized Indian sitting on an equally downcast horse. Some of the fictionalized speeches, in slightly altered form, have found their way into later literature as examples of supposedly genuine Indian oratory.[100]

Another popular theme was the dying Indian's stoic endurance under torture or misfortune, expressed in a death song or oration. At least half a dozen poems in this vein (three of them with the title *The Dying Indian*) appeared between 1792 and 1799.[101] Other common themes were the Indian's tenderness and steadfastness in love, his unswerving loyalty to his friends and people, his affection for the dead, and his bewilderment at the mysteries and seeming contradictions of Christianity.[102]

While the aforementioned poems were mostly fairly short, there were

98. Fairchild, *Noble Savage*, p. 94.
99. Bissell, *American Indian in English Literature*, pp. 205–206.
100. See for example Annette Rosenstiel, *Red & White* (New York, 1983), pp. 111–113, 125–126.
101. Bissell, *American Indian in English Literature*, pp. 183–189. For further discussion of this genre see Fairchild, *Noble Savage*, pp. 461–469, and Frank E. Farley, "The Dying Indian," *Kittredge Anniversary Papers* (Boston, 1913), pp. 251–260.
102. Bissell, *American Indian in English Literature*, pp. 190–202; Fairchild, *Noble Savage*, pp. 470–474.

also longer, narrative works on the Indians, and more particularly on the theme of Indian-White conflicts. Especially popular around the end of the eighteenth century were poems dealing with the Spanish conquests of Peru and of Mexico, sounding the same themes as did the "Peruvian" dramas that had already been popular for some time.

Perhaps the quintessential poetic expression of Primitivism is to be found in the affecting tale of the pure and simple Indian maiden Yariko, who is abused and finally deserted by her greedy and faithless European lover Inkle. The original source of the story–supposedly factual–was Richard Ligon's *True and Exact History of the Island of Barbadoes,* published in 1657.[103] It was repeated, with considerable elaboration, in a *Spectator* essay by Addison and Steele in 1712, and thence became the subject of more than a dozen poems and at least one opera over the next century. Yariko and Inkle are, obviously, perfect metaphors for the purity of Indian society and the corruption of European society, respectively.

A few poems were simply lyric or heroic depictions of Indian life, in which the contaminating European did not intrude. This genre included a few works by Wordsworth and Coleridge and a larger number by Southey,[104] but it reached its fullest development in the hands of the American romantics, whose work will be discussed in the next section.

ROMANTIC PRIMITIVISM IN AMERICA

It is a melancholy fact that Primitivism has never flourished on the frontier; that is, among persons in actual, day-to-day contact with natives. Not surprisingly, then, Romantic Primitivism did not achieve the same popularity in North America as it had in eighteenth and nineteenth century Europe. It was not wholly absent, for Euro-Americans were never immune to literary and philosophical influences from abroad. As Pearce observes, "Towards the end of the eighteenth century, budding American poets lined up, in a not very orderly fashion, either on the primitivistic or antiprimitivistic side. They pictured the Indians as distinguished upstanding warriors, now dead.... Or they pictured them in their sadistic mercilessness...."[105]

American Primitivism had to contend not only with the anti-Indian sentiment prevalent in the frontier districts, but also and more generally with the spirit of bumptious Progressivism that from the beginning was a

103. See Fairchild, *Noble Savage,* p. 82.

104. See ibid., pp. 172–228.

105. Pearce, *Savagism and Civilization,* pp. 178–179.

feature of American national character. Quoting again from Pearce:

> The specifically literary idea of the pitifully noble savage had to be accommodated to that larger idea of savagism which made possible not only pity but censure.... The literary history of the Indian in America is one in which the idea of savagism first compromised the idea of the noble savage and then absorbed and reconstituted it. What came into being in this reconstitution was the savage whom Americans had been seeking from the start, and he served them as they willed.[106]

The reconstituted savage of American Primitivism was the Vanishing Redman, who had been simple and noble in his time, but whose day was past. He must now, unfortunately but inevitably, bow before the inexorable march of progress and civilization. This idea was to find expression not only in primitivist literature, but equally in works of ethnography and history. It provided the motivation for much of the salvage ethnography that preoccupied both the Bureau of American Ethnology and the early Boasians, as we will observe in Chapters 5 and 6. The idea of the Vanishing Redman so fixed itself in the imagination of Americans that they were very slow to notice when Indians ceased to vanish, demographically speaking, after about 1890.

In literature, the tension between Primitivism and Progressivism was resolved in two ways. One was to leave the White Man out, and to portray the idyllic Indian world of the remote, prehistoric past. The other was to write adventure tales of Indian-White contact in which the actors on both sides were heroic. These two solutions are perfectly exemplified in two of the most famous works of American primitivist literature: the first in Longfellow's *Song of Hiawatha* (1855) and the second in Cooper's *Last of the Mohicans* (1826). In both cases the moral dilemma of the Primitive/Civilized conflict was removed.

In sum, the tenor of American primitivist literature was lyric or heroic; it was not philosophic. It is no accident that the works of the American romantics were frequently compared, by reviewers, not with those of Dryden or Southey but with those of Walter Scott.[107]

106. Ibid., p. 170.

107. Cf. William Charvat, *The Origins of American Critical Thought* (Philadelphia, 1936), p. 143.

Drama

In the early nineteenth century there was much earnest discussion about the need to develop an indigenous American literature, which would not simply emulate the classicist traditions of Europe. Among other things, it was frequently asserted that American literature should draw upon American historical materials.[108] This injunction seems to have been heeded especially by the primitivist playwrights, for nearly all of the American-produced dramas on Indian themes had some measure of historical basis. An especially popular theme was the story of Pocahontas, recounted in at least four plays produced between 1802 and 1848.[109] The backdrop in all cases was the contest between heroic Indians and equally heroic colonists, with the civilization and then the death of Pocahontas symbolizing the final, inevitable triumph of the latter.

Other dramas dealt with the lives of Pontiac and of Tecumseh.[110] Probably the most popular of all Indian dramas, however, was John Augustus Stone's *Metamora; or, the Last of the Wampanoags,* first performed in 1829.[111] It was one of a large number of dramas, novels, and poems that epitomized the Vanishing Redman theme by recounting the fate of the last member of this or that tribe; presumably they were all inspired by the enormous success of Fenimore Cooper's *Last of the Mohicans* in 1826. The Metamora of the title is better known to history as King Philip of King Philip's War (1675–76), and the story deals with his unsuccessful and ultimately disastrous war against the English, at the end of which he kills his wife and himself (the last Indian survivors) to prevent their enslavement. Pearce writes that "Stone wrote *Metamora* for Edwin Forrest, who specialized in noble savages of all sorts; and the title role became one of Forrest's favorites. It is probable that the popularity of the play is mainly responsible for the great number of like plays which followed it. There were some thirty-five in twenty years, mostly unpublished, mostly recorded as being well received."

108. For fuller discussion on this, see William Sedgwick in *Harvard Studies and Notes in Philology and Literature,* vol. XVII (1935), pp. 141–162, and John McCloskey in *Publications of the Modern Language Association of America,* vol. L (1935), pp. 262–273.

109. See Pearce, *Savagism and Civilization,* pp. 172–175.

110. Ibid., pp. 175–176.

111. See ibid., pp. 176–178. For dramatic purposes the author transferred Metamora from his native Pokanoket tribe to the Wampanoags, who really were supposed to be extinct in 1829. This device was fairly common in early "Indian" fiction.

Indian novels enjoyed at least as much popularity as did Indian dramas in nineteenth century, even though their idealized portrayal of the Indian often provoked sharp criticism from frontiersmen and from opponents of romanticism more generally.[112] But the content and theme of the novels was for the most part quite different from that of the dramas. The great majority of them had purely fictional settings, and their predominant theme might be summarized in the well-known words of Kipling: "East is East and West is West, and never the twain shall meet." The novels portrayed, in many different ways, the tragic consequences or the impossibility of culture-crossing: either of Whites trying to "go Indian," or of Indians trying to be civilized. By implication it was the duty of each race to stay in the niche to which nature or history had assigned it, implying also that it was the duty of the Indian ultimately to disappear.

Primitivism

A few examples may serve to illustrate the genre. In Maria Child's *Hobomok* (1824) a lonely and oppressed Puritan woman gives herself in marriage to a Noble Redman, but finds in the end that she must go back to her own people and he to his. In the anonymous *The Christian Indian* (1825), even the ennoblement of Christianity does not save the convert from corruption and degradation when he settles among the Whites. In Karl Postl's *Tokeah* (1829) the White heroine is reared among Indians but instinctively holds aloof from them, and is ultimately restored to civilization by a White lover. In Timothy Flint's *The Shoshonee Valley* good Whites who live in peace with the Indians are nevertheless caught up and destroyed in an Indian war provoked by their evil brethren. In Robert Strange's *Eoneguski* (1839) the title character, a Cherokee chief, befriends the Americans and fights alongside them in the War of 1812, but in the end he and his people become outcasts, driven west in the general Indian removal of the 1830s.[113]

The theme of "never the twain shall meet" was most fully and clearly developed in the short stories and novels of William Gilmore Simms. In *The Yemassee* (1835) the chief Sanutee disowns his son Occonestoga, who had gone over to the English and been corrupted and enslaved.[114] In *The Cassique of Kiawah* (1859) the son of a powerful chieftain is given as a kind of hostage to be brought up among the Whites, the secret hope being that

112. Cf. Charvat, *Origins of American Critical Thought*, pp. 143–144.

113. For additional detail, see Pearce, *Savagism and Civilization*, pp. 214–215.

114. Ibid., p. 217.

he will gain information that will later enable him to lead a surprise attack on them. But the son falls in love with the daughter of a colonist, and is torn between his old and his new loyalties. In the end he "discovers that he can have neither the love of his people nor the proprietor's daughter."[115]

All these works seem to reflect that propensity of the human mind that has been so much remarked by structuralists: the insistence on the maintenance of categorical boundaries.[116] The same inclination surely accounts for the sinister role so commonly assigned to the partly acculturated Indian, but even more to the half-breed, in American fiction.[117] The best-known example, among scores, is undoubtedly Injun Joe in *The Adventures of Tom Sawyer.*[118]

In view of prevailing American sentiment in the later nineteenth century, it is extraordinary to note how consistently antiassimilationist, at least by implication, were the novels of the earlier part of the century. It was suggested that the Indian should not and could not attempt to follow the White Man's ways; he was merely corrupted by civilization, and even by Christianity. The point is clearly made in M.C. Hodges's novel, *The Mestico* (1850): "[The Indians] were doubtless in their pristine state more entitled to the noble epithets which poesy has liberally bestowed, but in the contact with the whites, the savage unfortunately evinced an aptitude for the vicious teaching of the race of strangers. . . ."[119]

Yet this attitude does not seem to have been rooted in racial bias; it was sustained rather by the persisting ideal of the Noble Savage. It was the Indian's proper role to be Noble Savage or to be nothing. Not coincidentally, the antiassimilationism of the novels was mirrored in America's official Indian policy, which until the 1870s consistently emphasized the separation of Indians and Whites into physically distinct spheres, and the recognition of Indian sovereignty within their own sphere. Hodges's *The Mestico* was actually a novelized defense of the Indian Removal policy of the 1830s, which was part and parcel of the more general policy of Indian–White separation.

115. Ibid., p. 219.

116. See, among many other sources, Mary Douglas, *Purity and Danger* (London, 1966); id., *Natural Symbols* (Harmondsworth, 1970), pp. 173–201; Victor Turner, *The Forest of Symbols* (Ithaca, N.Y., 1967); and Edmund Leach in J.S. LaFontaine, ed., *The Interpretation of Ritual* (London, 1972), pp. 33–36.

117. For discussion, see esp. William J. Scheick, *The Half-Blood* (Lexington, Ky, 1979).

118. Mark Twain, *The Adventures of Tom Sawyer* (New York, 1876).

119. *The Mestico; or, The War-Path and its Incidents* (New York, 1850), pp. 55–56.

The American compromise between Primitivism and Progressivism found perfect expression in the work of Philip Freneau, the country's first major poet as well as a noted essayist and editor. He was a leading advocate of French Enlightenment ideals, a passionate supporter of the American Revolution, and at the same time an admirer of the Noble Redman, whom he celebrated in a number of poems published between 1772 and 1822. In one of his earliest poems, *The Indian Village* (1772), he described the idyllic and virtuous world of preconquest America, yet in another work of the same year he lauded *The Rising Glory of America* in his own time. *The Prophecy of King Tammany* (1789), probably his best known Indian poem, was also one of the first that clearly sounded the theme of the Vanishing Redman. Tammany (according to tradition, the first Indian to welcome William Penn to America) laments the fallen glory of his people, but also realizes the futility of Indian resistance to the advance of the white man. At the end of the poem he prepares his own funeral pyre:

Primitivism

Yes, yes,–I see our nation bends;
The gods no longer are our friends....

But in one of his last poems, published in 1822, Freneau showed that the tension between Primitivism and Progressivism was never really resolved. Called *On the Civilization of the Western Aboriginal Country,* the work began with a general philosophical consideration of the mutability of nature, including human nature, and concluded that the Indians are but another changeable form of unchanging matter. Later in the poem he enjoined civilized man to

Go, and convince the natives of the west
That *christian* morals are the first and best;

yet this was followed a few lines later by

Take all, through all, through nation, tribe, or clan,
The child of nature is the *better* man.

Freneau's last poem was similar to a great many others published in the same general period. These works were partly descriptive, partly historical, partly prophetic, and partly didactic.

> There is… a whole series of miscellaneous narrative and descriptive poems, ranging from the crude to the innocuously competent, which celebrate the death of the noble savage and the coming of civilization. The pattern of these poems is uniform enough to constitute a received way of imagining American relations with the Indians. The Indian is described for what he is, a noble savage. The coming of the white man is described for what it is, the introduction of agrarian civilization. And the Indian is shown dying or moving west, often with a vision of the great civilized life which is to come after him….[120]

The other accepted way of avoiding the Primitive/Civilized dilemma was, as we saw earlier, to leave civilized man out of the picture, and to describe only the pristine world of prehistory. This was the case in Freneau's *Indian Village,* but the genre was much more fully developed by poets a generation later. Indian poems with a strictly precontact setting included William Simmons's *Onea* (1820), Samuel Beach's *Escalala* of 1824 (although in this work the Mound Builders had to defend themselves against invading Norsemen), Isaac McClellan's *Fall of the Indian* (1830), and Henry Whiting's *Sannillac* (1831). But the Noble Prehistoric Redman surely reached his apogee in Longfellow's *The Song of Hiawatha* (1855).

Longfellow based his work on a thorough reading of the primitivist fiction as well as the ethnographic literature of his time; particularly on the monumental work of Henry Schoolcraft that will occupy us further in Chapter 5.[121] The plot was loosely based on a cycle of Chippewa myths recorded by Schoolcraft, but the hero was conflated with the Iroquois hero Hiawatha, the legendary founder of the League of the Iroquois, to heighten the dramatic possibilities of the narrative. In the poem, the hero, after undergoing hardships and travails, unites his warring people and ushers in a golden age of peace and plenty. What emerged was an authentic Indian hero refashioned for white rather than Indian tastes.[122] The work achieved such immediate popularity that it became required reading for generations of American schoolchildren, and it probably did more to keep alive the image of the Noble Redman than did any other work in the latter half of the nineteenth century.

120. Pearce, *Savagism and Civilization,* pp. 188–189.

121. *Information Respecting the History, Condition and Prospects of the Indian Tribes of the United States* (Philadelphia, 1854).

122. For discussion, see esp. Stith Thompson in *Proceedings of the Modern Language Association of America,* vol. XXXVIII (1922), pp. 128–143; also Pearce, *Savagism and Civilization,* pp. 191–194.

The plot of *Hiawatha,* following the parent myths, is laid almost entirely in the prehistoric era. Nevertheless the author felt it necessary to have Hiawatha live until the coming of the White Man, in order to foretell the vanishing of the Red Man. "One day the missionaries come and Hiawatha, according to Longfellow's understanding of the fate of the American noble savage, must welcome them. As they sleep that night, he slips quietly out and goes westward alone. Thus dies still another noble savage."[123]

An extraordinary exception to the general trend of American primitivist literature is represented by Sarah Morton's *Ouâbi; or, The Virtues of Nature,* a lengthy narrative poem published at Boston in 1790. It was one of the very few American works that echoed the general spirit of contemporary European Primitivism. The French Canadian hero, St. Castins, goes to live with the Illinois Indians and falls in love with Azakia, the wife of the chief. But the chief is captured by the Hurons and St. Castins leads a war party to rescue him, whereupon the grateful chief agrees to give up Azakia to him, and to take another bride in her place! But the chief nevertheless dies of grief over the loss of his beloved. "Breathing his last, he speaks to St. Castins, who has now proved that he can become a truly noble savage, and asks him to be chief in his place."[124]

It is obvious, in sum, that the tenor of Romantic Primitivism both in Europe and in America was overwhelmingly paternal, rather than historical or cultural. The authors, with few exceptions, made little effort to portray the institutions of primitive society or culture; it was the character of the Noble Savage himself that seized their imagination.

Latter-day Romantic Primitivism

By the later nineteenth century, the tide of American Romantic Primitivism had far receded. Ironically enough, a lingering admiration for the Noble Redman was evidenced more in the memoirs of certain frontier army officers and their wives than it was in popular fiction.[125] At the same time, these works also heralded the appearance of a new American compromise: the Melting Pot. The Indian, it was now suggested, had been appropriately noble in his time and circumstances, but it was now time for him to follow the path of civilization. Great hopes were held out for his com-

---

123. Pearce, *Savagism and Civilization,* p. 193.

124. Ibid., p. 186. For further discussion of the poem, see ibid., pp. 185–187, and Bissell, *American Indian in English Literature,* pp. 207–211.

125. For good examples, see Richard I. Dodge, *Our Wild Indians* (Boston, 1882) and Oliver O. Howard, *My Life and Experiences among our Hostile Indians* (Hartford, Conn., 1907); for more general discussion, see Sherry L. Smith, *The View from Officers' Row* (Tucson, 1990).

plete assimilation into the American mainstream, once the opportunities of education and of Christianization were laid before him, for it was continually asserted that "give him an education, and the Indian is just as good as we are." The literature of the later nineteenth century was, in short, overwhelmingly assimilationist, in keeping with the general Indian policy adopted by the U.S. Government at the same period.

In the early twentieth century, Primitivism found a new, highly esoteric voice in the novels of Conrad and D.H. Lawrence and in the poetry of Joyce, Yeats, and T.S. Eliot.[126] None of these, however, reached a large popular audience. For most Americans, the printed page gave way to the cinema as the most popular fictional medium. Here the image of the bloodthirsty and mostly ignoble Indian of the dime novels was perpetuated until well past the middle of the century through the medium of the cinema Western–one of the mainstays of the movie industry in its earlier years. After World War II the cinematic Indian began to regain a measure of nobility, and the classic Noble Savage staged a full comeback in Kevin Costner's *Dances with Wolves* (1989). This work represents in almost every sense a return to the themes and outlook of the eighteenth century primitivist novels, and even repeats many of their plot clichés. The enormous, even staggering popularity of *Dances with Wolves* demonstrates clearly that Primitivism was not dead but only dormant in the American spirit. As always, its revival was consequent on the return of troubled and self-doubting times.

PRIMITIVISM IN ANTHROPOLOGY

When anthropology claimed the territory of prehistory as its own, it inherited the traditions both of Progressivism and of Primitivism which had been developed by the earlier philosophers and literateurs. As Michael Bell notes, "Both anthropologists and creative writers have projected their versions of the primitive on to the strictly unknowable past…."[127] Since Primitivism is essentially a doctrine of the heart rather than of the head, however, it does not lend itself very readily to abstract theorizing. As a result Primitivism in anthropology persists much more as an emotional undercurrent than as a feature of overt theory.

As we saw in the last chapter, anthropology was born in the midst of, and as a result of, the great upsurge of Progressivism in the second half of the nineteenth century. The earliest anthropologists were, consequently,

126. For discussion see Bell, *Primitivism*, pp. 32–55.

127. Ibid., p. 65.

among the least primitivist, so fully were they wedded to the doctrines of Social Evolutionism, née Progressivism. An exception may be made in the case of certain particularistic ethnographers like Frank Hamilton Cushing, but they were definitely out of the anthropological mainstream.[128] It was not until the overthrow of Social Evolutionism as the dominant anthropological paradigm, at the beginning of the twentieth century, that a measure of Primitivism began to assert itself. Nevertheless, the prodigious program of salvage ethnography, which dominated ethnological fieldwork from about 1880 to 1940, was inspired directly by the persisting image of the Vanishing Redman.

The American historical anthropologists who came to the fore after 1900 were, as we will see later, very directly influenced by the German Idealist tradition. As such they were basically nonprogressivist and particularistic. For the most part, however, they were not overtly primitivist. Their mentor, the sternly honest Boas, always insisted that cultures, primitive or civilized, should be described "warts and all." It can be observed nevertheless that the warts are not very conspicuous in Boasian ethnographies; one learns very little about societal dissention, violence, or starvation among the Arapaho, Crow, Tsimshian, Navajo, or half a hundred other Native American peoples that were studied in the early twentieth century. The reader comes away from a Boasian ethnography with the distinct impression that life was good before the White Man came.[129]

One measure of the Primitivism of the Boasians may be obtained from a nearly forgotten book of fiction, *American Indian Life,* edited by Elsie Clews Parsons.[130] The contents are fictionalized short stories of life among particular North and Central American tribes, written by ethnographers who had studied those peoples. The list of contributors reads almost like a Who's Who of the great ethnographers of the Boasian Era: Boas, Kroeber, Lowie, Spier, Sapir, Wissler, Goldenweiser, Radin, and Swanton, to name only the most outstanding. Freed from the constraints of factual reporting, the authors could indulge to the full whatever romanticizing tendencies they had, and indeed many of the stories have a primitivistic flavor. Some of the tales read very much like contemporary juvenile fiction, though the book was not specifically intended for juveniles.

But Primitivism among the Boasians, as indeed among most anthropologists since that time, was largely a matter of personal rather than of

---

128. See esp. Joan Mark, *Four Anthropologists* (New York, 1980), pp. 96–130.

129. For further discussion, see Robert B. Edgerton, *Sick Societies* (New York, 1992), esp. pp. 1–15

130. New York, 1922.

disciplinary commitment. Paul Radin, at one extreme, had a distinctly romantic temperament, which shows through to some extent in all his published works, but especially in those which he wrote for the general public.[131] In *Primitive Man as Philosopher*[132] he emphasized, as did earlier writers of the Romantic era, the superior aesthetic and expressive powers of primitive man as opposed to civilized man. The book was written specifically to refute the then-popular idea that primitives have deficient intellectual powers. At the opposite extreme from Radin, his contemporary Leslie Spier produced a number of wholly dispassionate trait-list ethnographies without a hint of romanticization.[133] The work of Kroeber, too, is for the most part conspicuously lacking in Primitivism.

Primitivism in anthropology

The Configurationist paradigm of midcentury anthropology (sometimes called "Culture-and-Personality") was a latter-day outgrowth of the German idealist tradition, and as such will occupy us in Chapter 6. Configurationism shifted attention from the study of vanished aboriginal cultures to the study of primitive peoples in the here-and-now. Like the preceding historical school it was not overtly primitivist, except in implying that what is traditional is usually worth preserving. Nevertheless, Primitivism is fairly conspicuous in the earlier works of Ruth Benedict and of Margaret Mead, two of the pioneers of the configurationist school. By studying Samoan girls as a contrastive Other, Mead was able to show that the psychosexual problems of adolescence were a malaise of civilization, not to be found among the happy Samoans.[134] Mead however was by no means a pure primitivist, or indeed a pure anything; Primitivism, Progressivism, cultural relativism, and the belief in natural law all jostle for position throughout her enormous corpus of published work.

Among anthropologists of the recent past, the most outspoken primitivist by far is Stanley Diamond. His work introduces what for anthropology is a new departure: the classic Marxist vision of the Primitive utopia (see Chapter 7).[135] This is potentially significant, inasmuch as Marxism for the first time makes Primitivism theoretically as well as emotionally respectable. The Marxist version of Primitivism can also be found, in

---

131. In particular *The Story of the American Indian* (New York, 1927), and *Indians of South America* (New York, 1942). For discussion of Radin's primitivistic outlook, see Stanley Diamond in Sydel Silverman, ed., *Totems and Teachers* (New York, 1981), pp. 67–87.

132. Cleveland, 1927.

133. For example *Havasupai Ethnography. Anthropological Papers of the American Museum of Natural History*, vol. 29, no. 3 (1928).

134. Margaret Mead, *Coming of Age in Samoa* (New York, 1928).

135. See *Primitive Views of the World* (New York, 1969), and *In Search of the Primitive* (New Brunswick, N.J., 1974).

somewhat more tempered form, in Marshall Sahlins's *Stone Age Economics.*[136] But Sahlins and Diamond have attracted few followers, even among the Marxists, for the majority of them have rejected Marx's idealized vision of the Primitive. While Diamond continues unashamedly to flaunt the term "primitive," regarding it as a compliment, increasing numbers of his colleagues have abjured its use altogether.

If Primitivism can be said to represent in any sense a disciplinary rather than a merely personal commitment in anthropology, this is evident not so much in classical ethnographies as in the literature on culture contact, and particularly on the contact between White Americans and Indians. These works often resonate with the outlook and the themes of eighteenth-century Romanticism, and the primitivist's immemorial urge to self-castigation may be indulged to the full. The history of Indian-White relations is apt to be represented as a kind of timeless confrontation between the Noble Redman and the Brutal White; in effect between Good and Evil.[137] White massacres and atrocities may be recounted at considerable length, and are attributed to greed and cupidity. Indian atrocities, if recounted at all, are always accompanied by the apology that there was ample provocation.

Above all, however, disciplinary Primitivism finds expression in the earnest resolutions that are passed year after year at the annual meetings of the American Anthropological Association. These can be counted on to condemn any assimilationist or development policy that is proposed for tribal areas, either in the United States or abroad, and to call for the preservation of indigenous cultures from the corruptions of industrial civilization.

This propensity is much more conspicuous today than it was fifty years ago, when "acculturation" was one of the hot topics in anthropological discourse. The acculturation studies of Herskovits,[138] Linton,[139] Spicer,[140] and a host of others were mostly straightforward analyses of the contact situation, taking it for granted that native peoples—however noble their antecedents—had no choice but to accommodate themselves to the realities of twentieth-century civilization. Such works continued to reflect the nineteenth-century American compromise between Primitivism and Pro-

---

136. Chicago, 1972.

137. For some recent examples, see Rosenstiel, *Red & White*; Calvin Martin, ed., *The American Indian and the Problem of History* (New York, 1987), esp. pp. 3–34; and Jack Weatherford, *Indian Givers* (New York, 1988).

138. *Acculturation* (New York, 1938).

139. *Acculturation in Seven American Indian Tribes* (New York, 1940).

140. *Perspectives in American Indian Culture Change* (Chicago, 1961).

gressivism. The works of today, with their reiterated themes of regret, apology, and self-castigation, are much more nearly in the spirit of eighteenth-century Primitivism. Primitivism, as I remarked before, flourishes in disaffected times.[141]

Primitivism in anthropology

If Primitivism has never been a significant component of anthropological theory, in any overt sense, why does it remain nevertheless such a persistent feature of the anthropological ethos? The answer, I think, lies mainly in the kinds of people who are attracted to anthropology in the first place. The very choice of a career in this discipline implies a certain rejection of contemporary values and a preference for the contemplation of some exotic Other. Then, too, the typical anthropologist is the quintessential nature lover. Show me anthropologists; I'll show you backpackers, campers, whitewater boaters, rock climbers, conservationists–all the different kinds of outdoorspersons and nature-lovers. Primitivism simply goes with the turf; it is part of the ideological baggage that most of us carry into the discipline from our childhood.[142]

But if most American anthropologists are at least closet primitivists, I think it is largely an unconscious rather than a conscious commitment. They have not thought very deeply about the nature, the extent, or the bases of their commitment. As I suggested at the beginning of the chapter, Primitivism is an emotional undercurrent rather than an overt theoretical stance. The way to measure the Primitivism of anthropologists is not by reading their books but by talking to them "off the record," when their admiration for the peoples they study, and their disdain for their own time and culture, are most likely to find expression.

This makes it difficult to give a very precise characterization of anthropological Primitivism, which seems at times to involve elements of Historical Primitivism, at times of Cultural Primitivism, and at times of Paternal Primitivism. However, it is not easy for present-day anthropologists to be historical primitivists, when our image of the earliest hominid societies is a much cruder one than was that of the eighteenth-century romantics. It is also not easy to be a paternal primitivist when our experiences in the field have shown us that the primitive folk we study are fellow mortals with all the same vices and shortcomings as ourselves. Cultural Primitivism–an admiration not for the practitioners but for the institutions of primitive society–is left as the least problematic commitment, and I think it is in this direction that the feelings of anthropologists most clearly tend.

141. For further discussion of the extent of Primitivism in anthropological literature, see Edgerton, *Sick Societies.*

142. For further evidence of the persistence of primitivist thinking among American anthropologists, see Thomas Headland, and CA commentators, in *Current Anthropology* 38 (1997): 605–630.

SUMMARY

Primitivism is the other side of the coin from Progressivism. It is an ideology that views the development of civilization with regret rather than with approval, and that clings to an idealized image of Primitive Society and Primitive Man. It is very often a doctrine of self-castigation, as the Noble Savage is contrasted with modern man who has been corrupted by the luxuries and the self-indulgences of civilization. It is a doctrine that flourishes in unsettled and uneasy times, as surely as Progressivism flourishes in optimistic times.

Primitivism in Western thought, like Progressivism, had its beginnings in classical antiquity. It was especially prevalent in the corrupt and decaying world of the later Greek and Roman thinkers, reaching its most articulate development in the philosophies of the Cynics and Stoics. It was not a significant theme in medieval Christian philosophy, when living savages were viewed as godless and wicked, but it found expression of a sort in imagined utopias and Arcadias. Then, with the discovery of the Americas, a new and more satisfactory horizon opened for the primitivists. Arcadias no longer had to be imagined; they were actually being reported by the earliest explorers on the new continents. The Native American almost immediately took over the immemorial role of the Noble Savage, and in the minds of many he has continued to occupy that role down to the present day.

Because Primitivism is a doctrine more of the heart than of the head, it found only a very limited expression in overtly philosophical works of the medieval and modern periods. Its natural medium of expression was in literature and art, where it gave rise to a truly prodigious volume of plays, operas, novels, and paintings, most of them having a Native American setting. This trend, beginning almost immediately after Columbus's discovery, flourished for more than three centuries, reaching its apogee in the Romantic era of the late eighteenth and early nineteenth centuries.

European writing about the Indians was almost purely primitivistic, for it was easy and tempting to contrast the unspoiled conditions of aboriginal America with the chaotic social conditions and the endless wars of early modern Europe. The situation in America was more complicated, for here Primitivism had to accommodate itself to the bumptious optimism characteristic of the colonial era and the first decades of American independence. The distinctive American solution to this dilemma was the image of the Vanishing Redman: noble in his day and way, but finally doomed to give way before the inexorable march of civilization.

The pioneer theoretical anthropologists of the nineteenth century were far too wedded to Progressivism to have any leanings toward Primitivism. It was, nevertheless, the conception of the Vanishing Redman that motivated the early efforts at salvage ethnography undertaken by the Bureau of American Ethnology. Later, however, Primitivism proved to be quite compatible with German Idealism, the dominant ideology established in American anthropology by Boas and his students at the beginning of the twentieth century (see Chapter 6). There is a primitivistic undercurrent in many of the Boasian ethnographies, and even more in the studies of culture contact and change undertaken in the midcentury era. *Summary* This tendency waned noticeably with the revival of Progressivism after World War II, but appears to be once again somewhat on the rise.

Because Primitivism is mainly a doctrine of the heart, however, it finds expression much less in the published works of anthropologists than in their private discourse. It is this quality of emotional rather than of intellectual commitment that makes it possible for so many American anthropologists to be Progressivists and Primitivists at the same time.

CHAPTER 4

NATURAL LAW

WESTERN THOUGHT has always identified animals as part of the natural kingdom, and their habitual behaviors as part of nature's—or God's—intended order. But what about habitual human behaviors? Are widely observed social customs and laws also a reflection of nature's grand plan, or are they just man's attempts to impose his own order over what nature created? That question has been debated by philosophers, jurists, and theologians for over two millennia, and it has given rise to a voluminous literature in many languages.[1]

Some recurrent human behaviors are clearly responsive to biological or psychological imperatives; they are necessarily found in all human societies. These by common agreement can be assigned to the natural or the divinely ordained order. But many behaviors seem to be dictated not by obvious biological or psychological needs but simply by deeply ingrained ideas of what is right and wrong, and at least some of these ideas are also nearly universal from society to society. Here the issue of natural or divine intent becomes problematical. Can we say that universal or near-universal human beliefs about right and wrong—that is, moral ideas—are also part of the natural order? If so, what is it in nature that makes them right or wrong?

Throughout history, most Western thinkers have answered the first of those questions in the affirmative: universal moral dictates must be part of nature's or God's plan. The philosophers, jurists, and theologians have embodied this conviction in the doctrine of natural law. However, they have debated the second question endlessly, without coming to anything

1. The Library of Congress subject catalogue lists several thousand books and journals devoted primarily to the subject of natural law, and it is of course dealt with incidentally in a far larger number of works.

close to agreement as to what makes right right and wrong wrong. Concepts of natural law must derive from concepts of nature, but these are nearly as infinite as are concepts of God. There has however been a general line of progression in Western thinking about natural law from ancient to modern times, and this will provide the outline for discussion in the present chapter.

Obviously and importantly, the natural law discussed here–the natural law of the philosophers and jurists–is not the same as the laws of nature discussed by physicists and biologists. The latter are conceived to be universal and value-free; they operate inexorably and impartially on men, on animals, and on stones. Natural law on the other hand is value laden, and its operation is confined to the human sphere, or at most to the domain of humans and some of the higher mammals. The laws of nature are determinative: so far as we human beings are concerned, they specify what we can't help doing. Natural law on the other hand is only hortatory. It cannot force us to do or not do anything in a physical sense; it merely specifies what we will be rewarded for if we do it, or punished if we don't. In short and in simple, the laws of nature dictate what we must do; natural law indicates what we ought to do. Yet despite these fundamental differences, philosophers from Plato to the present have sought to reconcile the two principles, finding a basis for natural law in physical laws, or reducing the two to a common denominator. The fundamental problem, as David Hume observed (though he denied the possibility) is how to get from "is" to "ought." To avoid confusion in the discussion that follows, laws of nature will hereinafter be referred to as physical laws.

It must also be recognized at the outset that there is not, and never has been, a single, unitary conception of natural law. The doctrine seems rather to spring from a kind of innate conviction shared by most peoples and most philosophies, but interpreted by them in various different ways. Consequently, the natural law doctrine does not have any single "intellectual pedigree" in the same sense as do Progressivism and Primitivism; its history has been more diffuse and chaotic. Indeed, the reader may conclude in the end that there is no aspect of human customary behavior or belief that *cannot* be identified as natural law in one sense or another, so varied and diffuse have been the applications of the term. It may then be legitimately asked whether the concept has any practical utility, or whether there is anything "really there" to discuss under the heading of natural law. This is a vitally important ontological issue, but it is not one that I intend to pursue in the present work. My concern is not to consider whether there is or is not natural law, but to show how *the belief that there is natural law,* whether justified or not, has shaped the thinking of social and moral philosophers down through the ages, and has contributed to the basic conceptual framework of anthropology.

Natural law was an important and an honored concept in Western philosophy, theology, and jurisprudence for more than two thousand years. Only with the rise of social science in the nineteenth century did it come under attack; so much so that modern sociologists, anthropologists, and psychologists are reluctant to use the term. Yet the basic principle, that moral ideas have a natural basis, survives under other names in all of the social sciences, and it remains a source of unresolved moral dilemmas today. Any discipline that calls itself "social" must sooner or later consider the question of morality, since ideas of good and bad are part of the common property of all human societies. Anything that calls itself a science must consider the question of how ideas of good and bad come about. Finally, anything that calls itself a social *and* a natural science, as American anthropology does, must consider how common ideas of good and bad relate to the demands of the external environment. The problem for anthropologists remains what it was for the earliest Greek philosophers: to relate natural law to physical law.

THE DOCTRINE AND ITS VARIANTS

Natural law, then, refers not to recurrent behaviors as such but to codes of behavior: behavioral prescriptions and restrictions that are believed to be the common property of all nations and societies, and that must therefore reflect nature's, or God's, intent. Thus conceived, the concept necessarily has both behavioral and cognitive dimensions. It refers to acts–and avoidances–and also to the underlying ideas about right and wrong that give rise to those acts. Over the centuries some scholars have addressed themselves primarily to the behavioral and some to the cognitive dimension, but it is the latter that has proved endlessly fascinating, and controversial, first to philosophers, then to theologists and jurists, and finally to social scientists.

Clearly implied in the natural law doctrine is the belief that what is universal must be natural, and that what is natural must be right. The presumed universality of natural law has been attributed at times to the will of God, at times to the dictates of human reason, at times to the ordering of nature, and at times to the demands of Society. Summing up the concept, Dennis Schmidt has written that

> the fundamental presupposition of all natural law has been that there is an essential unity between what is right and what is the

highest expression of nature. All natural law theories hold that there is some natural standard independent of and above the positivity of existing conditions that provides the normative basis... for any legitimate critique of existing conditions. The metaphysical models for these normative principles have ranged from physical nature, to God, to reason, to human nature.... In every case, though, natural law theories have represented this principle as universal and immutable....[2]

The doctrine and its variants

The most essential feature of the natural law concept, in addition to universality, is its rationality. Even though its ultimate source may be non human, the dictates of natural law are always conformable with the dictates or the understandings of human reason. This has led many thinkers to suggest that human reason is itself a part of the natural law; it has been implanted in the human mind so that we may understand and obey the requirements of nature or of God. It is because of this quality of rationality that natural law cannot simply be equated with divine decree, even by those who regard its ultimate source as divine. An all-powerful God is under no obligation to be consistent or reasonable; in the case of natural law he has simply decided to do so. Even for theologians, therefore, natural law is essentially a mechanistic doctrine. The god of natural law theorists, if he exists at all, is a deus ex machina.

According to most definitions, natural law is neither revealed nor enacted. It thus stands in contrast on the one hand to scriptural law, and on the other to statute law. Although part of nature's (or God's) intention, it must be discovered by man.

The acceptance of "nature" as the source of moral norms is a principle common to Primitivism and to the belief in natural law.[3] While the primitivist makes invidious comparisons between the present and the past, or between the civilized Self and the primitive Other, however, the doctrine of natural law emphasizes the commonalities among peoples at all times and places. Far more than Progressivism or Primitivism, it is, or can be, a doctrine stressing the commonality of mankind. In terms of the distinction that was made in Chapter 1, it is a universalist doctrine, not a comparativist one.

The relationship between natural law and physical laws is highly prob-

2. In Ernst Bloch, *Natural Law and Human Dignity,* trans. Dennis J. Schmidt (Cambridge, Mass., 1986), pp. xiv–xv.

3. Cf. especially Arthur O. Lovejoy and George Boas, *Primitivism and Related Ideas in Antiquity* (Baltimore, 1935), pp. 103–116.

lematical, as we will see throughout the chapter. It has been conceived very differently in different ages. However, the trend of Western thinking throughout history has been predominantly monistic, and leading thinkers from Aristotle to the present have attempted to reduce natural law and physical laws to a single common explanatory principle.

Natural Law

In Western thought, natural law began as a philosophical doctrine and evolved successively into a juristic, a theological, and finally, in the eighteenth century, a sociological one. However, it did not outgrow its earlier mutations; it remains today a subject of discussion alike in philosophy, in jurisprudence, in theology, and in social science. Perhaps because of its theological and metaphysical associations, however, scientists, including anthropologists, have always been reluctant to call it by name or to confront some of the moral issues that it raises. I will argue nevertheless that, just as no natural science can operate without a concept of physical law, so no social or behavioral science can operate without a concept of natural law, by whatever name it is called. Social and behavioral sciences are concerned to discover regularities in human behavior, and to account for them in terms of some causal principle other than free human will. Anthropology and sociology go farther, attempting to discover not only recurring behaviors but recurring moral norms that govern behavior. These are nothing if not natural laws, according to most understandings of the term.

For all its popularity and its long history, the concept of natural law remains an elusive one; it is far more difficult to discuss than is either Progressivism or Primitivism. To begin with, the concept of natural law in one form or another is nearly universal: it has not been the product of particular times or places or circumstances. It may flourish equally well in ages of faith, when it is attributed to divine intent, in ages of reason, when it is attributed to the ordering of nature, or in ages of science, when it may be attributed to the inherent programming of the human mind.

There is surely no human group who do not believe that their most cherished customs are somehow inherently right, and at the same time there have always been critics to insist that certain customs or man-made enactments are inherently not right. Both positions require appeal to an authority higher than man's. The problem is: what authority? A great deal of human custom and law is directly traceable, through mythology or scripture, to the will of the gods, but a great deal is not. In the latter case even persons who believe that all law must be divinely ordained must appeal to something other than revelation or text to support their view. And there are always those who do not believe in the gods, or at least in the divine origin of law and custom, and who insist that the inherent rightness of laws and customs must be established on other than religious grounds. In these circumstances both believers and unbelievers have repeatedly appealed to "nature," yet there are as many and divergent ideas about nature as there are about the gods. In consequence, it has always been much easier to believe in natural law than to define it or to specify its content.

Issues and approaches

The doctrine and its variants

Philosophic and juristic discussions of natural law, insofar as I can follow them, seem to revolve around five issues: 1) Is there such a thing as natural law, above and beyond the domain of human enactments? 2) If so, what is its ultimate source? 3) How may it be discovered, or identified? 4) What is its specific content? 5) How does it relate to man-made laws, and vice versa?

A purely logical approach to the subject would seem to dictate that the above questions be tackled more or less in the order listed. That is, any consideration of natural law would have to begin with a clear understanding of what is meant by nature, or God, or both. Yet learned discussion has often proceeded from just the opposite direction: starting from the ideological conviction that certain of man's laws were or were not inherently right, and proceeding to support this view by appeals to this or that concept of nature or of God. Starting from that direction, the discussion often jumps over, or does not get down to, fundamental issues. The conveners of a conference on natural law a generation ago were forced to concede that "The outstanding characteristic of most contemporary discussions of the subject is that there are about as many definitions and concepts represented as there are participants. Often the discussion is concluded without agreement even on fundamental terms."[4]

In the centuries-long discussion of natural law that will occupy us in the present chapter, we can observe that some thinkers and schools have concerned themselves mainly with defining it, some with discovering its origins, and some with specifying its content. However, the question that most directly concerns us as anthropologists is the third one: how is natural law to be discovered, assuming that there is such a thing?

Amid the welter of ideas and opinions on this subject, it seems possible to recognize three fairly distinct threads of thought, or approaches, which for want of better terms I will call intuitive, teleological, and consensual. The intuitive approach, characteristic of the early Greeks, holds that human reason, operating in the light of day-to-day experience, will suggest

4. Arthur Harding in Robert N. Wilkin et al., *Origins of the Natural Law Tradition* (Dallas, 1954), p. vi.

to each individual what is and is not inherently right, hence natural. What this approach enjoins upon the individual is simply self-reflection. In the teleological approach, originated by Plato and Aristotle, nature is said to be endowed with purposes, and those laws and customs are natural which are in accord with nature's purposes. At least in theory this enjoins upon each individual the study of nature, in order to best understand its purposes. The consensual approach, dating from Roman times, abjures the question of origins, arguing instead that those customs which are common to all peoples must be natural, even though it may not be obvious why they are. This approach might also be called ethnographic, since by implication it enjoins the comparative study of peoples, to discover what customs are truly universal.[5]

Natural Law

The three approaches just named imply quite different conceptions of the relationship between natural law and physical laws. From the intuitive perspective, natural laws are logically deducible from physical laws. From the teleological perspective, natural laws and physical laws are coequal parts of a single grand system. From the consensual perspective, natural laws and physical laws are, at least potentially, two quite separate domains involving different "natures," the one human and the other physical.

Throughout the ages there has been a good deal of confusion as to whether natural laws should be regarded as prescriptive (like physical laws) or as purely descriptive of accepted norms.[6] Natural law from the teleological perspective has sometimes been regarded as prescriptive, there being no difference in theory between the laws to which men are subject and the laws to which physical matter is subject. In contrast, the intuitive and consensual approaches are more nearly descriptive, and a distinction is made between physical laws applicable to physical matter and the natural law embodied in human customs. I do not wish to suggest, however, that all thinkers and all schools can be conveniently identified with one or another of these approaches, for thinking on the subject of natural law has rarely been that precise. A great many thinkers have attempted to justify their belief in natural law on more than one ground.

Under the circumstances it comes as no surprise that the moral and political implications of the natural law concept are as ambiguous as are those of Progressivism and Primitivism. Like them, it has been invoked in support of all kinds of causes, from reactionary to radical. In the view of some ancient thinkers it required a life of strict moral rectitude, while oth-

5. For a more particularized classification of approaches, see Francis H. Eterovich, *Approaches to Natural Law from Plato to Kant* (New York, 1972), pp. 15–18.

6. Cf. Michael B. Crowe, *The Changing Profile of the Natural Law* (The Hague, 1977), p. 51.

ers believed that it justified prostitution, cannibalism, and suicide.[7] It was cited by medieval popes to justify the subjugation and enforced conversion of pagan peoples,[8] and by Anabaptists to support their doctrine of free love.[9] In the sixteenth century it was critical to the argument that Native Americans were fellow humans who could not be enslaved, while in the nineteenth century it was cited as justification for the enactment of segregation laws in the American South. In the recent past natural law has been invoked both in support of and in opposition to feminist and gay rights movements. The doctrine has occasionally even been turned on its head, to suggest that we civilized folk are really, at heart, still savages.[10]

The doctrine and its variants

Paradoxically, natural law may be seen as either relative or absolute. The progressivists of the eighteenth century believed that different laws were "natural" at different stages in the evolution of society, a point made very explicitly by Montesquieu in *Spirit of the Laws* (1748).[11] During the same era, primitivists insisted that the study of savage society would reveal the most basic laws that all mankind were meant to obey, at all stages of history.

As a philosophic doctrine, natural law does not necessarily require an empirical foundation, any more than do the doctrines of Progressivism or Primitivism. To some, like the founders of the American republic, it is simply "self evident, that all men are created equal, and that they are endowed by their creator with certain inalienable rights...."[12] These principles, in other words, do not require a cross-cultural search for exemplars. Nevertheless, the discovery of Native American cultures, and later the exploration and study of other tribal areas, provided for many thinkers a demonstration of the existence of natural law, insofar as certain beliefs and customs were found (or believed) to be universal among the newly discovered peoples. In other words, tribal societies provided unexpected support for the consensual approach to natural law, and this was to become one of the significant approaches to the subject in the seventeenth and eighteenth centuries. It is an approach that was to carry over, though without overt acknowledgment, into anthropology.

7. See ibid., p. 34.

8. See esp. James Muldoon, *Popes, Lawyers, and Infidels* (Princeton, N.J., 1979), pp. 3–27.

9. Cf. Bloch, *Natural Law and Human Dignity*, p. 29.

10. See, for example, Robert Ardrey, *African Genesis* (New York, 1961) and *The Territorial Imperative* (New York, 1966); Konrad Lorenz, *On Aggression*, trans. Marjorie Wilson (New York, 1966); Desmond Morris, *The Human Zoo* (New York, 1969); Lionel Tiger and Robin Fox, *The Imperial Animal* (New York, 1971).

11. English translation by Thomas Nugent (London, 1748), vol. 1, p. 7.

12. Preamble to the American Declaration of Independence.

As I have just suggested, the belief in natural law in one sense or another is surely universal. However, the same is not true as regards discussion and debate on the subject. In preliterate societies the concept is generally implicit rather than explicit. It only becomes explicit when natural law is placed in contrast to man-made law: *physis* versus *nomos*, as the Greeks originally termed them.[13] Thus, discussions and speculations about natural law are likely to emerge when human beings take it upon themselves to enact law, thereby usurping what had been the traditional prerogative of the gods. The question must then inevitably arise: how do the enactments of man relate to the will of the gods, or of nature? Not surprisingly, we find this question most prominently debated in legalistic ages and societies: in the Hellenistic and Roman eras, in the later Middle Ages, and intermittently in Western history from that time to the present.

Natural Law

In non-Western civilizations the legitimacy and the implications of natural law have been less overtly debated, though the concept itself is by no means lacking.[14] In Islamic jurisprudence it is clearly embodied in the *sunna*–the customary law of the Arab community that was followed, and therefore by implication endorsed, by the Prophet Muhammad, even though he is not known to have mentioned it.[15] In Confucian China it finds expression in the concept of *li*: the observance of traditions and rituals for their own sake, because they trace back to remotest antiquity and therefore must in the beginning have been divinely ordained.[16] As Needham has written,

> one would not appreciate the full force of the word *li* if one failed to recognize that the customs, usages and ceremonials which it summed up were not simply those which empirically have been found to agree with the instinctive feelings of rightness experienced by the Chinese people...; they were those which, it was believed, accorded with the 'will' of heaven, indeed with the structure of the universe.[17]

---

13. See Bloch, *Natural Law and Human Dignity*, p. 10.
14. See *Proceedings of the Natural Law Institute*, vol. V (Notre Dame, Ind., 1953), for discussions of the natural law tradition in Jewish, Muslim, Hindu, Buddhist, and Chinese thought.
15. See H.A.R. Gibb and J.H. Kramers, eds., *Shorter Encyclopaedia of Islam* (Ithaca, N.Y., 1965), pp. 552–553.
16. See esp. Joseph Needham, *Human Law and the Laws of Nature in China and the West* (Oxford, 1951), esp. p. 24.
17. Id., *Science and Civilization in China* (Cambridge, 1956), vol. 2, p. 526.

The Chinese contrast between *li* and *fa*–between accepted tradition and man-made decrees–corresponds in a general way to the early Greek contrast between *physis* and *nomos.*[18]

Historical contexts

In the West, at least since the time of Locke and Montesquieu, the doctrine of natural law has been invoked mainly in connection with the advocacy of universal human rights; so much so that there has been some tendency to think of the two as synonymous.[19] This however reflects only the overriding ideological preoccupation of the modern era, with its continual insistence on the rights of the individual. Historically, natural law has covered a much wider territory. For earlier thinkers the most fundamental concern of all law, including natural law, was with responsibilities, not with rights. Natural law like other law specified first and foremost what we must and must not do, and only incidentally what we are and are not entitled to.

GREEK NATURAL LAW: FROM *PHYSIS* TO *NOMOS*

It has been said, with reference to ancient philosophies, that the Hebrews made man independent of nature, and the Greeks made nature independent of man. This clever aphorism contains a germ of truth, but it is also misleading, for the Greeks did not by any means wholly separate man from nature. They achieved only a partial separation, and then debated endlessly what that might imply.

For the Hebrews, man's liberation from nature was the direct result of divine providence: he was given dominion over the beasts in the field from the moment of creation. The Greeks' vision of history however was evolutionary rather than creationist. They saw man's liberation from the limitations of nature as a very gradual process; a long upward climb involving the increasing triumph of human reason. Yet the separation of man from nature was incomplete. He was recognized to be an animal who had achieved a dominant position in the world through his superior intellect, but an animal all the same.

The Greeks were thus left to ponder the relationship between the natural order out of which man had arisen, and the man-made orders that he had created in his upward climb. Were the famous Athenian law codes, for example, purely and simply the products of human ingenuity, or were they somehow conformable to some larger design of nature? What was needed,

---

18. Cf. Needham, *Human Law and the Laws of Nature in China and the West.*

19. See, for example, Bloch, *Natural Law and Human Dignity,* and Richard Tuck, *Natural Rights Theories* (Cambridge, 1979).

in effect, was a unified theory that would account both for the natural and the man-made worlds; that would locate the human intellect and its workings within the grand scheme of nature. It was in the pursuit of that goal that the concept of natural law gradually emerged.

There are at least hints of a natural law concept in the work of many pre-Socratic philosophers; chiefly in their speculations about the nature and bases of justice, which they saw as necessarily proceeding from nature's ordering.[20] Thus in his famous funeral oration, Pericles alluded to "that code which, although unwritten, yet cannot be broken without acknowledged disgrace."[21] However, a systematic concern with law as such only became evident in the time of the Sophists, from the fifth to the third centuries B.C. It was they who developed the basic distinction between *physis* and *nomos*: the physical world and the world subject to human regulation.

The Sophist doctrines are known to the modern world mainly through the rebuttals that were launched against them by Plato, and are therefore not presented to us in a very sympathetic or in a systematic manner. At least four different versions of Sophistic natural law can be inferred from the different Platonic dialogues.[22] However, the doctrine that has received the widest currency among later scholars is that attributed to Protagoras: "Man is the measure of all things."[23] Obviously this is one interpretation of *nomos*: a thoroughly relativistic one. But other Sophists clearly had a different understanding of *nomos*. As critics of the existing social order, they sometimes referred to *nomos* as though it were nature's law, and cited it as a basis for attacking man-made laws and institutions.[24]

The celebrated *Dialogues* of Plato constitute, in their totality, a lifelong attack on the doctrines of the Sophists—the professional teachers of Athens who, he felt, bore a heavy responsibility for the sorry state of the community and polity in his time. Plato seems to have had no doubt that the Sophists were preaching moral relativism (and hence opportunism), and he set himself to show that there is an immutable natural order to which men and their laws must conform. As Sigmund notes,

20. Cf. Crowe, *Changing Profile of the Natural Law*, pp. 1–6; Eterovich, *Natural Law from Plato to Kant*, pp. 21–22; and Paul E. Sigmund, *Natural Law in Political Thought* (Washington, D.C., 1971), pp. 1–2.

21. Reported by Thucydides in his *History of the Peloponnesian War*, Book II, pp. 35–46.

22. Sigmund, *Natural Law in Political Thought*, pp. 2–4; see also Eterovich, *Natural Law from Plato to Kant*, pp. 22–26.

23. Sigmund, *Natural Law in Political Thought*, p. 3; Crowe, *Changing Profile of the Natural Law*, p. 8.

24. Sigmund, *Natural Law in Political Thought*, p. 9; Crowe, *Changing Profile of the Natural Law*, pp. 5–6.

the basic argument of the *Republic* amounts to an assertion that there is an order in nature and human nature which is universal, objective, and harmonious, in which the soul is the most fundamental principle, possessing a threefold internal structure (reason, spirit, and desire) which is the basis of moral obligation.... Corresponding to this natural order in man is a parallel hierarchical order in society... and in the universe....[25]

Greek natural law: from physis *to* nomos

Aristotle, whose range of interests was much wider than that of Plato, had less to say specifically on the subject of natural law, but his influence on the subsequent development of the doctrine was nevertheless far greater. Indeed he has sometimes even been called "the father of natural law."[26] This attribution of paternity is debatable, for Aristotle was by no means entirely clear or consistent on the subject. A certain concept of natural law seems implicit in much of Aristotle's *Politics,* but it was in the *Nicomachean Ethics* that he came closest to a clear articulation of the concept, in his distinction between natural and legal justice.[27] "Of political justice part is natural and part legal,–natural, that which everywhere has the same force and does not exist by people's thinking this or that; legal, that which is originally indifferent...."[28] An important qualification was the author's recognition that natural justice is nevertheless not immutable: "Things are just either by nature or by law. But we must not regard the natural as being something which cannot by any possibility change; for even the things which are by nature partake of change...."[29] But Aristotle, like Plato, did not translate his belief in natural justice into an attempt to spell out the details of natural law.

Aristotle's most lasting contribution, as it turned out, was to be his teleological view of nature.

> For Aristotle the essential nature of a thing can be discovered by determining its purpose or end. This in turn can be derived from its structure or normal functioning. *Physis* (nature) is related to *telos* (end); thus the teleological method can be used to discover nature's purposes and derive values from them. Aristotle uses this teleologi-

---

25. Sigmund, *Natural Law in Political Thought,* pp. 7–8.

26. Crowe, *Changing Profile of the Natural Law,* p. 19; Heinrich Rommen, *The Natural Law,* trans. Thomas R. Hanley (St. Louis, 1947), p. 16.

27. This work, more than any other by Aristotle, has been cited as a milestone in the development of natural law theory. See esp. Crowe, *Changing Profile of the Natural Law,* pp. 21–25.

28. Quoted in ibid., p. 21.

29. From the *Magna Moralia;* quoted in ibid., p. 23, n. 90.

cal analysis to demonstrate that man is naturally social and that government responds to needs which man has by nature.[30]

Attributing purpose (and thus, in a sense, will) to nature made it possible for the Stoics and later thinkers to decide what was and was not natural law in terms of what did and did not serve nature's purposes, and this has remained one of the major approaches to natural law down to the present day.[31]

Natural Law

Although Plato and Aristotle were clearly interested in natural law, it was by no means a cornerstone of their moral and political philosophies. That was left to the Epicureans and above all to the Stoics of later generations. These later schools largely abjured the metaphysical speculations that had preoccupied their predecessors, and concentrated their interest on moral philosophy. The definition and the pursuit of virtue became their overriding concern, and virtue lay in the understanding of, and obedience to, natural law.[32] Both schools made a clear distinction between natural and man-made law, insisting that the former must take precedence over the latter, and both were critical of the *polis*–the basic politicolegal institution of Greek society–as a man-made construct that was inimical to the purposes of nature. Epicureans and Stoics, however, conceived of the law of nature quite differently. To Epicureans it involved the pursuit of happiness; to Stoics it involved living in harmony with physical nature.

It is not easy to summarize the Stoic doctrines briefly, for the school endured for more than five hundred years, went through several developmental phases, and had both Greek and Roman adherents. Moreover the original writings of the Greek Stoics have largely disappeared, and are known to us only from later Roman commentaries.[33] However, the central thesis of the school, as characterized by Crowe, was that "We must know nature in order to follow nature's law; the universal law is the *law of nature* and the Stoic morality is epitomized in the maxim: 'Live according to nature'. . . ." [italics in the original].[34] But the Stoics could not specify a priori, any more than could Plato or Aristotle, exactly what it was that nature enjoined. Instead it became the lifelong duty of each individual to

30. Sigmund, *Natural Law in Political Thought*, p. 10.

31. Ibid., p. 12. For more extended discussion see Eterovich, *Natural Law from Plato to Kant*, pp. 30–35.

32. Crowe, *Changing Profile of the Natural Law*, p. 30.

33. Ibid., pp. 28–29.

34. Ibid., pp. 30–31. See also Eterovich, *Natural Law from Plato to Kant*, pp. 36–40, and Henry Sidgwick, *Outlines of the History of Ethics* (London, 1916), pp. 73–82.

study nature for himself, and thereby to discover how to live in conformity with it.

A radical feature of Stoicism, for its time, was its egalitarianism. Physical laws are uniform for all human beings, and therefore there can be no legal distinction of citizen and foreigner, freeman and slave, or man and woman. "The Stoics are citizens of the world, citizens of the human republic, and they are strongly inclined to propositions that are equally true and good in all parts of the world. After Plato and Aristotle they are the main founders of moral universalism," wrote Simon.[35] This conviction was clearly antithetical to the basic legal structure of the Greek city-state, based as it was on a whole series of hierarchical distinctions. Stoic egalitarianism has been cited as one of the foundation stones of the theory of natural rights.

Greek natural law: from physis *to* nomos

The Greek Stoics were not political reformers in any practical sense. They preferred to lead the life of detached contemplation and criticism that was always favored by Greek philosophers, and to condemn the society of their time without really trying to change it.[36] Moreover, the pursuit of virtue as they defined it was a personal rather than a collective quest—a conception that would later make Stoic philosophy clearly compatible with early Christian doctrine.[37] It was left to the Romans to attempt the application of Stoic principles in the sphere of practical affairs, a development that will be considered in the next section.

Three things may be said in summing up the Greek conception of natural law. First, it was largely nonempirical; it involved an understanding of nature that was intuitive, logical, and, at least in the case of Plato, mathematical, rather than observational. Second, the Greek perspective expressed more an ideal and an aspiration than a reality: many writers argued not so much that there *was* natural law observable in human affairs but that there ought to be. Finally, like so much of Greek philosophy, the concept of natural law was never translated into practice, in that none of the celebrated law codes of the city-states were based on this principle, though this was always the ideal of the philosophers.

ROMAN NATURAL LAW: FROM *NOMOS* TO *JUS GENTIUM*

From the earliest days of their republic,

35. Y.R.M. Simon, *The Tradition of Natural Law: a Philosopher's Reflections,* ed. V. Kunic (New York, 1965), p. 30.
36. On this, see esp. Bloch, *Natural Law and Human Dignity,* pp. 17–18.
37. Cf. Crowe, *Changing Profile of the Natural Law,* p. 36; Rommen, *Natural Law,* pp. 35–36.

> the Romans were determined that they would live under a government of laws, not of men. Such a commitment did not lead to an easy political life, but there is no more enlightening theme for an interpretation of Roman history than the essential devotion of the Romans to essentially legal politics, even under the emperors. It follows from this commitment, active and practical though it may be, that the intellectual history of the Romans will concern itself with the distinction between good and bad laws.[38]

Natural Law

No wonder, then, that the Stoic doctrines with their emphasis on natural law had a special and a practical appeal for the Romans that they never had for the majority of Greeks. The leading Roman adherents of Stoicism, far from being ivory tower intellectuals, were men active in public life, including such luminaries as the general Scipio Africanus, the orator-statesman Cicero, the moralist Seneca, and the Emperor Marcus Aurelius.

The fullest and most detailed account of Stoic doctrines in general, and of natural law in particular, that has survived from the ancient world is that of Cicero. By his own reckoning he was hardly more than a transmitter of older wisdom,[39] but the lofty eloquence of his language gave to Stoic doctrines–or his version of them–a special appeal that was to last for centuries. Early medieval writers on natural law relied far more on Cicero than they did on any other source.

Cicero's most famous dictum on natural law occurs in a passage that has survived from an otherwise lost book, *De Republica*: "There is in fact a true law–namely, right reason–which is in accordance with nature, applies to all men, and is unchangeable and eternal. By its commands this law summons men to the performance of their duties; by its prohibitions it restrains them from doing wrong...."[40] This passage has been acclaimed by one commentator as "one of the most memorable statements in all political literature."[41] Nevertheless, we lack the remaining portions of *De Republica* that would undoubtedly have amplified it, and given it a greater degree of concreteness. Modern scholars are obliged to rely instead on other works of Cicero, and particularly *De Legibus*, for a fuller understanding

38. Scott Buchanan, *Rediscovering Natural Law* (Santa Barbara, Calif., 1962), p. 14.
39. Cf. Crowe, *Changing Profile of the Natural Law*, pp. 36–37.
40. Quoted from Wilkin, *Origins of the Natural Law Tradition*, pp. 23–24. Slightly different translations are given by Sigmund, *Natural Law in Political Thought*, p. 22, and by Crowe, *Changing Profile of the Natural Law*, p. 37. The original text, with certain obviously Christian insertions, is preserved in the *Institutiones Divinae* of the fourth-century Christian writer Lactantius.
41. Cf. Wilkin et al., *Origins of the Natural Law Tradition*, p. 23.

of the author's ideas on natural law. Nowhere in the surviving works, however, is there any specification of the precise content of natural law, although at a minimum it clearly included a duty to contribute to society, a concern for justice, and respect for the life and property of others.[42]

The Romans' practical interest in law was not confined to the question of how best to govern themselves. Throughout most of their history they had also to govern an empire of highly diverse peoples; a challenge never faced by the Greeks. Although they were often forced to rely on arbitrary imperial decrees, they sought as much as possible to develop a rule of law for all their subjects no less than for themselves. In other words, they had to decide what were good and bad laws not just for Romans but for everyone, and this forced them to consider natural law from a very broad perspective. The laws of Rome and the laws of foreign lands had to be gathered together and distilled into a third law that was common to both.[43]

Roman natural law: from nomos *to* jus gentium

Out of their practical experience and necessity the Romans developed an entirely new approach to natural law: the *jus gentium,* or common law of all peoples.

> There were laws specific to a local community, civil laws, whose roots might reach far back into unique folkways and folk lore, the *mores.* But among these laws and between communities comparison revealed a matrix of common law, both customary and statutory, diverse in origin but identical in purpose and practice, laws of peoples, *ius gentium.* They revealed a body of principles upon which judges and administrators drew for reasons when they had to decide hard cases.[44]

This was something wholly different from the Greek conception of natural law, for the jus gentium was not revealed by intuition or deduced from personal experience of the world; it was discovered empirically by the cross-cultural study of peoples. The idea that the locus of natural law is embodied in laws already extant–in what is rather than in what should be –was to become one of the most powerful currents of philosophic thought on the subject. From this perspective the discovery of natural law entailed not the study of nature per se but the comparative study of peoples: in a word, ethnology. The Romans, in sum, were the originators of the consensual approach to natural law.

---

42. Ibid., pp. 22–23.
43. See esp. Bloch, *Natural Law and Human Dignity,* pp. 20–24.
44. Buchanan, *Rediscovering Natural Law,* p. 17.

In Roman hands, natural law thus moved from the domain of abstract philosophy to that of practical jurisprudence, and became the subject of a substantial and growing body of case law.[45] The jus gentium, assumed on the basis of experience to be common to all peoples, became also the basis for Roman dealings with barbarians beyond the imperial frontiers.[46] Natural law became, and to this day remains, the basis of international law.

Reference to jus gentium appears first in the writings of Cicero, but it was not a central feature of his doctrine. It was later Roman jurisconsults, particularly in the age of empire, who elevated jus gentium to a central position in the discourse on natural law. As Crowe has written,

> The importance of the classical Roman jurisprudence for subsequent juridical thought and philosophy of law can hardly be exaggerated. The writings of the second and third century jurisconsults, especially Gaius, Paulus and Ulpian, were enshrined in the *Corpus Juris Civilis,* compiled under the Emperor Justinian in the sixth century, and so had their authority confirmed and enhanced for centuries of legislators, jurists and philosophers. In particular, their definitions of natural law, *jus gentium* and civil law were to exert enormous influence.[47]

In sum, the Romans' interest in natural law, unlike that of the Greeks, was above all pragmatic. The requirements of imperial government led them to formulate a doctrine based on what is rather than on what ought to be; it was descriptive rather than prescriptive. In the process, natural law in effect moved from the domain of abstract philosophy to that of practical jurisprudence; it became a matter of interest more to the jurist than to the philosopher. The consensual definition of natural law never became wholly predominant, even in Roman times, but it has remained one of the important approaches to the subject down to the present day.

A fundamental weakness of all the ancient discussions of natural law—indeed of ancient philosophy in general—lay in the failure to establish definitions at the outset. The commentators never said precisely what they meant either by "nature" or by "law." It is apparent in fact that they used "nature" in two quite different senses, referring sometimes to the nature of physical matter and processes and sometimes to human nature.[48] Had

45. Cf. Crowe, *Changing Profile of the Natural Law,* p. 42.
46. Cf. Buchanan, *Rediscovering Natural Law,* p. 20.
47. Crowe, *Changing Profile of the Natural Law,* p. 41. For more detail on the historical development of jus gentium see ibid., pp. 41–43.
48. Cf. Sigmund, *Natural Law in Political Thought,* pp. 11–12.

they recognized this, they might have gone on to acknowledge that there may be more than one kind of natural law: that *jus naturale* and *jus gentium,* though fundamentally different, may both be natural.

Another problematical feature, which was to plague natural law theory for centuries to come, was the concept of "right reason." The term might at first glance suggest that there is such a thing as "wrong reason," but it is clear that none of the ancient writers really conceived of such a thing. The term seems rather to designate moral reason as distinguished from pragmatic reason. Finally, the ancient philosophers and jurists never distinguished between law and morality; they used the same term to refer both to what is and to what ought to be.[49]

Roman natural law: from nomos *to* jus gentium

NATURAL LAW IN THE EARLY CHURCH: FROM NATURE'S ORDER TO GOD'S WILL

In the development of law there was no sharp break between pagan and Christian tradition, as there was in philosophy and theology. The law of medieval Christians was still the law of Rome, compiled and codified under a Christian emperor but embodying largely pre-Christian concepts and practices. While Christian philosophers turned from ancient metaphysics to scripture as legitimation for their ideas, medieval jurists continued to cite the *Corpus Juris Civilis* of Justinian.

The Justinian code, becoming in time a semisacred text, had the effect of "freezing" the development of judicial philosophy for several centuries. There was, as a result, relatively little juristic debate over the meaning of natural law after the sixth century. But for quite other, theological reasons the idea of natural law was of great importance to early Christian philosophers, for whom it came to stand for the unspoken will of God. Thus, in early Christian times, natural law became once again more a philosophical than a judicial issue.

The central dogma shared by Christianity, Judaism, and Islam holds that the universe was created and is regulated entirely by the divine will. However, the nature and working of divine will are seen quite differently in the three faiths. Both the Hebrew and the Islamic god are very specific–indeed minutely detailed–about the obligations which their followers owe to them.[50] Christianity on the other hand is not primarily a religion

49. See esp. Rommen, *Natural Law,* p. 32; also Crowe, *Changing Profile of the Natural Law,* p. 51.

50. Cf. G.E. Von Grunebaum, *Islam,* pp. 66–67. *American Anthropological Association Memoirs,* no. 81 (1955).

of the law, despite the efforts of certain early church fathers to turn it in that direction. In Jewish tradition the Messiah was to be a reformer and savior, not a lawgiver, and this was the role given to Jesus. The result is that even Christian fundamentalists could never find in the teachings of Jesus all of the guidance needed for right living and for salvation. They always had to fall back on the Old Testament for behavioral prescriptions that are not to be found in the New Testament, even though the status of the Old Testament as holy writ was never clearly attested by Jesus himself.

Natural Law

But emergent Christianity also had to accommodate itself to the rationalistic tradition so long entrenched in Greek and Roman thought. Early Christian thinkers, while accepting the divine ordination of everything, continued nevertheless to believe in a rationally ordered and largely predictable universe. They therefore had to conclude that God himself had created the cosmic order: it was his will that certain things should be regular and rational and immutable. In effect, he created a cosmic law to which he bound himself along with everyone else. Yet very little justification for such a belief could be found in scripture.

It was here that the already existing doctrine of natural law found a place. Divine will was recognized to be incompletely revealed in Scripture, but it was revealed in the regularities that could be observed in nature, including in human behavior. For many Christian thinkers, from early times to the present, natural law became an essential element of a complete theology. It was able, moreover, to accommodate both the teleological, Stoic conception of natural law and the consensual notion of jus gentium. As Sigmund has observed,

> From inchoate beginnings in Greek thought, the Stoic philosophers developed a natural law theory which was the basis for most subsequent thinking on the subject. They viewed nature as permeated with reason, which was understood to be a moral force from which ethical norms could be derived.... A religious dimension was added to this rational conception of nature as the source of ethical norms, since a rational God was the source of the reason that permeated the universe. Christian belief combined this with a belief that God had written this law into men's hearts through the promptings of conscience.[51]

In other words, God created the inherent order in nature and then made men intuitively aware of it, and responsive to it.

51. Sigmund, *Natural Law in Political Thought*, p. 30.

Natural law in the early church

Discussions of natural law can be found in the work of many of the early church fathers, including Tertullian (c. 160–245), Clement of Alexandria (c. 158–215), Lactantius (d. 320), and Ambrose of Milan (c. 340–397).[52] Far more influential, however, were the writings of St. Augustine (354–431) and St. Isidore of Seville (570–636). Augustine's view, like that of most early church fathers, was essentially the Stoic one. However, he offered a conceptual distinction not previously made by Stoic philosophers, between what he called eternal law and natural law. Eternal law is the ordering of nature itself; it is inseparable from the divine will: "the divine reason or the will of God commanding that the natural order be preserved and forbidding its disturbance."[53] Natural law comprises those behavioral precepts that are clearly derived from or in harmony with eternal law: "participation of the eternal law in a rational creature"[54] Augustine several times cited the so-called Golden Rule, "do unto others as you would have them do unto you," as an example of natural law.[55] The Augustinian distinction between eternal law and natural law clearly corresponds to the distinction earlier made between physical laws and natural law.

Isidore of Seville was a legal encyclopedist, whose *Book of Etymologies* was a vast and uncritical compilation of judicial doctrines and usages current or known in his time. Like many a predecessor, including Cicero, the author was more a transmitter than an originator. But "tradition, the handing on of the achievements of the past, plays an all-important part in the formulation of a theory of natural law. For this reason Isidore of Seville has an importance out of all proportion to his personal achievement in that he preserved so much of antiquity."[56]

The original Christian contribution to natural law doctrine was not a large one, and can be regarded in most respects as a gloss on the previously extant Stoic doctrine. It consisted mainly in linking natural law to the will of God. The linkage was not really difficult to make, and had in a sense already been anticipated by the pagan philosophers. Since the time of Aristotle they had identified nature with purposes, which clearly implied the existence of a cosmic will. To this vaguely defined force they gave the name *logos,* but they did not attempt to explore its ontology in any detail. The Christian doctrine of divine will gave to the *logos* a very explicit ontology. Otherwise, however, the God whose will was invoked in early

52. For résumés of their ideas, see Crowe, *Changing Profile of the Natural Law,* pp. 57–62.
53. Ibid., p. 66.
54. Ibid., p. 65.
55. Ibid., p. 66.
56. Ibid., p. 72.

Christian doctrine was a wholly rational being, who had bound himself to obey his own laws, and in that respect he was hardly different from the generalized "nature" envisioned by the Stoics. The only determining role allowed to God within the Christian system was as its creator, or first cause.

NATURAL LAW, CANON LAW, AND THE SCHOLASTICS

Natural Law

The Western European Middle Ages witnessed the growing separation of church and state, reflected in the establishment of separate ecclesiastical and civil courts with their separate legal codes. The distinction between natural and man-made law thus acquired a kind of institutional framework, insofar as the law of the ecclesiastical courts could be identified as the law of God, while the law of the civil courts was recognized as the law of kings.

Various concepts and interpretations of natural law were employed, somewhat unsystematically, in both the civil and the ecclesiastical courts. By the twelfth century the accumulation of case law, papal decrees, and the like was such that there was a perceived need for synthesis and order in both civil and ecclesiastical (canon) law. In civil law this was achieved through the renewed study and exegesis of Roman law, and particularly of the *Corpus Juris Civilis.* The "glossarists" who undertook the task were practicing jurists rather than legal philosophers; their concern was to understand the letter rather than the spirit of the law.

In the field of canon law, order was achieved through codification, in the *Concordium Discordantium Canonum* produced by the Italian monk Gratian sometime in the first half of the twelfth century. This work, which became better known as the *Decretum Gratiani,* never received the official blessing of the church, but it supplied such an obvious practical need that it dominated discussion of canon law for centuries to come. Crowe has called it "possibly the most important document in the history of the canon law down to the codification of 1917."[57]

On the subject of natural law, however, the effect of the *Decretum* was to further confound the already existing confusion. The work opened with the assertion that

> The human race is governed in two ways, by natural law and by custom. Natural law is that which is contained in the law and the gospel, in virtue of which each is commanded to do to others what he

57. Ibid., p. 85.

would wish to be done to himself and is forbidden to do to another what he would not have done to himself.[58]

By identifying scripture as a source of natural law, Gratian undermined what had been one of the few generally accepted features of the concept: that it was nonscriptural. The definition was further muddied, in a later passage, by the assertion that "The natural law is contained in the law and the gospel; but not all that is to be found in the law and the gospel is shown to belong to the natural law."[59] To top off the confusion, Gratian asserted in another place that "natural law is common to all nations by reason of its universal origin in a natural instinct and not in any (positive) constitution."[60] In no more than three sentences, the canonist had managed to offer an intuitive, a consensual, and a scriptural definition of natural law.[61]

Natural law, canon law, and the Scholastics

For a century and a half after Gratian, canonical discussions of natural law were concerned almost entirely with attempts to reconcile and harmonize the differing conceptions found in the *Decretum Gratiani.* Hence the commentators have come to be called "Decretists."[62] Fortunately, it is neither necessary nor possible to review their voluminous and sometimes convoluted writings here, for after the thirteenth century they were to be superseded by the doctrines of St. Thomas Aquinas (1225–1274), which became the standard church teaching on natural law until well into the twentieth century.

Aquinas and his medieval predecessors lived in what has been called the Scholastic Age. The leading thinkers were cloistered monks, who had little opportunity and probably little desire to observe the everyday world at first hand. From their philosophical perspective there was no need to do so, for they believed that the sum of all attainable wisdom was contained in writings and dicta already in existence. The task of the philosopher and the jurist was to synthesize and harmonize the accumulated wisdom of the past, not to add to it. Aquinas, a Dominican monk, worked within this tradition, but his enduring achievement was to cast a much wider net than his predecessors, incorporating the wisdom not only of Scripture and of the early church fathers, but of the ancient philosophers as well, in a grand philosophical synthesis. More than any other individual, he is credited

58. Quoted from ibid., p. 75.

59. Ibid., p. 82.

60. Ibid., p. 75.

61. For detailed discussion of Gratian, see ibid., pp. 72–86; also Sigmund, *Natural Law in Political Thought,* pp. 36–38.

62. For a very detailed review of their work, see Crowe, *Changing Profile of the Natural Law,* pp. 93–135.

with reintroducing Aristotle into the mainstream of Western philosophy. On the subject of natural law, his contribution was "The fusion of Stoic and Roman Law ideas of natural law with Aristotelian notions of teleology and the incorporation of these concepts in a Christian framework. . . ."[63]

Aquinas produced no one work specifically devoted to natural law. Discussions or mentions of the subject are scattered through a great many of his writings but achieve their fullest expression in a section of his *Summa Theologica* that is devoted to law in general, and includes a quite specific discussion of natural law. Here and elsewhere, his doctrines were set down with a self-confident assurance that is rare in philosophical discourse, and that gives to many of his ideas a deceptive appearance of simplicity. In fact they are very far from simple, attempting as they do to reconcile a wide range of formerly conflicting doctrines. Inevitably, the work of Aquinas has given rise to an enormous body of interpretive literature and a fair amount of controversy. No brief précis can do proper justice to the Thomist (i.e., Aquinian) doctrine of natural law or the various interpretations of it; what follows here is mainly the interpretation of Paul Sigmund in *Natural Law in Political Thought.*[64]

Natural Law

According to Sigmund's interpretation, Aquinas distinguished, at least at times, four kinds of law: eternal law, divine law, natural law, and human law. Eternal law, following the doctrine of Augustine, is God's grand and unchanging plan for the universe. Divine law is that part of the eternal law that has been directly revealed to man through the scriptures. Natural law, again following Augustine, involves man's participation in eternal law through a special, innate quality of reason. A knowledge and understanding of eternal law has been implanted into the reason of every living person through a somewhat mystical process called *synderesis.*[65] Human law is the application of the precepts of reason, derived from natural law, in specific, contingent circumstances.

The place of jus gentium within the system of Aquinas is problematical, for like earlier thinkers he tried to reconcile two basically conflicting views. On one hand, Aquinas asserted that jus gentium cannot be natural

---

63. Ibid., p. 41.

64. *Natural Law in Political Thought,* pp. 39–54. More extended discussions of the Thomist doctrine of Natural Law, not always in agreement with Sigmund, are those of Crowe, *Changing Profile of the Natural Law,* pp. 136–191; Eterovich, *Natural Law from Plato to Kant,* pp. 49–60; Rommen, *Natural Law,* pp. 45–57; and Thomas E. Davitt in Wilkin et al., *Origins of the Natural Law Tradition,* pp. 26–47.

65. This concept first appeared in theological literature about a hundred years before the time of Aquinas. However, its meaning was never made very clear, and it disappeared from use after the Middle Ages. For extended discussion see Crowe, *Changing Profile of the Natural Law,* pp. 123–141.

law per se, since it is unique to mankind and is not shared with the lower animals. At the same time it is said to be "closely connected with" natural law because it is derived from natural law through the application of human reason. The locus of both natural law and jus gentium is within the realm of human reason, but natural law has been placed there by divine grace, while jus gentium has been developed through man's active exercise of his reasoning faculty. Jus gentium is nonetheless universal, and therefore does not fit the definition of human law. It is, in effect, a fifth category, standing somewhere between natural law and human law.[66]

Natural law, canon law, and the Scholastics

The heroic attempt of Aquinas to synthesize and harmonize so much earlier doctrine, pagan as well as Christian, was not and could not be entirely successful. As Sigmund observes,

> He could not admit the Aristotelian possibility that nature could provide fully for man's fulfillment. The theological doctrine of Original Sin and the Fall of Man compelled him to combine in his thinking two notions of nature–the first being man's uncorrupted nature in the state of innocence, and the second man's present sinful nature in which coercive government and property are necessary and slavery is useful. Similarly, his belief in the necessity of divine grace led Aquinas to assert that human nature could not arrive at its true goal–the direct vision of God–without divine assistance, and to combine a recognition of the necessity of the supernatural life of grace with the Aristotelian naturalism that pervades much of the rest of his theory.[67]

The grand philosophical synthesis of Aquinas, more comprehensive than anything that had been attempted since Aristotle, eventually became, and long remained, the official teaching of the Catholic Church. The Thomist conception of natural law was carried along with the remainder of the philosophical system, despite certain inherent difficulties that we have just noted. In the century after Aquinas there arose, nevertheless, a rather short-lived contrary tradition that has come to be called Nominalism. Its outstanding exponents were John Duns Scotus and William of Ockham; the first voices on theology to be heard from the British Isles.

In contrast to Aquinas, Scotus and Ockham asserted that God was not,

---

66. Sigmund, *Natural Law in Political Thought*, pp. 42–43. See also Davitt, in Wilkin et al., *Origins of the Natural Law Tradition*, pp. 59–60, and Crowe, *Changing Profile of the Natural Law*, pp. 149–155.

67. Sigmund, *Natural Law in Political Thought*, p. 46.

and could not be, bound by the constraints of the natural order he had created; he remained free to change it at any time. This doctrine was therefore sometimes called "voluntaristic." Natural law, especially for Ockham, consisted not of God's immutable decrees but of man's exercise of his reason in attempting to understand the divine will.

Ockham actually distinguished three different kinds of natural law, one of which was for all practical purposes jus gentium. Two features of his discussion on this subject are worthy of note here. First, in keeping with his insistence on the primacy of will, Ockham asserted that the legitimacy of any government depends on the will of the governed. Second, as regards jus gentium, he asserted that it derives its force as law not from its inherent reasonableness but simply from its universality; "the agreement of all men proscribing the contrary."[68] Both of these principles broke sharply with the ecclesiastical tradition that had prevailed for several centuries, anticipating in some ways the emergence of a separate, secularist tradition of natural law, which will occupy us in a later section.

The last of the medieval scholastics whose work requires consideration here is the Spanish theologian Francisco Suárez (1548–1617). In the best tradition of Scholasticism, he attempted to reconcile the Thomist and voluntarist doctrines. This is clear from his definition of the two basic requisites of law: that it be just and congruous with reason, and that it possess effective binding force, which can come ultimately only from the will of God.[69] The will of God nevertheless is the will of a rational being who cannot go against his own rational nature, nor can he grant man dispensation from it.[70]

Suárez distinguished, somewhat more clearly than had earlier thinkers, between rational human nature and natural law. Rational human nature does not furnish behavioral precepts; it merely defines right and wrong. Natural law involves behavioral precepts based on our perception of right and wrong.[71] The author devoted a good deal of study to the subject of jus gentium, which in his time had become a very practical issue in Spain (see next section). He followed Aquinas and earlier thinkers in placing jus gentium somewhere between natural and civil law, but followed Ockham in asserting that its force derives not from its inherent rationality but from its near-universality. Jus gentium cannot be absolutely immutable because even generally agreed customs may change in the course of

68. Ibid., pp. 56–57.
69. Eterovich, *Natural Law from Plato to Kant*, p. 71.
70. Ibid., pp. 73–74; Sigmund, *Natural Law in Political Thought*, p. 59.
71. Eterovich, *Natural Law from Plato to Kant*, pp. 71–73.

time; moreover, the "law of nations" is observed by almost all nations but not by all of them.[72]

In sum, the medieval conception of natural law differed from both the pagan and the modern doctrines in that nature was viewed as an intermediary between God and man, rather than as a first cause. This relieved the scholastics from two problems that have plagued the modern, secular theorists. First, they were not obliged to define nature very precisely, since it was whatever God had willed it to be. Second, they were not obliged to apologize for or to try and deny the essential teleology of the doctrine, which in both the medieval and the classical formulations was avowedly teleological.

Natural law, canon law, and the Scholastics

At this point we may take leave of the ecclesiastical doctrine of natural law, except insofar as it affected European understanding of the American Indians (to be considered in the next section). The subject continues to be studied and debated among theologians down to the present day,[73] but the concepts of natural law that have carried over into anthropology derive not from the churchmen but from a separate, secular tradition that arose beginning in the sixteenth century. This will mainly occupy us in remaining pages of the chapter.

NATURAL LAW AND THE AMERICAN INDIANS: THE SPANISH DEBATES

In 1495 Columbus sent back to Spain a number of Indian captives, hoping to sell them as slaves in the markets of Seville. However, Queen Isabella intervened and stopped the sale. Slavery at the time was commonplace in the Iberian Peninsula, and the queen was not greatly troubled about the morality of Columbus's action. She was, however, uncertain about its legality–a serious consideration in the highly legalistic world of the late Middle Ages. "We wish to be informed by civil lawyers, canonists and theologians whether we may, with good conscience, sell these Indians or not," she wrote. The verdict (which is not recorded) was apparently unfavorable, for in the following year the queen ordered that all Indian slaves in Seville be sent back to America.[74] This episode was to inaugurate a century of debate about the place of the Indians in relation to natural law–a

72. Ibid., pp. 74–76.

73. For discussion of the latter-day theological concepts of natural law, see Sigmund, *Natural Law in Political Thought,* pp. 180–194, and esp. Crowe, *Changing Profile of the Natural Law,* pp. 246–290.

74. Anthony Pagden, *The Fall of Natural Man* (Cambridge, 1982), p. 31.

debate that was to significantly transform European thinking both about the Indians and about the law.[75]

The discovery of America and its native inhabitants raised two immediate questions about natural law, which had both practical and theoretical implications. First, were the newly discovered peoples subject to natural law—hence to papal authority—in the same way as were all other peoples? Second, did the customs of the aborigines provide confirmation, in the form of jus gentium, for the universal existence of natural law? In the minds of many thinkers, the two questions were interlinked. Whether or not Indians were subject to the provisions of natural law would be determined by whether or not their customs showed an awareness of it.

The decision of Queen Isabella to return the Indian captives to America obviously did not resolve what came to be known as *las cosas de Indias* (best translated as "the Indian question"). In 1504, shortly after the Queen's death, King Ferdinand, the surviving Spanish monarch, called another convocation of civil lawyers, canonists, and theologians to debate the legitimacy of the Spanish occupation of the New World. The papal bull of Alexander IV in 1493 had granted to the Spanish king dominion over the whole of the Western hemisphere, with the exception of eastern Brazil, on the assumption that the Pope possessed jurisdiction over pagan as well as Christian lands. However, the legitimacy of this assertion of papal authority was questioned by a great many Spanish thinkers, ecclesiastical as well as temporal.[76] Ferdinand was therefore hopeful of finding a sounder legal basis for the Spanish conquests. His judicial consultants apparently found it for him in the doctrine of a Scottish theologian, John Mair (or Major), who cited the works both of Ptolemy and of Aristotle to prove that the Indians fell into the category of "natural slaves," a status that had been accepted by natural law theorists throughout the Middle Ages.[77] On this basis the council of 1504 had no difficulty in agreeing "in the presence and with the opinion of the archbishop of Seville... that the Indians should be given [to the Spaniards] and that this was in agreement with human and divine law."[78]

Because of continued outcry from missionaries, still another council

---

75. For a detailed discussion of the philosophical, theological, and practical problems arising from the discovery of the American Indians, and the efforts to administer them, see Lewis Hanke, *The First Social Experiments in America* (*Harvard Historical Monographs*, vol. V, 1935).

76. See Pagden, *Fall of Natural Man*, p. 30.

77. See ibid., pp. 38–39.

78. Quoted from ibid., p. 28.

was convoked by Ferdinand in 1512.[79] The question was once again the legitimacy of the conquest, and more specifically the forced conscription of Indian labor under the *encomienda* system. Only two of the submitted opinions, those of Bernardo de Mesa and Gil Gregorio, have survived. Both men cited the doctrine of Aristotle to support their contention that the Indians were barbarians and natural slaves. However, the king was still not satisfied with the outcome of the 1512 council, for shortly after its conclusion he asked two of its members, Juan López de Palacios Rubios and Matías de Paz, to draw up separate, more detailed opinions. Pagden has identified these as "the first full-length ethical and legal considerations of the justice of the conquest that have survived."[80] The *Libellus de insulanis oceanis* of Palacios Rubios is by far the longer and more interesting of the two documents. Curiously, the author began by painting a highly romanticized, primitivistic picture of the Indians as they had evidently been represented by certain missionaries and philosophers. He went on to show that this idyll was an illusion, for the Indians were without society and without religion. In particular he cited the matrilineal descent of the Arawaks (which he evidently took to be characteristic of all Indians) as evidence that they did not understand the proper organization of society. Nevertheless, the Indian did not quite fit the Aristotelian definition of a natural slave, for he was not born to be a slave. He retained a certain freedom of will and a will to be free, whereas Aristotle's natural slave had no other desire but to serve his master. This led to a paradoxical conception of the Indian as at once a slave and a free man, which was to persist in Spanish thinking for quite a long time.

The jurists' successive verdicts in support of the encomienda policy did not still the dissenting voice of the missionaries. Bartolomé de Las Casas returned from the Indies to Spain in 1515 to begin his lifelong crusade on behalf of Indian rights. Although he was only intermittently in Spain until 1547, he continued to speak out energetically whenever the occasion presented, and by the middle of the century he could unquestionably command the king's ear. Other missionaries who spoke or wrote on behalf of the Indians, and in opposition to their enslavement under the encomienda, were Domingo de Santo Tomás, Domingo de Betanzos, and Juan de Zumárraga.[81]

Meanwhile there grew up, independently of royal consultation, a group

---

79. See ibid., pp. 30–31, and Lewis Hanke, *Aristotle and the American Indians* (Chicago, 1959), pp. 14–15.

80. Pagden, *Fall of Natural Man*, p. 50.

81. Hanke, *Aristotle and the American Indians*, pp. 23–24.

of theologians who took it upon themselves to examine the "Indian question" from the standpoint of natural law. Most of them had been trained or had taught at the famous theological college at Salamanca, and they came to be known as the School of Salamanca. They took the position that the "Indian question" lay clearly outside the jurisdiction of civil law, and could only be discussed in terms of natural law, which is to say divine law. Therefore, said the theologians, they and not the civil jurists were the only ones qualified to discuss it. They questioned the citation of ancient philosophers by the jurists, whom they felt were insufficiently schooled to understand the doctrines they invoked.

Natural Law

The approach which the Salamanca theologians followed in elucidating the natural law was basically consensual–the study of jus gentium.

> If what the whole society of men, or even the largest part of it, considers to be true is, in fact, not so, then God must be at fault for it was he who first implanted in man's mind the clear and simple principles by means of which he is able to reach his understanding of the world: "Our intellect is from God," said Vitoria, "and if it were to have a natural inclination toward falsehood then this would have to be attributed to God." Any such hypothesis is evidently untenable, therefore "knowledge is that thing on which all men are in agreement."[82]

The founding genius of the Salamanca school was Francisco de Vitoria, who held the principal chair of theology at Salamanca from 1529 until his death in 1546. His views in regard to the Indians were frequently expressed in lectures throughout his career, and then, after his death, were collected and published in a work called *De Indis.* Although not printed until 1557, it was widely circulated in manuscript before that date, and had a lasting influence on all subsequent discussion of the "Indian question."[83]

Vitoria began *De Indis* by disposing of most of the arguments that had previously been advanced for enslaving the Indians, and then proceeded to develop his own theory. This was presented in two parts. The first was in effect a comparative ethnography, in which the author marshaled all of the evidence that could be adduced to show that the Indians were not really barbarians. One by one he reviewed what today we would call the basic categories of culture–cities, family life, rule by an elite, laws, judicial institutions, manufactures, trade, and religion–showing in each of these areas

82. Pagden, *Fall of Natural Man*, p. 63.
83. Ibid., pp. 65–66.

that the Indians had well-developed cultural institutions. His ethnographic examples were of course drawn, deliberately, from the most culturally advanced groups of which he had knowledge: the Mexica and the Inca.[84]

In the second part of *De Indis,* Vitoria took a different and somewhat contrary tack. He had proven that the Indians had all the basic, necessary institutions of civil society, but he had not proven that they were sound institutions. In fact, Indian civil life was disorderly or chaotic, as evidenced for example by the "twin horrors" of human sacrifice and cannibalism that were so repeatedly cited by European commentators.[85] These were not sufficient, in Vitoria's view, to establish that the Indians were barbarians, but they indicated that the natives had a very imperfect understanding of natural law. He compared them not to the wild men imagined by Ptolemy or Herodotus but to European peasants: "Even among our own people we can see many peasants who are little different from brute animals."[86] "'I believe,' he said, 'that if they seem so insensate and foolish... this comes, for the most part, from their poor and barbarous education.'"[87] Vitoria concluded in the end that both Indians and peasants were not natural slaves but natural children: too ignorant to be left to manage their own affairs, but capable of education until they were able to do so.

Vitoria has been cited by later historians both as an apologist for the existing order and as a major crusader for Indian rights. Either view involves a misreading of his character. He was first and last a theologian, and his interest in the Indians was at best juristic rather than humanitarian.[88] His major and important contribution however lay in applying the concept of jus gentium for the first time on a worldwide scale, to primitive as well as to civilized peoples.[89]

Other prominent members of the Salamanca school, whose views closely followed those of Vitoria, were Melchor Cano and Diego de Soto. Their writings, as well as the persistent pro-Indian propaganda of the missionaries, provoked a violent reaction from Juan Ginés de Sepúlveda, who was chaplain and official chronicler to the Spanish king. At the instigation of the president of the Council of the Indies, he wrote a work called *Democrates secundus sive de justis causis belli apud Indios* ("principles supporting the just cause of wars against the Indians") which was, in the words of

84. For a more detailed synopsis see ibid., pp. 60–79.
85. Cf. ibid., pp. 80–90.
86. Quoted from ibid., p. 97.
87. Ibid.
88. Cf. ibid., pp. 64–65.
89. See esp. Eterovich, *Natural Law from Plato to Kant,* pp. 64–67; also Crowe, *Changing Profile of the Natural Law,* pp. 215–216.

Pagden, "the most virulent and uncompromising argument for the inferiority of the Indians ever written."[90]

The virulence of Sepúlveda's language caused unease both to the Council of the Indies and to the king, and of course it infuriated Las Casas, who had just returned permanently to Spain. The Council refused to approve the publication of *Democrates secundus*, and, largely at the instigation of Las Casas, it was instead referred for judgment to the theologians at Alcalá and Salamanca. After considerable deliberation they recommended against its publication, on the ground that its doctrine was unsound. In the ensuing year so much outcry was raised both by Sepúlveda and by Las Casas that the king and Council of the Indies ordered that there should be a public disputation between the two men. The stage was thus set for the celebrated Valladolid debates of 1550–51.[91]

The topic set for debate was: "Is it lawful for the king of Spain to wage war on the Indians before preaching the faith to them in order to subject them to his rule, so that afterwards they may be more easily instructed in the faith?"[92] Sepúlveda naturally took the affirmative, and Las Casas the negative. Both men based themselves on their particular interpretations of natural law, Sepúlveda relying mainly on Aristotle and Augustine, and Las Casas citing the ethnographic evidence of jus gentium. But after three separate sessions, beginning in August of 1550 and ending in May of 1551, the outcome was inconclusive. Both protagonists claimed a victory of judgment, but there was no significant change in existing colonial policy.[93]

From the standpoint of history, however, there was one important consequence. Las Casas was stimulated by the Valladolid debates to set down on paper the ideas that he had been developing during a lifetime of advocacy for Indian rights. Shortly after the final debate he produced his *Argumentum apologiae... adversus Genesium Sepulvedam theologicum cordubensem*, an expanded version of the document he had read before the Valladolid judges. A little later came the *Apologética historia*, a massive comparative ethnography of American Indians, apparently written also in 1551. Finally, in 1566, came his comprehensive *Historia de las Indias*, a work on which he had labored for nearly forty years.

It is chiefly the *Apologética historia* that is of interest to us here. Essentially it followed the same format as the first part of Vitoria's *De Indis*, but with the second, more negative part, omitted. That is, the author reviewed

90. Pagden, *Fall of Natural Man*, p. 109.

91. See esp. Hanke, *Aristotle and the American Indians*, pp. 28–37.

92. Ibid., p. 38.

93. Ibid., p. 74. For a more detailed account of the debates see ibid., pp. 38–43.

an enormous mass of Native American ethnography to demonstrate that the Indians were not and should not be slaves–period. The missionary cited all kinds of historical and ethnographic evidence to show that the preconquest Indian communities fulfilled all of Aristotle's requirements for a true civil society. The historical method employed by Las Casas was to juxtapose short descriptions of ancient primitive cultures, like those of the Celts and Iberians, with descriptions of parallel institutions or customs among the American Indians. In sum, the *Apologética historia* was, in the words of Anthony Pagden, "an expansive piece of comparative ethnology, the first, so far as I am aware, to be written in a European language."[94]

José de Acosta published his major works a generation after those of Las Casas, at a time when the "Indian question" was no longer a subject of political dispute. The Spanish king had issued, in 1572, a new set of laws for the Indies which in theory if not in practice ended both the military conquests of the Indians and the encomienda system. There remained nevertheless a fundamental division of opinion in Spain between those who in effect adhered to the Sepúlveda view and those who adhered to the Las Casas view in regard to the Indians.[95] Two of Acosta's major works, *De procuranda indorum salute* (1588) and the much more comprehensive *Historia natural y moral de las Indias* (1589), were in the largest sense addressed to persons of the Sepúlveda persuasion. They aimed at quashing the "common and ignorant contempt in which the Indians are held by Europeans who think that these peoples have none of the qualities of rational men."[96]

Acosta was a Jesuit rather than a Dominican, but he was nevertheless strongly influenced by the Salamanca school. He was familiar in detail with the works of Vitoria, although he does not seen to have been familiar with those of Las Casas. But the *Historia natural,* although philosophically akin to *De Indis* and *Apologética historia,* was a far more ambitious work than anything attempted by either of the earlier defenders of the Indians. It was meant to provide, for novice missionaries and also for a wider audience, a complete system of knowledge about the New World, including both its natural features and its native peoples. The author saw himself as the heir to the great naturalists of antiquity, and one of his translators called him "the Herodotus and the Pliny of the newly discovered world."[97]

The works of Acosta were of course no more successful in putting to rest the "Indian question" than were those of Vitoria and Las Casas. In Spain and in Latin America, the spirit of the Valladolid debates has continued to

94. Pagden, *Fall of Natural Man*, pp. 121–122.
95. Cf. Hanke, *Aristotle and the American Indians*, pp. 86–88.
96. Quoted from Pagden, *Fall of Natural Man*, p. 157.
97. Ibid., p. 151.

rage right into the twentieth century, with champions of Sepúlveda and Las Casas still extolling the virtues of their respective heroes and damning their opponents as zealots, fascists, or communists.[98] As Hanke concludes,

> The problem discussed at Valladolid over four centuries ago concerning the proper relations between peoples of different cultures, religions, customs, and technical knowledge, has today a contemporary and sonorous ring. Sepúlveda and Las Casas still represent two basic and contradictory responses to the question posed by the existence of people in the world who are different from ourselves.[99]

The works of Vitoria, Las Casas, and Acosta comprise a unique chapter in the history of natural law, for they were at once learnedly theoretical and immediately practical. They constitute, in effect, the first instances of applied natural law. The Spanish theologians (with the partial exception of Vitoria) were concerned not to develop or improve the theory of natural law per se, but to apply the existing theory to a practical administrative and political problem which had moral roots. They systematically reviewed and cited far more ethnographic data than did any other natural law theorists before or since, but their purpose was not, like that of some later thinkers, to improve their understanding of the law itself. On the contrary, they used the law to improve their understanding of the peoples they studied; that is, of the American Indians.

For rational-minded Europeans of the sixteenth and later centuries, natural law succeeded where Scripture and history had failed. That is, it placed the Native Americans within an acceptable framework of understanding with respect both to ancient philosophy and to medieval theology. From being nature's slaves, the Indians were redefined as nature's children.[100] Nearly all subsequent European writing and thinking about the Indians reflected that perspective.

For essentially similar reasons, the works of Vitoria, Las Casas, and Acosta are landmarks in the history of ethnology. They illustrate how, long before anthropology, one particular natural law doctrine–that of jus gentium–provided a rational framework for the understanding both of cultural similarities and of cultural differences on a worldwide scale. It is a framework that, albeit under other names, has largely persisted to the present day.

98. See esp. Hanke, *Aristotle and the American Indians*, pp. 88–95.
99. Ibid., p. 95.
100. Cf. Pagden, *Fall of Natural Man*, p. 3.

THE REEMERGENCE OF A SECULAR DOCTRINE: FROM DIVINE WILL TO SOCIAL CONTRACT

According to Alexander d'Entrèves, the modern doctrine of natural law is rationalist, individualist, and radical, differing in all these respects from the medieval and earlier traditions.[101] "Natural Law in the modern period, frees itself from its close association with theology and the medieval church; it breaks with the hierarchical and group-oriented aspects of medieval theory; and it becomes a revolutionary ideology or justification for the transformation of political, economic, and social relationships."[102]

Like so many other rationalist and secularist traditions, the modern doctrine of natural law was a stepchild of the Protestant Reformation, and of the political conflicts it unleashed. Since the interpretation of Scripture –no longer the monopoly of an established church–had become problematical, all religious factions from Roman Catholics to radical sects like the Anabaptists and Mennonites sought to legitimize themselves on the basis of their own interpretations of natural law. The number of such interpretations was, consequently, legion.

We have already seen that some of the doctrines of William of Ockham anticipated the secularist tradition of natural law, though he was in fact a devout churchman. A more clearly transitional figure between the medieval and the modern traditions was Richard Hooker, whose *Laws of Ecclesiastical Polity* was published in 1593. Hooker, an Anglican, was in most respects a Thomist, but he was much more explicit than either Aquinas or Ockham in insisting that government must rest on the consent of the governed. Reviving the ancient tradition of conjectural prehistory, he imagined an original state of nature in which government did not exist. Government arose gradually and consensually from the perceived need of people to get along with one another and avoid conflict, in obedience to the commandment that we should love one another.[103]

Hugo Grotius, a Dutch Protestant theologian of the seventeenth century, has been acclaimed ever since his own time as the true founder both of modern natural law theory and of international law theory.[104] His *On the Law of War and Peace* (1625) was written during the height of the Thirty Years' War (1618–1648), and was intended to try and find a solution

101. A. P. d'Entrèves, *Natural Law* (London, 1951), pp. 49–62.

102. Sigmund, *Natural Law in Political Thought*, p. 55.

103. Ibid., p. 76. For fuller discussion see ibid., pp. 74–76, and esp. John S. Marshall in Wilkin et al., *Origins of the Natural Law Tradition*, pp. 48–68.

104. Cf. Sigmund, *Natural Law in Political Thought*, p. 61; d'Entrèves, *Natural Law*, p. 50; Rommen, *Natural Law*, p. 70; Crowe, *Changing Profile of the Natural Law*, p. 223.

for that incredibly barbarous conflict. "Throughout the Christian world I observed a lack of restraint in relation to war, such as even barbarous races should be ashamed of; I observed that men rush to arms for slight causes or for no cause at all, and that when arms have once been taken up there is no longer any respect for law, divine or human..." he wrote.[105] The starting point of Grotius's approach to natural law is a conception that dates back to Aristotle–that of man as an inherently social animal. All natural laws derive from man's need to live in society and to get along. All international laws derive from the need of societies to get along with each other.

Natural Law

Natural law for Grotius, as for many earlier thinkers going back to Stoic times, was "the rule of human acts as they agree or disagree with human nature according to right reason's dictates."[106] He set out to prove the existence of natural law in two ways:

> Proof a priori consists in demonstrating the necessary agreement or disagreement of anything with a rational and social nature [of man]; proof a posteriori, in concluding, if not with absolute assurance, at least with every probability, that is in according to the law of nature which is believed to be such among all nations, or among all those that are more advanced in civilization.[107]

The first "proof" hardly differs from that of the Stoics except for the emphasis on man's *social* as well as his *rational* nature–an important addition to the original doctrine. The second "proof" invokes the familiar concept of jus gentium, but only in a probabilistic sense.

Grotius's tendency to reify Society–that is, to invest it with a rational will of its own–clearly anticipates the thought of many Enlightenment thinkers. It shows through most clearly in his treatment of international law, which he saw not as a set of pragmatic arrangements between kings but as a set of immutable principles that govern the relations between societies, because societies like individuals must live together in peace. "If no association of men can be maintained without law..., surely also that association which binds together the human race, or binds many nations together, has need of law...."[108]

Purely on the basis of its content, Grotius's conception hardly satisfies

105. Quoted from Eterovich, *Natural Law from Plat to Kant*, pp. 78–79.
106. Ibid., p. 83.
107. Quoted from ibid., p. 81.
108. Quoted from ibid., p. 84.

the definition of modern natural law proposed by d'Entrèves. As the latter author observes, "It is not in its content that Grotius' theory breaks away from Scholasticism. It is in its method.[109] . . . Grotius' aim was to construct a system of laws which would carry conviction in an age when theological controversy was losing the power to do so. He proved that it was possible to build up a theory of laws independent of theological presuppositions. His successors completed the task."[110]

The reemergence of a secular doctrine

One of those who "completed the task" was Thomas Hobbes (1588–1679), famous for his description of primitive life as "solitary, poor, nasty, brutish, and short." Hobbes's ideas on natural law were set out in three works, but most completely in *Leviathan* (1651). According to Hobbes' view, the single drive that motivates all human conduct is self-preservation. Therefore, self-preservation through rational conduct is really the only natural law.[111] However, the instinct of self-preservation often brings men in conflict with their fellows, and it is for this reason that society (or rather, government) was developed: it ensures the preservation of all. Hobbes followed Hooker in imagining an original state of mankind in which there was no government; this was the "war of all against all" in which life was "nasty, brutish, and short." Government originated when people recognized that the best way to preserve oneself is to also let others preserve themselves. For this purpose a man should "lay down his right to do all things; and be contented with so much liberty against other men, as he will allow other men against himself."[112]

This line of thinking obliged Hobbes to distinguish between natural law and natural right; a distinction subsequently rejected by most other theorists. Natural right is only the right of self-preservation; natural law is the series of behavioral precepts that will best assure self-preservation. Hobbes enumerated these in considerable detail: they included seeking peace, sacrificing a degree of liberty for the sake of peace, honoring covenants, showing gratitude, getting along with others, pardoning offenses, punishing criminals, avoiding contumely, acknowledging the equality of others, generosity, dispensing equal justice when in office, equally sharing common property, disposal of indivisible property by lot, the right of primogeniture or first occupancy, guaranteeing safe conduct to envoys, and submission of disputes to arbitration. All of these rules were said to be, in one way or another, aspects of the Golden Rule.[113]

---

109. d'Entrèves, *Natural Law*, p. 51.
110. Ibid., p. 52.
111. Sigmund, *Natural Law in Political Thought*, pp. 79–80.
112. Quoted from Eterovich, *Natural Law from Plato to Kant*, p. 104.
113. Ibid., pp. 106–109.

As Eterovich observes, Hobbes's position involved a drastic reversal of the traditional view regarding the relationship between law and right. Previous thinkers had assumed that natural law flows from human nature and encompasses the totality of man's obligations and expectations, while natural right flows in turn from natural law. Hobbes reversed the proposition, insisting that natural right is fundamental to human nature, while natural law developed to protect it.[114] While most later thinkers rejected Hobbes' specific vision of natural law as deriving from the right of self-preservation, the emphasis on right rather than on duty as the primary focus of natural law was to become a cornerstone of most later thinking on the subject.

Hobbes's highly authoritarian doctrine, attributing to man a wholly self-interested nature, ran counter to the rising groundswell of liberal thinking in Europe, and it provoked a considerable, largely unfavorable reaction. It was in that context–the effort to develop a more liberal and more a optimistic doctrine–that natural law theory became almost inextricably blended with Progressivism, as we will see in the next section.

Niccolò Machiavelli has usually been regarded as the great dissenter on natural law; one of the few thinkers of his time who had no use for the doctrine.[115] Nevertheless, as Geerken has pointed out, a certain Ciceronian or Stoic conception of natural law is implicit in much of his writing.[116] The central concept of Machiavelli's philosophy is *ordine,* the consistent and orderly exercise of power by those who have power. He applied the term both to the ordering of the universe and the ordering of human affairs, and he clearly asserted that the order of man must imitate the order of nature: "he who imitates nature cannot be rebuked."[117] Whatever its specific natural law implications, Machiavelli's doctrine contributed greatly to the secularization of political and social thought in the early modern era.[118]

The lasting achievement of the early modern theorists was to conceive of natural law in an entirely new frame of relationship: not between man and nature or between man and God, but between man individually and man collectively, or in other words between the individual and society. It

---

114. Ibid., p. 102.
115. Cf. Heinrich Rommen in A. L. Scanlan, ed., *University of Notre Dame Natural Law Institute Proceedings* (Notre Dame, Ind., 1949), p. 90; Isaiah Berlin in Myron P. Gilmore, ed., *Studies in Machiavelli* (Florence, 1972), p. 194; and John H. Geerken in Harold J. Johnson, ed., *The Medieval Tradition of Natural Law* (Kalamazoo, Mich., 1987), p. 37.
116. Geerken in Johnson, *The Medieval Tradition in Natural Law,* pp. 37–65.
117. Ibid., p. 42.
118. Ibid., p. 39.

was a formulation that for the first time left both God and physical nature out of account; society itself became the determining force. Natural law was embodied in the "contractual" relationship between the society and its members. "To neither Hobbes nor Locke is natural law an expression of a cosmic moral order; it is a protection of individual human rights, a doctrine conformably concomitant with the emergence of modern science and philosophy and of democratic capitalism," wrote Douglas Sturm.[119]

The reemergence of a secular doctrine

The effect of this development was, in the long run, nothing less than revolutionary, for it converted natural law from a theological doctrine into a political one. In place of the age-old divine right of kings, the early modern theorists substituted the notion of social contract. It took some time however before the radical or reformist implications of the doctrine were realized. Hooker, Grotius, and Hobbes all believed that the citizenry from the beginning had granted virtually unlimited power to their sovereigns, so that the practical implications of social contract were hardly different from those of divine right. Importantly, they did not believe that the consent of the governed, once given, had to be periodically reaffirmed; in effect the social contract was not renegotiable. It was left to the thinkers of the Enlightenment to complete the job of transformation, converting natural law into a radical and reformist doctrine.

THE ENLIGHTENMENT: FROM SOCIAL OBLIGATION TO UNIVERSAL RIGHT

By any practical reckoning, the eighteenth century was the triumphal age of natural law: the time when it reached its climactic expression in the American and French Revolutions. Yet, paradoxically, the role of natural law in Enlightenment philosophy is ambiguous. Nearly all the leading thinkers believed devoutly both in a continually improving society and in an unchanging natural law, and it is not easy to reconcile these two aspects of their thought, which seem to involve quite different conceptions of the relationship between man, society, and nature. As believers in inevitable social progress, independent of any human will, the Enlightenment thinkers placed society quite unambiguously within the natural order. Social progress was itself a fundamental law of nature. Yet their natural law theory pictured society as a man-made institution created by the consensus of its members, and therefore outside the domain of nature. This contradiction was never wholly resolved in the eighteenth century.

119. Douglas Sturm in Mircea Eliade, ed., *The Encyclopedia of Religion* (New York, 1987), vol. 10, p. 322.

Nearly all Enlightenment theories, including those on natural law, show the influence of two powerful ideological currents: Utopianism and Deism. Like their Stoic forebears, the Enlightenment thinkers sought to be both realist philosophers and utopian reformers. Thus, progress and natural law stood both for historical realities and for utopian aspirations. The continuity of social progress, now accepted as historical fact, showed that human nature was ultimately perfectible: a notion dear to the hearts of nearly all eighteenth-century thinkers. Natural law had determined the course of progress, and it indicated the way in which perfection could be achieved.

A great many of the Enlightenment thinkers were either avowed or closet deists. That is, they continued to accept the divine origin and ordering of the universe while rejecting Scripture and revelation as evidence of the divine will. Science had shown that everything in nature, from planets to microbes, was consistently and logically ordered.

> What had science revealed? Everywhere design, order, and law, where hitherto there had been chaos. Whether one contemplated the infinitely great through the optic glass of the Tuscan artist, or the infinitely little through the microscope of Malpighi, one received at every turn new assurance that all was 'according to the Ordainer of order and mystical mathematicks of the city of heaven.'[120]

The study of nature, rather than of Scripture, thus became the only reliable clue to God's great plan.

Natural law was, of course, one manifestation of God's plan. This idea was hardly new; it had been a basic theological doctrine throughout the Middle Ages. But while the theologians accepted natural law as only one of several evidences of God's will, along with Scripture and revelation, the deists rejected all evidence except that of observed nature. They were scientific rationalists whose theories required a deity only as a prime mover to set the natural order in motion.

The metamorphosis of social contract theory

Basic to the Enlightenment doctrine of natural law was the notion of the "social contract," a concept often attributed to Rousseau but in fact tracing back at least to the time of Hooker. According to this conception, human beings had originally lived in isolation and without rules, but had

120. Quoted from Basil Willey, *The Eighteenth Century Background* (London, 1946), p. 5.

later come together in council and agreed to live as a community, their agreement being regarded as the "social contract." It was clear, from this perspective, that society was based on the consent of its members, and on no other authority.[121]

It is important to note that the "contract" was conceived in two senses. In the beginning it was the agreement between individuals to set up a government. Once that was done, however, the contract was between the government or state itself, and the individuals who had created it: it specified what the government and its subjects owed to each other. In that sense it was not unlike the Covenant between Yahweh and the Hebrews.

Their dual roles as historical theorists and as social activists also required the Enlightenment philosophers to think of natural law in two senses, one absolute and the other relative. Natural law in the absolute sense was embodied in the unchanging principle of the social contract: it specified what all societies had always owed to their members, since the beginning of "civil society." Natural law in the relative sense referred to the kinds of social regulation that were "natural" at each of the successive stages of evolutionary development.

The dualistic approach to natural law is clearly apparent in the work of Samuel Pufendorf, whose book on the history of law was briefly mentioned in Chapter 2.[122]

> An institution may be described as part of natural law in two senses; first, because it derives from some principle of natural law that something should be done or not done; and secondly, because it proceeds from some institution suggested by natural law for the betterment of society. An institution of natural law in the first sense existed even in the state of nature. An institution in the second sense was introduced [later] because right reason, out of consideration for the condition of social life, had shown the need for it.[123]

Pufendorf was a disciple and admirer of Grotius, and like Grotius he based his theory of natural law on man's inherent sociability. However, he rejected the empirical approach recommended by Grotius. The manners and customs of nations were so numerous that they could not possibly all be studied, and, importantly, there was no moral justification for restrict-

121. Peter Stein, *Legal Evolution* (Cambridge, 1980), p. 1.

122. *De Jure Naturae et Gentium,* published in English as *The Law of Nature and Nations* (1672).

123. Stein, *Legal Evolution*, pp. 5–6.

ing observation to the more "advanced" societies. "What nation will set itself up as a standard for others? Innocence and integrity may indeed be more readily found in the less highly polished nations than in the more advanced. The usual practices [of advanced societies] can easily be mistaken for the dictates of natural reason."[124] On this latter point Pufendorf foreshadowed the later thinking both of progressivists and of primitivists, who argued that the most basic institutions of natural law were likely to be discovered in those societies that were closest to original nature. However, Pufendorf himself eschewed the ethnographic approach, relying instead on philosophic contemplation of the nature, condition, and desires of man, in the tradition of the Classical philosophers.

Sigmund says of Pufendorf's writings that they

> combined the individualism and pessimism about human nature of Hobbes with the belief in man's potential rationality and sociability of the older tradition. During the century after its publication, his theory was one of the best-known systematic presentations of Natural Law. It was translated into English and French, used by Locke, criticized by Rousseau, and quoted by the American revolutionists. Yet after the middle of the eighteenth century Pufendorf's influence declined sharply while that of one of his readers, John Locke, continues to excite interest and controversy to the present day.[125]

Locke's *Two Treatises on Government* was published in 1690. It is accounted by nearly all commentators as the single most influential work of the Enlightenment, at least on the subject of natural law. This was certainly true in a practical sense; Locke's doctrines were cited more often than any others by the authors of the American and French Revolutions. In a purely theoretical sense, however, his contribution was less original than were those of his immediate predecessors. His special contribution was not so much to elaborate as to reinterpret the existing doctrine of the social contract, as it had been developed especially by Hooker, Grotius, and Pufendorf. Where they had discussed the contract mainly in terms of the obligations of individuals toward society, Locke was concerned almost wholly with the duty of society toward individuals. In his hands natural law became virtually synonymous with universal human rights. It is this view that has largely prevailed among political thinkers down to the present day.

---

124. Ibid., p. 5.
125. Sigmund, *Natural Law in Political Thought*, p. 81.

Like most of his contemporaries, Locke was not quite able to leave God completely out of account. He asserted that pleasure and pain–not salvation and damnation–are the natural sanctions underlying the law. However, these are the self-interested considerations that impel men to follow the law, not the reasons why the laws themselves are inherently just. It was still, ultimately, divine ordination that had identified some acts as inherently good and others as inherently evil. Throughout his writing he affirmed "the existence of a perfect parallel between the calculus of rationally apprehended truths and the divinely furnished system of hedonistic [i.e. self-interested] sanctions."[126]

Virtually all conceptions of natural law from ancient to early modern times had at least implied the existence of innate ideas of right and wrong that were present in the human mind at birth. Locke was perhaps the first to challenge this conception, insisting that the mind at birth is a "blank slate," or tabula rasa. For that reason he is often identified as one of the founders of modern social science theory.[127] Yet at first glance the tabula rasa doctrine would seem to negate the possibility of natural law. Locke was aware of the seeming contradiction, which he resolved by observing that "There is a great deal of difference between an innate law and a law of nature; between something imprinted on our minds in their very original and something that we, being ignorant of, may attain to the knowledge of, by the use and due application of our natural facilities."[128] In other words we are not endowed at birth with innate ideas but we are endowed with a reasoning faculty that will lead us all to the same conclusions–essentially the "right reason" that the philosophers had spoken of since ancient times. If this is true, however, then the tabula rasa doctrine seems to mean a good deal less than it says.

The French libertarians

From the middle of the eighteenth century onward, the doctrines of the social contract and of universal rights were developed most fully and most radically by French theorists. First among them was Charles Louis Montesquieu, whose work was cited in his own time just about as often as that of Locke, though his *Spirit of the Laws* (1748) was concerned primarily with civil law rather than with natural law per se. His most original contribution to natural law theory was to introduce a degree of relativism, and

---

126. Ibid., p. 88.
127. Cf. Marvin Harris, *The Rise of Anthropological Theory* (New York, 1968), pp. 10–12.
128. Quoted from Sigmund, *Natural Law in Political Thought*, p. 87.

by implication of empiricism, into the doctrine. Pufendorf and Locke had recognized that natural laws were different at different levels of social development, for new laws were introduced as the evolving needs of society dictated. Montesquieu added the recognition that the needs of society are not the same even among societies existing in the present. The central thesis of his work was the assertion that the civil laws of every society must be formulated in accordance with the natural law of that society. This relativism made necessary an empirical, ethnographic approach to the study of natural law which will concern us a little later.

In the popular mind today, the doctrine of natural law is associated more with the name of Jean-Jacques Rousseau than with any other. However, his ideas on the subject are not easy to ascertain clearly, partly because they evolved over time and partly because in any case they were never wholly consistent. The primitivist and the progressivist were always at war within Rousseau, as we saw in Chapter 3. Moreover, he did not explicitly employ the term natural law. "Knowing nature so little, and agreeing so poorly on the meaning of the word law, it would be very difficult to agree on a good definition of natural law," he wrote.[129] But almost the whole of his writing was devoted in one way or another to the topic of the social contract, and it seems clear enough, at least by implication, that he identified this with natural law just as did Locke, Hobbes, and Hooker. On the other hand his vision of how the contract had come about was substantially different from theirs.

All natural law theorists since Hobbes had based their doctrines on an imagined "original state of nature" from which society had sprung, but the state imagined by Rousseau was something far removed from the "nasty, brutish, and short" life imagined by Hobbes. It was a time of innocence, before virtue and vice, before pride, and above all before reason. Men's actions were guided entirely by sentiments. We saw in Chapter 3 how the Noble Savage of popular imagination was transformed, in the eighteenth century, from a primitive rationalist into a creature of heightened emotional and aesthetic sensibilities, and this quality of character was the starting point for Rousseau's understanding of natural law. Primitive man was driven by two instincts: self-preservation, and compassion for his fellow man. He felt "an innate repugnance to see his fellow man suffer," and this was the wellspring of all the social virtues such as generosity, humanity, benevolence, and friendship.[130]

---

129. In *Discourse on the Origin and the Foundations of Inequality among Men* (1755); quoted from Eterovich, *Natural Law from Plato to Kant*, p. 136.
130. Eterovich, *Natural Law from Plato to Kant*, p. 129.

But the original state of nature was much like that of childhood. It was not without drawbacks, for the competition of individuals led to rivalries that in time became fixed inequalities, and these in their turn led to wars. The time came when there was a felt need to reduce inequalities and to substitute justice for violence in the settlement of disputes: this was the original social contract and the origin of civil society. The rationale for the creation of civil society was therefore, in the beginning, a commendable one, and the consequences should have been wholly beneficial. In fact, almost from the beginning they were disastrous, for the social pact was devised by those who, in the state of nature, had become rich and powerful, and it was designed to favor their interests. The poor and disadvantaged followed along simply in the hope of finding some measure of protection in the newly constituted society; in effect they sacrificed freedom for protection.

It was clear to Rousseau at all events that the present state of society, in Europe and throughout the world, was hopelessly corrupt. "Man is born free, and everywhere he is in chains" he wrote as the opening sentence of *The Social Contract* (1762). At the same time Rousseau believed fervently, as did all the Enlightenment thinkers, in the perfectibility of human nature. But was this to be achieved by going forward or by going backward, and, if the latter, how far backward? The solution, in a sense, was to go forward by going backward: people should be enlightened enough to realize and correct the mistakes they had made.

There are many passages in Rousseau that could be interpreted to suggest that mankind should discard all social institutions and go back to the original, innocent state of nature–"the very best man could experience."[131] At the same time he recognized clearly that a return to the original state of nature, however idyllic in theory, was no more practicably possible than was a return to the Garden of Eden. What he really wanted was to have the best of both worlds, the original state of nature and the original state of society. The problem was "how to retain the advantages of society and government while avoiding the attendant evils of inequality, exploitation, self-deception, and falseness in society."[132] The problem was hardly a novel one; it has confronted just about every political and moral philosopher from ancient to modern times. Rousseau had no more success than had his predecessors or successors in figuring out how to have his cake and eat it too.

In purely practical terms, then, Rousseau's contribution to natural law theory was not a large one, nor was it wholly coherent. His rhetoric and

131. Quoted from Sigmund, *Natural Law in Political Thought*, p. 122.
132. Ibid., p. 123.

hyperbole have provided a rich source of revolutionary slogans, from his own time to the present, but no revolutionary regime has attempted to build a government based on his principles.

The Scottish moralists

While the French and Scottish Enlightenment thinkers were closely similar in their ideas about universal progress, they were less so on the subject of natural law. For all their intellectual fervor, the Scots were not radical reformers. They were concerned less with liberty than with morality, and it was their search for the objective bases of morality that led them to formulate their own concept of natural law, though they did not often use the term. They followed the older, theological tradition in linking natural law with morality, but followed the new, empirical tradition in searching for the bases of morality in human experience rather than in divine revelation. Their doctrine was secular without being particularly individualist or radical, and they continued to see natural law largely as a matter of duties rather than of rights.

The characteristic of Scottish natural rights doctrine which set it most clearly apart from the French was its antirationalism. The Scots believed firmly in the primacy of emotion over reason. The immediate locus of natural law–hence of morality–was to be found not in the universal power of reason but in universal human sentiments. David Hume put the matter most forcefully when he wrote that "Reason is, and ought only to be the slave of the passions, and can never pretend to any other office than to serve and obey them."[133] The morality of an action is determined not by its conformity to reason but simply by the sentiment of approval on the part of the actor and the community. This perspective was so frequently asserted in Hume's two major works, *A Treatise on Human Nature* (1740) and *An Enquiry Concerning the Principles of Morals* (1751) that the author has often been identified as an opponent of natural law theory.[134] But Hume did in fact develop his own theory of natural law, which will occupy us a little later.

The Scottish approach, from Hume onward, was more psychological than sociological. It was developed most fully by Francis Hutcheson, who asserted that a precise theory of morals could be derived from "proper observations upon the several powers and principles which we are conscious

---

133. David Hume, *A Treatise on Human Nature,* ed. L.A. Selby-Bigge (Oxford, 1888), Book II, part III, p. 415.
134. Cf. Rommen, *Natural Law,* pp. 110–113.

of in our own bosoms," and from "a more strict philosophical inquiry into the various natural principles or natural dispositions of mankind, in the same way that we inquire into the structure of an animal body, of a plant or of the solar system."[135] What Hutcheson singled out for observation was not actual codes of conduct, but men's feelings about conduct. His view generally echoed that of Hume: "The rights obtaining in natural liberty are indicated by the feelings in our hearts, by our automatic approval of what is of advantage to us and of no harm to others. After observing our natural feelings, we should consider the general feelings of society. That will tend to confirm what we have felt."[136] To the extent that they concerned themselves with natural law, the later Scottish thinkers (most of whom had been pupils of Hutcheson) generally followed Hutcheson's lead.[137]

The German legalists

In eighteenth-century Germany, a more narrowly legalistic conception of natural law was developed by the successors of Grotius and Pufendorf; especially Christian Thomasius and Christian Wolff.[138] The two men, like Grotius and Pufendorf, were primarily historians of law, and they were much more specifically concerned with the reform of existing legal systems than were the French or the Scottish thinkers. Both men worked out idealized systems of jurisprudence based on their own notions of natural law. They followed Pufendorf in rejecting the empirical approach recommended by Grotius, believing that natural law can be discovered only a priori, by deducing it logically from the rational and social nature of man. Thomasius insisted that every man can feel within himself whatever is necessary to understand the moral nature of man. It was up to enlightened rulers or legislators to enact these understandings into law, for the promptings of nature were not law in themselves; they only became law, *sensu stricto*, when backed by the command of a ruler. Wolff was not quite so insistent on this point, but he asserted that "No law exists without a moral obligation which precedes it, in which it is rooted, and from which it flows."[139]

Although their subject was the history of law, neither Thomasius nor Wolff was a trained jurist, nor were they historians in a narrow sense. In

135. Francis Hutcheson, *System of Moral Philosophy* (London, 1755), vol. I, pp. xiii–xv.
136. Quoted from Stein, *Legal Evolution*, p. 10.
137. See also Gladys Bryson, *Man and Society* (Princeton, N.J., 1945), pp. 25–29.
138. For discussion, see Stein, *Legal Evolution*, pp. 51–52.
139. Ibid., p. 52. For much more extended discussion of Thomasius, see Bloch, *Natural Law and Human Dignity*, pp. 281–314.

developing their idealized legal systems they eschewed altogether the study of existing systems, believing that reason alone could provide an appropriate basis for behavioral norms. Unlike nearly all true jurists, they had no respect at all for the force of tradition. Their proposals nevertheless had great appeal to some of the more enlightened rulers in eighteenth-century Germany, and they led directly to the adoption of revised legal codes in Bavaria, in Prussia, and in Austria.[140]

The empirical dimension

The so-called comparative method, discussed at length in Chapter 2, was employed by Enlightenment philosophers in support of their natural law doctrines as well as in support of universal progress. As Hildebrand has written,

> much effort in the eighteenth century was given to illustrating the supposed uniformity of human nature among the peoples of the world, past and present. The objective of these researches was the discovery of *similarities* in customs and practices among different peoples widely separated in space and time, a type of inquiry that was stimulated by the accumulation of a rich body of literature during the period of exploration and colonization [emphasis in the original].[141]

Properly considered, such an inquiry should have contributed more to the universalist doctrine of natural law than to the comparativist doctrine of progress.

As we saw earlier in the chapter, the comparative method did not originate in the Enlightenment. It was employed in everything but name by Las Casas and Acosta, two centuries earlier. The two Spaniards were not abstract theorists, however, and their writings had little influence on the subsequent development of European thought. It not until the seventeenth and eighteenth centuries that the comparative method became a programmatic feature of natural law theory. Its use was recommended by Grotius, and nearly all of the social contract theorists from Hobbes onward drew on ethnographic materials, especially from America, to support their doctrines. For Hobbes and Locke this was more a luxury than a

140. Stein, *Legal Evolution*, p. 52.

141. George H. Hildebrand in Frederick Teggart, compiler, *The Idea of Progress* (Berkeley, Calif., 1949), p. 13.

necessity, since their theories rested ultimately on a nonempirical foundation. Moreover, they cited ethnographic data from the Americas more to support their Progressivism than to support their natural law doctrines. On the other hand, Montesquieu's relativist approach to natural law made an appeal to ethnographic data mandatory.

Montesquieu's approach entailed, inescapably, the objective study of societies in their differing environmental, historical, and political settings, to determine which laws are "natural" in which circumstances. Following the earlier example of Lafitau,[142] he was the first of the Enlightenment theorists to buttress his doctrines with both historical and ethnographic case examples. As Stein writes,

> *De l'esprit des lois* is remarkable for its emphasis on the particular, the concrete, and it is this feature which, in part at least, accounted for its popularity. The work shifted the focus of legal speculation from the rules that governed men naturally, irrespective of the society in which they lived, to the rules that actually existed as specific [i.e. historical] phenomena in specific societies, past and present.[143]

The most nearly empirical of all Enlightenment thinkers was Antoine Yves Goguet, whose *On the Origin of Laws, Arts, and Sciences, and Their Progress among Ancient Peoples* (1758) was briefly mentioned in Chapter 2. Goguet largely followed Montesquieu in tracing out a general history of law, and in suggesting that different laws are "natural" at different stages of cultural development. He also believed that some laws are fundamental to all peoples at all times; these included laws related to marriage, to movable property, and to the punishment of offenses.[144] But Goguet's major innovation in the study of natural law, as in the study of universal progress, was his insistence that his method was inductive. In developing his theories he incorporated historical materials from the Babylonians, Hebrews, Egyptians, Persians, and Greeks, as well as ethnographic materials from China, India, and many contemporary primitive societies. Like all thinkers of the time, he had to rely on the ethnography of contemporary primitives to supply the otherwise missing earliest stages of human history.[145]

The empirical approach of Montesquieu and Goguet brought jus gen-

---

142. Whose work he ignored, and perhaps did not know. See Stein, *Legal Evolution*, pp. 17–18.

143. Ibid., p. 17.

144. See ibid., p. 21.

145. Ibid., p. 20.

tium once again to the fore, as the primary manifestation of natural law. Whatever was unchanging in the relationship between man and society would be revealed by those notions of right and duty that are common to all peoples. This approach also brought primitive society to the fore, at least for many thinkers, who felt that the earliest surviving version of the social contract could be studied in those societies that had advanced the least distance from the original state of nature. In that sense, primitive society became a touchstone for the discovery of natural law for progressivists and primitivists alike.

The psychological approach of the Scottish thinkers was also avowedly empirical, but it involved a different kind of empiricism from that of the French thinkers. The objects of study were the feelings of individuals, not the customs of societies. The sources of morality were to be discovered from "proper observations upon the several powers and principles which we are conscious of in our own bosoms," and from "a more strict philosophical inquiry into the various natural principles or natural dispositions of mankind,"[146] as Hutcheson had written. In other words the Scottish approach, like most psychological theories, was universalist rather than relativist. It entailed the study of ourselves and of our fellows, but not necessarily a cross-cultural survey. As a result the Scots did not place nearly the same emphasis on ethnographic evidence as did the French.

Summary of the eighteenth century

As we have just seen, the natural law theory of the Enlightenment sages was by no means unitary. On the contrary, we can witness in the eighteenth century the beginnings of three separate national traditions of thought: the British, the French, and the German. The differences between them were to exert a very strong influence on the subsequent development of anthropology in the three countries, as we will see especially in Chapter 7.

The two major streams of thought were the sociological and essentially rationalistic approach most fully developed by the French, and the psychological and partly antirational approach of the Scots. They shared in common the characteristics of secularism and, purportedly, empiricism, but the French approach was radical and individualistic while the Scottish was more traditionalist. The approach of the German legalists fell somewhere between the two, sharing the rationalism of the French but the emphasis on morality and duty of the Scots. All of the approaches involved

146. Hutcheson, *System of Moral Philosophy.*

internal contradictions that were not fully resolved in the eighteenth century; contradictions that provided a basis for opposition to the whole idea of natural law in the following century.

All of the leading Enlightenment thinkers believed both in universal progress and in natural law, yet they never fully reconciled these two strains of thought in a philosophically satisfactory manner. A continuing weakness was the lack of a fully articulated concept of society, in the modern sense. Society was still seen as essentially equivalent to government, whose only "will," or purpose, was either the will of the ruler or the consensus of the individual members. Yet the social progressivist theory of the Enlightenment thinkers clearly implied something much more: a social organism or community that evolves according to laws that are independent of the will of either rulers or governed, and must therefore in some sense have a will or purposes of its own. This "organic concept" of society did not develop until the nineteenth century, and when it did, it was accompanied by a challenge to the very legitimacy of natural law theory.

THE BEGINNINGS OF DISSENT: HUME AND KANT

From ancient times to the Enlightenment, the single most consistent feature of natural law theory was its rationalism. Whatever the ultimate source of the law–nature or God–its immediate locus was in the human power of reason. However, as we saw in Chapter 3, the pervasive rationalism of the eighteenth century began to be challenged, even its own time, by Romanticism and other antirational currents of thought. Rationalistic theories of natural law, which had been largely unchallenged since ancient times, were not immune from this attack. The critics did not initially question the idea of natural law itself; they questioned the long-accepted notion that its locus was in the human reasoning facility. We have just seen that a certain antirational thread runs all through the work of Rousseau, as well as through the Scottish approach to natural law. However, the most direct attacks on rationalistic natural law, and indeed on rationalism in general, were mounted by two other thinkers whom we have now to consider, David Hume and Immanuel Kant. Both of them lived and wrote in the eighteenth century, but the antirational trend of their thought sets them clearly apart from the mainstream of Enlightenment philosophy.

Hume was the first and by far the most insistent of the Scots in asserting the primacy of feelings over reason. Moreover and more importantly, he insisted that it is impossible to derive the one from the other by any logical process. Reason identifies what is, while feelings identify what ought to be.

In Sigmund's paraphrase, "a statement of value, an 'ought,' cannot be derived from a statement of empirical fact or logical deduction, an 'is.' The assertion that there are values inherent in nature or man is a logical fallacy. There are empirical observations and logical relationships perceived in the senses and reason, but they cannot tell us anything about what is good."[147]

Hume was an outspoken critic of the rationalistic natural law theories of his own time. He pointed out that the term "natural" was never precisely defined. It was used in at least three different senses: in opposition to "supernatural," in opposition to "artificial," and to designate something frequent or common. None of these meanings provided any guidance in determining what is moral.[148]

Natural Law

As a result of this critique, Hume has often been identified as an opponent of natural law theories in general.[149] But he did in fact develop a kind of natural law theory, which had at least two points in common with other Enlightenment theories. First, it asserted that natural law was related to the needs of society, and second, it identified natural law largely with the institution of private property.

Hume anticipated modern anthropological thinking in his belief that society arose when men recognized that they could achieve more by their collective efforts than they could individually. But living in society brought only limited benefits because men are naturally selfish, and moreover there is never enough wealth to satisfy everyone's desires. It was out of this circumstance that law necessarily arose; if it were not for human greed and the shortage of material goods there would be no need of laws. "It is only from the selfishness and confin'd generosity of men, along with the scanty provision that nature has made for his wants, that justice derives its origin."[150] It followed, in Hume's view, that all natural law was related to property. Human understanding of the laws, however, had come about only gradually and through experience; it was not implanted in man's consciousness from the beginnings of civil society. Hume's work laid the foundation for the later, much more sweeping rejection of natural law theory by the utilitarians, which will occupy us in the next section.

A more comprehensive attack on natural law theory as it existed in the eighteenth century was mounted by Immanuel Kant. The titles of his two best-known works, the *Critique of Pure Reason* (1781) and *Critique of Practical Reason* (1788) are sufficiently indicative of his attitude toward the pre-

147. Sigmund, *Natural Law in Political Thought*, p. 141.
148. Cf. ibid.
149. Ibid., pp. 141–145; Rommen, *Natural Law*, pp. 110–113.
150. Hume, *Treatise on Human Nature*, p. 495.

vailing rationalism of his century. Like Hume he was an outspoken critic of existing natural law theories, yet at the same time developed a kind of natural law theory of his own.

The beginnings of dissent

Unlike most eighteenth century thinkers, Kant was a philosophic system-builder. He inaugurated the philosophy known as Transcendentalism, which attempted to overcome and to eliminate the teleology characteristic of Western philosophy since the time of Aristotle. His theory was essentialist, insisting that things have to be judged by what they are, not by what purposes they serve. As applied to morality, this meant that the morality of any action was wholly independent of the outcome of that action; it was determined by some abstract principle of what is inherently good or bad.

For Kant, the "nature" that decrees natural law is simply rational human nature, and at the heart of human nature is the autonomous will of each individual.[151] Thus, unlike nearly all earlier theorists, Kant found the locus of natural law neither in reason nor in the emotions, but in the will. The will of each individual is autonomous, and cannot be subjugated to any other will. In that sense, the individual will was for Kant essentially what divine will was for earlier natural law theorists.

From Kant's perspective, behavioral maxims are rationally derived from the one basic moral law that we must do good, to which we are impelled by our natural will.[152] At various times and in various places, the philosopher laid down behavioral maxims that were derived from the imperative to "do good." All of these appear in one way or another to be variations on the Golden Rule: "Act only on that maxim through which you can at the same time will that it should become a universal law;" "Act as if the maxim of your action were to become through your will a universal law of nature;" "Act in such a way that you always treat humanity… never simply as a means, but always at the same time as an end;" "Every rational being must so act as if he were through his maxims always a law-making member in the universal kingdom of ends;" etc.[153] The essential circularity of Kant's reasoning is evident in the assertion that we must act in accordance with law and at the same time as though we were making law.

In his last major work, *The Metaphysics of Morals,* Kant retreated to a position more nearly in keeping with earlier, rationalist theory.

The state of nature is an expression for the absence of agreed legal

151. Cf. Sigmund, *Natural Law in Political Thought,* p. 163.
152. Ibid., pp. 174–175.
153. Quoted from Eterovich, *Natural Law from Plato to Kant,* pp. 147–148.

> and moral restraints; the term natural law is applied only to external coercive legislation which is universally and rationally necessary for a legal system; and the social contract is an analytic construct signifying the recognition by the people that they can find a higher freedom in a civil state regulated by law if they give up 'the wild lawless freedom of the state of nature.' As for natural rights, there is only right which man has by nature, that of moral freedom; all other rights are derived from it.[154]

It will be apparent from what has been said here that Kant's theory of morality is complex and abstruse, and certainly no brief synopsis can do it proper justice.[155] The theory will not be explored further here, however, because it is not particularly important as a contribution to doctrine. Its importance lies in the fact that, in the following century, it opened a second avenue of attack on the concept of natural law itself.

Obviously, the theories of Hume and of Kant were not closely similar. At first glance it might appear that their main similarity lay in their rejection of the prevailing rationalism of their times. In fact, neither man could really escape from that tradition, which had dominated Western thinking for more than two millennia. Hume made emotions rather than reason the locus of natural law, but went on to argue that the emotions are fundamentally reasonable. Similarly, Kant made will rather than reason the source of the law but argued that "good will is not to be looked upon as separate from practical reason."[156] Reason, then, became simply the servant of the emotions for Hume, and the servant of the will for Kant, just as for earlier thinkers it had been the expression of divine will. It lost its status as the ultimate source of natural law, but remained as the immediate source. In that respect, the antirationalism of Hume and of Kant was more apparent than real.

Both Hume and Kant were moralists rather than natural law theorists per se, and were sharply critical of the natural law theories of their own time. In rejecting scriptural tradition and in searching for an objective basis for morality, however, they found the basic idea of natural law inescapable. Nevertheless, their lasting influence was negative rather than positive. Their critiques of rationalistic theories brought the whole doctrine of natural law into question, and opened the door to a much more general attack in the nineteenth century.

---

154. Sigmund, *Natural Law in Political Thought*, p. 163.
155. For a much more detailed synopsis, see ibid., pp. 140–163.
156. Ibid., p. 144.

By the year 1800 the concept of natural law had had an honored place in philosophical and juristic discourse for well over two thousand years. It had been given all kinds of interpretations by all kinds of thinkers, but almost no one had seriously questioned that there was such a thing. Then, in the nineteenth century, the doctrine came under attack seemingly from all directions at once. It was denounced by romantics for its rationalism, by utilitarians for its assumption of moral absolutes, by Marxists for its mentalism, by social scientists for its teleology and its lack of determinism, and by religious traditionalists for the seeming godlessness that it had acquired in the Enlightenment.[157] Except for the latter group, most of these critics shared in the general spirit of radical agnosticism that was an important part of the nineteenth-century *Zeitgeist.*

The utilitarian critique

The most outspoken and the most immediately damaging criticism of natural law theory came from the utilitarians. This was a philosophical school founded near the end of the eighteenth century by Jeremy Bentham, and later embraced and enlarged by James Mill and by his more famous son John Stuart Mill. During the first half of the nineteenth century, Utilitarianism achieved a very considerable popularity in the British Isles, chiefly because of its association with popular measures of political reform. The doctrine had a certain indirect influence on the later development of British anthropology, and from that perspective will be further discussed in Chapter 7.

Simply stated, the utilitarian philosophy was hedonistic, and bore some resemblance to the ancient doctrine of the Epicureans. Utilitarians argued that the only rational guide in human conduct is to seek the greatest good for the greatest number, good being identified simply with happiness or pleasure, and evil with unhappiness or pain. All other theories of morality and politics could in practice be reduced to this principle, whatever their claims to divine or natural legitimation. "We distinguish among the many moral precepts in Scripture on this basis, and the legitimate insights of the natural law theory are derived not from an understanding of the purposes of nature, but from generalizations based on utility," as Sigmund has put it.[158]

157. Cf. Crowe, *Changing Profile of the Natural Law,* p. 245, and Allen W. Wood in Eliade, *Encyclopedia of Religion,* Vol. 4, p. 323.
158. *Natural Law in Political Thought,* p. 146.

From a strictly philosophical standpoint, the concepts of natural law and natural right were not so much antithetical as irrelevant to the utilitarians. Bentham and Mill found no need to make use of the two concepts, but they also had no particular theoretical reason to attack them. However, the philosophical doctrines of the utilitarians cannot be fully understood without reference to their political activism. Utilitarian philosophy was not an armchair enterprise; it was meant to provide a rationale, acceptable to the British, for very practical reforms that the adherents hoped to achieve in such matters as the penal code, public education, and the electoral system.

Although they were imbued with a reformist spirit, the utilitarians, like nearly all Britons, were appalled by the excesses of the French Revolution. They felt, with some justice, that British revulsion against the French revolutionary excesses was hindering the efforts at reform in England. This was the basis for Bentham's violent denunciation of the doctrines of natural rights and of the social contract, which had been rhetorical cornerstones of the French revolutionaries. But at the other extreme, Bentham also recognized that natural law doctrines were often invoked in support of the status quo, and in that guise also they inhibited the enactment of needed reforms. In other words, the doctrines of natural law and natural rights were either too radical or too conservative to be helpful in the cause of reform, to which the utilitarians were dedicated.[159]

The utilitarian critique was damaging to natural law theory not so much because of its inherent power as because of the extraordinary popularity that Utilitarianism enjoyed for a time in nineteenth-century Britain. This was due in turn to the very considerable successes achieved by the utilitarians in various areas of political and legal reform. "Throughout the middle portion of the nineteenth century," writes Bertrand Russell, "the influence of the Benthamites on British legislation and policy was astonishingly great, considering their complete absence of emotional appeal."[160]

Despite the strident disavowals of Bentham and the more moderate disavowals of the two Mills, a substantial element of natural law theory was clearly implied in their philosophy. Bentham's conception of human nature as dedicated exclusively to the maximization of pleasure and the minimization of pain certainly constitutes a kind of natural law in the Kantian sense. John Stuart Mill developed a somewhat loftier and less hedonistic conception of happiness as the pursuit of self-development in advancing the causes of human freedom and diversity, but again the echoes

159. Ibid., p. 147.

160. *A History of Western Philosophy* (New York, 1945), p. 777.

of earlier natural law theories are obvious.[161] Like other critiques of the nineteenth century, that of the utilitarians did not so much destroy natural law theory as force it to change its name.

Legal relativism

The nineteenth century

In nineteenth-century Germany, another kind of critique developed within the field of judicial philosophy. It came from the historical school of law, founded by Gustav Hugo and further developed especially by Friedrich von Savigny and Rudolf von Jhering. The historical school arose chiefly in reaction against the rationalistic legalism of Thomasius and Wolff, discussed earlier, although it too was stimulated partly by revulsion against the French Revolution, and the rhetoric that accompanied it.[162]

The legal philosophy of the German school was wholly derived from, and in keeping with, the more general philosophy of German Idealism, which will occupy us in Chapter 6. Its central doctrine was that of legal relativism: the law, like everything else in culture, is a historical product of historical circumstances that may be different for each people. Unlike the earlier Scholastics, the German jurists did not treat the codes of Justinian as sacred texts but as historical documents, which could not be understood without a study of the social and political contexts in which the law had developed. They recognized three stages in the evolution of Roman law: first the "primitive" period governed exclusively by customary law, then the "classic" period when customary law was enacted into statute law, and finally the "scientific" period when law and jurisprudence became subject to systematic study.[163]

Like the utilitarians, the German relativists strongly condemned the individualist natural law doctrines of the French revolutionaries. Yet their own philosophy was suffused with a kind of consensual natural law doctrine. Customary law, which was in existence prior to the beginnings of state legislation, was regarded as the "highest" kind of law, such that the state may not enact statute laws that are foreign to it. "Both the genius of jurisprudence and the genius of legislation must seek to find the law where it resides par excellence, that is, in the general legal consciousness of the people," as Rommen has put it.[164] In this sense the law is "found" rather than

161. Cf. Sigmund, *Natural Law in Political Thought*, pp. 148–149.
162. Rommen, *Natural Law*, p. 115.
163. Ibid., pp. 116–117; Stein, *Legal Evolution*, pp. 55–56. Stein points out that Hugo actually derived this idea from the forty-fourth chapter of Gibbon's *Decline and Fall of the Roman Empire.*
164. Rommen, *Natural Law*, p. 117.

enacted by the state. But there is, of course, a separate jus gentium to be found among each people, and no one jus gentium common to all peoples.

The Marxist attack

At one point or another in his writing, Karl Marx was critical of all forms of natural law theory, classical, theological, and sociological. To him, the doctrines of natural law theory were inseparable from ideology, which meant that, like religion, they were instruments of control by the ruling class. "The selfish misconception that induces you [the bourgeoisie] to transform into eternal laws of nature and reason the social forms springing from your present mode of production... you share with every ruling class that has preceded you," he wrote in the Communist Manifesto.[165] According to Marxist theory, all so-called laws were generated out of, and in support of, whatever mode of production (Oriental, Feudal, or Capitalist, for example) prevailed at a given moment in history.[166] Different rights were acquired by individuals at different stages of socioeconomic evolution, but this did not justify the retention of outmoded forms of social or economic organization. The original social contract, if there ever was one, related to a form of society that had long since been outgrown. It was merely "a door, of which no stone remains standing."[167]

At first glance, the Marxist theory of human nature and human history would appear to be wholly relativist. Yet the unresolved paradox of Marxist theory has always been its utopianism–the vision of an ultimate, classless society in which the agelong struggle of classes will finally cease, and government and law will wither away.[168] In this second Eden, the final relative state of society will become absolute, and the disappearance of class-formulated, class-serving civil law will allow natural law finally to reassert itself. Essential human nature, which has been suppressed and distorted throughout history by the inequitable division of labor, will be free to express itself. "Man's natural behavior has become human for him... and... his human nature has become nature for him... Communism... is the final resolution of the antagonisms between man and nature and between man and man."[169] There is after all, then, a natural law which has been

165. Quoted from Sigmund, *Natural Law in Political Thought*, pp. 164–165.
166. See esp. Karl Renner in Tom Bottomore, ed., *Karl Marx* (Oxford, 1973), pp. 123–127.
167. Bloch, *Natural Law and Human Dignity*, p. 189.
168. For discussion of this problematic. see Maurice Bloch, *Marxism and Anthropology* (Oxford, 1973), pp. 16–19. See also Chapter 7.
169. Quoted from Erich Fromm, trans., *Marx's Concept of Man* (New York, 1961), pp. 126–127.

suppressed throughout history by human greed, but which will win out in the end. (Marxism, as one of the philosophical roots of anthropology, will be further discussed in Chapter 7.)

The rise of Positivism

In the 1830s and 1840s, Auguste Comte launched the new discipline of sociology as a part of his more general philosophy of Positivism. Since that time, a high percentage of social scientists have been willing to acknowledge Comte as one of their founding fathers, while at the same time disavowing any allegiance to Positivism.[170] As early as 1865, John Stuart Mill wrote that

> though the mode of thought expressed by the terms Positive and Positivism is widely spread, the words themselves are, as usual, better known through the enemies of that mode of thinking than through its friends; and more than one thinker who never called himself or his opinions by those appellations, and carefully guarded himself against being confounded with those who did, finds himself, sometimes to his displeasure, though generally by a tolerably correct instinct, classed with Positivists, and assailed as a Positivist.[171]

This paradox arises, as usual in such cases, from conceptual ambiguity. Comte himself was far from clear or consistent as to what he meant by Positivism, and this has left the field open for a variety of interpretations. The ambiguities of positivist theory will occupy us more fully in Chapter 7; here it is sufficient to recognize that Positivism can be understood in two rather distinct senses, as a methodology and as a philosophy. As Rommen observes, "we must distinguish two forms of positivism: first, positivism as a consequence of an empiricist narrowing of reality, as a method; and secondly, positivism as a philosophy of life, as a conception of the universe and of man's place in it, as a Weltanschauung."[172]

In its most extreme form, the positivist method can be interpreted as an attempt to banish all forms of apriorism from philosophy and from science. The only acceptable evidence is that of the senses; the only acceptable

170. See Chapter 2 for fuller discussion.

171. John Stuart Mill, *Auguste Comte and Positivism* (Ann Arbor, Mich., 1965), p. 2; originally published in the *Westminster Review* in 1865.

172. Rommen, *Natural Law*, p. 125.

theory is that which can be adduced from the evidence of the senses. From this perspective, Comte was quite correct in recognizing that all natural law theory involves an element of apriorism. He based his criticism of natural law on both methodological and philosophic grounds: methodological, because notions of natural law did not have a solid empirical basis; philosophical, because (according to his scheme) anything to be called a law must be absolute, not relative to time and place. In effect, Comte's Positivism carried natural law theory all the way back to its beginnings in pre-Socratic Greece. That is, natural law was either part and parcel of physical law or it was nothing. "Human freedom and will were... dissolved into the natural laws that govern the inorganic and organic realms of existence...," in the paraphrase of Gertrud Lenzer.[173]

Positivist methodology, which almost everyone repudiates, is attributable quite specifically to Comte. Positivist philosophy, which most scientists at least tacitly endorse, follows logically from positivist methodology, but its origins are much less specifically Comtean. It represents the culmination of a trend of thought that had been developing for more than a century previously: an assertion that mankind is wholly part of nature, and must be studied on the same basis as the rest of the natural world, without reference to principles or assumptions that do not apply to other species. In this broader sense practically all of the social scientists of the later nineteenth and early twentieth centuries were positivists.

The result of this development was not so much to destroy the natural law concept as to halt its further development. Removed from the realm of metaphysical speculation, natural law became something to be studied and talked about (mostly under other names) but not really reflected on. It survives in all the social sciences as a series of unexamined propositions and unacknowledged legacies, and social scientists continue to employ what are essentially natural law concepts without reflecting on either their ontological or their moral significance. This will become particularly apparent when we come to consider the role of natural law theory in anthropology.

The triumph of agnosticism

It should be apparent, from the foregoing discussion, that the demise of natural law theory in the nineteenth century was more apparent than real. The utilitarians, the legal relativists, the Marxists and the positivists all propounded what were essentially natural law theories, even while dis-

173. Gertrud Lenzer, ed., *Auguste Comte and Positivism* (New York, 1975), p. lvi.

avowing the term. Natural law theory was thus not so much destroyed as driven underground. It was forced to assume a number of aliases, under which for the most part it still persists today. There can be no doubt, however, that the doctrine of natural law became unpopular by name, and, at least among scientists, it largely remains so.

The nineteenth century

The reason for this unpopularity has, I think, less to do with any specific criticisms than with the general spirit of radical agnosticism that came to the fore in the nineteenth century. It was a spirit in which nearly all of the critics of natural law theory shared. While Positivism and other philosophic doctrines did not by any means banish all forms of apriorism, they did finally banish the most a priori of all apriorisms: the belief in God as an active force in the natural world.

The nineteenth-century skeptics cannot quite be called atheists, since most of them continued to profess a belief in God, even while denying him any role in the affairs of the present world. Moreover, unlike most true atheists, they were not by any means critics of the church or of the institution of religion, which many of them considered necessary for the proper functioning of society. But, by general agreement, their theories were formulated without any reference to a divine will. We might say, turning orthodox Christian doctrine on its head, that God was banished back to the Garden of Eden. This was the essence of the scientific method, as it was understood in the nineteenth century.

Since the time of Augustine, natural law doctrines had been closely associated with theology and with metaphysics. Throughout the Middle Ages they were expounded almost exclusively by churchmen, and even the secularists of the early modern and Enlightenment periods had left a place for God, as the ultimate creator of human reason or of the emotions or of the will. It should be noted too that the older, theological tradition of natural law was not supplanted by the rise of secular theories. Thomist natural law continued to have an important place in Catholic thinking, and it was taught as part of the Moral Philosophy curriculum in most universities. It was in that guise that most of the nineteenth-century theorists had probably encountered it in their youth and had later come to reject it.

I suggest, then, that the historical association of natural law with theology and metaphysics was mainly responsible for the disavowal of the doctrine by the nineteenth-century skeptics. It was banished along with God, because of its perceived close association with him. But, in spite of the best hopes (and frequent claims) of the positivists, the banishment of God and of philosophy did not really succeed in banishing teleology from the study of man and nature, or in banishing the natural law doctrines that are inevitably implied in teleology.

NATURAL LAW IN ANTHROPOLOGY

The nineteenth century

As we saw in Chapter 2, many of the pioneer anthropologists of the later nineteenth century were jurists and/or historians of the law, who were led into anthropology through their search for the origins of law. Without quite acknowledging it by name, they had a very keen interest in natural law; particularly in the worldwide comparative study of jus gentium, in the fashion that had long since been recommended by Grotius. Maine and McLennan, in particular, made this the cornerstone of their progressivist theories. *Natural Law*

With their backgrounds both in law and in ethnology, and their special interest in jus gentium, the jurist-anthropologists were in a privileged position to introduce significant new insights into the concepts and the theories of natural law. In fact, they did not do so. They were also, in the best nineteenth-century tradition, positivists and agnostics, and like other thinkers of the time they abandoned the use of the term natural law, calling it instead by a variety of other names. The result was that they never really stopped to examine the legitimacy or the implications of the natural law concept itself from a jurist's perspective. They studied natural law, in the guise of jus gentium, as an empirical phenomenon without reflecting on it as an ontological problem. Moreover, virtually all anthropologists since their time have followed their lead. Because of this development we cannot really speak of the persistence of natural law *doctrines* within anthropology, but only of the survival, under other names, of natural law concepts and approaches.

Herbert Spencer, one of the few pioneer social evolutionists who was not a jurist, represents a partial exception to the foregoing generalization. He was also the only one of the pioneer evolutionists who can legitimately be called (and called himself) a philosopher. In the broad philosophical sense of the term, he was also the quintessential positivist of the later nineteenth century. He was at least as doctrinaire as Comte in his insistence that *Homo sapiens* must be studied as part of the larger natural order. As we saw in Chapter 2, he proposed a unitary theory of evolution that involved all matter, animate as well as inanimate. Yet Spencer not only developed a theory of ethics; he regarded it as the crown of his philosophical system.[174] Moreover and more importantly, he believed in absolute as well as relative ethics. "My ultimate purpose, lying behind all proximate

174. Cf. Frederick Copleston, *A History of Philosophy,* Book Three, vol. VIII, p. 136.

purposes, has been that of finding for the principles of right and wrong in conduct at large, a scientific basis."[175]

Although it was Spencer who first coined the phrase "survival of the fittest," he did not regard this as a true natural law, for it was the governing principle of imperfectly evolved minds. In perfectly evolved societies and minds, competition between individuals and societies would give way to mutual cooperation and aid. Absolute ethics is "an ideal code of conduct formulating the behaviour of the completely adapted man in the completely evolved society."[176] This was obviously a kind of natural law theory; it was similar in some respects to the social contract theories of the eighteenth century, in some respects to the progressivist theories of his fellow evolutionists, and in other respects to the utopianism of Marx.[177]

Natural law in anthropology

Modern anthropology: the legacies

I suggested at the beginning of the chapter that a concept of physical law is indispensable for all natural sciences, and a concept of natural law–under whatever name–is equally indispensable for all social and behavioral sciences. But it should be abundantly evident by now that there is no single, unitary doctrine of natural law. There is only a rather diffuse body of ideas whose common denominator is the belief that certain customs and beliefs are common to all mankind, that they are inherently reasonable, and that they have their origin in some force external to the human will. That force, as we have seen, has been variously identified as nature, as God, and as society–which from a teleological perspective may turn out to be three words for the same thing.

As there is no unitary doctrine of natural law in general, there is of course no unitary natural law doctrine in anthropology, and the term itself remains unfashionable. But anthropology has nevertheless inherited not one but several legacies from the long tradition of natural law theory that preceded it, and that contributed to its beginnings as a discipline. From the earliest Greeks (and more directly from eighteenth-century natural history) it has inherited the challenge of interpreting man's behavior in biological terms, while from eighteenth-century moral philosophy it has inherited the challenge of interpreting the same behavior in social terms. These two challenges have given rise, respectively, to naturalistic

---

175. Herbert Spencer, *The Data of Ethics* (London, 1907), p. v.

176. Ibid., p. 238.

177. For further discussion of Spencer's (unacknowledged) conception of natural law, see Arthur L. Harding in Wilkin et al, *Origins of the Natural Law Tradition*, pp. 76–81.

and to consensual approaches to natural law. In addition, the structuralists have revived the ancient intuitive approach, which was perhaps the oldest of all theories of natural law.

Natural law theory manifests itself in anthropology not only in different ways, but with varying degrees of explicitness and centrality. At the most implicit level, it may be said that nearly all anthropological theories at least assume the existence of natural law, insofar as they assume that common behaviors and beliefs have a rational basis outside of the human will. These theories do not necessarily involve a search for natural law; they simply take its existence for granted. At a more explicit level, cross-cultural surveys may involve an actual search for natural laws, in the form of cultural universals. At a still more explicit level, Structuralism and some other doctrines offer specific, a priori theories of natural law, although not under that name.

The legacies of natural law in anthropology are sufficiently fragmented so that they can only be considered here in a fragmented manner. In the following paragraphs I will first discuss what I take to be the most fundamental and enduring of legacies: the basic categorical framework that we have always assumed to be common to all cultures. I will then consider a number of specific domains of twentieth-century theory and practice in which I think natural law concepts are at least implicit. My concern, as I stated earlier, is not to argue the validity or the invalidity of any particular approach, but simply to consider how natural law doctrines have affected and continue to affect anthropological thinking.

The basic framework of culture. Insofar as there is a direct link between anthropology and older, naturalistic doctrines of natural law, it is to be found in the traditions of eighteenth century natural science, which then included ethnology. The naturalist of those early years was not just a student of *Homo sapiens*, but also and simultaneously a zoologist, a botanist, a geologist, a paleontologist, and an antiquarian. And in his studies of the human species he was simultaneously a physical and a cultural anthropologist; probably without any conscious awareness of the difference.

The scientific description of any newly discovered species involved two components. First, a description of the creature's physical characteristics: external morphology, skeletal anatomy, musculature, and the like. Second, a description of its habitual behaviors in feeding, mating, nesting, grouping, and the like. In his character as ethnologist, the naturalist approached each new tribe in exactly the same way: as though it were a new species. That is, he sought to describe both the physical aspect and the habitual "manners and customs" of the people. It would not have occurred to him that the description of physical characteristics and the description of cultural behaviors were separate activities that ought to be undertaken by different specialists, for both were considered equally to be descriptions of nature. In the study of peoples, the naturalist could not of course shoot and dissect specimens, as he routinely did with animal species, but he made up for this as best he could by taking external measurements and above all by the excavation and measurement of skeletons.

Natural law in anthropology

The underlying assumption was that "manners and customs," at least of primitive peoples, were as much a part of the natural order as were racial characteristics. Moreover, as we saw earlier in the chapter, there was a strong interest in discovering customs that were common to all primitive peoples. It was this assumption that gave rise to a quite specific, categorical framework of ethnographic inquiry. Just as physical morphology in animals was described under a more or less standardized set of headings having to do with stature, coloration, skeletal anatomy, dentition, and the like, so also cultures were described under a set of standardized categorical headings that were believed to be universal.

The categorical description and analysis of cultures traces back at least as far as the cosmographies of the late Middle Ages. When Bernhardt Varen (or Varenius, as his name appears on the Latin title page) wrote his *Geographia generalis* in 1650, he listed the things that need to be considered for each country and people as

> (1) the stature of the Natives, as to their shape, colour, length of life, Original, Meat, and Drink, &c. (2) Their Trafficks and Arts in which the Inhabitants are employed. (3) Their Vertues, Vices, Learning, Wit, &c. (4) Their customs in Marriage, Christenings, and Burials, &c. (5) Their Speech and Language. (6) Their State-Government. (7) Their Religion and Church-Government. (8) Their Cities and most renowned Places. (9) Their memorable Histories. And (10) their famous Men, Artificers, and Inventions of the Natives of all Countries.[178]

Three-quarters of a century later, when Joseph Lafitau published his *Customs of American Savages Compared with Those of Earliest Times* (1724), the categorical inventory had arrived at a form very similar to that em-

178. Varen, *Cosmography and geography in two parts....* (London, 1682), p. 3. For more detailed discussion, see Margaret Hodgen, *Early Anthropology in the Sixteenth and Seventeenth Centuries* (Philadelphia, 1964), pp. 167–168.

ployed by twentieth-century ethnologists; it included religion; political government; marriage and education; occupations of men; occupations of women; warfare; commerce; games; death, burial, and mourning; sickness and medicine; and language.[179] Harris has pointed out that these correspond closely to the universal categories of culture proposed by Clark Wissler in 1926: speech, material traits, art, knowledge, religion, society, property, government, and war.[180]

Without pushing the point further, I think it is apparent that anthropology's traditional, categorical method of analyzing cultures represents a kind of natural law theory, and a specific legacy of late medieval and early modern natural science. In and of itself it is a heuristic, classificatory device, but I think most anthropologists would insist that it corresponds to a catalogue of specific, universal needs.[181] Properly speaking, of course, it is a way of thinking rather than an explanatory theory. It has largely disappeared from ethnographic description in the last two generations, but as an analytical framework it survives in nearly all elementary anthropology textbooks today. In other words, it is still the way that we choose to represent our basic mode of thought to outsiders.

Natural Law

This mode of thinking is fundamentally Aristotelian, insofar as it finds universalities in culture and attributes them to specific purposes in nature. It involves, in other words, a teleological conception of natural law.

Cultural Relativism and cultural universals: the Boasian approach. The arrival of Franz Boas, and his transplantation of German Idealist doctrines to American soil, brought about a genuine revolution in American anthropological thinking which will be discussed more fully in the Chapter 6. The central doctrine of the Boasians was Cultural Relativism, a doctrine that has been equated by a number of critics with particularism and even with antinomianism.[182] This, however, is an unwarranted charge, for none of the Boasians were total relativists or total particularists; indeed many of them expressed their disapproval of ethical relativism. The ultimate philosophic goal at least for most of the Boasians was to find, through empirical

179. Cf. Harris, *The Rise of Anthropological Theory*, p. 17.

180. Ibid.

181. Cf. esp. Bronislaw Malinowski, *A Scientific Theory of Culture and Other Essays* (Chapel Hill, N.C., 1944); and Abram Kardiner, ed., *The Individual and His Society* (New York, 1939), pp. 5–7.

182. Cf. Harris, *Rise of Anthropological Theory*, pp. 336–337; Leslie White, *The Science of Culture* (New York, 1949), p. 110; Robert Nisbet, *Social Change and History* (New York, 1969), p. 224.

search, the commonalities that lie beneath the plethora of cultural forms: the unity beneath diversity.[183] Boas himself wrote that "Observation has shown... that not only emotions, intellect, and will-power of man are alike everywhere, but that much more detailed similarities in thought and action occur among the most diverse peoples."[184] An attempt to identify specific cultural universals can be found in the work of a great many of the Boasians, if not of Boas himself.

Natural law in anthropology

For the Boasians, as also later for the structuralists, the impetus to believe in and to search for cultural universals came partly from linguistics. Most of the Boasians had been formally trained in linguistics by their mentor, and indeed much of their time was spent in collecting and recording native texts. Moreover and more importantly, most of them accepted the "linguistic analogy:" the idea that the core of culture, like that of language, is a set of learned codes, and that a culture can be studied and described in the much the same way as can a language. The systematic, comparative linguistic analyses of the nineteenth century had shown that there are undoubted universals in the structure of languages, and this reinforced the belief that there were structural universals in culture as well. And as no rational explanation could often be given for the universals in language, so also there need not be an obvious explanation for the universals in culture.[185]

A. L. Kroeber was perhaps the most wholly relativist of the Boasians; he argued that what are normally identified as cultural universals are essentially "sub-cultural:"

> Such more or less recurrent near-regularities of form and process as have to date been formulated for culture are actually mainly subcultural in nature. They are limits set to culture by physical or organic factors. The so-called "cultural constants" of family, religion, war, communication, and the like appear to be biopsychological frames variably filled with cultural content, so far as they are more than categories reflecting the compartments of our own Occidental logico-verbal culture.[186]

183. Having studied under Lowie at Berkeley and known him personally, I feel better qualified to generalize about the aims of the Boasians than are those critics who only know them through the written page. Cf. also Robert Redfield, *Human Nature and the Study of Culture* (Chicago, 1962), pp. 442–443.

184. Franz Boas, *The Mind of Primitive Man* (New York, 1911). Quoted from Clyde Kluckhohn in A. L. Kroeber, ed., *Anthropology Today* (Chicago, 1948), p. 511.

185. Cf. Harris, *Rise of Anthropological Theory*, pp. 419–421.

186. A. L. Kroeber in *Journal of General Education* 3 (1949): 182–188.

Conversely, Lowie, another of the most relativistic Boasians, acknowledged that culture is not "a region of complete lawlessness," and that the functional relationship of traits resulted in cultural recurrences in different parts of the globe.[187] Clark Wissler and Alexander Goldenweiser—good Boasians both—went into some detail in discussing the universals in culture, largely in functionalist terms.[188]

In the midcentury era, the new influences of Functionalism and of Configurationism led to an accelerated interest in the search for cultural universals. This is reflected in seminal works of Ralph Linton,[189] Melville Herskovits,[190] Clyde Kluckhohn,[191] and Julian Steward.[192] The motivations were not quite the same for functionalists and for configurationists: the former were interested in relating cultural institutions to social imperatives,[193] while the latter were more interested in the discovery of basic human nature through the study of cultural recurrences.[194] However, they came to agreement on a fairly specific list of cultural universals that included language, other forms of symbolic communication, art, mythology, various specific aspects of ritual, exogamy and the incest tabu, marriage, systems of kinship reckoning, property, inheritance rules, trade, political forms, warfare, treatment of the sick, sports and games, and of course many categories of material culture.[195] In the 1960s, "New Ethnologists" would complain that many items on the list are universals only in the eye of the beholder; they are simply classificatory categories that we may impose in describing culture, but which do not necessarily correspond to the way that people think about their own ideas and behavior.[196] While there is a good deal of justification in this charge, it is nevertheless true that not all of the supposed universals are categorical labels; some involve quite specific, recurring behavior patterns.

Natural Law

In the years since World War II, the more or less unsystematic search

---

187. Robert H. Lowie, *Culture and Ethnology* (New York, 1966), pp. 88–90. The original was written in 1917.

188. Wissler, *Man and Culture* (New York, 1923), pp. 73–98; Goldenweiser, *Early Civilization* (New York, 1922), pp. 235–270.

189. *The Study of Man* (New York, 1936); esp. pp. 132–270.

190. *Man and His Works* (New York, 1948); esp. pp. 229–240.

191. Quoted in Kroeber, *Anthropology Today*, pp. 507–523.

192. *Area Research: Theory and Practice* (Washington, D.C., 1950). *Social Science Research Council Bulletin* 63.

193. See esp. D. F. Aberle et al. in *Ethos* 60 (1950): 100–111.

194. Cf. Redfield, *Human Nature and the Study of Culture*, pp. 442–444.

195. See esp. Herskovits, *Man and His Works.*

196. Kroeber had previously hinted at the same thing, in the passage quoted earlier (in *Journal of General Education*). For the "New Ethnology," see Harris, *Rise of Anthropological Theory*, pp. 568–604.

for universals undertaken by the Boasians has largely given way to the much more rigorous methodology of holocultural survey, which will be discussed in a moment. Anthropology's continuing interest in universals meanwhile continues to be reflected in many recent works.[197]

Not all of the Boasians directly acknowledged that their search for cultural universals was an attempt to discover "oughts" from the study of "ises," but this was a clear implication of the enterprise. Insofar as the method was genuinely empirical, it represents a consensual approach to natural law in keeping with the recommendations of Grotius, and even with the practice of the Roman jurisconsults.

Natural law in anthropology

Universal equality and universal rights. The Boasians' search for cultural universals was associated with, and largely motivated by, a passionate dedication to the principle of universal human equality. Much of this can be traced directly to the charismatic influence of Boas, himself–a man whose entire career was dedicated to demonstrating the racial, linguistic, and cultural equality of all peoples. Although he is often credited with major innovations in methodology and in theory, Boas was above all an idealogue–a fact that is attested to by his involvement in various social causes during the latter years of his career in New York.[198] His proper place in the history of anthropology will be more fully explored in Chapter 6; here it is sufficient to notice that his influence was at least as much ideological as it was theoretical. Indeed, egalitarianism may be the most enduring of the Boasian legacies in American anthropology.

For Boas and for many of his committed followers, like Lowie, Radin, and Herskovits, equality of man was beyond question an a priori natural law, as much as it was for Cicero, Augustine, and Aquinas. It was not a conclusion forced on them by their ethnographic researches, in spite of their supposed dedication to empiricism. It was a proposition that they set out to prove, not to test, by means of cultural as well as linguistic and biological evidence. Egalitarianism is the single natural law doctrine that underlies and informs nearly all of the prodigious and varied researches of the Boasians.

One should mention finally, in this connection, the passionate dedication of so many anthropologists to the cause of universal human rights,

---

197. For a review of these, as well as an excellent overview of the current "state of the art" in the search for cultural universals, see Donald Brown, *Human Universals* (New York, 1991), esp. pp. 54–87. For an example of universalist thinking, see Robert Murphy, *The Dialectics of Social Life* (New York, 1971).

198. See Marshall Hyatt, *Franz Boas, Social Activist: The Dynamics of Ethnicity* (New York, 1990).

and more particularly to the rights of native peoples. As in the case of Boasian egalitarianism, it is not a conviction that has arisen from empirical studies, but a part of the anthropological ethos.

Holocultural surveys. For all their commitment to the search for cultural universals, the Boasians, with their essentially qualitative methodology, were content to rest their convictions mostly on anecdotal evidence. A more rigorous approach was pioneered by G. P. Murdock through his statistical cross-cultural survey methodology, which led ultimately to the creation of the Human Relations Area Files. The methodology has been called by a variety of names; I will here follow Naroll in designating it as holocultural.[199]

Murdock was originally interested primarily in issues of social organization, and his first two holocultural surveys, both published in 1937, were on the sexual division of labor and on the social and political correlates of matrilineal and patrilineal descent.[200] In a much more sweeping 1945 article, he offered a list of seventy-two traits, from age-grading to weather control, that "occur, so far as the author's knowledge goes, in every culture known to history or ethnography."[201] Still more comprehensive and more methodologically systematic was his worldwide survey of social institutions published in *Social Structure.*[202]

Improvements in statistical methodology, as well as the advent of computers, have greatly enhanced the reliability of holocultural studies since their beginnings half a century ago. Naroll has classified the studies into three "generations": an early group that employed no sampling methods, but attempted to canvass all ethnographically reported cultures, and that employed no controls for extraneous variables; a second group that involved judgmental sampling and employed statistical measures of correlation but that still involved no control for data bias and parallels due to diffusion; and a third, ideal group that would hopefully overcome these remaining problems.[203] In the same article, Naroll also summarized the results of a large number of holocultural studies on such topics as kinship

199. Raoul Naroll in Raoul and Frada Naroll, eds., *Main Currents in Cultural Anthropology* (New York, 1973), p. 309.

200. In *Social Forces* 15 (1937): 551–553 and in G. P. Murdock, ed., *Studies in the Science of Society Presented to Albert Galloway Keller* (New Haven, Conn., 1937), pp. 445–470.

201. Murdock in Ralph Linton, ed., *The Science of Man in the World Crisis* (New York, 1945), p. 124.

202. New York, 1949.

203. Naroll and Naroll, *Main Currents in Cultural Anthropology,* pp. 318–319.

systems, kin avoidances, inheritance, marriage, divorce, and origin myths.[204] A more recent work that presents a universalist overview of human society and culture, based partly on holocultural surveys, is Naroll's *The Moral Order.*[205]

Holocultural surveys need not, of course, be undertaken exclusively for the purpose of discovering cultural universals. Their purpose may be to discover the correlation between different, functionally linked aspects of culture, as for example between religious beliefs and forms of social organization;[206] or they may be undertaken to discover patterns of regional diversity. Nevertheless, a great many holocultural surveys have involved a search for universals, and in those cases their fundamental aim is no different from that of the more intuitive Boasians. It may be noted too that their findings have very rarely disconfirmed the commonsense understandings or the anecdotally derived theories of earlier scholars, except to show that almost nothing is quite as universal as has commonly been thought. In general, however, holocultural surveys represent simply a more reliable means to the same basic goal sought by all consensual natural law theorists: that of discovering unity beneath diversity.

Structuralism. Structuralism is not a doctrine unique or original within anthropology, and it will be discussed as a separate philosophical tradition in Chapter 7. There are also disciplines or subdisciplines of structural linguistics, structural psychology, structural physics, structural biology, structural mathematics, and others, some of which are older than structural anthropology. Within anthropology the most persistent spokesman for the structuralist approach has been Claude Lévi-Strauss, who readily acknowledges the derivation of his ideas from those of the structural linguists Ferdinand de Saussure and Roman Jakobsen.

What all of the structuralisms have in common is some kind of belief in natural law. It is not, however, a uniform conception among the different disciplines. The structure envisioned by physicists is tantamount to what we have called physical law, while the structure envisioned by anthropologists and psychologists corresponds more closely to the Stoic and Aristotelian conceptions of natural law.

The basic assumption of structural anthropology is that human minds are somehow preprogrammed so that they all work in the same way. They perceive the external world in terms of inherent categorical systems, and

---

204. Ibid., pp. 328–332.

205. Beverly Hills, Calif., 1983.

206. On this topic, see Guy Swanson, *The Birth of the Gods* (Ann Arbor, Mich., 1974).

they develop mythologies to explain that world, and social systems to deal with it, in terms of their categorical perceptions. The objective of the structuralists has been twofold: to discover the inherent logic, common to all peoples, in man's mental programming, and to find some kind of purposive explanation for it. The first of these objectives involves essentially a search for universal mental categories; it has been a primary concern of the French structuralists. Meanwhile the British have been more concerned to try and relate recurring mental categories to the unchanging needs of society, mainly within the context of Durkheimian sociology. In general, the interest of American structuralists has been more nearly congruent with that of the French. In terms of the distinctions I made at the beginning of the chapter, it may be said that the French and American structuralists adhere to an intuitive conception of natural law theory, while the British are seeking to develop a teleological theory.

Structuralism has sometimes been dismissed as unscientific because of its belief in innate ideas (thereby rejecting the doctrine of Locke), while failing to explain how they come about, or even in some cases what purposes they serve.[207] The concern of structuralists, like that of many earlier thinkers, has not been to discover *how* human minds come to be preprogrammed, but *why*. Most of the explanations they have offered are either vaguely or explicitly sociofunctional, but they still account for only a fraction of the cross-cultural regularity that the structuralists claim to have identified. Structuralism thus continues to involve mainly an intuitive approach to natural law.

Human and primate ethology. Of all the different and diverse branches of anthropological enterprise, the study of human and primate ethology most clearly and unambiguously involves a search for natural law. In a narrowly professional sense it might be argued that these studies are not anthropological, since most of their practitioners were not trained as anthropologists and do not reside in academic departments of anthropology. But then, the same was true of Morgan, McLennan, and Frazer, to say nothing of the scores of pioneer field ethnologists who preceded them. The two important points about ethological studies are that their methodology, as far as it goes, is rigorously ethnographic, and their objectives are basically anthropological: to discover universals beneath diversity. In any case the findings of the ethologists, if not actually originated by anthropologists, are very frequently cited in the anthropological literature, usually in support of some general evolutionary or antievolutionary theory.

---

207. Cf. esp. Harris, *Rise of Anthropological Theory*, pp. 464–513.

Natural law in anthropology

Human ethology has very much in common with the spirit of eighteenth-century ethnology, insofar as it approaches man as an animal to be studied on the same basis as all other animals. As in the case of other animals, this means studying behavioristically, by observing and generalizing from actual behaviors rather than by asking questions. In principle it is a strictly etic study, rather than combining etic and emic observations as nearly all conventional ethnographies do.[208] The ultimate objective is to find commonalities not only between all human groups but between mankind and the rest of the animal kingdom; particularly between man and his nearer simian cousins.

While ethological doctrines have been proclaimed by a number of armchair theorists,[209] the single truly active field ethologist thus far has been Irenäus Eibl-Eibesfeld, who heads the Institute of Human Ethology at the Max Planck Institute in Germany. His methodology involves both primary and secondary research. He has done firsthand field work, including an enormous amount of "naturalistic" photography, among peoples all over the world. Like the American cross-cultural surveyors, he has also reviewed a truly prodigious amount of ethnographic literature and has subjected at least some of his findings to statistical analysis, in his search for human universals.

In general, the findings of Eibl-Eibesfeld tend to confirm the more impressionistic conclusions of anthropologists. Since he must work entirely from observed behaviors, however, he is largely precluded from investigating the cognitive areas of culture, such as mythology and cosmology, that have been of special interest to anthropologists. His most important and most interesting findings are all in one way or another related to social organization. Among his announced findings are that the family unit of husband-wife-children is basic in all societies, regardless of its embeddedness in larger household or kin structures; that marital bonding is always ideally for life, regardless of the actualities of divorce rates; that there are universalities in regard to courtship behavior, sexual modesty, and the limitation of sexual promiscuity; that the incest tabu is everywhere present; that there is a universal human tendency to aggregate in groups larger than are strictly necessary for subsistence; that there is a universal tendency to hierarchic ranking in such groups; that human groups always develop symbolic criteria of in-group and out-group identity; that all groups, at all levels of socio-economic complexity, exhibit some degree of territoriality; and that the

208. For the etic/emic distinction, see esp. Kenneth Pike, *Language in Relation to a Unified Theory of the Structure of Human Behavior* (Glendale, Calif., 1954).
209. For references, see n. 10.

institution of property is universal.[210] Eibl-Eibesfeld has also announced empirically discovered regularities in the areas of human conflict, communication, child behavioral development, and habitat exploitation,[211] and even in the field of aesthetics.[212]

Primate ethology involves the extension of ethological studies from the human sphere to that of our nearest nonhuman relatives. From the standpoint of human self-understanding it is perhaps the most exciting development of the last fifty years, revealing for the first time that culture is not, as we always thought, a uniquely human phenomenon. The discovery of behaviors among gorillas and chimpanzees that are analogous to some of our own social institutions has caused a rethinking of some of our most cherished ideas about human society, and especially about its natural bases. While most field studies of primates have not been carried out by anthropologists, their direct relevance to anthropology has been acknowledged by nearly everyone.

There are, of course, perfectly sound, particularistic or descriptive reasons for studying the social behavior of apes, just as there are in the case of elephants or of finches. Such studies are of interest in their own right, without having any necessary relevance to human self-understanding. In contrast, the undertaking of field studies of apes in order to learn more about *Homo sapiens* implies a belief in, and a search for, the broadest of all natural laws, which determine the behavior not only of all humans but of our nearest nonhuman neighbors as well. As always, there is an underlying assumption that such common behaviors (e.g. in food-sharing practices) must have some rational basis in the natural order, though it may not be clear in all cases what that basis is.[213] Unlike the approaches previously discussed, however, ethological studies do not constitute the direct survival of an older, prescientific tradition into the scientific era. They involve, on the contrary, a revival of a very ancient natural law concept; one that dates all the way back to the beginnings of Greek philosophy.

The anomaly of legal anthropology. If natural law concepts were to be explicitly discussed or employed anywhere within the modern anthropological literature, one might reasonably expect that it would be in the subdiscipline of legal anthropology. In fact, however, legal anthropology reflects

210. Irenäus Eibl-Eibesfeld, *Human Ethology* (New York, 1989), pp. 167–359.
211. Ibid., pp. 361–663.
212. As was earlier suggested by Raymond Firth, quoted by Kluckhohn in Kroeber, *Anthropology Today*, p. 511.
213. A recent study purports to show that moral ideas of right and wrong are present among chimpanzees and macaques as well as in humans; see Eliot Marshall in *Science* 271 (1996): 904.

exactly the same limitation as does the nineteenth-century writing of Maine, Morgan, and McLennan. Scholars like Hoebel, Gluckman, and Nader have contributed enormously to our understanding of the diversity of law in different societies, as well as to the problems of defining and studying law, but one looks in vain through the corpus of their work for any discussion of the fundamental issue of natural law. In a survey article in 1965, Laura Nader listed eight questions that have chiefly been of concern to legal anthropologists. Two of them were: "Is law present in all societies?" and "What are the universal characteristics of law wherever it is found?"[214] Missing, however, was the question, "Are there universal moral principles embodied in the law wherever it is found?"

Natural law in anthropology

The twentieth-century subdiscipline of legal anthropology remains not only positivist, but, for many of its adherents, behaviorist. That is, law is adduced from the empirical study of conflicts and how they are resolved; the "trouble-case method" as Hoebel has called it.[215] There are, it is true, formal and substantivist schools among the legal anthropologists, but the question at issue is not whether there is universal law, but whether the concepts and terminology of Western jurisprudence can appropriately be applied to non-Western societies.[216]

The enduring dilemma. The social and cultural anthropologists of Britain, France, and other European countries have long since severed whatever connection they had with physical anthropology. This has left them free to develop essentially dualistic perspectives, accounting for human behavior in the social world while leaving it to others to account, on different terms, for human behavior in the physical world. Not so in North American anthropology, where the marriage between physical and cultural anthropology, although shaky, remains intact. Far more than other anthropologies, the anthropology of North America remains both a social and a natural science in the fullest sense. Thus, for better or worse, it remains committed to the search for a monistic theory, which will reconcile natural law with physical laws. It is the same problem that faced the earliest Greek theorists at the dawn of philosophy.

The difficulty lies in the fact that the natural law doctrine is fundamentally a moral one, not a scientific or a logical one. Like Progressivism and Primitivism, it is an ideology involving inescapable value judgments. The belief that what is natural is right and what is right is natural does not stem

214. Laura Nader in *American Anthropologist* 67, no. 6, part 2 (1965): 4.
215. E. Adamson Hoebel, *The Law of Primitive Man* (New York, 1968), pp. 35–45.
216. Cf. Laura Nader, ed., *Law in Culture and Society* (Chicago, 1969), pp. 2–5.

from a clearcut understanding of nature; it stems from an instinctive conviction about what is right. The challenge for natural law theorists has always been to find logical, theological, or scientific justifications for what they believed intuitively to be right and wrong. In other words, natural law theory does not use nature to define right; it uses right to define nature. Such a procedure is inescapably teleological, since what is right can only be right with reference to some purpose, reflective in turn of a will. Plato and Aristotle made this very explicit when they defined nature in terms of purposes, and modern Western science has by no means escaped from the Platonic and Aristotelian view.

American anthropology, as we have seen, has inherited several different conceptions of natural law. It has largely abjured the intuitive conception, except in the case of pure structuralism, but it has derived ideas about normative human behavior both from the study of man and from the study of nature. But what happens when these studies lead to fundamentally different conceptions of what is nature, and what is natural law? This dilemma raises the much more fundamental problem: is monism really possible in the study of *Homo sapiens,* when all efforts not only to reconcile social and natural science, but even to reconcile the different social sciences, have thus far failed? It is a question far beyond the scope and intent of this book, but one that all social scientists must eventually ponder.

From a purely historical standpoint, two points may be made in concluding the discussion of natural law and anthropology. First, insofar as anthropology is a universalist rather than a comparativist discipline (and this varies greatly from one practitioner to another), its universalist perspective is at least partly derivable from, and is not fundamentally different from, older traditions of natural law theory. Second, natural law theory is the single philosophical root that traces back, unbroken, from the anthropology of the twentieth century to the earliest philosophies of classical antiquity. If it is not the stoutest of anthropology's roots, it is at least the deepest.

SUMMARY

Natural law is the only concept discussed in this book that is nearly worldwide in its distribution, and that has a continuous history from ancient to modern times. The idea that recurrent human behaviors and beliefs are part of some natural or divinely created order is found, in one guise or another, in just about every human society, and in the West it has been a subject of overt philosophical and theological speculation since very ancient times. Unlike the doctrines of Progressivism and Primitivism it was not suppressed or submerged in the Middle Ages; on the contrary it was a major concern of medieval Scholastics and jurists no less than of the philosophers who preceded them and of the social theorists who followed them.

If the basic concept of natural law is a very compelling idea, it is also a frustratingly elusive one. Over the centuries natural law has meant a great many things to many people; indeed it seems to have meant many things to most of the individuals who used the term. No one except perhaps Hobbes has ever offered an entirely unitary formulation. Others have combined intuitive, teleological, and consensual approaches, prescriptive and descriptive definitions, and a priori and a posteriori reasoning in a truly bewildering variety of combinations.

Summary

Nevertheless, it is possible to trace a definite, if somewhat meandering, course in the evolution of Western thought on the subject of natural law. The earliest Greek philosophers took it for granted as part of nature's ordering, and made no distinction between natural law and physical law. It was the Sophists who first made a distinction between the two, thereby separating out natural law as a distinct realm for speculation. But it was Plato and Aristotle who gave the doctrine its teleological dimension, insisting not only that there are innate ideas about right and wrong but that they can be related to discoverable purposes in nature. In late antiquity this idea was to become the cornerstone of Stoic philosophy.

The Romans were heavily influenced by Aristotelian and Stoic ideas, but out of their need to govern an ethnically diverse empire they also developed a practical, nonspeculative approach to natural law. They sought to discover it empirically, through the identification of customs and beliefs that were common to all peoples: the jus gentium. Implicit in this as in all conceptions of natural law was the assumption that whatever is universal must be right, whether or not we can discover the reason. It was jus gentium that provided the primary basis for the celebrated sixth-century Code of Justinian, which was to have an enormous influence on later juristic thinking.

By the end of classical antiquity there had thus developed three rather distinct approaches to natural law: the intuitive conception of the earliest philosophers, the teleological approach of Aristotle and the Stoics, and the consensual approach of the Romans.

The natural law doctrine did not die out in the Middle Ages; on the contrary it attained a heightened importance, both philosophically and practically. There were two reasons for this. First, the Code of Justinian, with its emphasis on jus gentium, continued to provide the foundation for all European civil law for a thousand years. Second, the Christian theologians sought to find, through the study of natural law, a fuller understanding of God's will than could be found in Scripture. Their approach was as teleological as that of the Stoics, by whom they were heavily influenced, but God's will was now substituted for nature's purposes as the ultimate explanation for recurring behaviors and beliefs. The medieval thinkers actually combined, or attempted to combine, all three of the earlier approaches to natural law: the intuitive, the teleological, and the consensual. This synthesis was never fully successful, but it came closest to realization in the works of Thomas Aquinas.

The natural law concept acquired a wholly new, practical importance following the discovery of the Americas. The question of whether Native Americans were or were not fellow human beings, and whether it was or was not lawful to enslave them, was hotly debated in Spain, and it was ultimately decided not by papal decree but by an appeal to natural law. It was successfully argued that the Indians must be fellow human beings because they had the same basic customs and the same ideas of right and wrong as did other peoples. The debates and their outcome not only had an influence on Spanish colonial policy; they also helped to shape the course of future thinking on the subject of natural law, and particularly its application in the field of international law.

The secularizing trend in early modern thought, already noted in Chapter 2, made itself felt in the field of natural law theory as well. Hugo Grotius produced in 1625 a work of fundamental importance, *On the Law of War and Peace*, in which for the first time he explained universal human behaviors and beliefs in terms neither of nature's purposes nor of God's will, but on the requirements of society. This elevation of society, rather than God or nature, to the role of prime mover in human affairs was to form the cornerstone of all later philosophical and juristic thinking on the subject of natural law, although it was of course rejected by theologians.

Gradually, among the successors of Grotius, there emerged the concept of the social contract. Human beings, originally living in isolation, had come together and agreed to live as a community, and their agreement, which restricted the liberties of the individual in the interest of the group, constituted a kind of contract. Society was constituted originally by the voluntary consent of the governed, but once constituted it became essential to human existence, and its preservation and smooth functioning were overriding necessities. Its demands upon the individual were then expressed in natural law. Ideas of right and wrong might not serve the self-interest of individuals, but they could be shown as necessary for the preservation of society.

However, the idea of the social contract was given a new and different emphasis during the eighteenth century, in keeping with the generally lib-

Summary

ertarian spirit of Enlightenment thinking. Stress was now placed on the fact that the original contract which created society was a voluntary one, which meant that societies could only continue to exist by the consent of the governed. They could not, therefore, make arbitrary and unreasonable demands on their members; the social contract must guarantee rights to the individual as well as requiring duties from him. In the hands of libertarians and revolutionaries, the doctrine of social contract, and therefore also of natural law, became associated more and more with the demand for universal rights rather than with the specification of duties, a manifestation that is particularly evident in the U.S. Declaration of Independence. It is this latter-day version of natural law theory—almost a complete inversion of the original doctrine—that is most often invoked by social thinkers and political activists in the present day.

Because of its assumptions about innate ideas, but even more because of its close association with medieval theology, the whole idea of natural law began to come under attack in the later eighteenth century. Both David Hume and Immanuel Kant condemned it for its philosophic rationalism. Then, with the demise of moral philosophy and the rise of the social sciences in the nineteenth century, the doctrine came under attack from several directions at once. Utilitarians saw it as a detriment to social reform, legal relativists and Marxists condemned its universalism, positivists decried its lack of empirical foundations, and agnostics dismissed it because of its historical association with theology. The result of these developments was to banish the term natural law from the vocabularies of social scientists. Yet it can be shown that Utilitarianism, Legal Relativism, Marxism, and Positivism all involve implicit natural law concepts in one sense or another, as indeed do all the modern social sciences.

Anthropology shares with the other social sciences the general avoidance of the term natural law, and therefore an inability or a disinclination to confront directly the issues that it raises. Yet natural law doctrines persist under other names in many areas of anthropological endeavor and thought. Our basic, categorical framework for analyzing culture, harking back as it does to Las Casas and Lafitau, at least implies an intuitive belief in human universals. Structuralism involves a much more explicit belief in universals, which may be either intuitive, in the case of linguistic structuralists, or teleological, in the case of Durkheimian structuralists. Cross-cultural surveys often involve an active, empirical search for universals, in the tradition of jus gentium. The anthropologist's traditional dedication to egalitarian doctrines reflects the Enlightenment equation of natural law with universal rights. But the belief in and the search for natural law is surely most unmistakable in the fields of human and primate ethology.

In this chapter I have traced the history of the natural law doctrine not so much to identify the source of specific anthropological ideas as to show the ubiquitousness of the doctrine. Some anthropological approaches and ideas, like the basic categorical framework and the egalitarian ideal, are clearly legacies of older philosophy, but others are simply new manifestation of a very old and deep-rooted idea, which at bottom is common to all the social sciences. This is the belief that there are basic commonalities in human belief and behavior; that what is common must be natural; and that what is natural must in one sense or another be right. If the concept of natural law implies a belief in innate ideas, it would seem that the idea of natural law is itself one of them.

CHAPTER 5

"INDIANOLOGY"

THE NATIVE AMERICAN has been cast in the role of Noble Savage so often and for so long, and has learned to exploit the role so effectively, that our interest in him might easily be dismissed as nothing more than Primitivism. This is largely true on the European continent, where Native American studies has a small but enthusiastic group of devotees. For North Americans, however, the matter is more complex. As I have written elsewhere, "It has been the peculiar fate of the Indian to become, for the great majority of us, a symbol and a metaphor for qualities in our national character and our national experience that we intermittently cherish and yearn to revive. For better or worse, the Indian's destiny is more bound up in that symbolic identity than in the practical realities of economics."[1] In popular American mythology, the Indian is a figure of our Heroic Age, rather than of any Golden Age of innocent simplicity. He plays the role of Homer's Trojans, not of Herodotus's Scythians.

America's special and complex attitude toward the Indian finds expression in many and sometimes surprising ways. Place names furnish one suggestive example. It is hardly an accident that all but ten of the thirty-seven states added to the union after 1783 have been given native names, or that one state took the name Indiana. This was not due just to the continuation of previously established usage; the names were often adopted after considerable debate, and from obscure sources. In my old home state, the first territorial legislature not only chose the generally little-used name Arizona, in preference to the suggested alternatives Gadsdenia and Gadsonia, but also decreed that all of the territory's counties should be named after Indian tribes—and this at a time (1863) when the Apache and Navajo wars

1. In Susan Abbott and John Van Willigen, eds., *Predicting Sociocultural Change, Southern Anthropological Society Proceedings*, no. 12 (1980), pp. 122–123.

were still raging.[2] The popularity of Indian emblems and motifs in advertising,[3] the Indian cultism in the Boy Scouts and in numerous American fraternal organizations,[4] and the totemic adoption of tribal names by athletic teams are additional testimony to what I will call popular Indianology. It finds expression most of all, however, in the truly extraordinary number of Americans who claim Indian ancestry or even Indian identity, often on quite dubious grounds. The number or persons who reported themselves as Indians in the 1990 U.S. census exceeds by more than 100% the actual enrolled membership of all the 530-odd federally recognized tribes, even though membership rolls often include persons having no more than 1/16 Indian blood.[5]

Importantly, too, the Indian is uniquely "ours," along with the grizzly bear and the Grand Canyon and the Rocky Mountains. He helps define what America is because he is something we don't have to share with Old World nations, who can only enjoy and appreciate and study him at a distance. For want of a better word, I will refer to this peculiarly American preoccupation with the Indian as "Indianology." It has a long history, beginning virtually at the moment of Columbus's first landing, and it remains an important feature not only of the general American ethos but more specifically of the ethos of American anthropology.

INDIANOLOGY AS A DISCIPLINE

Indianology as I define it is not just a popular ideology; it is also a field of study. It clearly differs from all of the doctrines previously discussed, however, in that it is not so much an articulate philosophy as a kind of intellectual and moral passion. In this respect it bears comparison to such older fields of thought and study as Egyptology and Sinology. These studies are not without moral implications, insofar as they reflect on the worthiness of the chosen Other, but they do not necessarily reflect favorably or unfavorably on ourselves. The interest in the Other is simply in his otherness, for better or worse. Indianology, Egyptology, Sinology, and similar hu-

---

2. Subsequent legislatures partially departed from this principle, so that today only ten of the state's fifteen counties are named after Indians.

3. See esp. Rayna Green in Wilcomb E. Washburn, ed., *History of Indian-White Relations* (Washington, D.C., 1988), pp. 593–596. *Handbook of North American Indians,* vol. 4.

4. Cf. Elizabeth Tooker in *American Anthropologist* 94, no. 2 (1992): 359.

5. The figure for those claiming Indian identity in 1990 is 1,959,234; see Bureau of Indian Affairs, *American Indians Today,* 3rd ed. (Washington, D.C., 1991), p. 9. For the blood quantum requirements for membership in particular tribes see C. Matthew Snipp, *American Indians: the First of this Land* (New York, 1989), pp. 362–365.

manistic disciplines offer a kind of escapism rather than expressed or implied moral judgment—a very personal and purely subjective preference for one people or age over others, and perhaps over our own. The Indianologist is an unabashed Indian-lover, the Egyptologist an Egypt-lover, and the Sinologist a China-lover.

As such, the historical roots of Indianology trace back much more to Renaissance humanism than to the moral philosophies of antiquity or of the Enlightenment. The Renaissance was par excellence an age of passions, including a passionate curiosity about everything connected with the newly expanding external world. Renaissance Man collected indiscriminately: seashells, coins, antiquities, exotic flora and fauna, and—not coincidentally—queer customs of savage peoples.[6] The shells, coins, and antiquities found their way into "cabinets of curiosities" (later to become museums), the flora into herbaria, the fauna into zoos, and the queer customs—since they could not be physically collected—into the pages of ethnographic compendia that were originally called cosmographies.[7] One of the first of these, the *Omnium Gentium Mores, Leges & Ritus*, was published by Johan Boemus in 1520.[8] It was followed by a host of others, and by the seventeenth century the cosmography had assumed a standard organizational format closely resembling that of a modern ethnography, with chapters on religion, government, marriage, education, occupations of men and women, warfare, commerce, games, death and burial, sickness and medicine, and language.[9]

In due course the Renaissance collecting mania gave birth to the natural sciences: the active and organized collecting of geological, paleontological, floral, faunal, and ethnographic materials by field workers. At first, the naturalists were as eclectic in their interests as were their noble or wealthy patrons; they collected fossils, rock samples, exotic plants and animals, antiquities, and whatever else struck their fancy as exotic. Later, specialization inevitably occurred, and the naturalists became respectively paleontologists, geologists, botanists, zoologists, and ethnologists. Ethnologists in turn became specialists in particular areas, and in the process one group of ethnologists became Indianologists. It is no accident that research in Indianology, no less than in classics and in Egyptology, was long associated with museums—the quintessential, institutional expression of Renaissance humanism.

6. See esp. Margaret Hodgen, *Early Anthropology in the Sixteenth and Seventeenth Centuries* (Philadelphia, 1964), pp. 111–161.
7. Ibid., pp. 162–206.
8. Ibid., pp. 131–132.
9. Cf. Marvin Harris, *The Rise of Anthropological Theory* (New York, 1968), p. 17.

Indianology derives also from another Renaissance passion: that of singling out for study a particular era or people, its culture and its history. The first such passion was of course for the study of classical antiquity, which led to the founding of the Society of Dilettanti as early as the sixteenth century.[10] Little by little it evolved into what today we call classical studies. Somewhat later came Egyptology, Assyriology, Indology, Sinology, and–though not by name–Indianology.

Indianology as a discipline

But Indianology in America, though clearly a field of study, never had a chance to establish itself as a separate academic discipline, as it did in some European countries.[11] At first it was subsumed under a generalized, highly nationalistic natural history; the Indian was studied along with the native American fauna, flora, and geology, by a corps of all-purpose naturalists. When a separate field of American ethnology finally emerged in the latter part of the nineteenth century, it was coopted almost at once into the fledgling discipline of anthropology, because of the key role that Native American ethnography played in the development of evolutionary theory. And there, for better and worse, it has firmly lodged ever since. It remained true in America, at least until the 1980s, that persons with a special leaning toward Native Americans, and who wanted to make a career studying them, had to become anthropologists; they had no other choice. Over the years this circumstance has attracted, or impelled, into American anthropology a substantial number of scholars who really cared nothing at all about Africans or Melanesians or, for that matter, about physical anthropology or linguistics; persons who would certainly have taken their degrees in Indianology if such an option had been available to them. These "closet Indianologists" helped give American anthropology a distinctly humanistic as well as a somewhat parochial character that has been, at least until the fairly recent past, one of its most distinctive characteristics.

The discipline of "Indianology," as I define it, is not precisely synonymous with Native American Studies, although there is large area of overlap. But Indianology has at its ideological foundation the conception of the Indian not merely as Other, but as a very special Other: always colorful, often spiritual, sometimes heroic and sometimes dastardly, but in any case somehow larger than life. The Indian, in short, has a special mystique, just as has the ancient Egyptian for the Egyptologist, and the Chinese for the Sinologist. When the Indian is viewed merely as a representative of a generalized non-Western Other, as he is in most recent anthropological studies, or when he is viewed as fellow *Homo sapiens* with the same basic problems as

10. Glyn Daniel, *A Hundred Years of Archaeology* (London, 1950), p. 17.

11. There are chairs and departments of "American Studies" (usually meaning Native American Studies) in a number of European universities.

the rest of us, as in psychological and economic studies, then the mystique is lost, and these studies cease to be Indianological in the sense that I have defined it. For Indianology, although it is certainly a field of scholarship, is basically a humanistic and not a scientific one. It is, or at least has been, the great humanistic branch of American anthropology. I will return to this issue at the end of the chapter.

THE BEGINNINGS OF INDIANOLOGY: EXPLORERS, CONQUERORS, AND COMPILERS

In the most literal sense, the birth of Indianology can be fixed in the year 1493, when Columbus wrote the first of his letters (since published) to Queen Isabella, describing his discoveries.[12] In the next half century, a great many other explorers and conquistadores, of several nationalities, wrote accounts of their discoveries which eventually found their way into print. Among the best known in their own time were the accounts of Amerigo Vespucci (1500–1506), Hernán Cortés (1522), and Jacques Cartier (1545). It must be acknowledged, however, that the first explorers and conquerors were not very keen or very accurate observers of the Native American scene. With the exception of Columbus they were mostly not well-educated men, and they seem to have lacked the kind of ethnographic curiosity that often comes from extensive reading or foreign travel. Then, too, the first of the explorers were not fully aware of the novelty of their discoveries. Believing themselves to be in a new part of the long-familiar continent of Asia, they assumed that the Indians were somehow akin to the Tartars, already made famous through the colorful accounts of Carpini, Rubruck, and Marco Polo.[13]

Two of the most ethnographically sensitive documents from the age of the conquests were not written by the expedition commanders or their official chroniclers, but by relatively humble foot soldiers. Bernal Díaz del Castillo accompanied Cortés on his march of conquest to Mexico City, and lived out the remaining sixty years of his life in Mexico and Guatemala. His *Verdadera historia de la conquista de la Nueva España* is rich in descriptive detail about the Mexico of the Aztecs, as the conquerors first observed it.[14] Pedro Cieza de León left Spain as a teenager, just after the conquest of Peru,

12. See Edward Bourne in Margaret Mead and Ruth Bunzel, eds., *The Golden Age of American Anthropology* (New York, 1960), pp. 18–20.
13. Cf. Lee Huddleston, *Origins of the American Indians* (Austin, Tex., 1967), pp. 3–13; for the accounts of the "Tartars" (actually Mongols) see David Morgan, *The Mongols* (Oxford, 1986), pp. 24–27.
14. See Genaro García in Bernal Díaz del Castillo, *The Discovery and Conquest of Mexico* (New York, 1956), pp. xix–xx.

and took part in the Spanish conquest of Colombia and in the civil wars in Peru before returning to Spain, where he died in 1554. He planned an extensive, four-part *Crónica del Perú,* of which one part dealt with the prehispanic kingdom of the Incas.[15] These works were not published until long after they were written, but they were widely available in manuscript, and were cited by many later compilers of ethnographic data.

The beginnings of Indianology

However, the true founders of Indianology as a scholarly discipline were learned compilers who, a generation after the first discoveries, began to synthesize the information provided by the actual discoverers into general works of natural history. By this time the identity of the Americas as a new world had been clearly established, and the ethnographic and other details of the new lands had begun to excite in European minds an interest that has never subsided. The first compilations to appear were the *De orbe novo* of Pedro Martir de Anglería,[16] published in four volumes between 1511 and 1530, and the *Sumario de la natural historia de las Indias* of Gonzalo Fernández de Oviedo, published in 1526.[17] The first was a history of the conquests and colonizations, which also included a substantial amount of ethnographic detail, while the second was essentially a work of natural history, combining botany, zoology, and ethnography. Both works were immediately translated into several European languages. Not very much later came the *Verdadera relación de la conquista del Perú* of Francisco Jérez (1534), the first volume of Oviedo's very much expanded *Historia general y natural de las Indias y Tierra Firme del Mar Océano* (1535), and López de Gómara's *Historia general de las Indias* (1552). Then, at the end of the sixteenth century, came a virtual flood of historical, naturalist, and ethnographic compilations, such as the massive *Historia general de los hechos de los castellanos en las Indias y Tierra Firme del Mar Océano* of Antonio de Herrera (1601–1613), and the *Los veinte i un libros rituales i monarchía indiana, con el origen y guerras de los Indios Occidentales* of Juan de Torquemada (1613).[18]

Spanish exploration in the New World did not of course end with the conquests of Mexico and Peru. Penetration into the North American bor-

---

15. It was known to and used by William H. Prescott when he wrote his *History of the Conquest of Peru* in 1847.

16. Often cited as Peter Martyr, because his work was originally published in Latin under that name. For discussion see Huddleston, *Origins of the American Indians,* pp. 6–8.

17. See ibid., pp. 16–19.

18. For extended bibliographies of early works on Peru, see John H. Rowe in Julian Steward, ed., *Handbook of South American Indians,* vol. 2, p. 330, and George Kubler in the same volume, p. 332. *Bureau of American Ethnology Bulletin* 143 (1946). For detailed discussion of individual works, see Raúl Porras Barrenechea, *Los Cronistas del Perú (1528–1650)* (Lima, 1986).

derlands in the seventeenth and eighteenth centuries resulted in an enormous number of additional *relaciones* continuing almost to the end of the colonial period, and these are of continuing value to ethnohistorians working in the U.S. Southwest and in northern Mexico.[19] There are many other *relaciones* from the Spanish explorations in Central America and in southern South America.[20] The information derived from these, like that from the earlier explorations, continued to find its way into general ethnographic compendia until the end of the colonial era. However, from the middle of the sixteenth century onward, the compilers relied far more on the ethnographic accounts of missionaries than they did on the explorers, and these will be considered separately in later paragraphs.

The first English voyagers to the New World generally made landfall to the north of the Spanish colonies, in areas where the native cultures were less advanced than in Central and South America. The Indians encountered along the Atlantic Seaboard seemed to the explorers to offer no potential either as tributaries or as slave laborers. As a result, the attitude of the first English explorers was almost wholly one of disappointment and scorn, expressed for example in Frobisher's assertion (1577) that they "live in Caves of earth, and hunt for their dinners or praye [prey], even as the beare and other wild beastes do."[21] But when the interest of the English turned eventually from exploration to colonization, their attitude necessarily changed. Much like Columbus, they had a vested interest in representing the Indians in a favorable light, as an inducement to potential settlers.[22]

The first indication of a genuine interest in the Indians by a British explorer may be seen in John White's *Map of Eastern North America from Florida to Chesapeake Bay* and *Map of Eastern North America from Cape Lookout to Chesapeake Bay,* both written in 1585–86. Both works included locations and information about Indian tribes and were accompanied by numerous drawings of Indians and Indian life. But it was Captain John Smith, attempting to plant the first successful English colony on Ameri-

---

19. For an extended list of references, see W. R. Swagerty, ed., *Scholars and the Indian Experience* (Bloomington, Ind., 1984), pp. 63–78. See also Adolph F. Bandelier, *Final Report of Investigations among the Indians of the Southwestern United States...* (Cambridge, 1892). *Papers of the Archaeological Institute of America, American Series,* vol. IV.

20. A great many of these are listed in Julian Steward, ed., *Handbook of South American Indians,* vol. 1, pp. 580–624. *Bureau of American Ethnology Bulletin* 143 (1946).

21. Richard Hakluyt, *The Principall Navigations, Voiages, and Discoveries...* (Glasgow, 1904), vol. vii, p. 224. For the English attitude generally, see Roy Harvey Pearce, *Savagism and Civilization* (Berkeley, Calif., 1988), pp. 4–6.

22. Cf. Benjamin Bissell, *The American Indian in English Literature of the Eighteenth Century* (New Haven, 1925), p. 3. *Yale Studies in English,* vol. LXVII.

can soil, who was obliged for the first time to take a practical interest in the Indians, much as the Spanish had had to do in the preceding century. This is clearly reflected in his *Generall Historie of Virginia, New England, and the Summer Isles*, first published in 1624, which differs markedly from all earlier English accounts in its detailed and generally sympathetic account of Indian life and customs. It remains the primary source of information about several long-extinct Algonquian peoples of the Atlantic Seaboard.

The beginnings of Indianology

However, Smith's optimistic view represents only a brief flash of light in the darkness, so to speak. After the Virginia Massacre of 1622, and until the end of the colonial period, the attitude of English travelers and settlers in the southern Atlantic colonies was generally as hostile to the Indians as had been that of the first explorers.[23] Among the works of English explorers, therefore, Smith's *Generall Historie* stands almost alone as a source of valuable ethnographic information.

For the most part, the firsthand *relaciones* of the explorers were in the *veni, vidi, vici* ("I came, I saw, I conquered") format popular since the time of Caesar's *Commentaries.* The works of the compilers, on the other hand, fall into two general categories: histories, and natural histories. The latter are of course somewhat more systematic and comprehensive than the former in their presentation of ethnographic data. It may be noted, however, that neither the explorers nor the compilers were in any true sense ethnographers. None of them had spent extended periods in contact with a particular native group, and none had mastered an Indian language. Lacking particularized information about individual groups, the tendency of the earliest commentators was to generalize about all Indians as though they constituted a single people. Moreover, the compilers had no particular reason, and apparently no desire, to present the Indians in a sympathetic light. They were portrayed simply as exotica, along with the indigenous fauna and flora.

MISSIONARY INDIANOLOGY

The official, legal sanction for the Spanish and Portuguese subjugation of the Indians, and their subsequent conscription under the *encomienda*, was to allow their conversion to the Christian faith. As a result, missionaries entered the New World virtually on the heels of the earliest conquistadores. But while they entered the same world as the conquerors, they saw it from the beginning through different eyes. Theological debate had established that the Indians were worthy of conversion precisely because they

23. See Pearce, *Savagism and Civilization*, pp. 8–16.

were fellow mortals; indeed, as we saw in Chapter 4, churchmen had been at pains to argue that, except for their lack of religion, the Indians had most of the institutions of civilization. Thus the missionaries approached them not as exotic wild species but as fellow humans whom they hoped to redeem to a state of Grace. Many of the evangelists spent long periods among particular native groups, and made a sincere effort to learn their languages. Whether or not they were sympathetic toward native customs, the missionaries were in a far better position to observe, describe, and interpret them than were the conquistadores and explorers.

The different missionary orders were somewhat variable in the degree of their interest in, and tolerance for, Native American customs. The Dominicans were first on the scene, as we saw in Chapter 4. Despite their notorious association with the Inquisition in Europe, they were relatively tolerant and interested observers of Indian society, as well as passionate defenders of Indian rights, as attested by the works of Vitoria and Las Casas discussed in Chapter 4. After 1570, however, the Dominicans rapidly gave place to the Jesuits and the Franciscans as the primary missionary orders in the New World.

By the time the new missionary orders became supreme, around 1600, the encomienda system of forced labor had nominally been abolished, the worst abuses of the early conquistadores had been curbed, and the question of Indian rights was less critical than it had been in the previous century. The Jesuits and Franciscans were therefore somewhat more narrowly concerned with the religious conversion of the Indians, and less with defending their character and their rights, than were the Dominicans. The first Jesuit missionaries were fairly sympathetic toward the Indians, but their ardor somewhat cooled as the years passed and the task of converting the natives and suppressing their native religious practices proved more difficult than they had first supposed.[24]

Notwithstanding their limited vision, the Jesuits' efforts at conversion always depended heavily on preaching and teaching in the native languages. If they did nothing else, the missionaries prepared a truly enormous number of vocabularies and grammars of Indian languages. In contrast, the Franciscans, who after 1767 replaced the Jesuit missionaries throughout nearly all of Spanish America, believed that the native languages only served the purposes of the Devil. They had a definite policy of eliminating the use of the Indian languages, and forbade their missionaries to learn or to speak them. The result is that the vast ethnographic and ethnohistorical archive contributed by missionaries in Spanish America

24. Cf. Edward H. Spicer, *Cycles of Conquest* (Tucson, Ariz. 1962), pp. 308–324.

was, after the sixteenth century, the work almost entirely of the Jesuits.[25] While failing in any real way to penetrate the Indians' point of view, it is nevertheless by far the richest descriptive archive that we possess on Indian "manners and customs" in the colonial period.

Missionary Indianology

Two of the immortal works of Spanish Indianology were, nevertheless, written by Franciscans. Of Diego de Landa's *Relación de las cosas de Yucatan* (1566), William Gates has said that "ninety-nine percent of what we know today of the Mayas, we know as a result either of what Landa has told us... or have learned in the use and study of what he told."[26] The vast *Historia general de las cosas de la Nueva España* of Bernardo de Sahagún, apparently completed in 1578, is similarly the source of most of what we know about the prehispanic Aztecs. Notwithstanding the disapproval of his superiors, Sahagún made extensive use of native texts dictated or written out for him by Indian informants–one of the reasons why his work never achieved publication until the twentieth century.[27] A work of comparable importance from South America is the *Historia del Nuevo Mundo* of the Jesuit Bernabé Cobo, originally completed in 1653 but not published until 1882. Most of this multivolume manuscript was lost in the intervening years; what has survived to publication is a volume of generalized observations on the Indians, and part of a second volume dealing specifically with the prehispanic history and ethnography of the Incas.[28]

The vast majority of missionary reports from Spanish America remain buried in the Archives of the Indies, and are accessible only to those who can travel to Seville to study them. Not so the reports of the French Jesuit missionaries in Canada, which were forwarded to the mother house in Paris and were annually published in the *Jesuit Relations* between the years 1632 and 1674, and intermittently thereafter until 1791.[29] The seventy-three published volumes remain today the primary if not the sole sources of information about numerous tribes of northeastern America that became extinct during the early historic period.

It is important to note that French colonial policy in Canada aimed at a minimum disruption of indigenous society and culture, since the undermanned French settlements increasingly required the help of Indian allies

25. Ibid., pp. 327–328.

26. William Gates in Diego de Landa, *Yucatan before and after the Conquest,* trans. William Gates (New York, 1978), p. iii.

27. See Ruth Bunzel in Mead and Bunzel, *Golden Age of American Anthropology,* pp. 47–48.

28. See Roland Hamilton in Father Bernabe Cobo, *History of the Inca Empire* (Austin, Tex., 1979), pp. xiii–xvi.

29. The best general synopsis of the Jesuit Relations is Camille de Rochemonteix, *Les Jésuits et la Nouvelle-France* (Paris, 1895–96 and 1906).

to maintain themselves against the ever-expanding English.[30] Thus the missionaries' sole objective was to convert the Indians to Catholicism, not to civilize them; it was a somewhat easier task than making them over into house-dwelling, town-dwelling, clothes-wearing farmers, as the Spanish missionaries sought to do.[31] Not surprisingly, the descriptions of Indian culture by the French Jesuits were generally more sympathetic toward Indian culture than were those of their Spanish confrères. It should be added too that the *Jesuit Relations* had a propagandistic purpose: they were intended to generate popular support for the missions, and for the French colonial enterprise more generally.[32] Deserving of special mention among the French Jesuits is Joseph Lafitau, whose *Customs of American Savages Compared with Those of Earliest Times* was extensively discussed in Chapter 2.

The role of missionaries in the English colonies was much more limited than in the colonies of France and Spain, despite the professed ideal of converting the savages that was incorporated in some of the colonial charters.[33] For most of the colonial period neither the British Crown nor the Church of England had an overt evangelization policy, and whatever missionary efforts were to be made were left to the initiative (and the expense) of the colonists themselves. In general they were either very slow in getting started, or did not start at all. The Puritans in Massachusetts and the Quakers in Pennsylvania were active at times in their missionary efforts, but their success was largely undone by the periodic interruptions of the Indians wars as well as by the dying off, out-migration, or forcible eviction of their Indian converts. The most active and most successful missionaries in colonial Anglo-America, as well as in the early period of American independence, were not the colonists themselves, but members of the German-based Moravian order.[34] Outstanding among them was John G.E. Heckewelder, whose *An Account of the History, Manners, and Customs of the Indian Nations, Who Once Inhabited Pennsylvania and the Neighboring States* (1819) and *A Narrative of the Mission of the United Brethren among the Delaware and Mohegan Indians* (1820) are unrivaled in the annals of missionary Indianology from the early nineteenth century. In general, however, neither the mentalities of the missionaries nor the circumstances of colonial life, especially in the Northeast, were very conducive to ethnographic reporting, and the missionaries of colonial Anglo-America

30. See Mason Wade in Washburn, *History of Indian-White Relations*, p. 20.
31. See Spicer, *Cycles of Conquest*, pp. 281–282.
32. Wade in Washburn, *History of Indian-White Relations*, p. 25.
33. See R. Pierce Beaver in Washburn, *History of Indian-White Relations*, p. 420.
34. Ibid., pp. 430–436.

contributed little of enduring value to the literature of Indianology except for grammars and vocabularies of a few now-extinct languages.[35]

Missionary Indianology

While in Spanish America missionary activity largely ceased at the end of the colonial era, the opposite was true in Anglo-America. The American government for three-quarters of a century exhibited the same indifference toward Indian conversion as did the British Crown, but this policy was reversed after the Civil War. As a result, large-scale missionization took place for the first time on all the western reservations.[36] The missionaries were given the task of converting the Indians not only to Christianity, but to all aspects of contemporary "civilized" life and values, and at the same time of extirpating whatever remained of the native cultures.

It has to be said on behalf of the missionaries that they took up the cause of Indian rights, in a political sense, as zealously as had their Dominican and Jesuit forebears in Spanish America.[37] Given their assigned task of educating and "Americanizing" the Indians, however, it is hardly surprising that few of them took any interest in the native cultures that they were supposed to extirpate. There were nevertheless a few exceptions that are worthy of note. Missionaries, responding to questionnaires, furnished a great deal of the information incorporated in Lewis Henry Morgan's *Systems of Consanguinity and Affinity in the Human Family*[38] as well as in the early publications of the Bureau of American Ethnology. Beyond that, a few missionaries took upon themselves the role of true ethnographers, out of personal interest. James O. Dorsey, originally an Episcopal missionary, contributed a very large number of ethnographic studies of the Ponca, Omaha, and other tribes of the plains in the last quarter of the nineteenth century.[39] During the same period Myron Eels, a Congregational missionary in the state of Washington, published a steady stream of articles about the tribes of the Puget Sound area.[40] Perhaps most outstanding of all, in terms of its lasting value, was the work of the Franciscan Berard Haile, who devoted a lifetime to the study of the Navajo language and religion.[41]

In summing up the Indianological contributions of the missionaries, a distinction must be made between those that were and were not intended for public circulation. Writing only to their ecclesiastical superiors or to the colonial authorities, the missionaries could and did express disappointment and frustration with their Indian charges. When writing for

35. See Elizabeth Tooker in Washburn, *History of Indian-White Relations*, p. 5.
36. See esp. Francis Paul Prucha, *American Indian Policy in Crisis* (Norman, Okla., 1976).
37. See ibid., pp. 132–168.
38. See Chapter 2.
39. See Washburn, *History of Indian-White Relations*, p. 640.
40. See ibid., pp. 641–642.
41. Ibid., pp. 647–648.

the general public, however, their works can generally, though not universally, be characterized as apologetics. That is, they were designed to present the Indians in as favorable a light as possible to European readers, and above all to allow the reader to identify with them as fellow mortals. Although the evangelistic zeal of the missionaries—the unshakable conviction that "we are right and they are wrong" in matters of faith—imposed a definite limitation on their ethnographic insight, it is nevertheless true that the Indianology of the missionaries came much closer to true anthropological literature than did any other works of the preanthropological era, despite the longstanding, mutual antipathy between anthropologists and missionaries.

THE FRONTIERSMEN: TRAVELERS, SETTLERS, SOLDIERS, AND TRADERS

While the accounts of conquistadores and of missionaries differed substantially in their portrayal of the Indians, they had in common the fact that they were designed to inform, or to influence public opinion, rather than to entertain. At the time they were written there was not yet a mass popular press or a large reading public in Europe. Indeed, many of the works existed only in manuscript form until their publication in the nineteenth or even the twentieth century. By the eighteenth century, nevertheless, both printing and literacy were widespread in Europe, and new kinds of Indianological literature made their appearance: works designed less to inform than to entertain, titillate, or in some cases horrify a large popular audience. Such were the innumerable firsthand accounts of life among the Indians, or encounters with them, that were published by travelers, settlers, soldiers, and traders. From the sixteenth to the nineteenth century, it was largely these works that fed the seemingly insatiable popular appetite for information about the Indians. They form a kind of progression, the travelers gradually giving place to the settlers and the settlers to the soldiers, as day-to-day observers of Indian life. The majority of traders' accounts came last of all in time, dating mostly from the twentieth century.

The travelers

The first published account of travel in the Americas, not written by a conquistador or missionary, was apparently the *Histoire d'un voyage fait en la terre du Brésil* of Jean de Léry, published in 1578.[42] Dating from about the

42. For a modern English translation, see *History of a Voyage to the Land of Brazil Otherwise Called America*, trans. Janet Whatley (Berkeley, Calif., 1992).

same time is an unpublished manuscript, *Histoire de André Thevet angoumoisin cosmographe du Roy de deux voyages par lui…* by André Thevet.[43] Both works provided extensive ethnographic information about Brazilian tribes. They were followed shortly by a host of others, in several European languages and dealing with various parts of Spanish and Portuguese America.

Most of the travel accounts reached their readers not in their original form, but as retold in popular collections like those of Ramusio (Venice, 1550–1559), Hakluyt (London, 1589), Purchas (London, 1625), and De Bry (Frankfurt, 1590–1634). The works of De Bry, in particular, achieved an enormous and lasting popularity, chiefly because of their many full-page illustrations depicting scenes from Indian life. These have often been cited as authentic ethnographic documents, and they continue to be reproduced in books on the Indians down to the present day.[44] In fact, the engravers had never seen an Indian, nor were they working from sketches brought home by the travelers. They simply used their own imaginations to portray the scenes and activities described by the travelers. As Bissell writes, "Although there is no slight element of realism in these earliest representations of American natives, a marked tendency developed in the course of the next two centuries to picture the Indians with all the beauty and grace of classical statuary…."[45] The result was a rather curious anomaly: depictions of physically beautiful Indians performing barbarous acts, as in De Bry's famous representation of a cannibal feast.[46]

It must be acknowledged, however, that the engravings accurately captured the spirit of the written accounts they accompanied; accounts that tended repeatedly to dwell on the bizarre and sensational aspects of Indian life. Like so many of the explorers' *relaciones*, they treated the Indians as exotica. But as more reliable information about the Indians accumulated, chiefly through the works of the missionaries, it became increasingly difficult to depict them in fantastic and sensational terms. Thus, the travelers' accounts of the seventeenth and eighteenth centuries achieved considerably more factual realism than did their predecessors, though they were still very much warped by preconceptions.[47]

---

43. It was finally published in Paris in 1953.

44. E.g., Oliver La Farge, *A Pictorial History of the American Indian* (New York, 1956), p. 64; Charles Hudson, *The Southeastern Indians* (Knoxville, Tenn., 1976), p. 227.

45. Bissell, *American Indian in English Literature*, p. 5.

46. It is reproduced on the cover of Anthony Pagden, *The Fall of Natural Man* (Cambridge, 1986). For numerous other early depictions of the Indians, see Rachel Doggett, ed., *New World of Wonders* (Washington, 1992).

47. Bissell, *American Indian in English Literature*, p. 7.

Europeans continued to visit the Americas, and to write of their travels, throughout the eighteenth and nineteenth centuries, but they visited an increasingly settled land, and their attention was claimed more and more by the life of the colonists rather than by the Indians.[48] The task of describing and interpreting the native inhabitants then fell instead to the permanent settlers.

The settlers

"Indianology"

From the beginning the attitude of permanent settlers in North America was hegemonic, not only toward the land and its resources but toward its native inhabitants.[49] They felt that it was for them, and not for temporary visitors, to tell the story of the Indians with whom they had to live as neighbors. Many of them had fought the Indians or been raided by them, and in the seventeenth century, most still had to live in fear of such raids. Their attitude toward the Indians was much less romantic than was that which prevailed in so much European fiction at the same period (see Chapter 3), and much of their writing was intended, quite deliberately, to counteract the romanticized picture created by the fiction writers.

In the Virginia colony, there was a brief "window of peace" between 1607 and 1622—the date at which the Indians rose and attempted a general massacre of the colonists. Practically all of the favorable descriptions of the Virginia Indians date from that fifteen-year interval. At least half a dozen settlers' accounts were published, in addition to John Smith's *Generall Historie of Virginia*, previously mentioned. Properly speaking, the reports were not so much favorable, in a descriptive sense, as optimistic. While painting a fairly uniform picture of Indian culture as backward and barbarous, they nevertheless gave a good account of the Indian's character, and held out hope of his pacification and civilization through the Christian faith. But after 1622 the attitude of the Virginia colonists quickly hardened. "The Indian became for seventeenth-century Virginians not a man in the grip of devilish ignorance, but a man standing fiercely and grimly in the path of civilization," writes Pearce.[50] Indian customs were generally deemed unworthy of notice, except to condemn them, and the settlers' accounts after 1622 contain little of ethnographic value.

With a few notable exceptions, the attitude of the New England settlers

48. For discussion of many of these works, see Marc Patcher, ed., *Abroad in America: Visitors to the New Nation 1776–1914* (Reading, Mass., 1976).
49. Cf. Pearce, *Savagism and Civilization*, p. 169.
50. Ibid., p. 11.

was comparable to that of the Virginians, except that the Puritans continued to phrase their condemnation of the Indians in Biblical terms. "The Puritans carried to its extreme the logic of seventeenth-century Christian imperialism," writes Pearce. "God had meant the savage Indians' land for the civilized English and, moreover, had meant the savage state itself as a sign of Satan's power and savage warfare as a sign of earthly struggle and sin. The colonial enterprise was in all ways a religious enterprise."[51] Although the enterprise was generally warlike, with respect to the Indians, there were periodic attempts to Christianize some of the New England tribes, as we saw earlier. It was in that context that Roger Williams produced his *Key into the Language of America* (1643), an ethnographic and linguistic guidebook for missionaries who would work among the Narragansets. Some sketchy ethnographic information was also included in descriptions of the New England colonies published by William Wood (1634)[52] and Thomas Morton (1637).[53]

The frontiersmen

Colonists in Maryland and Pennsylvania generally enjoyed better relations with the Indians than did their neighbors to the north and south, and during most of the seventeenth century their published accounts continued to reflect the same optimism toward the conversion and civilization of the Indians as was found in the earliest accounts from Virginia. However, neither group had much success in its missionary endeavors, and their accounts do not suggest a very close familiarity with Indian life and customs.[54]

In general, then, the accounts of the seventeenth-century settlers seem to confirm the adage that familiarity breeds contempt. Even those that were relatively favorable to the Indians were often poorly informed and incurious. By the eighteenth century, however, the Indians had been largely dislodged from settled coastal regions, and many colonists no longer had any real contact with them. Dwellers in the seaboard cities could begin to regard the Native Americans more dispassionately, and with a good deal more curiosity, than did the frontiersmen of earlier generations. As a result there appeared, in the eighteenth century, a number of noteworthy American works of Indianology, which combined firsthand observation with the scholarly study of older reports. The earliest of them, Robert Beverly's *History of the Present State of Virginia* (1705) was also the most comprehensive. It was the first attempt by an Anglo-American to provide a complete and relatively objective overview of Indian life, comparable to some of the best

51. Ibid., p. 20.

52. *Nevv England's Prospect: a True, Lively and Experimentall Description of that Part of the America, Commonly Called Nevv England...* (London, 1634).

53. *The New English Canaan, or New Canaan...* (Amsterdam, 1637).

54. Pearce, *Savagism and Civilization*, pp. 16–19.

work of the Spanish missionaries. Like them, the author drew on a combination of personal experience, interviews, and previously existing manuscript sources.[55] Three years later in time came John Lawson's *A New Voyage to Carolina* (1708), containing a mass of ethnographic detail based on the author's personal explorations. Lawson like Beverly attempted to steer a middle course between execration and admiration: "He does not wish to praise the Indians nor to condemn them; he is interested in seeing them for what they are."[56] Cadwallader Colden, a wealthy New York merchant who had extensive dealings with the Iroquois, published in 1727 the first edition of his *History of the Five Indian Nations Depending upon the Province of New York in America.* It was primarily a history of Indian-White relations, but it contained also a great deal of valuable ethnographic information. The author followed the lead of Beverly and Lawson in depicting the Indian as a "natural man," having all the savagery but also the wild freedom and the hardihood of character that are imparted by a life in nature.[57]

By the end of the eighteenth century, public opinion, at least in the colonial cities, had shifted even more in favor of the Indian. J. Hector Crevècoeur's *Letters from an American Farmer* (1782), briefly mentioned in Chapter 3, was the first work by a settler to express a genuinely romanticized, primitivistic view of the Indian.[58] Still more romantic and primitivistic was William Bartram's *Travels through North and South Carolina, Georgia, East and West Florida, and the Cherokee Country* (1791). The author offered a kind of panegyric on Cherokee character: "O divine simplicity and truth, friendship without fallacy or guile, hospitality disinterested, native, undefiled by artificial refinements."[59] John Filson's *Settlement and Present State of Kentucke* (1784) was, however, a much more straightforward exploration account, in the general spirit of Beverly and Lawson.

Settler descriptions of the Indians, then, underwent an evolutionary progression, reflecting partly the circumstances of history and partly the changing literary market. Like so much that has been written about the Indians, the earliest settler accounts have to be understood as a kind of propaganda. The authors had established themselves in America as competitors with the Indians for the land and its resources. There was, consequently, a certain truculence in their assertion of a divine right to colonize and expand, which was based on their cultural superiority to the barbarous natives. In contrast, the early eighteenth century accounts reflect a

55. See ibid., pp. 42–43.

56. Ibid., p. 44.

57. See ibid., pp. 45–46; Bissell, *American Indian in English Literature*, pp. 12–14.

58. See Pearce, *Savagism and Civilization*, pp. 139–142; Bissell, *American Indian in English Literature*, pp. 46–48.

59. Quoted in Pearce, *Savagism and Civilization*, p. 142.

kind of progressivist tolerance. The Indians were still generally depicted as barbarous, but this was now seen as appropriate and inevitable for people at their stage of development. They were children of nature, and nature was recognized to be "red in tooth and claw." By the end of the century, the Indian menace was sufficiently distant in time and space so that the authors could indulge in the same kind of nostalgic Primitivism that had become wholly dominant in European fiction.

The frontiersmen

However, many settler accounts from the eighteenth century, and most of those from the nineteenth century, were narratives of captivity, and these were anything but sympathetic toward the Indians. They stand so clearly apart from all other Indianological literature that they will be discussed later under a separate heading.

The soldiers

The first soldiers to write about the Indians were, of course, the conquistadores. In the centuries that followed, other military commanders occasionally wrote of their campaigns against the Indians, but their accounts contain almost nothing of ethnographic value. It was not until the latter half of the nineteenth century, when garrison forces were stationed on most of the western reservations in North America, that soldiers were brought into close and prolonged contact with Indians, and could describe them as something more than simply enemies.

Popular literature portrays the relations between Indians and the U.S. Army as entirely hostile, but this is a very inaccurate picture. Many of the garrison officers who served in the West after 1848 never saw combat, and most of their contacts with Indians were entirely peaceful. Moreover, one has only to think of the number of Indian agencies that are still named "Fort something-or-other" (Fort Apache, Fort Defiance, Fort Duchesne, Fort Hall, Fort Washakie, and innumerable others) to appreciate the role that the U.S. Army once played on the Indian scene. The army post, with its resident "sutlers" (traders) and its distributions of rations, was for fifty years the primary nexus of contact between the Indian and the Anglo-American worlds. As Sherry Smith observes, "the U.S. Army was the largest national organization in substantial contact with Indians in the trans-Mississippi West between 1848 and 1890."[60]

A fair number of the soldiers occupied their time by getting to know their Indian neighbors. Their published memoirs, as well as those of their wives, became part of the popular Indianological literature of the nineteenth century. Some of the memoirs were pure campaign accounts, but a

60. Sherry L. Smith, *The View from Officers' Row* (Tucson, Ariz., 1990), p. xiv.

rather surprising number were at least partly ethnographic in content. The notorious Custer undoubtedly spoke for many of his fellow officers when he wrote that "In studying the Indian character, while shocked and disgusted by many of his traits and customs, I find much to be admired and still more of a deep and unvarying interest."[61] Like nearly all Indianological literature after the middle of the nineteenth century, the soldiers' memoirs were written mainly for the Eastern intelligentsia, who had long since lost any contact with the Indians but still thirsted to hear about them.[62]

As might be expected, the soldiers' attitudes toward the Indians varied from sympathetic to hostile, yet certain consistent features appear again and again in their accounts. They give the Indian credit for physical hardihood and for indifference to pain; they speak repeatedly of the noble character of individual chiefs like Joseph and Cochise, while many ordinary Indians are represented as treacherous; they characterize the Indian woman as an overworked drudge who never experiences the joys of romantic love; they recognize the Indians' bravery in battle but also their chaotic lack of discipline; they acknowledge that most Indian wars were provoked by White encroachment; and almost without exception they believe that Indians could and should be civilized, and absorbed into the mainstream of American life.[63]

The soldiers were, of course, professionally interested in all things military. They had the opportunity not only to fight the Indians on occasion but also and more importantly to query them about their military tactics and objectives, and to listen to their war tales. Perhaps the single most outstanding virtue of the soldiers' memoirs, or at least the best of them, is the information they give about Indian warfare, seen as it were from both sides.

Whatever his other characteristics, the Indian that emerges from the soldiers' accounts is above all colorful. While a great many officers decried the romanticized image of the Redman as depicted by James Fenimore Cooper,[64] a surprising number went on to create their own rather romantic image. Indeed, there is an unexpected note of Primitivism running through many of the memoirs; it is evident that army officers were no more immune than were other educated Americans from the dominant romanticism of the Victorian age.

Among more than 150 published letters, diaries, and reminiscences,[65] two are deserving of individual mention because of their ethnohistorical

61. Quoted in ibid., p. 15.
62. Ibid., pp. xvi–xvii.
63. See ibid., pp. 15–181.
64. Ibid., p. 16.
65. For a bibliography, see ibid., pp. 234–244.

value. Colonel Richard I. Dodge's *Our Wild Indians* [66] is surely the single most detailed ethnographic compendium ever produced by an American military man. It bears a typically Victorian subtitle, "Thirty-three years' personal experience among the Red Men of the Great West; a popular account of their social life, religion, habits, traits, customs, exploits, etc., with thrilling adventures and experiences on the great plains and in the mountains of our wide frontier," and this effectively captures the content and style of the book, as well as the credentials of its author. Similar in content but more specifically autobiographical is General Oliver O. Howard's *My Life and Experiences among Our Hostile Indians.* [67]

The frontiersmen

The soldiers' reminiscences can in one sense be characterized as racist, and in another sense as antiracist. They were racist in a purely classificatory sense; that is, in their extraordinary tendency to generalize about all Indians as though they were a single people.[68] But the officers were antiracist in their continued insistence that Indians were inherently just as good as the rest of us, lacking only a proper education to make them into proper and fully participating American citizens. At the conclusion of *Our Wild Indians,* Colonel Dodge observed: "Look at the numbers of educated, cultivated Indians now in the Territory; and recollect that but for the indomitable courage, perseverance, and brains of Juarez, a full-blood Indian, our sister republic [Mexico] would now be groaning under the tyranny of a foreign emperor."[69] It is worth remembering that these opinions were expressed at a time when segregation laws, based on a theory of racial inferiority, were being enacted all over the American South.

Notwithstanding their necessarily limited perspective, the memoirs of army officers and their wives comprise an invaluable ethnohistorical record. They were written at the same time as the first formal ethnographic inquiries were being undertaken by scholars, yet their special value lies precisely in their lack of what at the time was the prevailing ethnographic perspective. While the scholars were diligently probing memory culture and attempting to reconstruct the indigenous cultures of a bygone age, the soldiers were describing Indian life exactly as they saw it in their own time, with its guns, horses, and store-bought finery as well as the ceremonies and social customs surviving from an earlier age. Collectively, the soldiers' accounts are the best record that we have of North American Indian life as it was actually lived in the second half of the nineteenth century.

---

66. Hartford, 1882.
67. Hartford, 1907.
68. Smith, *View from Officers' Row,* p. 15.
69. Dodge, *Our Wild Indians,* p. 652.

Considering the important role that traders have played almost throughout the history of Indian-White relations, it is surprising how few of them left any account of their activities, apart from letters and journals that were not published until long after their own times.[70] This may be explained partly by the fact that traders were often not well-educated men, and many of them no doubt had the proverbial businessman's contempt for book-learning. Nevertheless, the handful of published memoirs from before the twentieth century include two classics: James Adair's *History of the American Indians* (1775) and Josiah Gregg's *Commerce of the Prairies* (1844). Adair traded all over the Southeast but lived mainly with the Chickasaws, and had married a Chickasaw wife. As the title suggests, his book is not about trading per se, but it is a rich mine of ethnographic information based on firsthand observation over a long period of time. In this respect it compares with the best of the early missionary accounts, and is perhaps more insightful into the Indian mentality.[71] Gregg's *Commerce* is more specifically concerned with trading and is essentially autobiographical, detailing several of his trading expeditions from St. Louis to the Southwest between 1831 and 1840. The book is only incidentally about the Indians, since Gregg was trading mainly with the Mexican settlements in Santa Fe and Chihuahua, but it is by far the best and most detailed account of the Santa Fe trade in its heyday. Also important, for the Great Lakes area, is John Long's *Voyages and Travels of an Indian Interpreter and Trader Describing the Manners and Customs of the North American Indians* (1791).

By the twentieth century, Indian trade had virtually disappeared as a distinct form of commerce everywhere except among the Navajo. There are, however, at least eight published accounts of Navajo trading in the twentieth century either by traders or by their wives.[72] Some of these provide valuable information about details of Navajo religion and mythology, but their primary value is that they take up the story of day-to-day Indian-White relations just where the soldiers leave it, and carry it through to the middle years of the twentieth century.

---

70. A number of the early traders are listed, and the published editions of their letters cited, in Washburn, *History of Indian-White Relations*, pp. 617–702.

71. See esp. Wilcomb E. Washburn in Lawrence H. Leder, ed., *The Colonial Legacy*, vol. III (New York, 1973), pp. 91–120; also Washburn, *History of Indian-White Relations*, pp. 617–618.

72. For a partial listing of these, see William Y. Adams, *Shonto, a Study of the Role of the Trader in a Modern Navaho Community* (Washington, D.C., 1963), pp. 7–8. *Bureau of American Ethnology Bulletin* 188. For a very extensive bibliography on Navajo trading and traders, see Frank McNitt, *The Indian Traders* (Norman, Okla., 1962), pp. 363–369.

The trading post obviously offered a different window for observation than did the army post, and this is reflected in the content of the traders' accounts. The traders were in a better position than anyone else to measure the full extent and nature of Indian dependency on Anglo-American goods, and the Indians' complex interweaving of traditional and modern economic practices, and this is the single greatest virtue of their accounts. It is worth noting too that most traders necessarily had some command of an Indian language. However, the twentieth-century accounts were written at a time when the Indian wars and the threat of them were long over, and the preoccupation with warlike activity that is so prominent in the soldiers' accounts is entirely missing.

The lack of a professional ethnographer's perspective is both a strength and a weakness in the accounts left by travelers, settlers, soldiers, and traders. Although these individuals were for the most part sympathetic observers, very few of them made any attempt to "get inside" the Indian world or to project the Indian's point of view, nor do they seem to have felt any urge to do so. The strength of their accounts lies in their lack of any concept of "ethnographic present," other than the present that was actually experienced by them. Without attempting to recover a bygone past, they simply provided a detailed and sometimes intimate outsider's view of Indian life as it was actually lived, day-to-day, from the eighteenth to the twentieth century. While the narrowly ethnographic value of their accounts may be limited, their ethnohistorical value is enormous.

THE CAPTIVES

Standing clearly apart from all other forms of Indianological literature are the published accounts of persons who suffered temporary captivity among the Indians. These tales enjoyed an enormous popularity in the eighteenth and especially in the nineteenth century. As Frederick Drimmer writes, "For our ancestors, these remarkable tales had all the suspense and romance that the historical novel, the science-fiction tale, and the detective story hold for us today, with one important difference–these stories were *real*. . . . A large number of the captivity narratives were reprinted time and again, in both the United States and Europe. Some were among the great best sellers of their day."[73]

According to a recent survey there are around two thousand published

73. Frederick Drimmer, ed., *Captured by the Indians* (New York, 1961), p. 10. For extended discussion of the captivity narrative as a literary genre, see ibid., pp. 8–21, and James Levernier and Hennig Cohen, eds., *The Indians and Their Captives* (Westport, Conn., 1977), pp. xiii–xxx.

captivity tales, dealing with more than five hundred separate episodes of captivity.[74] The earliest appears to be the narrative of Juan Ortiz, who was captured and enslaved from 1529 to 1539 by Indians in the Tampa Bay area.[75] The latest whose authenticity can be verified was the adventure of Nat Love, better known as Deadwood Dick, a Black cowboy who was briefly captured by either Apaches or Pimas in 1876.[76] Infinitely the best known to the general public is the captivity of Captain John Smith among the Powhatans, related in his *Generall Historie of Virginia.*[77]

According to Levernier and Cohen, the captivity narratives as a literary genre exhibit a definite evolutionary progression, reflecting the changing literary appetites of their times.[78] The earliest tales were those of captured explorers, and like other explorers' accounts they were intended at least partly to supply factual information about the Indians at a time when they were still relatively unknown ethnographically. Often the period of captivity forms only one episode in a longer narrative of exploration. There is relatively little sense of indignation in the explorers' accounts, for the possibility of capture in warfare had always existed, and the explorers knew perfectly well that they risked it.

The early settlers who followed the explorers, and who furnished most of the captivity tales after the sixteenth century, also knew that they risked captivity, but they had convinced themselves that they had a legitimate title to the land they occupied. They regarded the Indian raids in which they were carried off as unjust and unprovoked, and their narratives are permeated by a sense of outrage. The stories focus much more exclusively on the physical and spiritual sufferings of the captive, and less on the description of Indian customs, than do those of the explorers. There is, nevertheless, a certain sense of guilt, or at least of divine punishment, in the earliest accounts of the settler-captives. "Indian captivity was a spiritual affliction that God, for some inscrutable reason, had chosen to visit upon his servants," as Levernier and Cohen put it.[79] The ultimate moral lesson, which the authors seldom failed to point out, was that steadfast faith will triumph over any adversity.

The captivity tales from the middle of the eighteenth century onward

---

74. See Levernier and Cohen, *Indians and Their Captives*, p. xiv. For partial bibliographies, see ibid., pp. 275–278 and esp. Newberry Library, *Narratives of Captivity among the Indians of North America* (Chicago, 1912).

75. The narrative was first published in Portuguese in 1557, and in English in 1609. For an excerpt, see Levernier and Cohen, *Indians and Their Captives*, pp. 3–11.

76. For a published excerpt, see ibid., pp. 200–205.

77. For a published excerpt, see ibid., pp. 12–19.

78. Ibid., pp. xiii–xxx.

79. Ibid., p. xvii.

reflect the increasing secular-mindedness of their times. They were frequently propagandistic, intended to generate antagonism toward either the French or the English (as the instigators of Indian raids in which the captives were taken). At a later date, the narratives from the early period of American independence, dwelling especially on the barbarities of the Indians, were often intended to provide support for the Indian Removal policy of that period. "A few narratives presented a sympathetic picture of Indian life," write Levernier and Cohen, "but most of them were shaped by publishers exploiting a mass market that thrived on sensationalism, in a natural alliance with land speculators who wanted to implement a policy of Indian extermination in the interest of real estate development."[80] In marked contrast, most of the captivity narratives published after 1850 presented the Indians in a relatively favorable light. Most, however, were secondhand retellings of older captivity episodes, revived and reinterpreted as part of a general literary effort to recreate and to romanticize a vanished American past. It was in the nineteenth century also that the Indian captivity became a staple of novels, plays, and poems, as we saw already in Chapter 3.

Most of the captivity narratives were, by intention, horror stories, which dwelled with lurid fascination on such practices as scalping and the torture of prisoners. Very few of the authors made any effort to see the world through Indian eyes, even while sharing their life and livelihood sometimes for years at a time. Yet precisely for the latter reason, the accounts are rich in ethnographic detail, much of which is unavailable from any other source. Whatever their revulsion may have been, the captives had an opportunity vouchsafed to no one else before or since: that of living the Indian life in the fullest sense, day in and day out, and through good times and bad. Indeed, the contrast between life in good times and life in bad times is one of the most striking features of many of the tales. The picture that emerges is of a much less evenly regulated round of life than one might gain from reading standard ethnographies. In discussing the purely material aspects of life, the captives often expressed a genuine appreciation or admiration for Indian ingenuity, recognizing that the natives were able to wrest a living from the land and to create the material necessities of life in circumstances in which they themselves would have been helpless.

The captivity narratives are now almost wholly forgotten by the general reading public, but they remain as the single most unique genre of Indianological literature. So far as I know, there is nothing comparable in the literatures dealing with any other native peoples of the world.

---

80. Ibid., pp. xxi–xxii.

POPULAR INDIANOLOGY: LITERATURE, ART, AND EXHIBITIONS

In the early accounts of conquerors, missionaries, travelers, and naturalists, the Indians were variously portrayed as barbarous or civilized, brave or cowardly, strong or weak.[81] In the Romantic era, however, they acquired a new character that was very soon to overshadow all others: that of colorfulness. It is a theme that pervades nearly all popular writing about the Indians, as well as art, photography, and cinematography, from the eighteenth century to the present. In the popular imagination, seemingly worldwide, the American Indians stand alone as the most colorful of native peoples. Books and movies about the Indians have an enormous popularity on every continent, and in my own extensive travels in Africa and Asia I have found myself continually bombarded with questions about the Indians, once it became known that I had lived among them.[82]

Fictional and artistic representations cannot be dismissed simply as peripheral or unimportant aspects of Indianology. For one thing, the sheer volume of printed and painted material is enormous, far surpassing the volume of material on all other native peoples combined. More importantly, most of mankind still forms its lifelong impressions of the Indians through fictional and artistic media rather than through the reading of factual reports. I know of no other people in the world of whom this is true to the same degree. An earlier generation of English and American readers might perhaps have formed their impressions of Africans from reading Rider Haggard and similar romances,[83] but no one reads those works today. In contrast, fictional representations of the Indians—especially cinematic representations in the present era—continue to reach and to fascinate an enormous, worldwide audience.

The Indian in literature and film

Lewis Hanke has observed that, from the sixteenth century to the present day, a great deal of Spanish writing about the Indians has carried on the debate begun by Las Casas and Sepúlveda in 1550 (described in Chapter 4).[84] That is, the authors are either strongly pro-Indian or anti-Indian.

---

81. For an extended review of conflicting ideas on these points, see Antonello Gerbi, *The Dispute of the New World*, trans. Jeremy Moyle (Pittsburgh, 1973).

82. When I offered courses in anthropology at Peking University in 1989, and again when I taught at Almati State University in Kazakhstan in 1995, the first course requested in both places was North American Indians!

83. For discussion, see esp. Brian V. Street, *The Savage in Literature* (London, 1975).

84. Hanke, *Aristotle and the American Indians* (Chicago, 1959), pp. 88–95.

But Hanke could have said the same about practically all other Indianological literature as well. The symbolic identities that have been attached to the Indians, almost from the moment of their discovery, have seemingly rendered it impossible to be wholly detached and objective about them. Western thought identified them from the beginning as the quintessential Other, and in that guise just about everything written about them, whether factual or fictional, is loaded with expressed or implied moral judgments. Almost the entire literature on the Native Americans can therefore be divided into "good Indian" and "bad Indian" representations. Whether good or bad, however, the Indian is always colorful, and a source of endless fascination for both writers and readers.

Popular Indianology

So long as Great Britain remained sovereign in the American colonies, the Indian continued to be a subject of intellectual, artistic, and moral concern to British novelists and poets. After American independence, however, he became almost exclusively a matter of American concern. There are virtually no important British works of fiction dealing with Indians between Tobias Smollett's *The Expedition of Humphrey Clinker* (1794) and D.H. Lawrence's *The Plumed Serpent* (1926).[85] But, as Leslie Fiedler observes, "there is scarcely a major figure in American literature, especially in the realm of the novel, who has not been concerned with the White-Red encounter."[86] The adventure and the trauma of winning the land away from its native inhabitants was, for well over two centuries, at the very core of American historical consciousness, and many of its resonances are still with us today.

A kind of class distinction can be detected between "good Indian" and "bad Indian" representations in American fiction. The major writers like Emerson, Thoreau, Melville, Hawthorne, and Whitman, who wrote for an educated eastern intelligentsia, all sounded the theme of the noble but doomed Redman, which was discussed at length in Chapter 3. Mark Twain was perhaps the only major American author of the nineteenth century who did not take a favorable view of the Indians; his attitude was colored by his personal experiences on the frontier.[87] At the same time as Emerson, Thoreau, and Melville were writing, however, there grew up an enormous popular literature aimed at a larger and less fastidious audience, which reveled in accounts of violence and slaughter. Such were the dime novels of the later nineteenth century, and their twentieth-century successors in the pulp magazines and the movies. In these works, as

85. See Leslie Fiedler in Washburn, *History of Indian-White Relations*, pp. 574–575.

86. Ibid., p. 587.

87. Ibid., pp. 575–577.

Fiedler observes, "the undercurrent of White nostalgia and guilt, everywhere present in Cooper, is replaced by a celebration of violence and a simple-minded joy in the victory of White civilization. And it was acted out in Wild West shows, even as it was being frozen into classic form in the standard Western of the early twentieth century, best represented perhaps by Zane Grey's *The Vanishing American* (1925)."[88]

The dime novel has long vanished from the literary scene, and twentieth-century literary representations of the Indian are overwhelmingly in the "good Indian" category. Very frequently they are primitivistic, using the Indian as a symbolic figure to castigate modern American life. A few have moved from straightforward romanticism into deliberate absurdity, as in such well-known works as Ken Kesey's *One Flew over the Cuckoo's Nest* (1962), Thomas Berger's *Little Big Man* (1964), Dorothy Johnson's *A Man Called Horse* (1965), and Arthur Kopit's play *Indians* (1969).[89] In an altogether separate and indeed unique category are the immensely popular Navajo detective stories of Tony Hillerman.[90] These works are hardly different in plot structure from a great many other detective stories, but their Indian characters and setting have given them an almost unprecedented worldwide popularity.[91]

In addition to works in English, there are also substantial bodies of Indian fiction in French and, especially, in German. However, very few "major" or serious writers concerned themselves with the Indian; the published works are mostly those of incredibly prolific hack writers. In France, Paul Duplessis produced sixty volumes between 1856 and 1866,[92] and in Germany, according to Christian Feest, more than a hundred authors produced approximately one thousand titles of Indian fiction in the last quarter of the nineteenth century.[93] Indian literature in other European languages, although extensive, consists mainly of translations from English-language classics. However, there are several original Eskimo novels in Danish.[94]

A special and voluminous domain of Indianological literature, which exists in many languages, is that of children's fiction. Here again there is a

88. Ibid., pp. 575–576.

89. Ibid., p. 579.

90. E.g., among many others, *The Blessing Way* (New York, 1970), *Skinwalkers* (New York, 1986), and *A Thief of Time* (New York, 1988).

91. When I have told friends in England and on the European Continent that I had lived among the Navajos, I have been asked again and again if I read Hillerman, and what I think of him.

92. See Christian Feest in Washburn, *History of Indian-White Relations*, p. 582.

93. Ibid., p. 584.

94. Ibid., p. 586.

clear dualism of presentation. In nineteenth-century adventure tales, and in comic books and movies of the early twentieth century, the Indians were commonly represented as bad guys. But for more than a century there has existed also a very large genre of books about Indian children, which invite the modern American or European youngster to identify with the Indian and to step back with him or her into a noble and pristine world of the past. In these works the Noble Savage lives on perhaps more fully than anywhere else in modern literature. A great many Americans and Europeans of my generation–probably including most anthropologists–acquired their first acquaintance with Indians, and formed their first impressions of them, from reading books of this kind. As a result their impressions were, and largely remain, both highly favorable and highly romanticized.

Popular Indianology

Since the 1930s, movies and television have increasingly replaced the printed page as the chief fictional media in which the Indian is represented. Since the outstanding characteristic of the fictional Indian is colorfulness, film provides the ideal medium for its portrayal, and it is hardly surprising that stories involving the Indians were mainstays of the early cinema industry. However, the cinematic Indian differs in no important respect from the novelistic one, and he need not be considered under a separate heading here.[95]

The Indian in pictures

The popularity of the Indian as a subject of artistic representation goes back at least to Theodor De Bry's travel compilations, published between 1590 and 1634.[96] The enduring popularity of those works was due in no small measure to their numerous, highly fanciful illustrations of scenes from Indian life. As Bissell observes, they set the standard for idealized and romanticized European depictions of the Indians for the next two centuries.[97] During the Romantic era of the eighteenth and nineteenth centuries, painters no less than illustrators seized upon the Indian as the embodiment of romantic ideals. The peaceful Indian village, set against an appropriately idyllic landscape, was a favorite theme. Very few of the illustrators or painters before the nineteenth century had actually seen an Indian; their works were based either on the interpretation of published

95. For more extended discussion of the Indians in cinema and television, see Michael T. Marsden and Jack Nachbar in Washburn, *History of Indian White Relations*, pp. 607–616.

96. Cf. Oliver La Farge, *A Pictorial History of the American Indian* (New York, 1956), p. 64; Charles Hudson, *The Southeastern Indians* (Knoxville, Tenn., 1976), p. 227.

97. Bissell, *American Indian in English Literature*, p. 5; see also Doggett, *New World of Wonders*.

accounts, or, very often, purely on the artist's imagination. This romantic tradition has continued, in one form or another, to the present day, although the latter-day romantics have nearly always painted from life rather than from imagination. The very numerous paintings of Plains Indians from the later nineteenth century, and of Southwestern Indians from the twentieth century, exemplify the continued appeal of the romantic genre.

A new tradition of ethnographic realism was inaugurated by the highly popular paintings of George Catlin, completed mostly between 1830 and 1836. During those years Catlin visited most of the tribes of the northern Plains and produced several hundred portraits, landscapes, and scenes of Indian life, portrayed in vivid colors that contrasted with the generally rather muted tones of the earlier romantics. Eventually, the painter gathered together a large number of his best works and opened Catlin's Indian Gallery in Albany, New York. The exhibition was an instant success, and the author took it successively to Washington, Philadelphia, and Boston, and subsequently to London and Paris. Catlin in fact created a new genre of Indian painting that was widely imitated in the middle years of the nineteenth century.[98]

After Catlin's time, and thanks to his influence, the favorite subjects for nearly all nineteenth-century painters of Indians were the tribes of the northern Plains. It was no longer possible to portray generalized Indians; an increasingly sophisticated public demanded more ethnic specificity. Most Indian painters continued in the romantic tradition, but with the insertion of more realistic ethnographic detail than was commonly employed by the earlier romantics. Among the better-known artists who worked in this genre were John Mix Stanley, Karl Bodmer, Paul Kane, Henry Farny, and, toward the end of the nineteenth century, Frederick Remington. In addition to these, a great many other painters of western landscapes placed diminutive Indian figures in the middle ground of their pictures—a very common device in nineteenth-century romantic painting everywhere.

As in literature, so also in art, there arose a kind of vernacular or proletarian genre of Indian representation side-by-side with the work of the "serious" artists. Some of the most widely known visualizations of the Indian are found in the paintings of a host of untrained and long-forgotten artists. Depictions of popular scenes like Pocahontas saving Captain John Smith and Custer's Last Stand were widely reproduced on calendars and

98. See Marjorie Halpin in George Catlin, *Letters and Notes on the Manners, Customs, and Conditions of the North American Indians* (New York, 1973), pp. vii–xiv. The original work was published in London in 1844.

cheap prints, and huge mural versions of them served often as circus posters. Indian portraits and scenes might also be applied as decoration to mirror backs, hotpads, and other artifacts.[99]

In the years after the Civil War, Indian photographs came to enjoy almost as much popularity as did Indian paintings. Among the great photographers of the Indians were William H. Jackson, John K. Hillers, James Mooney, and Edward S. Curtis.[100] So popular were Indian photographs that John Wesley Powell, the first director of the Bureau of American Ethnology, was said to have paid off the mortgage on his Washington home through the sale of photographs from his western explorations.[101] Given the primitive state of photographic technology, it is hardly surprising that the most artistically sophisticated of the photographs are actually studio portraits, which bear a marked resemblance to Catlin's paintings. The Indian subject is usually seated on an artificial rock, in front of a painted backdrop of western scenery, is arrayed in buckskins and/or blankets, and holds a drum, peace pipe, tomahawk, or some other item commonly associated with Indians. However, the best photographs of Jackson, Hillers, and Mooney were all taken in the field.

The Indian on exhibition

Very soon after the first American conquests, Indian captives were exhibited as curiosities in Europe. They always attracted so much interest that, in later times, the exhibition of Indians, as well as of their crafts, evolved into a regular industry. In the nineteenth century, when Indians were no longer familiar to eastern Americans, "Indian shows" of one kind and another became highly popular in the United States as well.

Although Native Americans were brought to Europe, voluntarily or involuntarily, all through the seventeenth and eighteenth centuries,[102] the first strictly commercial exhibition may have been that of Samuel Hadlock, who toured England and Germany with an Eskimo couple from 1822 to 1826.[103] Also in the year 1822, a family of Botocudo Indians from Brazil

---

99. Green in Washburn, *History of Indian-White Relations*, pp. 596–598.

100. For examples of their work, see Johanna Cohan Scherer and Jean Burton Walker, *Indians* (New York, 1973), and Paula R. Fleming and Judith Luskey, *The North American Indians in Early Photographs* (New York, 1986).

101. See William Culp Darrah, *Powell of the Colorado* (Princeton, N.J., 1951), p. 182. A close examination of the photos will show that a great many of Powell's Indians are wearing the same set of buckskins, which the photographer loaned to his subjects in order to make them look appropriately "Indian."

102. For accounts of some of these, see Christian F. Feest, ed., *Indians and Europe* (Aachen, 1989), pp. 61–193.

103. For extended discussion, see Robin K. Wright in ibid., pp. 215–241.

was briefly exhibited in London by a certain X. Chabert, who insisted that they were exhibiting themselves of their own accord and for their own profit.[104] In 1835 a group of Ojibwas, who had been lured to England under false pretenses, was induced to put on a spectacle called *Rifle-Shot, or the Michigan Chief* for London audiences. It was perhaps the archetypical Wild West show, and included "a native American Indian festive dance by the real Indian warriors... furious combat with tomahawk & scalping knife... preparations for sacrifice and dance of death... [and a] complete picture of American Indian life & habits."[105]

The first really successful Indian show in Europe was apparently that of George Catlin, created in New York in 1837 and taken to Europe in 1840. In his New York Indian gallery Catlin exhibited only his famous paintings and a collection of artifacts, but in Europe he added performing Ojibwas, Ottawas, and Iowas to his show. In the latter half of the nineteenth century, and indeed up to World War II, Indian shows became commonplace in the major European cities as well as in the United States.[106] A common feature of these shows was the *tableau vivant,* in which a group of costumed Indians acted out a brief scene "from Indian life": "The Camp Fire," "The War Dance," "The Scalping of a Prisoner," and the like.[107] In addition there were usually Indian craft exhibits, and sometimes Indian dancers, at the international exhibitions that proliferated all over Europe in the later nineteenth century.[108]

In 1884 the Indian show took on a dramatic new form with the appearance of Buffalo Bill's Wild West Show and Congress of Rough Riders. It became the prototype for at least ten other major shows in the late nineteenth and early twentieth centuries, and achieved an enormous popularity both in Europe and America. Cowboys, soldiers, and Indians mixed in a wild panoply of drama that included cavalry charges, attacks on forts, trick riding and roping, Indian dances, and, after Sitting Bull joined the show, a reenactment of Custer's Last Stand.[109] The central dramatic focus of the Wild West show, in contrast to earlier Indian shows, was its equestrian performances. The Buffalo Bill show remained popular for more than half a century, and was not finally disbanded until 1938.

---

104. See J. C. H. King in ibid., pp. 243–251.
105. Quoted from J. C. H. King in *European Review of Native American Studies* 5, no. 1 (1991): 36.
106. For accounts of some of these see Feest, *Indians and Europe,* pp. 337–401; also Johanna Riegler in *European Review of Native American Studies* 2, no. 1 (1988): 17–20.
107. See H. David Brumble III, *American Indian Autobiography* (Berkeley, Calif. 1988), pp. 69–70.
108. See King in *European Review of Native American Studies* 5, no. 1 (1991): 37–39.
109. See Green in Washburn, *History of Indian-White Relations,* p. 601.

Another once-popular form of entertainment, which usually included an Indian component, was the traveling medicine show. It drew its inspiration from the very widespread American folk belief that Indians possess arcane medical knowledge, which can be of benefit to all those who can learn the "recipes." Thus, the self-proclaimed doctor peddled his patent remedy, "based on an old Indian formula," out of the back of a traveling show-wagon. The actual sales pitch was preceded by a show that commonly featured a strong man performing feats of strength (made possible of course by daily doses of The Remedy), sometimes jugglers, acrobats, or magicians, and very often an elaborately costumed Indian "chief" who danced, played the drum, and performed feats to illustrate his strength and health. At the peak of their popularity, in the last quarter of the nineteenth century, there were more than eighty "Indian" folk remedies on the market, peddled mostly through the medium of traveling shows.[110]

In the twentieth century, the Wild West show and the medicine show have given way to the "pow-wow," or dance festival, as the great, popular Indian show. At these events, dance teams from many tribes come together to perform relatively short dance routines, often but not always taken from longer, traditional ceremonies. The costumes seem to become more elaborate each year, with much garish use of poster-paint colors and reflecting metal and glass. "Pow-wows" are held all over Indian country, in large towns and small, during the summer months.

In addition to the Indian entertainments just discussed, there were Indian craft exhibits, usually accompanied by performing craftsmen and women, at all the major U.S. world's fairs from Chicago in 1892 at least until the New York and San Francisco fairs of 1939–40. And every summer there are performing Indian dancers, singers, and craftspersons at dozens of federal and state parks as well as in local Fourth of July celebrations, harvest festivals, and the like. In sum, it is surely safe to say that no other people in history has become so accustomed to being exhibited, and to exhibiting themselves, as have American Indians. While this is understandably resented by a good many of today's activists, for whom the Indian's role as a curiosity is demeaning, it has nevertheless provided a substantial economic opportunity–a kind of acting career–for many Indians in the nineteenth and twentieth centuries.

GOVERNMENT INDIANOLOGY

Several of the original English colonies in North America had announced

110. Ibid.

policies of converting the Indians to Christianity, but none otherwise manifested any interest in studying them. However, almost from the founding of the American republic, the systematic investigation and recording of Indian cultures, languages, and antiquities became a major commitment of the United States government. I do not know of any other country which, before the twentieth century, had a similar policy, and certainly no other native peoples have been the subject of so much continuous government interest as have the North American Indians. Above all, it was government involvement that converted Indianology from a purely literary and aesthetic preoccupation into a scientific and scholarly discipline. In the process, it laid some of the most important foundations for twentieth-century American anthropology.

Like so many other enlightened aspects of U.S. government policy, this one is attributable in considerable part to the genius of Thomas Jefferson. His commitment to Indianology arose from the conjunction of three passions: natural history, Nationalism, and Progressivism. His enthusiasm for natural history is attested by his membership in at least two natural history societies,[111] and by his sponsorship of paleontological excavations in Kentucky, while his scientific Nationalism is evident in his assertion that American natural history should be studied by American institutions.[112] His Progressivism is attested in his belief (shared with nearly all Enlightenment thinkers) that American Indians were especially requiring of study because they exemplified the beginning stage of all human cultural development.

Jefferson's specific interest in all things Indian is evident in the chapter on Aborigines in his *Notes on the State of Virginia,* published in 1785. Here he gave not only a detailed enumeration of all the Virginia tribes, with their locations, populations, and chief settlements, but also a more general enumeration of all the tribes of the Eastern Seaboard, from Quebec to Florida.[113] He also speculated at length on the probable Asiatic origin of the Indians, lamented that they had been so little studied in any systematic way, and finally, reported on the results of his own excavation of an Indian burial mound.[114] Elsewhere in the *Notes on Virginia,* Jefferson recommended that the College of William and Mary should establish a professorship de-

111. He was a member and onetime president of the American Philosophical Society and an Honorary Member of the Société Linnéanne de Paris. He was also at one time a member of the Royal Academy of Inscriptions and Belles Lettres in Paris.

112. Quoted in Dumas Malone, *Jefferson and the Rights of Man* (Boston, 1951), pp. 84–85.

113. Thomas Jefferson, *Notes on the State of Virginia,* ed. William Peden (New York, 1954), pp. 94–95, 103–107.

114. Ibid., pp. 98–102.

voted specifically to the Indians, whose goal would be "to collect their traditions, laws, customs, languages, and other circumstances which might lead to a discovery of their relation with one another, or descent from other nations."[115]

The early explorations and surveys

Government Indianology

After his election as president and the purchase of the Louisiana Territory, Jefferson was able to inaugurate the field program in natural history (including Indianology) that he had so long dreamed of, when he sent forth the Lewis and Clark exploring expedition (1804–1806). Of his instructions to the explorers, Clark Wissler has written that

> He gave full directions for the recording of ethnographic data, surprisingly modern in tone, which might even now serve as a guide to a field worker. This document is not famous like Jefferson's draft of the Declaration of Independence but it shows the same masterful grasp of fundamentals, for he fully sensed the modern field worker's job. He went even farther in anticipating the practical value of such knowledge in promoting the acculturation of the Indians.[116]

The Lewis and Clark expedition set a precedent followed by many later U.S. exploring expeditions, which generally included a naturalist and an artist, one of whose duties was to record Indian life. For example Samuel Seymour, who accompanied the Long exploring expedition to the Rocky Mountains in 1819–20, was instructed to "paint miniature likenesses, or portraits if required, of distinguished Indians, and exhibit groups of savages engaged in celebrating their festivals or sitting in council. . . ."[117] Other naturalist/artists accompanied the exploring expeditions of John C. Frémont in 1845 and 1848.

A pioneer Indianologist in his own right was Swiss-born Albert Gallatin, who served as Jefferson's secretary of the treasury and subsequently on a number of U.S. diplomatic missions. He was a founder and the first president of the American Ethnological Society, and a lifelong student of Indian languages. In 1826 he published *A Table of the Indian Languages in the United States*, which included the first attempt at a classification of the

---

115. Ibid., p. 151.

116. Clark Wissler in *Proceedings of the American Philosophical Society* 86 (1943): 196. For a summary review of the contribution of Lewis and Clark to ethnography, see Verne F. Ray and Nancy O. Lurie in *Journal of the Washington Academy of Sciences* 44 (1954): 358–370.

117. Quoted from A. Irving Hallowell in Frederica de Laguna, ed., *Selected Papers from the American Anthropologist 1888–1920* (Washington, D.C., 1960), p. 20.

languages and the first tribal language map. In 1836 he published a much enlarged *Synopsis of the Indians within the United States east of the Rocky Mountains and in the British and Russian Possessions in North America,* and in 1848 a final summation of his linguistic researches.[118] Gallatin's work was not sponsored by the U.S. government in a financial sense, but it had the enthusiastic support and encouragement of Jefferson, and the collaboration of the War Department (then in charge of Indian affairs) in providing vocabularies of many Indian languages.[119]

An important figure in the development of early government Indianology was Lewis Cass, who served as governor of the Michigan Territory, and unofficial superintendent of Indian Affairs, from 1813 to 1831. In his earlier years Cass was very much interested in Indian affairs, and published several articles that had a major influence on the development of U.S. Indian policy.[120] Most importantly for future research, he developed a 64-page questionnaire, involving more than 350 separate questions, that was to be followed in the investigation of Indian customs and languages. Already in 1820, he had observed that "The time for collecting materials to illustrate the past and present condition of the Indians is rapidly passing away."[121] Field research on the Indians was thus conceived primarily as a task of ethnographic salvage before it was too late, and this was to remain the predominant concern in government Indianology until well into the twentieth century. Cass's questionnaire was published in 1823,[122] and copies were immediately sent to Indian agents, traders, and military men, with the request that they supply information for any tribe with which they might be familiar. Not many replies were received, and no overall summation of the results was ever published, but the questionnaire method initiated by Cass was to remain an important feature of government Indianological research under Henry R. Schoolcraft, Lewis H. Morgan, and John Wesley Powell.[123]

Henry Schoolcraft was a contemporary and friend of Cass who from

---

118. It was published as the Introduction to Horatio Hale's *Indians of North-West America, Transactions of the American Ethnological Society,* vol. 2 (1848).

119. Hallowell in de Laguna, *Selected Papers from the American Anthropologist 1888–1920,* p. 29. For extended discussion of Gallatin's contribution, see Robert E. Bieder, *Science Encounters the Indian, 1820–1880* (Norman, Okla., 1986), pp. 16–54.

120. See Washburn, *History of Indian-White Relations,* p. 628.

121. Quoted by Hallowell in de Laguna, *Selected Papers from the American Anthropologist 1888–1920,* pp. 40–41.

122. Under the title *Inquiries Respecting the History, Traditions, Languages, Manners, Customs, Religion, Etc. of the Indians, living within the United States.*

123. For discussion of Cass, see Hallowell in de Laguna, *Selected Papers from the American Anthropologist,* pp. 39–41; Bieder, *Science Encounters the Indian,* pp. 147–155; and Elizabeth S. Brown in *Michigan History* 37, no. 3 (1953): 286–298.

1822 to 1841 served as Indian agent in the Great Lakes area. During this time he began the systematic collection of information, especially about the Ojibwa, following essentially the guidelines of the Cass questionnaire. He was above all a pioneer in the collection of myths and folktales, which he published in a two-volume work with the title *Algic Researches* in 1839.[124] After leaving his government post he moved to New York City and supported himself by writing popular books about the Indians; he was also, along with Gallatin, a founding member of the American Ethnological Society.

Government Indianology

In 1846, having learned of the impending foundation of the Smithsonian Institution, Schoolcraft submitted to its regents a comprehensive "Plan for the investigation of American Ethnology." This was not immediately acted upon, and the author therefore turned to Congress, urging a similar plan of investigation to be carried out by the War Department (still in charge of Indian affairs until 1849). This second proposal was duly approved and funded, with Schoolcraft designated as the chief investigator. He spent the rest of his life compiling, from personal investigations and from questionnaires, the massive *Historical and Statistical Information Respecting the History, Condition, and Prospects of the Indian Tribes of the United States…*, which appeared in six folio volumes between 1851 and 1857.[125] The work was poorly organized and contained a great deal of misinformation, especially about the tribes of the newly acquired Oregon and New Mexico territories, but it was the first attempt at a comprehensive, government-sponsored survey of all available information about the Indians of the United States.[126] Since Schoolcraft was employed full-time for several years in its compilation, he may perhaps be identified as the first fully professional government Indianologist. His work set a precedent, if not a model, that continues to be followed today, in that it was the precedent for the two-volume *Handbook of American Indians North of Mexico* published by the Bureau of American Ethnology in 1907–1910,[127] and more recently for the twenty-volume *Handbook of North American Indians,* published by the Smithsonian Institution and still in process of completion.[128]

124. "Algic" was his term for the Algonquian linguistic family.

125. It was published by Lippincott, Grambo & Co. of Philadelphia, with funding from the Bureau of Indian Affairs.

126. See Hallowell in de Laguna, *Selected Papers from the American Anthropologist,* pp. 42–47, and Bieder, *Science Encounters the Indian,* pp. 146–193.

127. *Bureau of American Ethnology Bulletin* 30, edited by Frederick W. Hodge.

128. Edited by William C. Sturtevant. Ten volumes have been published to date; the first two appeared in 1978.

America presented a unique opportunity for the student of cultural history, in that there was no gap in time between the prehistoric past and the ethnographic present. Thus, Indianology was seen from the beginning as encompassing archaeology no less than ethnology and linguistics; a fact attested by Jefferson's excavation of an Indian mound. In later years, government exploring expeditions were regularly instructed to report on antiquities as well as to collect ethnographic information.[129] *"Indianology"*

Before the acquisition of the Mexican Cession, by far the most conspicuous antiquities within American territory were the great earthen mounds scattered all over the midwestern and southeastern states, and these began to excite interest at a very early date. Because no Indians had been observed to build mounds in the historic period, and because living Indians could give no information about them, the popular belief arose that the mounds were the work of a vanished earlier race, the Mound Builders. It was that belief that stimulated most of the earliest antiquarian researches in North America. General Rufus Putnam, who served under Washington in the American Revolution, surveyed and mapped the mounds at Marietta, Ohio, in 1788; his work has been cited as "the genesis of the science of archaeology in the United States."[130] The American Antiquarian Society was founded in 1812, with the primary objective of investigating the mounds, and shortly afterward Caleb Atwater was appointed Ohio State Archaeologist (albeit without salary) for the same purpose. Atwater carried out an extensive surface survey of mounds in Ohio and neighboring states, which was published in 1820 as volume 1 of the *Transactions and Collections of the American Antiquarian Society.*[131] Schoolcraft also became interested in the "mound problem," publishing several papers and a full-length monograph on mounds that he had visited in Virginia, Ohio, and Michigan. He was one of the first to suggest that the mounds were the work of ordinary Indians, ancestral to the present-day tribes, and not of a vanished earlier race.[132]

Much more extensive and systematic than the work of Putnam or At-

129. For discussion, see esp. John R. Cole in John V. Murra., ed., *American Anthropology, the Early Years,* pp. 111–125. *1974 Proceedings of the American Ethnological Society,* 1976.
130. Henry C. Shetrone, *The Mound-Builders* (New York, 1930), p. 13.
131. With the title *Description of the Antiquities Discovered in Ohio and other Western States.* For more on Atwater see Hallowell in de Laguna, *Selected Papers from the American Anthropologist,* p. 79, and Mead and Bunzel, *Golden Age of American Anthropology,* pp. 100–105.
132. See Hallowell in de Laguna, *Selected Papers from the American Anthropologist,* pp. 46–47, 81.

water was that of Ephraim G. Squier and E.H. Davis, who between 1845 and 1847 carried out excavations in over two hundred mounds, and collected information about scores of others throughout the whole region of the Midwest. They attempted the first classification of the mound sites, although it was found to be unsatisfactory by later researchers. Squier, like Schoolcraft, accepted the idea that the mounds were the work of Indians and not of an earlier race; on the other hand he believed that there was a cultural connection between the mounds of the Mississippi Valley and the temple mounds of Mexico. The work of Squier and Davis was not carried out under direct government sponsorship, but it was published at government expense, as the first publication of the newly founded Smithsonian Institution.[133]

The postwar western surveys

Government Indianology received a fresh impetus after the Civil War, from the four great governmental surveys that were sent forth to explore and map the newly acquired territories of the Far West. The ethnological contribution of the surveys was relatively modest, but their effect on archaeological research was revolutionary. It was the western surveys–in particular the Geological and Geographic Survey led by Ferdinand Hayden and the Survey West of the 100th Meridian led by Lt. George Wheeler –that first brought to public attention the great cliff dwellings and other ruined pueblos of the Southwestern territories. *The Eighth Annual Report of the Hayden Survey* (1876) included the "Report of W.H. Jackson on Ancient Ruins in Southwestern Colorado," accompanied by some of Jackson's spectacular photographs of cliff dwellings near Mesa Verde.[134] Three years later the Wheeler Survey published an entire volume on archaeology, which included reports on archaeological collections from Southern California as well as descriptions of many ruins in Arizona and New Mexico.[135] In spite of its title the volume was not purely archaeological; it included also the first descriptions in English of several of the contemporary

133. *Ancient Monuments of the Mississippi Valley. Smithsonian Contributions to Knowledge,* vol. 1 (1848). For more on the archaeological work of Squier and Davis, see Hallowell in de Laguna, *Selected Papers from the American Anthropologist,* pp. 80–81, and Thomas G. Tax in Timothy H.H. Thoresen, ed., *Toward a Science of Man* (The Hague, 1975), pp. 99–124.

134. *Eighth Annual Report of the United States Geological and Geographic Survey of the Territories* (1876), p. 373. For more on the Hayden Survey see Richard A. Bartlett, *Great Surveys of the American West* (Norman, Okla., 1962), pp. 3–120.

135. *Report upon United States Geographical Surveys West of the One Hundredth Meridian,* vol. VII.

Pueblo Indian villages,[136] a classification of Western Indian dialects, and a comparative table of forty Indian vocabularies.[137] Thanks to these discoveries and publications, the spectacular puebloan remains of the Southwest soon displaced the eastern mounds as the main focus of American archaeological interest, and they remained so for nearly half a century.

The least productive of the four western surveys, from a purely scientific standpoint, was the survey of the Colorado Plateau directed by Major John Wesley Powell from 1869 to 1879.[138] Yet it was to have the most far-reaching influence of all on the subsequent development of Indianology. *"Indianology"* In the course of surveying the Plateau, "The Major" (as Powell was always called) had developed a strong interest in the ethnography of the Ute and Paiute Indians–at that time among the least acculturated tribal groups remaining in the United States. When the four western surveys were combined into the permanent United States Geological Survey in 1879, it was Powell who persuaded the government to create simultaneously a Bureau of American Ethnology, attached to the Smithsonian Institution. It became the primary institutional home of Indianology for the remainder of the nineteenth century, and in every sense the embodiment of Jefferson's dream.

The Bureau of American Ethnology

The Bureau of American Ethnology (always BAE to anthropologists) was created by act of Congress in March, 1879, with Major Powell as its first director. As Hinsley writes, "The BAE was Powell's personal creation, the culmination of his experiences in science, politics, and exploration during the 1870s; it emerged from the Survey tradition and in every important respect continued the pattern of structure, procedure, and purpose of the Survey years. The BAE was to be a permanent anthropological survey."[139] The early Bureau staff included many veterans of the western surveys, including William H. Holmes (later to become director) and Cyrus Thomas from the Hayden Survey, Henry W. Henshaw and Harry C. Yarrow from the Wheeler Survey, and John Pilling and J.K. Hillers from Powell's own Colorado Plateau Survey.

Powell was a friend and an enthusiastic admirer of Lewis Henry Mor-

136. Ibid., pp. 325–336.
137. Ibid., pp. 403–485. For more on the Wheeler Survey see Bartlett, *Great Surveys of the American West*, pp. 333–372.
138. See Bartlett, *Great Surveys of the American West*, pp. 219–329; also Darrah, *Powell of the Colorado*, pp. 108–176.
139. Curtis M. Hinsley, Jr., *Savages and Scientists* (Washington, D.C., 1981), p. 147.

gan, whose *Ancient Society* appeared just two years before the BAE was formed (see Chapter 2). In the first Annual Report of the Bureau (1881), the new director announced an ambitious scheme "to organize anthropologic research in America" in such a way that the systematic study of American Indians would enhance and illustrate the development of progressivist theory.[140] It was, in the words of Darrah, "a dazzling introduction to a new science of man,"[141] which Powell liked to call the "New Ethnology."[142] In keeping with that vision, he consistently interpreted both ethnological and archaeological findings in progressivist terms, following as far as possible the evolutionary schema proposed by Morgan.[143] But Powell never really imposed his own views on the Bureau's research program, partly because of a firm belief that scientific strictures must not inhibit individual creativity, and partly because most of the BAE researchers were in any case unpaid amateurs, whose views could not be coerced.[144] In fact, the Bureau simply continued for more than half a century the task begun by the western surveys: that of amassing and systematizing any and all information about the American Indians. It was in the truest sense a Bureau of Indianology, not a Bureau of Anthropology in any theoretical sense.

Government Indianology

Nevertheless, the Bureau's rubric from the beginning embraced what were to become the traditional four subfields of anthropology: ethnology, linguistics, archaeology, and physical anthropology. In the study of American Indians, the dividing lines between the first three of the subfields were not perceived to be sharp. Ethnological field work nearly always included the collection of texts and vocabularies, while in the Southwest (where so much of the Bureau's early field work was carried on) the puebloan ruins were recognized as the immediate antecedents of the currently inhabited Pueblo villages. Most of the early BAE staffers had been trained, in the nineteenth-century tradition, as all-purpose naturalists, and they saw nothing inappropriate in carrying out ethnographic and linguistic researches in one season, and archaeological investigations in the next. Physical anthropology fell into a rather separate category, since Powell was profoundly skeptical of nineteenth-century physical anthropology with its emphasis on racial differences.[145] "The study of man is demotic, not biotic," he liked to insist.[146] It was not until Ales Hrdlicka joined the

140. *First Annual Report of the Bureau of American Ethnology, 1879–80*, pp. xi–xxxiii.
141. *Powell of the Colorado*, p. 269.
142. See Hinsley, *Savages and Scientists*, pp. 125, 137–138.
143. For Powell's evolutionary views, see esp. ibid., pp. 125–143.
144. Cf. Ibid., pp. 152–155.
145. Cf. his contribution in the *First Annual Report* of the BAE (1881), pp. 71–86.
146. Quoted from Hinsley, *Savages and Scientists*, p. 137.

staff, at the beginning of the twentieth century, that the BAE began publishing monographs in physical anthropology.

Like nearly all anthropological research before and since, the Bureau's field work was carried out mostly by lone researchers pursuing their own individual interests.[147] With an annual budget of $20,000, the BAE could obviously fund only a limited amount of research by its own staffers. But Powell's promotional genius showed itself in his ability to search out and to provide encouragement, and sometimes field funding, for a host of amateur and part-time Indianologists–and most importantly to provide for the publication of their work. Another of the director's tactics was to provide office space and a small stipend for recognized scholars whose field work was already largely complete, such as Garrick Mallery, James Mooney, and Albert Gatschet, to allow them to write up and publish their material. Among the many distinguished field workers who were recruited and/or aided in this way were James O. Dorsey, Frank Hamilton Cushing, Washington Matthews, the brothers Cosmos and Victor Mindeleff, Matilda Coxe Stevenson, Gerard Fowke, and Stewart Culin.[148]

"Indianology"

With such a proliferation of individual field researches, the obvious needs at the headquarters level were for organization, coordination, and synthesis. It was in these activities that Major Powell's genius showed itself most fully. He was in addition a man of prodigious energy, as attested by the fact that for more than ten years (1881–1894) he served as director both of the Bureau of American Ethnology and the U.S. Geological Survey. (He continued to direct the BAE up to the time of his death in 1902.) Finally he was a consummate politician, whose status as an authentic Civil War hero (he lost an arm at Shiloh) was a major political asset in post-Civil War Washington. Powell did not hesitate to make use of that cachet when, year after year, he wheedled special funds from Congress to support the work of field investigators like Cushing and the Mindeleffs.[149]

Powell's enduring monument is to be found in the forty-eight Annual Reports of the BAE issued between 1881 and 1933,[150] and the two hundred Bulletins issued between 1887 and 1971.[151] The early Annual Reports were massive, quarto affairs each of which included major scientific papers as

147. Cf. ibid., p. 152.

148. For a fuller list, see Hallowell in de Laguna, *Selected Papers from the American Anthropologist*, p. 57.

149. For biographies of Powell, see Darrah, *Powell of the Colorado*, and Wallace Stegner, *Beyond the Hundredth Meridian* (Boston, 1954).

150. *Annual Reports* continued to appear until 1965, but after 1933 they no longer contained scientific contributions.

151. For complete lists see *Bureau of American Ethnology Bulletin* 200 (1971).

well as the Director's operating report. The Bulletins, published in octavo size, were mostly full-length monographs that were considered too long for inclusion in the regular annual reports. Only a handful of the contributions were of Powell's personal authorship, but few of them, before 1902, would have been published without his active support and funding. Indeed, as Hallowell observes, "One wonders what the history of American anthropology in the late nineteenth century would have been if the Bureau as he conceived and directed in had never come into existence."[152]

Government Indianology

Powell's training as a naturalist had convinced him that the continued amassing of empirical data must sooner or later be followed by classification, and this he saw as the overriding need in the study of American Indians. Reports of all kinds had been accumulating, unsystematically, for well over two centuries, and they seemed to provide information on literally thousands of "tribes." It was clear, however, that some of the would-be "tribes" were no more than subtribes or even individual villages, and also that some peoples, like the Iroquois and the Chippewa, were known in the literature under a variety of names. At the other extreme, single terms like Sioux and Apache were applied to what were in effect many different tribes. If existing literature were to be synthesized in any useful way, the first requirement was to figure out "who was who" among the Indians. This task was to occupy, and in some respects to plague, the BAE headquarters staff throughout the first quarter-century of its existence.[153] After more than a decade of compilation, Powell had to confess in 1897 that "the work is of such character as not soon to be completed, since each new investigation yields additional information."[154] The "synonymy" (as it was originally designated) finally achieved fruition with the publication of the two-volume *Handbook of American Indians North of Mexico* in 1907 and 1910.[155]

The synonymy was only one of several major projects of synthesis launched by Powell. The first to appear in print was his own classification of Indian linguistic families north of Mexico, published in the *Seventh Annual Report* in 1891.[156] Others, which did not appear until after the Major's death, included the *Handbook of American Indian Languages* (1911 and 1922),[157] the *Handbook of Aboriginal American Antiquities* (1919),[158] the

152. Quoted in de Laguna, *Selected Papers from the American Anthropologist*, p. 57.
153. Cf. Hinsley, *Savages and Scientists*, pp. 155–158.
154. *Fifteenth Annual Report of the Bureau of American Ethnology*, p. lxxix.
155. *Bureau of American Ethnology Bulletin* 30, edited by Frederick W. Hodge.
156. Pp. 1–142.
157. *Bureau of American Ethnology Bulletin* 40, by Franz Boas.
158. *Bureau of American Ethnology Bulletin* 60, by W. H. Holmes.

Handbook of the Indians of California (1925),[159] and finally the seven-volume *Handbook of South American Indians* (1946–1959).[160] The latter two works were not conceived in Powell's time, but they represent in every respect a continuation of the tradition of synthesis to which he had dedicated the BAE.

The research program of the BAE did not significantly change after the death of Powell, or indeed during the entire eighty-six years of the Bureau's existence. The main change was that the Bureau extended its field of interest to the Indians of Central and South America, although its main focus always remained on North America. However, the institution's role as the primary locus of Indianological research in North America was increasingly eroded after 1900 by the emergence of other research centers, first in museums and then in university departments of anthropology. Most of the twentieth-century Indianologists were in fact Ph.D. anthropologists based in these institutions. Many of new departments launched their own anthropological monograph series, so that field workers no longer had to rely so heavily on the BAE Bulletins and Annual Reports as outlets for their work. By midcentury the BAE was only one of a dozen active centers of Indianological research, although it remained almost the only one with an exclusively Indianological focus. *"Indianology"*

In 1965 the Bureau of American Ethnology was reconstituted as the Smithsonian Office of Anthropology (changed to Department of Anthropology in 1968). On paper, this marks the end of a significant era in government Indianology: first because the Office/Department of Anthropology does not have an overall, coordinated research focus, and second because its field of interest is now worldwide. Yet the publications of the department (now designated as *Smithsonian Contributions to Anthropology*) are still overwhelmingly Indianological, and are hardly different in style or content from the Bulletins of the BAE. Moreover, the Smithsonian's commitment to produce the vast, twenty-volume *Handbook of North American Indians* is clear evidence that the great old survey tradition of the BAE lives on.

The Bureau of Indian Affairs

The Bureau of Indian Affairs was created by executive order in 1824. Since that time it has been, during most of its history, the sole federal agency responsible for conducting relations between the U.S. government and the

159. *Bureau of American Ethnology Bulletin* 78, by A. L. Kroeber.
160. *Bureau of American Ethnology Bulletin* 143, edited by Julian H. Steward.

five hundred-odd tribes within U.S. borders, and for carrying out the terms of the innumerable treaties negotiated with the individual tribes. As Indian Commissioner Ross Swimmer recently observed, the Indian Bureau (BIA) has to perform for Indians all of the different functions that are performed for other Americans by all the various agencies of federal, state, and local government, except in the areas of public health and national defense.[161]

Government Indianology

It might have been supposed, therefore, that the BIA would have the strongest possible interest in the study of its Indian subjects. Individual agents in the field did indeed undertake studies, and provided information on the questionnaires that were sent to them by Cass, Schoolcraft, and Morgan. For most of the Bureau's history, however, it was directed and staffed by political hacks for whom the Indians held no intellectual interest at all. After the Civil War, the Indian Bureau became so corrupt as to constitute a national scandal.[162] A measure of its low public esteem can be seen in the fact that the newly created Bureau of American Ethnology was lodged in the Smithsonian Institution and not in the BIA, which might have seemed a more logical place. The worst abuses were corrected by the end of the nineteenth century, but it was not until the inauguration of Franklin Roosevelt's New Deal administration in 1933 that the Indian Bureau showed any serious interest in research on its own initiative.

Roosevelt appointed as Commissioner for Indian Affairs the dynamic John Collier; the first director of the BIA who had a scholarly as well as a humanitarian interest in the Indians, and who appreciated the importance of research as a basis for policy development. He was the first commissioner to bring anthropologists into the BIA, in both administrative and research roles. Among many other investigations, he launched the Indian Education Research Project, in collaboration with the Committee on Human Development at the University of Chicago. Its objectives reflect the central concerns of midcentury anthropology, which were at once scholarly and humanitarian: "to investigate, analyze, and compare the development of personality in five Indian tribes in the context of their total environment–socio-cultural, geographical, and historical–for implications in regard to Indian Service Administration."[163] Half a dozen of the leading anthropologists and psychologists of the time were commissioned to carry out long-range studies among the Sioux, Navajo, Zuni, Hopi, and

161. Statement read before the Subcommittee on Interior and Related Agencies, Committee on Appropriations, United States House of Representatives, October 27, 1987.

162. See esp. Prucha, *American Indian Policy in Crisis.*

163. Clyde Kluckhohn and Dorothea Leighton, *The Navaho* (Cambridge, Mass., 1946), p. vii.

Papago, with special focus on the socialization and enculturation of children within the tribal environments. The Education Research Project not only had a profound effect on the educational programs of the BIA; it also resulted in some of the most influential monographs of midcentury anthropology: *Warriors without Weapons,* by Gordon Macgregor,[164] *The Navaho*[165] and *Children of the People,*[166] by Kluckhohn and Leighton, *The Hopi Way,* by Thompson and Joseph,[167] *Culture in Crisis,* by Laura Thompson,[168] and *The Desert People,* by Joseph, Spicer, and Chesky.[169]

Unhappily, the Indian Bureau's interest in major research was short-lived. World War II diverted national attention to other and higher priorities, and all the anthropologists formerly employed in the Bureau went off to work in war-related agencies. After the war the BIA once again became politicized, and the research projects inaugurated under Collier were never resumed. In time a number of tribes hired anthropologists and commissioned studies on their own initiative, and some even took the studies into their own hands, but these were not policy initiatives of the BIA.

Latter-day government Indianology

The federal government continues to be heavily involved in the sponsorship of Indianological research, but its role since World War II has been largely reactive, and to some extent even involuntary. The major dam-building programs of the Tennessee Valley Authority, the Bureau of Reclamation, and the Army Corps of Engineers necessitated a great deal of salvage archaeology, in advance of the flooding, and the government was obliged to provide funding both for the field work and for publication of the results. Many of the early river basin survey reports were published in the series of Bulletins of the Bureau of American Ethnology; later, responsibility was taken over by the Office of River Basin Surveys, under the National Park Service.[170] The Park Service also carried out and published a good many other archaeological investigations, in sites that were being prepared for public exhibition.[171]

---

164. Chicago, 1946.
165. Cambridge, Mass., 1946.
166. Cambridge, Mass., 1948.
167. Chicago, 1944.
168. New York, 1950.
169. Chicago, 1949.
170. The publications are designated as Publications in Salvage Archaeology of the River Basin Survey Office, Lincoln, Neb.
171. Publications are mainly in the U.S. National Park Service, Archaeological Research Series.

Finally, the flood of Indian claims brought against the federal government as the result of a 1959 Supreme Court decision has resulted in a truly prodigious amount of archaeological, ethnohistorical, and ethnographic research.[172] Anthropologists, historians, and other scholars were employed in equal numbers by the tribes in preparing their claims (mostly for compensation for the loss of territory) and by the government in preparing its defenses.[173] In many cases the federal government was obliged to pay the costs on both sides, since the tribes had no resources of their own. More than three hundred volumes of testimony before the Indian Claims Commission have so far been published, and they constitute an invaluable ethnohistorical archive.[174]

Government Indianology

MUSEUM INDIANOLOGY

Although it now embraces no fewer than sixteen separate museums, the Smithsonian Institution was not conceived originally as a museum. It was chartered in 1846 "for the increase and diffusion of knowledge among men," and its original director, Joseph Henry, always insisted on that primary function. Throughout his long tenure (to 1877) he resisted all suggestions for the creation of a formally constituted national museum.[175] Meanwhile, however, the Smithsonian became, as the nearest equivalent to a national museum, the recipient of materials collected by the numerous government exploring expeditions as well as by a great many private donors. By the 1870s the institution had already a recognized "ethnological division" (also responsible for archaeological materials) with three paid assistants. Eventually the need for a properly organized and curated museum could no longer be ignored, and the U.S. National Museum was finally established as a branch of the Smithsonian in 1881.[176]

Because of its status as a kind of half-sister to the Bureau of American Ethnology–both lodged within the Smithsonian–the National Museum

---

172. See Charles F. Wilkinson, *American Indians, Time, and the Law* (New Haven, Conn., 1987), pp. 1–2.

173. For a description of typical proceedings, see the opening pages in any of the Garland American Indian Ethnohistory Series, cited below. For more general discussion of the Indian Claims Commission and its work, see Imre Sutton, ed., *Irredeemable America: the Indians' Estate and Land Claims* (Albuquerque, 1985).

174. They are published in the Garland American Indian Ethnohistory Series by the Garland Publishing Co., New York.

175. See esp. Wilcomb E. Washburn in *A Cabinet of Curiosities: Five Episodes in the Evolution of American Museums* (Charlottesville, Va., 1967), pp. 106–166.

176. For discussion of the gradual evolution of Smithsonian ethnology, see Hinsley, *Savages and Scientists*, pp. 64–79.

never developed a field research program of its own. It functioned in effect as the curatorial arm of the BAE. There was however a good deal of in-house study of existing collections, and a modest series of publications resulted.[177] The first Curator of Ethnology, Otis T. Mason, devoted the entire latter part of his career to the cataloguing, description, and above all the classification of the museum's collections. He was the first great taxonomist in the field of Indianology, publishing important monographs on harpoons, cradles, travel equipment, and traps.[178] However, he is best remembered for his monumental study, *Aboriginal American Basketry.*[179]

Although the Smithsonian's ethnology collections date back to the 1840s, the first formally established museum of Indianology in the United States was the Peabody Museum of American Archaeology and Ethnology at Harvard University, founded in 1866. In spite of its title, the interests of the Peabody were not exclusively Indianological; indeed its earliest acquisitions were archaeological collections from northern Europe.[180] Under the dynamic leadership of Frederick Ward Putnam (from 1875 to 1909), however, the Peabody became second only to the BAE as a center of Indianological research in America. Its focus was somewhat more heavily archaeological than that of the BAE, but Peabody research from the beginning also included ethnology, linguistics, and physical anthropology.[181] The museum early became involved in Mesoamerican excavations, and these have remained a major research focus down to the present day.[182]

Putnam was a protean figure, who ranks alongside John Wesley Powell in the development of Indianology in the later nineteenth century. The talents and the achievements of the two men were essentially complementary. Both were freewheeling promoters, but while Powell's influence was exerted mainly in the organization of research, that of Putnam was exerted above all in the organization of museums. In 1891, while still acting as curator of the Peabody, he went to Chicago to organize the archaeological and ethnological exhibits for the World's Columbian Exposition; exhibits

177. They were mostly published in the Annual Reports of the United States National Museum.

178. For a list of his publications, see Hinsley, *Savages and Scientists*, pp. 305–306.

179. Published in the *Annual Report of the United States National Museum for 1901–2* (Washington, D.C., 1904), pp. 171–548.

180. J. O. Brew, ed., *One Hundred Years of Anthropology* (Cambridge, Mass., 1968), pp. 13–14.

181. Most Peabody Museum researches are published in the series of Papers of the Peabody Museum of American Archaeology and Ethnology, Harvard University. For the early field researches of the Peabody, see Curtis M. Hinsley in George W. Stocking, ed., *Objects and Others*, pp. 49–74. *History of Anthropology*, vol. 3 (1985).

182. The Mesoamerican researches are published mostly in the Memoirs of the Peabody Museum of American Archaeology and Ethnology, Harvard University.

that afterward became the permanent nucleus of the Field Museum of Natural History collections.[183] At the beginning of the twentieth century he performed a similar function for the newly founded American Museum of Natural History in New York, an institution that deliberately modeled itself on the Field Museum. In 1903 he went on to California to found the Anthropological Museum and the Department of Anthropology at the University of California–while all the time retaining his positions both as Curator of the Peabody Museum and as Peabody Professor of American Archaeology and Ethnology at Harvard![184] The Field Museum, the American Museum, and the California Department of Anthropology each became a major center of Indianological research in its own right, and the publisher of an important monograph series.[185]

Museum Indianology

For obvious reasons a great deal of museum Indianology was collection oriented. Archaeological excavations were carried out especially in sites that gave promise of yielding objects for display; hence the proliferation of museum-sponsored digs in the Southwest, where attractive pottery, basketry, and other fine craft products could be expected. Ethnological studies were often carried out in conjunction with collecting expeditions, whose primary purpose was the acquisition of Indian costumes and material culture for display. One salutary consequence was that museum-sponsored ethnographies were often meticulously detailed in their description of native technological processes. Yet the "big four" in the field of museum Indianology–the Smithsonian, the Peabody, the Field Museum, and the American Museum–were all active in pure research as well as in the mounting of exhibitions, and they sponsored a good deal of field work, for example in linguistics and physical anthropology, that produced nothing for display.

Not quite one of the big four, but the most purely Indianological of all U.S. museums, is the Museum of the American Indian (Heye Foundation) in New York City, created in 1916 to house what had been the private collection of George F. Heye. Although it is not very active in field research, it has published a steady stream of small monographs and articles, mostly related in one way or another to its collections or else reprinted from other journals. Indian materials are also exhibited, of course, in scores of re-

---

183. The Field Museum was renamed the Chicago Natural History Museum in 1943, and then resumed its original name in 1965.

184. For biographical sketches of Putnam, see Joan Mark, *Four Anthropologists* (New York, 1980), pp. 14–61; Washburn, *History of Indian-White Relations*, pp. 677–678, and Christopher Winters, ed., *International Dictionary of Anthropologists* (New York, 1991), pp. 555–557.

185. Field Museum of Natural History, Anthropological Series (later designated Fieldiana); American Museum of Natural History, Anthropological Papers; University of California Publications in American Archaeology and Ethnology.

gional and local museums throughout the United States, and some of these developed important field research and publication programs of their own. Noteworthy in this regard are, or were, the Milwaukee Public Museum, the Logan Museum in Beloit, Wisconsin, the state museums of New Mexico and Arizona, the Museum of Northern Arizona in Flagstaff, and the Southwest Museum in Highland Park, California.

It was in the arrangement of materials for exhibition that the museums made their most signal contribution to the field of Indianology. At the U.S. National Museum, Otis T. Mason, like Powell at the BAE, was a devotee of Morgan's evolutionary theory. To the extent that he could, he tried initially to organize the exhibition of Indian materials in what he believed to be evolutionary sequences (following the example of the Pitt Rivers Museum at Oxford[186]), without regard to their place of origin. This procedure offended the young Franz Boas, who felt that it "decontextualized" the materials being exhibited. In an 1887 article published in *Science,* he urged that Indian materials should be displayed in such a way as to illustrate their historical and environmental contexts, and their interrelatedness.[187] In other words, articles made and used at the same time by the same peoples should be displayed together. Above all, Boas objected to the grouping of materials on the basis of classifications that ignored time and space: "classification is not explanation," he insisted.

Although Mason publicly defended his own system of exhibition,[188] by the 1890s he was beginning increasingly to display Indian materials in what he called "life-groups," which in effect coincided with the recommendation of Boas.[189] This procedure was especially congenial to William H. Holmes, who joined Mason at the National Museum in 1889.[190] The life-group was in effect a life-size diorama: a group of costumed wax figures portrayed in lifelike settings and engaged in daily activities, either within a cutaway tipi or wigwam, or against a painted outdoor backdrop showing appropriate scenery for the group displayed. This mode of representation reached its fullest fruition in the exhibits at the World's Columbian Exposition in 1894–95, which were to live on throughout the twentieth century in the ethnology section of the Field Museum of Natural History.[191] It was subsequently adopted also by the American Museum and by many local museums. As Hinsley writes, "After Chicago virtually every

186. Cf. William R. Chapman in Stocking, *Objects and Others,* pp. 15–48.
187. Volume 9, no. 224 (1887), pp. 485–486. See also Ira Jacknis in Stocking, *Objects and Others,* pp. 75–111.
188. Also in *Science* 9, no. 226 (1887): 534.
189. Hinsley, *Savages and Scientists,* p. 100.
190. For the career of Holmes see Mark, *Four Anthropologists,* pp. 131–171.
191. Hinsley, *Savages and Scientists,* pp. 108–109.

government anthropology exhibit featured primitive peoples working and playing in appropriately naturalistic environments."[192]

It was in the course of developing their display procedures that the museums made their most enduring contribution to Indianology: the concept of the culture area. It was obviously impossible to mount a separate display for each of the hundreds of tribes from which collections had been obtained; a judicious selection had to be made. A search for representative tribes to display led to a clear recognition that there was a strong similarity among the Indian cultures in particular environmental settings, but marked differences between one environment and another. In time it became a deliberate goal of the museums, beginning at Chicago, to present a life-group illustrating the basic cultural features of each area of North America. Mason himself was the first to grasp the implications of this discovery. He began speaking informally about "ethnographic regions" in the early 1890s, and in 1895 published the first formal delineation of American culture areas (both North American and South American).[193] The culture area concept was subsequently refined by Holmes, and was most fully elaborated by Clark Wissler in his pathbreaking *The American Indian,* in which the ethnography of North America was systematically described in terms of culture areas.[194]

Museum Indianology

The arrangement of ethnographic data in terms of culture areas has been followed in nearly all books about the North American Indian since Wissler's time, as well as in nearly all museum displays. The concept has obvious limitations, in that the boundaries between areas are not always sharp, and there is much more homogeneity among the cultures in some areas than in others, yet it continues to be the most effective and coherent way of organizing the vast diversity of North American Indian ethnography.[195] Curiously, the culture area concept has never proven equally useful in other parts of the world, in spite of efforts to apply it in South America, Africa, and Asia.[196]

From the standpoint of research productivity, museum Indianology enjoyed its heyday from about 1900 to 1930. During that period field re-

---

192. Ibid., p. 109.

193. *Annual Report of the United States National Museum for 1895,* pp. 639–665. He had proclaimed the same idea in somewhat more generalized form a year earlier in the *American Anthropologist* (old series) 7 (1894): 137–161.

194. New York, 1917.

195. For further discussion of the concept and its limitations, see Harris, *Rise of Anthropological Theory,* pp. 374–377.

196. For South America, see Julian Steward in *Handbook of South American Indians,* vol. 5 (1949), pp. 669–772. *Bureau of American Ethnology Bulletin* 143. For Africa, see Melville Herskovits in *Africa* 3 (1930): 59–77; for Asia, see Elizabeth Bacon in *Southwestern Journal of Anthropology* 2 (1946): 117–132.

search was increasingly taken up by university anthropologists as well, but as of 1930 the museums were still providing the most abundant funding. Then, the Great Depression of the 1930s caused a severe cutback in funding, while World War II virtually brought field research to a standstill. A number of museums, including the Smithsonian, the Peabody, and the Field, resumed active research in the Americas after World War II, but all of these are now heavily involved in research in other parts of the world as well. Meanwhile, the tremendous proliferation of university departments of anthropology has meant that, at least in quantitative terms, Indianological research has become much more a university than a museum enterprise. Yet museum research, tied as it is to considerations of display and to the culture area concept, remains truer to the traditional, particularistic spirit of Indianology than does university research.

INDIANOLOGY BECOMES ANTHROPOLOGY—AND VICE VERSA

Powell and Putnam had no doubt that what they were doing was anthropology. Long before the arrival of Boas, both men were using the term regularly, and Powell had played a major role in founding the Anthropological Society of Washington.[197] The idea that anthropology in America was "founded" by the young Franz Boas would therefore have struck them as absurd. Yet the word "anthropology" did not appear in the name of either institution headed by the two men, nor in the two academic chairs that had been established at Harvard and at Pennsylvania. It was Indianology, not anthropology, that was institutionalized in late nineteenth-century America. The achievement of Boas was to institutionalize anthropology, and to establish it in the universities as well as in the museums. From the beginning it was conceived by Boas—as indeed it was already by Powell and Putnam—as a comprehensive, worldwide discipline embracing the whole of Indianology and a great deal more besides.

When Boas began teaching anthropology at Columbia, therefore, he did not create a new discipline; he merely created a new *academic* discipline. In the domain of research, he simply brought professional organization and training to a diverse body of activities and theoretical interests that were already ongoing, under a variety of names. Most of those activities and interests revolved in one way or another around the study of the Indians, and Boas accepted this as the appropriate, primary focus for American anthropology as he taught and practiced it.

It is worth noting that, when Boas began teaching, there were already

197. Darrah, *Powell of the Colorado*, pp. 263–264.

established chairs of American archaeology and ethnology (that is, of Indianology) both at Harvard and at the University of Pennsylvania. Had the occupants of those chairs, Putnam at Harvard and Brinton at Pennsylvania, had the same interest in professionalization as had Boas, Indianology might well have emerged as an autonomous academic discipline, comparable to Egyptology and Sinology. But Putnam and Brinton had been educated in the gentlemanly tradition of nineteenth-century American universities, while Boas was a product of the continental European system with its heavy emphasis on graduate training and advanced degrees.[198] Thus it was Boasian anthropology, not the more particularized discipline of Indianology, that was professionalized by Boas. And when, in the early twentieth century, the need for professionalization in the social sciences came to be generally recognized, it was Boas alone who was ready with a graduate training program and with a supply of newly minted Ph.D.'s to fill the shoes of the retiring amateurs.

Indianology becomes anthropology & vice versa

Boasian Indianology

In 1900 the study of Indianology was still largely in the hands of all-purpose naturalists and of out-and-out amateurs. Thirty years later, it was almost wholly in the hands of university-trained anthropologists, all but a handful of whom had been trained by Boas or by one of his students. The anthropologists had not only created new centers of Indianological research at a dozen major universities; they had also moved in increasing numbers into the museums and the BAE as the older scholars died or retired. Although there had been some initial hostility between the BAE researchers and the Boasians,[199] by 1930 the Bureau itself was staffed entirely by professional anthropologists.

As we saw in Chapter 2, the Boasians are often credited with bringing about a revolutionary (though not a salutary) paradigm shift in anthropology. However, this is true at best only in a theoretical sense, and American anthropology has never been primarily a theoretical enterprise. It is above all a field discipline, and on this point the Boasians were in complete agreement with their Indianological predecessors. When, at the beginning of the twentieth century, they launched the so-called fieldwork revolution, they simply took over and made their own what had been the ongoing program of Indianological research for half a century. Thus, so far as Indianol-

198. For Brinton's career, see Washburn, *History of Indian-White Relations*, p. 625, and esp. Regna Darnell in Murra, *American Anthropology in the Early Years*, pp. 69–98.
199. See Hinsley, *Savages and Scientists*, pp. 283–284.

ogy was concerned, the so-called revolution was not a revolution but a takeover. It would be true to say, moreover, that Indianology had more impact on anthropology than vice versa.

The most profound and most lasting impact of nineteenth-century Indianology on twentieth century American anthropology can be seen in the persistence of the "four-field model:" the conception of anthropology as embracing ethnology, linguistics, archaeology, and physical anthropology. Given that the four-field concept was also prevalent in England at the turn of the century,[200] and given the personal proclivities of Boas, it might be argued that he would have introduced four-field anthropology into the curriculum at Columbia, whether or not there were Indians and Indianology. However, I think this is debatable, particularly as regards archaeology. Neither Boas nor any of his early students had any personal interest in archaeology, and, so far as I know, none of them except Fay-Cooper Cole ever conducted excavations in the field. It is also true that few of Boas's students shared their mentor's interest in physical anthropology. Yet when they went forth from Columbia to found the anthropology departments at California, Washington, Michigan, Illinois, Northwestern, and half a dozen other schools, they included archaeology and physical anthropology in the curriculum as a matter of course. I think this can only be interpreted as a bow to the already established paradigm of Indianology.

It seems clear, in sum, that Boas found in America an ongoing enterprise that in most respects was congenial to him, and to which he quite willingly adapted himself. This was surely a major consideration in his decision to settle permanently in the United States. What was mainly lacking, from his European perspective, was professionalization, and this he set about correcting by the institution of university graduate training. Since he was first in the field in that respect, it was he and his students who became the professional Indianologists of the early twentieth century.

Above all, the Boasians agreed on the overriding need for ethnographic salvage. Indianologists from Cass to Powell had urged the importance of recording Indian cultures and languages before it was too late, and this became the dominant concern of the early Boasians as well. It was no accident that so many of them did their dissertation fieldwork among the tribes of the Northern Plains and the Columbia Plateau—the areas where traditional cultures had been most drastically affected by the disastrous Dawes Allotment Act of 1887.[201] Equally noteworthy was their general ne-

200. Cf. A. C. Haddon, *History of Anthropology* (London, 1910).

201. See esp. Mead and Bunzel, *Golden Age of American Anthropology*, pp. 340–343.

glect of the Southwest; the area where traditional cultures were seemingly least at risk.[202]

Indianology becomes anthropology & vice versa

Although the Boasians rapidly moved Indianology from the museum to the university, as the discipline's main institutional base, the universities had little in the way of research funds of their own. For the better part of a generation, museums remained the chief source of funding for both ethnological and archaeological field work. Thus, it was mainly through his continuing connection with the American Museum of Natural History that Boas was able to send his earliest students into the field. Much of their ethnological research was done in the context of what were nominally collecting expeditions, and this had a certain influence on the focus of their inquiries, which were heavily preoccupied with details of material culture and technology.

As anthropologists, many of the great Boasians pursued interests that carried them far beyond the conventional boundaries of Indianology. Boas himself studied the head forms of European immigrants and their children, and used his findings to attack racial anthropology. Kroeber studied women's dress fashions and Japanese drama, and engaged in philosophical discourses with Arnold Toynbee and Pitirim Sorokin. Lowie became the foremost American authority on social organization, and Sapir practically rewrote the book on linguistic theory. These were works that probably could not have been written by the Indianologists of an earlier generation, except perhaps for Morgan. Yet in their investigations of Native Americans, the Boasians stayed comfortably within the established paradigm of Indianology. Wissler's *The American Indian*[203] and Kroeber's *Handbook of the Indians of California*[204] and *Cultural and Natural Areas of Native North America*[205] are all within the great survey tradition of the BAE. Lowie's *The Crow Indians*[206] exemplifies the one-tribe ethnographic monograph at its best, while Sapir's *Time Perspective in Aboriginal American Culture*[207] is the best programmatic statement of Indianological research methodology that was ever written. And there were other early Boasians, like H. K. Haeberlin, Leslie Spier, Erna Gunther, and Gladys Reichard, who worked entirely within the Indianological paradigm.

---

202. The main exceptions were the Yuman-speaking tribes of the Southwest, and these indeed were extensively studied, by both A. L. Kroeber and Leslie Spier.
203. Clark Wissler, *The American Indian* (New York, 1917).
204. *Bureau of American Ethnology Bulletin* 78 (1925).
205. *University of California Publications in American Archaeology and Ethnology*, vol. 38 (1939).
206. New York, 1935.
207. *Geological Survey of Canada, Memoir* 90 (1916).

The early Boasians shared with all other Indianologists an exclusive concern with traditional, precontact cultures. Their basic field technique was to find and interrogate elderly informants who could recall the great days of the war parties and the tribal councils and the sun dances, either from personal recollection or from what they themselves had been told as youths. The anthropologists showed virtually no interest in the cultural transformations and adaptations that had taken place under the conditions of White contact, or in the transformed cultures that existed in their own times. Indeed, the most serious charge that can be leveled against the early Boasians, and all other Indianologists before about 1930, is that they showed so little concern for the welfare of living Indians.

The writings of the Boasians on public policy questions show that they were not insensitive men and women.[208] I think their moral myopia as regards the Indians can only be explained by the fact that when they "bought into" the ideology of Indianology, they also "bought into" what for a century had been its dominant myth: that of the Vanishing Redman. Boas, Kroeber, and Lowie were as convinced as were Schoolcraft, Morgan, and Powell that Indians cultures must inevitably disappear, and that the overriding need was to study them while there was still a chance. They might have disagreed as to the reason why the cultures would disappear–whether due to evolutionary progress or to diffusion from the dominant civilization–but the result in any case was foregone, and beyond any control by the Indianologist.[209]

The fifty years from 1880 to 1930 were surely the Golden Age of Indianology as a research discipline. Beginning with the great western surveys, it became institutionalized in the BAE and the Peabody Museum, and from there spread to other museums and then increasingly to universities in every part of the United States. It was carried on first by all-purpose naturalists and by amateurs, and then in the twentieth century was taken over increasingly by anthropologists, but all of them worked within a single, well-established research paradigm. Within American anthropology it was not the only paradigm, but it was almost the only research paradigm. And it was, as it had always been, basically a humanistic rather than a genuinely scientific enterprise. From 1900 to 1930 (and to a considerable extent until after World War II), Indianology was the great humanistic dimension of American anthropology.

---

208. See, for example, Marshall Hyatt, *Franz Boas, Social Activist* (New York, 1990).
209. Cf. Nancy O. Lurie in Washburn, *History of Indian-White Relations*, pp. 549–550.

Indianology becomes anthropology & vice versa

Among the myopic tendencies that are exhibited in published histories of anthropology, none seems more extraordinary or more pernicious than the tendency to treat all American anthropology before about 1960 as exemplifying a single, Boasian paradigm. Certainly Boas and his students, and their students, cast an enormous shadow over the whole era, but their interests underwent a significant shift around 1930, as did those of the non-Boasian anthropologists who were entering the field in increasing numbers. These changes profoundly affected the attitude of anthropologists toward the Indians.

Many factors were involved in the change. First of all, there were not many tribes left that were wholly unstudied, and from that perspective the need for salvage could be regarded as a fait accompli.[210] Moreover, the dying off of elderly informants meant that in any case the chance to recover genuinely "traditional" culture was at an end, at least in most parts of the country. Perhaps most importantly, the anthropologists belatedly recognized that the "Vanishing Redman" was not in fact vanishing, either in a demographic or in a cultural sense. Demographically, his numbers had been increasing steadily since the beginning of the century.[211] Culturally, the highly influential Meriam Report of 1928 made it plain that the assimilationist policies pursued by the Bureau of Indian Affairs for fifty years were not having their desired effect.[212] The Indian cultures of the early twentieth century might have come a long way from their precontact origins, but they were still also far removed from the American mainstream. Whether or not this was seen to be desirable, it was evident in any case that something basically Indian was stubbornly persisting.

At the same time, the impact of British Functionalism began to be felt in America, largely through the teaching of A. R. Radcliffe-Brown at Chicago (1931–1936). This was a non-Boasian paradigm, and one that could be successfully applied only to the study of present-day, observable societies. Finally, it should be recalled again that the 1930s were an era dominated by ideologies of social concern. The Western world was plunged into economic depression and social turmoil, and Fascism, Communism, and the New Deal all flourished as ideologies dedicated to improving the lot of the common man. Within that intellectual climate it was simply not possible

---

210. Morris Opler once informed me that he was advised to do his doctoral research (1931–1937) among the Apache because they were the last major tribe that had not been studied.

211. See Snipp, *American Indians*, pp. 63–66.

212. Lewis Meriam et al., *The Problem of Indian Administration* (Baltimore, 1928).

for educated scholars to pursue an interest in the Indian past while shutting their eyes to the severe social, economic, and psychological problems besetting the Indians in the present. Belatedly, American Indianology developed a social conscience.

The upshot of all these developments was to refocus the interest of ethnologists from the past to the present. Ethnology at that point ceased to be primarily a culture-historical discipline, as it had been since its beginnings, and became much more a sociological one. This was to prove a far more important turning point in the history of American anthropology than was the so-called Boasian revolution of 1900, in terms of its impact not only on theory but on research activity as well.

From their altered perspective, the American anthropologists of the 1930s found new questions to ask about the Indians: in what ways had their cultures changed and not changed, what were the mechanisms of change, and what were the factors that inhibited change? Those questions gave rise to the two dominant lines of research in midcentury American Indian studies, which I have called the sociocultural and the configurationist. The sociocultural school focused on the processes of culture change, which were subsumed within the concept of acculturation. The configurationists focused on cultural persistence, and sought to identify the core values, themes, and cultural personality that persisted from generation to generation even while the more surficial aspects of culture were undergoing rapid change. Both kinds of study were seen to be important in the development of Indian policy for the future, and it was out of these researches that the subdiscipline of applied anthropology was born.[213]

But while ethnology shifted its focus from the past to the present, linguistics and archaeology did not follow along. Linguists continued to collect vocabularies and to write grammars of traditional Indian languages, as they had done for more than a century. Archaeologists until after World War II continued historically oriented researches, whose aim was to compile a comprehensive, continent-wide schema of Indian prehistory.[214] Meanwhile physical anthropology, at the insistence of Boas, had abandoned its preoccupation with race, and found itself without a central organizing concept or a clearcut research mission, especially with reference to the Indians.[215] The result of these developments was a conspicuous drawing apart of the four traditional subdisciplines, each of which from

213. Lurie in Washburn, *History of Indian-White Relations*, p. 552.

214. See Gordon R. Willey and Jeremy Sabloff, *A History of American Archaeology* (San Francisco, 1974), pp. 88–130.

215. See esp. George W. Stocking, Jr., *Race, Culture, and Evolution* (New York, 1968), pp. 161–194.

about 1930 to 1960 was pursuing a somewhat different research agenda. Only archaeology and linguistics remained genuinely Indianological in the old sense. Ethnologists were still mostly studying the Indians, but had in effect demystified them, and relegated them to the category of a generalized non-Western Other. From the 1930s onward, Indians were more of theoretical than of humanistic interest. Acculturation studies, community studies, and values studies were not in any way special to the Indians; they were studies that increasingly were carried out among all kinds of non-Western peoples.

Indianology becomes anthropology & vice versa

Anthropology bows out

America emerged from World War II with a vastly transformed and aggrandized self-image, and this transformation affected the image of the Indian as well. The United States was now a world power with worldwide responsibilities, the most immediate of which was to rebuild the war-shattered nations of Europe. Another, even more pressing responsibility was soon to emerge: the perceived need to oppose the worldwide spread of Communism. From that global perspective the problems of the Indians seemed to be very small potatoes indeed; especially since Indians like other Americans had generally prospered under the economy of the war years.

The new global outlook of the nation at large was, as usual, reflected in the outlook of anthropologists. The transformed postwar world was not only a subject of engaging interest; it also presented unique, undreamed-of new opportunities for field work. It must be recalled that the nations of Western Europe, though economically shattered at home, still held most of the Third World in colonial subjugation at the end of World War II: the empires of Britain, France, Belgium, the Netherlands, and Portugal were all substantially intact. And while the colonial powers had looked with a suspicious eye on anthropological research—especially by nationals other than their own—before the war, they could hardly refuse entry to American anthropologists at a time when their governments at home were receiving massive infusions of American aid. Suddenly, the entire colonial worlds of Africa, India, Southeast Asia, and Oceania were opened up to the Americans. Once again there were scores of unstudied tribes to be investigated; peoples far less culturally transformed and far more colorful than the Indians had now become available for study.[216]

In almost no time, Indians ceased to be the main focus of American ethnological research. On the reservations, most of the sociologically ori-

216. Cf. Lurie in Washburn, *History of Indian-White Relations*, p. 553.

ented studies launched during the 1930s had been suspended during the war for lack of funds, and many were never resumed. Nearly all of the anthropologists who had worked for the Indian Bureau during the Collier years were drawn initially into war-related research, and then, after the war, went off into overseas development programs and research. And the research that was resumed among the Indians continued the gradual process of demystification and routinization that had begun in the 1930s. As Nancy Lurie writes, "Many established anthropologists who had begun careers as North Americanists took advantage of postwar research opportunities to begin new research interests in more exotic, untouched areas. Thus, circumstances conspired to deflect intensive social and intellectual interest from the American Indians during a period when they could ill afford this kind of neglect."[217]

Meanwhile archaeology and linguistics also, rather abruptly, moved away from their Indianological roots. Some American prehistorians also fanned out overseas, though not in anything like the same numbers as did the ethnologists. The majority of them continued to work on North American sites, but with an entirely new perspective after the 1960s. Under the self-proclaimed "paradigm revolution" of New Archaeology, they announced that they were no longer interested in the Indians and their history; the only legitimate aim of archaeological research must be to test general, theoretical propositions that were independent of historical considerations.[218] The excavation of Indian remains was viewed as a means to an end, rather than an end in itself.

Linguists, led by Noam Chomsky, began searching for deeper levels of linguistic understanding than can be obtained from the study of imperfectly mastered Indian languages, and turned their attention to the deep analysis of their own mother-tongues.[219] Meanwhile physical anthropology for all practical purposes transformed itself into human biology.[220] Thus, in their different ways, all of the traditional subdisciplines of American anthropology cut themselves off from a tie to any particular data base, and became essentially theory-driven. Humanistic anthropology was not

217. Ibid.

218. Cf. Kent V. Flannery in *Scientific American* 217, no. 2 (1967): 119–122; Lewis R. Binford in Sally R. Binford and Lewis R. Binford, eds., *New Perspectives in Archaeology* (Chicago, 1968), pp. 5–32; and Paul S. Martin in *American Antiquity* 36, no. 1 (1971): 1–8.

219. See, e.g., Noam Chomsky, *Transformational Analysis* (Cambridge, Mass., 1955); id., *Current Issues in Linguistic Theory* (The Hague, 1964); id., *Language and Mind* (New York, 1968).

220. See Donna J. Haraway in George W. Stocking, ed., *Bones, Bodies, Behavior*, pp. 206–259. *History of Anthropology*, vol. 5 (1988).

wholly abandoned, but it now survived in the form of distinct, semipoetic modes of ethnographic expression rather than in the particularistic study of particular peoples. It was now the anthropologist rather than the subject people that was endowed with a mystique.

The Indians take exception

Indianology becomes anthropology & vice versa

If the 1930s witnessed a rapid change in the attitude of anthropologists toward Indians, the 1960s witnessed an equally profound (though perhaps not so rapid) change in the attitude of Indians toward the anthropologists.[221] This is not an easy movement to chart, because it is almost impossible for anyone to survey Indian public opinion, if indeed there is such a thing. American Indians today still belong to more than 500 tribes, still speak more than 200 languages, and reside on hundreds of reservations as well as in towns and cities across the United States. In the Southwest alone – the only region that is personally familiar to me – there are more than 20 tribes on more than 30 reservations, and on each reservation there is a wide divergence of attitudes toward Whites, including anthropologists. Among the Hopi, whole villages have split apart over this issue.[222] Under the circumstances no one, either Indian or White, can really speak for Indian opinion with any claim to authority. The generalizations that I offer here are as much intuitive as anything else; they are based on conversations with Indians of my acquaintance as well as on a certain amount of published literature, none of which can be regarded as authoritative.

Indian disenchantment was certainly in part a direct reaction to anthropological demystification. The Indians resented the loss of their special claim on the attention and the interest of the anthropologists, and the fact that they were now subjects merely of theoretical rather than of humanistic interest. But there were more pragmatic considerations as well. A very important factor was the termination policy adopted by the Bureau of Indian Affairs in 1952, and the anthropologists' perceived failure to speak out against it.[223]

The termination policy was another indirect consequence of America's new, global thinking. It was felt that, if we could put the nations of Europe back on their feet in a few short years, and end their dependence on us, we could surely do the same for the Indians who had been under our care for

---

221. See esp. Lurie in Washburn, *History of Indian-White Relations*, pp. 552–556.
222. See, among many sources, Mischa Titiev, *Old Oraibi*, pp. 69–96. *Papers of the Peabody Museum of American Archaeology and Ethnology*, Harvard University, vol. 22, no. 1 (1944). See also Laura Thompson and Alice Joseph, *The Hopi Way* (New York, 1965), pp. 46–48.
223. See esp. Lurie in Washburn, *History of Indian-White Relations*, pp. 552–553.

a century. All that was required was massive infusions of monetary aid, and this was freely forthcoming. But Indians immediately recognized the policy (which was in force only from 1952 to 1960) as a threat to their sovereignty, while anthropologists with a few exceptions did not. Indeed, many anthropologists had been accustomed to hear the Indians complain so insistently about the Indian Bureau for so many years that they took it for granted that the Indians would be happy to be free of the Bureau. They failed to recognize that Indians might complain about the Bureau, but they emphatically did not want to end the special status they had always enjoyed under the treaties and executive orders, and that was now threatened under the termination policy.

In the largest sense, however, Indian resentment against anthropologists can only be understood as part of a much more generalized resentment against Whites, which has been growing steadily since the decade of the 1950s. And this in turn is part of a still larger social phenomenon: the movement on the part of all American minority groups to assert themselves in their own voice, to demand more attention to their problems, a larger share of the nation's resources and opportunities, and a greater degree of cultural and social autonomy than they have been accorded in the postwar world. This too is an unintended but inevitable by-product of the new, global American outlook. It reflects a deeply held conviction on the part of minorities that the nation has been giving far too much of its attention–and resources–to the problems of peoples overseas, while neglecting equally needful and disadvantaged groups at home. Anthropologists, who rushed overseas and largely abandoned the Indians, stood accused in this respect along with the rest of the nation.

It is my impression, then, that Indian disenchantment is not so much with Indianology itself as with post-Indianological anthropology. Most of the Indians of my acquaintance are highly appreciative of the early ethnographic work that was done among them, and rely on the BAE and the Boasian ethnographies for an authentic record of their own earlier traditions.[224] What they resent is that anthropologists took over this time-honored ground and then abandoned it, relegating Indians to the status of a "mere" non-Western Other: a subject of theoretical rather than of humanistic interest. Similarly, I think that the New Archaeologists, who dug up Indian remains while professing no interest in the Indians, bear a heavy responsibility for the antipathy that Indians now feel toward all forms of archaeology.[225] And I think the significant growth of what I can only call

224. Cf. ibid., pp. 550–551.
225. Cf. Vine Deloria, Jr., in *American Antiquity* 57, no. 4 (1992): 595–598.

"Indigenous Indianology" in the latter part of the twentieth century represents in essence an attempt on the part of Indians to reclaim the ground that the anthropologists abandoned; to reestablish (or reinvent) the Indian mystique very much in the same terms as it was originally established by the Indianologists. This issue will be briefly considered at the end of the chapter.

The legacies

Indianology becomes anthropology & vice versa

Regardless of its theoretical pretensions, every science is shaped to a considerable extent by the special characteristics of its subject matter. American anthropology is no exception, nor are the anthropologies of Britain, France, and Germany. When, at the beginning of the twentieth century, American anthropology adopted the Indians as its primary subject matter, it did not fall heir simply to the body of Indianological scholarship that had accumulated during the nineteenth century. In a larger sense it fell heir also to the entire, complex body of literary, artistic, and ideological traditions surrounding the Indians, that had been accumulating for four centuries. Such a heavy intellectual and emotional baggage was bound to have a major imprint on the discipline, above all for those numerous American anthropologists who were attracted into anthropology from an earlier, particularistic interest in the Indians, and who entered the discipline with their attitudes already formed.

Some of the legacies of Indianology in present-day anthropology are obvious and will hardly be disputed by anyone. The most obvious, and surely the most permanent, is a vast and richly diverse ethnographic, linguistic, and archaeological archive. We recognize today, as many of the original authors did not, that this is not the record of a timeless aboriginal past. Just as every archaeological site report is the record of a community only at a certain moment in its existence, so every ethnography is a snapshot of a culture at one moment in its development. It cannot be taken as representative of the same culture a hundred years earlier, just as it emphatically is not a portrait of the culture a hundred years later (that is, in the ethnographer's own time). But the site reports and the ethnographies and the grammars–along with the older reports of the conquistadores, missionaries, and travelers–record whole chapters in Indian cultural history that would otherwise be lost to us. In sum, our ethnographic understanding of the Indians is based on a far richer and more complete historical (and prehistoric) record than is true for any of the other peoples we have studied.

The vast archive of Indianology, encompassing all the different kinds of literature discussed in this chapter, provides the empirical foundation for the flourishing subdiscipline of ethnohistory, sometimes now referred to as the "fifth subfield" of American anthropology. It is not uniquely American; there are ethnohistorians at work also in Africa, Indonesia, and other regions. But the subdiscipline originated, so far as I know, in North America, and certainly it is far more highly developed here than elsewhere. Although the ethnohistorians have occasionally attempted to define their enterprise in terms of a theoretical paradigm rather than of any particular database, this has not been very successful.[226] Ethnohistory is, on the contrary, the one subfield of American anthropology that remains genuinely Indianological.

Another legacy that seems obvious to me is the four-field tradition, which today is virtually unique to North America. During most of this century Europeans have not conceived of a close connection between ethnology, linguistics, archaeology, and physical anthropology, and they have occasionally ridiculed the Americans who do.[227] However, the connection becomes intelligible when the four subfields are seen as part of the total effort to define the American Indian in relation to the known worlds of nature and culture: something that became an overriding concern for Western thinkers from the moment when the New World was discovered.

Other legacies of Indianology are more subtle, and perhaps more controversial. I think it is safe to say that a great many American anthropologists, including many who have never worked among the Indians, nevertheless retain a kind of proprietary/paternalist attitude toward them. Thus, the profession can be counted on to speak out, in the form of newspaper articles or letters or resolutions of the American Anthropological Association, on almost any policy issue that affects Indians, whether or not it has anthropological implications. For fifty years the enterprise of studying and teaching about the Indians was almost wholly monopolized by anthropologists, and there arose an understandable tendency to feel that anything connected with the Indians was somehow "anthropological" by definition, because Indianology was wholly subsumed within anthropology. I think many anthropologists still resent the fact that the field of Indian studies has been so much invaded by psychologists, economists, and historians in the recent past.

I think too that, as a legacy of Indianology, Americans have tended to feel closer to their subjects, and to identify with them, more than have other anthropologists. This was partly a consequence of propinquity. Unlike

226. See Bruce G. Trigger in *Ethnohistory* 29 (1982): 1–19.
227. Cf. Åke Hultkrantz in *Current Anthropology* 9, no. 4 (1968): 289–310.

Africans and Polynesians, the Indians did not live a world away from their investigators; sometimes they lived in the next county. Without undue expense they could be visited and studied during summer vacations, on weekend trips to the reservations, or even in a nearby city workplace. There was, in addition, a sense of shared identity and shared experience. In many contexts the anthropologist and the Indian could identify with one another as fellow Americans. They endured the same weather, they paid the same taxes, they used the same highways, they saw the same movies, and they rubbed shoulders in many situations outside the research context. Very importantly, they fought side by side in the same wars, and this was a source of pride to both. The propensity to refer to "my people" is by no means unique to American anthropologists, but I think it is more common among them than it is among anthropologists of other nationalities.

Indianology becomes anthropology & vice versa

Paradoxically, the sense of involvement has very often been accompanied by a sense of guilt. As I noted in Chapter 3, the anthropological profession seems determined to take upon itself the burden of guilt and of atonement for the nation's past sins, where Indians are concerned. This becomes clear when we contrast the writing of anthropologists with that of historians on the subject of Indian-White relations. Historians seem able to approach this topic with a degree of detached objectivity, recognizing that there were no good guys and no bad guys, that is very rare in anthropological writing.[228] Historians have consistently recognized also that the relationship between Indians and Whites was an evolving, dynamic one, presenting new challenges and new opportunities in each generation, where anthropologists have been more prone to represent it is a kind of timeless confrontation between Good Indians and Bad Whites. In short, anthropologists to a very considerable extent continue to perpetuate the Good Indian/Bad White Man myth that is one of the most enduring legacies of Indianology. It is, of course, only one manifestation of the more general philosophy of Primitivism, discussed in Chapter 3.

Finally, I think it is fair to say that many anthropologists still retain in their minds, at least unconsciously, a kind of generalized model of Primitive Man. It is an unintended legacy of Progressivism, in which the model of Primitive Man was quite explicit from the time of Locke onward. The point I want to make here is that, insofar as American anthropologists have such an unconscious model in mind, it is nearly always the lengthened shadow of the American Indian. I think this is one of the most important points of distinction between American and European anthropologists, whose model of Primitive Man tends to wear an African or an

228. For discussion see Swagerty, *Scholars and the Indian Experience.*

Oceanian face. And our distinctively American vision may have been shaped, for many of us, less by anthropological reading than by the books we read and the films we saw in our early youth: the basic, popular literature of twentieth-century Indianology.

THE INDIAN VOICE

No discussion of Indianology would be complete without some mention of the Indians' own contribution to the subject. Until recently the Indian voice was a very muted one, yet there have always been, almost since the time of the first conquests, a few educated Indians who sought to make the Indian point of view known to a White audience. Both in Peru and in Mexico, histories of the Spanish conquest, as seen through Indian eyes, were written within a century after the conquests themselves.[229] In North America, where for a long time there was no literate Indian tradition, the voice of the Native American was heard largely in the form of oratory. Indian oratory was already celebrated for its rhetorical power in the time of Jefferson,[230] and a great many examples of Indian speeches were recorded and published by their White hearers simply because of their literary appeal.[231] In the later nineteenth century there also developed, in North America, a genre of Indian "autobiography," which now includes more than six hundred published works.[232] All but a handful of these were actually the work of White compilers, who stitched together into a connected narrative the scattered reminiscences of an Indian informant.[233] The few published autobiographies that are purely of Indian authorship were of course written by highly educated individuals, and they nearly all sound the "Up from Savagery" theme.

It is only in the twentieth century, and indeed largely in the last generation, that a genuine literary tradition has developed among North American Indians. As a result the Indian voice now has a very considerable power, not only among anthropologists and Indianologists but among the American public more generally, and indeed even in the halls of Congress.

229. See esp. Steve J. Stern, *Peru's Indian Peoples and the Challenge of Spanish Conquest* (Madison, Wis., 1982); Karen Spalding, *Huarochirí* (Stanford, Calif., 1984), pp. 106–167; and Scott O'Mack in *Ethnohistory* 40, no. 3 (1993): 488–489.

230. Cf. Jefferson, *Notes on the State of Virginia*, p. 63 and p. 227.

231. Many examples have been compiled in Annette Rosenstiel, *Red & White* (New York, 1983).

232. See H. David Brumble III, *An Annotated Bibliography of American Indian and Eskimo Autobiographies* (Lincoln, Neb., 1981), and Brumble, *American Indian Autobiography*, pp. 211–257.

233. Brumble, *American Indian Autobiography*, pp. 11–13.

It is heard today in many different forms: in poetry, in novels, in revisionist histories, in revisionist ethnographies, in political manifestos, and in outright polemics.

Although there are some distinguished Indian anthropologists, a good many of the Indian authors have been at pains to distance themselves from the traditional anthropological enterprise and from traditional anthropological representations. "It is for us to tell our own story, not for you to tell it," is the message that resonates through much of their work.[234]

The Indian voice

It is this insistence that has led to the establishment of Departments of Native American Studies in many North American universities; departments that privilege the Indian voice over the anthropological one.

But if Indian authors have distanced themselves from anthropology, they have not really distanced themselves from the older and broader traditions of Indianology. It is noteworthy that their works are virtually all written for a White audience, not for fellow Indians, and they seek, as did their predecessors back to the time of the Spanish conquests, to present the Indian not in his own traditional terms but in terms that the White Man can understand and appreciate. In so doing, they continue to sound the immemorial themes of Indianological literature: the Indian as Noble Savage, the Indian as Mighty Warrior, the Indian as a person of heightened aesthetic sensitivity, the Indian as Nature-lover and conservationist, and–especially in recent years–the Indian as Victim. Indians have increasingly appropriated Indianology, as did the anthropologists a century earlier, but they have changed it no more than did the anthropologists. They did not repudiate Indianology; they simply reclaimed it.

SUMMARY

Indianology is a term I have coined to describe a humanistic discipline, focused on the study, understanding, and appreciation of Native Americans. It is comparable in every respect, except in its subject matter, to the more familiar disciplines of Egyptology, Sinology, and Classics. Its origins, like theirs, trace back in the broadest sense to Renaissance humanism, and more specifically to the moment when the New World was discovered.

Indianology is not an ideology in quite the same sense as are Progressivism, Primitivism, and the doctrine of natural law, for it involves no assumptions about universal human nature or about history. It is, if anything, a particularistic ideology, which attaches special virtue not to

234. For discussion see esp. Lurie in Washburn, *History of Indian-White Relations*, pp. 552–556.

any abstract idea but to a particular people. However, it is probably best described as a passion, which demands no intellectual or rational justification.

Whether seen as noble or as monstrous or as merely childlike, the Native American captured the romantic imagination of Europeans as have no other peoples before or since. Within a century of Columbus's landing there arose an ever-growing body of literature, devoted to describing and interpreting the Indian for European readers. At first, information was derived from accounts written by the explorers and conquerors, which were sometimes brought together in great ethnographic compendia. A little later, missionaries came to settle for long periods among the Indians and to study their languages and customs; their reports vastly expanded and also in many ways corrected the vision of the conquistadores. After them came, in time, travelers, settlers, soldiers, and traders, who recorded their own experiences and impressions from their own particular perspectives. A special class of observers were the captives, whose years of forced residence among the Indians–made known in time in more than two thousand published accounts–provided a unique opportunity to observe native life a close range.

"Indianology"

Although the conquerors, missionaries, settlers, and others held widely differing views about Indian character, they all agreed on one characteristic: that of colorfulness. It was due to that special quality that the Indian became, and has ever since remained, an enormously popular figure in literature, in art, and in exhibitions. He came especially to be celebrated in children's literature, which had a strong formative influence on the minds of many young Europeans and Americans.

The Indian became for the first time a subject for systematic and objective study, rather than just for literary depiction, concurrently with American independence, and thanks in very large part to the genius of Thomas Jefferson. Jefferson insisted that study of all aspects of American natural history, including ethnology and archaeology, should be one of the basic objectives of the newly formed national government–a commitment that is reflected in the instructions that he gave to the Lewis and Clark exploring expedition. It was Jefferson's vision that inspired the early government-sponsored researches of Lewis Cass and Henry Schoolcraft, the work on Indian languages by Albert Gallatin, and the archaeological and ethnological investigations that were undertaken by the great surveys of the American West, after the Civil War. Finally, Jefferson's vision reached full fruition in 1879 with the founding of the Bureau of American Ethnology (BAE), a government institution devoted wholly to the scientific study of the Indians. The Bureau almost from the beginning was equally committed to ethnographic, linguistic, archaeological, and physical anthropological studies, since all of these were seen as contributing to our overall understanding of the Native American.

Summary

The Bureau of American Ethnology remained the main locus of Indianological research for more than a quarter-century, although there were also ethnological museums, involved to some extent in research, at Harvard and at the University of Pennsylvania. None of these however were connected with professional training programs, and their field workers were either all-purpose naturalists, or out-and-out amateurs. It was left to Franz Boas and his students, at the turn of the twentieth century, to found the first academic departments of anthropology in North America, with emphasis on professional training. Yet while these men and women created a new academic and professional discipline, the field research program that they undertook was almost wholly Indianological, and different in no important respect from the earlier work of the BAE.

As anthropology departments proliferated in universities, the Indianological enterprise at first came to be shared between universities and museums, and then to find its primary home in universities. However, there was very little change in research orientations and objectives until the 1930s, when for the first time anthropologists began to look upon their discipline less as a historical and more as a sociological one. As a result, emphasis among university anthropologists shifted from the attempted recovery of bygone Indian cultures to the study of present-day Indian communities, their problems and their adaptations. This development, however, affected mainly the ethnologists, while archaeologists and linguists continued to pursue what were essentially historical studies.

Simply as a "target of opportunity," the Indian remained not only the main but almost the sole focus of American anthropological research until after World War II. Then, America's new status as a world power with worldwide interests opened up whole new fields for ethnographic investigation in Africa, Asia, and Oceania, at the same time when most of the American tribes had seemingly been studied. Indian studies did not cease, but they came to be regarded as something of an intellectual backwater, while exciting new insights were coming from the ethnologists in Africa and New Guinea. Meanwhile, for other reasons, archaeologists, linguists, and physical anthropologists also turned away from a primary interest in Indians. For those who did continue the study of Native Americans, they had largely lost their special mystique, and become simply one of many possible objects of study.

But the long identification with Indianology played a critical role in shaping North American anthropology, and it has left many legacies. The most important, surely, is the vast archive of ethnological, linguistic, and archaeological information about the Indians that was compiled in the days when this was seen as the primary objective of the discipline. The most conspicuous legacy, professionally, is the four-field tradition: the continuing insistence that proper anthropology must include components of ethnology, archaeology, linguistics, and physical anthropology.

Finally, the defection of anthropologists has left the domain of Indianology free for Indians themselves to reclaim. The time-honored themes of Indianological literature today resonate more fully in the works of Indian writers and artists than they do in anthropology, or anywhere else.

CHAPTER 6

GERMAN IDEALISM

Unlike the philosophic traditions discussed in Chapters 2–4, the philosophy of German Idealism cannot be traced back to classical antiquity. Nevertheless, it was not without antecedents in the ancient world. The Greeks before Alexander, like the Germans before Bismarck, were neither an ancient civilization (in comparison to Egypt and Mesopotamia) nor an organized state. They were a collection of petty, frequently warring principalities, and were very conscious of their role as latecomers on the stage of civilization. Yet they had a powerful sense of their common Greekness, in contrast to the surrounding barbarians–a sense based not on polity or history but on their possession of a common language and common intellectual and cultural achievements. For many Greek thinkers the sense of Greekness conveyed also a sense of cultural superiority, as expressed in the boast of Pericles that "all of the world's culture had reached its culmination in Greece, and all Greece in Athens."[1] However, this feeling was not universally shared. On the contrary, a certain cultural relativism is evident in Herodotus: "if one were to offer men to choose out of all the customs in the world such as seemed to them the best, they would examine the whole number, and end by preferring their own; so convinced are they that their own usages far surpass those of all others."[2] This relativistic outlook was to be characteristic also of the German idealists.

THE HISTORICAL SETTING

What was true of Greece in the time of Socrates was true also of Germany

1. Pericles' Funeral Oration, as quoted by Spencer Harrington in *Archaeology* 45, no. 1 (1992): 34.
2. Quoted from Clyde Kluckhohn, *Anthropology and the Classics* (Providence, R.I., 1961), p. 30. The original is from the *Histories*, Book III, chapter 38.

up to the middle of the nineteenth century: it was a collection of petty principalities lodged uncomfortably between the superpower of France on the west and the despised Slavic "barbarians" on the east. Importantly, too, Germany until the last quarter of the nineteenth century was neither an imperial nor a colonial power,[3] and was therefore not committed to that ideology of cultural or religious or racial superiority that is virtually a political necessity for colonial powers. Sentiments of superiority were certainly not lacking among the German intelligentsia, but they were not a requirement of the political situation.[4] As Kroeber and Kluckhohn have written,

The historical setting

> In the decades following 1770 Germans for the first time began to contribute creatively to the general European civilization abreast of France and England, and in certain fields even more productively; but at the same time they remained a nationality instead of an organized or unified nation. Being politically in arrears, their nationalism not only took solace in German cultural achievement, but was led to appraise culture as a whole above politics. . . .[5]

Thus situated, the Germans developed a body of philosophical tradition which reflected their special historical situation, and which I will designate collectively as German Idealism. Its central and most distinctive feature was the separation of mind from matter, and the insistence on the primacy of mind. Beginning in the so-called German Enlightenment (*Aufklärung*) of the eighteenth century, this doctrine was developed successively through the philosophies of Kant, Herder, Hegel, and Windelband, among many others. It was brought to America, at least in part, by Franz Boas in 1887, although by the time of his arrival it had already taken root also in the large German-American community in which so many of Boas's first students were reared. Between them, Boas and his students fashioned in the early twentieth century a distinctive, idealist American anthropology that owed far more to the intellectual traditions of Germany than it did to England, France, or any other foreign source.[6]

German Idealism became, in the works of Kant and Hegel, an all-em-

---

3. Excepting, of course, Austria. It is significant that none of the German idealist philosophers were Austrian.

4. For discussion see Dorothy M. Figueira in *Comparative Civilizations Review* 25 (1991): 1–27.

5. A. L. Kroeber and Clyde Kluckhohn, *Culture, a Critical Review of Concepts and Definitions* (New York, n.d.), pp. 51–52.

6. Cf. Richard Handler in *Current Anthropology* 32, no. 5 (1991): 609.

bracing, world-system of philosophy, but we will be concerned here only with those aspects of the idealist tradition that were relevant to history and to culture. Four specific features of the tradition may be noted at the outset. First, because their major accomplishments before 1870 were intellectual and philosophical rather than political or technological, the Germans developed a kind of progressivist theory that emphasized the successive liberation of the human mind, or spirit (*Geist*), rather than the development of social institutions or technology. This enabled the German philosophers to place themselves at the summit of their own particular evolutionary scenario, as all proponents of progressivist theory have always done (cf. Chapter 2).[7] I will refer to this later as the tradition of Historical Universalism. Second, because the Germans had suffered a succession of foreign invasions and religious wars but had never been successfully conquered, their progressivist theory emphasized the theme of success through struggle (*Sturm und Drang*). As Frank Manuel puts it, "the education of the human race was no lark. There is throughout these writings a sense of the pain and anguish of growth."[8] Third, because they defined themselves in cultural and linguistic rather than in political terms, the Germans took a strong interest in the cultural differences between peoples, which they explained partly in environmental and partly in historical terms. Central to this perspective were the concepts of the *Volk* and the *Volksgeist*; the former designating a group of people united by language and culture, the latter the unique and enduring spirit embodied in the language and the culture. I will refer to this later as the tradition of Historical Particularism, which existed side by side with the tradition of Historical Universalism in German philosophy. Finally, because they remained a deeply religious people, the philosophical outlook of the Germans remained highly moralistic, emphasizing the duties rather than the rights of the individual as a member of society. In all these respects, the German philosophical outlook of the eighteenth and nineteenth centuries differed profoundly from that of the French, which we discussed extensively in Chapter 2.

German Idealism

It must be observed, before going further, that the term "Idealism," as applied to German philosophy, has no very precise or generally agreed definition. In the narrowest sense it has been used to label a specific, relatively brief period in the development of German thought, beginning with Kant (c. 1770) and ending with Hegel (1831). In its broadest sense it identifies a

7. This idea was most clearly articulated by Hegel; see W.H. Walsh, *Philosophy of History* (New York, 1960), p. 144.
8. Frank E. Manuel, *Shapes of Philosophical History* (Stanford, Calif., 1965), p. 118.

tendency toward mentalism and idealism that is conspicuous in nearly all German philosophy from the Enlightenment to the present. Idealism in the broad sense was not confined to the academic philosophers; it was embodied also in the liberal and humanistic poetry, fiction, and essays of Lessing, Schiller, Goethe, and a host of others–works that were known and revered by just about every educated German in the nineteenth century. In the end the general prevalence of Idealism among the German intelligentsia surely owed more to the poets than it did to the philosophers, who mostly wrote for one another rather than for a general audience.[9]

The historical setting

In the present chapter the term Idealism will be employed mainly in the broader sense. It must be repeated again, however, that the chapter will be concerned only with those aspects of German Idealism that are relevant to the study of history, culture, and society. It will not deal with theories of knowledge, truth, morality, or aesthetics, though all of these were also propounded by the great German system-builders.

One further word of terminological explanation is in order. The word "German" as employed here necessarily applies not to the citizens of a single country, but to all of the German-speaking inhabitants of central Europe. Before 1870 they were subjects of more than a dozen nations and principalities, and since that time they have still been divided between Germany, Austria, and Switzerland, to say nothing of the large German populations in Czechoslovakia and Russia. "German" therefore means German-speaking, and I hope that Austrian and Swiss readers will not be offended at being included under this umbrella term.

THE GERMAN ENLIGHTENMENT AND THE PHILOSOPHY OF HISTORY

German idealist philosophy had its roots in the movement that called itself the German Enlightenment (*Aufklärung*), and that began at about the same time as did the cognate movements in France and Scotland. Its acknowledged founders were the legal philosophers Christian Thomasius and Christian Wolff, whose work was briefly discussed in Chapter 4.[10] As we saw in that chapter, Thomasius and Wolff shared the general optimism and rationalism of their French and Scottish confrères. Toward the middle of the eighteenth century, however, Aufklärung philosophy began to take a somewhat different tack, retaining the idealism of the founders but in-

9. Cf. ibid., pp. 116–117.

10. See Frederick Copleston, *A History of Philosophy* (New York, 1985), Book Two, vol. VI, pp. 101–120.

creasingly rejecting their particular kind of pragmatic rationalism.[11] Germany at the time had still not fully recovered from the devastation of the Thirty Years' War (1616–1648), and this was reflected in the intellectual as well as in the political life of the country. The German thinkers lacked both the bumptious self-confidence of the French and the moral certitude of the Scots. They were less inclined to take anything for granted, and, far more than their French and Scottish contemporaries, they were given to metaphysical speculations about the nature and the meaning of things. As Manuel puts it, "Political dormancy made the Germans more speculative and imaginative, less cut-and-dried, and often less sensible than their French counterparts."[12] The theme of metaphysical speculation continues to resonate through nearly all German philosophy down to the present day.

German Idealism

One of the things about which the Germans liked to speculate was history. As Peter Reill writes, "The accepted model of historical understanding was an unstable mixture of classical, medieval, and humanist elements circumscribed by and crammed into the traditional Christian interpretation of universal history. Universal history provided both a means of interpreting and selecting facts and a convenient framework for periodizing time."[13] The Germans like the French recognized the obsoleteness of this model, yet they also recognized that elimination of the traditional Christian interpretation left the recorded facts of history with no obvious meaning. Moreover, in marked contrast to the French, they were mostly devoutly religious men, who felt that there must be some moral lesson or pattern in history.[14]

The French and Scottish thinkers were also preoccupied with understanding history in a new light, as we saw in Chapter 2. However, their philosophy of history can be summed up in a single word: progress. They got around the problem of facts by inventing their own; that is, by writing conjectural scenarios of prehistory in keeping with their faith in progress. But the Germans, at least in this area of their philosophy, were much less apriorist. Rather than imposing order *on* history, as the French and Scots had done, they sought to find order *in* history, partly through empirical study and partly through the exercise of abstract logic. As Bury has written, their enterprise was one of "fitting into a connected narrative, the histories of various peoples who came into relations with one another, within a given range, so that they are drawn out of their isolation and recognized to have

11. Ibid., pp. 135–149.
12. *Shapes of Philosophical History*, p. 117.
13. Peter Hanns Reill, *The German Enlightenment and the Rise of Historicism* (Berkeley, Calif., 1975), p. 9.
14. Ibid., p. 43.

meaning... in the common history of man."[15] For this reason conjectural prehistory never figured prominently in the formulations of the Germans, as it did in those of the French and the Scots.

The German Enlightenment

It is not necessary in this work to give further consideration to individual thinkers of the German Enlightenment,[16] for at the end of the eighteenth century their influence was very largely supplanted by the new, transcendental philosophical system propounded by Immanuel Kant. It is sufficient to note that, in a very general way, the Aufklärung philosophers prepared the ground for the later historical philosophy that developed partly out of, and partly in reaction to, their particular version of rationalism. Their single most lasting contribution was perhaps their recognition that "societies were regulated by the feelings, the beliefs, the ideas, the habits of heart and mind of the men who compose them. These shared communal feelings, embodied in custom, language, and law, formed the character, or spirit, of the times."[17] In other words, history for the Germans encompassed the history of culture, or of mind, much more than it did the development of society or of polity.

THE DUALISTIC PRINCIPLE

As we saw in Chapter 4, the overwhelming trend in Western philosophic thinking has been monistic. *Homo sapiens* has been regarded as part of the natural order, and the effort has been made to develop or discover laws that would explain both man and nature (i.e., mind and matter) according to a single set of principles. But the essence of German philosophy from the Enlightenment to the present has been dualistic: the conception of mind and matter as separate realms governed by different principles. The study of history was the study of mind; the study of nature was the study of matter. The separation of history from nature was a theme repeatedly emphasized by the German philosophers.[18]

It is important to recognize, then, that when the Germans philosophized about history, they were talking about much more than we would understand by the term today. History for the Germans embraced not only all human events, but all human institutions. Having set history apart from nature, they were left with no way to understand society, polity, or

15. J. B. Bury, *Ancient Greek Historians* (New York, 1958), p. 45.

16. For much more extended and individualized discussion, see Reill, *German Enlightenment and the Rise of Historicism*; also Copleston, *History of Philosophy*, Book Two, vol. VI, pp. 101–149.

17. Reill, *German Enlightenment and the Rise of Historicism*, p. 161.

18. See esp. R. G. Collingwood, *The Idea of History* (New York, 1956), pp. 165–166.

culture except as historical phenomena. It should be recalled too that in the eighteenth and earlier nineteenth centuries the various social sciences had not yet taken shape as independent disciplines. Thus, the German philosophy of history embraced not only what today we would call history, but nearly all of what we would call sociology, political science, economics, and cultural anthropology. In that respect the historical philosophy of the Germans was equivalent to the moral philosophy of the Scots; both were in effect the study of man.[19]

German Idealism

While the Germans drew a clear distinction between the natural sciences and what they called history (i.e., the human sciences), within the latter category they did not make a distinction between what today we would call the social sciences and the humanities. Both were viewed as aspects of a kind of generalized study of mind, which later came to be called *Geisteswissenschaft.* This conflation was inevitable in the eighteenth century, when the special quantitative methods and the probabilistic theories of social science had not yet developed. However, the German conflation of the social sciences and the humanities persisted right through into the twentieth century, and it exerted a considerable influence on the early anthropology of the Boasians, as we will see later.

The philosophy of history developed by the Germans has been labeled both as rationalist and as progressivist, inviting comparison in both respects with the Enlightenment traditions of France and Scotland. But the comparison obscures more than it clarifies, for both rationality and progress meant something very different to the Germans than they did to the French and the Scots. The historical outlook of the French, and to a lesser extent of the Scots, was societal, pragmatic, and to a considerable degree materialist, while that of the Germans was individualist and mentalist. The French located man clearly within the natural order, while the Germans set him apart from it. As a result the Germans viewed history as a process of human mental development having its own internal dynamic, and without much reference to external influences. Progress for the French was measured by the advancement of society, while for the Germans it was measured by the increasing enlightenment of the individual mind. In the French and Scottish schemes reason was primarily a means to practical ends, while to the Germans it was always an end in itself.

The difference was also, and importantly, one between a world in being and a world in becoming–a philosophical distinction originally noted by the Germans themselves.[20] The rational world of the French, especially,

19. Cf. Walsh, *Philosophy of History,* p. 123.
20. Cf. Copleston, *History of Philosophy,* Book Three, vol. VII, p. 177.

was a world in being. Man had always been a rational creature, and had employed his reasoning power to achieve an increasing mastery over nature, and to construct increasingly effective social and economic systems. For the Germans, however, man had not always been rational; he was evolving toward rationality as his mind gradually freed itself from the trammels of tradition and mythology. Thus, where the triumph of reason to the French and Scots was measured by man's increasing mastery over nature, to the Germans it was measured simply in his mastery over himself. Utopia, for the French and Scots, was to be a world characterized by an ideally democratic social order; for the Germans it was to be a world in which all human minds were totally free to exercise the individual will of the thinker. The freedom of the mind became, in effect, the watchword of German Idealism.

The dualistic principle

German philosophy thus embodied a kind of logical paradox. When reason was conceived as an end in itself, it became itself a somewhat mystical concept, rather like the *logos* of the ancients. Rationalism, as embraced in German philosophy, involved not so much the exercise of reason as the worship of reason. Thus German philosophy can be, and has been, identified both as rationalist and as mystical, or in other words as rational and anti-rational. It is this paradoxical quality, I think, that makes German historical philosophy so difficult to access by pragmatic-minded British and American thinkers, not excluding the present author.

THE IDEALIST HISTORICAL TRADITIONS: UNIVERSALIST AND PARTICULARIST

The philosophy of Immanuel Kant, partly discussed in Chapter 4, is usually taken as marking the end of the German Enlightenment and the beginning of Idealism, narrowly defined.[21] Its author has sometimes been identified as a revolutionary figure in the history of philosophy in general; one whose *Critique of Pure Reason* (1781) and *Critique of Practical Reason* (1786) broke cleanly with the Progressivism of the Enlightenment, clearing the way for the development of transcendental and romantic philosophies. But while his philosophy marked a revolutionary break with respect to the pragmatic and teleological Progressivism of the French and Scottish enlightenments, his general perspective, and in particular his philosophy of history, had much in common with the mentalistic and idealistic traditions that were already at least clearly implicit in earlier thinkers of the Ger-

21. Walsh, *Philosophy of History*, p. 122; Bertrand Russell, *A History of Western Philosophy* (New York, 1945), p. 703.

man Enlightenment. His work does not really represent either the final end of the Aufklärung or the earliest beginning of Idealism, but rather the pivotal transition point between the two.

Kant was the first of a series of comprehensive system-builders, some of whom had been his pupils, and all of whom were heavily influenced by him. Of their work and outlook in general Bertrand Russell has written:

German Idealism

> The critique of knowledge, as a means of reaching philosophical conclusions, is emphasized by Kant and accepted by his followers. There is an emphasis on mind as opposed to matter, which leads in the end to the assertion that only mind exists. There is a vehement rejection of utilitarian ethics in favour of systems which are held to be demonstrated by abstract philosophical arguments. There is a scholastic tone which is absent in the earlier French and English philosophers; Kant, Fichte, and Hegel were university professors, addressing learned audiences, not gentlemen of leisure addressing amateurs.[22]

It may be said in sum that German Idealism was quintessentially the philosophy of mind, whose collective manifestation was culture.

Although the overall philosophical systems of the German idealists had much in common, their philosophies of history developed along two rather different lines. In one group were the universalists, from Kant to Hegel, who continued the Enlightenment tradition of *Weltgeschichte*–that is, of constructing universal histories of mankind, without regard for regional differences. They were interested in cultural differences only between one age and the next, not between one people and another: in *culture* rather than in *cultures*. In the other group were the particularists, exemplified especially by Herder, who were interested in the differences in culture from age to age, but even more in the differences from one people to another. These two historical traditions were to influence later anthropological thinking in quite different ways, and they will be considered separately here.

Historical Universalism

Kant was somewhat unusual among German philosophers in that he was not greatly interested in history, which occupied only a small place in his overall philosophical system. Indeed he was one of the few idealists who

22. Russell, *History of Western Philosophy*, p. 704.

cannot be identified primarily as a philosopher of history. He did nevertheless propose a certain approach to history in an essay, *An Idea for a Universal History from the Cosmopolitan Point of View*, published in 1784. Like his Aufklärung predecessors he was an out-and-out universalist and was not concerned with the explanation of cultural differences. Although he was the first writer to use the term anthropology in the title of a book,[23] he meant by it the study of universal human nature, not the study of particular cultures.[24]

The idealist historical traditions

Kant had argued, with respect to natural law, that the assumption that nature has purposes cannot be proven either empirically or philosophically. Nevertheless, nature is unintelligible unless the existence of a purpose or purposes is presupposed. He took exactly the same position with regard to history: it could only be intelligible if some overriding purpose was assumed in advance. The task of the philosopher was therefore to devise some schema that would make the known facts of history both philosophically meaningful and morally defensible. He had, as Walsh puts it, "to show that, first appearances notwithstanding, history is a rational process in the double sense of one proceeding on an intelligible plan and tending to a goal which moral reason can approve."[25]

Kant proceeded to demonstrate this by purely philosophical, and teleological, arguments. Then, having persuaded himself that history does indeed involve a law of progress, he had to explain why this should be so, and how it came about. From a moralistic standpoint the problem was a serious one, since Kant shared the common, primitivistic view that the earlier, prerational state of human society was the happier one.[26] His explanation for progress was a surprising one, departing markedly from the optimistic idealism of the French and Scottish thinkers. The force driving progress, in Kant's view, was not man's conscious drive toward wisdom, virtue, and rationality, but rather his baser impulses of pride, ambition, and greed. These evil elements made the continuation of a stagnant and peaceful society impossible: they gave rise to conflicts between each individual's desire for a peaceful and friendly life with his neighbors and his desire to dominate and exploit his neighbors. It was the resulting discontent with his place under the status quo that drove man to overthrow it and to build new institutions in place of the old.[27] Therefore, "the force which serves as

---

23. *Anthropologie in pragmatischer Einsicht abgefasst von Immanuel Kant* (Königsberg, 1798).
24. Cf. Copleston, *History of Philosophy*, Book Two, vol. VI, p. 311.
25. Walsh, *Philosophy of History*, p. 123.
26. On this point see esp. Collingwood, *Idea of History*, pp. 99–100.
27. Ibid., pp. 100–101.

mainspring of [progress] cannot be human reason but must be the opposite of reason, that is, passion: intellectual ignorance and moral baseness."[28] This last proposition was to have enormous consequences for the later development of German historical philosophy, for it is clearly the wellspring of the dialectical tradition later elaborated and made famous by Fichte, Hegel, and Marx.

The dialectical element

German Idealism

Like the concepts of *Volk* and *Geist*, to be discussed later, the dialectic was a uniquely German contribution to philosophy, and one that was rooted in special historical circumstances. Germany since the early seventeenth century had been swept over by a seemingly endless succession of wars and foreign invasions. The Germans, like the ancient Greeks, had come to regard war at the very least as an inevitable part of the human experience, and at best as a cleansing and strengthening experience that could lead to cultural and moral progress. This outlook found expression in the philosophy of *Sturm und Drang* (storm and stress)–the perception of the natural world not as a peaceful kingdom but as a place where mighty, opposing forces were always in contention. The *Sturm und Drang* motif was already well developed in German romantic literature of the eighteenth century,[29] and it was also at least foreshadowed in the philosophical writing of the German Enlightenment. That is, the Aufklärung philosophers believed that history was propelled forward by the dynamic tension or conflict between the spirit of the times (*Zeitgeist*), the spirit of particular peoples (*Volksgeist*), and the spirit of groups or corporations (*Gesellschaftsgeist*).[30]

The dialectical concept was to find much more articulate expression in the work of Kant, and even more in that of his successors, Fichte and Hegel. In time it became a component both of German Progressivism and of German Primitivism. The progressivists, led by Fichte and Hegel, saw progress as arising out of the conflict between opposing ideas, while primitivists, exemplified by Nietzsche and Wagner, harked back nostalgically to a heroic age of conflict between titans. Throughout most of the nineteenth century, German Idealism had to accommodate itself in one way or another to the *Sturm und Drang* motif.

28. Ibid., pp. 101–102; italics in the original.
29. See esp. Edith Runge, *Primitivism and Related Ideas in Sturm und Drang Literature* (Baltimore, 1946); also Oskar Walzel, *German Romanticism*, trans. Alma Lussky (New York, 1932), pp. 3–15.
30. See Reill, *German Enlightenment and the Rise of Historicism*, pp. 180–181.

The man usually, though erroneously, credited with introducing *Sturm und Drang* into German philosophy was Johann Gottlieb Fichte, a onetime pupil of Kant. He, and most of the other early idealist philosophers, followed the example of Kant in attempting to develop a single, unified system embracing all the different domains of human knowledge and experience–something which they believed that Kant had failed to do. Fichte's specific vision of history was set forth mainly in *The Characteristics of the Present Age,* published in 1806. His outlook, like that of Kant, was universalistic and wholly mentalistic. He went well beyond Kant, however, in the specificity of his dialectic theory. Fichte believed that each stage of history was characterized by the dominance of a particular idea, which affected every detail of life. But every dominant idea necessarily generated opposition to itself, resulting in a struggle that culminated–always temporarily–in the dominance of a new idea, setting the stage for a new struggle. It was Fichte who first introduced the terms thesis, antithesis, and synthesis–later made famous by Hegel and Marx–to describe the dialectic of ideas in history.

The idealist historical traditions

The philosophical system of Friedrich von Schelling showed affinities both with the universalism of Fichte and with the particularism of Herder (to be discussed later).[31] Schelling's historical outlook was basically universalistic, and he accepted in somewhat modified form the dialectical theory of Fichte. The earlier stage of history, in Schelling's view, was one in which men conceived themselves passively as part of nature, and worshipped nature; in the second they passed on to a stage of historical self-consciousness in which they worked out their own destinies in accordance with their consciousness of the absolute. The relationship between the two stages was dialectical, in that historical self-consciousness arose as a natural opposition to the unreflective acceptance of nature.[32]

German Idealist philosophy, in the narrower sense, reached its culmination in the work of Georg W. F. Hegel, published between 1801 and 1831. Hegel is generally acknowledged as the greatest of the idealists,[33] and one whose influence for a time reached far beyond the borders of Germany.[34] Taken as a whole, his philosophical system was the most complex, the most purely mentalistic, and, by general consensus, the most obscure of all the German philosophies–which is saying a good deal on all three counts.[35]

---

31. For a résumé of his works see Copleston, *History of Philosophy,* Book Three, Vol. VII, pp. 94–97.
32. See esp. Collingwood, *Idea of History,* pp. 111–113.
33. Copleston, *History of Philosophy,* Book Three, Vol. VII, p. 159.
34. See Russell, *History of Western Philosophy,* p. 730.
35. Cf. ibid.

Even Goethe, who greatly admired Hegel, confessed that he could not understand him,[36] while Sutton insists that he has been seriously misunderstood by nearly all of his most devoted followers.[37]

Hegel's philosophy of history was implicit at many points in the vast corpus of his writings, but it was spelled out systematically only in a course of lectures that were not published until after his death.[38] Apart from its highly abstruse metaphysics the system really contained relatively little that was new, and it would merit little attention except for the enormous influence that it exerted on Karl Marx and Friedrich Engels. Hegel took over in toto the dialectical theory of Fichte, with its recurring triads of thesis-antithesis-synthesis. Believing that reason is the only reality, however, he felt obliged to "prove" the reality of the dialectic not by reference to the facts of history but by arguments from abstract logic. As Malefijt has written, "Hegel began by stating that the moving power of history was its own spirit, its *Weltgeist,* by which he meant that history possessed an inherent predisposition to move and develop in a certain given direction. This predisposition was "reason" and the direction it took was toward the increase of human freedom."[39] By "human freedom" Hegel (like Kant and Fichte) meant not liberty of the person but the free exercise of reason, untrammeled by custom or religion.

German Idealism

Hegel was somewhat inconsistent when he asserted that, although abstract reason is the only reality, the dialectical theory must nevertheless find confirmation in the actual facts of history before it can be accepted.[40] He found seeming confirmation in the progression of "world" history through four stages–Oriental, Greek, Roman, and German–each dominated by a basic idea, or *Geist,* which nevertheless contained within it the seeds of its own destruction. The dialectical progression of the four "world-historical" stages involved at each stage an increasing liberation of the human spirit. This formulation was to provide the foundation for the later periodization of history by Marx and Engels–a component of their general theory that has proven troublesome ever since, as we will see in Chapter 7.

The idealist tradition of *Weltgeschichte* did not by any means end with Hegel. Indeed it reached its widest popularity in the works of the so-called

36. Claud Sutton, *The German Tradition in Philosophy* (New York, 1974), p. 58.

37. Ibid., p. 59.

38. Originally as *Vorlesungen über die Philosophie der Weltgeschichte,* edited by Edward Gans (Berlin, 1837); trans. by J. Sibree as *Lectures on the Philosophy of History* (London, 1861).

39. Annemarie deWaal Malefijt, *Images of Man* (New York, 1974), p. 103.

40. Cf. Walsh, *Philosophy of History,* pp. 141–142; Sutton, *German Tradition in Philosophy,* pp. 59–60.

postidealists, especially Schopenhauer, Nietzsche, and Spengler.[41] In contrast to their pedantic predecessors, these authors wrote in an overtly romantic and at times an apocalyptic style, making no pretense to intellectual rigor. It was surely for that reason that they were much more widely read and discussed in intellectual circles, especially outside Germany, than were Kant and Hegel. It was probably for the same reason, however, that they had almost no influence on the later development of anthropological thought, and they need not be further considered here.

The idealist historical traditions

Historical Particularism

German Historical Particularism exerted a much greater influence on the subsequent development of anthropological thinking than did Universalism. As with so many other aspects of idealist thought, the earliest roots of this tradition trace back to the Aufklärung. The way was actually led by historians of religion, the so-called neologists, who sought to retain a deep Christian faith while at the same time redefining the church as a purely human institution and the product of historical circumstances.[42] From this perspective all Christian doctrines and sects were recognized as being valid for their own times and places, and in the broader sense so too were all religions. And since many of the neologists treated religion and society as interdependent phenomena, their religious relativism became in effect a more general cultural relativism.[43]

The concept of *Geist* (usually translated as "spirit") was widely employed by the Aufklärung philosophers, but they never attempted to define it systematically. They used it variously to mean the spirit of the times (*Zeitgeist*), national character (*Volksgeist*), the spirit of groups or corporations (*Gesellschaftsgeist*), the spirit of events (*Geist der Begebenheiten*), or the overall driving force of human creativity (unmodified *Geist*). As we saw a little earlier, it was the dynamic tension between these sometimes conflicting forces that was seen as propelling history forward.[44]

The Geist concept was invoked by the German Enlightenment philosophers mainly in their attempt to define the German Self: to identify the essential factor that made Germans different from other Europeans.[45] They did not apply it in a systematic way to anyone but themselves and their own historical predecessors. They nevertheless laid the foundation for a more

---

41. See esp. Sutton, *German Tradition in Philosophy*, pp. 77–99.
42. Reill, *German Enlightenment and the Rise of Historicism*, p. 162.
43. Ibid., pp. 165–172.
44. Ibid., pp. 180–181.
45. See esp. ibid., pp. 180–189.

general cultural particularism and relativism, when later philosophers began to apply the Geist concept to all of the world's peoples and cultures.

Historical Particularism also drew some of its inspiration from Kant, but it owed less to his specific philosophy of history than to his more general Transcendentalism. His doctrine of "the thing in itself"–the idea that everything and everyone most be understood on its own terms, and without reference to anything else or to any purpose–laid both the epistemological and the moral foundation for later German particularism. In the study of mankind, Kant had insisted that the autonomous will of each individual is fundamental, and this could easily be extended by his successors to the idea that the autonomous will of each *Volk* is fundamental. In that sense Kant can be held responsible both for the cultural particularism and for the cultural relativism that became essential features of German ethnology.

German Idealism

However, the undoubted father of German Historical Particularism as an articulate philosophy was Johann Gottfried Herder, another onetime pupil of Kant. Herder's contribution to the subsequent development of German Idealism has been vastly underrated, both in his own country and abroad. There are probably several reasons for this neglect. To begin with, his published oeuvre is massive, muddled, and frequently obscure: Rationalism and Mysticism, Progressivism and Primitivism, Deism and Agnosticism seem to tumble over one another in a disorderly progression in his pages. There is, consequently, no one clearcut philosophical message. It is possible to cite specific passages to show that Herder was for or against almost anything. Boas, for example, identified him as a geographical determinist,[46] while Calabrese denies that this was an important element in his thinking.[47] To make matters worse, Herder had the temerity to quarrel both with his mentor Kant and with his pupil and erstwhile friend Goethe–two of the sacrosanct figures of German philosophy. Nevertheless, as Kroeber and Kluckhohn have written,

> Herder's scope, his curiosity and knowledge, his sympathy, imagination, and verve, his enthusiasm for the most foreign and remote of human achievements, his extraordinary freedom from bias and ethnocentricity, endow his work with an indubitable quality of greatness. He sought to discover the peculiar values of all peoples and cultures....[48]

46. *The Mind of Primitive Man* (New York, 1938), p. 32.
47. John Calabrese, *Herder and Anthropology* (MS in the author's possession), p, 70.
48. Kroeber and Kluckhohn, *Culture*, p. 39.

Herder's main ideas that are relevant to us here were set forth in his four-volume *Ideen zur Philosophie der Menschengeschichte* (Ideas about the Philosophy of the History of Mankind), published between 1784 and 1791. Here, as everywhere in his writing, his message was not entirely clear or consistent, so that he has been identified at times both as a racist and an antiracist, a progressivist and an antiprogressivist. He was adamant in condemning the conventional racial typologies of his time, yet he believed at least to some extent in the genetic inheritance of cultural characteristics –the Geist of each culture.[49] Herder was also outspokenly critical of the three-stage models of evolution, based on modes of subsistence, that were proposed by the French and Scottish progressivists, discussed in Chapter 2. He was far ahead of his time in recognizing that most of the world's primitive peoples lived by a combination of foraging, animal husbandry, and agriculture, so that these could not really be viewed as successive stages of development.[50] But Herder proposed instead his own, highly original three-stage version of history, which owed almost nothing to the French and Scottish traditions of conjectural history.

The idealist historical traditions

In Herder's scheme, the first, relatively brief stage of history was the time between the first appearance of man and the emergence of regionally differentiated cultures; the time when there was, in effect, a single, worldwide prehistoric culture. The second and by far the longest stage, which Herder called the *Volk* stage, comprised the familiar world divided into separate peoples with separate languages and traditions. The third stage, brief and as yet incomplete, was marked by the gradual worldwide spread of modern Western civilization, which would eventuate once again in a single, worldwide culture. Herder called this the Historical stage because, in his view, Volk cultures were in a state of timeless equilibrium, and therefore had no historical self-consciousness.

Whatever Herder's historical vision may have been, it was always the Volk that captured his strongest sympathies and interest.[51] His use of the term, as of most other terms, was not entirely clear or consistent. It referred to all of the world's peoples before the rise of Western industrial civilization, but also at times to the less educated elements that persisted within the European societies of his own time.[52] In other words, the Volk concept lumped together primitives, peasants, and proletarians–a conjunction that was also commonly made by progressivists in the eighteenth century,

49. Gottfried Herder, *Outlines of Philosophy of the History of Man*, trans. T. Churchill (London, 1803), Book VIII, Chapter 2.

50. Ibid., Book VIII, Chapter 3, p. 202.

51. For additional discussion, see Malefijt, *Images of Man*, pp. 99–102.

52. See esp. Georgiana Simpson, Herder's Conception of "Das Volk." Unpublished Ph.D. dissertation, Department of Germanics, University of Chicago, 1921.

as we saw in Chapter 4. We may also note here that Herder's Volk corresponded rather closely to the conception of folk culture formulated by Robert Redfield in the middle of the twentieth century—a theoretical development that will occupy us later in the chapter.

In sum, Volk-ness was an evolutionary stage defined not by material circumstances but by a particular mind-set, which had been characteristic of all mankind during most of its history, and which still persisted among all but the educated elites in European countries. It was the mind-set characterized by a timeless, nonreflective adherence to traditions—the Volksgeist—that had arisen through the conjunction of man's creative imagination and the environmental and climatic conditions peculiar to each region. Herder's distinction between the Volk and the "historic" mindsets clearly anticipates the distinction later made by Ferdinand Tönnies between *Gemeinschaft* and *Gesellschaft,*[53] and also Lévy-Bruhl's distinction between the prelogical primitive mentality and the logical civilized mentality.[54]

At the heart of the Volk mind-set was the Geist particular to each people. This term, too, was never very precisely defined. It clearly did not embrace the whole of culture, but only that portion of the culture that was unique to each Volk—essentially what twentieth-century anthropologists would call the culture core. The Geist was unchanging through time and was transmitted from generation to generation mainly through the education of children, but perhaps also to some extent by genetic inheritance. Herder anticipated Durkheim and Weber, as well as Tönnies and Lévy-Bruhl, in assigning priority to myth and ritual among the components of the Geist.[55]

If Herder's theoretical and moral contribution is problematical, his role as a concept giver is not. He did not actually originate the concepts either of the Volk or of the Geist, but it was he who made them the basic organizing concepts of German particularism.[56] Collingwood states that "Herder, so far as I know, was the first thinker to recognize in a systematic way that there are differences between different kinds of men, and that human nature is not uniform but diversified. Herder is thus the father of anthropology, meaning by that the science which (*a*) distinguishes the various physical types of human beings, and (*b*) studies the manners and customs of these various types. . . ."[57]

While the identification of Herder as the father of anthropology has

53. In his *Gemeinschaft und Gesellschaft* (Leipzig, 1887).
54. Initially in *Les Fonctions Mentales dans les Sociétés Inférieures* (Paris, 1910).
55. Herder, *Philosophy of the History of Man,* Book VIII, Chapters 3 and 4.
56. See esp. Simpson, Herder's Conception of "Das Volk."
57. Collingwood, *Idea of History,* pp. 90–91.

not been widely acknowledged within the profession, he undoubtedly deserves recognition as the modern-day father of Cultural Relativism. Indeed his commitment to this doctrine was adamant: he spoke out repeatedly and vehemently against all forms of colonialism, imperialism, and slavery. "O man, honor thyself; neither the pongo nor the gibbon are thy brother: the american and the negro are: these therefore thou shouldst not oppress, or murder, or steal; for they are men, like thee...."[58] More broadly, Herder may be identified also as the father of the concept of *cultures* in the specific, plural sense, as opposed to *culture* in the generic sense. This issue will occupy us again later in the chapter.

The idealist historical traditions

Historical Particularism was almost wholly absent in the works of Fichte and Schelling, but then resurfaced to a modest degree in Hegel. Unlike Fichte and Schelling, and even Herder, Hegel did not believe that history would culminate in the emergence of a single civilization or of a single state. He believed–following Herder–that the creative force of the world as a whole was manifest in the *Volksgeister* of individual peoples, and that these were part of history's purpose. "Every nation has its own characteristic principle or genius, which reflects itself in all the phenomena associated with it.... And every nation has a peculiar contribution which it is destined, in its turn, to make to the process of world history. When a nation's hour strikes, as it does but once, all other nations must give way to it, for at that particular epoch it, and not they, is the chosen vehicle of the world spirit."[59] This was, however, in obvious contradiction to the generally universalistic tone of Hegel's philosophy.

In the later nineteenth century German Historical Particularism developed in two rather different directions, which I will here call German Nationalism and Ethnic Idealism. German Nationalism was the ideology driving the unification of the many German kingdoms in the 1860s and 70s. It was a thoroughly statist and chauvinist doctrine, emphasizing not only the distinctness of the Germans but also their superiority over other peoples, and their historically ordained destiny to rule over non-Germans. This doctrine evolved through Hegel, Nietzsche, and Kossina into the excesses of Nazism.[60] Ethnic Idealism on the other hand was egalitarian and nonstatist: the Germans served merely to exemplify the historical and cultural uniqueness of all *Völker*. If the cultural autonomy of the Germans entitled them to aspire toward political unity and autonomy, so also did the cultural autonomy of all other peoples. Evolving through the

58. Herder, *Philosophy of the History of Man*, vol. VII, part I, p. 166.

59. Walsh, *Philosophy of History*, p. 144; see also Sutton, *German Tradition in Philosophy*, pp. 73–74.

60. For discussion, see esp. Figueira in *Comparative Civilizations Review*, pp. 1–6.

works of Herder, Windelband, and Dilthey, the ethnic idealist position gave birth in time to the morphological school of biology, to Gestalt psychology, to the historicist movement in history, and to the semisacred doctrine of Cultural Relativism in anthropology.

Throughout the nineteenth century German particularism found expression not only in the tomes of the philosophers, but also in the work of the German ethnologists and ethnographers, to which we will turn a little later.

THE NEO-KANTIAN "SCIENCE OF MIND"

The dualistic philosophy of the Germans consistently set history apart from nature, as we have seen earlier. Up to the time of Hegel this dualism was simply taken for granted, or was defended on the basis of purely metaphysical arguments. In the latter part of the nineteenth century, however, there arose a new philosophical movement, called the Neo-Kantian, that sought to explicate more clearly the distinction between the historical and the natural realms. The so-called Marburg School of philosophy explored the logical foundations of the natural sciences, while the Baden School concerned itself with the philosophy of values, culture, and history.[61] By this time, however, philosophy *qua* philosophy had largely fallen into disfavor, as it did everywhere with the triumph of practical science in the latter half of the nineteenth century. Thus, the Neo-Kantians of the Baden School sought to justify the study of history not as metaphysical philosophy but as a legitimate kind of science, while at the same time retaining the traditional distinction from natural science.

Like all their German predecessors, the Neo-Kantians meant by "history" a great deal more than we understand by the term today. They were really discussing the differences between the natural sciences and what today we call the social sciences, although the Germans preferred to think of these latter as cultural sciences. The philosophers themselves recognized the need for a new and more comprehensive term for their field of study; thus Wilhelm Windelband recommended that the old-fashioned term *Geschichte* (history, in the narrow sense) be replaced by *Kulturwissenschaft* (the study of Culture).[62] A little later Wilhelm Dilthey coined the term Geisteswissenschaft, which is incapable of precise translation, but has sometimes been translated figuratively as the "science of the mind."[63] According to Dilthey it embraced "history, national economy, the sciences of

61. See Copleston, *History of Philosophy*, Book Three, vol. VII, pp. 361–364.
62. Collingwood, *Idea of History*, p. 168.
63. Copleston, *History of Philosophy*, Book Three, vol. VII, p. 369.

law and of the State, the science of religion, the study of literature and poetry, of art and music, of philosophical world-views, and systems, finally psychology."[64]

It is apparent from the foregoing list that Geisteswissenschaft in Dilthey's usage embraced aspects both of social science and of the humanities, without attempting to differentiate between the two.[65] The list makes it clear, however, that the primary emphasis was humanistic: on aspects of mind and culture rather than on society or institutions. Subsequent German usage has distinguished, as the Neo-Kantians did not, between *Gesellschaftswissenschaft* (social sciences) and Geisteswissenschaft (roughly, humanities). In sum, then, the Neo-Kantians perpetuated the traditional German distinction between the natural and the human sciences, but also the traditional failure to distinguish between the social sciences and the humanities.

The Neo-Kantian "Science of Mind"

Four of the leading members of the Baden School were Wilhelm Windelband, Heinrich Rickert, Georg Simmel, and Wilhelm Dilthey, whose major works on historical philosophy were all published initially in the last two decades of the nineteenth century.[66] Although there were some differences of perspective among them, they were agreed on three fundamental points. First, they accepted the basic, twofold division between the natural sciences and the human sciences, thus perpetuating the dualistic tradition that had prevailed in Germany since the Aufklärung. Second, they asserted that natural science involved the search for laws, or governing principles, while the study of history must concern itself with particulars, or in other words with differences as much as with similarities. To express this difference, Windelband characterized the natural sciences as *nomothetic,* and the study of history as *ideographic.*[67] Third, they all agreed that the study of natural science must be as objective as possible, while the study of history cannot be other than subjective, since it involves an attempt to understand the Self. That is, the facts of history cannot be comprehended except in the light of our own personal experiences of the world.[68]

The special contribution of Wilhelm Windelband was embodied in his Philosophy of Values.[69] He asserted that the most basic components of

---

64. Quoted from ibid.

65. See esp. H. P. Rickman, ed., *W. Dilthey Selected Writings* (Cambridge, 1976), pp. 11–12.

66. Copleston, (*History of Philosophy,* Book Three, pp. 368–373) argues that Dilthey cannot really be classified as a Neo-Kantian, but his historical outlook seems to me generally in harmony with the Baden School. For other Neo-Kantians, see ibid., pp. 366–368.

67. See Collingwood, *Idea of History,* p. 166.

68. Copleston, *History of Philosophy,* Book Three, vol. VII, pp. 370–371.

69. First expressed in a rectorial address, *Geschichte und Naturwissenschaft,* delivered at Strasbourg in 1894.

human cognition are not perceptions but value judgments as regards the true, the good, and the beautiful. These are in fact the most fundamental components of the Volksgeist of each people, as conceived by Herder.[70] Heinrich Rickert went on to elaborate Windelband's conception into a more specific and concrete theory of history, in which each people and age was distinguished primarily by its values.[71] Windelband and Rickert thus came very close to articulating the concept of cultural values that was to become a central concern of configurationist anthropologists a century later.

German Idealism

Georg Simmel carried the dualistic perspective a step further in recognizing that the "facts" studied by the historian are something very different from the facts of the natural scientist.[72] They are merely the man-made records of vanished happenings, which can never be observed empirically or reproduced experimentally. He also asserted that the philosopher cannot really "discover" a coherent pattern in history; rather, he imposes upon it his own personal philosophy.[73] This assertion of subjective relativism was to have a considerable influence on twentieth century philosophies of history, and it resonates as well in much current thinking about ethnography.

The subjectivist position taken by Wilhelm Dilthey generally agreed with that of Simmel. Starting from the proposition that we can only understand history (or culture or society) in the light of our own experiences (*Erlebnisse*) as human beings, he went on to argue that we should try to see the times of Caesar or Napoleon as much as possible through the eyes of Caesar or Napoleon; to imagine the world as they would have seen it on the basis of experiences that they would presumably have had: their *Nacherleben.*[74] Dilthey therefore concluded that the understanding of human societies (or historical ages) was a matter of hermeneutics (interpretation), while the understanding of natural phenomena was a matter of explanation.[75]

The Neo-Kantians were contemporaries as well as fellow-countrymen of Franz Boas, but their major works were not published until after he had completed his university studies, and it is not certain that he read them in any systematic way. Although he mentioned Dilthey a couple of times in one of his published lectures,[76] he had a general distaste for all forms of

70. Copleston, *History of Philosophy,* Book Three, vol. VII, p. 364.
71. Rickert's ideas were first published in 1896, but they were more fully developed in his *System der Philosophie* published in 1921.
72. In *Die Probleme der Geschichtsphilosophie* (Leipzig, 1892).
73. For discussion see esp. Collingwood, *Idea of History,* pp. 170–171.
74. Ibid., pp. 171–173; Copleston, *History of Philosophy,* Book Three, vol. VII, pp. 368–373.
75. Sutton, *German Tradition in Philosophy,* p. 130.
76. *Anthropology, a Lecture Delivered at Columbia University...* (New York, 1908).

philosophical speculation, and there is no good evidence that he was much influenced by contemporary trends in historical philosophy.[77] The same was not true of Boas's early students in anthropology, several of whom acknowledged specific debts to Windelband, Rickert, and Dilthey.[78] This influence must, then, be attributed not to Boas personally but to the prevailing intellectual climate of the German-American community in which so many of the first Boasian anthropologists were nurtured. I surmise, therefore, that the influence of the Neo-Kantians was exerted upon the early Boasians prior to their formal exposure to anthropology; indeed it may have been one of the factors that later influenced their decision to become anthropologists. The more general question of how German idealist philosophy found expression in the work of the Boasian anthropologists will be discussed later in the chapter.

The Neo-Kantian "Science of Mind"

THE ENVIRONMENTAL FACTOR

Paradoxically, as it would seem, German Idealism from the beginning included a certain element of Environmental Determinism. The particularists had to explain how one culture came to be different from another, and they could hardly ignore the factor of environment when mankind occupied such a diversity of physical surroundings. Starting in a limited way in the Aufklärung, Environmental Determinism grew into a major element in German thinking in the later nineteenth century.

At first glance, the doctrine of Environmental Determinism would seem to be at odds with the out-and-out mentalism of the idealists. The influence of environment is usually thought of in materialist terms: that is, in terms of available food and other resources, and their inevitable impact on the shape of society and economy. But the environmental determinism of the Germans, at least in the beginning, was actually a mentalist rather than a materialist perspective. It was not the subsistence resources of the environment that shaped the development of human cultures, but the sensory and aesthetic *gestalts* of landscape, climate, flora, and fauna. It was due to these factors that, for example, mountain-dwellers were fiercely independent, dwellers in river valleys were easygoing and lethargic, and seafaring peoples were restless. Environment, like so many other components of German philosophy, became a semimystical concept.

The earliest hints of environmental causality can be found in the work

77. *Contra* Marvin Harris, *The Rise of Anthropological Theory* (New York, 1968), pp. 268–271.
78. See Robert H. Lowie in *American Anthropologist* 58 (1956): 995–1015; Ruth Benedict, *Patterns of Culture* (New York, 1934), p. 2; Harris, *Rise of Anthropological Theory*, pp. 268–271.

of a few of the German Enlightenment thinkers, including Johann Michaelis, Johann von Mosheim, and Isaak Iselin. These writers, citing Montesquieu as their authority, placed more emphasis on climate, and its supposed influence on human temperament, than they did on other environmental factors (cf. Chapter 2). Material resources were considered important primarily to the extent that they accelerated or retarded the course of cultural development for each people, rather than because they determined its direction.[79]

The extent and nature of Herder's environmental determinism has been debated, like everything else in his philosophy. He devoted most of one volume of the *Ideen* to a discussion of the influence of climate on history,[80] and it may have been this that led Boas to assert, certainly incorrectly, that he "believed that natural environment was the cause of the existing biological and cultural differentiation."[81] In fact, Herder always saw individual cultures as arising from the interplay of environment and the genius, or Geist, of each people, without being very clear about which was the stronger influence. Moreover, his conception of the physical environment, and the nature of its influence, was at least as mystical and mentalistic as that of his Aufklärung predecessors. He spoke of peoples as having an "organic" relationship to their native soils. "Man is as a tree, which once planted in the soil, 'produced leaves and fruit adapted to the climate.'"[82] Like the *Aufklärers,* Herder placed proportionately more emphasis on climate than on other environmental factors.

Environmental Determinism did not really become a "hard," or materialist doctrine, until the latter part of the nineteenth century, mainly in the work of the German geographers. The primary exponents of the doctrine were Karl Ritter, Theobald Fischer (Boas's teacher), and Friedrich Ratzel. However, the geographers drew their inspiration not from the idealist tradition but from the work of the English historian Henry Thomas Buckle, which we discussed in Chapter 2. Indeed the geographers were outspoken critics of the idealist position, regarding their own doctrine as a corrective to it.[83]

Franz Boas in his university days was a student of Fischer, and later, at the Berlin Ethnographic Museum, was associated with Ratzel. It is fairly clear that, when he undertook his first field expedition in 1883, he was something of an environmental determinist in the hard sense. It is equally

79. See Reill, *German Enlightenment and the Rise of Historicism,* pp. 133–134.
80. Herder, *Philosophy of the History of Man,* Book VII, Chapters 2–5.
81. Boas, *Mind of Primitive Man.*
82. Quoted from Calabrese, Herder and Anthropology, p. 13.
83. See Harris, *Rise of Anthropological Theory,* pp. 265–266.

clear that, partly as a result of his experience among the Eskimos, he soon retreated from the materialist position, and it was certainly not part of the "Boasian doctrine" that he passed on to his students in America.[84] Insofar as the Boasians were environmental determinists, it was at least as much in the Herderian sense as in the Ritterian.

THE GERMAN ETHNOGRAPHIC TRADITION

In the eighteenth and nineteenth centuries German Idealism found many different avenues of expression; in poetry, drama, and art history no less than in philosophy and history. One of its most distinctive manifestations was in the German ethnographic tradition, which for a time had no close parallels in other countries. Germany ethnography always stood outside the mainstream of historical philosophy, but there was a definite cross-influence.

The special role that comparative ethnography enjoyed in nineteenth-century Germany clearly relates to the centrality of the Volk concept, not only in historical philosophy but also in the German self-image. Indeed it was a unique feature of German ethnography that from the beginning it involved an attempt to define the German Self as well as to define the Other. Lacking a unified nation or a national history, the Germans, as we saw, attached special importance to language and to culture as criteria of self-identity. This led to the systematic, comparative study of Germanic-speaking peoples–especially the Scandinavians–in an effort to reconstruct a kind of proto-Germanic *Urkultur,* or ancestral culture, which could be accepted as a national prehistory. (This tradition would later find dramatic expression in the operas of Wagner.) "The central problem," writes Hans Vermeule, "was the origin, descent, and migrations of the diverse nations of the Nordic world."[85] It was in that spirit that August Schlözer wrote his *Allgemeine Nordische Geschichte* (General Nordic History) in 1771, and it was in that book that he first introduced the term *Ethnographie,* as well as its German equivalent, *Völkerkunde.*[86] It was only a short step from the comparative study of Nordic peoples to the comparative study of peoples more generally, and the step was soon taken.

The distinction between ethnography and ethnology is at best a fuzzy one, and it has been conceived in different ways by different authors. Some have described ethnography as the field-research dimension of ethnology, while others, including myself, prefer to think of it as the empirical, de-

84. Ibid., pp. 265–267.

85. In *History of Anthropology Newsletter* XIX, no. 2 (1992), p. 7.

86. Ibid., pp. 6–9.

scriptive-comparative dimension of ethnology. Consistent with this latter usage, I will here refer to the German tradition, both in literature and in field work, as ethnographic, because it was preeminently descriptive rather than theoretical.

The literary aspect

The German ethnographic tradition was first of all a literary tradition. In the broadest sense its origins can be traced back to the cosmographies of the sixteenth century: those encyclopedic compendia of "queer customs" that so delighted European readers in the age of exploration. It is a curious fact, however, that by the nineteenth century the cosmographic tradition had died out just about everywhere except in Germany. The encyclopedic, multivolume ethnographic compilations of Meiners, Klemm, Waitz, and Ratzel had no parallels in other countries. When E.B. Tylor published his *Researches into the Early History of Mankind* (1865) and *Primitive Culture* (1871), he was obliged to draw most of his ethnographic case materials from the German works,[87] because there was simply nothing comparable in English.[88]

All of the earliest German ethnographic compendia were cast in the form of "world histories," and were written to a progressivist schema. That is, the cultures of the world were grouped and classified on the basis of their supposed degree of progress, rather than geographically. From a consideration of their titles alone it might be thought that these works belonged to the universalist tradition of Weltgeschichte which we discussed earlier. In fact however there was an important difference. The Weltgeschichte of the universalists were conjectural histories of *culture* in the singular, and they were highly speculative, making little use of empirical ethnographic data. The ethnographic compendia on the other hand were studies of the evolution of cultures in the plural, and progressivist theory, although not absent, was always secondary to the presentation of ethnographic detail. The compilers sought to explain how cultures had progressed over time, but also and more importantly how and why cultures had come to be different from one another. In other words, these works were in the particularist rather than in the universalist tradition of idealist philosophy. Like the cosmographies that preceded them, the ethnographic compendia were above all collections of queer and fascinating customs.

Robert Lowie took Carl Meiners's *Grundriss der Geschichte der Mensch-*

87. Leipzig, 1843.

88. See Edward B. Tylor, *Researches into the Early History of Mankind*, ed. Paul Bohannan (Chicago, 1964), p. 8.

heit (Foundations of the History of Mankind), published in 1785, as the starting point for his *History of Ethnological Theory.*[89] This was probably appropriate, insofar as the *Grundriss* involved the first systematic effort not only to describe but to classify all the world's peoples, at least partly on the basis of their cultural characteristics. But the classification reflected the typical "ethnological" thinking of the time in that it conflated cultural, linguistic, and racial data indiscriminately, treating them as interdependent. Perhaps the most noteworthy feature of Meiners' approach was its holism: he pleaded for "a view of man as he has been at all times and in all places."[90]

The German ethnographic tradition

Much more influential than the work of Meiners was that of Gustav Klemm, whose *Allgemeine Cultur-Geschichte der Menschheit* (General Cultural History of Mankind) was published in 1843. It was followed by the much expanded, two-volume *Allgemeine Culturwissenschaft* (General Science of Culture) in 1854 and 1855. The author still accepted uncritically the three-stage progressivist schema of the French Enlightenment thinkers, but this merely served as an organizing framework within which he presented a mass of ethnographic detail from all parts of the world. The works of Klemm were the source of much of the ethnographic case material included by E. B. Tylor in his *Researches into the Early History of Mankind* (1865) and *Primitive Culture* (1871) – the first two major ethnographic compendia in English. Klemm also provided a definition of culture which anticipated and possibly inspired that of Tylor, and of subsequent anthropologists down to the present day. It was composed, he said, of "customs, information, and skills, domestic and public life in peace and war, religion, science, and art."[91]

The six-volume *Anthropologie der Naturvölker* (Anthropology of Primitive Peoples) of Theodor Waitz (1858–1871) was apparently the first ethnographic compendium that broke with the "world history" format, surveying the cultures of the world from a geographical rather than from a historical perspective. The work was mainly a treatise on primitive mentality, and it sounded the same egalitarian note as had Herder half a century earlier. Native intelligence, according to Waitz, was roughly the same among all peoples and at all times in history. Cultural differences were due to the vicissitudes of history rather than to innate differences in mental ability. In the early twentieth century this was to become one of the dogmas of Boasian anthropology.[92]

89. Lowie, *The History of Ethnological Theory* (New York, 1938), pp. 10–11.

90. Ibid., p. 11.

91. Quoted from ibid., p. 16.

92. For further discussion of Waitz, see ibid., pp. 16–18.

The three-volume *Völkerkunde* of Friedrich Ratzel (1885–1890) was the first of the German compendia to show the influence of the newly founded ethnographic museums of Germany and neighboring countries (see below). In compiling this worldwide ethnographic survey, the author drew heavily on museum collections, especially from Berlin and Vienna. As a result the work, far more than any predecessor, was heavily weighted on the side of material culture: it was a veritable treasure trove of information about weapons, containers, food-preparing apparatus, pottery, musical instruments, clothing and ornaments, and similar items of material culture that were regularly exhibited in ethnographic collections. Indeed, the numerous and detailed woodcut illustrations made the *Völkerkunde* a kind of printed museum in its own right, and this surely was one reason for its enduring popular appeal.[93] It was also, as Lowie has observed, the last of the worldwide surveys to be compiled by a single author.[94]

The concept of a pictorial museum was carried still further in the vast *Bilder-Atlas*, a multivolume pictorial encyclopedia of the arts and sciences published at Leipzig in 1885.[95] The volume on ethnography had chapters on each of the main regions of the world, written by the geographer Georg Gerland, but the main content of the work consisted of 112 plates comprising more than 1200 individual woodcut figures. They were generally similar to the illustrations of Ratzel, illustrating the physical appearance and dress of tribal peoples, scenes of outdoor activity, household interiors, and all kinds of items of material culture. Ratzel's *Völkerkunde* and the *Bilder-Atlas* remained the standard ethnographic surveys in German until the appearance in 1910 of *Illustrierte Völkerkunde* (Illustrated Ethnography), a multiauthored and multivolume work edited by Georg Buschan.[96]

The fieldwork aspect

It has become a commonplace to say that ethnology in the nineteenth and twentieth centuries marched hand-in-hand with colonialism.[97] However, this was much less specifically true in Germany than in Britain, France, or the United States. German ethnographic inquiry began long before that country acquired its overseas possessions, and indeed even before it was

93. It went into a second edition only six years after the completion of the first.

94. Lowie, *History of Ethnological Theory*, p. 122.

95. The American edition, published in Philadelphia in 1886, had the title *Iconographic Encyclopaedia of the Arts and Sciences.* The ethnology volume in this edition had an added section, "Anthropology and Ethnology," written by D. G. Brinton of the University of Pennsylvania.

96. See Lowie, *History of Ethnological Theory* (n. 89), p. 122.

97. Cf. esp. Talal Asad, ed., *Anthropology & the Colonial Encounter* (London, 1973).

politically unified. Moreover, it was never concentrated within the German-ruled territories. Indeed a great deal of German field ethnography was carried out in South America, where Germany never had colonial interests.[98]

We have already noted the beginnings of German ethnography in the attempt to define a German cultural Self, resulting in the publication of Schlözer's *Allgemeine Nordische Geschichte* in 1771. The beginnings of a more comprehensive German ethnographic enterprise may perhaps be traced to the prodigious travels and explorations of Alexander von Humboldt, between 1799 and 1829. The great all-around naturalist published altogether more than thirty volumes covering nearly every aspect of natural history, but the five-volume *Kosmos* (1845–1862) was his magnum opus. Although ethnography played only a minor role in the work of Humboldt, he did make cultural observations on the Indians of Central and South America, and also brought back collections of artifacts and pictorial manuscripts from Mexico. Moreover, the enormous prestige enjoyed by Humboldt–exceeding that of any other scientist in Europe in the mid-nineteenth century–laid the foundations for future ethnographic research in Germany. In his last years he drew up the initial plans for the Berlin Ethnographic Museum, although the institution was not formally established until some years after his death.[99] Humboldt's *Kosmos* was one of the early influences on the young Franz Boas and is regarded by some as providing the foundation for Boas's own personal philosophy of science.[100]

The German ethnographic tradition

Three other German naturalist-explorers from the earlier nineteenth century who deserve brief mention for their ethnographic contributions are Mungo Park, Heinrich Barth, and Georg Schweinfurth. All of them published multivolume accounts of their African travels, which were to find a permanent place in the ethnographic literature.[101]

98. See, for example, the numerous examples cited in the bibliography of Julian H. Steward, ed., *Handbook of South American Indians,* vol. 3 (Washington, D.C., 1948), pp. 909–986. *Bureau of American Ethnology Bulletin* 143. See also Timothy J. O'Leary, *Ethnographic Bibliography of South America* (New Haven, Conn., 1963).

99. See Berthold Riese in Christopher Winters, ed., *International Dictionary of Anthropologists* (New York, 1991), pp. 314–315.

100. See Clyde Kluckhohn and Olaf Prufer in Walter Goldschmidt, ed., *The Anthropology of Franz Boas,* pp. 11–13. *American Anthropological Association Memoir* 89 (1959). See also Matti Bunzl in George W. Stocking, Jr., ed., *Volksgeist as Method and Ethic,* pp. 17–78. *History of Anthropology,* vol. 8 (Madison, Wis., 1996).

101. The English editions of their works are: Mungo Park, *Travels in the Interior Districts of Africa,* 2 vols. (London, 1817); Henry Barth, *Travels and Discoveries in North and Central Africa,* 5 vols. (London, 1857–1858); and Georg Schweinfurth, *The Heart of Africa,* 2 vols. (London, 1874).

The career of Adolf Bastian (1826–1905) marks a turning point in the history of German ethnography in a number of respects. He was the first of the German field researchers who was specifically and exclusively an ethnographer, rather than an all-purpose naturalist. But he was also a prodigious scholar and an institution-builder, who in effect brought together and integrated the literary, the fieldwork, and the institutional aspects of the German ethnographic tradition. At the end of his life it was said that "No German scholar has traveled more, none read more, none written more."[102]

German Idealism

Bastian eventually published more than a dozen ethnographic volumes based largely on his own travels and observations.[103] But Bastian also incorporated ethnographic material from other authors in his publications, so that they belong both to the realm of field ethnography and to the encyclopedic tradition which we discussed earlier. He published in addition several theoretical works, setting forth his distinctive views on ethnological theory.[104] His outlook–highly unusual for its time–was strongly opposed to the theory of biological evolution, while at the same time espousing a kind of modified theory of cultural evolution, based on the concept of the psychic unity of mankind.[105] That is, cultural development everywhere was thought to proceed in more or less the same way because all human minds worked in the same way. This was almost certainly the inspiration for the Psychic Unity doctrine later proclaimed in English by E.B. Tylor.[106] It seems probable too that Bastian's opposition to evolutionary theory and to racial determinism exerted a considerable influence on Boas, who was Bastian's assistant at the Berlin Museum in 1885 and 1886.

Bastian in his later career was also active as a curator and an editor. He was appointed curator of the ethnology section in the Berlin Museum in 1868, and then, in 1886, founded the Royal Museum for Ethnology in Berlin. Under Bastian's direction, this became for several decades the premier ethnographic museum in the world. Bastian was also instrumental in founding the Berlin Society for Anthropology, Ethnology, and Prehistory (1869), and for a number of years he served as one of the editors of the *Zeitschrift für Ethnologie.*[107] This prodigious panoply of activities closely

---

102. Quoted from Lowie, *History of Ethnological Theory,* p. 31.

103. Among them *Der Mensch in der Geschichte* (Mankind in History, 1860); *Völker des östliches Asiens* (Peoples of East Asia, 1866–1871); *Culturländer des alten America* (Cultural Regions of Aboriginal America, 1878–1889); and *Indonesien* (Indonesia, 1884–1894). All but the first of these were multivolume works.

104. For a list of these, see Robert B.M. Ridinger in Winters, *International Dictionary of Anthropologists,* p. 37.

105. See esp. Lowie, *History of Ethnological Theory,* pp. 35–38.

106. Ibid., pp. 72, 76–78.

107. Ibid., pp. 30–31.

paralleled the roles that Boas was later to play in North America, and it can hardly be doubted that, at least in the area of professional activity, Bastian was one of Boas's chief role models.

After Bastian's time, and up to the beginning of World War II, a veritable army of German and Austrian ethnographers went to work among tribal peoples in just about every part of the world.[108] Many were collecting materials for the ethnographic museums that were burgeoning all over Germany and Austria; others were associated with universities, where ethnology came increasingly to have an honored place in the curriculum. It appears that some ethnographic fieldwork was even sponsored by newspapers; for example, Franz Boas's expedition to Baffinland in 1883–84 was largely financed by the *Berliner Tageblatt,* to which he promised to contribute a series of articles.[109] This is surely testimony to the wide popular appeal that ethnography had among the German reading public.

The German ethnographic tradition

Most of the German field studies (like nearly all ethnographic field studies then and since) were highly particularistic, and for that reason they have not been translated into other languages. As in the museum-sponsored studies in America, discussed in the last chapter, there was always a heavy emphasis on material culture. A few of the German and Austrian ethnographers whose work has become well known outside the German-speaking world were Hermann Baumann, Leo Frobenius, Walter Hirschberg, Felix von Luschan, Carl Meinhof, Richard Thurnwald, and Diedrich Westermann in Africa, Felix von Luschan in the Near East, Stephen Fuchs and Christoph von Fürer-Haimendorf in India and Nepal, Berthold Laufer in East Asia, Robert von Heine-Geldern and Paul Schebesta in Southeast Asia, Richard Thurnwald and Diedrich Westermann in Melanesia, Karl von den Steinen in Polynesia, Walter Krickeberg in North and Middle America, Paul Kirchoff and Edouard Seler in Middle America, Walter Lehmann and Theodor Preuss in Middle and South America, and Martin Gusinde, Curt Nimuendajú, and Karl von den Steinen in South America.[110]

The diffusionist perspective

Insofar as German ethnography had a theoretical program, it was basically historical and particularistic, in keeping with the general spirit of His-

108. See Melville Jacobs, *Pattern in Cultural Anthropology* (Homewood, Ill., 1964), p. 22.

109. See A.L. Kroeber in *Franz Boas 1858–1942*, pp. 8–9. *American Anthropological Association Memoir* 61 (1943).

110. For biographical sketches, see Winters, *International Dictionary of Anthropologists*, passim.

torical Particularism that had flourished in Germany since the time of Herder. While the progressivist ethnologists of England, France, and the United States were still mainly interested in discovering similarities between cultures, and attributing them to the workings of a general process of evolution, the Germans were equally concerned with the ways in which cultures differed from one another. Bastian, as we saw, still adhered to a kind of mentalistic progressivist theory, based on the notion that cultures evolve in similar ways because human minds work in the same way. He was, as a result, a great believer in independent invention, asserting that cultural parallels should not be attributed to diffusion or culture contact unless it could be proven historically.[111]

German Idealism

A generation later, Friedrich Ratzel and Fritz Graebner turned this doctrine completely on its head. They were both convinced of the basic uninventiveness of mankind, and believed that cultural parallels should always be attributed to diffusion unless it could specifically be ruled out by historical and geographic circumstances. In the paraphrase of Lowie, "The uninventive human beings that were constantly migrating hither and yon simply transported what they had picked up as their cultural inventory.... Ratzel dropped the requirement that diffusion can... be inferred only by a continuous or otherwise traceable distribution. Bows on the Kassai [in Central Africa] may be affiliated with those from New Guinea irrespective of whether the path of migration is ascertainable."[112] Ratzel was first and foremost a geographer, and like all the German geographers of his time he attributed cultural differences mainly to the influence of environment, while cultural similarities were nearly always attributed to diffusion.

While Ratzel was content to proclaim a general faith in diffusion, it was his disciple Leo Frobenius who laid the foundations for what was to become a concrete theory of diffusion. In his *African Culture* (1898) he pointed out a number of cultural parallels between Africa and New Guinea, and suggested that these were too specific to have evolved by chance; they must be due to diffusion from a common source. He further suggested that a systematic study of the geographical distribution of the traits might make it possible to identify their place of origin.[113] A little later, Fritz Graebner and Wilhelm Schmidt elaborated the idea of Frobenius into the *Kulturkreis* (literally, culture-circle) theory of diffusion, which envisioned diffusion as occurring in successive waves from a few fixed points of special cultural

---

111. Lowie, *History of Ethnological Theory*, pp. 35–36.
112. Ibid., p. 123.
113. Cf. H. R. Hays, *From Ape to Angel* (New York, 1958), p. 272.

creativity.[114] What *Kulturkreislehre* (culture-circle theory) attempted to do in effect was to convert a purely historical principle (diffusion) into something like a determinist one.

The German ethnographic tradition

Most of the German and Austrian ethnographers after about 1880 were in one sense or another disciples of Ratzel, Graebner, and Schmidt, and many of their field researches were undertaken specifically to study trait distributions. They interpreted their findings consistently in terms of diffusionist theory, just as Powell, Morgan, and other progressivists in England and America consistently interpreted ethnographic findings in terms of progressivist theory. However, the theoretical predilections of the German and Austrian ethnographers did not prevent them from carrying out excellently detailed descriptive studies, and compiling a rich ethnographic archive.[115]

Kulturkreislehre did not emerge as an articulate theory of diffusion until the early twentieth century; after the time when Boas had begun training the first generation of American anthropologists. Its rigidly formulaic character was never congenial to Boas or his students, and indeed the theory never attracted any significant adherents outside the German-speaking world. However, the Boasians shared completely with the Germans the belief in diffusion as the primary driving force in cultural change. Their diffusionism, however, remained a purely historical rather than a determinist theory of cultural development. That is, culture change was seen as resulting from the unpredictable accidents of culture contact and borrowing, rather than from any predictable process. Culture was, in Lowie's words, "a planless hodgepodge, a thing of shreds and patches."[116] This historicist perspective was in keeping especially with the thinking of Herder.

The institutional base

It should be apparent from the foregoing that ethnography occupied a privileged place not only in idealist thinking, but also in the German popular mind. It comes as no surprise, then, to find that ethnography found an institutional home–indeed several institutional homes–in Germany long

---

114. See Fritz Graebner, *Methode der Ethnologie* (Heidelberg, 1911) and Wilhelm Schmidt, *The Culture Historical Method of Ethnology* (New York, 1939). For commentary see esp. Clyde Kluckhohn in *American Anthropologist* 38, no. 2 (1936): 157–196; Jacobs, *Pattern in Cultural Anthropology*, pp. 21–22; and Lowie, *History of Ethnological Theory*, pp. 177–195.

115. Jacobs, *Pattern in Cultural Anthropology*, p. 22. For a detailed and perceptive review of German and Austrian diffusionist ethnography in Africa see, Jürgen Zwernemann, *Culture History and African Anthropology. Uppsala Studies in Cultural Anthropology*, vol. 6 (Uppsala, 1983).

116. Robert H. Lowie, *Primitive Society* (New York, 1920), p. 441.

before it did in other countries. The first ethnographic collection (Sammlung für Völkerkunde) was assembled at Göttingen as far back as 1780, while the Royal Ethnographic Collection was created at Vienna in 1806. However, the great heyday of ethnographic museum development was in the last third of the nineteenth century. Museums were founded at Munich in 1868, Leipzig in 1869, Berlin in 1873, Dresden in 1876, Vienna (the first officially constituted public museum in that city) in 1876, Hamburg in 1879, Stuttgart in 1884, Bremen in 1896, Cologne in 1901, and Frankfurt in 1904. It is important to note that all of the aforenamed institutions were purely ethnographic museums; they were not ethnographic sections in larger natural history museums, as were nearly all the ethnographic collections in England and the United States.[117] The only purely ethnographic (and archaeological) museum in the United States before the twentieth century was the Peabody Museum at Harvard University, founded in 1866.

The most numerous and also the finest ethnographic museums in the world today are still to be found in Germany, Austria, and German-speaking Switzerland. As of 1990 there were, in the three countries, no fewer than ninety-one major and minor ethnographic museums—probably more than in the rest of Europe combined. There were in addition twenty-two research institutes devoted largely or entirely to the study of ethnology.[118]

The proliferation of learned societies provides another measure of the importance of ethnography and ethnology in the German-speaking world. The two earliest societies, in Berlin and in Vienna, were founded respectively in 1869 and 1870, and these remain the major national associations today. However, there are also local ethnological societies in more than a dozen German, Austrian, and Swiss cities, as well as societies specializing in the ethnography of Africa, Asia, and Latin America. The total number of ethnological societies in the three countries in 1990 was thirty-six.[119]

Summary

Far more than the French or the British, the Germans were interested in ethnography as an end in itself, rather than as an aid in the building or the substantiation of progressivist theories. Their interest represents one of

117. I am heavily indebted to private communications from Professors Christian Feest and Andreas Kronenberg, both of the Johann Wolfgang Goethe University in Frankfurt, for information contained in this section.

118. Figures from G. Baeck and R. Husmann, eds., *Handbuch der deutschsprachigen Ethnologie* (Göttingen, 1990), pp. 194–240. The figures do not include institutions in the French- and Italian-speaking cantons of Switzerland.

119. Ibid., pp. 244–249.

the many manifestations of the particularist tradition in German philosophy. It was a by-product not of colonial expansion, but of the attempt to define a German Self, on the basis of cultural and linguistic rather than of political criteria.

The German ethnographic tradition

The German ethnographic tradition clearly had many points in common with the tradition of Indianology that developed independently in the United States. There are, however, some important differences to note. First of all, German ethnography was never proprietary, or hegemonic. It was carried on in all parts of the world, regardless of political sovereignty, and it was not fueled by any special sense of responsibility toward, or interest in, any particular peoples. Second, it was not a government-backed enterprise; it was a reflection purely and simply of popular interest on the part of the German people, or at least of the intelligentsia. This is probably why, much earlier than Indianology, it found an institutional home in museums, which were designed to appeal to the general public rather than simply to a community of scholars.

Most importantly, German ethnography never had an ulterior agenda. Primitive peoples were not studied because they provided support for an evolutionary theory, or because of a sense of national responsibility, or in the hope of assisting their eventual assimilation; they were studied simply because the Germans found them interesting. This was the essence of German ethnographic particularism, and it clearly echoes the Kantian insistence on understanding "the thing-in-itself."

THE TRANSPLANTERS: TYLOR AND BOAS

In the latter part of the nineteenth century, important aspects of the German idealist and the German ethnographic traditions were transplanted to England and to the United States. The two key figures in this transfer were, respectively, E. B. Tylor and Franz Boas. They were to become two of the most influential figures in the history of anthropology, but in a purely theoretical sense they were not so much innovators as importers, bringing the concepts and the outlook of German Idealism into the English-speaking world.[120] Although Tylor's impact was mainly in Great Britain, and although it did not last much more than a generation, he is important for Americans as well because it was he who formulated, in English, the basic concept of culture that became central to American as well as to British anthropological theory.

120. For extended discussion of the commonalities in outlook and influence between Tylor and Boas, see Elvin Hatch, *Theories of Man and Culture* (New York, 1973), pp. 13–73.

Tylor and Boas are perhaps two of the most widely misunderstood figures the history of anthropology. Tylor is repeatedly classified simply as a pioneer evolutionist, and his name is linked with that of Lewis Henry Morgan.[121] He was indeed a matter-of-course evolutionist, as was nearly every other anthropologist in the English-speaking world at the end of the nineteenth century, but unlike Morgan, McLennan, and other social evolutionists he was neither a system-builder nor a drum-beater.[122] Like Klemm and other German predecessors, he simply used evolutionary theory as a convenient way of organizing his ethnographic materials, rather than using the ethnographic materials to build a theory of evolution. His *Researches into the Early History of Mankind* (1865) and *Primitive Culture* (1871) are much more nearly in the tradition of the great German ethnographic compendia than they are in the social evolutionary tradition of Maine, Morgan, and McLennan. In these works, Tylor in effect transplanted onto British soil the German ethnographic tradition.

German Idealism

It is conspicuous too that the highly mentalistic and rationalistic evolutionism of Tylor is conceptually far removed from the materialistic, socially oriented evolutionism of Morgan. The difference in perspective between the two men is clearly reflected in the titles of their respective magnum opera: *Primitive Culture*,[123] and *Ancient Society*.[124] In the latter work Morgan never spoke of culture. He used the older term "civilization," but it is clear that, as in nearly all earlier writing, the word referred to a society of people as well as to its customs: society and culture were not yet conceptually differentiated. Tylor for his part had little to say about society. *Primitive Culture* has the subtitle "Researches into the Development of Mythology, Philosophy, Religion, Language, Art and Custom": a highly mentalistic catalogue that conspicuously excludes social organization and kinship. Moreover, in the very first sentence of the book, Tylor provided for the first time (in English) a definition of culture as something conceptually separable from society, and capable of study in its own right. It was, he said, "that complex whole which includes knowledge, belief, art, morals, law, custom, and any other capabilities and habits acquired by man as a member of society."[125] The definition has proved so serviceable that it is continually quoted down to the present day, and has really never been

121. E.g., in Harris, *Rise of Anthropological Theory*, pp. 142–216.
122. Cf. Lowie, *History of Ethnological Theory*, pp. 83–84.
123. London, 1871.
124. New York, 1877.
125. Tylor, *Primitive Culture* (London, 1871), p. 1.

much improved on. As we saw a little earlier, it owed its inspiration at least partly to Gustav Klemm.

There can be little doubt that Tylor's conception and definition of culture, and indeed his whole position in anthropology, derives largely from the German idealist tradition.[126] It is often forgotten that Tylor's self-education as an anthropologist, following upon his return from Central America, took place partly in Germany, and that the ethnographic materials cited so copiously in *Researches into the Early History of Mankind* and in *Primitive Culture* are mostly derived not from English but from German sources; especially from the voluminous works of Klemm.[127] In short and in sum, it was Tylor who gave to the English-speaking world its central organizing concept of culture, which had already been developed in everything but name by the German idealists. This, rather than his somewhat intellectualized evolutionism, represents his most signal contribution to the development of anthropological thought.[128]

The transplanters: Tylor and Boas

Franz Boas

The giant figure of Franz Boas looms so large in the history of American anthropology that his name and his work have already been cited repeatedly in this as well as in earlier chapters. He was not a great innovator or an original thinker but a great transplanter, who brought to America the German traditions of idealist philosophy, particularist ethnography, and professional education. The story of his life and career have been told so often in anthropological literature[129] that they must be part of the folklore that "every student anthropologist knows and every grownup anthropologist must at least have forgotten," to borrow a phrase from R. R. Marett.[130] A few details must nevertheless be repeated here, insofar as they are relevant to understanding Boas's early background and his later influence in American anthropology.

---

126. See esp. Joan Leopold, *Culture in Comparative and Evolutionary Perspective: E. B. Tylor and the Making of Primitive Culture* (Berlin, 1980).

127. See Tylor, *Early History of Mankind*, p. 8, and *Primitive Culture*. See also George W. Stocking, Jr., *Victorian Anthropology* (New York, 1987), pp. 157–158, 161.

128. This is to some extent disputed by Stocking, *Victorian Anthropology*, pp. 302–304.

129. Among many other sources see Lowie, *History of Ethnological Theory*, pp. 128–155; Melville Herskovits, *Franz Boas* (New York, 1953); Kroeber in *Franz Boas, American Anthropological Association Memoir* 61, pp. 8–9; Kluckhohn and Prufer in Goldschmidt, *Anthropology of Franz Boas*, pp. 11–13; Abram Kardiner and Edward Preble, *They Studied Man* (Cleveland, 1961), pp. 134–159; Marshall Hyatt, *Franz Boas, Social Activist* (New York, 1990).

130. Marett used the phrase in referring to J. G. Frazer's *Golden Bough;* see Kardiner and Preble, *They Studied Man*, p. 92.

Boas was born in 1858, into a well-to-do family of freethinking Jews in the small German city of Minden. He studied physics, mathematics, and geography at the Universities of Heidelberg, Bonn, and Kiel, taking his doctorate at Kiel in 1881. His major thesis was in physics. Subsequently he did a year of military reserve service, and in the following year made the acquaintance of the psychologist Wilhelm Wundt, an experience that may have shaped his thinking more than has commonly been recognized.[131] In 1883 he persuaded a Berlin newspaper to finance him for a year's field study on Baffin Island, off the northeast coast of Canada, on the promise of submitting a series of popular articles. His intention was to study the influence of environment on the seasonal migration and subsistence habits of the Eskimos, a project that reflected the environmental determinism prevailing among German geographers at the time. Boas joined a German scientific expedition that was already in the field, but remained in Baffinland after the departure of the other members, spending a complete year among the Eskimos. It was this experience, resulting ultimately in his *Central Eskimo* monograph,[132] that launched his career as an ethnologist.

After leaving Baffinland in 1884 Boas spent a few months in New York City, where he had already become engaged to a German-American girl. He then returned to Germany, where he was appointed an assistant in the Museum für Völkerkunde under Adolf Bastian. In 1886 he also received an appointment as docent in geography at the University of Berlin. These appointments brought him into close association with the physiologist-ethnologist Rudolf Virchow and the geographer-ethnographer Friedrich Ratzel, both of whom apparently had a strong influence on his ethnological thinking.[133]

In 1886, before actually taking up his duties at the university, Boas set out for the field again, this time to study the culture of the Bella Coola Indians in British Columbia. His interest in this group had been aroused when he encountered a group of Bella Coolas who were "on exhibition" in Berlin. He promptly threw himself into the study of the existing ethnographic literature, and by the time he took the field he had already published two articles on the Bella Coola language and two on Bella Coola culture. Boas's second field expedition lasted for about six months, and inaugurated his lifelong involvement with the ethnography of the Northwest Coast Indians.[134] At the end of this second field expedition the young ethnographer

131. See Kluckhohn and Prufer in Goldschmidt, *Anthropology of Franz Boas*, p. 11.

132. Published in the *Sixth Annual Report of the Bureau of American Ethnology, 1884–1885* (Washington, D.C., 1888), pp. 399–669.

133. Kroeber in *Franz Boas, American Anthropological Association Memoir* 61, p. 9.

134. See esp. Ronald P. Rohner, *The Ethnography of Franz Boas* (Chicago, 1969).

stopped off again in New York, married his fiancée–and settled down. He had already made up his mind to leave Germany because of growing anti-Semitism, and the offer of an editorship of *Science* magazine made the move economically possible.

Boas's arrival in America was fortuitous both for him and for his adopted country, for he arrived at a time when the need for graduate, professional education was just beginning to be recognized in American universities. Clark University in Worcester, Massachusetts, was a new institution that was consciously patterning itself on the German university model, and in 1888 Boas was invited to be its first docent in anthropology, and to offer graduate training. Here, in 1892, he awarded the first American Ph.D. in anthropology, to A.F. Chamberlain.[135] Meanwhile Boas, who was always conscious of the need for professional associations and networking, had established a connection with the British Association for the Advancement of Science, and its Committee on the Northwestern Tribes of Canada sponsored several additional field trips to the Northwest Coast.

In 1892 Boas left Clark University to become an assistant to F.W. Putnam in setting up the Department of Anthropology at the World's Columbian Exposition (later Field Museum of Natural History), an event related in Chapter 5. From Chicago he went on to a similar role at the American Museum of Natural History in New York, and in 1896 was also appointed lecturer in physical anthropology at Columbia University. In 1899 he was promoted to a full professorship at Columbia, and the rest, so to speak, is history. During the thirty-eight years of his tenure at Columbia he awarded more than twenty Ph.D.'s, and for two decades these were almost the only anthropology doctorates awarded in the United States. As anthropology began to achieve a certain academic respectability–largely through the efforts of Boas himself–his students went forth to found many of the leading anthropology departments at other institutions. It was almost wholly through the influence of Boas that academic professionalism was introduced into American anthropology, and the discipline moved from the museum to the university as its primary institutional base.

Boas's lasting legacy is represented primarily in the work of his students. He wrote only a few books, none of which reached a very wide audience. He also published more than six hundred articles, but they were nearly all narrowly particularized in scope, for, as Leslie White has correctly observed, Boas was always preoccupied with details.[136] As a scholarly

135. See Kroeber in *Franz Boas, American Anthropological Association Memoir* 61, p. 12.

136. See esp. Leslie White, *The Ethnography and Ethnology of Franz Boas*, pp. 34–67. *Texas Memorial Museum, Bulletin* 6 (1963).

organizer, however, his influence was immense, for in his time he founded and/or edited nearly every one of the major anthropological journals in the United States. In this regard he ranks alongside J.W. Powell and F.W. Putnam as one of the three great organizers in American anthropology.

German Idealism

Despite the enormous output of his writing, and the enormous amount that his been written about him, Boas remains one of the most misunderstood and misrepresented figures in the history of anthropology. He has been variously identified as the founder of a school, a great methodological innovator, a rigorous empiricist, and an anarchic opponent of all systematic theory–none of which is entirely true. Properly speaking, he was neither a major theorist nor a methodologist, but an ideologue. His lifelong dedication to the equality of man–racial, cultural, and linguistic–is the single message that resonates through all of the vast and diverse body of his published work. He foreshadowed that dedication in the diary he kept in his early youth, while wintering on Baffin Island: "What I want to live and die for is equal rights for all, equal possibilities to learn and work for poor and rich alike! Don't you believe that to have done even the smallest bit for this, is more than all of science taken together?"[137]

Boas's egalitarian ideology had behind it the force of an almost superhuman moral passion. Kroeber has written that

> So decisive were his judgments, and so strong his feelings, that his character had in it much of the daemonic. His convictions sprang from so deep down, and manifested themselves so powerfully, that to the run of shallower men there was something ultra-human or unnatural about him: he seemed impelled by forces that did not actuate them.[138]

It is important, in conclusion, to recapitulate briefly the factors in Boas's background that were to play a major part in shaping the subsequent development of American anthropology. First, as a member of the liberal intelligentsia, he was unquestionably steeped in the general philosophical tradition of German Idealism. This was seldom specifically acknowledged in his writing, but it shows through, above all, in his passionate, lifelong dedication to the cause of human equality. Second, he had been educated in the Continental European system, with its emphasis on

137. See Douglas Cole in George W. Stocking, Jr., ed., *Observers Observed,* p. 37. *History of Anthropology,* vol. 4 (Madison, Wis., 1983). The second-person form of address is explained by the fact that the diary was in the form of a long, continuing letter to his fiancée in New York.

138. Kroeber in *Franz Boas, American Anthropological Association Memoir* 61, p. 23.

graduate training and advanced degrees. This was at a time when graduate education still hardly existed in England and America, where the university was viewed mainly as an institution for the creation and maintenance of an educated gentry class rather than for the production of a corps of trained professionals.[139] Third, he retained the holistic nineteenth-century conception of natural science, including the natural science of man, which took for granted the conjunction of physical anthropology with ethnology. Fourth, through his association with Bastian and Virchow at the Berlin Museum, he was thoroughly imbued with the particularistic and relativistic outlook of German ethnography. Fifth, through his association with Ratzel as well as his earlier studies in geography, he had become something of an environmental determinist. Finally, his prolonged and continuous contact with the Baffin Eskimos had enabled him to see the interconnectedness of cultural traits, and had left him at least an incipient functionalist.

This, then, was the baggage that Boas carried with him to America, and that he bequeathed to the first generation of professional American anthropologists. It remains to consider in a later section how much of it they absorbed, and how they built upon it.[140]

KLEINDEUTSCHLAND IN NEW YORK: THE GERMAN-AMERICAN MILIEU

The New York City to which Boas removed in 1887 has been cited by one author as the third-largest German city in the world, with an estimated German-speaking population of well over a half million.[141] They were still, at that date, a cohesive ethnic community, referring to themselves and their neighborhoods as *Kleindeutschland* ("Little Germany").[142] They were residentially clustered in Lower Manhattan and in outlying enclaves in Williamsburg, Brooklyn, and Hoboken, New Jersey, and they had their own sporting clubs, fraternal organizations, political clubs, and cultural centers; their own German-language newspapers and theater.[143] What they did not have, unlike all the other ethnic minorities in New York, was a

139. See esp. Clark Kerr, *The Uses of the University* (Cambridge, Mass., 1963), pp. 12–18.

140. For a thorough exploration of the German idealist influences on the young Boas, see George W. Stocking, Jr., ed., *Volksgeist as Method and Ethic: Essays on Boasian Ethnography and the German Anthropological Tradition,* esp. pp. 3–184. *History of Anthropology,* vol. 8 (Madison, Wis., 1996). However, this volume does not sufficiently acknowledge the contribution of Boas's students to the development of idealism in American anthropology.

141. Stanley Nadel, *Little Germany* (Urbana, Ill., 1990), p. 1.

142. This term was applied both to the German-American residential district in Lower Manhattan, and more broadly to the whole German-American community in the greater New York area. I will use it in the latter sense here.

143. For extended discussion, see Nadel, *Little Germany.*

community of religion. They were Catholics, several kinds of Protestants, Jews, and freethinkers. Also, they came from nearly all of the states and principalities of Germany and Austria.[144] Germanness in Kleindeutschland was, as it had been in the old country, a matter of common culture and language, not of religious or political allegiance.

In 1887 at least 10 percent, and perhaps as much as 20 percent, of the German-American population was Jewish.[145] For most, however, this was not a primary self-referent. Unlike their coreligionists from eastern Europe, a high percentage of the German-American Jews were freethinkers, or at least were nonpracticing. As Robert Murphy put it, "their dedication to learning, political liberalism, and professional attainment was their only devotion."[146] Although they occasionally joined with other Jews in supporting philanthropic and community improvement projects,[147] they were separated from the east European immigrants by both language and culture, and they felt a strong sense of cultural superiority in respect to their non-German coreligionists.[148] In most contexts they identified much more strongly with their fellow Germans than with their fellow Jews, and they were active in nearly every aspect of the community life of Kleindeutschland.[149] There was, inevitably, some prejudice against the Jews among German-American gentiles, but it was widely condemned in the German press and among the community leaders of Kleindeutschland.[150]

German Idealism

Kleindeutschland was, it seemed, a world in which one could move comfortably between a German, a Jewish, and an American identity, or be simultaneously all three.[151] Rabbi Felsenthal of Chicago put the matter eloquently:

> Racially I am a Jew, for I have been born among the Jewish nation. Politically I am an American as patriotic, as enthusiastic as devoted an American citizen as it is possible to be. But spiritually I am a Ger-

144. Ibid., pp. 165–167.
145. Ibid., p. 100.
146. Robert F. Murphy, *Robert H. Lowie* (New York, 1972), p. 10.
147. Cf. Irving Howe, *World of Our Fathers* (New York, 1976), p. 230.
148. Cf. ibid, pp. 417–554; Nadel, *Little Germany*, pp. 101–102. It was the German Jews who coined the pejorative epithet "kike" for the eastern Jews, reflecting the fact that so many of their surnames ended in "-ki." See Moses Rischen, *The Promised City* (New York, 1970), p. 98.
149. See esp. Rudolf Glanz, *Jews in Relation to the Cultural Milieu of the Germans in America up to the Eighteen Eighties* (New York, 1947); also Eric E. Hirschler, *Jews from Germany in the United States* (New York, 1955), pp. 42–45.
150. Nadel, *Little Germany*, p. 102.
151. For additional discussion, see ibid., pp. 99–103; see also Theodora Kroeber, *Alfred Kroeber, a Personal Configuration* (Berkeley, Calif., 1970), pp. 24–27.

man, for my inner life has been profoundly influenced by Schiller, Goethe, Kant and other intellectual giants of Germany.[152]

In particular, the rabbi's statement illustrates how deeply German Idealism had struck a responsive chord among the Jews, in America as well as in the old country. Kroeber has described the cultural ethos of Kleindeutschland as "the mellow golden sunset of the German civilization of Kant and Goethe, translated to a late afterglow among congenial and harmonious American institutions...."[153]

Kleindeutschland *in New York*

Franz Boas married into the society of Kleindeutschland when he wed Marie Krackowizer in 1887, and he entered almost at once into the social and cultural life of the German-American community. He lectured at the German cultural centers and wrote articles for the German-language magazines.[154] As one of the very few members of the community who could boast a doctorate from a German university, and as an editor of *Science* magazine, he enjoyed enormous intellectual prestige.

The Kleindeutschland into which Boas settled was also the community in which nearly all of his earliest students had grown up. Most, though not all, were of German-Jewish extraction, and at least some were the offspring of well-to-do burghers. They did not follow their fathers into trade, however, for the German immigrants, though not themselves university-educated, had that special veneration for higher education that has always characterized the German bourgeoisie.[155] They saw to it that their sons and daughters got the best available education, in the arts and literature as well as in history and science. Some were sent to private schools or were educated at home by private tutors, others went to elite public schools like the Horace Mann School and the Bronx High School of Science.[156] We may take it for granted that they were thoroughly imbued with the spirit of German Idealism, whether specifically from their schooling or more generally from the ethos of their home community. Later, the German-American sons and daughters were encouraged to enter the university–which usually meant Columbia or Barnard–and to pursue the learned professions that had been beyond the reach of their immigrant parents.

It is important to notice that none of Boas's earliest students went to

152. Hirschler, *Jews from Germany*, p. 51.

153. Theodora Kroeber, *Alfred Kroeber*, p. 27.

154. Some of these are cited in Theodora Kroeber, *Alfred Kroeber*, pp. 68–72.

155. See esp. Lenore O'Boyle in *Comparative Studies in Society and History* 25, no. 1 (1983): 3–25.

156. For Kroeber's education as an example, see Theodora Kroeber, *Alfred Kroeber*, pp. 14–29, and Julian Steward, *Alfred Kroeber* (New York, 1973) pp. 3–5, 19–20.

Columbia specifically to study with him, or to study anthropology, for they had probably never heard of either one. Otherwise, we may assume, they would have declared an anthropology major from the beginning. As it was, Goldenweiser and Lesser majored initially in philosophy, Haeberlin and Wissler in psychology, Herskovits, Radin, and White in history, Lowie and Reichard in classics, Benedict and Kroeber in literature, and Chamberlain and Sapir in modern languages. Several of the early Boasians had already changed majors more than once before they discovered anthropology. But when these individuals encountered Boasian anthropology, near the end of their student careers, they became virtually instant converts. What happened, it seems clear, is that they found what they had really always been looking for: the perfect disciplinary embodiment of German Idealism. Psychology, literature, and philology had offered partial fulfillment for idealist visions; Boasian anthropology offered complete fulfillment.

German Idealism

Boas offered something else that was otherwise lacking in American higher education: a mentor in the German tradition. At this time German university education was still, as all medieval education had been, essentially a patron-client system, and it was much more important to have a mentor than to have a major. One did not enroll in a German university, at least at the graduate level, to study a particular subject; one enrolled to study under a particular professor. If the professor dabbled in a number of different subjects, as many Germans did, so also did his students. And if the professor moved from one university to another, as many also did, the students followed along as a matter of course, for in reality it was the professor and not the institution that conferred a degree. In the end, it became the personal responsibility of the professor-patron to find employment for his student-clients, when their student days were over.[157]

Boas became just that kind of professor-patron for his German-American students. He was not a guru, as has sometimes been asserted;[158] the idealist outlook had already been implanted in the students long before they came under his tutelage. Very few of them took more than one or two basic courses from him, for by the time they encountered him they had already completed their residence and unit requirements. Most spent no more than one or two years with him, during which time he set them individually tailored reading programs, and sometimes sent them on field research projects.[159] But his most important contribution was to set his

157. The German professors have been referred to as "academic mandarins"; see Fritz K. Ringer, *The Decline of the German Mandarins* (Cambridge, Mass., 1969).

158. Cf. Kardiner and Preble, *They Studied Man*, p. 157.

159. See Herskovits, *Franz Boas*, pp. 22–24; Kroeber in *Franz Boas, American Anthropological Association Memoir* 61, pp. 14–16.

students in the direction to which their idealism had been tending all along; he made them realize that they had really always wanted to be anthropologists. In that role he served as a guide rather than as a guru. He was also, in the German academic tradition, a point of reference: a fixed position in an intellectual pedigree.

Kleindeutschland *in New York*

Paradoxically, it appears that at least some of Boas's students were more deeply grounded in the literature of German Idealism than was the master himself. This seems particularly evident in the writing of Kroeber, Lowie, Goldenweiser, Sapir, and Benedict. They, like nearly all of Boas's students, came to him from earlier backgrounds in the social sciences or humanities, whereas Boas himself had studied primarily physics and geography. Moreover, three of his most important mentors and colleagues, Fischer, Bastian, and Virchow, had been outspoken critics of the Idealist philosophical tradition.[160] The point is important because, as I will suggest a little later, the so-called Boasian paradigm in anthropology actually owed as much to the students as it did to Boas himself.

In sum, it is important to recognize what Boas did and what he did not do. He did bring with him, and transplant to America, the tradition of academic professionalism that in the late nineteenth century was a special feature of continental European higher education.[161] He also brought the German ethnographic tradition, though, as we saw in the last chapter, it was hardly different in spirit from the tradition of Indianology that had developed independently in America. He did not bring, or rather did not initiate, the philosophy of German Idealism, which was already deeply rooted in the German-American community before his arrival.[162] He found German-American students who were steeped in that philosophy, and convinced them that anthropology was their proper calling. What he achieved on American soil, therefore, was the merger of professionalism, ethnography, and idealist philosophy into what, in the first years of the twentieth century, became a uniquely American anthropology.

EARLY BOASIAN IDEALISM: THE AMERICAN HISTORICAL SCHOOL

As we saw in Chapter 5, an important distinction must be made between the work of the Boasians before and after about 1930; the watershed date

160. Cf. Lowie, *History of Ethnological Theory*, p. 31.
161. On this, see Kerr, *Uses of the University*, pp. 12–18.
162. However, for Boas's specific contribution to the Culture concept, see George W. Stocking, Jr., *Race, Culture, and Evolution* (New York, 1968), pp. 195–233.

when American anthropology shifted its primary focus of interest from the past to the present. I will refer to the period before 1930, with which I am concerned here, as the early Boasian period, and to the anthropologists of that time as early Boasians.

The theoretical and research paradigm that was developed by the early Boasians, and that was dominant between about 1900 and 1930, has usually been designated as the American Historical School, and its origins have been attributed quite specifically to Boas himself.[163] The title is appropriate, but the attribution is not, for Lowie was quite correct in recognizing that Boas was more a functionalist than a culture historian.[164] The American Historical School was the creation of the early students of Boas, and their historical preoccupation came much less from their mentor than from their general background in the German idealist tradition. Both Kroeber and Radin were to assert, long after their student days, that Boas was not really a historian,[165] while Boas on his part condemned some of the historical reconstruction methods of Kroeber and Wissler as unscientific.[166]

German Idealism

The research program

In discussing American Historical Anthropology, it is necessary to distinguish between its research program and its theoretical orientations. The field research program of the early Boasians was thoroughly consistent with the German ethnographic tradition, but it was not in fact an importation from Germany. As we saw in the last chapter, the Boasians simply took over and made their own the program of Indianological research that had been ongoing for more than a generation in the hands of the Bureau of American Ethnology, the Peabody Museum at Harvard, and one or two other institutions. They had really no other choice, since they had no independent research funding. Until at least the 1920s their field work was funded by the Smithsonian Institution, the American Museum of Natural History, the Field Museum of Natural History, and other institutions that were already in existence, and they necessarily conformed their investigations to the general research objectives of those institutions.

163. Harris, *Rise of Anthropological Theory*, pp. 250–289; Malefijt, *Images of Man*, pp. 225–233; Allen W. Johnson and Timothy Earle, *The Evolution of Human Societies* (Stanford, Calif., 1987), p. 2.

164. Lowie, *History of Ethnological Theory*, pp. 142–144.

165. A.L. Kroeber in *American Anthropologist* 37 (1935): 539–569; Paul Radin, *Method and Theory in Ethnology* (New York, 1933), pp. 14–20.

166. Cf. Lowie, *History of Ethnological Theory*, pp. 153–154.

At the heart of the research program was the commitment to cultural salvage, an urgent need on which the Boasians were in complete agreement with their Indianologist colleagues and predecessors.[167] Essentially, the American Historical research program came to involve the following components:

Early Boasian Idealism

Salvage ethnography. As we saw in the last chapter, it was the consideration of ethnographic salvage that directed the steps of so many early Boasians to the northern Plains and the Pacific Northwest, and a little later to California and the Great Basin. Like the Indianologists who had preceded them, they were interested wholly in the recording of "traditional culture" or in other words precontact conditions, which they investigated by querying the most elderly informants who were still mentally alert. They continued to employ, either formally or informally, the questionnaire methodology that had been in use among Indianologists for more than half a century (and that was generally also employed at this time by British, French, and German ethnographers). Their endeavors culminated in the compilation and publication of trait-list ethnographies that were often minutely particularized in their enumeration of traits, but conveyed no overall impression of what it was like to be an Arapaho or a Havasupai. The ethnographies were always, by convention, expressed in the "ethnographic-present" tense, even though the customs that were described had often disappeared generations earlier, and could not actually be observed by the ethnographers. The trait-list approach to ethnography was, of course, essential as a basis for trait-distribution studies, which were one of the major preoccupations of the American Historical School, as they were also of the German ethnographers in the early twentieth century (see Chapter 7).

A methodological innovation of the Boasians, at least in theory, was the insistence on a long field sojourn, which would ideally involve learning the language of the subject people. For at least a generation, however, this ideal was honored much more in theory than in practice. The reasons were mainly pragmatic: research funding was simply not available for extended field stays, and without funding the museums or universities in which the anthropologists were employed would not grant them extended leaves for research. It should be noted in any case that the trait-list, questionnaire-type ethnography undertaken by the early Boasians did not really require either long field sojourns or command of the native language; it could be done just as well in a succession of short visits, or even by bringing Indian informants to the campus.

167. See Margaret Mead and Ruth Bunzel, eds., *The Golden Age of American Anthropology* (New York, 1960), pp. 340–343.

Linguistics. A great many of the early Boasians undertook to record Indian languages along with other aspects of culture. Their linguistic research program was another legacy of Indianology, and before the 1920s it differed in no important respect from the work of the earlier American scholars. What the fieldworkers mainly undertook was the phonetic recording of native, mostly mythological texts, which were then subjected to both interlinear and figurative translation. In a few cases the anthropologists also produced vocabularies and grammars, although in these endeavors they had very often been preceded by missionaries and Indian agents. Before the great analytical innovations of Sapir in the 1920s, however, the Boasians had few analytical tools at their disposal. Their competence as linguists was limited to their mastery of the International Phonetic Alphabet, and their hours of field practice in using it. For that reason, they are more accurately termed language recorders rather than true linguists.

The Boasians had two basic motivations for recording Indian languages, both of which they shared with the earlier Indianologists. One, as in the case of ethnography, was simply salvage, for Indian languages were disappearing as rapidly as were other aspects of indigenous culture, and hundreds had already become extinct. The other motivation was a recognition, which had been common in comparative philology since the eighteenth century, of the importance of language as a key to the reconstruction of prehistory. Speakers of related languages could be assumed to be descended from a common ancestral people, and the distribution of language families over nations and continents gave a clue to ancient migrations and to original homelands.[168]

Physical anthropology. The study of physical anthropology was not a specific component of Indianology, at least until the early twentieth century. It was however a regular feature of German ethnography, reflecting the common nineteenth century view that racial, ethnic, and linguistic differences were interconnected. The paradox of Boas's position was that he accepted the relevance of physical anthropology to the study of man, while at the same time vehemently denying the interconnection between racial, ethnic, and linguistic data.[169] That is, he accepted physical anthropology as an appropriate and necessary part of the anthropological discipline, and at the same time destroyed what had always been its central organizing concept: the concept of race.[170]

168. For discussion see esp. Edward Sapir in David G. Mandelbaum, ed., *Selected Writings of Edward Sapir* (Berkeley, Calif., 1949), pp. 432–460.

169. For the background of Boas's involvement in, and commitment to, physical anthropology, see Benoit Massin in Stocking, *Volksgeist as Method and Ethic*, pp. 79–154.

170. See esp. Stocking, *Race, Culture, and Evolution*, pp. 161–194.

The result was that physical anthropology was left without a very clearcut mission within the framework of Boasian anthropology; it was never quite certain what it was supposed to contribute. This is undoubtedly the reason why so few of Boas's students followed their mentor into this particular field of investigation. So far as I know, Melville Herskovits was the only one of the Boasians who undertook significant researches in physical anthropology.

Early Boasian Idealism

Archaeology. Considering the basically historical preoccupation of the early Boasians, it comes as a surprise to observe that archaeology was not a part of their research program. In the broadest sense, this may reflect the general lack of interest in prehistory that was characteristic of the German philosophy of history. The Boasians did nevertheless take a particularistic interest in the prehistory of the Indians; they simply did not see this as accessible through archaeology. So little real, systematic archaeology (as opposed to artifact-collecting) had been done in North America in the early twentieth century that the Boasians did not recognize its possibilities.

Prehistoric archaeology, then, was the one component of Indianology that the Boasians did not take up.[171] It was left to other, non-German anthropologists, working within the older tradition of Indianology, to construct the entire time-space grid of North American prehistory that took shape between about 1920 and World War II.[172] Like the Indianologists who had preceded them, a great many of the outstanding archaeologists of the early twentieth century came from small-town or rural backgrounds in the Midwest, and their work grew out of a boyhood interest in the Indians.

Their lack of personal involvement does not mean that the Boasians considered archaeology unimportant. They recognized the essential role that archaeological data had played in the reconstruction of Old World prehistory, and that our entire understanding of human cultural evolution before about 3000 B.C. was based on no other evidence.[173] They taught about archaeology in their introductory classes and wrote about it in their

171. An exception was Fay-Cooper Cole, who is now best remembered for his archaeological work in Illinois. But Cole was a Midwesterner who had his earlier college education at Northwestern and Chicago before going on to a final degree with Boas; he represents a bridge between the Boasian and the older Indianological traditions.

172. See esp. Gordon R. Willey and Jeremy A. Sabloff, *A History of American Archaeology* (San Francisco, 1974), pp. 88–130.

173. Lowie, for example, published an English résumé of Hugo Obermaier's scheme of Old World prehistoric sequences; see Stuart Rice, ed., *Methods in Social Science* (New York, 1931), pp. 266–274.

textbooks,[174] and later, when departments expanded, they added full-time archaeologists to their faculties. So far as North America was concerned, however, they accepted the near-universal belief that the Indians were latecomers to the continent, whose cultures had subsequently evolved only in the sense of adapting to particular habitats. Neither they nor anyone else, in the first quarter of the twentieth century, had any real idea of how much lay under the North American soil, or how much it had to teach.

German Idealism

The theoretical and philosophical perspectives

If the research program of the early Boasians was basically American in its origins, the theoretical and philosophical perspectives that they brought to their work were not. To begin with it is noteworthy that none of Boas's early students were, so far as I know, attracted to anthropology by a previous interest in the Indians for their own sake. They were thoroughgoing urbanites who probably had never seen an Indian, and they were not brought up on Indianological lore to the same extent as were Anglo-American youth. It may thus be suggested that the Boasians' interest in the Indians flowed from a more general interest in anthropology, whereas for the majority of Anglo-Americans the reverse was true.

The theoretical perspectives of the Boasians, then, were not inherited from an earlier American tradition, as was their research program. On the contrary, they were derived in large measure from the German idealist tradition. It was those perspectives that, collectively, gave a distinctive character to the American Historical School of Anthropology. Essentially the following components were involved:

Culturology. It is commonly and correctly asserted that the basic organizing concept of twentieth-century American anthropology has been the concept of culture.[175] Less often recognized is the fact that there are really two culture concepts, one generic and the other specific, both of which are important in the American anthropological tradition. The generic concept in all its essentials is the one articulated by Tylor more than a hundred years ago: the definition of culture as a set of learned, shared behaviors and beliefs. It derives from the German universalist tradition, and is basic to our understanding of generalized cultural evolution, or in other words

174. Cf. Clark Wissler, *Man and Culture* (New York, 1923), pp. 212–246; A.L. Kroeber, *Anthropology* (New York, 1923), pp. 137–179; 393–506.
175. Cf. Kroeber and Kluckhohn, *Culture*, pp. 1–8.

of the differences between peoples at different points in time. The specific concept is the concept of *cultures*, in the plural, which owes its inspiration to the German particularist tradition; it is basic to our understanding of the differences between peoples at the same point in time.[176]

Early Boasian Idealism

Both the generic and the specific concepts of culture were important elements in the German idealist tradition, represented respectively by *Kultur* (generic) and *Volksgeist* (specific). Neither was exclusively German: the Indianologists before Boas had spoken of the "civilization" of the Indians in general, and of the differences between one Indian "nation" and another in particular. It was the German achievement, however, to separate culture clearly both from society and from the state; a consequence of the fact that in the early nineteenth century there was a German culture but there was no single German society or state. And the separation of culture from society made possible the examination of culture as an entity for study in its own right (Kroeber's "Superorganic"[177]), without reference to any specific social or political context. This is the perspective that Leslie White would later call culturological.[178]

Since they were not very much concerned with the study of evolution, or of Native American prehistory, the Boasians (except for Kroeber) were generally more interested in cultures in the specific sense than they were in culture in the generic sense. In this they followed the lead of the German particularists, and specifically of Herder, who was much more interested in discovering what made Germans different from French and Slavs than he was in defining the commonalities of modern European culture that were shared by Germans, French, and Slavs. For the Boasians, this particularizing tendency went hand-in-hand with the rejection of the evolutionist (i.e., progressivist) theoretical framework, and with the consequent belief that one culture was as important as another.

The linguistic analogy. An important component of the *Kultur* concept (generic sense) that was distinctly German in its origins was the linguistic analogy: the conception of culture not as behavior but as a set of socially learned behavioral codes, analogous to the grammatical rules of a language. This meant that cultures could be studied in essentially the same way as were languages: not by observing and analyzing a mass of behaviors, but by eliciting the rules underlying the behaviors. As Ward Goodenough

---

176. See Stocking, *Victorian Anthropology*, pp. 302–304.

177. A. L. Kroeber in *American Anthropologist* 19 (1917): 163–213.

178. Leslie White in *Southwestern Journal of Anthropology* 1 (1945): 221–248; id., *The Science of Culture* (New York, 1949).

put it, "Culture... consists of standards for deciding what is, standards for deciding how one feels about it, standards for deciding what to do about it, and standards for deciding how to go about doing it."[179]

Such an approach did not require extensive field observation or a large body of informants; the rules either of language or of culture could be learned by interviewing a few well-informed respondents. The fundamental assumption, in the case of both language and culture, was that there was only one set of rules for everybody.[180] Moreover, just as lexical or grammatical elements could be freely borrowed from one language to another, without affecting the basic integrity of either, so also could culture traits. Culture could therefore be envisioned as a set of infinitely separable traits, comparable to vocabulary items, though there was necessarily an underlying "grammar," or cultural blueprint, that held them together. This "paralinguistic" conception of culture may help to explain why, in the minds of the Boasians, there was always a close connection between ethnographic and linguistic research.

German Idealism

Cultural particularism. As we have already seen, the concept of cultures, in the specific, Herderian sense, provided the basic Boasian framework for organizing and understanding the ethnography of native North America. In the broadest sense, the basis for this conception can be traced back both to Herder's emphasis on the *Volksgeist* and to Kant's insistence on "the thing-in-itself"; an entity to be understood and respected without reference to any external context and relationship. But Boasian particularism also had another basis, in the methodology of natural science. When the Boasians made culture their central organizing concept, it necessarily meant also that they made cultures, rather than societies or nations, their basic units of analysis, comparison, and classification. That is, Native North America was seen to be made up of a panoply of *cultures* (not peoples per se), which could be grouped into culture areas. From this perspective, every culture had to be treated as a bounded, inclusive unit for purposes of comparison and classification.[181] Here, once again, the linguistic analogy came into play. Each Indian "belonged" to one and only one culture in the same way that he or she was a speaker of one and only one mother-tongue.

179. *Cooperation in Change* (New York, 1963), p. 259.
180. Disregarding, of course, a few special cases where different forms of speech were prescribed for men and women.
181. For the epistemological assumptions underlying systems of classification, see esp. William Y. Adams and Ernest W. Adams, *Archaeological Typology and Practical Reality* (Cambridge, 1991), pp. 76–90.

Boasian particularism, combined with the trait-list approach to ethnography, resulted in a distinctive literary product: the comprehensive one-tribe ethnography. This was not, it must be added, a strictly Boasian innovation. Morgan's *League of the Ho-De-No-Sau-Nee, or Iroquois,* published in 1851, may perhaps be regarded as the archetypical tribal ethnography. But the attempt to describe the complete culture of a single tribe in terms of a basic categorical blueprint–an itemized list of traits–was not only a special emphasis of the American Historical School; it was regarded by the members themselves as their paramount ethnographic achievement.

Early Boasian Idealism

Cultural determinism. According to the Boasian perspective it was culture that mainly caused the behavior of individuals, so that individual performances could be disregarded once the "rules" of culture had been learned. This was the essence of culturology: an outlook that clearly reflects the prevailing mentalism in all German philosophy.

Cultural relativism. Treating each culture as a discrete, bounded unit is not the same thing as saying that all cultures are of equal value. It was on this latter point that the Boasians differed most sharply from their Indianologist colleagues, and where they showed most overtly the influence of German Idealism. The leading Indianologists of the nineteenth century were nearly all disciples of Morgan, as we saw in the last chapter; they had no more doubt than had the Enlightenment progressivists that there were "lower" and "higher" cultures. But Boas was as passionately opposed to any such conception as was Herder, and nearly all his students concurred. In their different ways, Lowie, Goldenweiser, Radin, and Herskovits[182] all became impassioned spokesmen for the doctrine of Cultural Relativism, and it remains to this day the single most powerful ideological legacy of German Idealism in American anthropology.

Environmental adaptation. The concept of environmental adaptation was one to which nearly all of the Boasians paid lip service. This point of view was imprinted upon Boas through his association with the German geographers Fischer and Ratzel and is very much apparent in his study of the Baffin Eskimo.[183] Later, however, he moved away rather markedly from environmental determinism, placing more emphasis on the impor-

182. A collection of Herskovits's essays was published under the title *Cultural Relativism* (New York, 1972).

183. *Sixth Annual Report of the Bureau of American Ethnology* (1888), pp. 399–669.

tance of historical trajectories in the development of cultures.[184] In this he was followed by nearly all his students; indeed he may actually have been influenced by the students, since, as I suggested earlier, some of them were apparently more grounded in the idealist tradition than was Boas himself. Considering their apprenticeship under Boas, what is extraordinary in the work of the early Boasians is not their insistence on the importance of environment but their lack of it. They really saw cultures much more as products of their own special histories of development than as shaped by environmental circumstances. Even the culture area phenomenon, which seems clearly to carry an implication of environmental determination, was seen by Kroeber as resulting more from processes of diffusion than of adaptation.[185] It may be suggested, in sum, that the thinking of the early Boasians was considerably more in harmony with that of Herder than it was with that of Ratzel.

Historicism. The Boasians agreed with virtually all other anthropologists at the turn of the century in regarding their discipline as basically a historical science. Maitland's oft-quoted dictum, that "By and by anthropology will have the choice between being history or nothing,"[186] was not at all inappropriate in the context of its time (1902). But the Boasians brought to their study the particularly German conception of history, as being very largely concerned with the growth and spread of cultures. And, according to Kroeber, "Edouard Meyer, by some considered the greatest historian of our time, assigns to anthropology the task of determining the generic or universal features in human history."[187]

The Boasians believed, in theory, that the shape of every culture was determined by the combination of its environment and its own individual history of development. However, as we have just seen, in practice they placed a good deal more emphasis on the latter than on the former. No culture could be fully understood without taking its history of development into account, and history must therefore be studied as a basic component of any ethnographic inquiry. By the same token, to the extent that the Boasians attempted to place individual cultures within larger contexts of understanding, they were first of all historical contexts, and only secondly environmental contexts.

---

184. Franz Boas, *Race, Language and Culture* (New York, 1940), p. 306; see also Harris, *Rise of Anthropological Theory*, pp. 265–267, and Malefijt, *Images of Man*, p. 227.
185. Cf. Steward, *Alfred Kroeber*, pp. 53–54.
186. Quoted here from the flyleaf of Radin, *Method and Theory in Ethnology.*
187. A. L. Kroeber, *Configurations of Culture Growth* (Berkeley, Calif., 1963), p. 3.

Diffusionism. Cultural diffusion was, for the Boasians, the driving force of cultural change, as evolution had been for the progressivists. And although they did not go to anything like the same lengths as did the Austrian *Kulturkreis* theorists, who liked to think of diffusion as occurring in orderly and retrodictable waves,[188] they nevertheless hoped to find macropatterns within the seemingly random and chaotic mass of cultural borrowings. Hence, the study of culture trait distributions became one of the major research preoccupations of the American Historical School.

Early Boasian Idealism

The distribution studies were not an end in themselves. They would supposedly make it possible to reconstruct general patterns of prehistoric diffusion, and to trace particular trait-complexes to their region of origin. The sum of all such waves of diffusion would add up to a prehistory of America, according to the German conception of history. In fact, no macropatterns of diffusion were ever discovered by the Boasians, except insofar as they were implicit in the culture area concept. All of the published studies of diffusion and distribution turned out to be highly particularized surveys of specific traits, such as Harold Driver's survey of the distribution of girls' puberty rites,[189] and Kroeber's very brief essay on the distribution of salt, dogs, and tobacco.[190]

Qualitative methodology. Considering the theoretical and methodological advances that had taken place in sociology, political science, economics, and experimental psychology by the end of the nineteenth century, the absence of statistical methodology and of probabilistic theory in the work of the early Boasians is striking. Their methodology and their outlook were strictly qualitative and normative, or in other words humanistic. Indeed, both Kroeber and Radin questioned the legitimacy of the social science concept itself.[191] On the whole, too, the Boasians were conspicuously more interested in customs than in institutions; in mind rather than in society. In these respects as in so many others, they continued in the well-worn tradition of German idealist philosophy. It was not until the middle of the twentieth century, with the advent of social functionalism, that the quantitative methodology of the social sciences made a belated appearance in American anthropology.[192]

---

188. See esp. Kluckhohn in *American Anthropologist* 38, no. 2 (1936): 157–196, and Jacobs, *Pattern in Cultural Anthropology*, pp. 21–22.

189. *University of California Anthropological Records* 6:2 (1941).

190. *University of California Anthropological Records* 6:1 (1941).

191. A.L. Kroeber in *Journal of Social Psychology* 1 (1936): 317–340; Radin, *Method and Theory in Ethnology*, esp. pp. 168–182.

192. Cf. George C. Homans, *The Nature of Social Science* (New York, 1967); Pertti J. Pelto, *Anthropological Research* (New York, 1970), pp. 154–212.

Summary. In sum, the approach of the American Historical School to the study of cultures was historicist, culturological, atomistic, and mentalist. It was historicist in that culture was approached largely as a historical phenomenon, and culturological in that cultures and not individuals were the units of study and comparison. Individuals were treated as mere carriers of cultural traditions. It was atomistic in that, although all the Boasians paid lip service to the concept of cultural integration, they never identified the integrating factor that held cultures together. On the contrary they treated them much more as congeries of separable parts, any one of which might at any time be replaced through a process of diffusion. Finally, their outlook was mentalistic in that the concept of adaptation was largely lacking. Cultures were shaped by their histories more than by their environments.

By the later 1920s, some of the Boasians, apparently including Boas himself, began to be troubled by the limitations of this approach. It was not, as they saw it, inherently wrong; there was simply too much that it failed to account for, or even to consider. A serious limitation, which we discussed in the last chapter, was the exclusive concern with "traditional" culture of the past, ignoring altogether the present-day Indian cultures. Another was the lack of a genuine theory of cultural integration. Still another was the lack of any concern for the relationship between cultures and the individual actors who were their bearers. All of these deficiencies were supposedly to be remedied in the later Boasian paradigm of Configurationism, which made its appearance at the end of the 1920s.

MIDCENTURY IDEALISM: THE CONFIGURATIONISTS

The factors that brought about a major shift of emphasis in American anthropology around 1930 were discussed in the last chapter. It is sufficient to recall here that the discipline belatedly developed a social conscience, and the interest of ethnologists was diverted from "traditional" (precontact) cultures to those of the present day, and from the study of history to the study of factors affecting cultural change and persistence. Two somewhat different midcentury paradigms emerged: the sociocultural school, which concentrated on the processes of culture change, and the configurationist school, which sought to discover the bases of cultural persistence.

The sociocultural school was essentially non-Boasian. Its earliest proponents, like Robert Redfield, Sol Tax, and W. Lloyd Warner, had been students or colleagues of A. R. Radcliffe-Brown during his years at Chicago (1931–1936), and they were more influenced by the traditions of British Utilitarianism than they were by German Idealism.[193] On the other hand

193. See George W. Stocking, Jr., *Anthropology at Chicago* (Chicago, 1979), pp. 21–29.

the configurationist school was pioneered by Boasians, especially Edward Sapir, Ruth Benedict, and Margaret Mead. Its popularity soon spread to other anthropologists like A.I. Hallowell, Morris Opler, Cora DuBois, and Clyde Kluckhohn, who had not been students of Boas, but their work and outlook nevertheless conformed closely to the German idealist tradition. Configurationism in the broadest sense represents not only a latter-day Boasian paradigm but the apogee of German idealist influence in American anthropology, even though many of its leading practitioners were neither Boas's students nor German-Americans.

Midcentury idealism

In addition to its preoccupation with here-and-now cultures, Configurationism also reflected a growing interest in psychology, which was common both to anthropologists and to the general public. There was, for the first time, an emphasis on the study of the individual, and more particularly on the study of individual personalities. In marked contrast to Freudian psychologists, however, the anthropologists saw personality almost purely in culturological terms: that is, the personality of each individual was imprinted by the core values and interests of his or her culture. The configurationists could therefore speak of the "cultural personality" of the Zunis, for instance, as something characteristic not only of most individual Zunis, but of Zuni culture itself. The cultural personality was therefore something very close to the traditional Geist of the German idealists.

Because of its preoccupation with personality, the configurationist paradigm has often been referred to in literature as the "Culture and Personality" school or approach,[194] but this term is unsatisfactory for several reasons. To begin with, personality as conceived by anthropologists was something much more inclusive than the personality conceived by psychologists; it included nearly every habit of mind acquired by individuals that could be attributed to cultural conditioning. Moreover, some of the anthropologists were much more interested in the "personality" of whole cultures than they were in the personality of individuals within the culture; their approach would have to be designated as Personality *of* Culture rather than Personality *in* Culture. More importantly, very few of the anthropologists at midcentury were interested in personality for its own sake; they saw it as a projection of what they called the core values, attitudes, sentiments, and themes that persisted from generation to generation, and these were the real objects of their interest.

The basic perspective

What the midcentury anthropologists were interested in discovering,

194. See, for example, Harris, *Rise of Anthropological Theory*, pp. 393–463.

then, was the Geist of each culture, even though without exception they shied away from the use of the term. Their avoidance was perhaps due to the highly mystical connotations that the Geist had acquired at the hands of writers like Nietzsche, and to its frequent use by jingo German nationalists. In its place, Ruth Benedict and A.L. Kroeber introduced the term Configuration, and I have followed their lead in designating the midcentury paradigm as Configurationism.

Essentially, the configurationist paradigm involved the following propositions:

German Idealism

1. The enduring heart of every cultural system is composed of a set of core values, interests, and sentiments, that for individuals within that system are a priori definitions of the true, the good, and the beautiful.

2. The set of core values, interests, and sentiments constitutes the integrating force that holds each society and culture together. All other culturally patterned beliefs and behaviors are consistent with them, and they will largely determine what innovations are accepted or rejected in situations of culture contact.

3. The core values, interests, and sentiments are imprinted on each "member" of the culture from birth onward, through processes of enculturation, child socialization, and personality formation that are unique to each culture.

4. As a result of these processes, the special character (Configuration) of the culture as a whole will be reflected in the personalities of its individual "members," making it possible, for example, to characterize Germans as authoritarian, English as undemonstrative, and Americans as materialistic.

5. It is the processes of childhood indoctrination that largely assure the continuity of each culture from generation to generation. As a result, values, interests, and sentiments persist over time, even while surficial features like subsistence, material culture, and technology undergo profound changes. This explains why three generations of forced education had failed to make over the Indians into mainstream Americans, even while converting them from their traditional subsistence practices into freehold farmers and mechanics.

Configurationist research

Consistent with the propositions just discussed, Configurationism came to have three basic research agendas:

1. To discover what are the core values, interests, and sentiments of each culture.

2. To study empirically the processes of enculturation, socialization,

and personality formation through which the cultural core is imprinted on each individual member.

3. To define the normative "cultural personality" of individuals in each culture; that is, that part of each person's total personality that could be attributed to the molding influence of the culture itself.

A configurationist ethnography, such as Laura Thompson's and Alice Joseph's *The Hopi Way*,[195] would ideally combine all of these components. The core values and themes would provide a *leitmotiv* for the description of the culture as a whole, as well as explaining the behavior and the personality of individuals. This kind of ethnography obviously remedied one of the most conspicuous deficiencies in earlier Boasian ethnography, by identifying the integrating force in each culture. This analytical approach came to be known as descriptive integration.[196]

Midcentury idealism

Among the configurationists there were some, like Benedict and Kluckhohn, who were primarily interested in the first of the research agendas; that is, in characterizing whole cultures (the personality-of-culture school). Others, like Mead and Hallowell, were more interested in the second and third issues; that is, in characterizing individuals within cultures, and in studying the processes through which they were enculturated (the personality-in-culture school). This was largely a matter of research emphasis, however, for all the configurationists agreed that the normative personality of individuals was a reflection of the overall personality of the culture, and that neither could be studied without reference to the other.

While there was clearly a chicken-and-egg relationship between cultural configuration and individual personality, the configurationists differed to some extent on the question of primary causality. Kroeber and Benedict believed strongly in a superorganic Geist, meaning that culture could be said to exist in its own right, independently of the beliefs and actions of individuals.[197] Other, more psychologically oriented anthropologists, like Sapir and Spiro, questioned the validity of the Superorganic concept, arguing that culture has no existence apart from the beliefs and actions of individual persons.[198] From this perspective, cultural regularities or patterns can be said to exist only to the extent that individuals have been taught to think and act in the same way. In a figurative way it might be suggested that Kroeber and Benedict believed that culture "causes" individual personalities, while Sapir and Spiro believed that individuals "cause" the cultural personality.

195. New York, 1965.

196. A. L. Kroeber, *The Nature of Culture* (Chicago, 1952), pp. 63–65; for discussion see also Benedict, *Patterns of Culture*, pp. 45–56.

197. See esp. A. L. Kroeber in *American Anthropologist* 19 (1917): 163–213.

198. See Edward Sapir in *American Anthropologist* 19 (1917): 441–447.

The earliest pioneer of Configurationism was Edward Sapir, an early student of Boas who from the beginning had always had a strong interest in psychology.[199] He laid the foundations for the configurationist paradigm in two 1927 articles, "Speech as a Personality Trait"[200] and "The Unconscious Patterning of Behavior in Society."[201] However, it was two latter-day Boasians, Ruth Benedict and Margaret Mead, who popularized the new paradigm, in a series of books that found a wide popular audience. It was largely through their works that the American intelligentsia formed an impression of what anthropology was all about. However, writing as they did for popular audiences, Benedict and Mead never achieved, and indeed never attempted, anything like conceptual rigor. It was another group of midcentury anthropologists, inspired originally by the neo-Freudian psychologist Abram Kardiner, who first introduced a measure of conceptual formality into the configurationist paradigm.[202]

Between 1936 and 1940, Kardiner conducted a series of seminars in cross-cultural psychology at Columbia University, in which Sapir, Benedict, Ruth Bunzel, Cora DuBois, Ralph Linton, and Carl Withers all took part at one time or another. Later, Kardiner induced Linton, DuBois, and Withers to submit ethnographic materials that they had collected in the field, respectively among American Indians, Melanesians, and Midwestern Americans, for formal psychological analysis, including for the first time the analysis of projective tests (Rorschach and Thematic Apperception).[203] In the resulting publication, *The Psychological Frontiers of Society,*[204] Kardiner was able to establish a clear link between the cultural institutions and the normative individual personalities among each of the three groups.

In the 1950s, Clyde Kluckhohn emerged increasingly as the primary champion of Configurationism, at least within the social science community. In a long series of articles, published in a wide variety of journals and conference proceedings, he explored the relationships among culture, society, and personality, and between anthropology and psychology.[205] Kluckhohn was interested above all in values, and in the 1940s and 1950s he

---

199. See esp. Mandelbaum, *Selected Writings of Edward Sapir,* pp. 507–508.

200. *American Journal of Sociology* 32 (1927): 892–905.

201. In E. S. Dummer, ed., *The Unconscious: a Symposium* (New York, 1927), pp. 114–142.

202. For Kardiner's role in the development of midcentury Psychological Anthropology, see esp. William C. Manson in George W. Stocking, Jr., ed., *Malinowski, Rivers, Benedict and Others,* pp. 72–94. *History of Anthropology,* vol. 4 (Madison, Wis., 1986).

203. See ibid., pp. 84–86.

204. New York, 1945.

205. For his complete bibliography, see Talcott Parsons and Evon Z. Vogt in *American Anthropologist* 64 (1962): 148–161. For a collection including a few of his theoretical articles, see Clyde Kluckhohn, *Culture and Behavior,* ed. Richard Kluckhohn (New York, 1962). For a vol-

designed the ambitious "Comparative Study of Values in Five Cultures," carried out among Navajo and Zuni Indians, Spanish-Americans, Mormons, and Texans, living close together in the high, dry environment of the Upper Southwest.

Midcentury idealism

The Comparative Values Study,[206] was the most ambitious interdisciplinary project in which anthropologists had been involved up to that time, and eventually no fewer than sixty-eight publications and eleven unpublished theses resulted from the project.[207] Yet the Comparative Values Study never achieved more than a fraction of its expected potential, and its failure to live up to expectations probably helped contribute to the general loss of interest in Configurationism in the 1960s. In retrospect, however, the study can be seen as representing the high tide of German Idealism as an active, rather than merely a latent, influence in anthropological field work.

Even more ambitious, and certainly more pretentious, than the Comparative Values Study were the "national character" studies that enjoyed a brief popularity after World War II. During the war itself, Ruth Benedict had been engaged by the Office of War Information to collect information about Japanese character and culture, which would aid in the expected forthcoming invasion and the subsequent military occupation of the Japanese islands.[208] She eventually used the information collected from newspapers, histories, novels, movies, art, and other materials to write *The Chrysanthemum and the Sword*, a kind of national ethnography that emphasized above all the traits of the Japanese cultural personality, as Benedict conceived it.[209]

Benedict's work enjoyed a considerable popularity, resulting in a short-lived vogue for "the study of culture at a distance."[210] Within a few years it

---

ume of essays evaluating Kluckhohn's contributions in many different fields, see Walter W. Taylor, John L. Fischer, and Evon Z. Vogt, eds., *Culture and Life* (Carbondale, Ill., 1973).

206. Many of the project's publications appeared in the series of *Papers of the Peabody Museum of American Archaeology and Anthropology, Harvard University.* The earlier publications were designated as "Reports of the Ramah Project," while later ones were designated as "Reports of the Rimrock Project," after it was decided to use pseudonyms in place of the actual community names.

207. See Evon Z. Vogt and Ethel M. Albert, eds., *The People of Rimrock* (Cambridge, Mass., 1966), pp. 299–305.

208. For the wartime development of National Character studies, see Manson in Stocking, *Malinowski, Rivers, Benedict, and Others*, pp. 86–89.

209. Ruth Benedict, *The Chrysanthemum and the Sword* (Boston, 1946). For description of the methodology employed, see esp. pp. 1–19.

210. See Margaret Mead and Rhoda Métraux, eds., *The Study of Culture at a Distance* (Chicago, 1953).

was followed by similarly conceived studies of England,[211] France,[212] Russia,[213] and the United States,[214] all of which focused primarily on the issue of national character, and its causes. The popularity of these studies was brief, for it was simply not in the tradition of anthropology to work on so grand a scale or to paint with so broad a brush. Above all, it was not in the tradition of anthropology to write ethnography without doing fieldwork. But the national character studies, while they lasted, represented the supreme manifestation of German idealist thinking in American anthropology, inasmuch as "national character" was hardly to be distinguished from the Volksgeist of Herder and Hegel.

German Idealism

FOLK CULTURE AND PEASANT SOCIETY

Robert Redfield was not a Boasian, nor was he brought up on the traditions of German philosophy. Yet, paradoxically, he became in time one of the most original and influential idealist thinkers in the history of American anthropology. His outlook was shaped neither by teachers nor by traditional literature, but by his personal experiences in the Mexican Indian village of Tepoztlán, where we went to do dissertation research. Redfield went to Tepoztlán expecting to find "traditional" Indian culture; what he found instead were what he would later characterize as folk culture and peasant society. The people of Tepoztlán were certainly Indians, but theirs was not an isolated and self-contained world; their institutions of economy, government, law, and religion were all at least partly integrated with those of the Mexican nation. Yet he also found many cultural and social survivals from the Aztec past, which were not shared with other Mexicans. From this experience arose the twin concepts of peasant society and folk culture, which would become two of the most important conceptual breakthroughs in midcentury anthropology.[215] Redfield's initial concepts were refined by him in a series of pathbreaking studies in the Yucatán peninsula,[216] and then by a host of other midcentury anthropologists who followed in his footsteps.

Peasants, in Redfield's formulation, were the agricultural proletariat upon which all the great world civilizations depended, but who participated in the institutions of civilization in only a limited way. They were one-

211. Geoffrey Gorer, *Exploring English Character* (London, 1955).
212. Rhoda Métraux and Margaret Mead, *Themes in French Culture* (Stanford, Calif., 1954).
213. Geoffrey Gorer and J. Rickman, *The People of Great Russia* (London, 1949).
214. Geoffrey Gorer, *The American People* (New York, 1948).
215. See Robert Redfield, *Tepoztlan, a Mexican Village* (Chicago, 1930).
216. Published most comprehensively in *The Folk Culture of Yucatan* (Chicago, 1941).

time tribesmen who had been drawn into the economic and political orbit of the civilized powers, but at the same time had been excluded from most of the benefits of civilization. Of necessity, they had retained many elements of their traditional, precivilized culture: folk social organization, folk medicine, folk religion, folklore, and the like. Moreover, they had commonly reinterpreted the legal and religious traditions of the urban elites to meet their own, local needs.[217] These various cultural manifestations were designated as "Little Traditions," in contrast to the "Great Traditions" of the urban elites which were largely inaccessible to the peasants. Redfield went on to formulate the concept of the "folk–urban continuum," a scale of development on which particular peoples, or communities, could be ranked in accordance with how far they had progressed from the folk toward the urban, or from Little Traditions toward Great Traditions. The folk–urban concept was developed initially in *The Folk Culture of Yucatan,* in which Redfield showed how four different Maya communities lay at different points along the continuum.[218]

Folk culture and peasant society

Although Redfield's outlook was originally sociofunctional rather than historical, he came increasingly to recognize that the folk–urban continuum was really an evolutionary theory, and that all mankind, regardless of local circumstances, was progressing along a common trajectory of development from the folk to the urban.[219] He came also, increasingly, to view this progression in idealist rather than in functionalist terms. The differences between the peasant and the urbanite, but also between one civilization and another, were first and foremost questions of world-view, a concept that acquired increasing centrality in Redfield's later writing.[220]

Although Redfield acknowledged his debt to Ferdinand Tönnies's concepts of *Gemeinschaft* and *Gesellschaft,*[221] he does not seem to have recognized how much Tönnies in turn owed to Herder. In fact, Redfield's conceptions of folk society and culture were extraordinarily close to Herder's conceptions of the Volk and the Volksgeist–terms that were equally applicable to tribesmen and to peasants. It is therefore possible to locate Redfield within the general stream of German idealist tradition,

217. These ideas were most fully developed in *Peasant Society and Culture* (Chicago, 1956).

218. *Folk Culture of Yucatan,* esp. pp. 338–369. For the most succinct summary of the folk-urban scheme, see Horace Miner in *American Sociological Review* 17 (1952): 529–537.

219. This perspective was most fully developed in *The Primitive World and its Transformations* (Ithaca, N.Y., 1953).

220. See Redfield, *Tepoztlan,* pp. 60–79, and *The Little Community and Peasant Society and Culture* (Chicago, 1960), pp. 81–95.

221. Cf. *Tepoztlan,* p. x, and Redfield, *The Little Community and Peasant Society and Culture,* pp. 141–142.

even while recognizing many of his ideas undoubtedly came to him independently, as a result of his field researches.

Redfield's conceptual contributions had an enormous practical impact on anthropological research in the midcentury era. For the first time, peasants were brought together with primitive tribesmen within a single conception of the noncivilized Other, making it possible to study them through the traditional lens of anthropology. The result was that the whole peasant world was opened up to ethnographic study, and this at a time when genuine tribesmen were becoming scarce, while peasants still constituted at least 75 percent of the world's population. Following in the pioneering footsteps of Redfield, anthropologists fanned out in ever-increasing numbers, first through the villages of Latin America and then, after World War II, throughout Mediterranean Europe, the Near East, India, China, and Southeast Asia, in search of peasant society and culture. The peasant community study rapidly replaced the tribal ethnography as the basic ethnographic document of the midcentury era. Not all the ethnologists were as idealist as was Redfield, but it was nevertheless true that, for about a generation, anthropology's basic conceptions of peasant society and of folk culture were predominantly mentalistic and idealistic.

THE DECLINE AND FALL OF IDEALISM

The idealist perspective remained virtually unchallenged in American anthropology through the first third of the twentieth century. Although it was formulated by the Boasians, it was generally congenial also to the Indianologists like Cushing, Holmes, McGee, and Putnam, who were already on the scene. It was congenial even to the archaeologists, who, as we saw, stood entirely outside the Boasian circle. During the early part of the century they were mainly occupied in creating a classificatory grid for the prehistoric cultures of North America by means of cultural sequences and artifact typologies.[222] Their analytical approach was therefore necessarily both culturological and historical, like that of the Boasians, and like them also the archaeologists tended to attribute culture change very largely to diffusion.

The first serious challenge to Idealism occurred when the British social functionalist A.R. Radcliffe-Brown arrived to teach at the University of Chicago in 1931.[223] Radcliffe-Brown always insisted that "he was not opposed to history; only to conjectural history."[224] But in any case cultural

222. See Willey and Sabloff, *History of American Archaeology*, pp. 88–130.

223. See Stocking, *Anthropology at Chicago*, p. 21.

224. Fred Eggan, personal communication.

history was irrelevant, from Radcliffe-Brown's functionalist perspective. Cultural institutions existed not because of past historical developments or of environmental constraints, but because they fulfilled the needs of society in their own time. The essential premise was that the cultural institutions of any particular time and place could be understood with reference to the social needs of that time and place, and without reference to past events.[225]

The decline and fall of Idealism

Radcliffe-Brown soon gathered around him a group of devoted students and disciples at Chicago, and they became one of the most potent and vital theoretical forces in midcentury American anthropology. It was they, especially, who took the lead in refocusing the main interest of American anthropologists from cultures of the past to cultures of the present–a development we discussed both in Chapter 2 and in Chapter 5. Yet Radcliffe-Brown did not ultimately succeed in extinguishing the historical and idealist traditions of the Americans. Some of his most devoted students and colleagues, like Robert Redfield, Edward Spicer, and Morris Opler, were won over initially to the social pragmatism of their teacher, yet in their later work they reverted increasingly to the idealism and the historicism of their predecessors. The last major works of Redfield, Spicer, and Opler were all basically culture-historical, and idealist.[226]

The Radcliffe-Brownian attack failed, in America, because functionalist theory was never able to account for cultural forms. Functionalism could explain *why* certain kinds of ritual or of kinship institutions existed, but it could not explain why Hopis impersonated their gods while Navajos did not, or why Navajos lived in hogans while Apaches lived in wickiups. By and large the Americans were unwilling to accept this limitation, for American anthropology, both Indianological and idealist, had always placed heavy emphasis on the study of cultural forms.[227]

Another line of attack was opened by Leslie White, a one-time student of Boas who soon became one of his most persistent and severe critics.[228] White was one of the very few mid-century anthropologists courageous enough to proclaim an allegiance to Marxism, and he insisted that Social Evolutionism must always be at the heart and core of anthropological theory. He attacked the Boasians unmercifully for their rejection of evolu-

---

225. See A.R. Radcliffe-Brown, *Structure and Function in Primitive Society* (Glencoe, Ill., 1952), pp. 1–15, and Adam Kuper, ed., *The Social Anthropology of Radcliffe-Brown* (London, 1977), pp. 25–41.

226. For discussion see William Y. Adams in *Journal of the Southwest* 32, no. 1 (1990): 18–26.

227. See Stocking, *Anthropology at Chicago*, p. 21.

228. See esp. White, *Ethnography and Ethnology of Franz Boas*, and id., *The Social Organization of Ethnological Tradition*, pp. 3–28. *Rice University Studies*, vol. 52, no. 4 (1966).

tionary theory. Yet White's perspective was in many ways less different from that of the Boasians than might be supposed today. He was always a doctrinaire Marxist in the nineteenth-century sense, and, as we have seen, the theories of Marx were themselves a by-product of the German historical tradition. A.L. Kroeber was surely the quintessential American idealist, yet both he and White agreed that their basic views on culture were very similar.[229] They were both (as were many Boasians) out-and-out culturologists, who approached culture as a distinct class of phenomena, independent not only of biology and psychology, but to a large extent also of environment. In that respect White was not really a materialist in the same sense as were the Marxist anthropologists of a later generation; he was as much a cultural determinist as were the Boasians. The main difference of perspective between him and them was simply that he saw culture as the product of evolutionary forces, while they saw it as the product of historical forces.

Still another attack on idealism, of a different kind, was launched by Oscar Lewis, who in 1943–44 and in 1947 restudied the village of Tepoztlán. The picture that met his eye was very different from that depicted by Redfield. Wrote Lewis: "Our findings... would emphasize the underlying individualism of Tepoztecan institutions and character, the lack of cooperation, the tensions between villages within the municipio, the schisms within the village, and the pervading quality of fear, envy, and distrust."[230] Redfield subsequently acknowledged the legitimacy of Lewis's portrayal, while at the same time insisting that his own was not inaccurate. The community was, he said, "a combination of opposites."[231] Lewis, however, never conceded the legitimacy of Redfield's perspective, which he considered to be romanticized.[232]

In a series of later works, Lewis went on to develop the concept of the "Culture of Poverty," an attenuated, stress-filled, and generally unrewarding kind of culture that was shared by rural peasants as well as urban underclasses.[233] The "Culture of Poverty" idea enjoyed a considerable vogue during the 1960s, when it was congruent with the "war on poverty" that dominated America's social consciousness at that time. Later most an-

229. Leslie White in *Southwestern Journal of Anthropology* 1 (1945): 221–248; A.L. Kroeber in the same journal, 2 (1946): 1–15, and in *American Anthropologist* 50 (1948): 405–414.

230. Oscar Lewis, *Life in a Mexican Village* (Urbana, Ill., 1951), pp. 428–429.

231. Redfield, *Little Community and Peasant Society and Culture*, pp. 132–148.

232. For more on Redfield's romanticized perception see George W. Stocking Jr., ed., *Romantic Motives*, pp. 229–235. *History of Anthropology*, vol. 6 (Madison, Wis., 1989).

233. Oscar Lewis, *Five Families* (New York, 1959); *The Children of Sanchez* (New York, 1961); *Pedro Martinez* (New York, 1964); *La Vida* (New York, 1966).

thropologists came to repudiate it, because it was seen to be denigrating to the poor. There can be no doubt nevertheless that Oscar Lewis's work largely destroyed the idealist vision of peasant life and culture that had been constructed by Redfield, and that had prevailed among American anthropologists in the midcentury era. The image of peasantry that prevails today is largely that which has been formulated by Eric Wolf.[234] It draws heavily on Marxist materialist theory, and places far more emphasis on economic and systemic constraints than on world-view in explaining the special characteristics of peasant life and culture.

The decline and fall of Idealism

The most serious, and ultimately fatal, attack on Idealism began in the 1960s with the rise simultaneously of Cultural Materialism, Neo-evolutionism, and Marxism. These three closely interrelated developments were seen by many anthropologists as combining in a single, materialist paradigm, which we discussed at length in Chapter 2. The proponents of the new doctrine launched a severe and at times polemical attack on the Idealism of their predecessors, which in their view had made anthropology "unscientific"–the most damning of all accusations in the intellectual climate of the 1960s.[235]

Cultural Materialism for the first time introduced the concept of adaptation as a significant factor in the evolution of culture, which meant that it brought cultural theory closer into line with biological theory. Biological and cultural evolution were seen alike as reactions to environmental possibilities and environmental constraints. Thus the dualistic tradition, which had persisted with or without formal acknowledgment since the time of the German Enlightenment, was finally eliminated: mind and matter were reunited as parts of a single system of nature.

But in the end it was surely pragmatic considerations of research funding that drove the final nail into the coffin of idealist anthropology. By the 1970s the National Science Foundation was funding more anthropological research than all other sources combined,[236] and in the eyes of that institution idealist anthropology was "unscientific," and not entitled to NSF funding. Idealism had shown that it could hold out against the attacks of rival, functionalist and materialist paradigms; it could not hold out against the need for money.

---

234. Especially in *Peasants* (Englewood Cliffs, N.J., 1966).

235. See esp. Harris, *Rise of Anthropological Theory*, pp. 250–372; also Marshall D. Sahlins and Elman R. Service, *Evolution and Culture* (Ann Arbor, Mich., 1960), pp. 1–3; Johnson and Earle, *Evolution of Human Societies*.

236. For partial confirmation, see Thomas C. Patterson in *American Anthropologist* 88 (1986): 16.

"NEW ETHNOGRAPHY": THE LAST GASP

The triumph of materialism and of "scientific anthropology" after World War II did not quite end the German idealist tradition in American anthropology. It had yet one more mutation to undergo, in the movement that initially called itself the "New Ethnography."[237] Although it never became dominant paradigmatically in the same way as were the earlier historical and configurationist schools, it nevertheless achieved a certain popularity in the 1960s and '70s.

German Idealism

The central emphasis in New Ethnography was not merely on seeing the world through the native's eyes, as configurationists had also aspired to do, but in describing it in terms that a native might have used. That is, a "new ethnography" of any given people should employ the descriptive concepts and categories of the people themselves, rather than those traditional in ethnographic literature; it should read as though written by and for a member of the culture and society under investigation. In the words of Ward Goodenough, such a document should provide "whatever it is one has to know or believe in order to operate in a manner acceptable to [the members of the society described] and to do so in any role that they accept for any one of themselves."[238] The New Ethnography was necessarily pioneered by linguistically oriented ethnographers, since the key to accessing the native's system of thought could only be through his or her language.

The basic point of departure for New Ethnography was the conceptual distinction between "etic" and "emic" understandings of culture, first propounded by Kenneth Pike in 1954.[239] The two terms were derived from the concepts of phonetics and phonemics in linguistics, where phonetics refers to sound differences within a language that can be recognized by any hearer, without knowing the language, but that may have no semantic significance to speakers of the language, while phonemics refers to sound differences that have semantic significance to speakers of the language. The latter are of course peculiar to each individual language, and cannot be determined without studying the language itself. In similar fashion Pike used "etic" to designate categorical distinctions made by the ethnologist, for example between law and religion, that might have no meaning for members of a given society, while "emic" referred to understandings and distinctions meaningful to the members themselves.

---

237. See William Sturtevant in *American Anthropologist* 66, part 2 (1964): 99–131.

238. Ward Goodenough in *Bulletin of the Philadelphia Anthropological Society* 9, no. 3 (1956): 3–4.

239. *Language in Relation to a Unified Theory of the Structure of Human Behavior* (Glendale, Calif., 1954).

"New Ethnography": the last gasp

The aim of New Ethnography, then, was to depart from the traditional format that had been employed in ethnographies since the time of the medieval cosmographies, and to describe each culture in terms of categories and distinctions meaningful to its members.[240] Obviously, such an approach represents the quintessence of ethnographic particularism, as well as the quintessential application of the linguistic analogy to the study of culture. Indeed, Pike had even spoken of "behavioremes," or minimal units of behavior that should be analogous to the phonemes in a language.[241] It is not surprising, then, that the new ethnographers concentrated heavily on the study of indigenous categorical systems, and indeed nearly all of their enduring contributions are in this area.[242] Today's studies of ethnobotany, ethnozoology, ethnoentomology, and all of the other specialties that collectively are called ethnoscience are all based on the methodology of the New Ethnographers.

In the effort to free themselves from the presuppositions of Western categorical thinking, the New Ethnographers developed a quite rigorous methodology for eliciting the meaning of native terms. A linguistic "frame" (i.e., usually a sentence) was created in which one of the terms was treated as a variable to be investigated; for example, "the things that you can see in the sky at night are __________." The ethnographer then elicited all the different native terms that could occur in this linguistic context. The next step was to take all of the different terms that might occur in that context (equivalents of "star," "planet," "moon," "comet," etc.) and try them over in other "frames," such as for example "the [stars] cause things to happen in the village." A native hearer would in each case indicate whether or not the suggested usage was meaningful and appropriate. This would lead ultimately to the discovery of the indigenous system of astronomy.

The rigorous methodology of the New Ethnographers seemingly overcame the major objection that had been launched against earlier forms of idealist anthropology, namely that they were unscientific. The new approach has been characterized by a former colleague of mine[243] as "Humanism in jackboots." Yet in the end it was also the undoing of New Ethnography as a serious approach to comprehensive ethnography. The methods of elicitation were so cumbersome and time-consuming that it would have taken several lifetimes just to a complete a study of the material inventory of most peoples, let alone their systems of social relations.

---

240. For the methodology, see esp. Stephen A. Tyler, ed., *Cognitive Anthropology* (New York, 1969); and Ward H. Goodenough, *Description and Comparison in Cultural Anthropology* (Chicago, 1970).

241. Pike, *Language in Relation to a Unified Theory of the Structure of Human Behavior*, p. 57.

242. See esp. Tyler, *Cognitive Anthropology*, pp. 28–90.

243. James Boster, now at the University of California (Irvine).

What the New Ethnographers achieved were a series of highly particularized studies in a few domains of culture, which never came close to adding up to a comprehensive ethnography.

New Ethnography was in time to devolve into the less pretentious subfields of ethnoscience and cognitive anthropology, both of which continue to flourish in a modest way. Insofar as these are offshoots of New Ethnography, which in turn grew out of Configurationism, they can still be linked to the intellectual pedigree of German Idealism. But they are research specializations that make no claim to comprehensiveness, and that imply no philosophical commitment to Mentalism or Idealism as opposed to other theories of culture. As an informing and a comprehensive philosophy in American anthropology, German Idealism did not outlive the New Ethnography of the 1970s.

German Idealism

THE LEGACIES

Notwithstanding what has just been said, mentalism in the broadest sense is far from dead in American anthropology. In fact, it seems at the moment to be making a substantial comeback, in the movements that are variously called Reflexive Anthropology, Hermeneutics, Deconstructionism, and Postmodernism. There is even some revival of interest in, and appreciation for, the Boasians.[244] But the new movements cannot really claim intellectual descent from the German idealist tradition, for they retain almost nothing of its philosophical perspective. They are mentalist without being idealist, insofar as they see culture not as enduring tradition, or *Volksgeist,* but as the calculated creation of individuals and groups pursuing their self-interests. Unlike earlier idealists, moreover, the new movements overtly deny the legitimacy of traditional scientific methodology. They are, in the broadest sense, reactions against the excessive materialism and scientism of the last generation; they represent another of the inevitable pendulum swings of intellectual fashion in anthropology.

The German idealist tradition has nevertheless left three enduring legacies in American anthropology. First is the culture concept itself, which remains firmly fixed as the basic organizing concept of the American discipline. There are of course over a hundred proposed definitions of culture in the anthropological literature, but nearly all of them can be traced back directly or indirectly to German origins.[245] The definition that appears most commonly in elementary anthropology textbooks is that of

244. Cf. Jane H. Hill and Bruce Mannheim in *Annual Review of Anthropology* 21 (1992): 381–406.

245. See Kroeber and Kluckhohn, *Culture.*

Tylor, but, as we saw earlier, its inspiration is certainly to be found in earlier German philosophy.

A second legacy is the continuing insistence of virtually all American anthropologists on the importance of cultural history, whether or not it is relevant to their particular research specializations. It is unthinkable to most Americans that cultural institutions should be investigated or explained with no reference to the history of their development.

The legacies

Finally, and perhaps most importantly, there is the persistence of Egalitarianism: the ideology that in the literature has usually been labeled as Cultural Relativism. The latter term is not really satisfactory, for two reasons. First, the Egalitarianism of anthropologists is not confined to the realm of culture; it extends equally to the realms of race and language. Second, the implications of the term "relativism" are ambiguous, and have been much debated both within and outside the discipline. Opponents of the doctrine often equate Cultural Relativism with Ethical Relativism, while anthropologists deny such an identification.[246] A much less problematical term for the anthropologists' commitment is simply Egalitarianism, and its basic implication is that of equal legitimacy. No culture is conceived to be superior to another because it is more in harmony with nature's supposed intention, or because it has superior moral sensibility, or because it has advanced higher on the evolutionary ladder.

But while the ideological commitment of American anthropologists to Egalitarianism is almost universal, it is not always consistent either with their theoretical doctrines or their personal moral convictions. As I have suggested in earlier chapters, there remain a great many closet progressivists as well as closet primitivists in the ranks of American anthropologists. The former continue to believe, or feel intuitively, that civilized societies are more advanced than primitive ones, and the latter that primitive societies are morally superior to civilized ones. These conflicts between ideology and theory, and between professional and personal commitments, are among the many unresolved tensions in American anthropology that will occupy us in the final chapter.

---

246. For discussion, see Lowie, *History of Ethnological Theory*, p. 25; Benedict, *Patterns of Culture*, pp. 45–47; Kroeber and Kluckhohn, *Culture*, pp. 344–354; Kardiner and Preble, *They Studied Man*, p. 153; Harris, *Rise of Anthropological Theory*, pp. 163–164; Melville Herskovits, *Cultural Relativism* (New York, 1973), pp. 1–68. For reference to writers opposed to the relativist position, see Donald Campbell in Herskovits, *Cultural Relativism*, p. v. For recent discussion of the problematical nature of the doctrine, see Wilcomb E. Washburn in *American Anthropologist* 89, no. 4 (1987): 939–943.

SUMMARY

German Idealism

German Idealism was not so much an overt philosophy as an all-pervasive world-view, arising out of the special historical circumstances in which German-speaking peoples found themselves in the early modern period. They were politically divided and technologically somewhat backward, yet their intellectual and artistic achievements were on a par with those of other European nations. As a result, they developed a philosophical outlook that placed primary emphasis on cultural and artistic rather than on political or physical attainments; they insisted on the primacy of Mind over Matter. The Germans were also preoccupied with the question of their own identity, which was not, as in most European countries, defined by the possession of a common state or even a of common religion. Germanness was a matter of culture and language, and these became overriding preoccupations for the German thinkers. From a combination of their Mentalism with their ethnic Nationalism, they developed the concept of the Volksgeist: the distinctive and enduring spirit that was characteristic of each people.

The earliest German idealist philosophers were interested in universal history in much the same way as were their French and Scottish confrères, with the difference that they measured human progress in terms of mental achievements rather than of political or material ones. They also insisted that progress could only come about through struggle and stress, reflecting again the particular history of Germany. This line of reasoning found expression especially in the works of Fichte and Hegel, and finally of Marx. In keeping with the Volksgeist concept and with German Nationalism more generally, however, there were also historical philosophers who were more interested in the differences between cultures than in the similarities. They thought not in terms of culture but of *cultures,* each being the product of its own distinctive history. This particularistic conception of history found early expression in the work of Herder, and it was later further elaborated in the "Science of Mind" as developed in the works of Dilthey, Windelband, and Simmel; works that were very widely read by the German intelligentsia at the end of the nineteenth century.

Historical Particularism was not just a movement in philosophy and literature; it also led, in the nineteenth century, to an active ethnographic tradition. Not content just to define the special qualities of their own culture, the Germans were interested in discovering the special qualities of other cultures as well. Their interest led to the compilation of vast, multivolume ethnographic encyclopedias, detailing the "manners of customs" of peoples all over the world, and later also to active ethnographic field investigations in North and South America, Africa, and Oceania. Before the end of the nineteenth century several ethnographic museums and several ethnographic societies had already been founded. In all these respects German ethnographic inquiry was well in advance of that in other European countries.

Summary

The German ethnographic tradition, with its emphasis on culture history and on cultural particularism, was transplanted to England by E.B. Tylor and to America by Franz Boas. At Columbia University, Boas gathered around him a group of students who were drawn almost entirely from the New York German-American community, and who were already steeped in the literary traditions of German Idealism. Boas and his students together fashioned what has been called the American Historical School of Anthropology, which became the dominant American paradigm for a quarter of a century. It was heavily permeated by the spirit of German Idealism, as manifest in its emphasis on culture rather than on society as the unit of study, its cultural particularism, its Cultural Relativism, its basically historical outlook, and its emphasis on diffusion as the primary engine of cultural change.

In the 1930s anthropologists, like other thinkers, became preoccupied with the social problems of their own time, and they turned their attention from the past to the study of existing societies. German Idealism now found a new outlet in the work of the configurationists, who sought to discover in each native culture the core of beliefs and values that persisted from generation to generation, and that gave the culture its distinctive and enduring quality, even while society, polity, and technology were undergoing rapid and sometimes disastrous change. In referring to this core they generally used the term Configuration, but the concept in all its essentials was identical to the Volksgeist of earlier idealists.

After World War II the idealist perspective came under attack from several directions at once: from social anthropologists inspired by the British tradition of Radcliffe-Brown, from orthodox Marxists, and above all from the newly dominant paradigm of Cultural Materialism. The latter-day movements of Postmodernism, Hermeneutics, and the like also depart from the idealist perspective, insofar as they accord no determining power either to culture or to history. Yet German Idealism has left important legacies that can still be detected in American anthropology. Among these are the continued emphasis on culture as the basic organizing concept of the discipline, the continuing appreciation for the importance of history, and above all the continued commitment to the doctrine of Cultural Relativism.

CHAPTER 7

OTHER ROOTS; OTHER TREES

IN PREVIOUS CHAPTERS I have discussed at length the five philosophical and/or ideological influences that I believe have played the largest part in the shaping of American anthropology, below the level of conscious theory. In terms of my original metaphor, they are the major roots of the discipline. Two tasks remain in the present chapter: to consider briefly some of the discipline's lesser roots, and to consider the ways in which American anthropology differs from the anthropologies of other lands, which might appropriately be called neighboring trees.

SOME LESSER ROOTS

The subject matter of anthropology, embracing so many different aspects of human belief and behavior, inevitably leaves the field open to just about any kind of philosophical or ideological influence. Over time there have, consequently, been many other influences besides the five considered in Chapters 2–6. Some, like Rationalism and Marxism, have been powerful in their own right, but I have not treated them in separate, individual chapters, because in the stream of anthropological thought they cannot be "factored out" in pure form. That is, they have been largely combined with or implicit in other doctrines, which I have already discussed. Other traditions like Utilitarianism, Socialism, and Structuralism have not been given separate treatment either because they have not influenced the mainstream of American anthropological thought, or because their influence was short-lived. Yet the impact of these doctrines has been felt at times and in places, and they deserve at least a brief mention in the present chapter.

Rationalism

We have seen in earlier chapters that the label "rationalist," applied to philosophies, can have more than one meaning. It can refer to the belief in a logically ordered universe, to a universe accessible to understanding through human reason alone, to a belief in the successive growth over time of the human reasoning power, or simply to the "worship" of reason as a kind of manifestation of the divine. All of these different "rationalisms" can be identified in different areas of anthropological or preanthropological thought.

Some lesser roots

The belief in an ordered universe, whose governing laws are conformable to the understandings of human reason, has surely been the single most powerful current in Western philosophical thought. The Greeks believed from the beginning in an ordered universe, whose immutable governing laws could be apprehended through the exercise of human reason because they were inherently reasonable laws. In the Middle Ages this kind of rationalism was tempered by a belief in the supremacy of divine will, but it was nevertheless the will of an inherently rational god, who had bound himself to obey his own laws.

In the seventeenth century, Rationalism freed itself from theology and burst forth once again as an autonomous and all-embracing philosophy, especially in the works of Descartes, Spinoza, and Leibniz.[1] At least in principle, their philosophical systems were wholly apriorist, envisioning a universe accessible to understanding through reason alone. A kind of debate then ensued between the rationalists and the empiricists, led by Locke, Berkeley, and Hume, who believed that reality must be apprehended through sensory experience rather than through reason.[2] The dispute between rationalists and empiricists was identified by Bertrand Russell as "one of the great historical controversies in philosophy,"[3] but in the practical sphere of scientific study, including the Study of Man, the lines between the two were never sharply drawn. Nearly all Western science has rested from the beginning upon a combination of Rationalism and Empiricism, holding that the universe must be apprehended through a combination of reason and sensory observation. In science, as opposed to philosophy, Rationalism has never been and really cannot be an autonomous and self-sufficient doctrine.

In anthropology, with its traditionally strong emphasis on empirical observation, the role of Rationalism has been mostly ancillary. It has manifested itself in combination with other philosophic doctrines like Progressivism and the belief in natural law; doctrines that are asserted by their

1. Among many sources, see esp. John Cottingham, *The Rationalists* (Oxford, 1988).
2. See ibid., pp. 1–11.
3. Quoted from R. S. Woolhouse, *The Empiricists* (Oxford, 1988), p. 1.

adherents to be correct because they are conformable to reason as well as to observation. Since Rationalism and Progressivism are both essentially optimistic doctrines, which flourish in prosperous times, it is not surprising that these two have been most frequently coupled. But Rationalism has also exerted a certain influence, in one way or another, on most of the other philosophic doctrines described in earlier chapters, though some, like Primitivism, do not appear at first glance to be rationalistic.

Among anthropologists, at least four different kinds of Rationalism can be observed in different areas of theory. We can make an initial distinction between those theories that locate rationality primarily in the cosmos, and those that locate it within the human mind. Borrowing the terminology of Kenneth Pike, I will refer to these respectively as Etic Rationalism and Emic Rationalism.[4] But a distinction can also be made, in the ranks of emic rationalists, between those who think of human rationality as something always in being, and those who think of it as something in the process of becoming. Finally, there are scholars who find rationality not so much either in nature or in the human mind as in the processes of history itself. I will refer to thinkers in this latter category as historical rationalists. It should not be supposed however that the different kinds of anthropological rationalism are always or necessarily in conflict; they can and do occur in varying combinations.

Etic Rationalism. Despite frequent protestations to the contrary, Etic Rationalism is teleological, involving the belief that all human cultural behavior makes sense in terms of the purposes or the laws of nature.[5] From this perspective, the reasons why people really do things may be quite different from the reasons they give for doing them, since their actions are ultimately dictated not by their own understanding but by nature's reason (sometimes referred to facetiously as "the great ecologist in the sky"). As Marvin Harris phrases it, there are no "stupid customs," regardless of how bizarre certain practices like Aztec cannibalism or the Indian sacred cow may appear at first glance, to ourselves or even to those who practice them.[6] Most etic rationalists will concede that not all human customs are yet understandable in rational terms, but it is assumed that they all will be when once we fully understand the grand design of nature.

Nearly all natural law theory is rationalistic, as we saw in Chapter 4.

4. *Language in Relation to a Unified Theory of the Structure of Human Behavior* (Glendale, Calif., 1954).
5. See esp. Marvin Harris, *Cultural Materialism* (New York, 1980), pp. 46–76.
6. *The Rise of Anthropological Theory* (New York, 1968), pp. 168–169.

Most of it is also etic, finding the locus of rationality in nature's order or in the will of God. Etic Rationalism is also evident in most forms of Progressivism. It surely reaches its extreme in the twin doctrines of Cultural Ecology and Neo-evolutionism, popular since the 1950s. From the perspective of these doctrines every important cultural practice makes ecological sense, whether or not the actors realize it, and every enduring cultural change is adaptive, according to Spencerian and Darwinian principles of natural selection. Unlike some other forms of Rationalism, to be discussed in a moment, Etic Rationalism does not necessarily impute greater reasoning power to modern than to primitive man; it only imputes superior reasoning power to the properly enlightened anthropologist, who can understand other people's customs even when the people themselves cannot.

Some lesser roots

Another form of Etic Rationalism is found in Durkheimian Functionalism, propagated in France by the school of Émile Durkheim, and in England and the United States most fully by A. R. Radcliffe-Brown and his adherents. From the perspective of these scholars, all cultural institutions are conformable to the needs of society, rather than to the dictates of nature. Durkheimian Functionalism and Cultural Ecology have in common their disregard for man's own reasoning capabilities, holding that many cultural institutions exist for reasons that the people themselves don't understand. But the Durkheimians accord a central position to religion in their theoretical scheme, seeing it as the ideological cement that holds society together, while the cultural ecologists tend to dismiss it almost as epiphenomenal. The Durkheimian vision of society, moreover, is essentially a static one, in which change takes place only to the extent necessary to maintain equilibrium within a society. Thus, "*plus ça change, plus c'est la même chose.*" In contrast, the world-view of the cultural ecologists is a dynamic one, with culture change seen as necessary adaptation to an ever-changing external environment.

In either case, the cultural ecologists and the Durkheimian functionalists see culture and culture change as governed by laws that are independent of human will or cognition. This relatively mechanistic perspective has allowed the adherents of both doctrines to insist that they are more "scientific" than are other anthropologists—a claim they have not been slow to assert.[7]

---

7. Most insistently in the work of Marvin Harris; see *The Nature of Cultural Things* (New York, 1964); *Cows, Pigs, Wars and Witches* (New York, 1974); *Cannibals and Kings* (New York, 1977); and *Cultural Materialism* (New York, 1980). See also A. R. Radcliffe-Brown, *A Natural Science of Society* (New York, 1948).

Emic Rationalism. Emic Rationalism locates rationality within the human consciousness. It sees culture not as adaptive to nature's or society's purposes but as the conscious formulation of human reason, acting to serve man's own purposes. A distinction must be made, however, between those who, like Tylor, believed that man has always been rational, and those who, like Frazer and Lévy-Bruhl, saw him as becoming increasingly rational over time. The Tylorian perspective, which may be termed Rationalism-in-being, has been especially prevalent among primitivists, including many Indianologists. They have been at pains to show that the customs of primitive peoples are at least as sensible as our own, and that the people themselves understood this.[8] Central to this perspective is the concept of primitive man as thinker, or the Cerebral Savage,[9] whose culture has been fashioned through centuries of reasoned attempts to overcome his problems.

In contrast to the Rationalism-in-being theorists are the believers in Rationalism-in-becoming, a view found especially among idealist progressivists. From their perspective, primitive culture is narrowly bound by the constraints of myth and tradition, which provide behavioral guidelines for the unthinking, but which serve as deterrents to progress. In the course of the centuries, however, man increasingly overcomes these limitations and is governed instead by his own reasoning powers, with the result that progress accelerates at an ever-increasing rate. The whole of prehistory and history is thus seen as a process of human rationalization. This view was perhaps most fully embodied in the work of the German idealists of the eighteenth and nineteenth centuries, but it was not inconsistent with Durkheimian Functionalism, and in fact was very explicitly espoused by Lévy-Bruhl.[10] In the twentieth century it has been vehemently disavowed by the adherents of Cultural Relativism, but it has retained a certain currency among nonanthropologists, partly through the influence of Max Weber and Sigmund Freud.

Historical Rationalism. Historical rationalists are those who find rationality not so much in nature or man as in the processes of history itself. This outlook was at least implicit in the thinking of the French and Scottish

8. See, for example, Paul Radin, *Primitive Man as Philosopher* (Cleveland, 1927), esp. pp. 229–388; Stanley Diamond, *In Search of the Primitive* (New Brunswick, N.J., 1974), esp. pp. 116–175; Stanley Diamond, ed., *Primitive Views of the World* (New York, 1969).

9. Cf. Clifford Geertz in *Encounter* 28, no. 4 (1967): 25–32.

10. In *Les Fonctions Mentales dans les Sociétés Inférieures* (Paris, 1910), and several later works.

progressivists, as well as their successors McLennan and Morgan, insofar as they all believed in a more or less inexorable law of progress. However, it was given much more explicit formulation by the German idealists, beginning with Kant, who asserted that "history is a rational process in the double sense of one proceeding on an intelligible plan and tending to a goal which moral reason can approve."[11] Hegel went further, making the whole of history an inherent property of Cosmic Reason itself.[12] The perspective of the Germans was more overtly teleological than that of the French or Scots, insisting that history moves always and inexorably toward an ultimate goal: the complete liberation of the human will, which they called the absolute (see Chapter 6).

Some lesser roots

Twentieth-century anthropologists have very largely abandoned the faith in progress and in the freedom of the human will, both of which were dominant ideas among their predecessors. On one hand, the particularists and diffusionists see culture history as resulting from a series of accidental contacts between peoples. On the other hand, the evolutionists of today have substituted adaptation for progress as their central organizing concept, thus also making culture change and history responsive to external impulses rather than to any internal dynamic. There is not, from either of these perspectives, any necessary directionality in cultural development or history.

It might therefore be suggested that Historical Rationalism is extinct in modern anthropology, were it not for its survival in the classical doctrines of Marxism. Marx and Engels took over wholesale, from Hegel, the notion of an inexorable, internal dynamic in history, and those anthropologists who continue to adhere to the Marxist formula must still plead guilty to the charge of Historical Rationalism. Meanwhile other forms of Rationalism, both etic and emic, continue to flourish in anthropology, although at the moment they are under frontal attack from the adherents of Postmodernism and other antinomian doctrines that reflect the troubled and pessimistic spirit of the 1990s. It seems unlikely however that the popularity of these doctrines will last, given the extraordinary persistence of Rationalism as the core feature of Western philosophical and scientific thinking for two and a half millennia.

Positivism

Auguste Comte's philosophy of Positivism has often been cited as an important current in anthropological thought, but this is true only insofar as

11. Quoted from W. H. Walsh, *Philosophy of History* (New York, 1960), p. 123.
12. See Annemarie deWaal Malefijt, *Images of Man* (New York, 1974), p. 103.

"Positivism" is used as a kind of surrogate label for what is more broadly called Empiricism, or even the scientific method. So far as Comte's specific doctrine of Positivism is concerned, its philosophical import has never been clear, as we noted in Chapter 4. Moreover, almost no one since the middle of the nineteenth century has identified himself or herself as a positivist; the term is always applied, usually disparagingly, to someone else. Andreski puts the matter succinctly: "this term has continued to be bandied about in all sorts of possible and impossible senses; the latest fashion prevailing at the time of writing [1974] enjoins us to be anti-positivists, without worrying too much what a positivist is. In Comte's first formulation 'positivism' was... used as the opposite of 'negativism,' to distinguish between a positive and negative attitude to science as the ultimate source of knowledge. Unfortunately, no sooner had he made this distinction than Comte began to twist it, and apply it to everything he happened to assert or approve of."[13] In fact, John Stuart Mill had said virtually the same thing as early as 1865.[14]

It seems clear that Comte thought of Positivism mainly as the antithesis of metaphysical philosophy. The doctrine seems to reduce, in essence, to three propositions: 1) facts are facts, and can be established incontrovertibly through observation, experimentation, and the "comparative method" (see Chapter 2). 2) There is no fact except in relation to some theory. 3) The positivist method consists first of ascertaining facts and then of propounding laws.

Comte's use of the terms "fact," "theory," and "law" was far from consistent, but it appears that the core of meaning in each of them was something different from what most scientists would understand today. "Facts" for Comte corresponded to what today we would call "data." We can all acknowledge that a great deal of what we observe in the field goes unrecorded by us–i.e., does not become data–not because it isn't true but because it has no relevance to whatever question we are investigating. Data, then, consists not of all facts, but of those facts that are relevant to our purposes. It seems equally clear that "theory" for Comte was not confined to explanatory propositions; it appears to encompass models, classifications, measures, generalizations, and just about any frame of thought into which "facts" can be fitted. The author's meaning is perhaps best understood if for "theory" we substitute "scientific purpose." The essence of his first and second propositions can then be stated: "What is, is, but it only becomes significant with reference to some purpose." Comte's understanding of "law" was also much broader than is our usage today. Indeed,

13. Stanislav Andreski, ed., *The Essential Comte*, trans. Margaret Clarke (New York, 1974), p. 9.
14. See Gertrud Lenzer, *Auguste Comte and Positivism* (Chicago, 1975), p. xix.

it seemed to include any observable or inducible process, whether descriptive or prescriptive.

It should be clear at this point that Positivism is not properly a philosophy as we would understand it, but a methodology.[15] It is, moreover, a methodology that had already been in more or less regular use among normative scientists for more than a century,[16] and has continued so down to the present day. If I understand Comte correctly, Positivism is simply observation plus induction or deduction, but guided necessarily by and toward some purpose. There is nothing in this that cannot be found in Bacon or Descartes except its application to the human sphere. But the latter had itself already been practiced if not articulately advocated throughout the preceding century, and it continues to be practiced by anthropologists and most other social scientists down to the present day.

Some lesser roots

To clarify our historical understanding I think we have to separate the importance of Comte the man from the importance of his doctrine. Comte *is* important, mainly because, by his repeated and doctrinaire insistence, he made a place for the study of man among the sciences. He completed the transition from moral philosophy to social science that had been begun by Saint-Simon. But there is nothing new in Comte's doctrine of Positivism that obliges us to recognize it as an important innovation. He gave a name to a social science methodology that was already well established, yet the name itself never really caught on, and few subsequent thinkers have ever identified themselves as positivists. If there remains nevertheless a very substantial component of Positivism in anthropological theory and method, it is the legacy not of Comte but of the generations of Enlightenment thinkers who preceded him.

Marxism

Marxism, or Dialectical Materialism, is quintessentially a form of progressivist theory, and very much a product of the same forces that shaped much of the Enlightenment thinking. However, it is markedly distinct from other progressivist theories, and its influence in anthropology has been unique; for that reason I have set it apart for separate consideration in the present chapter.

Marxism differs from all of the doctrines heretofore discussed in that it also is, or has been, an organized, self-proclaiming sect. Like other sects it has its founding prophets, its sacred scriptures, its exegesis, and, arising

15. Cf. Andreski, *The Essential Comte*, p. 11.
16. Cf. E. E. Evans-Pritchard, *A History of Anthropological Thought* (New York, 1981), p. 42.

therefrom, a body of officially proclaimed dogma. Like other sects also it is exclusivist: in the eyes of true believers you are either a Marxist or you aren't, and you may not adulterate the official doctrine with other, non-Marxist ideas.

All this makes Marxism both easier and more difficult to discuss than other philosophical schools. Easier, because one can start from a body of very concrete and specific literature; more difficult, because the self-proclaimed boundaries of the sect do not begin to measure the true extent of Marxist influence, in anthropology or elsewhere. Thinkers like Marvin Harris and Eric Wolf have played a leading role in popularizing Marxist ideas within anthropology, yet to speak of them as Marxists is to risk the accusation by true believers that you aren't really talking about Marxism, but about some kind of bastard revisionism.[17] Too, Marxism has always been a political as well as an intellectual movement; it involves not only belief but a very specific action agenda. This means that individuals can and do enlist in the action agenda without necessarily accepting the whole intellectual package, and vice versa. At times, in discussing American anthropology, it will be necessary to distinguish between political Marxism and intellectual Marxism.

Purely as a historical philosophy, Marxism is itself a blend of much older traditions. In fact, it achieves the quite considerable feat of combining Progressivism and Primitivism. It offers a scenario of history with a utopia at both ends: primitive stateless communism at the beginning, and utopian stateless communism at the end. This seeming paradox has created a dilemma that continues to plague orthodox Marxists down to the present day. If class conflict is the necessary catalyst for all social progress, how can we have advanced beyond the original, classless society of Marxist imagination?[18] As Maurice Bloch puts it, "Marxists stopped being Marxist when they turned to primitive society."[19] Bloch has explained the anomaly by reminding us that all of the writings of Marx and Engels are part history and part propaganda. They used their idealized, Morgan-derived vision of primitive society as a rhetorical club to castigate modern Capitalism—the traditional practice of the primitivist. Also and perhaps more importantly, they wanted to argue that utopia can be regained at the end of history because it existed at the beginning.[20]

To recapitulate the Marxist schema briefly, Marx and Engels envisioned

17. Cf. Maurice Bloch, *Marxism and Anthropology* (Oxford, 1983), pp. 130–135.
18. See esp. ibid., pp. 16–19.
19. Ibid., p. 19.
20. Ibid., pp. 16–19.

the progress of all human society through a series of fixed evolutionary stages, each defined by a distinctive mode of production. The names that the two authors attached to their stages changed to some extent in the course of their successive writings; in modern translations they are most often rendered as Tribal (sometimes given as Gentile or Lineal), Asiatic (sometimes Oriental), Ancient (sometimes Slave-holding), Feudal, and Capitalist, with Communism as the ideal, as yet unrealized stage to come.[21] Each of the stages was marked by the appearance of a new system for the mobilization of labor, resources, and technology, in order to produce needed goods and services. In the Tribal stage the mobilizing force was kinship networks; in the Asiatic stage it was theocratic monarchies; in the Ancient (i.e., Greek and Roman) it was the Mediterranean system of chattel slavery; in the Feudal it was the bonds of medieval master-serf obligation; in the Capitalist it was the mobilization of capital in the hands of entrepreneurs. Each stage saw the appropriation of power and resources by a new "have" class, and the dispossession of one or more new "have-not" classes. The resulting, inevitable conflict between "haves" and "have-nots" eventually led to the overthrow of old systems and the establishment of new ones. The Marxist series of stages was actually taken over in somewhat modified form from Hegel, as was the theory of conflict (thesis-antithesis-synthesis) resulting first in the establishment and then the overthrow of each stage (see Chapter 6).

Some lesser roots

Marxism and American anthropology. For obvious reasons, the Marxist vision of social evolution never had much appeal for American anthropologists. With its rigid developmental schema, its fixed stages, and its utopianism, it remains very close to the eighteenth- and nineteenth-century Progressivism which twentieth-century anthropology has so consistently disavowed. Then too, most Americans have not found the concept of class struggle very useful in the study of societies that Marx himself acknowledged to be classless. Throughout the middle years of the twentieth century Leslie White's was just about the sole, lonely voice raised on behalf of intellectual Marxism,[22] and even he never allowed Marxist theory to influence his ethnographic field studies of Pueblo villages.[23]

21. For discussion, see ibid., pp. 32–62.

22. Most conspicuously in *The Science of Culture* (New York, 1949) and *The Evolution of Culture* (New York, 1959).

23. *The Pueblo of San Felipe* (*American Anthropological Association Memoir* 38, 1932); *The Pueblo of Santo Domingo, New Mexico* (*American Anthropological Association Memoir* 43, 1935); *The Pueblo of Santa Ana, New Mexico* (*American Anthropological Association Memoir* 60, 1969); *The Pueblo of Sia, New Mexico* (*Bureau of American Ethnology Bulletin* 184, 1962).

Political Marxism had slightly more appeal for anthropologists than had intellectual Marxism during the midcentury era. In the 1930s Marxist organizations were just about the only ones in America speaking out against the abuses of Nazism; as such they enlisted considerable support especially from Jewish intellectuals in the New York area. Anthropologists at Columbia, at City College of New York, and at the New School for Social Research—even including the great Boas—lent their support to Marxist causes,[24] while at the same time introducing scarcely a hint of Marxist theory in their anthropological writings.

In the end, nevertheless, it was political Marxism that opened the way for a more general consideration of Marxist theory among American anthropologists. The catalyst was the Vietnam War, when for the first time in modern American history it became intellectually acceptable and even fashionable to be "unpatriotic," in the view of the general public. The fact that Marxism had long been declared unpatriotic gave it an appeal among the young radicals that its intellectual content alone could not have done. Reading and discussing Marx was one way of registering one's discontent with the Vietnam War, and with imperialism in general. And since the young radicals were very much on the cutting edge of anthropological development in the 1960s, thanks in large part to the explosive growth of the discipline, the older anthropologists found for the first time that they could not afford to ignore Marx.

Once they got beyond the bizarre evolutionary schema, which few anthropologists can accept even now, both the young radicals and their older colleagues found much more in Marx than they had expected, and much that was serviceable to their analytical needs. Most importantly they were liberated from the sterile doctrines of so-called classical economics, which at the beginning of the twentieth century had decoupled economics from political and social structure. As a result, economics was virtually eliminated from the list of cultural categories that anthropologists routinely surveyed.[25] But Marxism placed the economy firmly back within a historical, political and social context, or rather within a series of them; it reconnected "political" and "economy." As a result, anthropological studies published since the 1960s are far more economically sophisticated than were any earlier works.

However, the outstanding contribution of Marxism was undoubtedly

24. See Melville Herskovits, *Franz Boas* (New York, 1953), pp. 103–122; Marshall Hyatt, *Franz Boas, Social Activist* (New York, 1990), pp. 143–153; Jonathan Friedman in *Current Anthropology* 28, no. 1 (1987): 109–110.
25. For discussion, see esp. Marshall Sahlins, *Stone Age Economics* (Chicago, 1972).

its unabashed focus on exploitation as a basic feature of economy and society. The term had of course been in use for a long time in its ecological sense, as describing man's use of his environment. But Marxism showed that socioeconomic systems are, much more importantly, a matter of man exploiting man; of people arranging to benefit from the labor of others. Exploitation in this sense usually is, but need not always be, pernicious, because the system of exploitation need not always be asymmetrical. But human nature (which according to Marx is the product and not the cause of economic systems) is such that all parties in a system of exploitation will seek to maximize their own advantage, and, because power is very seldom equally distributed, an asymmetrical relationship will usually develop.

Some lesser roots

At its most doctrinaire, Marx's economic and political doctrine amounts to a sweeping conspiracy theory, in which the ruling classes are always contriving by whatever means they control to squeeze everything they can from the proletariat. Anthropologists have varied enormously in the extent of their agreement or disagreement with Marx on this point, depending partly on their individual, optimistic or pessimistic temperaments, and partly on the Zeitgeist of their immediate times. But almost all of them have accepted the basic idea of exploitation as the central feature of socioeconomic systems, whether for better or for worse.

This general acceptance has provided a foundation not only for new modes of ethnographic analysis but for several kinds of "liberation anthropology," the most currently active of which is feminist anthropology. Only a minority of feminist anthropologists can in any strict sense be called Marxists, and perhaps only a minority are conspiracy theorists, but all of them start from the basic premise that social relations are systems of exploitation, in which, most of the time, men are unequally exploiting the labor (and often the sexuality) of women.

In many ways the acceptance of Marxist exploitation theory marks the end of anthropology's age of innocence. Marxism stands alone in challenging the notion of innate human goodness, which in one way or another is implicit in all of the philosophical schools that I have previously discussed. Even Primitivism does not question basic human goodness; it sees man as corrupted through frailty rather than through an innately evil nature. Marxism also allows basic goodness to primitive man, but from that point onward sees the course of history as dictated by man's urge, or need, to succeed at the expense of others. This vision of all human societies (always excepting the primitive) as systems of exploitation in turn undermines the optimistic voluntarism so characteristic of earlier anthropology: the belief that peoples had the cultures they wanted to have. According to Marxism, people mostly have the cultures that have been forced upon them.

For the most part, Marxism (or selected aspects of it) have been accepted by anthropologists not as a progressivist theory but as a universalist theory. The evolutionary schema from ancient communism to capitalism to utopian communism is rejected, while the basic concepts of dominance, inequality, and exploitation are now applied to the analysis of primitive societies as freely as they have always been used in criticizing our own society. In this usage the basic distinction between Self and Other disappears; we are all self-seeking humans engaged in exploiting, or trying to exploit, other self-seeking humans.

Through the ages, Western thought has vacillated between an image of man as inherently good and an image of man as inherently evil. Marxism denies any such ascription, but, at least in contrast to the naively idealistic theories that preceded, it seems to come down predominantly on the side of evil. In that respect it conforms well with the pessimistic Zeitgeist of the present age, and this may account for some of its popularity.[26]

Utilitarianism and Socialism

The same circumstances that gave birth to Marxism in nineteenth-century Germany led in England to the development of a more genteel, uniquely British tradition, at once philosophical and pragmatic, that came to be known as Radicalism.[27] The movement demanded, first and foremost, sweeping reforms in the law, in government, and in education, to bring the society and polity of England into conformity with the new industrial order that was emerging. The radical and reformist spirit found expression initially in the philosophy of Utilitarianism, and later in the more activist doctrine of Socialism.

The utilitarian doctrine. Utilitarian philosophy was almost exclusively a British phenomenon. It had its roots in the moral philosophies of Anthony Shaftesbury, Francis Hutcheson, and Joseph Priestley, and to some extent in Locke, but was first articulately proclaimed (and named) by Jeremy Bentham in the closing decades of the eighteenth century.[28] In the nineteenth century it was further developed by James Mill, and then reached its fullest development in the philosophy of John Stuart Mill; particularly

26. For a modern revision of Marxist historical and social theory, see Adam Schaff, *A Philosophy of Man* (New York, 1963).
27. For an excellent general survey of Radicalism in England, see Bertrand Russell, *Freedom versus Organization 1814–1914* (New York, 1934), pp. 51–175.
28. See esp. Ernest Albee, *A History of English Utilitarianism* (London, 1902), pp. 52–63; also Bertrand Russell, *A History of Western Philosophy* (New York, 1945), p. 775; Frederick Copleston, *A History of Philosophy* (New York, 1985), Book Three, Vol. VIII, pp. 3–17.

in his Utilitarianism (1863). In the later nineteenth century it rapidly lost popularity, although it exerted a considerable influence on the social theories of Herbert Spencer as well as on the English socialists. The utilitarian doctrine never had much influence in other lands, but in the British Isles it was one of the most powerful intellectual currents in the first half of the nineteenth century.[29]

Some lesser roots

Utilitarianism was quintessentially a political rather than a historical philosophy. Throughout its rather brief history it was closely associated with movements for electoral, educational, and penal reform. Indeed it was the espousal of those practical objectives, many of which were eventually achieved, that accounted for much of the popular appeal of Utilitarianism. It became, for a time, the chief philosophical expression of Radicalism, until at the end of the nineteenth century it was supplanted by Socialism.[30]

Unlike nearly all of the other doctrines discussed in these pages, the utilitarian philosophy was wholly ahistorical. It offered no scenario of past human development, but focused its attention entirely on a hoped-for future. In Kantian terms it was a philosophy of *ought* rather than of *is*. Simply stated, the utilitarian philosophy argued that the only rational guide in human conduct is to seek the greatest good for the greatest number, good being identified simply with happiness or pleasure, and evil with unhappiness or pain.[31] All other theories of morality and politics could in practice be reduced to this principle, whatever their claims to divine or natural legitimation.

Unlike the French and German philosophers of his time, Bentham did not equate happiness either with personal liberty or with the emancipation of human reason. On the contrary, he condemned the doctrine of the Rights of Man as nonsense.[32] He measured happiness largely in material terms, based on considerations of subsistence, abundance, security, and equality, and saw it as the obligation of the state to provide those things.[33] In that sense his doctrine was much more statist, and less libertarian, than were those of most Enlightenment thinkers. Indeed, Bentham was a kind of legal determinist: he firmly believed that just and moral laws would result in a just and moral populace, and legal reform was therefore at the very heart of his utilitarian program. The challenge faced by all governments was to balance off the happiness of individuals against the collective well-

---

29. See esp. Russell, *History of Western Philosophy*, p. 777.
30. Ibid.
31. An idea expressed most clearly and succinctly by John Stuart Mill in *Utilitarianism* (London, 1864), pp. 9–10.
32. Russell, *History of Western Philosophy*, pp. 775–776.
33. Ibid.

being of the community; this was to be achieved through the enactment of laws that would make the interests of individuals coincide with those of the community.[34]

James Mill, a close associate of Bentham, did much to publicize the ideas of his friend, and he remained all his life a fairly doctrinaire Benthamite. Not so his son John Stuart Mill, the last and by general consent the greatest of the utilitarians. The younger Mill was bothered by the accusations of hedonism and egoism that had been leveled against Utilitarian philosophy, and he undertook to show that "true happiness" was something other than the pursuit of individual gratification. He criticized Bentham's belief that all forms of happiness are equally good, arguing instead that the best kind of happiness is that which is grounded in the individual's social feelings. It results from acts that promote the happiness of the whole community, and not just of the actor. John Stuart Mill also departed to some extent from the total rationalism of Bentham and of James Mill, insisting that happiness is generated by aesthetic feelings as well as by rational thought, and that such feelings should be actively promoted. As a consequence of this broadened perspective, the Utilitarianism of the younger Mill was much less specifically tied to programs of legal and institutional reform than were the doctrines of his predecessors, although as an active politician and member of Parliament he was always a supporter of reform measures.[35]

The development of philosophical Socialism. Toward the end of the nineteenth century, it became apparent to many radicals that the reforms advocated by the utilitarians were not sufficient to address the problems created by industrialization. Utilitarianism then rapidly gave way to Socialism as the chief expression of radical thought. The socialist doctrine retained many of the features, both philosophical and practical, of Utilitarianism, but was more extreme in its economic program. It broke completely with the principle of laissez-faire capitalism, which up to then had been semisacred in British liberal thought, and had been largely accepted by the utilitarians. In terms of its economic program British Socialism had the same ultimate goal as had Marxist Socialism, but in Britain the goal was to be achieved through reform and through democratic processes rather than through revolution. As a result, British Socialism was always

34. Ibid., p. 775. For more extended treatment of Bentham and Benthamite doctrine, see esp. William L. Davidson, *Political Thought in England* (New York, 1916), pp. 30–113; and Russell, *History of Western Philosophy*, pp. 82–118.

35. For the Utilitarianism of John Stuart Mill, see esp. Albee, *History of British Utilitarianism*, pp. 191–267; Copleston, *History of Philosophy*, Book Three, Vol. VIII, pp. 25–92; and Davidson, *Political Thought in England*, pp. 133–234.

closely associated with the trade union movement, which Marxists regarded as a bourgeois deception.[36] Also and importantly, the British Socialist doctrine remained ahistorical, in marked contrast to the dialectical Progressivism that was central to Marxist doctrine.

Some lesser roots

In sum, both Utilitarianism and Socialism were ahistorical, functionalist doctrines that focused on the relationship between society and the individual. They held that societies exist to provide for the needs of their members, but at the same time the members have necessarily to identify their personal interests with the needs of society at large. Both doctrines reflected a kind of optimistic, pragmatic reformism that was a special characteristic of British social thought throughout the nineteenth century. Rejecting both the *Sturm und Drang* outlook and the historical determinism of the Marxists, they firmly believed that enlightened societies could perfect themselves through the enactment of properly enlightened laws.[37]

The connection with British Functionalism. There are obvious points of resemblance between the general outlook of the utilitarians and socialists, and the ahistorical Functionalism that became dominant in British anthropology in the middle years of the twentieth century. The development of British Functionalism is usually associated with the names of Malinowski and Radcliffe-Brown, but the two men were clearly building, whether knowingly or unknowingly, on an already well-established philosophical tradition in the British Isles. Their specific ideas may or may not actually have derived from the reading of Bentham or Mill or Robert Owen, but the ready reception of those ideas among British intellectuals is surely attributable to the persisting outlook of nineteenth-century radicalism. It is noteworthy too that the functionalist theory of Malinowski, Radcliffe-Brown, and their successors, like the Utilitarianism that preceded it, was largely a British phenomenon, and never achieved much currency in other lands.

It is not possible to trace a direct connection between either Malinowski or Radcliffe-Brown and the utilitarians, since Malinowski was educated in Continental Europe, while Radcliffe-Brown received his education at a time when utilitarian ideas were largely passé in England. I think however that Socialism provides, in the case of each man, a connecting link with the philosophical radicalism of the nineteenth century. Radcliffe-Brown was a youthful adherent of political radicalism (he was known to his schoolfellows as "Anarchy Brown"), and had adopted from the anarchist Peter Kropotkin the conception of society as a self-regulating sys-

36. For discussion see Russell, *History of Western Philosophy*, pp. 146–175.

37. On this, see esp. Henrika Kuklick, *The Savage Within* (Cambridge, 1991), pp. 4–20.

tem.[38] Malinowski after his arrival in England became a familiar of the Bloomsbury intellectual set, which was heavily imbued with socialist ideas.[39] Although Radcliffe-Brown always attributed his functionalist leanings to Durkheim rather than to British antecedents,[40] his ahistorical perspective certainly did not derive from Durkheim, whose theory was nothing if not evolutionist.

The somewhat variant doctrines of Functionalism developed by Malinowski and by Radcliffe-Brown were not, of course, simply anthropological versions of Utilitarianism or of Socialism. Neither man spoke of individual happiness per se as a significant desideratum, and certainly neither regarded control of the economy as one of the most important obligations of the state. What anthropological Functionalism shared with the earlier British doctrines was a more general, functionalistic perception of the relationship between society and the individual, within which each had an obligation to maintain the other. It was a perception that rendered history irrelevant, since social forms (including the structure of the state) were determined by pragmatic, present-day needs and not by the inertia of tradition.

In their different ways, Utilitarianism, Socialism, and British Functionalism were all quintessentially voluntaristic. Since historical tradition carried no special weight, all peoples had, or could have, whatever culture and society they chose. Reasonable men could pass whatever laws they chose to improve their society and culture. There was, as a result, a spirit of optimistic reformism that passed from Utilitarianism to Socialism, and then in turn to British Functionalism. It is noteworthy that E. B. Tylor, the acknowledged founder of British anthropology, often spoke of anthropology as a "reformer's science," whose findings would enable "great modern nations to understand themselves, to weigh in a just balance their own merits and defects, and even in some measure to forecast... the possibilities of the future."[41] In the heyday of Functionalism, Malinowski was to assert that the findings of anthropology compelled "intelligent and even drastic reform" in the institutions of Western society.[42]

---

38. See Alan Barnard in Christopher Winters, ed., *International Dictionary of Anthropologists* (New York, 1991), p. 563, and Adam Kuper, *Anthropologists and Anthropology* (London, 1973), p. 55. For the evolution of Radcliffe-Brown's ideas in the course of his career, see esp. George W. Stocking, Jr., in *History of Anthropology,* vol. 2 (1984), pp. 131–191.
39. See Kuper, *Anthropologists and Anthropology,* pp. 32–37.
40. Ibid., pp. 53–54; see also Robert H. Lowie, *The History of Ethnological Theory* (New York, 1937), pp. 221–229.
41. E. B. Tylor in his Introduction to the English translation of Friedrich Ratzel, *The History of Mankind* (London, 1896), p. v.
42. Malinowski in V. W. Calverton and Samuel D. Schmalhausen, eds., *The New Generation* (New York, 1930), p. 168.

The optimistic outlook of the reformers remained prevalent in Britain until the end of World War I, when a general disillusionment and pessimism became evident in many domains of social and historical thought.[43] Anthropologists, however, were active in colonial settings rather than in the British Isles, and they continued throughout the 1930s and 1940s to believe that their researches could and would lead to more enlightened colonial administrations—retaining in that respect the spirit of optimistic reformism of earlier generations.[44] It was undoubtedly because of that same naive optimism that so few anthropologists foresaw the rapid end of the colonial era after World War II.

Some lesser roots

In sum, British Functionalism was not in any direct way an anthropological expression of either Utilitarianism or Socialism. Nevertheless, it built upon a broad philosophical foundation laid by the nineteenth century radicals, involving a voluntaristic preoccupation with the present and the practical hope for a better future, while largely dismissing the past as irrelevant.

The American connection. In a book that is largely concerned with American anthropological thought, it would be possible to ignore Utilitarianism and Socialism altogether, were it not for the historical accident of Radcliffe-Brown's five-year teaching stint at Chicago (1931–1936).[45] During that brief interval he exerted an extraordinary influence on a small group of colleagues and students, who (as we saw in Chapter 5) established the nearest thing to a sociofunctionalist school in American anthropology. Robert Redfield, Sol Tax, Fred Eggan, W. Lloyd Warner, Edward Spicer, and Morris Opler all at one time or another proclaimed themselves followers of Radcliffe-Brown, and they were among the most influential thinkers of the midcentury era. The "Chicago School" was the first wholly non-Boasian movement in twentieth-century American anthropology, and it exerted a major influence within the discipline for about twenty years.[46] Although it drew heavily on earlier sociological traditions at the University of Chicago, reflecting especially the work of Charles H. Cooley, Robert E. Park, and Ernest W. Burgess, the school would almost certainly not have come into existence without the catalytic influence of Radcliffe-Brown.

In America, then, much more specifically than in Britain, it is possible

43. See esp. Kuklick, *The Savage Within*, pp. 20–26.

44. See esp. Kuper, *Anthropologists and Anthropology*, pp. 46–48; Harris, *Rise of Anthropological Theory*, p. 540; and Kuklick, *The Savage Within*, pp. 182–241.

45. As nearly as I can determine, Malinowski's somewhat shorter stint at Yale (1938–1942) had almost no influence on mainstream anthropological thought in America.

46. See George W. Stocking, Jr., *Anthropology at Chicago* (Chicago, 1979), pp. 21–25.

to identify Radcliffe-Brown as the source of anthropological ideas that trace back to the utilitarians. To a very considerable extent, it was those ahistorical and functionalist ideas that helped to refocus the interest of American anthropologists from the study of the past to that of the present, a development that we considered at length in Chapters 5 and 6. And it was that development in turn that made possible the development of applied anthropology, which first began to flourish in the 1930s.

Yet the intellectual influence of British Functionalism in America was to be fleeting. Radcliffe-Brown's appeal seems to have been based largely on personal charisma, and it did not long outlive his departure from Chicago and return to England.[47] Moreover his teaching, doctrinaire and indeed dogmatic though it was, could never wholly suppress the American traditions of Cultural Idealism and of Historical Determinism, even in his own most dedicated students. As I have written elsewhere in regard to Edward Spicer, he "reconciled the antithetical traditions of social pragmatism and cultural idealism, as did Linton and Redfield, by being a pragmatist at the theoretical level, but an idealist at a deeper and more philosophical level."[48] With the passage of time, not only Spicer but also Redfield, Opler, and Tax reverted increasingly to a historical and an idealist perspective.

Today, the general spirit of British Functionalism, and indeed of Utilitarianism, lives on most fully in the subdiscipline of applied anthropology. Despite occasional protestations to the contrary, the outlook of applied anthropologists remains heavily ahistorical and functionalist. Development anthropology, in particular, continues to exhibit much of the optimistic reformist spirit that was characteristic of British thinkers from Bentham to Malinowski.[49] Indeed, applied anthropologists often acknowledge Malinowski as one of the founders of their subdiscipline,[50] and have named their annual achievement award in his honor.

Structuralism

The anthropological doctrine of Structuralism was discussed briefly in Chapter 4, as one of the several manifestations of natural law theory in

47. Ibid.

48. William Y. Adams in *Journal of the Southwest* 32, no. 1 (1990): 24.

49. See, for example, Roger Bastide, *Applied Anthropology*, trans. Alice L. Morton (New York, 1971), pp. 105–120; Erve Chambers, *Applied Anthropology* (Englewood Cliffs, N.J., 1985), pp. 81–100; John van Willigen, *Applied Anthropology* (South Hadley, Mass., 1986), pp. 79–109.

50. Cf. Bastide, *Applied Anthropology*, pp. 7–21; Kuper, *Anthropologists and Anthropology*, pp. 46–48.

anthropology. It remains here to place the doctrine in a somewhat wider historical context, for Structuralism is not wholly or even originally an anthropological doctrine. It burst upon the public consciousness in the 1960s, due almost entirely to the insistent promotion of Claude Lévi-Strauss, and this has given rise to a common perception that the doctrine originated at that time.[51] In fact, it has antecedents tracing back at least to the nineteenth century. Lévi-Strauss himself has regularly acknowledged his debt to the structural linguists Ferdinand de Saussure and Roman Jakobson, but earlier antecedents of Structuralism can be found in the works of Karl Marx and Sigmund Freud, among others.

Some lesser roots

Since Structuralism is a self-proclaiming and a recently fashionable doctrine, it should in theory be easier to discuss than, say, Rationalism or Positivism. In fact it is not, for there are as many versions of Structuralism as there are of Rationalism. Richard and Fernande De George have observed that

> Structuralism has been described as a method, a movement, an intellectual fad, and an ideology. Each of these characteristics is in part valid. For structuralism is a loose, amorphous, many-faceted phenomenon with no clear lines of demarcation, no tightly knit group spearheading it, no specific set of doctrines held by all those whom one usually thinks of as being associated with it. It cuts across many disciplines–linguistics, anthropology, literary criticism, psychology, philosophy. For some it gives hope of uncovering or developing a common basic approach to the social sciences, literature, and art which would unify them and put them on a scientific footing, much as the "scientific method" grounds and unifies the physical sciences.
>
> To the extent that structuralism is a movement, it is multidimensional with several independent leaders, each disowning any relation to the others and each carrying along with him a group of devoted and enthusiastic followers.[52]

This last observation reflects the special, anarchic quality of French intellectualism, in which modern Structuralism is largely embedded.

What all of the structuralists have in common is the belief in a structured universe; or to be more accurate, a belief that the particular part of

51. Cf. Richard T. De George and Fernande M. De George, *The Structuralists* (New York, 1972), p. vii.
52. Ibid., p. xi.

the universe which is their own field of study exhibits an inherent and a coherent structuring that is part of nature's order, and not a mere imposition of the human observer. Thus, structural anthropologists and psychologists believe that the structures they encounter in thought and behavior are universal, not variable from culture to culture or from individual mind to mind. What reason is to the rationalist, structure is to the structuralist: an essential feature of nature itself.

Structuralism, like Rationalism, may or may not be overtly teleological. The recurring social structures observed by Lévi-Strauss, for example, are clearly related to the requirements of society to maintain itself, according to Durkheimian theory.[53] The same is at least equally true of the social theories propounded by Mary Douglas, Victor Turner, and other British structuralists.[54] However, the cognitive structuring which, according to Lévi-Strauss, leads all of mankind to perceive the world in terms of binary oppositions, is less obviously related to any purpose in nature.[55] Recurring linguistic structures are also difficult to explain in terms of any specifiable need. It is this apparent lack of causality that has led Marvin Harris and other proponents of "nomothetic anthropology" to dismiss Structuralism as unscientific.[56]

Forerunners. As we observed in Chapter 4, the concern of anthropologists has been with recurring structures in culture and language, which are presumed to reflect universal ways of thinking. These in turn are presumed by many structuralists to reflect either nature's purposes or evolutionary laws, or both. From this perspective, Karl Marx has been identified as one of the first structuralists, exemplified by his assertion that "Life is not determined by consciousness, but consciousness by life."[57] By "life" he meant the conditions inherent in each of his successive evolutionary stages, which, in his view, more or less automatically generated appropriate modes of thought. Marx's Structuralism was thus basically evolutionary rather than universalistic, with ways of thinking dictated by economic imperatives that changed from age to age. This approach has

53. Claude Lévi-Strauss in A. L. Kroeber, ed., *Anthropology Today* (Chicago, 1953), pp. 524–553.
54. Cf. Mary Douglas, *Purity and Danger* (London, 1966); id., *Natural Symbols* (London, 1970); Victor Turner, *The Ritual Process* (Chicago, 1969); id., *Dramas, Fields, and Metaphors* (Ithaca, N.Y., 1974); Edmund Leach, *Culture and Communication* (Cambridge, 1976).
55. Cf. esp. Claude Lévi-Strauss, *The Raw and the Cooked* (New York, 1969)
56. Harris, *Rise of Anthropological Theory*, pp. 464–513.
57. From *The German Ideology*, quoted in De George and De George, *The Structuralists*, p. xii.

latterly served as the basis for a school of Structural Marxism, pioneered by Louis Althusser.[58]

While Marx concerned himself exclusively with group thought, or ideology, Sigmund Freud sought to find a structural basis for individual thought. As is well known, he attempted to account for all human behavior, both normal and neurotic, on the basis of unconscious motivations that are common to all humans, and are largely related to sexuality. His theory, in its way, was as rigidly deterministic as that of Marx, asserting "that even the smallest detail of mental life is determined and that the determining psychical factors are discoverable."[59] But where Marx's Structuralism was evolutionary, that of Freud was universalist: the psychological factors determining human thought were the same for all peoples at all times. The structuralist aspects of Freud's theory have been especially emphasized in the work of the modern structural psychologist Jacques Lacan.[60]

Some lesser roots

Although Claude Lévi-Strauss has identified Marx and Freud as two of his "three mistresses" (along with geology),[61] his distinctive version of structural anthropology certainly owes far more to the linguist Ferdinand de Saussure than it does to any other predecessor.[62] Saussure's contribution, unlike that Marx or Freud, was methodological rather than theoretical, and it involved no expressed or implied teleology. He was simply the first linguist to concentrate on meanings rather than on linguistic forms, and to treat language as a system of signs. He was the acknowledged creator of semiology: the comparative study of signs and symbols not only in language but in religion, social organization, and other areas of cultural behavior. The analogy between language and culture had been employed, at least tacitly, by cultural idealists for a long time (see Chapter 6), but it was Saussure who first suggested explicitly the possibility of studying language and culture according to the same basic approach. Linguistics, in his view, provided the "master pattern" for the study of meaning in all areas of culture.[63]

It was Saussure also who formalized the distinction between *langue* (language) and *parole* (speech), pointing out that acts of speech are sur-

---

58. Cf. his *Reading Capital* (New York, 1970).

59. De George and De George, *The Structuralists*, p. xvii.

60. Cf. Jacques Lacan, *Écrits* (Paris, 1966).

61. See De George and De George, *The Structuralists*, pp. xvii–xviii.

62. His magnum opus was *Course in General Linguistics*, first published in 1916 and translated into English in 1959 (trans. Wade Baskin; ed. Charles Bally and Albert Sechehaye; New York, 1959).

63. De George and De George, *The Structuralists*, pp. xviii–xx.

face phenomena that are determined by deeper, partly unconscious linguistic structures. These latter are very imperfectly comprehended in the rules of grammar that are taught to schoolchildren, for all linguistic performance exhibits a great deal of structuring that is not accounted for by conventional grammatical rules. The linguist can only study actual acts of speech (*parole*) but his or her task is to try and uncover the deep structure (*langue*) that determines the form of the acts. It was a common assumption of Saussure, and later of structural linguists in general, that at the deepest level, all languages exhibit a common structure, despite the obvious differences in grammatical rules that are apparent at the surface.[64] Carried beyond the domain of language, this became a basic assumption of structural anthropology as well: the idea that, below the obvious surface differences, all cultures exhibit certain common patterns that are the result of common ways of thinking.

Another linguist who exerted a major influence on the development of structural anthropology was Roman Jakobson, originally a member of the Prague Linguistic Circle and later a professor at Columbia, Harvard, and M.I.T. It was he who first suggested that all phonemic distinctions that are made in any given language are based on a conception of binary opposition: e.g., between *b* and *p*, between voiced and unvoiced *th*, and so on.[65] Extended from language to other areas of culture, the theory of binary oppositions became one of the cornerstones of Lévi-Strauss's structural anthropology. That is, he believes that all mankind understands the world of experience in terms of binary oppositions: between hot and cold, raw and cooked, nature and culture, and so on.

Lévi-Strauss and structural anthropology. If Lévi-Strauss is not the founder of Structuralism per se, he is the undoubted founder of structural anthropology as we know it today. Looking below the surface variability of cultural behavior, he has attempted to find regularities in such matters as language, cooking, dress, table manners, art, myths, and social organization. He shares with Marx and Freud the belief that much that appears to be accidental is actually determined, and that the determining laws are the same for all peoples. The ultimate aim—acknowledged even by Lévi-Strauss to be still far from achievement—is to define basic human nature.[66] Few other anthropologists have attempted to apply structural the-

64. Cf. De George and De George, *The Structuralists*, pp. 7–17. For a very lucid discussion of Saussure and his work, see esp. Jonathan Culler, *Ferdinand de Saussure* (Harmondsworth, 1977).

65. Cf. De George and De George, *The Structuralists*, p. xix.

66. See ibid., pp. xxiii–xxvii.

ory on so grand a scale as has the French master, but he has nevertheless had a substantial following, especially among British social anthropologists. His appeal in North America has been somewhat more limited, as will be seen a little later.

Some lesser roots

Although Structuralism, as we have just seen, has roots tracing back a century and more, its great popularity belongs to the era immediately following World War II; above all in France. The doctrine eventually spread to many countries, but nearly all of the structuralist gurus of the postwar era, whether in linguistics, anthropology, psychology, psychoanalysis, literary criticism, or philosophy, were and are French, or French-Swiss.[67] The movement and its popularity cannot in fact be fully understood without reference to the general intellectual climate in postwar France.

The debacle of World War II and the humiliation of Nazi occupation had destroyed a good many of the traditional foundations of French Nationalism. The postwar intellectuals were looking for new moorings; doctrines conformable to the general traditions of French philosophy but untainted by association with the institutions and regimes of the recent past. In that rather chaotic and volatile intellectual climate, three major philosophic doctrines contended for adherents. Marxism had already had a certain following in France before the war, but it had gained a new respectability and appeal as a result of Russia's contribution to the German defeat, and of the major role that the Soviet Union was obviously destined to play in the postwar world. However, Marxism left almost no room for that independence of thought and disputation that has always been dear to the French intelligentsia; even worse, perhaps, its origins were wholly non-French.

At the opposite extreme from Marxism was the philosophy of Existentialism, proclaimed by Jean-Paul Sartre.[68] It was a highly abstruse doctrine, derived in part from German Idealism, which tended to locate reality within the realm of human consciousness. It was antitheoretical in the sense of asserting that if a thing has existence (i.e., is perceived to exist), then its existence requires no explanation (hence the name, Existentialism). The doctrine had a certain appeal because its chief proponent was unmistakably French, it was conformable to the somewhat anarchic spirit of the times, and it certainly left plenty of room for disputation. However,

---

67. See ibid., p. xi.

68. Sartre liked to proclaim himself a follower of Marx, and in later writings did indeed attempt to reconcile his theories with those of Marxism. It is clear nevertheless that he had no use for the materialist aspects of Marxism. See Copleston, *History of Philosophy*, Book IX, pp. 340–343.

its anti-empirical basis was more in keeping with the general traditions of German than of French thought, and indeed Sartre readily acknowledged the influence of Hegel, Husserl, and Heidegger.[69]

Between the dogmatic rigidity of Marx and the antinomian resignation of Sartre, Structuralism seemed to offer a reasonable middle ground. By comparison with the other two it seemed an eminently empirical doctrine, in keeping with the general tradition of French philosophy since the time of Descartes. It repudiated equally the apriorism of the Marxists and the moral abdication of the existentialists. Its message was rather that there *are* ultimate realities and certainties, which await discovery empirically. If the world seems a confused and uncertain place, it is because the realities lie so deep below the surface that they have mostly not yet been discovered, but by the application of the proper methodology they eventually will be. Structuralism therefore appeared as a doctrine of hope and also as a doctrine of science–and it had the further appeal of being quintessentially French.

Other Roots; Other Trees

What was true of Structuralism in general was true of structuralist anthropology in particular: it seemed to keep its feet on the empirical ground at a time when other doctrines did not.[70] This will not be apparent to anyone who reads only the later works of Lévi-Strauss, which exhibit a good deal of obfuscation and calculated ambiguity.[71] Like so many French intellectuals, the author delights in word games and double entendres. But the earlier works, like "Social Structure"[72] and *Anthropologie structurale*[73] exhibit a much more straightforward quality, and will explain why Structuralism in the beginning appeared to be a respectably scientific doctrine, and one that did not contravene the earlier and still respected teachings of Descartes and Comte, and of Durkheim and Mauss.

Structural anthropology in England and America. If the appeal of Structuralism in postwar France has to be understood in reference to Marxism and Existentialism, the same is not true in England or America, where neither Marx nor Sartre had much of a following among anthropologists in the

69. Ibid. For a much more extended and critical discussion of Existentialism than is possible here, see ibid., pp. 340–389.

70. In *La Pensée sauvage* (Paris, 1962) and other works, Lévi-Strauss launched a spirited critique of Sartre and Existentialism. See esp. Lionel Abel in E. Nelson Hayes and Tanya Hayes, eds., *Claude Lévi-Strauss, the Anthropologist as Hero* (Cambridge, Mass., 1970), pp. 235–246.

71. Cf. Harris, *Rise of Anthropological Theory,* pp. 510–512.

72. Lévi-Strauss in Kroeber, *Anthropology Today,* pp. 524–553.

73. Paris, 1958.

immediate postwar years. Lévi-Straussian structural anthropology nevertheless gained a very substantial following in England in the 1950s and 1960s, and secured the adherence of such once-devoted functionalists as Raymond Firth and Edmund Leach. This can be attributed partly to the generally Francophile leanings of the British intellectuals, who were always receptive to new influences from across the Channel.[74] The success of the doctrine was aided, too, by the charismatic, almost messianic character of Lévi-Strauss himself. As Adam Kuper has written,

Some lesser roots

> Not only was there a certain boredom with conventional theory, but the Empire was falling apart and with it, some felt, the traditional laboratory of the discipline. Many were ready to shift their interest from norms and action to symbolic systems.... 'structuralism' came to have something of the momentum of a millennial movement, and some of its adherents felt that they formed a secret society of the seeing in a world of the blind. Conversion was not just a matter of accepting a new paradigm. It was, almost, a question of salvation.[75]

From an American perspective, however, the paradigm shift from Radcliffe-Brownian (i.e., Durkheimian) Functionalism to Lévi-Straussian Structuralism was more apparent than real; it involved more a shift of research interest than a change of theoretical orientation. Nearly all of the British structuralists were able to make their studies conformable to Durkheimian interpretation; that is, they showed that recurring structures in social organization, classification, and ritual served the interests of society, in maintaining its cohesion and its boundaries.[76] Thus, Structuralism in British anthropology really involved the extension of functionalist analysis in a new direction.

Structuralist anthropology gained a following in England even before the translation of Lévi-Strauss's major works into English, since one of the distinguishing characteristics of the British intelligentsia has always been its ability to read French.[77] Not so in America, where the great majority of anthropologists have always been functionally monolingual. It was not until the publication of the English translations of *The Savage Mind* (1966), *Structural Anthropology* (1968), and *The Elementary Structures of Kinship* (1969), that Structuralism gained much of a foothold west of the Atlantic,

---

74. Cf. Kuper, *Anthropologists and Anthropology*, pp. 52–53.
75. Ibid., p. 206.
76. For references, see n. 54.
77. See Kuper, *Anthropologists and Anthropology*, pp. 206–207.

and it was always a more purely Lévi-Straussian and less Durkheimian version of Structuralism than that which flourished in Britain.

American Structuralism built upon the earlier foundations of Boasian Mentalism and Configurationism, and it flourished (to the extent that it did) as a conscious alternative to the dominant Cultural Materialism of the 1960s. It is not surprising, therefore, that Americans were generally more interested in Lévi-Strauss's studies of mythology and other mental phenomena than they were in his earlier works on social organization. To a very considerable extent the American structuralists were mere disciples, who, unlike their British colleagues, added nothing new or original to the Lévi-Straussian canon. It is notable too that Structuralism in America gained a foothold only in a small number of elite schools, like Harvard, Chicago, and California, which prided themselves on intellectual sophistication. At the same time, the doctrine was often regarded as a suspicious foreign import by rank-and-file American anthropologists.

Nationalism and Imperialism

No discussion of ideological currents in the Western world can wholly ignore the phenomenon of Nationalism. At least in the political sphere it has been perhaps the single most powerful ideology of the last three hundred years, and has been a major contributing factor to any number of wars. Inevitably, its impact has been felt in intellectual life as well, even if the impact has been largely unacknowledged and often unintended. Nationalism surely offers one explanation for why the anthropologies of America, Britain, France, and Germany are so different from one another; more so, I believe, than is true in the case of any other social science, and certainly far more so than is true in the natural sciences.

To my mind, the most overtly nationalistic anthropology is that of France. It has developed in a more or less unbroken line from Comte to the present, and has been largely impervious to influences from abroad. There has been, I believe, at least an unconscious feeling that France has a special responsibility, or historic mission, to take the lead in the development of social and political theory, following in the footsteps of Montesquieu, Turgot, and Condorcet. In keeping with this general trend in intellectual life, French anthropology has always emphasized the social and political aspects of the human condition, and it has been imbued with a sense of the anthropologist's political responsibility.[78]

German anthropology too has followed its own distinctive course,

78. See, for example, Anthony Giddens, *Émile Durkheim* (Harmondsworth, 1978), pp. 15, 69–85.

which has been largely guided by general trends in German philosophy. It has concerned itself with the cultural and the historical rather than the social and political aspects of life, and has emphasized the anthropologist's detachment from, rather than involvement in, the activities and responsibilities of the political arena. In both France and Germany, then, anthropology has conformed itself, more or less as a matter of course, to the larger philosophical trends distinctive of each nation.

Some lesser roots

One of the most conspicuous features of the French and German anthropologies is the extent to which they have ignored one another; a development that surely reflects the general state of relations between the two countries. I think something of the German intellectual chauvinism may have carried over, however unwittingly, to the German-oriented Boasians in America. How else to account for their almost total lack of attention to the work of Durkheim and his school, at a time when it was exerting a major influence not only in France but in England as well? As we saw earlier in the chapter (and in Chapter 6), ideas inspired by the French school really took root only at the non-Boasian University of Chicago.

The histories of anthropology in England and in America are, for various reasons, more complicated than in France or Germany. For one thing, philosophers and philosophy in general have never had the same prestige in the Anglo-Saxon world as they have had on the European Continent; they have not provided the beacons for other disciplines to follow. Many Anglophone anthropologists have not been widely read outside their own field, and they have felt no special urge to march in step with philosophers, sociologists, psychologists, and other intellectuals. As a result, the development of anthropology has been a good deal more intellectually autonomous, and for the same reason more erratic, in Britain and America than in France and Germany.

British anthropology can certainly not be accused of hypernationalism, in view of its extraordinary receptivity to influences from Continental Europe. In a certain sense it had its beginning when Tylor introduced the perspectives of German Idealism into Britain, and it has been periodically subject to influences from across the Channel ever since. Two of the founders of modern social anthropology at the London School of Economics were the Finnish-born Edward Westermarck and Polish-born Bronislaw Malinowski, and the later popularity of the ideas of Durkheim and of Lévi-Strauss is also noteworthy.

In view of their receptivity to Continental influences, the seemingly insistent refusal of British anthropologists to take seriously the work of their American colleagues is at least equally extraordinary. Louis Henry Morgan is, so far as I know, the only American anthropologist whose work has ever been given serious attention by British Scholars.[79] The major and most original later developments in American anthropology, like Configurationism, cultural ecology, and ethnoscience, have had almost zero impact on the other side of the Atlantic. Configurationists like Clyde Kluckhohn, Anthony Wallace, and Clifford Geertz made important conceptual advances in the study of religion,[80] yet one looks in vain for any serious consideration of their work in the writings of Mary Douglas, Victor Turner, I.M. Lewis, and other British students of religion.[81] The principal trends that American and British anthropology have shared in common are either those, like Social Functionalism, that Americans have borrowed directly from Britain, or those, like Structuralism, that both have borrowed from a continental source.

There is, moreover, almost no familiarity in Britain with the vast and rich ethnographic literature on American Indians. There seems to be, indeed, a tendency to look upon the Native Americans as "storybook" peoples–proper subjects for the Indianologist but not for the anthropologist. This is reflected, for example, in Aidan Southall's observation that "American sociology [i.e., anthropology] can do wonderful things perhaps for America, but its data base is so massively huge that no American sociologist however well-meaning can hope to get out from under this pile and see straight into the Other, our anthropological Other."[82] It is clear indeed from the whole of his discourse that Southall's anthropological Other is the African, and that Indians do not qualify.[83] I am bound to conclude that the general British disregard for American anthropology and its findings represents a kind of chauvinism, whose roots no doubt go back to the colonial period.

American anthropology is by no means free from the charge of provincialism, as I have suggested here and there in earlier pages. However, I do not believe that American anthropology with all its shortcomings can be accused of deliberate nationalism–at least not at the level of theory. There is hardly a development in British or French anthropology, in particular, that has *not* had its adherents on this side of the Atlantic. Indeed it is precisely the receptivity of American anthropology to just about any kind of

79. Cf. Meyer Fortes, *Kinship and the Social Order* (Chicago, 1969), and Adam Kuper, *The Invention of Primitive Society* (London, 1988), pp. 42–75.

80. E.g., Kluckhohn, *Navaho Witchcraft* (Boston, 1967); Wallace, *The Death and Rebirth of the Seneca* (New York, 1970); Geertz, *The Religion of Java* (Glencoe, Ill., 1960).

81. See, e.g., Douglas, *Purity and Danger* and *Natural Symbols*; Turner, *The Ritual Process* and *Dramas, Fields, and Metaphors*; I.M. Lewis, *Ecstatic Religions* (Baltimore, 1971).

82. Interviewed by John W. Burton in *Current Anthropology* 33, no. 1 (1992): 81.

83. Ibid., pp. 67–83.

influence, indigenous or foreign, that has given it the rather diffuse and incoherent quality so often derided by foreign scholars.[84]

Imperialism. Imperialism is not the same thing as Nationalism, despite the frequent association of the two during the last three hundred years. But imperialism is a much older phenomenon, tracing back to the earliest civilizations, and when all is said and done it is a practical strategy for exploitation rather than an ideology or a philosophy. Thus, its influence in anthropology has been at the level of field practice rather than of theory.

Some lesser roots

The fact that field ethnography developed hand-in-glove with colonial or imperial expansion has been too often remarked to require further elaboration here.[85] France, Britain, and the United States all had their colonized territories, where subject natives were uniquely "theirs" to study. This was in the beginning a matter of practical opportunity, but in time both the colonial powers and the ethnographers became decidedly possessive about their anthropological turf. The colonial administrators may or may not have encouraged ethnological studies by their own nationals, but in general both they and the ethnographers were strongly resistant to field studies by outsiders.

Americans were perhaps a bit less possessive in this respect than were the European powers; that is, they were willing to "share" the Indians with European ethnographers. This was partly because anthropological studies, no matter how critical of American policy, never posed a practical threat to American control over the Indians. But if American anthropologists have not been possessive, they have been conspicuously expansionist. The expansion of American ethnographic studies, first throughout Latin America in the 1930s and 1940s, and then throughout virtually the whole world after World War II, has sometimes been viewed as reflecting a kind of anthropological empire-building, taking advantage of America's unquestioned economic dominance. This has certainly been the view of a fair number of Latin American anthropologists,[86] and of some European anthropologists who saw their once-private colonial domains invaded by Americans to whom entry could no longer be refused.[87]

Because of the close association between anthropology and colonialism, it has become fashionable to suggest that ethnographic studies pro-

84. Cf. Åke Hultkrantz in *Current Anthropology* 9, no. 4, (1968): 289–310.

85. See Talal Asad, ed., *Anthropology & the Colonial Encounter* (London, 1973); Kuper, *Anthropologists and Anthropology,* pp. 123–149.

86. As I am told by several colleagues who have done fieldwork in various Latin American countries.

87. I often heard this idea expressed or at least implied by British anthropologists working in Africa.

vided a kind of intellectual rationale for imperialist expansion and colonization.[88] However, this thesis will not really stand up to historical scrutiny, for at least three reasons. First, Europe's avid curiosity about the Primitive Other dates back to a time long before the scramble for colonies, and it was gratified by travelers' accounts and cosmographies long before genuinely ethnographic field studies were undertaken. Second, the ethnographic studies that are most commonly criticized as "colonialist" were undertaken in nearly every case after colonial regimes had already been established, and the question of whether to colonize or not to colonize was moot. Moreover, they very commonly were critical of existing policies toward the natives. Third and most importantly, the makers of colonial policy in England and America cared little about philosophical justification; they rationalized their actions and policies on the pragmatic grounds of national self-interest, or else of "Manifest Destiny."

It is surely correct to state, on the other hand, that ethnographic field studies were encouraged–when they were–in the hope that they would contribute to the development of more effective and more enlightened colonial regimes.[89] Indeed this was one of the specific rationales given for the establishment of the Bureau of American Ethnology in 1879.[90] But it was a hope that was to be almost wholly disappointed, both in the United States and in Britain. Anthropologists were no more able than were the politicians and administrators to foresee an end to the colonial era, and to that extent they had a practical as well as a moral interest in promoting the development of enlightened colonial policies. Yet it was a continual complaint of administrators that the anthropologists furnished them with nothing of practical value, and their field reports were much more often critical than supportive of colonial policies and officials.[91] Anthropologists were the opportunistic beneficiaries, not the promoters or propagandists, of Imperialism.

SOME NEIGHBORING TREES

The five doctrines discussed in Chapters 2–6 are not unique to American anthropology, but they are woven into a combination that is surely unique to America. The same doctrines, and others, have combined in different ways and at different times in other countries, to shape a distinctive national anthropology in each. It remains here to consider, albeit briefly,

88. Cf. Asad, *Anthropology & the Colonial Encounter*; Marianna Torgovnick, *Gone Primitive* (Chicago, 1990).

89. Cf., for example, Kuper, *Anthropologists and Anthropology*, pp. 123–127.

90. See Curtis M. Hinsley, Jr., *Savages and Scientists* (Washington, D.C., 1981), pp. 147–151.

91. See Kuper, *Anthropologists and Anthropology*, pp. 127–130.

some of the other national anthropologies and their ideological underpinnings. I must necessarily cast them in the role of anthropological Other, for I cannot speak with an insider's authority about any of them, and my knowledge of their literatures is limited.[92] My concern in any case is not to explore them in detail, but simply to consider how and why they differ from the anthropology of America.

Some neighboring trees

It must be acknowledged at the outset that comparisons between American anthropology and other anthropologies are, at best, problematical. The boundaries of the discipline are not as sharply demarcated in other countries, especially in Europe, as they are in North America, and there is no general consensus as to who is and is not to be called anthropologist. In Britain the title is claimed only by a limited number of academic professionals, yet the Royal Anthropological Institute for a long time included also a great many amateurs, who legitimately considered their contributions to be anthropological. In France the term was not used at all (except by physical anthropologists) before the 1950s, and is still claimed chiefly by a small cohort of mainly armchair scholars. Yet there is at the same time a substantial population of practicing field ethnologists who are not designated in France as anthropologists, but whose work certainly fits the North American definition of the term. At the other extreme are lofty philosophical pundits like Foucault and Derrida, who are also not anthropologists in a professional sense, yet who exert a powerful philosophical and theoretical influence within the discipline, both in their own country and abroad. In Germany and Russia the name anthropologist is still applied almost exclusively to physical anthropologists, while students of culture continue to sail under the older banners of ethnology and prehistory.

This difficulty throws into relief the special nature of American four-field anthropology, with its persisting conjunction of ethnology, archaeology, linguistics, and physical anthropology (discussed at some length in Chapter 5). The same conjunction existed briefly in the British Isles, but came unstuck in the 1920s. It never really existed on the European continent, although there were (and still are) rudimentary leanings toward the four-field conjunction in several European countries, as well as in the Third World.[93] Shall we, then, designate as "French anthropology" (for example) only the work of those scholars who call themselves and are called anthropologists, or shall we include also those individuals like Foucault

92. However, having spent two sabbatical years in residence at Cambridge University, I can at least claim an acquaintance with British anthropology that goes beyond the published literature.

93. See, for example Wilhelm Mühlmann, *Geschichte der Anthropologie* (Bonn, 1948), esp. pp. 148–182; Josef Wolf, *Integral Anthropology* (Prague, n.d.); L. P. Vidyarthi, *Rise of World Anthropology* (Delhi, 1978).

and Derrida who are not anthropologists in a professional sense, but who exert a powerful influence in our discipline? Or, finally, should we include everything, ethnological, archaeological, linguistic, or physical anthropological, that would be called anthropology if it were carried on in North America?

I have not really attempted to resolve this dilemma, preferring instead to point out that comparisons depend necessarily on what is being compared. In other words, the differences between American anthropology and other anthropologies are larger or smaller depending on what is and is not included under the term. Since philosophical influences have exerted themselves much more strongly in ethnological and social studies than they have in other branches of anthropology, however, my primary concern must be with the ethnologies and the social anthropologies of Britain, France, Germany, and Russia, whatever they may choose to call themselves. For simplicity I have referred to the disciplines under consideration as anthropology in all cases, whether or not they are so designated in the countries where they are found.

It must be said too that it is much easier to generalize about the anthropology of any country as it existed a generation ago than it is today. The discipline was everywhere relatively small until after World War II, and therefore reasonably cohesive. Since that time it has undergone enormous growth, with the inevitable diversification that takes place as a result. What is so conspicuously true in present-day America is true to some extent in other countries as well: that anthropology has largely abandoned its traditional center, while galloping off simultaneously in many new directions. My generalizations are therefore more accurate from the perspective of historical overview than they are as characterizations of the present-day state of the discipline in Britain, France, Germany, or Russia.

Anthropology in Britain

British and American anthropology followed a common course of development, dominated by progressivist thinking, throughout the latter half of the nineteenth century. The dialogues of McLennan, Morgan, and Tylor, although they involved disagreements, were those of men who recognized that they were engaged in a common intellectual enterprise on the two sides of the Atlantic.[94] All of them thought of anthropology as embracing the subdisciplines of prehistory, ethnology, linguistics, and

94. See, for example, Harris, *Rise of Anthropological Theory*, pp. 180–216; Thomas R. Trautmann, *Lewis Henry Morgan and the Invention of Kinship* (Berkeley, Calif., 1987), pp. 179–204; Adam Kuper in *Journal of the History of the Behavioral Sciences* 21 (1985): 3–22.

physical anthropology. Early in the twentieth century, however, the anthropologies of the two countries began to diverge rapidly and sharply, as the Americans succumbed to German philosophical influences and, a little later, the British succumbed to French influences. Both for a time turned their backs on Progressivism, but in different ways and for different reasons.

Some neighboring trees

As late as 1909, the Board of Studies in Anthropology at the University of London proposed a guide for the study and teaching of anthropology. It embraced: A, physical anthropology, with subdivisions of (a) zoological, (b) paleontological, (c) physiological and psychological, and (d) "ethnological" studies,[95] and B, cultural anthropology, with subdivisions of (a) archaeological, (b) technological, (c) sociological, (d) linguistic, and (e) ethnological studies.[96] This was the same schema followed by A. C. Haddon when he published his *History of Anthropology* in 1910,[97] and essentially by R. R. Marett when he published *Anthropology* a couple of years later.[98] In short, the Britishers endorsed, at least in principle, the four-field schema that by now was well institutionalized in America. Haddon indeed was an ardent admirer of the U.S. Bureau of American Ethnology, as was his adopted countryman Max Müller. Both of them urged Britain to fund a similar research institute, to concentrate especially on the anthropology of the British overseas colonies.[99] Yet the suggestion was not acted upon, and in fact four-field anthropology never really became professionally institutionalized in the British Isles as it was in America. Its only comfortable home was, and to some extent still is, in the Royal Anthropological Institute, which until after World War II was largely an amateur institution.

As I suggested especially in Chapter 5, the four-field conception which dominated and motivated British and American anthropology in the later nineteenth century was a direct consequence of the triumph of Evolutionism, both Darwinian and Spencerian. The newly proclaimed science of anthropology involved a sometimes uncomfortable conjunction of four previously existing disciplines, each of which was believed to provide support in a different way for evolutionary theory. In particular, the marriage of physical anthropology (formerly comparative anatomy) and cultural anthropology (formerly ethnology) was based on the supposed analogy

95. I.e., in this context, the comparative study of racial characteristics. Note that ethnology was also included as a subdivision of cultural anthropology, where it referred to the comparative study of cultures.

96. See Alfred C. Haddon, *History of Anthropology* (London, 1910), pp. xiii–xv.

97. Ibid.

98. London, 1912.

99. G. W. Stocking, Jr. in *History of Anthropology Newsletter* XXI, no. 1 (1993): 20–21.

between biological and cultural evolution. But when Evolutionism ceased to be the dominant paradigm in anthropology, the four-field schema lost its basic sanction, and in Britain it did not outlive the generation of Haddon and Marett. In the United States, as I have suggested earlier, its continued survival is best explained by the special circumstances and needs of Indianology.

It is an extraordinary and well-documented fact, discussed already in previous chapters, that the shape of British anthropology in and after the 1920s was set not by Marett at Oxford and Haddon at Cambridge, but by Malinowski and Radcliffe-Brown, teaching at the London School of Economics and at various overseas institutions. The ahistorical Functionalism proclaimed in different ways by these two pioneers was much more in keeping with the general philosophical currents of their time than was the optimistic Progressivism which always lay just below the surface of evolutionist theory. It seems to have had a special appeal to a number of bright young men and women from the overseas dominions, who became the most devoted apostles of the new anthropological dispensation.[100] Under their hands, British anthropology shed almost the whole of its historical baggage: not only progressivist and diffusionist theory, but the subdisciplines of archaeology, linguistics, and physical anthropology that had supported them. The four-field concept, which had never been systematically institutionalized in teaching and research programs, ceased to exist even as an ideal.

When Evolutionism was dethroned and the four-field package came unstuck, the subdisciplines of prehistoric archaeology, linguistics, and physical anthropology did not of course go out of existence. All of them pursued their independent courses of development, as indeed they had done before they were swept into the anthropological net. Meanwhile the general title "anthropologist" was wholly coopted by the functionalists, who claimed it as their exclusive prerogative. They distinguished themselves not merely from the archaeologists, linguists, and physical anthropologists, but also from the ethnologists, whose interests continued to be mainly historical.

Thus, self-proclaimed anthropology in Britain in the 1920s became a discipline far more narrowly focused than it had been a generation earlier.[101] It had in the process become something so different from the anthropology of America in so many ways that the two should probably have been called by separate names–a suggestion that was actually put forward in

100. See Kuper, *Anthropologists and Anthropology*, pp. 90–91; and Edmund Leach in *Annual Review of Anthropology* 13 (1984): 11.
101. Cf. Kuper, *Anthropologists and Anthropology*, p. 168.

Britain by both Malinowski and Radcliffe-Brown.[102] Such a difference of nomenclature might perhaps have avoided the invidious comparisons that have subsequently been made between the two anthropologies, each accusing the other of going about its job in the wrong way. The British accuse the Americans of being "all over the map," and of lacking any coherent focus, while the Americans accuse the British of parochial smugness, and of being too narrowly focused on the social dimensions of culture.[103] In fact, the two groups of self-proclaimed anthropologists were and are simply not interested in the same things.

Some neighboring trees

One of the distinctive features of British anthropology during most of the twentieth century has been the absence both of Progressivism and of Primitivism—two themes that continue to resonate strongly on the American side. Social Evolutionism, née Progressivism, was banished by Malinowski and Radcliffe-Brown in the name of Functionalism in the 1920s, and this perspective was adopted by nearly all the British anthropologists of the midcentury era. It is noteworthy that while Radcliffe-Brown, as a functionalist, acknowledged a primary debt to Durkheim,[104] he ignored altogether the Progressivism that was a central feature of the Frenchman's own philosophical system.

Beginning in the 1950s, British Functionalism gave way to, or was tempered by, Structuralism, but the orientation remained basically nonprogressivist and indeed ahistorical. At the time of present writing there are a few signs of a revival of social evolutionist thinking in the British Isles,[105] but it has not yet moved back into the anthropological mainstream, as it did in America in the 1950s.

As we saw in Chapters 2 and 3, the decline or repudiation of Progressivism in the past has often been counterbalanced by a florescence of Primitivism. However, this did not happen in British anthropology. It might be argued that the philosophical implications of Primitivism are inconsistent with the self-confident superiority that has always characterized the British intellectual classes,[106] yet at the same time it must be remembered that Primitivism flourished in England in the eighteenth century. Indeed,

---

102. Malinowski coined the term Social Anthropology; Radcliffe-Brown suggested that it was just a kind of Sociology.

103. Cf. George P. Murdock in *American Anthropologist* 53 (1951): 465–473; Southall in *Current Anthropology* 33, p. 81.

104. See Kuper, *Anthropologists and Anthropology*, pp. 32–37.

105. See, for example, Tim Ingold, *Evolution and Social Life* (Cambridge, 1986); C.R. Hallpike, *The Principles of Social Evolution* (Oxford, 1988); Ernest Gellner, *Plough, Sword and Book* (London, 1988).

106. Cf. Leach in *Annual Review of Anthropology*, p. 10; John Messenger in *Inis Beag Revisited* (Sheffield, 1989), pp. 117–119.

no country was more affected by the movement of literary Romanticism, and none contributed more to the enormous body of primitivist novels, poems, and plays that were discussed in Chapter 3. It is worth noting, however, that British Primitivism in the eighteenth century drew most of its inspiration from the Native American peoples, many of whom at that time were still under British colonial rule. Since American independence, on the other hand, British literateurs and British anthropologists alike have eschewed the American Indian as subject matter.

Other Roots; Other Trees

From the beginning, the British anthropologists drew mainly upon Oceanic and African case materials, which means that they studied societies far more complex than were those of most North American tribes. In the twentieth century, unlike the eighteenth, it was sometimes the Polynesian or Melanesian, but above all the African, who occupied the role of Savage Other for the British. But while the African has been cast in the role of Savage, it has always been difficult for Europeans (at least since ancient Greek times) to see him as Noble Savage. This is no doubt partly a function of latent or overt race prejudice, but it is a reflection also of the complexity of most indigenous African cultures. Many of the societies studied by the functionalists were chiefdoms or states (as current jargon would have it), and their conspicuous social stratification ran counter to the ideal of Egalitarianism that is so dear to primitivists.

For obvious reasons, then, the dimension of "Indianology" is also missing in Britain, to be replaced at least in part by a kind of "Africanology."[107] And the British, as we have seen, drew much of their theoretical inspiration in the twentieth century from French sources, while the Americans drew more of theirs from the Germans. This leaves natural law as the only major philosophical doctrine that is shared in any significant measure between the two Anglophone schools of anthropology. No wonder, then, that they feel so little affinity for one another.

There is, perhaps, a difference of national character to be noted as well. As a race, the British are often accused of *sangfroid* and of lacking moral passion, and these qualities seem indeed to be reflected in British anthropology. Notwithstanding its utilitarian and socialist antecedents (discussed in an earlier section), British anthropology exhibits a certain lofty detachment from the political arena, and anthropologists have not enlisted in activist causes to anything like the same extent as they have done in

107. It became at least partly institutionalized in the International Institute of African Languages and Cultures (later called simply the International African Institute), founded in 1926. Although nominally international, the great majority of its active members were always British. See Kuper, *Anthropologists and Anthropology*, pp. 130–133.

America or on the European continent. British anthropology would seem to be the most purely academic of anthropologies; it speaks much more exclusively from the head, and less from the heart, than do the anthropologies of other lands.

However, the generalizations about British anthropology so confidently asserted by both Britons and Americans really apply only to British *academic* and professional anthropology; i.e., to those functionalists and structuralists who have claimed for themselves the title "anthropologist." Yet their work until after World War II comprised only a fraction of the total anthropological enterprise in the British Isles. Before the 1960s there were fewer than thirty professional anthropologists in the whole of Great Britain,[100] virtually all of whom had been students of Malinowski, Radcliffe-Brown, or, very frequently, both. But side by side with the professional Association of Social Anthropologists (ASA), there has always existed the older and much larger Royal Anthropological Institute of Great Britain and Ireland (RAI), many of whose members until the recent past were amateurs.[109] Their numbers included colonial officials, missionaries, and travelers, who regularly contributed anthropological articles to *Man*, the *Journal of the Royal Anthropological Institute, Sudan Notes and Records, Tanganyika Notes and Records, The Uganda Journal*, the *Journal of the Royal Central Asian Society, Man in India*, and doubtless many others. These works encompass not only social anthropology but the wider aspects of ethnology, as well as a certain amount of prehistory, linguistics and physical anthropology. The outlook of the authors has frequently been progressivist or diffusionist, occasionally also primitivist, showing in any case a strong historical orientation. If, then, the designation "British anthropology" is allowed to encompass the work of the nonprofessionals as well as of the academics, the differences from American anthropology become much less conspicuous than is usually supposed. The academics have nevertheless insisted that theirs is the only "true," or legitimate, British anthropology,[110] and Americans seem by and large to have taken them at their word.

Some neighboring trees

108. Ibid., p. 151.

109. It was founded as the Anthropological Institute of Great Britain and Ireland in 1871, and became the Royal Anthropological Institute after receiving a royal charter in 1900. For the circumstances attending its founding see George W. Stocking, Jr., *Victorian Anthropology* (New York, 1987), pp. 235–273. For a review of its history and a discussion of its nature see esp. Kuklick, *The Savage Within*, pp. 58–71.

110. Cf. Kuper, *Anthropologists and Anthropology*, p. 108.

When speaking of French anthropology, it is important first of all to notice a major institutional difference from the anthropologies of the English-speaking world. Anthropology *soi-disant* is a purely academic discipline, heavily theoretical and philosophical, which is taught in a few universities by learned sages who are primarily scholars rather than field researchers. At the same time ethnology, linguistics, prehistoric archaeology, and physical anthropology are all separate and unconnected research disciplines carried on mainly by narrowly focused specialists who are based more often in research institutes than in universities. There is not, as a result, the same close conjunction between teaching and research that has usually been insisted on in the English-speaking world. The ethnologist or archaeologist may give an occasional course of lectures on his or her specialty at the local university, but is not expected to have a broader command of the anthropological field. The anthropologist on the other hand is a teacher and thinker who is not expected to do fieldwork. There may at times be a certain sense of alienation between the two groups, much as exists between the practitioners of "pure" and "applied" science. This same institutional differentiation exists in many other parts of continental Europe, where research is traditionally the province of institutes rather than of academe.[111]

Prior to about 1950 there was no self-labeled anthropology in France except physical anthropology. Studies of culture and society belonged to two other, quite distinct disciplines, designated respectively as ethnology and comparative sociology. Ethnology was the province of the Musée de l'Homme, the Institut Français de l'Afrique Noir, and other research institutes that were not university-based; latterly they have all been superseded by the all-encompassing Centre National de la Recherche Scientifique. French ethnology was and is quintessentially a field discipline, and its theoretical orientations, like those of ethnologists in most other countries, remained largely historical. Comparative sociology on the other hand was and largely is the province of university-based armchair *philosophes.* It was renamed anthropology by Lévi-Strauss in the 1950s, but still remains essentially a philosophical enterprise, and it conspicuously has not merged with the discipline of ethnology. In France as in Britain, therefore, one must make a distinction between a small group of theoretical movers and shakers, whose work is widely read and admired abroad, and a much

111. Many institutes, especially in Germany, are nowadays lodged within universities, but they are administratively separate from the teaching departments.

larger cohort of field workers whose work reaches only a limited audience, and is very rarely translated into English or German. It is, here again, the work of the theoreticians that Americans (and British) think of as the essential French anthropology.

Some neighboring trees

I will follow the lead of Lévi-Strauss in designating as anthropology what was known to Durkheim, Mauss, and Lévy-Bruhl as comparative sociology. This field from its beginnings has followed a much more consistent, linear pattern of development that did the anthropologies of England and the United States, for it has been almost impervious to influences from abroad. As I suggested earlier in the chapter, this is surely the consequence in part of intellectual nationalism. French anthropology was, and remains, a direct outgrowth of the French Enlightenment, and French anthropologists continue to acknowledge a debt to Montesquieu and Turgot far more regularly than their British or American colleagues acknowledge a debt to Tylor or to Morgan. Comte considered himself a disciple of the Enlightenment masters (especially Condorcet); Durkheim acknowledged the influence of Comte; Lévi-Strauss is avowedly a follower of Durkheim. Each naturally added new dimensions to the edifice of French philosophical thought, without however breaking overtly with the work of predecessors.

The acknowledged founder of what today is called French anthropology, as well as of modern French sociology, was of course Émile Durkheim. His outlook was strongly, even dogmatically, sociofunctionalist, drawing on the earlier work of Comte and Spencer.[112] Like them, he attributed most cultural institutions and developments to the overriding need of society to maintain itself. He exerted also a very strong influence on a generation of British social anthropologists, as we saw a little earlier. Yet Durkheim's brand of Functionalism was something very different from the ahistorical Functionalism of Radcliffe-Brown and his disciples, for it was superimposed over a progressivist schema that was a direct legacy of the French Enlightenment.[113] Although Durkheim never proposed a formal stage theory, it is clear, especially in *The Elementary Forms of the Religious Life*,[114] that he regarded Primitive Man (exemplified by the native Australians) as a type category, and the starting point for a continuing process of social evolution. His distinction between "mechanical" and "organic" solidarity, the organizing bases respectively of primitive and of advanced so-

---

112. See Abram Kardiner and Edward Preble, *They Studied Man* (Cleveland, 1961), pp. 115–118.

113. Ibid., p. 117.

114. Paris, 1912.

ciety, was nothing if not a progressivist theory.[115] The same outlook is reflected also in the work of all his close associates, notably including Marcel Mauss, Maurice Halbwachs, and Lucien Lévy-Bruhl. All of them related cultural institutions to social needs, and cultural changes over time to the changing needs of an evolving and ever more complex social order. Lévy-Bruhl went perhaps farthest in developing an overtly progressivist schema, focusing on the evolution of cognition and reason.[116]

The Progressivism of the French was at the same time something quite different from that of their British and American colleagues, for it was noteworthy for the absence of Darwinian influence. It never occurred to Durkheim or his collaborators to include biological evolution (and therefore physical anthropology) within the compass of their interests, for they thought of evolution strictly in terms of evolving society, rather than of the evolving human species. It would perhaps be accurate to say that they were progressivists without being evolutionists; their Progressivism was an unalloyed survival of the eighteenth-century Enlightenment tradition.

Other Roots; Other Trees

From Montesquieu through Comte to Durkheim and his school, the dominant philosophical themes in French social thought were thus Progressivism and natural law. After World War II, however, Lévi-Strauss initiated the first major change of direction of French anthropological thought, retaining the belief in natural law but at least partially ignoring the Progressivism of his predecessors. His Structuralism is in theory a universalist doctrine, which seeks to identify what is common to the thinking of all peoples everywhere. Yet his theories in regard to commonalities in kinship systems, exchange systems, and mythology are nearly all derived from the comparative study of tribal peoples, and it seems clear that he continues to think of Primitive Man as a type category in much the same way as did Durkheim and Lévy-Bruhl.

But if there are clear residues of Progressivism in the work of Lévi-Strauss, there are also certain undertones of Primitivism in his purely ethnographic descriptions of Brazilian natives.[117] Structuralism–an aspect of natural law theory–nevertheless remains at the heart and core of his work, and provides the strongest philosophical link between French and American anthropology today. Progressivism and Primitivism are sec-

115. See esp. Steven Lukes, *Émile Durkheim, His Life and Work* (London, 1973), pp. 147–167.

116. In a series of works published between 1912 and 1938, of which the best known are *Primitive Mentality* (1922; English translation 1923) and *How Natives Think* (1912; English translation 1926). For a full list and discussion of his works see Evans-Pritchard, *History of Anthropological Thought*, pp. 119–131.

117. As in *Tristes Tropiques* (Paris, 1961).

ondary, rather weak links, while Indianology and German Idealism are not conspicuous features of French anthropological thought.

Marxism must be mentioned as another important influence in postwar French anthropology, as it has been also in the United States. However, it has made itself felt in quite different ways in the two countries. While in America Marxism has been linked mainly to the dominant paradigm of Cultural Materialism, in France it has blended instead with the equally dominant paradigm of Structuralism. The absence of Materialism is indeed one of the most conspicuous and surprising features of French Marxism; one that would surely have horrified Marx himself.

Some neighboring trees

Notwithstanding the early and brief field experiences of Lévi-Strauss and of Pierre Bourdieu, French anthropology as a theoretical and intellectual enterprise remains just about as much an armchair exercise as it was in the days of Montesquieu and Turgot. Durkheim was, by his own reckoning, a rigid empiricist,[118] and he regularly acknowledged his debt to the British and American ethnographers upon whom he drew so heavily in developing his theories of social organization and of religion.[119] Yet it never seems to have occurred to him or to other members of his circle to carry out fieldwork at first hand. This tradition of lofty detachment has if anything increased in recent years. Indeed the currently popular and influential theorists, like Foucault, Bourdieu,[120] Sperber, and Derrida, are mostly all-purpose philosophers rather than specifically anthropologists, whatever their academic labels may be.[121] They spin out their grand theories from a magisterial height, and from an encyclopedic overview of other peoples' work, just as did Durkheim and Mauss in the *Année Sociologique* eighty years ago.[122] If British anthropology is the most academic of anthropologies, French anthropology is surely the most cerebral.

But in France as in England, there are also field ethnologists whose work must be considered separately from that of the theoreticians, for it sometimes shows quite different philosophical orientations. Much of it, especially in Africa, remains strongly historical in its orientations. There is in addition a small handful of Francophone ethnologists who bridge the gap between ethnology and philosophy, and who have become well known

118. Cf. esp. *The Rules of Sociological Method* (Paris, 1895).

119. See esp. Lukes, *Émile Durkheim*, pp. 450–453.

120. Although Bourdieu is a self-proclaimed ethnographer who has published several works on the ethnography of Algeria, Derek Robbins has shown that the actual scope of his field experience was as limited as was that of Lévi-Strauss in Brazil. See Robbins, *The Work of Pierre Bourdieu* (Boulder, Colo., 1991), pp. 10–28.

121. Foucault and Derrida are commonly identified as philosophers, Bourdieu as a sociologist, and Sperber as an anthropologist.

122. See Kardiner and Preble, *They Studied Man*, pp. 110–111.

to American audiences through their more philosophical works. Among this group are Marcel Griaule, Louis Dumont, Luc de Heusch (actually a Belgian by nationality), and Claude Meillassoux. These individuals have spent extensive time in the field, but they are known outside their own country mainly for sweepingly theoretical or philosophical writings that are as universalistic in scope as are those of Lévi-Strauss or Foucault.

One further characteristic of the French, and indeed of most Continental European scholarship, is worthy of note. One can observe not only a kind of disciplinary consistency, but a high degree of personal consistency in the work of each individual scholar. A European scholar is expected to stake out an intellectual and philosophical position early in life, and to stick to it thereafter. The consequence is that many Europeans, like Lévi-Strauss and Griaule, are rather self-consciously laboring on a lifelong oeuvre, or monument, in which each successive publication is seen as a building block. They may perhaps still be hoping that, after death, the entire body of their work will be published in uniform and comprehensive editions, as was routinely done in the eighteenth and nineteenth centuries. In any case their work seems to reflect a degree of intellectual self-consciousness that is rare in American anthropology, where each field project is likely to be treated as self-contained, and where individuals move freely and unabashedly between different fields of interest and different philosophical orientations. It is not uncommon for Americans to expressly repudiate their earlier philosophical positions, whereas in Europe such an admission may be regarded as rather shameful, or at least as an admission of personal defeat.

Anthropology in German-speaking lands

The question of who should and should not be called an anthropologist is even more problematical in the German-speaking world than it is in England and France. As in France before World War II, the term is applied only to physical anthropology, while the field of cultural studies continues to be called either *Ethnologie* or *Völkerkunde.*[123] My discussion will therefore concern the work of people who call themselves ethnologists, but are called anthropologists by their colleagues in other lands. With apologies to Austrian and Swiss colleagues, I must continue to use "Germany" and "German" in the broad sense, to encompass all of the German-speaking lands and peoples of central Europe.

German anthropology, as I am calling it, resembles French anthropolo-

123. It is noteworthy for example that the *Handbuch der Deutschsprachigen Ethnologie* (Göttingen, 1990) has the translated English title *Guide to German-Speaking Anthropology.*

gy only in its intellectual nationalism. That is, it has developed in a logical and unbroken progression from the work of eighteenth- and nineteenth-century German philosophers, and has been largely impervious to influences from abroad. Its outlook always has been and remains basically mentalistic and historical, rather than functionalist or structuralist. Following especially in the tradition of Herder, it has emphasized the importance of cultural differences, and the doctrine of Cultural Relativism. Above all it has emphasized the importance of minutely detailed ethnographic data, and therefore of fieldwork—a circumstance that is reflected in the truly extraordinary number of German ethnographic museums and societies (see Chapter 6). In these respects it is not markedly different from the ethnologies of France and of Britain, but whereas ethnology (in the old-fashioned sense) in France and Britain stands rather outside the theoretical mainstream, in Germany it is and has always been the theoretical mainstream. There is no tradition of ivory-tower theorizing independent of ethnographic fieldwork; German anthropology is nothing if not down-to-earth. While theory is not absent, it must always be buttressed by masses of ethnographic data. As nearly as I can tell, the German ethnographic tradition, discussed in Chapter 6, remains at the heart of German anthropology down to the present day.

Some neighboring trees

At the turn of the twentieth century, all anthropology was regarded, and regarded itself, as a historical discipline, reflected in F.W. Maitland's dictum that "By and by anthropology will have the choice between being history or nothing."[124] But in Britain and America, as we have seen, anthropology eventually turned away from historical interests, to concentrate upon the analysis of present-day situations and problems. German anthropology on the other hand never developed a social conscience; the discipline has always remained basically historical, devoted to the reconstruction of past cultural developments and population movements through the study of ethnographic trait distributions.

As we saw in Chapter 6, the German historical and culturological outlook was shared by Boasians in America during the early part of the twentieth century. At the heart of German ethnographic theorizing, however, was a belief not shared by the American culture historians: a belief in the basic uninventiveness of the primitive mind, or "*urdummheit*" as K.T. Preuss rather facetiously called it.[125] Friedrich Ratzel and Fritz Graebner, the founding fathers of German ethnology, both believed in the principle of uninventiveness. This outlook ran directly counter to one of the most

124. Quoted here from the flyleaf of Paul Radin, *The Method and Theory of Ethnology* (New York, 1933). I have seen variant renderings of the quotation in other works.
125. See H.R. Hays, *From Ape to Angel* (New York, 1958), p. 284.

fundamental though unstated assumptions of the progressivists, who held that what man has invented in one place he can and eventually will invent in another. That is, the progressivists assume that when peoples everywhere reach a certain level of social development, they will come up with similar institutions and similar inventions, whether or not they have any contact with one another. The Germans on the other hand believed that cultural parallels must in all cases be treated as evidence of diffusion or migration, unless it can be categorically proven that no such movements occurred.[126]

The ethnographer's task, then, was first to discover cultural parallels, through meticulously detailed field studies, and then to posit the prehistoric migrations or diffusions that had produced them. This was the basic German approach to "ethnographic prehistory," ("conjectural history" as it had been called in the British Isles), and it was spelled out in exhaustive and rigorous detail by Graebner in his *Methode der Ethnologie,* published in 1911. It should be noted incidentally that the Germans, strictly speaking, were migrationists rather than diffusionists; that is, they attributed cultural parallels much more often to actual population movements than to the diffusion of ideas across cultural borders. The notion that "ideas have wings" and can be spread by word of mouth from neighbor to neighbor and from land to land was one of the mainstays of the twentieth-century American diffusionists, but it was surprisingly slow in finding a place in German culture-historical thought.[127]

Methode der Ethnologie became the Bible for two generations of German and Austrian ethnographers. Like Boas in America, Graebner expressed his vehement opposition to all forms of speculative theory–a category that necessarily included evolutionary theory. He pointed out, with justice, that the schemata of the social evolutionists depended on arranging culture traits from different parts of the world in a logically neat progression, rather than on any real chronological evidence. It might be true that hoe cultivation had preceded plow cultivation, but there was no way of proving it. (Like almost all his colleagues at the time, Graebner had no appreciation for the possibilities of archaeology.)[128] In place of evolutionary theory, Graebner offered the concept of the *Kulturkreis,* or culture-circle. The idea had actually originated with Leo Frobenius, who had been

126. See ibid.

127. For discussion on this, see esp. William Y. Adams in P. G. Duke *et al.*, eds., *Diffusion and Migration: Their Roles in Cultural Development* (Calgary, 1978), pp. 1–5; and William Y. Adams, Dennis P. Van Gerven and Richard Levy in *Annual Review of Anthropology* 7 (1978): 482–533.

128. See Hays, *From Ape to Angel,* p. 283, and Jürgen Zwernemann, *Culture History and African Anthropology,* pp. 44–53. *Uppsala Studies in Cultural Anthropology,* 6 (1983).

Some neighboring trees

struck by certain close (and still unexplained) cultural parallels between West Africa and Oceania. He hypothesized that these represented the outer fringes of what had originally been an area of continuous cultural distribution, the intervening, central area having subsequently been modified by later waves of diffusion or migration.[129] But Frobenius was never a very systematic or orderly thinker, and it was left to Graebner to work up the Kulturkreis into a formal theory, which could account for cultural distributions all over the globe. The idea was enthusiastically championed also by Wilhelm Schmidt at the University of Vienna, who in time became the grand guru of Kulturkreis theory. As a result, the Kulturkreis approach came to be known as the Vienna School, though it always had adherents in Germany as well.

Several features of Kulturkreis theory may be briefly noted here. First, the movement of culture is generally ascribed to migration rather than to simple diffusion. Second, culture does not evolve on its own; peoples continue to have their original cultures, unmodified through the centuries, until some new migration comes along to change them. Third, culture moves from place to place, and subsequently survives, in the form of trait-complexes rather than individual elements, even though there may be no logical interconnection among the traits involved. Graebner's "Melanesian bow culture," for example, involved a conjunction of pile dwellings, coiled pottery, specially hafted adzes, and spoons; Frobenius's African Kulturkreis included shields, bows, knives, throwing clubs, throwing knives, musical instruments, and house forms.[130] Finally, there is a very heavy emphasis on items of material culture rather than social organization, mythology, or other more abstract forms of culture. This probably reflects the museum orientation of so many of the German ethnographers, but also Graebner's belief that tangible objects represent the "hardest" and most reliable kind of ethnographic evidence, because no observer bias is involved. This particular emphasis was a blessing in one respect, for German ethnographers in the field continued to observe, record, and collect material culture long after it had ceased to interest the more socially oriented anthropologists in Britain and the United States.

One of the signal virtues of Kulturkreis ethnology was indeed its continuing emphasis on fieldwork. As Melville Jacobs has written, "the field research enthusiasm of Boasian diffusionists was paralleled in the numerous field researches of devotees of Viennese layer-cake historicism. Today an impressive percentage of the ethnographic archives about nonwestern societies and cultures comes from dedicated people whose primarily his-

129. In his book, *Der Ursprung der afrikanischen Kulturen* (Berlin, 1898), pp. 270–298.
130. See Zwernemann, *Culture History and African Anthropology*, p. 34.

torical and diffusionist orientation of *Kulturkreis* persuasion frequently did little to refine or damage their field perceptions. But the mainstreams of twentieth century behavioral sciences were little attended to by *Kulturkreis* disciples.... *Kulturkreis*... remained rigidly nineteenth century in its fabric of method and historicist aims."[131]

Kulturkreislehre was, of course, the very antithesis of Functionalism, for the emphasis was entirely on cultural forms, without any consideration of their functional context or meaning. Similarly shaped adzes or spoons were important evidence of culture contact, regardless of the fact that they might have been used for quite different purposes in different areas. In the end, this total disregard for context proved fatal. The Kulturkreis approach was already under attack in both Germany and Austria in the years just before World War II,[132] and after the war it was rapidly and to all intents and purposes completely abandoned.[133]

The disavowal of Kulturkreislehre did not, however, spell the end of the German ethnographic tradition, which apparently continues to flourish throughout the German-speaking world. The orientations of the German ethnographers and ethnologists remain basically culture-historical, but they now tend to attribute culture change much more to diffusion than to migration. They have reverted to more narrowly particularistic or regionally focused studies, without attempting to fit them into worldwide schemata. Josef Haekel, one of the most influential of the postwar German ethnographers, admonished that "It is... recommended that... research on historical relationship be restricted to geographically limited areas. It is then easier to give full consideration to the local data, and there is more possibility for control and for a better understanding of intertribal communications."[134]

German anthropology was thus becoming more narrowly particularized in its focus at the same time when anthropology in France was becoming increasingly rarefied. As a result the German philosopher Jürgen Habermas seems to have exerted virtually no influence on the anthropology of his own country, although his performance theory of language (the Theory of Communicative Action) has had a considerable vogue among anthropologists in the United States.[135]

---

131. Melville Jacobs, *Pattern in Cultural Anthropology* (Homewood, Ill., 1964), p. 22. For an extended critique of *Kulturkreislehre*, see also Clyde Kluckhohn in *American Anthropologist* 38 (1936): 157–196.

132. See Zwernemann, *Culture History and African Anthropology*, pp. 86–119.

133. See ibid., pp. 109–127; Jacobs, *Pattern in Cultural Anthropology*, pp. 21–22.

134. Haekel in *American Anthropologist* 61 (1959): 868.

135. See esp. Habermas, *The Theory of Communicative Action*, trans. Thomas McCarthy (Boston, 1981).

Some neighboring trees

There can be no doubt that the dominant philosophical influence in German anthropology, from its beginnings to the present day, has been German Idealism. Primitivism is also at least an undercurrent, for the German ethnographers have shown a special preference for the world's simpler cultures, both in the Old World and the New.[136] In South America, for example, they have given special attention to the peoples of Amazonia and of Tierra del Fuego. Indianology might indeed be mentioned as another, partially separate undercurrent, for the Native American seems always to have had a special fascination for German-speaking peoples. This is reflected not only in the truly prodigious amount of fictional literature about Indians that is published in Germany (cf. Chapter 5), but also in the extensive field researches of German ethnographers, especially in South America. No other European nation has sponsored anything like the same amount of ethnographic fieldwork among the peoples of the New World.

As we saw in Chapter 6, German Idealism, Primitivism, and Indianology were also the dominant philosophical influences in American anthropology during the first third of the twentieth century. During that interval of time there was certainly a closer affinity between the anthropologies of the United States and of Germany than there was between American and British or French anthropology. It was further enhanced by the German backgrounds of so many of the early Boasians, who could and did read the German-language literature at a time when it was simply ignored by scholars in Britain and France. Yet the Americans never "bought into" the Kulturkreis principle; on the contrary they were some of its severest critics.[137] On their side the Germans, preoccupied as they were with cultural forms, never developed the psychological interests that increasingly preoccupied the Boasians after about 1930.

As the American anthropologists shifted their attention from the past to the here-and-now, and as the discipline passed into the hands of non-Boasians who were not of German ancestry, the spiritual affinity between Americans and Germans rapidly diminished, and in time virtually disappeared. American anthropology today has no one dominant philosophical orientation, but in the aggregate it is probably closer in spirit to the anthropologies of both Britain and France that it is to that of Germany. The single bond that continues to unite Americans and Germans is perhaps that of Indianology, though today it is not a dominant interest in either country.

---

136. Cf. Jacobs, *Pattern in Cultural Anthropology*, pp. 21–22.

137. Cf. Lowie, *History of Ethnological Theory*, pp. 177–195; Jacobs, *Pattern in Cultural Anthropology*, pp. 21–22.

The term "anthropology" in the Soviet Union was applied exclusively to physical anthropology, as it was also in other European countries until a generation ago. The whole panoply of enterprises that in America and England are variously call ethnography, ethnology, social anthropology, and linguistics were all subsumed under the single term *Etnografia.* This has sometimes caused confusion in translations, since in English the term "ethnography" has much more narrowly specific connotations.[138] Once again, I will consider all of the various components of Russian and Soviet ethnography to fall within the scope of anthropology.[139]

As in so many other countries, Russian ethnography was a byproduct of imperial expansion. It began with an interest in the more primitive tribal peoples of Eastern Siberia, who came under Russian rule in the seventeenth and eighteenth centuries. By the later nineteenth century the Academy of Sciences in St. Petersburg was regularly publishing ethnographic and linguistic articles about these peoples, contributed mainly by learned political exiles like Waldemar Bogoras and Waldemar Jochelson. Both men were active in the field between 1895 and 1897 as members of an exploring expedition sponsored by the Russian Geographical Society, and both subsequently worked for a number of years with the Jesup North Pacific Expedition, directed by Franz Boas and sponsored by the American Museum of Natural History.[140] The early Russian ethnographic researches were highly particularistic and were not seen as part of a broader anthropological enterprise, for the new theoretical discipline of anthropology was, with some reason, regarded as godless and subversive by the Tsars. In keeping with that circumstance, there was no specifically anthropological society; the Russian Geographical Society continued to be the main institutional home of Russian ethnography down to the time of the 1917 revolution.

Paradoxically, the revolution of 1917 elevated anthropology for the first time to the status of an important theoretical discipline, and at the same time bound it in a theoretical straitjacket: that of Marxist orthodoxy. As a result, Soviet anthropology remained theoretically stagnant for over sixty years. The works not only of Marx and Engels but even of Morgan were treated as sacred documents, which might perhaps be ignored but could not be criticized or amended. The academic teachers of anthropology

138. For discussion, see esp. Ernest Gellner in Ernest Gellner, ed., *Soviet and Western Anthropology* (New York, 1980), pp. x–xii.

139. I gained some familiarity at least with the traditions and the legacies of Soviet Anthropology while teaching at Almati State University, in Kazakhstan, in 1995.

140. See Winters, *International Dictionary of Anthropologists*, pp. 71–72 and 327–328.

simply used them as classroom texts, while the ethnographers in the field often ignored them, continuing to pursue largely particularist and historical interests. Slezkine suggests that in the early years of the Soviet regime the ethnographers took refuge in a kind of nostalgic Primitivism as an escape from the rigidities of Marxist doctrine.[141]

Some neighboring trees

Curiously enough, ethnographic particularism was itself encouraged by political circumstances. If theoretical anthropology (in the guise of Marxist theory) acquired a new political relevance under the Soviet regime, so also, in a very different way, did old-fashioned, particularist ethnography. It became the handmaiden of the famous, or infamous, Soviet Nationalities Policy.

It is axiomatic, under Marxist theory, that Communist governments must be seen to represent the free will of the masses. In support of that image, the Soviet government solemnly maintained a great many democratic fictions, one of which was the fiction that the Soviet Union was a voluntary association of culturally autonomous peoples, united only by a common class-consciousness and a devotion to Communism. The doctrine of cultural and ethnic autonomy was first proclaimed as a practical policy by Lenin in the 1920s, as a way of inducing the subject populations of Central Asia–always rebellious under Tsarist authority–to support the new regime. In time, it became the basic Soviet framework for dealing with all of the scores of ethnic minorities that are scattered throughout the Russian Empire. "Autonomy" meant, in principle, that each of the Soviet Union's myriad peoples was organized as a separate, self-governing administrative unit, allowed to elect its own soviets and cadres. Culturally, it included the guarantee that each ethnic unit might use its own language, wear its own national costume, and in theory practice its own religion. However, the cadres and other officials had in all cases to be members of the Communist Party, answerable to superiors in Moscow, and the amount of actual self-determination that was allowed in the various republics and *nagornoi* was usually small.[142] Each self-governing unit had, of course, a specifically demarcated territory within which its authority ran.

Under the Nationalities Policy, the Soviets in time developed a kind of nested hierarchy of nominally self-governing units. At the top of the pyramid were the so-called union republics, like Lithuania, Ukraine, and Kazakstan–in theory sovereign nations that had entered into a voluntary union. At the next level were the "autonomous republics," like Yakutia and Karakalpakia, most of which were non-Russian enclaves within the huge

141. Yuri Slezkine in *Current Anthropology* 32, no. 4 (1991): 476–484.

142. For discussion, see esp. Geoffrey Wheeler, *A Modern History of Soviet Central Asia* (New York, 1964), pp. 123–131.

Russian Federated Republic. They were partially but not wholly free from control by the union republics in which they were located. Then came "autonomous regions," or *nagornoi*, many of which were enclaves within enclaves, as for example of Armenians in Nagorno-Karabakh, within the Republic of Azerbaizhan. Finally, at the lowest level, were "autonomous districts," which again were mostly enclaves within enclaves.[143]

No matter how it may have originally been conceived, the Nationalities Policy with its proliferation of ethnically differentiated units soon became an instrument to "divide and rule." It served especially to prevent the various Turkic-speaking and Muslim peoples of Central Asia from making common cause.[144] Within this framework it became one of the major tasks of the Soviet ethnographers and linguists to decide who were and were not legitimate ethnic groups, entitled to some degree of autonomy; the field workers were therefore encouraged to pursue highly particularistic studies that should emphasize the differences rather than the similarities between peoples. The task presented little difficulty in the case of huge, linguistically distinct and self-recognizing groups like the Lithuanians and Ukrainians, but it became much more troublesome in the case, for example, of the scores of Turkic-speaking peoples scattered in groups large and small throughout Central and East Asia.[145]

No wonder, then, that the study of ethnic groups and the problem of ethnic identity became among the chief preoccupations of Soviet ethnography. Much of the work undertaken was necessarily classificatory rather than theoretical, and hewed closely to the traditions of nineteenth-century ethnology. There was nevertheless a lively debate over the definition of ethnicity, as there was also for a time in the West.[146] Indeed this was probably the single most controversial issue among Soviet ethnographers, even though the debate was always somewhat constrained by the requirements of policy.[147] For example, ethnic groups in Soviet usage had to have a historically defined territory,[148] which precluded consideration of diaspora

143. Ibid.

144. See esp. Muriel Atkin in Jo-Ann Gross, ed., *Muslims in Central Asia* (Durham, N.C., 1992), pp. 46–72.

145. See, for example, Shirin Akiner, *Islamic Peoples of the Soviet Union* (London, 1983).

146. Cf. George De Vos and Lola Romanucci-Ross, eds., *Ethnic Identity* (Palo Alto, Calif., 1975); Ronald Cohen in *Annual Review of Anthropology* 7 (1978): 379–403; and William Petersen in William Petersen, Michael Novak, and Philip Gleason, *Concepts of Ethnicity* (Cambridge, Mass., 1982), pp. 1–26.

147. For extended discussion, see esp. Teodor Shanin in *Comparative Studies in Society and History* 31, no. 3 (1989): 409–424; Julian Bromley and Viktor Kozlov in the same volume, pp. 425–438; and Yu. Bromley and T. Dragadze in Gellner, *Soviet and Western Anthropology*, pp. 151–170.

148. Bromley and Dragadze in Gellner, *Soviet and Western Anthropology*, p. 162.

minorities like the Gypsies. The Soviets, however, pioneered in the study of ethnogenesis–the processes through which self-recognizing ethnic groups come into being. They remain today the world leaders in this important and neglected field of investigation, which has a special relevance in the case of pastoral nomads.[149]

Some neighboring trees

Since there was a heavy emphasis on fieldwork in Soviet *Etnografia,* there was not the same division between the armchair theoreticians and the field practitioners that existed in some other European countries. Field workers were expected to incorporate Marxist theory, or at least Marxist terminology, in their published reports, and teachers were expected to buttress theory with ethnographic facts in the classroom. As nearly as I can discover, however, anthropology never developed very far as an autonomous teaching discipline or as a subject for philosophical speculation, any more than it did under the Tsars; it was a subject taught only to would-be ethnographers. The locus of teaching and the institutional home of virtually all Soviet ethnography was in the various institutes of ethnography and anthropology (meaning physical anthropology) that were established in Moscow and in some of the republics. However, the emphasis on fieldwork has significantly declined in the recent past, perhaps because all the "ethnic groups" had now been officially demarcated for political purposes, and there was no further need for field research to sustain the Nationalities Policy.[150]

It is somewhat surprising to find the four-field conception of anthropology persisting, at least on paper, in the Soviet Union and in the several republics that have succeeded it. The reasons appear to have been partly theoretical and partly practical. Linguistics–important for the delineation of ethnic groups–was always treated as a dimension of ethnography. The central research institution, as we have just noted, was the institute in Moscow that combined ethnography with physical anthropology, while research in the Armenian Republic was under the aegis of the Institute of Archaeology and Ethnography. The four-field conjunction (except in the case of ethnology and linguistics) seems to have existed mainly as an administrative convenience, but it nevertheless probably reflects the continuing centrality of evolutionary theory in Marxist thought.

In 1980 Ernest Gellner–a sympathetic observer–summarized the content of Soviet *Etnografia* in terms of four characteristics: first, an emphasis on modes of production as basic to the classification of peoples; second,

149. See contributions by T.A. Zhdanko, K. Shanijazov, R.G. Kuzeev, S.G. Agadzhanov, A. Karryev, and S.M. Abramzon in Wolfgang Weissleder, ed., *The Nomadic Alternative* (The Hague, 1978), pp. 137–197.

150. See Valery Tishkov in *Current Anthropology* 33, no. 4 (1992): 374.

classification in terms of a universal evolutionist schema, with little attention to cultural diffusion; third, a heavy emphasis on ethnicity; fourth, the differentiation of ethnic groups on the basis of cultural rather than specifically social characteristics.[151] The first two of these were of course dictated by the requirements of Marxist theory, while the latter two reflected the practical needs of the Nationalities Policy. Kirghiz and Kazakh, for example, could hardly have been differentiated on the basis of social organization; it was relatively minor differences of language and aesthetic culture that justified their division into separate republics.[152] From the standpoint of imperial control, however, it was essential to keep these two traditionally warlike peoples from uniting.

At first glance, there would appear to be a contradiction between the Universalism of Marxist evolutionary theory and the particularism dictated by the Nationalities Policy. If all peoples are moving along the same evolutionary path toward the same goal, and if there is a need to inculcate in all of them a common class-consciousness, why is it necessary to emphasize ethnic distinctions based on characteristics that, according to Marx, are unimportant features of the cultural suprastructure? Some Soviet ethnographers attempted to answer this criticism with a thoroughly Hegelian argument that was not, in substance, very different from that used by advocates of cultural pluralism in the West. They argued that ethnic diversity was necessary for evolutionary advance in history in the same way as was biodiversity in the biological world: it provided a starting point for the development of class conflict.[153]

It should not be supposed that there was complete uniformity of perspective among the Soviet "ethnographers," whose numbers included linguists, demographers, and sociologists in addition to more traditional ethnographic recorders. The extreme diversity of their field experiences and activities was sufficient in itself to produce some differences of outlook. Moreover, although none took anti-Marxist positions, there was considerable variation in the extent to which they introduced Marxist analysis into their writings.[154]

---

151. Gellner, *Soviet and Western Anthropology*, pp. xiii–xvi. The author might not wholly agree with my choice of terms; for some reason he seems determined to avoid characterizing Marxist theory as evolutionist.

152. In literature before the late nineteenth century, the Kazakh were always designated as Kirghiz, with the result that the so-called Kirghiz Steppe lies wholly within Kazakhstan.

153. See Gellner, *Soviet and Western Anthropology*, p. xv; Yu. I. Semenov in the same volume, pp. 29–58.

154. See Meyer Fortes in ibid., p. xi. Fortes claims that "Soviet ethnographers, linguists, demographers, and sociologists are as diverse in their interests and in their approaches as are anthropologists the world over," but this is clearly belied by the Soviet-authored chapters in the same volume.

Some neighboring trees

However, Karl Marx is now dead throughout the former Soviet lands, and this has precipitated a crisis in Soviet ethnography that is rather different from the malaise currently afflicting the discipline in the West. As Valery Tishkov (Director of the Institute of Ethnology[155] and Anthropology in Moscow) writes, "The recalcitrance of the subjects of our discipline and especially ethnic violence and the politicization of ethnicity in our country have highlighted unexpected discrepancies in our interpretation of past experience and posed a challenge to the academic community, but the depth of these discrepancies and the response to this challenge are both still far from being understood."[156] In other words, reading between the lines, the chickens of Soviet ethnic policy have come home to roost, and the ethnographers who contributed to the development and maintenance of that policy are left at a loss. Tishkov calls for a reemphasis on prolonged fieldwork (which he calls the "repatriation of ethnography"), an improved dialogue with the peoples being studied, a redefinition of "ethnicity" that will free it from the constraints both of policy and of evolutionary theory, and a critical self-analysis of the scientific community itself.[157] He ends by quoting Foucault to the effect that the intellectual must never say, "Here is what you must do."[158]

It is difficult to talk about commonalities between Soviet and other anthropologies, given the special political circumstances in which the Soviets were always forced to operate. If the British discipline is the most academic of anthropologies, the French the most cerebral, and the German the most down-to-earth, the Soviet was assuredly the most politicized. The extent of resemblance between the Soviets and their colleagues abroad can be measured almost entirely by the extent to which other anthropologies have been interpenetrated by Marxist theory–which indeed is fairly significant in some instances, as we saw earlier. However, Soviet anthropologists differ from their foreign counterparts in that they have always given primary emphasis to the specifically evolutionary dimension of Marxist thought, whereas this has probably been the least influential aspect of Marxism for American, British, and French anthropologists. Cultural Materialism might be mentioned as a further bond of affinity between Soviet and

155. Its name has recently been changed from "Ethnography" to "Ethnology" as part of Tishkov's own attempt to reform the discipline.

156. Tishkov in *Current Anthropology* 33, p. 371.

157. Ibid., pp. 371–382. Most of Tishkov's Russian colleagues have agreed with his criticisms of their discipline, but have been more overt than he in blaming shortcomings on the Soviet system rather than on internal shortcomings of the ethnographic discipline. See ibid., pp. 382–393.

158. Ibid., p. 382, quoting Michel Foucault, *Power/Knowledge*, trans. C. Gordon (New York, 1980), p. 62.

American anthropologists, but the Soviet version of Materialism, constrained as it was by the rigidities of Marxist theory, has always lacked a genuinely ecological dimension.

Anthropology in other lands

The Netherlands and Scandinavia. Outside of the countries previously discussed, European anthropology has flourished chiefly in the Netherlands and in Scandinavia. The Dutch until 1946 had extensive colonial holdings in Indonesia, and a large, highly specialized field of Indonesian studies was developed. It was, however, a particularistic discipline like Sinology or Indology. Like them it was in part philological, involving the study of ancient and medieval scriptures, and like them it was seen more as a branch of Orientalism than of anthropology. At the same time there developed, at the University of Leiden, a highly theoretical school of anthropology, more or less on the French model and heavily influenced by French Structuralism.[159]

Scandinavian anthropology until after World War II was wholly dominated by the German ethnographic tradition, though not specifically by Kulturkreislehre. Having no overseas colonies, the Swedish and Norwegian ethnographers were active among European folk populations, but also to some extent in Africa. They published their results in German, and attended German ethnographic congresses. The European researches were carried out under the aegis of university departments of European or Nordic ethnology; those in Africa mainly by museum-based personnel. There were no university departments of anthropology as such.[160]

Developments in Denmark took a slightly different direction because of the Greenland connection. The Danes, under the leadership of Knud Rasmussen and Kaj Birket-Smith, became world leaders in the study of the Eskimos, not only in their Greenland colony but in Canada and Alaska as well. They published in English rather than in German, and attended the quadrennial International Congresses of Americanists. The Danish researches belonged, and belong, clearly within the tradition of Indianology, and it is from that perspective that so many Americans are familiar with them.

After World War II, all of the Scandinavian countries felt an understandable desire to break away from the German tradition. Departments of social anthropology (or, in one case, cultural anthropology), modeled

159. See, for example, Winters, *International Dictionary of Anthropologists*, pp. 330–331.

160. For a brief survey of the status of Swedish Anthropology in 1959, see K.G. Izikowitz, Carl-Axel Moberg, and Albert Eskeröd in *American Anthropologist* 61, no. 4 (1959): 669–676.

initially on those of the British, were established eventually in all of the major universities. There was a deliberate shift to English as the language of publication, and consequently a growing influence of English-language publications. The Norwegian Frederik Barth, trained originally in the British tradition, became one of the internationally recognized leaders in the field of social anthropology; one whose investigations of ethnicity added a whole new dynamic to the field.[161] Meanwhile the older, particularistic ethnographic tradition waned as its practitioners died or retired. There are still, at the present time, separate university departments of European ethnology and of anthropology, but the kind of anthropology that is taught seems to be pretty much the same in both cases.

Some neighboring trees

In the 1960s and 1970s Structuralism and structural Marxism enjoyed a certain vogue, just as they did in Britain, but there was at the same time some influence from cultural ecology. Today Scandinavian social anthropology has become a good deal more eclectic than it was earlier, thanks in part to the flood of published material coming from America. There is not however any semblance of a four-field tradition: archaeology is taught in departments of European prehistory, linguistics in departments of linguistics, and physical anthropology, if at all, in departments of biology.[162]

India. Outside the Western world, anthropology is probably more deeply rooted and more fully developed in India than in any other country.[163] This results from a historical peculiarity, in that India was virtually the only nonwestern country that had a well-developed indigenous civilization and a huge native intelligentsia, yet remained under European colonial rule for a very long time, and until the recent past. Under these circumstances the Western sciences, including anthropology, were early transplanted to India, and were embraced by Indian scholars, many of whom went to England for advanced education.[164] By the time of Indian independence in 1948 anthropology was already being taught in many universities, and several anthropological journals had made their appearance. Today the subject is offered in at least two dozen Indian universities, many of which offer graduate degrees, and there is an active publication

161. See, among many works, Frederik Barth, ed., *Ethnic Groups and Boundaries* (Boston, 1969).

162. For information about Scandinavian Anthropology I am especially indebted to my colleague Tomas Håkansson.

163. Among other things, Indian anthropology exhibits a surprising degree of historical self-consciousness. More than half a dozen authors have reviewed the historical development of the discipline. For a list and discussion of these, see L. P. Vidyarthi and Bina Kumar Ray, *The Tribal Culture of India* (New Delhi, 1985), pp. 4–9. See also L. P. Vidyarthi, *Applied Anthropology in India* (Allahabad, 1984), pp. i–xxviii.

164. See Gopala Sarana and Dharni S. Sinha in *Annual Review of Anthropology* 5 (1976): 210.

program, mainly in English. In addition the Anthropological Survey of India, the country's chief research institution, employs more than 400 anthropologists–the largest number employed by any single institution in the world.[165]

According to Vidyarthi and Rai, the history of Indian anthropology began with the establishment of the Asiatic Society of Bengal in 1774.[166] The two aforementioned authors divide the subsequent history of the discipline into three phases: the Formative from 1774 to 1919, the Constructive from 1920 to 1949, and the Analytical from 1950 onward. During the Formative Period highly particularized studies of tribal peoples were carried on mainly by British colonial officials, though near the end of the period a few ethnographic monographs were published also by Indian scholars. The Anthropological Survey of India had its beginnings in this era. During the Constructive Period–which corresponded to the heyday of Functionalism in Britain–the first university departments of anthropology were established, large numbers of Indian scholars went to England for graduate study, and the anthropology of India took on very strongly the coloring of British social anthropology. In the Analytical Period after independence, the flood of American social anthropologists who came to do village studies in India exerted a considerable influence on Indian scholars. One consequence was that the main focus of interest shifted from exotic, non-Hindu tribes to Hindu castes.[167] Nevertheless, the overall character of anthropology in India still reflects more influence from Britain than from America.

As in so many countries already discussed, it is still necessary in India to make a distinction between social anthropology and ethnology. The nomenclature, however, is different, for here social anthropology generally comes under the rubric of sociology, while ethnology, linguistics, and physical anthropology are all called anthropology, retaining the conjunction that was created in Britain and America at the end of the nineteenth century, and was transplanted to India by British colonial administrators. Archaeology however stands apart; it is carried on within the ideological framework of national culture-history, or in other words Indology.

Social anthropology has generally taken the form of traditional village studies of the midcentury type, a surprisingly high percentage of which have been undertaken by Americans. Why British social anthropologists have so largely avoided the Indian subcontinent remains something of a

165. For much of the information in this section I am indebted to my colleagues Satish Kedia and John van Willigen.

166. *Tribal Culture of India*, p. 4.

167. Ibid., pp. 12–19; see also Sarana and Sinha in *Annual Review of Anthropology*, pp. 210–212, 220–221.

mystery; it may be because the village never really supplanted the tribe as the main unit of analysis for British anthropologists. However, there has been a substantial number of village studies by native Indians, notably including British-trained G.S. Ghurye,[168] M.N. Srinivas,[169] and their students. These individuals teach mostly in university departments of sociology and consider their work to be sociological. Their philosophical orientations are definitely functionalistic rather than historical, and are generally close to those of their British colleagues.[170]

Some neighboring trees

In another category altogether are the particularistic and historically oriented ethnographic studies of tribal peoples, carried on by the Anthropological Survey of India as well as by many university departments. The Survey is a continuing legacy of the colonial era, and retains much of the outlook of the Formative Period; that is, of early twentieth-century British anthropology. It was perhaps the nearest that the British ever came to establishing a research institution comparable to the Bureau of American Ethnology; like the latter its mandate was to collect all kinds of ethnographic, linguistic, and physical anthropological information about all of India's peoples. Long after social anthropologists had eschewed any interest in biological studies, the Survey continued to collect anthropometric and serological data from all over India.[171] The Survey of India serves also in an advisory capacity to the Ministry of Human Resources, which is responsible for the administration of tribal peoples. There are, in addition, several tribal research institutes maintained by state governments.[172]

The traditional cleavage between social anthropology and the other anthropological subdisciplines appears today to be breaking down, due in part to the three-field conjunction that is maintained in most university departments. As social anthropologists are engaged to teach in departments of anthropology rather than of sociology, there is inevitably a certain convergence of perspective between them and the more traditional ethnologists.[173] Another contributing factor has been a growing American influence, reflected both in the number of Indian anthropology students who now go to America for graduate training, and the adoption of American-published textbooks for many undergraduate anthropology courses.

---

168. See Winters, *International Dictionary of Anthropologists*, pp. 234–235.
169. Ibid., pp. 661–662.
170. See, for example, McKim Marriott, ed., *Village India* (Chicago, 1955), which has contributions by both American and Indian scholars.
171. See Clarence Maloney, *Peoples of South Asia* (New York, 1974), p. 49.
172. See Sarana and Sinha in *Annual Review of Anthropology*, pp. 211–212.
173. Ibid., pp. 214–218.

China. China, like India, had a flourishing indigenous civilization and a huge literati class, but it was spared both the curses and the blessings of colonial domination, at least in the intellectual sphere. Western sciences were, as a result, rather late in finding a home in China. Anthropology nevertheless made a promising beginning in the 1930s and 1940s, with the pathbreaking village studies of Fei Hsiao-Tung,[174] Martin Yang,[175] Francis L. K. Hsu,[176] and others.[177] All of the authors had been trained partly in the United States or in Britain, and their work reflects the general orientation of Chicago (and British) social anthropology at midcentury. However, the anthropological enterprise was brought to a standstill by the chaotic conditions prevailing after World War II, and more particularly by the Communist victory in 1949. Hsu and Yang emigrated, while Fei, who remained in China, was assigned by the state to relatively minor and innocuous researches among tribal peoples. Intellectuals in general were regarded with suspicion throughout the Mao years, and the "Great Proletarian Cultural Revolution" of 1965–1977 brought a temporary end to nearly all forms of research and scholarship.

Anthropology in China today is making a modest comeback. Departments have been established in three southern universities, though not at prestigious Peking University, and visiting scholars have been engaged to teach anthropology courses in other institutions.[178] However, the main locus of ethnographic field research is the Institute of Nationalities (*Minzuxueyuan*), which owes its existence to China's adoption of a nationalities policy based on that of the Soviet Union. In the Chinese administrative hierarchy there are autonomous regions (provinces), autonomous counties, and autonomous prefectures, which are granted varying degrees of self-determination depending on the shifting whims of the central government in Beijing.[179] The Institute of Nationalities, located in Beijing, is both a university and a research institute; it has the interesting triple mandate of educating the youth of China's fifty-five recognized ethnic minori-

174. *Peasant Life in China* (London, 1939).
175. *A Chinese Village* (New York, 1945).
176. *Under the Ancestors' Shadow* (New York, 1948).
177. For a partial listing see Malinowski's preface to Fei, *Peasant Life in China*, p. xvii, note.
178. I was invited to teach three anthropology courses in the Department of Archaeology at Peking University in the spring of 1989. Much of my information about present-day Chinese anthropology is derived from my personal experiences and inquiries at that time and subsequently.
179. For evidence of China's mercurial policy shifts toward the minorities, see George Moseley, *A Sino-Soviet Cultural Frontier*, which details the adventures and misadventures of a Chinese Kazakh commune under Communist rule. *Harvard East Asian Monographs*, 22, 1966.

ties, of carrying out ethnographic and linguistic field researches among the minority peoples, and of advising the government in regard to minorities policy. Institute members are active in carrying out fieldwork, mainly of a descriptive and culture-historical nature, especially in Xinjiang (Chinese Turkestan) and in the southwestern provinces of Guangxi and Yunnan. As in the Soviet Union, and for the same reason, their focus is highly particularistic.

Some neighboring trees

Mexico. The United States, the Colossus of the North, always casts a shadow over developments south of the border, and this is conspicuously true in the case of Mexican anthropology. The first anthropological researches in Mexico were undertaken by North Americans, and the development of an indigenous Mexican anthropology was in the beginning largely nurtured through collaboration with colleagues from the north. Since that time and down to the present, Mexican anthropology continues to be heavily interpenetrated by North American researchers, teachers, and collaborators.

The four-field approach, diffused from North America, remains basic in all of the many Mexican universities where anthropology is taught. It is noteworthy however that here, as nowhere else to my knowledge, archaeology is the most prominently featured of the subdisciplines; the tail that wags the dog of Mexican anthropology. This is partly a matter of national policy, since archaeological research is closely associated with tourism, so important to the Mexican economy. It also reflects the fact, however, that Mexico, far more than any other Latin American country, has attempted to build a national consciousness and a national pride, on the basis of her indigenous cultural heritage. This is abundantly demonstrated in the great National Museum of Anthropology–surely one of the world's premier museums of both archaeology and ethnology.

It follows that the strongest philosophical bond between Mexican and North American anthropologists today is that of Indianology, which in Mexico is officially designated as *Indigenismo.* While in the United States and Canada it is now no more than an undercurrent, it remains at the very heart and core of Mexican anthropology. It is not inappropriate that the main research institute in the country is the National Institute of Anthropology and History (INAH), a conjunction reflecting the fact that anthropology continues to be viewed mainly as a historical discipline.

Mexico was once regarded also as a fertile field for ethnographic researches, both by outsiders and by Mexican scholars. However, ethnological research seems these days to be very much in abeyance. This may possibly reflect the fact that many Mexican anthropologists, like other anthropologists throughout Latin America, are philosophical Marxists. The present government is fairly conservative, and may look with disfavor on field investigations by persons whose loyalty is considered suspect.[180]

Peru. Anthropology in Peru today is just about as well established as it is in Mexico. It has been taught at the University of San Marcos–the country's oldest and most prestigious university–for a good many years, and in the last generation anthropology departments have been established also in most of the country's other leading universities, both in Lima and in the provinces.[181]

Peruvian anthropology appears to differ in just about every respect from the anthropologies of North America and Mexico. To begin with, there is no semblance of a four-field tradition. Anthropology here means ethnology and social anthropology, while archaeology is treated as a wholly separate discipline and a branch of history, and physical anthropology hardly exists. Moreover, the discipline looks much more to Europe than to North America for theoretical inspiration. There is a particularly strong influence from British social anthropology, which results in a generally close liaison between university departments of anthropology, of sociology, and of economics. Although many and perhaps most Peruvian anthropologists are intellectual and political Marxists, their published works do not seem to show a heavy Marxist theoretical influence.

Active field research is carried on both among Quechua- and Aymara-speaking Indian villagers in the highlands, and among tribal peoples in the Montaña and Amazonia. There is a considerable tradition of regionalism in field research, such that studies among the highlanders are carried out mainly by anthropologists in the highlands universities, while studies of the Amazonian peoples have been undertaken more often by anthropologists from the several universities in Lima. Research among the highlanders, who have been heavily Hispanicized for many centuries, tends to be in the present-oriented tradition of social anthropology, while research among the rainforest peoples conforms much more to the old tradition of salvage ethnography. As in so many countries, there is a certain degree of intellectual alienation between the social anthropologists and the more historically oriented ethnographers.

---

180. For information on Mexican Anthropology I am indebted in part to my colleagues Kenneth Hirth and Michael Smythe, and I have also some measure of personal familiarity.

181. I am especially indebted to my friend and student Pierre Bidegaray for information about Peruvian anthropology.

Other Latin American countries. Anthropology has been fairly well established in both Argentina and Chile since World War II. The four-field approach is found in a few of the major city universities, like Buenos Aires and La Plata in Argentina and the University of Chile, partly because of the large role that North Americans have played in developing those departments. Provincial universities, however, generally have separate departments of ethnology and archaeology, while linguistics and physical anthropology are unrepresented. Archaeology is the most active field discipline in both countries, and there is nowadays the same emphasis on high-tech archaeology that prevails in North America. Ethnology tends to stay within in the historically oriented tradition, with a special emphasis recently on ethnohistory.[182]

Some neighboring trees

I am unable to comment with any certainty about the situation in Brazilian anthropology. The country has a long tradition of salvage ethnographic and linguistic studies among its numerous Amazonian tribes, and also of social anthropological studies among Afro-American and mixed populations in the coastal states, but I do not know what kind of relationships obtain among these specialties, or between them and archaeology. In other countries of Central and South America anthropology either has not been established or is very much in its infancy, and it is not possible to speak of national traditions.

Some summary reflections

The foregoing tour of world anthropologies gives rise to three summary reflections that are worth stating:

1. The four-field conception of anthropology was very largely a British and American phenomenon, and was conceived initially in the service of the doctrine of Social Evolution. It did not gain a foothold in Continental Europe because the evolutionary doctrine either was not important or did not require empirical confirmation in the minds of continental thinkers. It remained intact in England only as long as Social Evolutionism was the dominant anthropological paradigm, after which it was discarded. It has survived in North America, and latterly also in Mexico, more because of its relevance to Indianology than to Evolutionism. It has survived in India as a three-field conjunction (that is, with the omission of archaeology) as a legacy of the colonial era, reflecting the outlook of British administrators in the early twentieth century. In the Soviet Union it existed largely on

182. I am indebted to my colleague Tom D. Dillehay for information on Argentinian and Chilean Anthropology.

paper, but perhaps reflected the continuing importance of evolutionary theory to Marxists.

2. In much of Continental Europe anthropology, so-designated, is an academic and a theoretical discipline, while ethnology, archaeology, linguistics, and physical anthropology are research disciplines. The home of anthropology is in universities; the home of the four "subdisciplines" (which are often not regarded as such in Europe) is more commonly in research institutes, which may or may not be connected with universities. As a result, many of the major theoreticians are not field workers, while the field workers are not primarily teachers. The "subdisciplines," and more particularly ethnology, provide grist for the anthropologists' mill, but anthropological theory does not usually guide or influence ethnographic practice. Field anthropology tends to be theory-driven, for better and worse, only in North America and in England. Fieldwork in the Soviet Union was, strictly speaking, more policy-driven than theory-driven.

3. The relationship between tradition-oriented ethnology and present-oriented social anthropology has been and remains tendentious. They represent distinct philosophical traditions, the one primarily historical, the other primarily sociological. Ethnology is very much the older discipline, and is often regarded by social anthropologists as an anachronism, yet it remains surprisingly alive and well in a great many countries. It has not been pushed into oblivion, as some Britons appear to believe, nor has it simply evolved into social anthropology, as some Americans have suggested. It lives on in many places for the simple reason that its historical mission, that of salvaging traditional cultures while there is still time, is far from completely fulfilled, and it is still considered important both by the public and by anthropologists themselves. The home of salvage ethnology today is mainly in museums and research institutes, rather than in universities, but in Continental Europe (and India) these continue to play a far larger role in the research schema than they do in England or America. The two traditions of ethnology and social anthropology thus co-exist in an uneasy and ill-defined relationship in many countries, neither fully acknowledging the legitimacy of the other. The nearest thing to a genuine merger, such as it is, appears to have taken place in the United States.

CHAPTER 8

IN SEARCH OF THE ANTHROPOLOGICAL SELF

THROUGHOUT THE previous chapters I have attempted, within reason, to refrain from editorializing, believing that any ideas or ideologies that have exerted a major influence upon anthropological thinking are worthy of a respectful hearing. As I said in the Introduction, however, I did not write the book simply as an exercise in historiography. The history that appears in these pages is meant to be a means to an end, not an end in itself. My ultimate goal has been to help anthropologists to a deeper understanding of, and respect for, their discipline, through a better understanding of the ideological forces that have helped to shape it. In pursuit of that goal, I will try in this final chapter to draw the lessons that I think can and should be drawn from our history, and I will editorialize without apology.

Some colleagues have suggested that this work would benefit from a final chapter, which would pull together and synthesize the various and disparate currents of thought that have been discussed in previous chapters. To do that, however, would be to achieve what anthropology itself has never been able to do. American anthropology has indeed claimed within its boundaries Progressivism, Primitivism, natural law doctrine, Indianology, and German Idealism. It has never truly synthesized them, nor is it possible to do so–and that is precisely my point. There is not and cannot be any uniform or monistic anthropological identity; there is a whole panoply of available identities, among which individuals must choose for themselves, as indeed they always have. Inevitably and necessarily, each anthropologist forges his or her own unique compromise among the different ideologies that contend within the discipline.

THE DILEMMA

The situation of anthropology today presents an extraordinary paradox. Never, at least in this century, has the discipline enjoyed wider popularity as well as academic acceptance, and never has it been more self-doubting. History, psychology, sociology, political science, and various humanistic fields routinely employ what were originally anthropological concepts and theories, with full acknowledgment of their source. In particular the concept of culture, in its anthropological sense, has become part of the working vocabulary of every educated man and woman–not least among the erstwhile "primitives" whom it was once used to describe. Both ethnological and archaeological films are shown with great frequency not only on Public Television but even on the commercial networks, and in them we hear anthropological theories presented as though they were received truth. And just about everyone I meet, above the age of fifty, tells me that, if they had had their choices, they would have liked to be an anthropologist or an archaeologist. How many anthropologists do we meet who say that they would have wished to be something else?

Yet never has the discipline of anthropology seemed less certain of its own mission or its own legitimacy. Gone is the confident search for evolutionary or historical or behavioral laws that preoccupied earlier generations; we are now told by a few individuals that the laws have all been discovered, by many more that they are undiscoverable because of faulty and subjective human judgment, and by a few that there are no laws. Ethnographic description is seen variously as literary criticism, as self-revelation, or as propagandism for this or that political agenda, with no reality save in the eye of the beholder. Archaeology, when not blown elsewhere by the winds of intellectual fashion, has retreated into sheer methodological virtuosity: digging as an end in itself rather than as a means.

Why this disciplinary malaise, at the very moment when we should be enjoying our popular acceptance? Certainly it is a reflection in part of the generally nervous and peevish spirit of the times, when America's days of glory are visibly fading. Anthropology has always been far more influenced by the Zeitgeist, and susceptible to the intellectual currents and fashions of the moment, than its practitioners have cared to admit, as I have suggested repeatedly in earlier pages. Sociology, psychology, and other social sciences are no different, and it is noteworthy that they too are now assailed by self-doubts.[1] But the malaise in anthropology cannot be attributed to ex-

1. For the crisis in sociology, see esp. Dennis Wrong in *Comparative Studies in Society and History* 35, no. 1 (1993): 183–196.

ternal causes alone; it arises also, I am certain, from the deficiency and myopia of our self-understanding.

The situation is admittedly not a simple one, for our profession is confronted simultaneously with a congeries of partly interlocking problems: economic, political, institutional, and ideological. The economic and the political problems have, for obvious reasons, largely claimed our attention in the recent past, but their solution is not really going to resolve our identity crisis. In any case, the solution to those problems is not in our hands. The economic problem will take care of itself when the next upswing in the business cycle brings a renewal of abundant funding, and the political problem will be at least partially resolved when nonwestern peoples and other Others become more receptive to our attentions than they are at present. This again is not likely to be much influenced by any efforts of ours, for we have not proven, in general, to be very good salespersons for our discipline, partly because we don't properly understand it ourselves. I propose here, however, to discuss just those aspects of anthropology's problems over which I think we do have some control: the institutional and above all the ideological. Both of these relate, in different ways, to the problem of self-identity, which to my mind is the most profound of the crises we face.

The crisis of identity in anthropology is not unique to America; there seems to be a general sense of malaise nearly everywhere. Yet the nature of the problem is not entirely the same from country to country. As we saw in the last chapter, many countries have spawned their own national anthropological traditions out of a combination of intellectual, practical, and historical circumstances, and each may have its own problems in a rapidly changing world. In the former Soviet Union, the collapse of the Communist system presents a special set of practical as well as theoretical problems, while elsewhere the general eclipse of Marxism has caused mainly theoretical discomfort. In Britain the problem seems to be one of finding a new guiding philosophy in place of dethroned Functionalism and Structuralism, while at the same time, as always, avoiding undue influence from America.

In America we have a specially complex identity problem because of the four-field tradition. As I have noted in the last chapter, the tradition is found also in Mexico, the former Soviet Union, and a few other countries, but it is nowhere so central to anthropology's self-image as it is in the United States. If British anthropology has always been at some pains to distance itself from the American discipline, the reverse is also at least to some extent true. The four-field tradition represents, I believe, one of our ways of distancing ourselves from our British colleagues. The depth of our commitment to this particular self-definition is reflected not only in the organizational structure of most anthropology departments, but in a great deal of recent correspondence in the *Anthropology Newsletter* published by the American Anthropological Association.[2] In those pages many of our leading practitioners spoke out strongly for four-field anthropology, while no one to my knowledge spoke against it, yet in all of the letters (including my own) I could find no very compelling arguments except historical ones.

The dilemma

The problem is clearly not one of definition. In our textbooks we offer all sorts of definitions of anthropology, all of which are true but not sufficient. In fact, no brief statement could begin to encompass the complexity of what we think and do. It is worth noting in any case that the so-called "hard sciences," which we profess to admire and emulate, are all defined by their subject matter and not by theories, methods, or approaches: geology, physics, chemistry, astronomy, and so on. On the same terms we have sometimes defined our own discipline just by literally translating its title: the study of man. Obviously, however, this provides no basis for differentiating ourselves from all the other social and behavioral sciences. Even if we define ourselves as the Study of Other Man, *Homo sapiens alter*, as I think we properly should, we are still far from explaining what the anthropological enterprise is all about.

It is essential to recognize, before going further, that there is not just one identity problem in American anthropology, there are two: one collective and the other personal. This point seems to have been poorly understood by many anthropologists, and it unnecessarily confounds our dilemma. There has been a tendency to equate the search for a personal identity with the search for a collective identity, as though the one were subsumed within the other. Most Americans today, including most younger anthropologists, seem to be other-directed, to use David Riesman's term: they take their behavioral cues and their identity cues from those around them.[3] I find that many of my students are anxious to be whatever anthropology is, if they can just figure out what it is. Yet in the past, the shoe was sometimes on the other foot. Inner-directed[4] anthropologists as diverse as Boas, Malinowski, and Marvin Harris have wanted to insist that anthropology should be whatever they were; they have sought to narrow the discipline down to just those things that they were personally interested in. Both they and the young people of today made the common mistake of attempting to

2. See *Anthropology Newsletter* 34, nos. 1–3 (1992–1993).

3. David Riesman, *The Lonely Crowd* (New Haven, Conn., 1961), pp. 19–24.

4. Again, Riesman's term; see ibid., pp. 14–17.

conflate disciplinary and individual identities, as if to say in effect, "l'Anthropologie, c'est moi."

It is undoubtedly this conflation of disciplinary and individual identities that accounts for the persistent trend toward Monism in anthropology; the assertion that there should be one and only one anthropological doctrine.[5] The individual must indeed, for the sake of intellectual integrity and consistency, be something of a monist, but it does not follow that the discipline as a whole should adhere to one and only one doctrine, any more than is the case in philosophy.

Fortunately for anthropology, any attempt at disciplinary monism is bound to be futile, since we cannot control or alter the past. Anthropology is not just the sum of what is going on at the moment; it is the sum of everything that has been done, taught, and written in its name for the last century and a half; like every other human institution it is the growth of time. Its future may be shaped, but its past cannot be altered or expunged, by the decisions or preferences of individual practitioners. No one person can hope to command more than a fraction of its accumulated store of wisdom and unwisdom, nor should anyone be obliged to defend all of it. The challenge to the individual anthropologist is first to understand all of the discipline's possibilities and then to chart a course among them, without at the same time suggesting that his or hers is the only right path for others to follow.

In short and simple, the search for a collective identity for anthropology must be separated from the search for an individual identity for each anthropologist, and I intend to pursue the two issues separately in the pages that follow. My concern, as always in this book, will be mainly with the collective identity of North American anthropology. While it might be theoretically possible to discover an even more comprehensive identity, embracing all of the anthropologies of the world, such an effort would require more knowledge of the anthropological Others than I possess.

THE SEARCH FOR A COLLECTIVE IDENTITY

Since I have insisted that anthropology is the study of the Other, it follows that we cannot really study ourselves in the traditional anthropological way. I think this is amply apparent in our efforts at self-analysis, which nowadays are replete with breast-beating, finger-pointing, and self-parody: indulgences that we do not allow ourselves in the study of the Other. But we can at least accord ourselves the recognition that we, like all Others,

5. For discussion, see Murray J. Leaf, *Man, Mind, and Science* (New York, 1979), pp. 180–336.

are neither more nor less than human, with all the virtues and vices inherent therein. Whatever cultural, social, or historical universals we may have discovered in the study of the long ago and the far away must inevitably apply to us also. We can try also to recognize that to the vast majority of mankind we ourselves are Other, and we have to give at least some consideration to how others see us, for that too is part of our identity.

The search for a collective identity

In the recent past there has been more than adequate recognition of the humanness of the individual anthropologist; indeed our human frailties have sometimes been emphasized to such an extent as to suggest that everything we do in the field is suspect. I certainly agree that it is the responsibility of each researcher to be aware of his or her biases and limitations, and as much as possible to make readers aware of them also;[6] but my concern at the moment is with collective rather than with individual strengths and weaknesses. If it is the responsibility of individuals to know their individual capabilities and limitations, it is at least equally incumbent on them to know the capabilities and the limitations of their discipline as a whole, for disciplinary character is much more than the sum of individual characters. Just as individual anthropologists have all the same qualities that are common to other human beings, so also anthropology collectively has all the same qualities that inhere in all human institutions. Like all the rest of them it is at once a historical phenomenon, a cultural phenomenon, a social phenomenon, a political phenomenon, and an ideological phenomenon. All of these dimensions make their contribution to our collective identity, and each will be considered briefly in the next pages.

The historical dimension

Anthropology, like everything else we study, cannot be understood independently of cultural and historical contexts. Self-understanding demands that we recognize not only the internal growth dynamic of our discipline, but also the cultures and the times in which it has been developed, and the social systems in which it has been embedded. We are not required to approve or endorse all of the things that were done and said in the name of anthropology in past years, but we need to understand that they were done and said by intelligent and well-intentioned men and women who had good reasons, at the time, to do the things they did and to say the things they said. If the anthropologies of yesteryear differed in many ways from those of today, it was mostly because the earlier anthropologists were interested in different things, and were therefore asking different ques-

6. I have attempted this in all my own published work; see Preface, note 11.

tions. Careful reanalysis will often disclose that the methodologies of the past were entirely appropriate for answering the questions of the past. If one's interests remain primarily historical, for example, it is still difficult to improve upon the traditional methods of the salvage ethnologist–one reason why salvage ethnology continues to flourish in many countries despite the fact that social anthropologists have declared it passé.

Anthropology in our own eyes may be limited to what anthropologists do nowadays, but in the public eye it includes also everything we have done since the middle of the last century. As I suggested earlier, our past accomplishments are a legacy for which we have to accept responsibility. Not only are they in the public domain, but older works in general are much more widely read by the general public than are the tomes of the present day. Fifty years after his death, Malinowski is surely still the most widely read of British anthropologists, and Margaret Mead probably remains the most widely read of Americans. And since we cannot disavow their works, or delete them from the public record, it behooves us to know and understand them, and to appreciate them for what they are and are not. We should be prepared to explain them to the public and to our students not as timeless classics, but as appropriate products of their times and circumstances. At all events we can't afford to say simply that they are not worth reading, or that we ourselves have never read them.

There is of course more than one historical perspective open to us in studying ourselves. If we insist on viewing the growth of our discipline from the perspective of unilinear evolution, as nearly all historians of anthropology have so far done, we may perhaps look upon the anthropologies of the past as imperfect evolutionary stages along the road to our present enlightenment. (Note for example that Robert Lowie has a chapter entitled "Progress,"[7] and Marvin Harris speaks of The *Rise* of Anthropological Theory.[8]) But I hope I have said enough in earlier pages to make it clear that the history of anthropology may be viewed also from the perspectives of diffusion, of Structuralism, of Marxism, of intellectual Nationalism, and probably several others. I do not argue for any particular perspective here; I merely insist that anthropology is a historical phenomenon whose nature cannot be fully understood without reference to *some* historical context.

Whatever perspective we adopt, I think our history is nothing to be ashamed of; on the contrary, to be ashamed of anthropology's history is necessarily to be ashamed of the discipline itself. We took advantage of the

7. Robert H. Lowie, *The History of Ethnological Theory* (New York, 1937), pp. 86–127.
8. Marvin Harris, *The Rise of Anthropological Theory* (New York, 1968).

colonial umbrella in precisely the same way as did the colonized peoples themselves. They may have heartily resented foreign domination, but since they could do nothing to change it, they took what advantage they could of it by seeking education and wage jobs and other possibilities offered within the system. Anthropologists did the same, and at the same time were often just as critical of colonial regimes as were the subject peoples themselves.[9]

The search for a collective identity

I do not think we should be unduly disturbed by the fact that much of our earlier work no longer meets the approval of the people we purported to study; or rather of the grandchildren and great-grandchildren of the people we purported to study. They live in a world vastly different from that of their progenitors, and they seek a different self-identity. For example, many Native Americans today seem anxious to assure themselves and us that their ancestors were not really warlike; that this was a fiction invented by anti-Indian propagandists, or a reaction to White encroachment. But I can assure them that their great-grandfathers–the ethnographic informants of yesteryear–were equally anxious to assure us that they *were* warlike, in a time when they had been forcibly pacified and disarmed. We took them at their word, and recorded the war tales that they told us, whether real or imagined. The classic ethnographies may not meet the spiritual needs of today's Lakota or Kiowa, but they were not meant to; they were snapshots of another moment in cultural time. The only question that should be of concern to us is: would they have met the approval of those who actually furnished the information, and whose world we tried to preserve on paper?

The currently fashionable notion that "legitimate" ethnography and history can be written only by those whose ancestors actually experienced it runs counter both to established conventions of historiography and science, and to common sense.[10] It is a basic assumption of psychology that the individual can see things in himself or herself that no one else can, but so also can the analyst. The same is assuredly true of human societies collectively: they have to be seen both from the inside and from the outside, as Self and as Other. The fact that the Lakota and the Kiowa do not appear to themselves as Self in the same guise as they appear to us as Other does not necessarily indicate that either of our understandings is more privileged than the other.

---

9. On this see Talal Asad in George W. Stocking, Jr., ed., *Colonial Situations,* pp. 314–324. *History of Anthropology,* vol. 7 (Madison, Wis., 1991).

10. For one such argument, see Roy Willis in Luc de Heusch, *The Drunken King,* trans. Roy Willis (Bloomington, Ind., 1982), p. xii.

If we properly understand the contexts of our history, there is much in our past that we can and should regard with pride. Salvage ethnography, which dominated the ethnological enterprise for more than half a century, has produced a vast descriptive archive of cultures that have since disappeared. However imperfect that record may be, it is the only one that is now left. Moreover, the continued practice of salvage ethnology, wherever in the world there are still tribal cultures to be salvaged, is evidence enough that the world still attaches high priority to this uniquely anthropological enterprise. The same consideration applies to salvage archaeology. A generation ago it was condemned as unscientific;[11] today it consumes more research funding than do all other kinds of archaeology, simply because, in times of threatened destruction of sites or cultures, the world at large recognizes that salvage must be our highest priority. And anthropological linguistics, as opposed to "pure" linguistics, is still very much a salvage enterprise also.

But anthropology in its century and a half of existence has done much more than salvage data; it has also generated a distinctive philosophical vision of the human species that was once regarded as subversive, but is now almost universally prevalent among the intelligentsias of the Western world. As a result, much of our once-esoteric conceptual vocabulary has become part of the everyday discourse of educated men and women. The present heavy emphasis on, and demand for, Cultural Pluralism surely owes much to the anthropological way of thought. Anthropologists may not have initiated the movement, but it is notable that the pluralists look to anthropologists and anthropological literature for legitimation.

Under the circumstances, it is surely time to lay aside the self-defeating burden of guilt that seems to afflict so many anthropologists, who wish somehow to atone for past injustices done to tribal peoples. It is entirely appropriate that our discipline should be the conscience of the world in regard to the treatment of tribal and peasant peoples in the present and future, but it is pointless to beat our breasts over what was done in the past. Guilt and shame benefit no one and atone for nothing, and unless we can find a better way to account for Wounded Knee than to suggest that White Americans are intrinsically evil, we are surely untrue to the principles of our own calling. In my view the relative detachment of professional historians, in examining the record of Indian-White relations, often makes them better ethnohistorians than are anthropologists.

11. See, for example, Frank Hole and Robert F. Heizer, *An Introduction to Prehistoric Archaeology* (New York, 1966), p. 32.

Anthropology arose in specific, nineteenth-century cultural circumstances to meet nineteenth-century cultural needs. Our anthropologist forefathers confirmed, scientifically, the confident belief of Victorian men and women that theirs was the apogee of human civilization. Those ideological convictions have changed over time, and anthropology has changed with them. We are not wholly governed by external, cultural conditions, but we are never immune from them. The cultural embeddedness of our discipline is unmistakably evident in the different national anthropologies that have developed in the United States, Britain, France, and Germany, each reflecting the special cultural traditions of that country. There may be a certain practical necessity in this, insofar as public acceptance (and therefore funding) may depend on conformity with the prevailing Zeitgeist, but it is also the case that anthropologists, like other people, are prone to follow the crowd. Indeed our basic culture concept draws nearly all its explanatory power from just this human propensity to conform.

The search for a collective identity

No paradigm in twentieth-century anthropology has remained dominant for more than a generation, and—with apologies to Thomas Kuhn—this is due at least as much to external as to internal causes.[12] Paradigm shifts in anthropology are historically the result of three factors: a changing cultural and political climate in the nation at large, the need to find new questions to ask when we have exhausted the possibilities of the old ones, and generation gaps. Only the second of these really confirms Kuhn's theory of scientific revolutions. But paradigm shifts occur more or less predictably with each new generation of anthropologists, and they are nearly always initiated by young people. In considerable part, they reflect the need of each rising generation to make its own place in the discipline.

The inclination to follow the crowd means that we are always susceptible to intellectual fads. If the times in general are fad-ridden, as they are at present, so also is anthropology apt to be. The enthusiasm with which we rush to embrace each new dispensation is in some ways heartening; it shows at least that anthropologists have not become world-weary cynics. But the confident belief of the enthusiasts that they have finally discovered the Eldorado that we have always been seeking indicates not only naiveté but an ignorance of history. The enthusiasts should be encouraged in their enthusiasm but at the same time would do well to consider the old Chinese maxim: "And this, too, shall pass."

---

12. In *The Structure of Scientific Revolutions* (Chicago, 1962) Kuhn attributes paradigm shifts primarily to internal developments within each discipline.

Cultural contexts, in the real world, are inseparable from social contexts, and anthropology is no less socially than culturally embedded. It has always existed, and can only exist, within a framework of public acceptance and expectation. From the standpoint of social theory, we have and must have both a Status to occupy and a Role to play.[13] The former provides us with a public identity; the latter involves behavioral expectations. We may not always be comfortable with the public's image or its expectations, but we have to acknowledge that for the most part they are well founded historically. That is, they correctly reflect what we have done and said in the past. In any event, continued public acceptance and support depends at least in part on our doing what the public expects us to do, and knowing what the public expects us to know.

In my experience, the public image of anthropology is defined less by what we think, or even by what we do, than it is by what we know. The public asks what we do mainly out of curiosity; it often asks what we know out of a genuine need for the information. Applied anthropologists are very rarely hired in the belief that they can do things that other people can't do; it is nearly always on the assumption that they know things other people don't know–a fact that is not always fully appreciated by the applied anthropologists themselves.[14]

In the classroom and in our books we appear above all as purveyors of esoteric knowledge, telling the public sometimes what we believe and sometimes what we do, but most of the time what we have learned. Early on, we demarcated certain fields of investigation as uniquely ours–often resenting the attempted intrusion of other disciplines–and the public unhesitatingly turns to us for knowledge about those fields, as we feel that it properly should. If we want to continue occupying the socially accepted role we have forged for ourselves, we really can't afford not to have the knowledge that is expected of us. For more than a century we made Tribal Man our private domain of investigation, and it won't do now to tell the public that we are no longer interested in him, or that he didn't really exist. We can afford to admit all kinds of past errors of perception, but not to ad-

13. For the distinction, and a discussion of role theory in general, see Ralph Linton, *The Study of Man* (New York, 1936), pp. 113–131; also Kingsley Davis in *American Sociological Review* 7 (1942): 309–321, and Marion Levy, *The Structure of Society* (Princeton, N.J., 1952), pp. 159–160.

14. I always felt that our applied anthropology training program at the University of Kentucky placed too much emphasis on doing and not enough on knowing, but this may be changing.

mit plain ignorance or indifference. For the sake of playing our self-created and now expected role, I think every anthropologist should know at least the broad outlines of hominid evolution and the main stages of prehistoric cultural development. And I have already suggested more than once that an American anthropologist who doesn't know at least the major Native American culture areas is like a professor of English who has never read Shakespeare.

The political dimension

John Stuart Mill observed long ago that production is an economic process, but distribution is a political process.[15] We can recognize today that his dictum applies to the distribution of academic rewards and of research funds just as much as to other commodities. As long as anthropology must compete for those things with other disciplines, it cannot help but be politicized.

A century ago anthropology's main institutional home was in museums. Today, in the United States, it is largely in universities, but at the same time it has to rely almost entirely on external agencies for research funding. In Europe, anthropology is divided between universities and research institutes. All of these instrumentalities, at home and abroad, are political arenas in which we compete with other disciplines for resources and recognition. In so doing we have to represent ourselves to best advantage to our would-be patrons, and at times to dance to their tunes.[16] For the sake of National Science Foundation funding we must sometimes claim major theoretical significance for field studies that are in fact statistically trivial; for the sake of university resources we must sometimes make exaggerated claims about our contribution to the university's overall mission. These practical necessities cannot help but affect our self-image, since we sincerely try to be what we claim to be, difficult though that sometimes is.

If the discipline is politicized with respect to its external relationships, it is internally politicized as well. This is evident in the continuing proliferation of our disciplinary and subdisciplinary associations, which number more than thirty by latest count. The associations exist not merely to facilitate communication between specialists, but also to achieve a certain degree of empowerment for anthropologists and for the practitioners of the

---

15. See *Principles of Political Economy,* ed. J. Laurence Laughlin (New York, 1888), pp. 155–156. The original edition was published in 1848.

16. For discussion, see William Y. Adams, "Archaeology: Natural and/or Social Science?" Paper read at the Third American-Soviet Archeology Symposium, Washington, D.C., May 8, 1986.

various subdisciplinary specialties. And the presidency and other high offices in the American Anthropological Association, which used to go more or less routinely to the most senior and distinguished anthropologists as a kind of honorific, now go instead to those individuals who have "paid their dues" in the service of the organization.

To my mind, however, the political dimension of American anthropology is most conspicuous at our annual meeting, when for a week the entire profession resolves itself into a vast patronage network, in which nearly everyone is seeking to make contact with someone at a higher level. This is when, as a friend of mine put it, we become accustomed to talking to "faces without eyes," as those we talk to are simultaneously on the lookout for someone with whom conversation might prove more advantageous. I assume that people at the very top of the prestige ladder–the big guns of our profession–are spared this rather disconcerting experience.

The ideological dimension

We come now to what I think is the crux of our identity search: the dimension of ideology. I hope that earlier chapters have sufficiently established that this is not only an important but an inescapable feature of anthropology. When we staked out the Other as our exclusive domain of investigation, we necessarily fell heir to the moral problematic that is inherent in the concept of otherness. As a result, we have absorbed or at least been influenced by all of the different philosophical traditions through which, over the centuries, Western man has attempted to comprehend the non-western Other.

It is necessary at this point to reassert two things categorically: that anthropology is basically, if not exclusively, the study of the Other, and that otherness is always morally problematical. As I have said more than once before, to compare is to judge. It follows that anthropology can never escape a moral dimension, and therefore it cannot be a purely neutral science. This is not to suggest, as some now do, that it cannot be a science on any terms; the issue of what science is and how it relates to anthropology will be considered later.

There will surely be some who will dispute my contention that cultural anthropology must be the study of the Other.[17] To my mind, however, the few and often trivial anthropological attempts to investigate present-day

17. Throughout the remainder of this chapter I will use "anthropology" to mean cultural anthropology. The question of where physical anthropology properly fits into our enterprise is a highly complex one, and is outside the scope of the present book.

American society are the proverbial exceptions that prove the rule. First of all, the number of such studies is infinitesimally small, in comparison to our studies of other peoples. A book on *Anthropology and American Life* published in 1974 lists only 118 such studies–just about one-tenth the number of titles that have been published on the Navajo alone.[18] Moreover, a fair number of the listed titles are actually by sociologists.[19] Most importantly, though, a high percentage of the studies carve out for examination some small, off-center segment of modern American society that we, the mainstream bourgeoisie, can readily identify as Other. Cocktail waitresses; carnival barkers; locomotive engineers; street corner gangs: these are the indigenous exotica we have chosen to constitute the anthropology of America.[20] A modern textbook on urban anthropology has major chapters dealing respectively with Chicano prisoners, black families in Chicago, Portland longshoremen, and residents of a California retirement community; can anyone believe that these add up collectively to a portrait of American urban life?[21] Even when we purport to study mainstream American behavior we often seem compelled to redefine it as exotica, as for example in the oft-quoted Nacirema parodies[22] and in Jack Weatherford's study of congressional politics, which has the suggestive title "Tribes on the Hill."[23]

The search for a collective identity

A further point, and one that is not always fully appreciated by anthropologists, is that ours is the most insistently proletarian of the social sciences. Everyday life–however boring and monotonous to the participants –is the stuff of anthropological inquiry, and the common man and woman, not the governing elites, are always the foci of our interest. Anthropological archaeologists give their attention to everyday dwelling-sites, rubbish dumps, and workshops, pooh-poohing the Egyptologist and the classical archaeologist with their exclusive concern for temples and royal tombs. Ethnographic descriptions, which tend to be highly normative, portray the daily life of ordinary men and women–the folk with whom we ourselves identify, since most of us come from relatively undistinguished origins.

---

18. The latest edition of the *Ethnographic Bibliography of North America*, ed. George P. Murdock and Timothy J. O'Leary (New Haven, Conn., 1975) lists 1,127 titles on the Navajo (vol. 5, pp. 287–327).

19. See Joseph G. Jorgensen and Marcello Truzzi, eds., *Anthropology and American Life* (Englewood Cliffs, N.J., 1974), pp. 517–524.

20. These studies are listed in ibid.

21. George and Louise Spindler, eds., *Urban Anthropology in the United States: Four Cases* (New York, 1978).

22. For the original, see Horace Miner in *American Anthropologist* 58, no. 3 (1956): 503–508.

23. South Hadley, Mass., 1985.

This means, quite simply, that anthropological description is and is meant to be the portrayal of the commonplace. But while the commonplace among other peoples is always fascinating and frequently informative, the commonplace among ourselves is just that. Anthropological studies that have genuinely attempted to portray mainstream American society have merely used new words to tell us what we already knew. As a result, who now reads the supposedly monumental Yankee City studies, for example?[24] Of course anthropologists can, and sometimes have, duplicated the methods and the results of the sociologists, but I see no evidence that they have achieved results that could not have been as readily attained by sociologists. My argument, then, is simply that anthropology has a unique contribution to make only in the study of the Other.

The assertion that otherness is always problematical will, I hope, be less contentious to anyone who has read the preceding chapters. The concept of Other is meaningless except with reference to the Self, which means that it cannot be other than subjective. All of the attempts to comprehend the Other that have occupied us in earlier chapters were and are at the same time part of our ongoing attempt to understand the Western, or Euro-American, Self. We have variously considered the Other-as-backward-predecessor (Progressivism), the Other-as-happy-child and the Other-as-moral-superior (Primitivism), the Other-as-ourselves (natural law), the Other-as-dramatic (Indianology) and the Other-as-perpetually-different (German Idealism). The fact that all of these interpretations have attracted some of history's best minds, and that no one of them has ever fully triumphed over the others, or probably ever will, should be sufficient evidence that comparisons between Self and Other can never be free of expressed or implied moral judgment.

This fact was more or less overtly recognized by the philosophers who preceded us, and who laid the intellectual foundations for our discipline. Progressivists and primitivists and believers in natural law all knowingly applied the same standards of moral judgment to the Other as to ourselves, and on that basis the progressivists decided that we were superior, the primitivists decided that the primitives were superior, the natural law proponents decided that we and the Other were fundamentally the same. For their part, the Indianologists and German idealists decided that we and the Other were meant to be different.

---

24. These studies, by William Lloyd Warner with various co-authors, are known collectively as the Yankee City Series, vols. 1–4, and were published by Yale University Press between 1941 and 1947. For fuller references, see Jorgensen and Truzzi, *Anthropology and American Life.* The pseudonymous "Yankee City" is actually Newburyport, Massachusetts.

However, there is a difference between philosophically contemplating the Other and systematically studying him, and this is anthropology's special dilemma. We claim to be a natural science rather than a branch of philosophy, and in deference to that ideal we attempt to suspend judgment in regard to the Other. As I noted especially in Chapter 4, we traditionally accept the concept of nature as norm; that is, we assume that whatever is normative in any given society is natural, and whatever is natural is right for that society. In taking this approach we are in effect placing *Homo sapiens* among the rest of the animal kingdom, who are similarly exempted from judgment when their anatomy and their mating and feeding habits are studied by biologists and zoologists. We do not condemn our subjects for cannibalism or endemic warfare or slavery on the same ground that the biologist does not condemn wolves for their predation or mosquitoes for their parasitism. Anthropology, in short, is the study of the Other as animal, and it is that perspective–in effect the perspective of the biologist–that accounts both for our sense of privilege as observers and for our suspension of moral judgment.

The search for a collective identity

Note, however, that we do not grant the same immunity to ourselves; anthropologists have been persistently severe critics of many aspects of American culture and society. We inherit a tradition, going back to Tylor and Malinowski, that anthropology should be a reformer's science.[25] Yet the asymmetrical relationship between Self-as-human and Other-as-animal–between the judged and the unjudged–should logically preclude any comparison between the two; it should render the Other irrelevant in our quest for self-understanding. Nevertheless, we make those comparisons all the time, and we insist that our studies of the long ago and the far away would be of no value if they did not contain lessons for us. But how shall we draw lessons from the unjudged to the judged?

We do it, unavoidably, by implication, and perhaps often unconsciously. The moment we make comparisons between the Other and ourselves we bring the Other, however unwittingly, under the same moral lens through which we view ourselves. And we continue, as we have done since time immemorial, to view the Other as some kind of yardstick by which to measure ourselves. In thirty years of teaching introductory anthropology and other undergraduate courses I have found that my students *always* make self-judgments, favorable or unfavorable, on the basis of what I tell them about other peoples, and so, I am convinced, do most anthropologists. Our discipline, in sum, is laden with moral implications that remain largely unstated because in strictly scientific terms they cannot be stated. The moral lessons of anthropology are apparently inescapable, yet they

25. See Henrika Kuklick, *The Savage Within* (Cambridge, 1991), p. 7.

have always to remain implicit. This does not mean however that we don't believe them, secretly or subconsciously, and it explains why the various philosophical views of the Other which trace back to remote antiquity still continue to resonate, and often to conflict, within our discipline today.

The aesthetic dimension

In deference to today's postmodernists and reflexive anthropologists, I am bound to acknowledge that anthropology has also its aesthetic dimension. That is, there are changing literary fashions in the way we represent the Other, which cannot be explained on other than stylistic grounds. But this is inherent in all cultural phenomena, and I will treat it as just one more evidence of anthropology's cultural dimension, already discussed.

Philosophy: the sum of the parts

The late Will Rogers liked to say that "I am not a member of any organized political party; I am a Democrat." It appears that anthropologists, at least American anthropologists, could say something analogous: "I am not a member of any organized scholarly discipline; I am an anthropologist." Certainly this accusation has been leveled against us more than once by our European colleagues.[26] Can we, in fact, find any common thread among all the things we say and do, and have said and done in the past, to justify calling them all anthropology?

I think we can, if we combine the two fundamental understandings I have suggested earlier: that our discipline is the study of the Other, and that its basic viewpoint is zoological. It is, in other words, the natural history of *Homo sapiens alter* in the fullest sense of the word, embracing both the biological and the cultural animal. Yet we exempt our own civilization and time from this study of man-in-nature, because we can't quite see ourselves from that perspective; our urban civilization has carried us too far from a direct articulation with nature.

It is important to notice that I use the term "natural history" rather than "natural science." Radcliffe-Brown and his followers liked to insist that anthropology was the natural science of man, but their conception of natural science was so narrowly parochial that it excluded the whole of man's biological nature, and much of his cultural nature as well.[27] What they meant, I assume, was that if anthropology is to be a science at all, it

26. See Åke Hultkrantz in *Current Anthropology* 9, no. 4 (1968): 289–310; Aidan Southall interviewed by John W. Burton in *Current Anthropology* 33, no, 1 (1992): 81.
27. See A. R. Radcliffe-Brown, *A Natural Science of Society* (New York, 1948).

must confine itself to those aspects of the human scene that can be investigated with scientific rigor. But this limitation does not apply to natural history, which includes the study of whatever can be observed in animal species, by methods rigorous or anecdotal. Radcliffe-Brown, moreover, started from the assumption that social organization was the prime mover in human affairs, and therefore the only thing that needed investigation, whereas natural historians make no assumptions about prime movers; they study and record everything on the chance that it might prove important.

The search for a collective identity

Whatever our discipline is, it is certainly not the orderly, coherent, and dispassionate science that some of our members aspire to. On the contrary, the historical evidence suggests that anthropology is both more and less than a science. More, because we cannot avoid moral issues that are traditionally outside the domain of science; less, because much of our investigation does not meet accepted standards of scientific rigor.

In summation of everything I have said heretofore, I think the only way to understand anthropology *at the highest and most abstract level* is to recognize that it is really a field of philosophy.[28] It has taken over what for centuries was one of the recognized and most important domains of the moral philosopher–the study of the Other–without really changing the terms of the discourse. The proof of this is that we have not wholly supplanted any of the earlier philosophical perspectives of the Other, but have simply, consciously or unconsciously, coopted them. To a very large extent, modern anthropology is still what Enlightenment moral philosophy was.

What price science?

But then, what price science? The notion that we are a science is dear to the hearts of modern anthropologists; for many it is at the heart of their self-image. In the minds of those individuals it is the quality that sets us clearly apart from the philosopher: to be a scientist is to be a nonphilosopher. This supposed dichotomy is one of the most enduring legacies of Comtean Positivism, with its insistence that there must be no speculation.

But the dichotomy is without historical foundation. Many of the greatest philosophers from Thales to Archimedes to Bacon and Newton were also scientists, and I think we are obliged to recognize that there is no inherent contradiction between science and philosophy. On the contrary there is, in my view, a necessary conjunction, since the great majority of or-

28. For a generally parallel view, see Elvin Hatch, *Theories of Man and Culture* (New York, 1973), esp. pp. 336–358.

ganizing theories in science are in fact philosophies, in the sense that they are derived only in part from empirical evidence. That is why so many of them have been discarded not only when new evidence accumulated, but also and perhaps more often when there was a change in the prevailing Zeitgeist. Certainly this applies in particular to anthropology, nearly all of whose "grand theories" are older philosophies renamed. This does not mean that they lack scientific credibility; they merely lack–so far–scientific provability. However, the fact that so many of them have persisted for so long suggests that they are probably right.

As I suggested in the Introduction, the question of what is and is not science is just about as tangled as is the question of what is and is not Christianity. But without pursuing that question further here, I think most people both within and outside the discipline would agree that if anthropology in toto is not a science, or not just a science, it nevertheless includes a good deal of science within its domain. To my mind, science in anthropology is to be found not at the level of theory but at the levels of data collecting and data processing; that is, in ethnology, archaeology, linguistics, and physical anthropology. At least at their best and most rigorous, these so-called subdisciplines (all of which existed before anthropology itself) may indeed safely be designated as sciences. Note, however, that they do not constitute *a* science, but a congeries of sciences involving quite different scientific procedures. Moreover, they are said to be scientific for different reasons.

Archaeology a generation ago defined itself as a science on the ground that it insisted on testing causal hypotheses,[29] but the epistemological weakness of that position has since become evident.[30] Today its claim to being scientific rests almost entirely on the employment of precise and high-tech field and lab procedures; that is to say, it is maximally scientific at the level of data acquisition. Indeed this has now largely become an end in itself; archaeological excavation is an exhibition of technical virtuosity, whatever the results may mean. In contrast, ethnology and linguistics continue to employ relatively crude methods of data acquisition; their claim to be scientific rests much more on the use of sophisticated statistical proce-

29. See Lewis R. Binford in Sally R. Binford and Lewis R. Binford, eds., *New Perspectives in Archaeology* (Chicago, 1968), pp. 5–32; John M. Fritz and Fred T. Plog in *American Antiquity* 35, no. 4 (1970): 405–412; Paul S. Martin in *American Antiquity* 36, no. 1 (1971): 1–8; Mark P. Leone, ed., *Contemporary Archaeology* (Carbondale, Ill., 1972), pp. 14–27.

30. See esp. L. Johnson in *American Anthropologist* 74 (1972): 366–367; D.H. Tuggle, A.H. Townsend and A.J. Riley in *American Antiquity* 37 (1972): 2–13; and Jane H. Kelley and Marsha P. Hanen, *Archaeology and the Methodology of Science* (Albuquerque, 1988). For extended discussion see also Adams, "Archeology: Natural or Social Science?"

dures in data processing. Physical anthropology has become so diverse as to be a congeries of sciences in its own right, but it has a much more concrete and scientifically provable organizing theory (biological evolution) that have the other subdisciplines, and may perhaps claim to be scientific on that ground alone.

Anthropology, then, embraces both philosophy and a congeries of rather disparate sciences. But the philosophy itself is far from unitary, as we have already observed in abundant detail. The only possible conclusion, to my mind, is that anthropology is a congeries of sciences overarched by a congeries of philosophies, and having in common only the pursuit of the natural history of *Homo sapiens alter.* The sciences are of recent development, but the philosophies are very much older; in other words, the sciences are new ways of answering old questions.

The search for a collective identity

By way of summary, I would say that our discipline is a domain of philosophy that relies largely but not exclusively on empirical evidence, and gathers empirical evidence largely but not exclusively by scientific means. This is of course a characterization and not a definition, and it is a characterization that I imagine many colleagues will find unsatisfactory. It is less explicit, and certainly less impressive, than our usual self-representations, and is not calculated to win support from deans or funding agencies. Worse still, it provides no starting point for individual self-definition–a separate issue that I will take up presently. But after fifty active years in the discipline, including twenty-four field seasons in both archaeology and ethnology, and after teaching thirty-four different courses encompassing all four of our traditional subfields, it is the only way I can characterize the totality of anthropology as I understand it today.[31]

No one condemns the discipline of philosophy because it embraces a wide variety of different and sometimes conflicting perspectives; on the contrary this is seen as one of the essential virtues of the field. Students, moreover, are expected to familiarize themselves with most of the major philosophical schools, not to accept them all but to be equipped to choose among them. As long as anthropology continues to deal in philosophical issues–as it unavoidably must–I think this must be true of our discipline as well. The philosophical and epistemological plurality that is so often derided not only by Europeans but even by many American anthropologists is in fact a virtue, not a defect. The burden is on the individual, not on the discipline as a whole, to decide what is true and not true within the compass of his or her individual understanding and experience. In the study of *Homo sapiens,* it can surely never be otherwise. As Ernest Gellner

31. See Hatch *Theories of Man and Culture,* pp. 336–358, for a generally concurring view.

has eloquently put it, "Science needs one world. It does not need one kind of man within it."[32]

To say that anthropology in its present state must necessarily embrace a wide variety of philosophical viewpoints is not to endorse the anarchic, postmodernist notion that "anything goes."[33] So long as our discipline is scientific as well as philosophical–as indeed it is–we remain committed like all sciences to the search for ultimate reality. Our investigations and discussions, we hope, bring us imperceptibly but nevertheless consistently closer to a grasp of that reality. If there is any value to our scientific endeavors at all, we should confidently expect that we will one day be better equipped to choose among philosophical alternatives than we are at present. In the meantime, it behooves us to keep our options open.[34]

THE SEARCH FOR INDIVIDUAL IDENTITIES

The immediate and critical problem that used to confront all anthropologists, at the outset their careers, was to decide if they were really cut out to be anthropologists or not, given the special rigors of fieldwork and the dubious career prospects of the discipline. But anthropology today is so broad and diversified that it is hard to imagine anyone who is not cut out to be some kind of anthropologist. The problem that confronts the individual today is rather to decide what kind of anthropologist to be, among the myriad theoretical possibilities. The choice, as I have suggested earlier, cannot be made just on the basis of the inherent appeal of this or that anthropological doctrine or activity; it has to be consistent with preexisting factors of background and temperament.

If anthropology at this stage of its development cannot afford to be monistic–*pace* Marvin Harris–it is nevertheless true that most individual anthropologists cannot afford not to be. In the present age of specialization it is increasingly difficult to practice more than one specialty, but, much more importantly, not one could espouse all the different doctrines that go by the name of anthropology without suffering a high degree of

---

32. Ernest Gellner in Martin Hollis and Steven Lukes, eds., *Rationality and Relativism* (Cambridge, Mass., 1982), p. 200.

33. I don't suppose that all self-styled postmodernists will agree with this characterization. In fact, I don't suppose that all postmodernists will agree on anything, given the extreme nebulousness of the movement. For discussion, by a sympathetic commentator, see Andreas Huyssen in Jeffrey C. Alexander and Steven Seidman, eds., *Culture and Society* (Cambridge, 1990), pp. 355–375.

34. For a holistic and pluralistic perspective generally parallel to mine, see Robert F. Murphy, *A Century of Controversy* (Orlando, Fla., 1985).

cognitive dissonance. The individual must make a choice not only of what to do, but also of what to think. A few individuals may unhesitatingly choose one and only one doctrine, and adhere to it lifelong; a larger number will probably do as I have done: take parts of several doctrines and create their own personal syntheses. These choices may be determined in part by what the individual is taught at the start of his or her career, but they should at least as prominently respond to much earlier conditioning factors.

The search for individual identities

I have argued elsewhere, and in another context, that "anthropologists are born and not made."[35] Of course I don't mean that literally, although I don't wholly rule out the possibility of genetic conditioning factors. What I really mean, however, is that we are preadapted to become anthropologists by conditioning factors in our experiences long before we ever heard of anthropology, just as were the students of Boas, to recall an obvious example discussed in Chapter 6. And we are preadapted not merely to become anthropologists, but to become particular kinds of anthropologists.

What to do?

It should be evident to anyone who knows the discipline well that the normative personality and world-view of archaeologists (at least, of prehistoric archaeologists) is quite different from that of ethnologists, and different again from that of linguists. Archaeology is a subdiscipline in which one must impose a considerable measure of order not only on the data, but often also on a team of unruly subordinates. Inevitably, archaeology appeals to law-and-order types, with a strong inclination toward monism. Archaeologists are conspicuously more doctrinaire in their theoretical and methodological pronouncements than are other kinds of anthropologists, and are very prone to insist that their own way of doing things is the only right one. As a result, the archaeological literature is full of preaching.[36]

Ethnologists on the other hand are forced to work in circumstances over which they can impose little control, and their work makes them

35. In *Archaeological Typology and Practical Reality* (Cambridge, 1991), pp. xx–xxi; and in Renée Friedman and Barbara Adams, eds., *The Followers of Horus* (Oxford, 1992), p. 1.

36. See Adams, "Archeology: Natural or Social Science," and in Friedman and Adams, *Followers of Horus,* p. 1. For a lengthier discussion of differing "normative personality types" in different branches of anthropology, see Murphy, *Century of Controversy,* pp. 287–319. His reference however is to the differences between ethnologists and social anthropologists, which I have not touched on here. For a related discussion, see also Stanley J. Tambiah, *Magic, Science, Religion, and the Scope of Rationality* (Cambridge, 1990), pp. 115–116.

acutely conscious (as archaeologists often are not) of the extreme complexity of the real-life human situation. The varied and frequently unsettling experiences of the field situation require a high level of personal tolerance, but ethnologists must also be prepared to accept a considerable amount of intellectual ambiguity. The subdiscipline, in short, appeals much more to tolerant personalities, and less to law-and-order personalities, than does archaeology. Radcliffe-Brown was an exception, but his very rigidity of outlook probably explains his singular lack of success as a field worker.[37]

My experience of linguists is somewhat limited, but my impression is that they generally have better developed mathematical minds than do either archaeologists or ethnologists, and I conclude that linguistics simply appeals to that kind of mind. One unfortunate consequence is that linguists are often rather verbally inarticulate, since there is a well-demonstrated negative correlation (statistically, not universally) between mathematical and verbalizing ability. Physical anthropology today is so diverse that I don't think it is possible to speak of a single normative personality; I assume that different fields of physical anthropology appeal to different types. The field of primate ethology nowadays seems to have a special appeal for female researchers with very strong bonding propensities.

The choice of a subdiscipline should be determined of course not merely by personality factors, but also by the kinds of activities one enjoys and/or is good at. Everybody enjoys digging as long as things are being found, but not many people enjoy it simply for the sake of moving dirt. Yet there are long periods on every dig when that is about all that is going on. When we read the diaries of distinguished ethnologists like Malinowski and Boas, we find them complaining repeatedly about days when they didn't get anything of value for their pains,[38] yet this happens all the time in archaeology. A considerable amount of patience is certainly required in all anthropological field work, but, having done both, I can assure readers that far more patience is required in archaeology than in ethnology. The happiest archaeologist, I am sure, is someone who simply enjoys digging; this may be one reason why, in the recent past, digging methodology has become so much an end in itself.

By contrast, the happiest ethnologist is surely a "people person;" someone who simply enjoys being around people for its own sake, and does not

37. For discussion see Adam Kuper, ed., *The Social Anthropology of Radcliffe-Brown* (London, 1977), pp. 1–7.
38. See Ronald P. Rohner, ed., *The Ethnography of Franz Boas* (Chicago, 1969); and Bronislaw Malinowski, *A Diary in the Strict Sense of the Term* (New York, 1967).

measure enjoyment only in terms of the amount of data elicited. From that perspective one of the most successful ethnologists I ever knew was the late Richard Van Valkenburgh, who through wholly informal interactions gained an extraordinarily deep insight into the Navajo world-view, most of which unfortunately never found its way into print.[39] Another such was the late Tom Hinton, who could sit all afternoon on a Mexican veranda in amiable silence, or just exchanging occasional chitchat with his informant-companions.[40] Both Van Valkenburgh and Hinton had the advantage of extreme linguistic fluency–a critical requirement for many kinds of ethnology–yet that in itself was the result of their overall receptivity to the cultures and the peoples around them; it was not acquired through formal study.

The search for individual identities

Yet Van Valkenburgh and Hinton published very little, for they were not driven by academic or scholarly ambition. They were content to enjoy cross-cultural interaction for its own sake, much as some archaeologists enjoy digging. I think in fact that the notorious nonpublishers in our discipline, who are fairly numerous both in ethnology and in archaeology, may be precisely those who enjoy fieldwork as an end in itself. Their extreme patience, which is ideal in fieldwork, is not always the best route to professional advancement.

The question of simple talent, whether inherited or acquired, also cannot be ignored. I know one archaeologist who, with the best of intentions, simply cannot tell pottery types apart, and another who cannot read stratigraphy; both essential qualifications in the kind of archaeology I do. A person who has great difficulty in learning second languages–a rather common condition among Americans–must stay away from many kinds of ethnography, and possibly also from linguistics. A person with no head for figures–also a common failing–will on the other hand probably be more comfortable in ethnology than in archaeology, and certainly more so than in physical anthropology.

We all recognize that the ability to learn second languages is a "gift" that is not readily susceptible to scientific analysis. One would suppose that this

39. With the approval of tribal officials he is now buried in the Navajo tribal cemetery near Fort Defiance, with a gravestone that reads simply *Diné bik'iis* (friend of the Navajo). His major published works are *Diné Bikéyah* [The Navajos' Country] (Window Rock, Ariz., 1941), and *A Short History of the Navajo People*, with John. C. McPhee (Window Rock, Ariz., 1941).

40. I found, in the course of personal visits to northern Sonora villages, that Hinton was known and loved just about everywhere; he was always referred to as "Tomasito." His major published works are two edited volumes, *Coras, Huicholes, y Tepehuanes* (Mexico City, 1972), and *Themes of Indian Acculturation in Northwest Mexico* (*Anthropological Papers of the University of Arizona*, no. 38, 1981).

was the single most important qualification for the anthropological linguist, but I am not sure that is actually the case. The linguists I have known, with one exception, have not been accomplished polyglots, and the late Carl Voegelin once assured me that Edward Sapir himself was a slow learner when it came to acquiring second languages. The special analytical quality that is required of linguists comes, I take it, from their mathematical competence rather than from language-acquisition skills. However, the ability to "pick up" languages rapidly may be essential for some kinds of ethnology.

The choice of a subfield may of course be forced on us by circumstances, as it was in my own case. That is, it may be a question of where we can find employment. This was fairly common half a century ago, and seems to be becoming so again, due in both cases to a restricted job market. One of the lessons we can learn from anthropology itself is that specialization is the road to extinction, and adaptability the road to survival; in that light I think all beginning anthropologists would be well advised to have more than one string to their bows. They may have to spend some "time in the wilderness," doing contract archaeology or public opinion surveying or some other uncongenial chore, but it is likely enough that, when economic conditions improve, they will eventually be able to find their ways back to their fields of preference.

What to think?

Given the intellectual diversity of our field, we anthropologists have to make choices not only in regard to what we do, but also in regard to what we think. That is, we have to choose among the many different philosophical and theoretical possibilities that have been discussed throughout this work, for no one could adhere to them all. Our choices here again will, or should, reflect our early conditioning. Whether or not we realize it consciously, many of us are already committed progressivists or primitivists or Indianologists long before we begin the study of anthropology. Indeed this may be precisely the reason we take up the study in the first place. During most of this century, for example, anthropology has been the only comfortable academic home for primitivists and Indianologists.

The choice of what to think, like the choice of what to do, may be influenced but should never be wholly determined by what our professors tell us to think. It has to be consistent also with what we like to think, just as the choice of a subdiscipline has to be consistent with what we like to do. It may even, in some cases, be determined by what we need to think. Those anthropologists who are genuinely religious (a rather rare breed, in my experience) will obviously have to choose doctrines that are not in conflict with their religious beliefs. But many other individuals will have intellectual or psychological needs that can be met by some anthropological or philosophical doctrines, but not by others.

The choice of what to think is influenced, but not wholly determined, by the choice of what to do. Given the inherent nature of archaeological evidence, it helps to be a good deal of a materialist, as indeed the great majority of present-day archaeologists are. The field ethnologist who works largely in a foreign language will, on the contrary, probably be drawn to those doctrines that emphasize the importance of cognitive factors in culture. The social anthropologist will obviously derive little satisfaction from fieldwork unless he or she can believe in the determining influence of social relations. There is a conspicuous tendency for different theoretical paradigms to be dominant in different subfields, just because they are most consistent with the kinds of evidence being gathered, or even with the research methodology employed. Yet no one philosophical or theoretical paradigm is inseparably linked to any one research specialty. Whether in archaeology, ethnology, or linguistics, there is always a choice of what to believe, and in the long run it is bound to be influenced by factors external to the subdiscipline itself.

The search for individual identities

The identity problem, then, is and can only be a highly individual one: not just "what is anthropology?" but more importantly "where do I fit in?" The search for a successful answer will lead in different directions for different persons, but it should in theory always begin from the Socratic precept: Know Thyself. Yet self-knowledge at the outset of one's career is apt to be relatively limited, and may often lead to initial missteps and wrong choices that become evident as self-knowledge increases. It is one of the signal virtues of American anthropology, above all others, that those youthful mistakes are relatively easy to correct. The discipline, like philosophy itself, is notably forgiving of changes of heart or interest, and indeed midcareer changes of direction are almost as much the rule as the exception. It is one of the delightful paradoxes of our profession, and its single most rewarding feature, that the study of the Other is at the same time a lifelong voyage of self-discovery.

AN ANNOTATED BIBLIOGRAPHY OF SECONDARY SOURCES

A FULL BIBLIOGRAPHY of the works that are cited in this book would list more than 700 titles, including at least 150 that I have not actually read. Particularly for the ancient and medieval periods I have depended heavily on a limited number of secondary sources that I believe to be reliable. The following is an annotated list of those sources, for the benefit of readers who may wish to pursue the topics I have discussed at greater length than I have done.

INTRODUCTION

McGrane, Bernard. 1989. *Beyond Anthropology.* New York: Columbia University Press. A very brief but valuable historical review of evolving Western concepts of the Other, from classical antiquity through the nineteenth century.

Pandian, Jacob. 1985. *Anthropology and the Western Tradition.* Prospect Heights, Ill.: Waveland Press. Another small book which discusses Western concepts of the Other, and their relation to anthropology. Thoughtful but somewhat disjointed.

PROGRESSIVISM

General

Hildebrand, George H. 1949. "Introduction," in Frederick Teggart, compiler, *The Idea of Progress.* Berkeley: University of California Press. A brief but very lucid introductory overview to accompany Teggart 1949, q.v.

Teggart, Frederick, compiler. 1949. *The Idea of Progress.* Berkeley: University of California Press. An encyclopedic compilation of short excerpts from progressivist works, from Hesiod to Darwin. Invaluable as a sourcebook but, except for the introduction by Hildebrand, there is almost no accompanying commentary.

Van Doren, Charles. 1967. *The Idea of Progress.* New York: Praeger. An exhaustive, minutely particularized analysis of the different meanings of "progress" in the works of philosophers and historians. Organized topically rather than chronologically, and therefore of limited value as a historical sourcebook.

Ancient Progressivism

Cole, Thomas. 1967. *Democritus and the Sources of Greek Anthropology.* American Philological Association, Philological Monographs, no. XXV. A very detailed work of source criticism, which seeks to trace the later progressivist traditions of Greece and Rome to their original, pre-Socratic sources.

Edelstein, Ludwig. 1967. *The Idea of Progress in Classical Antiquity.* Baltimore: Johns Hopkins Press. An excellently detailed, chronological review of ancient sources. Successfully refutes Bury's contention that the idea of progress is strictly a modern one.

Guthrie, W.K.C. 1957. *In the Beginning.* London: Methuen. A series of published lectures on Greek views concerning the origins of life and the early state of man. Particularly good in regard to the origins of life.

Lovejoy, Arthur O., and George Boas. 1935. *Primitivism and Related Ideas in Antiquity.* Baltimore: Johns Hopkins Press. Progressivism is one of the "related ideas" that is discussed at considerable length, with numerous directly quoted excerpts both in the original languages and in translation.

Medieval and Enlightenment Progressivism

Bryson, Gladys. 1945. *Man and Society: the Scottish Inquiry of the Eighteenth Century.* Princeton, N.J.: Princeton University Press. The most detailed source on the Scottish Enlightenment. However, the discussion is organized around themes rather than around the work of individual authors, which somewhat lessens its value as a historical sourcebook.

Bury, J.B. 1932. *The Idea of Progress.* New York: Macmillan. An erudite but rather selective review of the development of progressivist theory from the sixteenth through the nineteenth centuries. The value is somewhat diminished by lack of full documentation of many sources.

Evans-Pritchard, E.E. 1981. *A History of Anthropological Thought.* New York: Basic Books. The early chapters provide good, brief overviews of the work of Montesquieu, of Comte, and of several Scottish Enlightenment thinkers.

Meek, Ronald L. 1976. *Social Science and the Ignoble Savage.* Cambridge: Cambridge University Press. An excellently detailed review of the development of progressivist stage theory, mainly in the seventeenth and eighteenth centuries. By far the best available source on this topic. The title is misleading; the book is not concerned with works that disparage the savage.

Pollard, Sidney. 1968. *The Idea of Progress: History and Society.* New York: Basic Books. Excellent, thoughtful history mainly of eighteenth- and nineteenth-century progressivist thought.

Spadafora, David. 1990. *The Idea of Progress in Eighteenth Century Britain.* New Haven, Conn.: Yale University Press. Apparently a doctoral dissertation; much more detailed and meticulously analytical than previous works on eighteenth-century Progressivism, but lacks any central theme or focus.

Wagar, W. Warren, ed. 1969. *The Idea of Progress since the Renaissance.* New York: John Wiley. A collection of essays on a few outstanding progressivist thinkers, from Bodin to Toynbee.

Whitney, Lois. 1934. *Primitivism and the Idea of Progress, in English Popular Literature of the Eighteenth Century.* Baltimore: Johns Hopkins Press. Mainly about Primitivism, but also includes chapters on Progressivism.

Nineteenth-century Progressivism

Akirch, Arthur A. 1944. *The Idea of Progress in America, 1815–1860.* New York: Columbia University Press. Discusses the idea of progress as a cornerstone of American political and social ideology in the first half of the nineteenth century.

Progressivism in anthropology

Burridge, Kenelm. 1973. *Encountering Aborigines.* New York: Pergamon Press. A very erudite consideration of the role played by Australian Aborigines in the development of anthropological progressivist theory, mainly in the twentieth century.

Kuper, Adam. 1988. *The Invention of Primitive Society.* London: Routledge. A highly critical review of social evolutionist theory in anthropology, from Darwin to Lévi-Strauss. The author contends that anthropology's classic type-concept of the Primitive is an illusion.

Sanderson, Stephen K. 1990. *Social Evolutionism, a Critical History.* Cambridge, Mass.: Basil Blackwell. Concentrating mainly on the latter half of the twentieth century, this is the most comprehensive review of current progressivist theories in anthropology and sociology.

Stocking, George W., Jr. 1987. *Victorian Anthropology.* New York: Free Press. Excellently detailed and thoughtful review of the "proto-history" of anthropology in nineteenth-century Britain.

PRIMITIVISM

General

Bell, Michael. 1972. *Primitivism.* London: Methuen. A brief but elegant discussion of the general concept of the primitive and some of its implications, mainly with reference to literature.

Ancient Primitivism

Long, Timothy. 1986. *Barbarians in Greek Comedy.* Carbondale: Southern Illinois University Press. The author points out that barbarians are only rarely depicted in drama as Noble Savages, in marked contrast to their role in Greek philosophy.

Lovejoy, Arthur O., and George Boas. 1935. *Primitivism and Related Ideas in Antiquity.* Baltimore: Johns Hopkins Press. Excellently detailed survey of primitivistic writings, arranged partly chronologically and partly topically. Contains numerous direct quotations both in original languages and in translation.

Medieval Primitivism

Boas, George. 1948. *Essays on Primitivism and Related Ideas in the Middle Ages.* Baltimore: Johns Hopkins Press. Less comprehensive than his survey of Primitivism in antiquity, but still a wide-ranging survey, and the only available work on Primitivism in this period.

Enlightenment and Romantic Primitivism

Bissell, Benjamin. 1925. *The American Indian in English Literature of the Eighteenth Century.* New Haven, Conn.: Yale University Press. An excellent, comprehensive survey covering ethnography, social theory, fiction, drama, and poetry, with extensive direct quotations.

Fairchild, Hoxie N. 1928. *The Noble Savage.* New York: Russell & Russell. Very erudite and detailed survey of the Noble Savage convention, mainly in the context of Romantic literature and poetry. By far the best work on this subject, but value as a reference is somewhat diminished by incomplete citation of sources.

Feest, Christian F., ed. 1989. *Indians and Europe: an Interdisciplinary Collection of Essays.* Aachen: Alano Verlag. A delightful collection of thirty-three short essays discussing European reactions to the American Indian, from the early sixteenth century to the present. The reaction has been and remains overwhelmingly primitivistic.

Runge, Edith A. 1946. *Primitivism and Related Ideas in Sturm und Drang Literature.* Baltimore: Johns Hopkins Press. Shows that German literary Primitivism of the eighteenth century was largely a reaction against Enlightenment Rationalism, and a celebration of the irrational in human nature.

Whitney, Lois. 1934. *Primitivism and the Idea of Progress in English Popular Literature of the Eighteenth Century.* Baltimore: Johns Hopkins Press. The best discussion of Enlightenment and Romantic Primitivism as serious theory, and its relationship to other social theories of the eighteenth century.

American Primitivism

Pearce, Roy H. 1988. *Savagism and Civilization.* Berkeley: University of California Press. Excellently detailed and thoughtful survey of the impact of the American Indian on American social thinking and on popular literature, both progressivist and primitivist. Deals mainly with the period from 1777 to 1851.

Anthropological Primitivism

Diamond, Stanley. 1974. *In Search of the Primitive.* New Brunswick, N.J.: Transaction Books. A collection of Diamond's primitivist essays, mostly having to do with the place of Primitivism in anthropology.

Diamond, Stanley, ed. 1969. *Primitive Views of the World.* New York: Columbia University Press. A collection of short contributions by different authors, mostly intended to illustrate the primitive world-view. Originally a *festschrift* for Paul Radin.

Radin, Paul. 1927. *Primitive Man as Philosopher.* New York: D. Appleton. A book written to refute the thesis of Lucien Lévy-Bruhl, that primitive thinking is prelogical. Examples from mythology and ethnography are cited to show that primitives are capable of speculative philosophical thought.

Stocking, George W., Jr. 1989. "The Ethnographic Sensibility of the 1920s and the Dualism of the Anthropological Tradition." *History of Anthropology* 6: 208–276. Madison: University of Wisconsin Press. Discusses Romantic Primitivism especially in the work of some of the later Boasians.

Marxist Primitivism

Slezkine, Yuri. 1991. "The Fall of Soviet Ethnography, 1928–38." *Current Anthropology* 32, no. 4: 476–484. Describes how Soviet ethnographers invoked a kind of Primitivism as an escape from the rigidity of Marxist doctrine.

NATURAL LAW

General

Bloch, Ernst. 1986. *Natural Law and Human Dignity,* trans. Dennis J. Schmidt. Cambridge, Mass.: MIT Press. A compilation of highly expostulatory essays, originally published separately, on different natural law thinkers and doctrines from ancient times to the present. The essays are individually enlightening but do not add up to a single comprehensive work.

Crowe, Michael B. 1977. *The Changing Profile of the Natural Law.* The Hague: Martinus Nijhoff. A very erudite and particularized survey of natural law theory from ancient times to the present, mainly from the perspective of Christian theology. By far the best source on medieval theory, but not good for the secular modern traditions, which are regarded by the author as "false."

Eterovich, Francis H. 1972. *Approaches to Natural Law from Plato to Kant.* New York: Exposition Press. A much briefer survey than that of Crowe, but exceptionally lucid. Probably the best brief introduction to the subject. The book contains an extensive and categorically arranged bibliography of writings on natural law.

Rommen, Heinrich A. 1947. *The Natural Law,* trans. Thomas R. Hanley. St. Louis: B. Herder Book Co. The first half is a rather selective and discursive review of natural law theory from ancient to modern times; the second half discusses various philosophical implications of natural law theory.

Sigmund, Paul E. 1971. *Natural Law in Political Thought.* Washington, D.C.: Winthrop Publishers. A series of brief but lucid essays about natural law theory in the successive periods of its history, accompanied by excerpts from original writings from each period.

Wilken, Robert N., et al. 1954. *Origins of the Natural Law Tradition.* Dallas: Southern Methodist University Press. A collection of four short essays, by different authors, discussing the natural law doctrines of Cicero, Aquinas, Hooker, and the nineteenth century evolutionists.

Natural law in China

Needham, Joseph. 1951. *Human Law and the Law of Nature in China and the West.* Oxford: Oxford University Press. Discusses various Chinese doctrines in comparison to Western doctrines; concludes that the Confucian concept of *li* comes closest to the Western conception of natural law.

Needham, Joseph. 1956. *Science and Civilisation in China,* vol. 2, pp. 518–583. Cambridge: Cambridge University Press. Covers essentially the same ground as Needham 1951.

Natural law in antiquity

Lovejoy, Arthur O., and George Boas. 1935. *Primitivism and Related Ideas in Antiquity.* Baltimore: Johns Hopkins Press. Natural law is one of the "related ideas," discussed especially in Chapter 3.

Medieval natural law

Natural Law Johnson, Harold J., ed. 1987. *The Medieval Tradition of Natural Law.* Kalamazoo: Western Michigan University, Studies in Medieval Culture, XXII. A collection of brief, particularized essays on various medieval thinkers and doctrines. Obviously a conference proceedings; not very useful as an overview of the period.

Muldoon, James. 1979. *Popes, Lawyers, and Infidels.* Philadelphia: University of Pennsylvania Press. An excellently detailed review of the doctrine of natural law mainly as embodied in medieval canon law.

The Spanish debates

Hanke, Lewis. 1959. *Aristotle and the American Indians.* Chicago: Henry Regnery. The most detailed summary setting forth the basic arguments of Las Casas and Sepúlveda in the famous Valladolid debates of the sixteenth century.

Muldoon, James. 1979. *Popes, Lawyers, and Infidels.* Philadelphia: University of Pennsylvania Press. Chapter 7 reviews briefly the doctrines developed in sixteenth-century Spain in relation to the status of the Indians under natural law.

Pagden, Anthony. 1982. *The Fall of Natural Man.* Cambridge: Cambridge University Press. The definitive source on sixteenth-century Spanish theories about the Indians and their political context. There is an added chapter on Lafitau in the second edition.

The Enlightenment and Romantic eras

Stein, Peter. 1980. *Legal Evolution.* Cambridge: Cambridge University Press. A slim but elegantly clear and concise treatment of legal doctrines, mainly from the seventeenth to the nineteenth century. The first chapter is the best brief source on early modern natural law theorists.

Tuck, Richard. 1979. *Natural Rights Theories.* Cambridge: Cambridge University Press. Narrowly focused on natural rights theories rather than on natural law more generally, but a comprehensive survey of writings on that topic.

Whitney, Lois. 1934. *Primitivism and the Idea of Progress.* Baltimore: Johns Hopkins Press, 1934. Chapter 1 discusses natural law theories as part of the philosophical background of eighteenth-century Primitivism.

Natural law in anthropology

Greenwood, Davydd J. 1984. *The Taming of Evolution.* Ithaca, N.Y.: Cornell University Press. A rather disjointed series of essays, mostly dealing with natural law concepts of the pre-anthropological era (although not by name), and arguing that they persist beneath the surface of what are supposedly evolutionary theories in the present day.

"INDIANOLOGY"

General

Mead, Margaret, and Ruth L. Bunzel, eds. 1960. *The Golden Age of American Anthropology.* New York: George Braziller. Brief selections from the writings of explorers, conquerors, missionaries, scholars, and pioneer anthropologists, dealing with Indians, from the earliest conquests to the middle of the twentieth century, with commentary by the editors.

Swagerty, W. R., ed. 1984. *Scholars and the Indian Experience.* Bloomington: Indiana University Press. Mainly a bibliographic review of recent writing about the Indians, covering all periods of history from the conquests to the present.

Washburn, Wilcomb E., ed. 1988. *History of Indian-White Relations.* Washington, D.C.: Smithsonian Institution. *Handbook of North American Indians,* vol. 4. A superb, encyclopedic collection of articles dealing with all aspects of Indian-White relations, from the earliest times to the present.

Early travelers, settlers, soldiers, and traders

Bissell, Benjamin. 1925. *The American Indian in English Literature of the Eighteenth Century.* New Haven, Conn.: Yale University Press. See entry under Chapter 3.

Pearce, Roy Harvey. 1988. *Savagism and Civilization.* Berkeley: University of California Press. See entry under Chapter 3.

Smith, Sherry L. 1990. *The View from Officers' Row.* Tucson: University of Arizona Press. A very comprehensive review of writing about the Indians by nineteenth-century soldiers and their wives, arranged topically rather than regionally or chronologically.

"Indianology"

Captivity tales

[Ayer, Edward E.] 1912. *Narratives of Captivity among the Indians of North America.* Chicago: Newberry Library. An annotated bibliography listing several hundred titles. A modern facsimile reprint, undated, was issued by Maurizio Martino, New York.

Drimmer, Frederick, ed. 1961. *Captured by the Indians.* New York: Dover Publications. Excerpts from fifteen captivity tales, with a brief introductory essay by the editor.

Levernier, James, and Hennig Cohen, eds. 1977. *The Indians and their Captives.* Westport, Conn.: Greenwood Press. Excerpts from twenty-nine supposedly real, and nine fictional captivity tales, grouped chronologically and exemplifying different dominant themes in the literature of different historical periods, with an introductory essay by the editors.

Popular Indianology

Feest, Christian F., ed. 1989. *Indians and Europe.* Aachen: Alano Verlag. See entry under Chapter 3.

Washburn, Wilcomb E., ed. 1988. *History of Indian-White Relations.* Washington, D.C.: Smithsonian Institution. *Handbook of North American Indians,* vol. 4, pp. 522–616. The section titled "Conceptual relations" includes essays on Indians in literature, art, the movies, and in the counterculture of the 1960s.

Government and museum Indianology

Bartlett, Richard A. 1962. *Great Surveys of the American West.* Norman: University of Oklahoma Press. Detailed accounts of the four great surveys of the post-Civil War period, that collectively gave birth to the Bureau of American Ethnology.

Bieder, Robert E. 1986. *Science Encounters the Indian 1820–1880.* Norman: University of Oklahoma Press. Has critically perceptive chapters on the work of Gallatin, Morton, Squier, Schoolcraft, and Morgan.

Hallowell, A. Irving. 1976. "The beginnings of Anthropology in America," in Frederica de Laguna, ed., *Selected Papers from the American Anthropologist 1888–1920,* pp. 1–90. Washington, D.C.: American Anthropological Association. An excellent, concise review of the development of all the four subfields of American anthropology in the nineteenth century.

Hinsley, Curtis M. 1981. *Savages and Scientists.* Washington, D.C.: Smithsonian Press. A study of the role of the Smithsonian Institution in the development of American anthropology, from its founding in 1846 until 1910.

Indianology and anthropology

Lurie, Nancy O. 1988. "Relations between Indians and Anthropologists," in Wilcomb E. Washburn, ed., *History of Indian-White Relations,* pp. 548–556. Washington, D.C.: Smithsonian Institution. *Handbook of North American Indians,* vol. 4. A brief but very perceptive overview of changing relations between 1830 and the present, analyzed in terms of a succession of periods.

Indigenous Indianology

Brumble, H. David III. 1988. *American Indian Autobiography.* Berkeley: University of California Press. The book consists mainly of essays on five well-known works of Indian autobiography, but the three opening chapters are concerned more generally with the nature and the limitations of this literary genre.

Rosenstiel, Annette. 1983. *Red & White.* New York: Universe Books. The book is about Indian perceptions of the White Man, and contains numerous specimens of Indian rhetoric, excerpted from orations and letters, from the sixteenth century to the present. Historical value of the work is somewhat diminished by the fact that the cited passages have clearly been heavily edited, and the original source in most cases is not given.

GERMAN IDEALISM

General

Manuel, Frank E. 1965. *Shapes of Philosophic History*, pp. 115–135. Stanford, Calif.: Stanford University Press. Chapter 6 gives a brief but insightful overview of the main differences between German and French philosophy.

Sutton, Claud. 1974. *The German Tradition in Philosophy*. New York: Crane, Russak. A very brief but useful overview of the thought of a few leading German philosophers, from Leibniz to the present day.

The German Enlightenment

Reill, Peter Hanns. 1975. *The German Enlightenment and the Rise of Historicism*. Berkeley: University of California Press. A general overview of German Enlightenment thinking arranged topically rather than by the work of individual thinkers. A particularly good source for some of the relatively little-known predecessors of Kant and Hegel.

Copleston, Frederick. 1985. *A History of Philosophy*, Book Two, vol. VI, part II. New York: Doubleday. Chapters V–VI review and evaluate in detail the work of all the major and several minor German Enlightenment thinkers.

The major idealist philosophers

Copleston, Frederick. 1985. *A History of Philosophy*, Book Two, vol. VI, part IV, and Book Three, vol. VII, part I. New York: Doubleday. Very detailed, clear and insightful discussions of the work of Kant, Fichte, Schelling, and Hegel.

Post-idealists and Neo-Kantians

Collingwood, R.G. 1956. *The Idea of History*, pp. 165–183. New York: Oxford University Press. Brief but insightful discussion of Windelband, Rickert, Simmel, Dilthey, Meyer, and Spengler.

Copleston, Frederick. 1985. *A History of Philosophy*, Book Two, vol. VI, part IV, and Book Three, vol. VII, parts II and III. New York: Doubleday. Detailed discussions of Schopenhauer, Kierkegaard, and Nietsche, as well as a rather brief chapter on Windelband, Rickert, and Dilthey.

The German ethnographic tradition

Baeck, G., and R. Husmann, eds. 1990. *Handbuch der deutschsprachigen Ethnologie.* Göttingen: Edition Re. A detailed and very useful directory of ethnographic museums, research institutes, university programs, and societies in German-speaking countries of Europe.

Bunzl, Matti. 1996. "Franz Boas and the Humboldtian Tradition," in George W. Stocking, Jr. ed., Volksgeist *as Method and Ethic*, pp. 17–78. *History of Anthropology*, vol. 8. Madison: University of Wisconsin Press. A discussion of the work and ideas of the two Humboldt brothers, and their influence on the subsequent development both of German and of Boasian anthropology.

Lowie, Robert H. 1937. *The History of Ethnological Theory.* New York: Farrar & Rinehart. Chapters II and IV discuss briefly the pioneering work of Meiners, Klemm, Waitz, and Bastian.

Zwernemann, Jürgen. 1983. *Culture History and African Anthropology. Uppsala Studies in Cultural Anthropology* 6. Detailed survey of diffusionist studies by German and Austrian ethnologists in Africa and elsewhere, from 1882 to 1982.

Kleindeutschland in America

Nadel, Stanley. 1990. *Little Germany.* Urbana: University of Illinois Press. Discusses the social, political, cultural, and religious life of the German-American community in New York City from 1845 to 1880; the milieu in which nearly all of Boas's earliest students were reared.

The Boasians in America

Harris, Marvin. 1968. *The Rise of Anthropological Theory*, pp. 250–373. New York: Thomas Y. Crowell. Uneven and biased, but by far the most detailed study of the nature and content of Boasian Anthropology that is currently available. Has individual chapters on Boas, Kroeber, and Lowie as well as briefer discussion of many other Boasians.

Hatch, Elvin. 1973. *Theories of Man and Culture.*, pp. 13–161. New York: Columbia University Press. The arrangement of topics and authors is somewhat offbeat and dischronic, but this is nevertheless a penetrating analysis of the work and thought of some of the leading Boasians.

Stocking, George W., ed. 1996. Volksgeist *as Method and Ethic; Essays on*

Boasian Ethnography and the German Anthropological Tradition. History of Anthropology, vol. 8. Madison: University of Wisconsin Press. A collection of lengthy essays dealing variously with early influences on Boas during his German years, and with subsequent manifestations of German idealism in the ethnographic work of Boas and of Kroeber.

OTHER ROOTS; OTHER TREES

Other roots

Rationalism

Cottingham, John. 1988. *The Rationalists.* Oxford: Oxford University Press. Detailed discussion of the essential features of rationalist philosophy as reflected in the works of Descartes, Spinoza, and Leibniz.

Positivism

Andreski, Stanislav, ed. 1974. *The Essential Comte,* trans. Margaret Clarke. London: Croom Helm. Selections from Comte's *Course of Positive Philosophy,* paraphrased in such a way that they are much clearer and more intelligible than in the original.

Lenzer, Gertrud. 1975. *Auguste Comte and Positivism.* New York: Harper & Row. Selections from several of Comte's most important works, with a very perceptive introductory essay by the editor, tracing the historical development of Comte's thought.

Marxism

Bloch, Maurice. 1983. *Marxism and Anthropology.* Oxford: Clarendon Press. A brief but elegantly clear discussion of anthropological ideas in the works of Marx and Engels, and of the subsequent development of Marxist anthropology down to the present day. By far the best available work on this subject.

Russell, Bertrand. 1934. *Freedom* versus *Organization, 1814–1914,* pp. 176–221. New York: W.W. Norton. Very good discussion of the development of Marxist thought in its historical context.

Utilitarianism and Socialism

Albee, Ernest. 1902. *A History of English Utilitarianism.* London: Swan

Sonnenschein. A very detailed review of the work and thought of more than a dozen utilitarian thinkers. Almost half the book is devoted to the work of earlier English philosophers, who preceded the development of Utilitarianism as a recognized philosophical school.

Davidson, William L. 1916. *Political Thought in England; the Utilitarians.* New York: Henry Holt. Detailed discussion of specifically political and legal aspects in the thought of Jeremy Bentham, James Mill, and John Stuart Mill.

Mill, John Stuart. 1971. *Utilitarianism, with Critical Essays,* ed. Samuel Gorovitz. Indianapolis: Bobbs-Merrill. The original text of Mill's 1863 work, setting out the essential features of his own version of Utilitarianism, together with twenty-eight essays by modern authors, discussing and evaluating various aspects of utilitarian philosophy.

Russell, Bertrand. 1934. *Freedom* versus *Organization, 1814–1914,* pp. 75–175. New York: W. W. Norton. An especially good and insightful discussion of the political, social, and historical context in which both Utilitarianism and Socialism arose in nineteenth-century England.

Structuralism

De George, Richard T., and Fernande M. De George, eds. 1972. *The Structuralists: from Marx to Lévi-Strauss.* New York: Anchor Books. Selections from the writings of leading structuralists, with a brief but lucid introductory discussion by the editors.

Kuper, Adam. 1973. *Anthropologists and Anthropology,* Chapter 7. London: Allen Lane. Brief but good overview of the work of Lévi-Strauss and its impact in British Anthropology.

Other trees

British anthropology

Kuklick, Henrika. 1991. *The Savage Within.* Cambridge: Cambridge University Press, 1991. A somewhat uneven overview of the history of British Anthropology from 1885 to 1945. The author divides the history of the discipline into three phases, attributing each to the influence of contemporary social and political conditions.

Kuper, Adam. 1973. *Anthropologists and Anthropology.* London: Allen Lane. An excellent, detailed review of the history of British social anthropology in the era of Malinowski and Radcliffe-Brown and their students, from 1922 to 1972. The author is able to offer the perspective of a latter-day "insider," unlike Kuklick and Stocking who are both American outsiders.

Stocking, George W., Jr. 1984. "Radcliffe-Brown and British Social Anthropology," *History of Anthropology,* vol. 2, pp. 131–191. Madison: University of Wisconsin Press. A very detailed assessment of the mid-century era in British anthropology, and its intellectual and historical background.

Stocking, George W., Jr. 1987. *Victorian Anthropology.* New York: Free Press. A superb overview of the nineteenth-century institutional and intellectual background from which British anthropology emerged at the end of the century.

French anthropology

Considering its persisting and powerful intellectual influence, the history of French anthropology is scandalously neglected in American and British textbooks. The following are the best general overviews in English; both are biased and in several ways unsatisfactory.

Harris, Marvin. 1968. *The Rise of Anthropological Theory,* Chapter 18. Although the chapter is titled "Structuralism," it actually traces the development of French thought from Durkheim through Mauss and Lévy-Bruhl to Lévi-Strauss. A typically uneven but thoughtful and penetrating critique in the author's familiar, polemical style.

Lowie, Robert H. 1937. *The History of Ethnological Theory,* Chapter XII. New York: Farrar & Rinehart. Lowie's position is nearly as biased as that of Harris, but his is the only other history in English that attempts to discuss the work of Durkheim and his school from the perspective of anthropology rather than of sociology. As the work was published in 1937, it does not cover French Structuralism.

German anthropology

Lowie, Robert H. 1937. *The History of Ethnological Theory,* Chapters II, VIII, and XI. An invaluable source because Lowie, with his strong German bias, devotes far more space to the Germans than does any other American historian of anthropology. The 1937 publication date means that it does not cover developments since World War II.

Mühlmann, Wilhelm E. 1948. *Geschichte der Anthropologie.* Bonn: Universitäts-Verlag. Although this is meant to be a general history of anthropology from classical times to the present, it concentrates heavily on the work of the Germans. The 1948 publication date means that it does not cover developments since World War II.

Zwernemann, Jürgen. 1983. *Culture History and African Anthropology. Uppsala Studies in Cultural Anthropology* 6. By far the most comprehensive survey of German diffusionist research and thinking, from the late nineteenth century to the time of writing. In spite of the title the discussion is not confined to German research in Africa; Oceania is considered as well.

Russian and Soviet anthropology

Bromley, Julian, and Viktor Kozlov. 1989. "The Theory of Ethnos and Ethnic Processes in Soviet Social Sciences." *Comparative Studies in Society and History* 31, no. 3: 424–438. Reviews the Soviet debate over the meaning of Ethnicity in the 1960s and 1970s.

Gellner, Ernest, ed. 1980. *Soviet and Western Anthropology.* New York: Columbia University Press. A published conference proceedings in which both Soviet and Western scholars discuss various aspects of Marxist anthropological theory and of Soviet ethnographic practice. The volume does not really attempt an overview of Soviet anthropology.

Shanin, Teodor. 1989. "Ethnicity in the Soviet Union: Analytical Perceptions and Political Strategies." *Comparative Studies in Society and History* 31, no. 3: 409–424. Traces the historical development of Soviet ethnicity theory in response to changing political needs.

Tishkov, Valery A. 1992. "The Crisis in Soviet Ethnology," *Current Anthropology* 33, no. 4: 371–394. A penetrating insider's critique of the recent state of theory and practice in Soviet ethnology, emphasizing the need for a radical restructuring. There are appended comments by a number of other Soviet as well as non-Soviet scholars.

Indian anthropology

Sarana, Gopala, and Dharmi P. Sinha. 1976. "Status of Social-Cultural Anthropology in India." *Annual Review of Anthropology* 5: 209–225. An overview of the status of Indian anthropology in 1976, beginning with a very brief review of its history.

Vidyarthi, L. P. 1984. *Applied Anthropology in India.* 2nd ed. Allahabad: Kitab Mahal. The first chapter is a very detailed review of the history of applied anthropology in India.

Vidyarthi, L. P., and Binay Kumar Rai. 1985. *The Tribal Cultures of India.* 2nd ed. New Delhi: Concept. The first chapter reviews the history of anthropology in India, as well as some previously published accounts of it.

INDEX

A

Academy of Sciences 383
acculturation 109, 249–250
Acosta, José de 31, 144–145, 159
Adair, James 86, 213
Adam and Eve 76, 83
Adams, Ernest xiii
adaptation 66, 314–315, 328, 338, 340
Addison, Joseph 98
Aeschylus 80
Aethiopian 80–81
Africa, Africans
  culture traits 69–70, 292–294, 380
  ethnographic researches in 250, 260, 290–292, 371, 376, 389
  in fiction 93, 217
Afro-American 396
Age of Discovery 72
agnosticism 166, 171–173, 190, 277
Akirch, Arthur 427
Alaska 389
Albee, Ernest 438–439
Alexander the Great, 263
Alexander IV, Pope 139
Algonquian peoples 200
Althusser, Louis 356
amateurs 260, 366, 368, 372
ambiguity 420–421
Amazonia 382, 395–396
Ambrose of Milan 132
American Anthropological Association 109, 255, 402, 411
American Antiquarian Society 229
American Ethnological Society 226, 228
American Historical School 107, 306–317
American Indians
  see Indians, American
American Museum of Natural History 240–241, 246, 300, 307, 383
American Revolution 150, 153, 229
Anabaptists 120, 146
Anaxagoras 13
Andreski, Stanislav 45, 341, 438
animal-rights movement 75
anthropological identity 399–424
anthropological linguistics
  see linguistics
Anthropological Society of Washington 243
Anthropological Survey of India 391–392
antithesis 274–275, 344
Apache Indians 193, 215, 234, 326
apes 91, 185

applied anthropology 249, 353, 409
Aquinas, Thomas 134–137, 146, 180, 189
see also Thomism
Arabs 21, 121
Arapaho Indians 107, 308
Arawak Indians 140
Arcadia, arcadianism 81, 83–84, 90, 111
archaeology, archaeologists
American 229–230, 249–250, 310–311
contribution to evolutionary theory 50, 60–62, 68
early discoveries 60–61
European 60–61
Mesoamerican 394–396
methodology 251, 417–418, 421
role in anthropology 369
role in Indianology 229–230, 249–250
personality of archaeologists 420–421, 424
see also prehistory
Archimedes 15, 416
Archives of the Indies 202
Argentina 396
Aristophanes 80
Aristotle, Aristotelian
cited in reference to American Indians 139–140, 143
conception of natural law 124–125, 147, 188
influence on Aquinas 135–136
teleology 119, 124–125, 164, 177, 188
Arizona 193, 230
army officers 211–212
see also soldiers
Asia 217, 242, 260, 295
Asiatic Society of Bengal 391
assimilation, assimilationism 106, 109, 248
Association of Social Anthropologists 372
Assyriology 196
atheism 172
Athens 14, 123
Atlantis 83
Atwater, Caleb 229
Aufklärung 264–271, 273, 276, 282, 284–285
see also Enlightenment, German
Augustine 16, 132, 143, 172, 180
Australia 36
Australian Aborigines 59–60, 68–69, 374
Austria, Austrians 159, 266, 292, 295, 303, 377, 381
Avalon 83
Ayer, Edward 434
Aymara Indians 395
Aztecs 54, 142, 197, 202, 323, 337

B

Babylonians 160
Bachofen, Johan 52–53
Bacon, Francis 7, 17, 35, 41, 342, 416
Baden School of philosophy 281–282
BAE
see Bureau of American Ethnology
Baeck, G. 437
Baffinland 292, 299, 301, 302, 314
Barnard College 304
Barth, Frederik 290, 390
Bartlett, Richard 434
Bartram 87, 209
Bastian, Adolf 291–292, 293, 299, 302, 306
Baumann, Hermann 292
Bavaria 159
Beach, Samuel 104
Behn, Aphra 95–96
Beijing 393
Belgium 250
Bell, Michael 75, 106, 428
Bella Coola Indians 299
Benedict, Ruth 108, 305–306, 318–322
Bentham, Jeremy 166–167, 347–348, 350, 353
Berger, Thomas 219
Berkeley, George 336
Berlin 285, 289–291, 295, 299, 302

Berlin Ethnographic Museum 285, 290–291, 302
Berlin Society for Anthropology, Ethnology, and Prehistory 291
Betanzos, Diego de 140
Beverly, Robert 203
BIA
see Bureau of Indian Affairs
Bieder, Robert 435
binary opposition 355, 357
biological evolution 375, 410, 418
biology, biologists 328, 375, 414, 418
Birket-Smith, Kaj 389
Bismarck, Otto von 263
Bissell, Benjamin 95, 206, 220, 429, 433
Blessed Isles
see Isles of the Blest
Bloch, Ernst 430
Bloch, Maurice 343, 438
Bloomsbury intellectuals 351
Boas, Franz
early career in America 299–300, 304
early career in Germany 299
ideology 177–178, 180, 264, 298, 301, 314
methodology 241
professionalizing activities 243–244, 260, 298, 300–301, 305
teaching at Columbia 243, 300, 305, 334
theoretical positions 107, 285–286, 302
Boas, George 76–77, 81–82, 426, 428, 429, 431
Boasian anthropology
fieldwork 244–248, 307–311
ideology 107, 112, 305–306
theoretical perspectives 63–64, 288, 311–317, 362
Boasians
backgrounds 284, 302–306, 382
fieldwork 244–247, 307–311
ideology 107–108, 177–178, 180–182
theoretical perspectives 311–317
Bodin, Jean 17
Bodmer, Karl 221
Boemus, Johan 195
Bogoras, Waldemar 383
botany 40, 57
Botocudo Indians 222
Bourdieu, Pierre 376
Brazil, Brazilians 85, 89–90, 139, 205–206, 375, 396
Brezeale, Daniel xiii
bride capture 53
Brinton, Daniel G. 244
Britain, British 166–168, 203–204, 218
see also British anthropology, England, Scotland
British anthropology
absence of physical anthropology 186, 368–369
amateurs in 371
early development 367–369
fieldwork 371
Functionalism in 248, 350–353, 369–370
influence on Indian anthropology 390–391
overview of 367–372
parochialism 362–363, 369–370
personality of 371–372
Structuralism in 183, 359–360, 370
theoretical orientations 350–353, 359–360, 370, 401
British Columbia 299
Brixham Cave 60
Bromley, Julian 441
Brumble, H. David 435
Bryson, Gladys 426
Buckle, Thomas Henry 46–47, 285
Buddhism 78
Buffalo Bill's Wild West Show 223
Bunzel, Ruth 321, 433
Bunzl, Matti 437
Bureau of American Ethnology
fieldwork 99, 232–233, 235, 253, 259–260, 307
founding of 259, 365

overview of 231–238
personnel 231, 233
publications 204, 228, 233–235
theoretical orientations 58, 231–233
Bureau of Indian Affairs 235–237, 248–253
Bureau of Reclamation 237
Burgess, Ernest W. 352
Burnett, James
see Monboddo
Burridge, Kenelm 428
Bury, J. B. 17, 39, 46, 267, 427
Buschan, Georg 289
Bushmen 68–70

C

Caesar, Julius 200, 283
Calabrese, John 277
California 230, 240, 248, 308, 361
Canada 37, 90, 202, 299, 389, 394
cannibals, cannibalism 120, 142, 206, 337, 414
Cano, Melchor 142
canon law 133–138
Capitalism 76, 150, 343–344, 347, 349
captives, captivities 96, 214–217, 259
Carpini, Joannes 197
Cartier, Jacques 197
Carver, Jonathan 86–87
Cass, Louis 227, 236, 245, 259
Castillo, Bernal Díaz del 197
categorical analysis of culture 175–177
categories, categorical systems 183, 191, 329–330
Catholic Church 136, 146, 203
Catlin, George 221–223
Celts 144
Central America 199, 290, 292, 298
Central Asia 384–385
Centre National de la Recherche Scientifique 373
Chabert, X. 223
Chamberlain, A. F. 300, 305
Champlain, Samuel de 86
Charlevoix, Pierre 23
Charron, Pierre 89–90
Cherokee Indians 101, 209
Chesky, Jane 237
Chicago 239, 242, 248, 300, 317, 352, 361, 393
see also Field Museum of Natural History, University of Chicago, and World's Columbian Exhibition
Chickasaw Indians 213
chiefdoms 27, 371
Chihuahua 213
Child, Maria 101
children's literature 107, 219–220, 259
Chile 396
chimpanzees 185
China, Chinese 12, 76, 78, 121–122, 160, 325, 393–394
Chinese anthropology 393–394
Chinese Turkestan 394
Chippewa Indians 104, 234
see also Ojibwa Indians
Chomsky, Noam 251
Christianity, Christian doctrine 101, 111, 126, 130, 189, 207–208
Christianization 208
Christy, Henry 61
Church of England 203
Cicero 80, 127–129, 132, 149, 180
Cieza de Leon, Pedro 197
cinema 106, 217, 220, 257
City College of New York 345
Civil War, U.S. 204, 222, 230, 233, 236, 259
Clark University 300
Clarke, Samuel 89
class conflict 343–344, 387
Classical economics 345
Classics 195, 258
classification 234, 241, 360, 385, 387
Clement of Alexandria 132
Cobo, Bernardo de 202
Cochise 211
Code of Justinian 129–130, 133, 188–189
cognitive anthropology 331

cognitive evolution 43
Cohen, Hennig 215–216, 434
Colden, Cadwallader 86, 209
Cole, Fay-Cooper 245
Cole, Thomas 416
Coleridge, Samuel 98
Collier, John 236–237, 251
Collingwood, R. G. 279, 436
Colombia 198
colonial regimes
  and anthropology 250, 289–290, 352, 364–365, 372, 389, 406
  opposition to 280, 365
colonization 198, 209
Colorado Plateau 230–231
Columbia Plateau 245
Columbia University 243, 245, 300, 304–305, 321, 345, 357
Columbus, Christopher 8, 84, 86, 88, 111, 138, 197, 259
Commissioner for Indian Affair 236
Communism, Communist 169, 248, 250, 343–344, 384, 393–394, 401
community studies 250, 325
comparative anatomy 50
comparative ethnology 141, 143–144
comparative method 19, 34–38, 43–45, 68, 159, 341
comparative sociology 373–374
Comparative Values Study 322
compendia
  see ethnographic compendia
compilers 87, 198–200
computers 181
Comte, Auguste
  comparative method 34–35, 44–45
  founder of sociology 41–42, 170
  positivist philosophy 170–171, 340–342
  progressivist theory 42–45
  see also Positivism
Condorcet, Marquis de 22, 32, 41–42, 361, 374
Configurationism, configurationists
  early development 318, 321
  overview of 317–325
  research 249, 319–323
  theoretical orientations 5–6, 64, 108, 179, 318–319, 364
conjectural history 29–31, 48, 146, 267, 278, 287, 325, 379
conjectural prehistory
  see conjectural history
conquerors 54, 197–198, 200–201, 205, 210, 217, 254, 259
conquistadores
  see conquerors
Conrad, Joseph 106
consensual approach to natural law 118–119, 128, 168, 180, 182
  see also jus gentium
contract archaeology 423
Cook, Captain James 87
Cooley, Charles H. 352
Cooper, James Fenimore 99, 100, 211, 219
Copleston, Frederick 436
core values 249, 318–320
corporate kin groups 52
Corpus Juris Civilis
  see Code of Justinian
Cortés, Hernán 197
cosmographies 176, 195, 287, 330, 365
  see also ethnographic compendia
Costner, Kevin 79, 106
Cottingham, John 438
Council of the Indies 142–143
Crevècoeur, Hector 87, 209
cross-cultural surveys 34, 161, 175, 181, 184, 190
Crow Indians 107
Crowe, Michael 125, 129, 133, 431
Culin, Stewart 233
cultural determinism 314
cultural diffusion
  see diffusion
cultural ecology 65–68, 338, 390
  see also Neo-evolutionism
Cultural Materialism 328, 334
cultural particularism 313–314

cultural personality 249, 318–323
Cultural Pluralism 407
Cultural Primitivism 76, 81, 85, 110
Cultural Relativism 177–180, 280, 314–315, 332, 378
cultural themes 214, 318, 320
culturology 311–313
cultural values
see core values
culture area concept 242
culture of poverty 327–328
Culverwel, Nathaniel 90
Curtis, Edward 222
Cushing, Frank H. 325
Custer, General George 211, 221, 223
cyclical theories 17
Cynics 81–83, 111

D

d'Entreves, Alexander 146, 148
d'Holbach, Baron 22
Dakota Indians
see Lakota Indians
Dalrymple, John 24, 32–33
Daniel, Glyn 10, 29
Danish anthropology 389–390
Darrah, William 232
Darwin, Darwinism 47, 51, 338, 368–369, 375
Davenant, William 94
Davidson, William 439
Davis, E. H. 230
Davis, John 87
Dawes Allotment Act 245
DeBry, Theodor 206, 220
DeGeorge, Richard and Fernande 354, 439
de Heusch, Luc 377
de Léry, Jean 205
De Pauw, J. Cornelius 32
De Soto, Diego 142
Deadwood Dick 215
Declaration of Independence 190
decretists 134
Degenerationism 17, 77, 81
Degérando, J.-M. 36–37, 58
Deism 151, 277
Democritus 13, 16
Derrida, Jacques 366–367, 376
Descartes, Réne 17–18, 41, 336, 342, 359
descriptive integration 320
detective fiction 219
determinism 166, 356
dialectic theory 273–275
Dialectical Materialism 342
see also Marxism
Diamond, Stanley 108–109, 430
Dicaearchus 14, 16, 31, 33, 55, 68, 81, 88
diffusion, Diffusionism 61, 292–294, 315–317, 325, 340, 369, 372, 379–381, 405
Dilthey, Wilhelm 281–283
dime novels 106, 218
Diodorus Siculus 13
Diogenes 76, 79, 81, 84
distribution studies 316
divine will 84, 115, 130–137, 145, 151, 172, 189, 316, 336, 338
Dodge, Colonel Richard 212
Dole, Gertrude 71
Dominicans 201, 204
Dorsey, George 204, 233
Douglas, Mary 355, 363
Drake, Francis 86
drama 14, 92, 94–95, 100, 111, 286, 371
Drimmer, Frederick 214, 434
Driver, Harold 316
Dryden, John 92, 94, 99
dualism 268–270, 282, 328
DuBois, Cora 318, 321
Dumont, Louis 377
Duns Scotus, John 136, 137
Duplessis, Paul 219
Durkheim, Émile 43, 338, 351, 359, 362, 370, 374–376
Durkheimian theory 183, 190, 338–339, 351, 355, 360, 374–375
Dutch anthropology 389

E

Earle, Timothy 67
ecology, ecological 66–68
 see also cultural ecology
economics, economists 28, 255, 269, 345–346, 395
Edelstein, Ludwig 15, 426
Eels, Myron 204
Egalitarianism 77, 126, 180–181, 191, 301, 332, 371
Eggan, Fred 352
Egypt, Egyptians 12, 85, 160, 263
Egyptology 194–196, 244, 258, 412
Eibl-Eibesfeld, Irenaeus 184–185
Eliot, T. S. 105
Emerson, Ralph Waldo 218
emic 329
Emic Rationalism 337, 339
Empiricism, empiricists 155, 159, 161, 181, 336, 341, 359, 376, 418
encomienda system 140, 144, 200–201
enculturation 237, 319–320
Engels, Friedrich 41, 69, 275, 340, 343, 383
England, English
 anthropology in 362–363, 367–372
 functionalist doctrines in 350–353
 socialist doctrines in 349–350
 structuralist doctrines in 359–360
 utilitarian doctrines in 167, 347–349
 see also Britain, British
Enlightenment
 French 19–22, 160–161
 German 266–271
 natural law theory in 150–162, 189–191
 Progressivism in 12, 18–38, 161–162
 Scottish 22–29, 55, 157–158
environment
 in German Idealist philosophy 284–286
 in relation to natural law 115
 influence on cultural development 66–68, 242, 293, 314–315, 328
Environmental Determinism 284–286, 289
Epicureans 125, 166
Erasmus, Desiderius 89
Eskimos 219, 222, 286, 299, 302, 314, 389
Eterovich, Francis 149, 431
Ethical Relativism 177, 332
Ethiopian 77, 80–81
Ethnic Idealism 280–281
ethnicity 385, 387, 390
ethnobotany 330
ethnoentomology 330
ethnogenesis 386
ethnographic compendia 199, 212, 259, 297
 see also cosmographies
ethnographic museums
 see museums
ethnographic present 214, 229, 308
ethnohistory, ethnohistorians 211–212, 214, 238, 255, 396, 407
ethnological societies 58, 295
ethnoscience 331, 363
ethnozoology 330
etic 329
Etic Rationalism 337–338
eugenics 50, 64
Evans-Pritchard, Edward E. 23, 427
evolution, Evolutionism
 biological evolution 357
 evolutionist doctrine 5, 47–49, 196, 297, 324, 326–327, 368, 396
 Marxist Evolutionism 343–344, 355–356, 383, 386–388
 social evolution 47–49, 370, 375, 396
 see also Progressivism
evolutionary stages
 see stage theory
exhibitions 222–224, 240–241, 259
Existentialism 358–359
Exogamy 52–53
exploitation theory 346–347, 364
explorers, exploration 197–198, 201, 215, 226, 259

F

Fairchild, Hoxie 83, 87, 96, 429
Farny, Henry 221
Fascism viii, 248
Feest, Christian xiii, 219, 429, 434
Fei, Hsio-Tung 393
Felsenthal, Rabbi 303
feminism 77, 120, 346
Fenton, William 38
Ferdinand, Kind of Spain 139–140
Ferguson, Adam 24–26, 27, 33–34, 49, 53, 68
Fichte, Wilhelm 21, 271–275, 280, 333
fiction 78, 85, 92, 217–220, 266, 382
Fiedler, Leslie 218–219
Field Museum of Natural History 240–241, 243, 300, 307
films
  see cinema
Filson, John 209
Firth, Raymond 360
Fischer, Theobald 285, 306, 314
Fison, Lorimer 59
Flint, Timothy 101
Florida 209, 225
folk culture 279, 323–325
Folk–Urban Continuum 324
Fontenelle, Bernard de 18, 37
Forrest, Edwin 100
Foucault, Michel 366, 376, 377, 388
four-field tradition 6
  in American anthropology 245, 255, 261, 366, 368–369, 401–402
  in British anthropology 245, 366, 368–369, 396
  in Mexico 394, 396
  in the Soviet Union 386
  contribution to Indianology 6, 245, 255, 396
  contribution to evolutionary doctrine 62, 368–369, 396
four-stage theory 54, 67
  see also stage theory
Fowke, Gerard 233
France, French 219, 358–361, 373, 375–382
  see also French anthropology
Franciscans 201
Frazer, James 36, 56, 59, 97, 183, 339
Frémont, Lt. John C. 226
French anthropology 338, 354, 356–362, 373–382
French Enlightenment
  see Enlightenment
French libertarians 154–157
French Revolution 22, 39, 150, 153, 167–168
Freneau, Philip 103–104
Freud, Sigmund 53, 59, 339, 354, 356–357
Freudian psychology 318
Fried, Morton 67
Frobenius, Leo 292–293, 379–380
Frobisher, Martin 199
Fuchs, Stephen 292
Functionalism, functionalists
  features of the doctrine 64, 179, 249, 325–326
  in American anthropology 64, 179, 248–249, 324–326, 352–353, 360
  in British anthropology 350–353, 369–370
  in French anthropology 374–375
  in Indian anthropology 392–392
  origins of the doctrine 45
Fürer-Heimendorf, Christoph von 292

G

Gaius, Roman jurist 129
Gallatin, Albert 226–228, 259
Garden of Eden 80, 82, 156, 172
Gates, William 202
Gatschet, Albert 233
Gay, John 95
Geerken, John H. 149
Geertz, Clifford 363
Geist 265, 273–279, 285, 318–320
  see also Volksgeist
Geisteswissenschaft 269, 281–282
Gellner, Ernest 386–387, 418, 441
geology 40, 50, 57, 402
Georgia 209
Gerland, Georg 289

German anthropology 361–362, 377–382
see also German ethnographic tradition
German Enlightenment
see Enlightenment
German ethnographic tradition 286–296, 334, 380–381, 389
see also German anthropology
German Idealism
bibliography 436–438
historical background 263–266
historical rationalism in 340
influence in American anthropology 177, 297–334
influence in German anthropology 382
influence on E. B. Tylor 296–298, 362
legal relativism in 168
Primitivism in 77, 112
summary discussion 333–334
German legalists 158–159, 161
German nationalism 280, 289, 319
German particularism 279, 312
German Progressivism 273
German Relativism 168
German Universalism 311
German-Americans 63, 264, 284, 304
Germany, Germans 168–169, 219, 263–296, 377–382, 407
see also German anthropology, German Idealism, German-Americans
Gesellschaftsgeist 273, 276
Gesellschaftswissenschaft 282
Gestalt psychology 281
Ghurye, S. C. 392
Gillen, J. C. 59
Glanvil, Joseph 89
glossarists 133
Gluckman, Max 186
Goethe, Johann Wolfgang 266, 275, 277, 304
Goguet, Alphonse 32, 36, 160
Golden Age 75, 81, 247
Golden Rule 132, 148, 164
Goldenweiser, Alexander 63, 107, 179, 305–306, 314
Gómara, Lopez de 198
Goodenough, Ward 312, 329
gorillas 185
Graebner, Fritz 293, 378–380
Gratian, medieval jurist 133–134
Great Basin 65, 308
Great Britain
see Britain
Great Lakes area 213, 228
Great Proletarian Cultural Revolution 393
great traditions 324
Greece, Greeks
anthropological ideas ix, 29, 55
cultural nationalism 263
natural law doctrines 121–126, 174–175, 186, 188
Primitivism 75, 78–82, 111
Progressivism 12–16, 71
Rationalism 336
Greenland 389
Greenwood, Davydd 433
Gregg, Josiah 213
Gregorio, Gil 140
Grey, Zane 219
Griaule, Marcel 377
Grotius, Hugo 31, 33, 55, 146–148, 150–153, 158–159, 173, 180, 189
Guangxi 394
Guatemala 197
Gunther, Erna 246
Gusinde, Martin 292
Guthrie, W. K. C. 426
Gypsies 386

H

Habermas, Jürgen 381
Haddon, Alfred 368–369
Hadlock, Samuel 222
Haeberlin, H. K. 246, 305
Haekel, Josef 381

Haile, Berard 204
Håkansson, Tomas xiii
Hakluyt, Richard 206
Halbwachs, Maurice 375
half-breeds 102
Hallowell, A. Irving 234, 318, 320, 435
Hanke, Lewis 145, 217, 432
Harris, Marvin 47, 177, 337, 343, 355, 402, 405, 419, 437, 440
Harvard University 239, 243–244, 260, 307, 357, 361
Harvard Kalahari Group 69–70
Hatch, Elvin 437
Havasupai Indians 308
Hawkesworth's Voyages 87
Hawkins, John 86
Hawthorne, Nathaniel 218
Hayden Survey 230–231
Hebrews 80, 122, 152, 160
Heckewelder, G. E. 203
Hegel, Georg 21, 264–265, 271–275, 323, 333, 340, 344, 359, 387
Heidegger, Martin 359
Heine-Geldern, Robert von 292
Helvetius, Charles 21, 32, 91
Henry, Joseph 238
Henshaw, Henry 231
Herder, Gottfried 264, 271–274, 277–285, 293–294, 312–315, 323–324, 333, 378
hermeneutics 283, 331
Herodotus 16, 79, 144, 263
Heroic Primitivism 77
Herrera, Antonio de 198
Herskovits, Melville 109, 179–180, 305, 310, 314
Hesiod 81
Heye Foundation 240–241
Hiawatha 104–105
Hildebrand, George 9, 159, 425
Hillerman, Tony 219
Hillers, John K. 222, 231
Hindu castes 391
Hindu philosophy 80
Hinsley, Curtis 8, 231, 241, 435
Hinton, Thomas 422
Hipparchus 15
Hirschberg, Walter 292
Historical Determinism 353
Historical Particularism 265, 276–281, 292–293, 333–334
historical philosophy
see philosophy of history
Historical Primitivism 76, 81, 85, 110
Historical Progressivism 11, 13
Historical Rationalism 337, 339–340
Historical Universalism 265, 271–278
Historicism 281, 315, 317
historiography 406
Hobbes, Thomas 17, 25, 40, 148–150, 153, 155, 159
Hodges, M. C. 102
Hoebel, E. Adamson 186
Holmes, William H. 231, 241–242, 325
holocultural surveys 34, 180–181
see also cross-cultural surveys
Homer, Homeric 77, 80–81
hominid evolution 410
Hooker, Joseph 146, 148, 150–151, 153, 155
Hopi Indians 1, 236, 252, 320, 326
Horace, Latin poet 80
Houyhnhnms 79, 85
Howard, General Oliver 212
Howitt, A. W. 59
Hrdlicka, Ales 232
Hsu, Francis 393
Hugo, Gustav 168
human ethology 183–185
Human Relations Area Files 181
human rights
see universal rights
human universals 184
humanism, humanistic 17, 247, 251, 258, 282, 316, 330
Humboldt, Alexander von 290
Hume, David 23–24, 114, 157, 162–163, 165, 190, 336
Huron Indians 105
Husmann, G. 437

Husserl, Edouard 359
Hutcheson, Francis 23, 157–158, 161, 347

I

Iberians 144
Ibn Khaldûn ix, 24, 35, 37, 45, 46, 52
Idealist Progressivism 10–11, 13
identity, anthropological
  see anthropological identity
ideology, ideological
  in American anthropology xi, 62, 64, 110–112, 187, 248–249, 301, 314, 401, 408, 411–415
  in German thought 264, 280
  in relation to American Indians 6–8, 194, 248–249, 258–259
  in relation to natural law 118, 146, 169, 187
  in relation to philosophy and theory vii–viii, xi, 3–5, 169
  Structuralism as 354, 356
Idyllic Primitivism 77
Illinois 245
Illinois Indians 105
imperial, imperialism 128, 280, 345, 364–365, 383, 387
Incas 37, 142, 198, 202
  see also Peru
India 54, 160, 250, 292, 325, 337, 390–392, 396–397
Indian agents 210, 227, 309
  see also Bureau of Indian Affairs
Indian anthropology 390–392
Indian autobiography 257
Indian Claims Commission 238
Indian Education Research Project 236
Indian languages 226, 234, 259, 309
Indian oratory 97, 257
"Indian question" 139–144
Indian Removal Policy 102, 216
Indian rights 140–143, 201, 204
Indian warfare 203, 211, 214
Indianology 193–261
  bibliography 433–435
  early development 197–216
  government Indianology 224–238
  indigenous Indianology 257–258
  in anthropology 243–257, 363, 382, 389, 394
  literature 217–222
  museum Indianology 238–243
  summary discussion 258–261
Indian-White relations 209, 213, 256, 407
Indians, American 6–8, 34, 59–60, 85–87, 111–112, 193–261
Indology 196, 391
Indonesia 255, 389
Inkle and Yarico 95, 98
Innocent III, Pope 84
Institut Français de l'Afrique Noir 373
Institute of Ethnology and Anthropology, Russian 388
Institute of Human Ethology 184
Institute of Nationalities, Chinese 393
International Congress of Americanists 389
international law 129, 146–147, 189
International Phonetic Alphabet 309
intuitive approach to natural law 118–119
Iowa Indians 223
Iroquois Indians 37, 54, 104, 209, 234
Isabella, Queen of Spain 138–139, 197
Iselin, Isaak 285
Isidore of Seville 132
Islam 121, 130
Isles of the Blest 79, 84

J

Jackson, William H. 222, 230
Jacobs, Melville 380
Jakobson, Roman 182, 354, 357
Japanese 322
Jefferson, Thomas 225–226, 229, 257, 259
Jérez, Francisco 198
Jesuit Relations 86, 202–203
Jesuits 86, 198, 201–204
Jesup North Pacific Expedition 383

Jews, Jewish 131, 303–304, 345
see also Hebrews
Jhering, Rudolf von 168
Jochelson, Waldemar 383
Johnson, Allen 67
Johnson, Dorothy 219
Johnson, Harold 432
Joseph, Alice 211, 237, 320
Joyce, James 106
Juárez, Benito 212
Judaism 130
see also Hebrews
jurisprudence 115, 117, 129, 168
jus gentium 126–130, 131, 135–147, 160–161, 169, 173, 188–189, 191
Justinian Code
see Code of Justinian
juvenile fiction
see children's literature

K

Kames, Lord 23–24, 33
Kane, Paul 221
Kant, Immanuel 162, 163–165, 190, 264–273, 277, 304, 313, 340, 348
Karakalpakia 384
Kardiner, Abram 321
Kazakhs, Kazakhstan 384, 387
Keate, George 87
Kent's Cavern 60
Kentucky 209, 225
Kesey, Ken 219
Kiel 299
King Philip's War 100
kinship 27, 33, 50–54, 56–57, 91, 182, 297, 344, 375
Kiowa Indians 406
Kipling, Rudyard 101
Kirchoff, Paul 292
Kirghiz 387
Kleindeutschland 302–306
Klemm, Gustav 287–288, 297–298
Kluckhohn, Clyde 16, 65, 179, 237, 264, 277, 318–322, 363
Knight, Richard 38
Kopit, Arthur 219
Kossina, Gustav 280
Kozlov, Viktor 441
Krickeberg, Walter 292
Kroeber, Alfred
quoted 178, 264, 277, 301, 304, 315
publications 246
theoretical perspectives 26, 63, 108, 247, 306, 315–316, 320, 327
Kronenberg, Andreas xiii
Kropotkin, Peter 350
Kuhn, Thomas 408
Kuklick, Henrika 439
Kulturkreis, Kulturkreislehre 293–294, 316, 379–382, 389
Kuper, Adam xi, 360, 428, 439–440

L

Lacan, Jacques 356
Lactantius 132
Lafitau, Joseph 23, 37–38, 86, 160, 176–177, 190, 203
Lakota Indians 79, 406
see also Sioux Indians
Land of the Blest 83
language 245, 329, 356–357, 387
see also linguistics
Lartet, Henri 61
Las Casas, Bartolomé de 86, 94, 140, 143–145, 159, 190, 201, 217
Laufer, Berthold 292
Lawrence, D. H. 78, 106, 218
laws of nature 114, 337
Lawson, John 209
LeJeune, Paul 86
Leach, Edmund 360
Lee, Richard 69–70
legal anthropology 186
legal determinism 348
legal relativism 168, 170, 190
Lehmann, William 23, 292
Leibniz, Gottfried 336
Leighton, Dorothea 237
Lenin, Vladimir 384
Lenzer, Gertrud 171, 438

Lesser, Alexander 305
Lessing, Gotthold 266
Levernier, James 215–216, 434
Lévi-Strauss, Claude 182, 354–362, 373–377
Lévy-Bruhl, Lucien 43, 279, 339, 374–375
Lewis, I. M. 363
Lewis, Oscar 327–328
Lewis and Clark Expedition 226, 259
liberation anthropology 346
Ligon, Richard 98
linguistic analogy 178, 312–313, 330, 356–357
linguistics
 and "New Ethnography" 329–331
 and Structuralism 356–358
 in Britain 369, 372
 in France 373
 in India 392
 in the Soviet Union 384–386
 methodology 329–330
 personality of linguists 421, 422–423
 role in anthropology 62, 178, 251–252, 261, 309
 role in Indianology 232, 234, 249, 254, 309
Linnaeus, Carolus 49
Linton, Ralph 109, 179, 321, 353
literature 111, 217–220, 259, 304, 354, 358, 400, 415
 see also fiction
Lithuania 384–385
Locke, John 19, 37, 150, 153–155, 159, 336
Logan Museum 241
logos 132, 270
London School of Economics 362, 369
Long Exploring Expedition 226
Long, John 213
Long, Timothy 428
Longfellow, Henry Wadsworth 99, 104–105
Louisiana Territory 226
Lovejoy, Arthur 76–77, 81–82, 426, 428, 431
Lowie, Robert
 history of German ethnology 287–289, 293
 professional education 305
 publications 246, 437, 440
 theoretical perspectives 63–64, 107, 179–181, 247, 294, 306–307, 314
Lubbock, John 60–61, 68
Lucretius 15, 38
Lurie, Nancy 251, 435
Luschan, Felix von 292

M

Macgregor, Gordon 237
Machiavelli, Niccolo 17, 149
Maine, Henry Sumner 52, 173, 186, 297
Mair, John 139
Maitland, Frederick 315, 378
Malefijt, Annemarie 375
Malinowski, Bronislaw 350–351, 362, 369–372, 402, 405, 421
Mallery, Garrick 233
Malpighi, Marcello 151
Malthus, Thomas 39
Manifest Destiny 365
Manuel, Frank 19, 265, 267, 436
Marburg School of philosophy 281
Marco Polo 197
Marcus Aurelius 127
Marett, Robert R. 56, 298, 368–369
Marquette, Jacques 86
Marx, Karl
 doctrines 169–170, 174, 340, 343–346, 355–359, 387
 influences on 46, 273–275, 327, 333
 Primitivism of 109
 Progressivism of 41, 67, 69
Marxism, Marxists
 and natural law 169–170, 171, 190
 and Structuralism 376, 390
 doctrines 326–327, 328, 334, 340, 342–347, 358–359
 in Peruvian anthropology 395
 in Soviet anthropology 382–388, 396–397, 401

Primitivism in 108–109
Progressivism in 41, 66–67, 169
Maryland 208
Mason, Otis T. 239, 241–242
material culture 246, 289, 292, 319, 380
Materialism 15, 21, 28, 46, 269, 297, 327–328, 331, 424
see also Dialectical Materialism
matrilineal kinship 52–53, 140
Matthews, Washington 233
Mauss, Marcel 43, 359, 374–376
Maya Indians 202, 324
McClellan, Isaac 104
McGee, W. J. 325
McGrane, Bernard 415
McIlvaine, J. H. 54
McLennan, John 49, 51–53, 56, 173, 183, 186, 297, 340, 367
Mead, Margaret 108, 318, 320–321, 405, 433
medicine shows 224
Meek, Ronald 24, 26, 38, 427
Meillassoux, Claude 377
Meiners, Carl 287
Meinhof, Carl 292
Melanesia, Melanesians 292, 321, 371, 380
see also Oceania
Melville, Herman 218
Mentalism
in American anthropology 324, 317, 325, 331, 361
in British anthropology 297–298
in German anthropology 378
in German Idealist philosophy 265, 268–271, 274, 284, 293
in progressivist theory 21–22, 43, 46–47, 49, 293
Meriam Report 248
Mesa, Bernardo de 140
Mesa Verde 230
Mesoamerican excavations 239
see also Maya
Mesopotamia 12, 263
metaphysics 115, 117, 172, 267, 275, 281, 341
methodology 342, 356, 405, 420–421
Mexica
see Aztecs
Mexican anthropology 394–395
Mexico, Mexican
anthropology in 394–396, 401
archaeological studies in 230
conquest of 197
ethnographic studies in 199, 290, 323, 422
in literature 95, 98, 257
Meyer, Edouard 315
Michaelis, Johann 285
Michigan 227, 229, 245
Micronesian 87
Middle America
see Central America
migration, migrationism 54, 379
Mill, James 46, 166, 347, 349
Mill, John Stuart 45–46, 166–167, 170, 341, 347, 349, 410, 439
Millar, John 26–27, 33, 49, 53, 68
Mindeleff, Cosmos and Victor 233
minorities 253, 394
minorities policy 394
see also Nationalities Policy
missionaries 105, 139–144, 199–205, 213, 217, 254, 259, 309, 372
Mississippi Valley 230
mode of production 169, 344, 386
Modernism 11–12
modes of subsistence 14, 21, 31, 45, 49, 54, 68, 278
monastic movements 83
Monboddo, Lord 91–92
Monism 117, 186–187, 268, 399, 403, 419–420
Montaigne, Michel de 89
Montesquieu, Charles Louis
environmentalism 120, 285
influence on French anthropology 374–376
natural law theory 120, 122, 154–155, 160
progressivist theory 20, 31–32, 68, 120

Mooney, James 222, 233
moral philosophy 2–3, 7, 40–41, 47, 114–115, 172
moral relativism 123
moral universalism 126
More, Henry 89
Morgan, Lewis Henry
and Marxism 383
ethnographic researches 54, 227, 236
influence on American anthropology 56–57, 231–232, 314
influence on British anthropology 57, 362–363, 367
influences on 26, 54, 340
kinship studies 54, 204
materialism 54–55
progressivist theory viii, 38, 49–52, 53–57, 67–68, 294, 297
Morphological School of biology 281
Morton, Sarah 105
Morton, Thomas 208
Mosheim, Johann von 285
Mozart, Wolfgang 85
Mound Builders, mounds 104, 229–231
movies
see cinema
Muhammad 121
Mühlmann, Wilhelm 441
Muldoon, James 432
Muller, Klaus xiii
Müller, Max 368
multilinear evolution 27, 45, 66–67
see also Neo-evolutionism
Murdock, George P. 181
Murphy, Robert 303
Musée de l'Homme 373
museums
role in American anthropology 300
role in early anthropology 57, 195, 410
role in French anthropology 373
role in the German ethnographic tradition 395
role in Indianology 238–243
role in Mexican anthropology 394
role in salvage ethnography 397
Museum für Völkerkunde 299
Museum of Northern Arizona 241
Museum of the American Indian 240
Muslims 82, 385
see also Islam
Mysticism 270, 277
mythology, myths 117, 184, 228, 270, 279, 309, 339, 357, 361, 375

N

Nacirema parodies 412
Nadel, Stanley 437
Nader, Laura 186
Napoleon 39, 40, 41, 283
Naroll, Raoul and Frada 181
Narragensett Indians 208
national anthropologies 408
national character studies 322–323
National Park Service 237
National Science Foundation 328, 410
Nationalism 225, 361–364, 374, 378, 405
Nationalities Policy 384–387, 393–394
Native Americans
see Indians, American
Native American Studies 193, 195, 258
natural history 196, 198, 200, 225, 259, 290, 295, 415, 418
see also natural science
natural law 113–191
and American Indians 138–145
and Primitivism 89–91, 108
and Rationalism 336–337
and universal rights 148–162
bibliography 430–433
early modern conceptions 20, 146–450
Enlightenment theories 150–162, 272
features of the doctrine 115–120
historical contexts 121–122
in anthropology 173–187, 190–191, 371, 375
in antiquity 122–130

medieval conceptions 130–138
summary discussion 187–191
under attack 162–173
natural rights 126, 148–149, 157, 165–167, 348
see also universal rights
natural science 195, 281–282, 302, 313, 414
see also natural history
naturalists 217, 232, 244, 247, 260
Navajo Indians 1, 107, 193, 204, 213–214, 219, 236, 322, 412, 422
Nazis, Nazism viii, 280, 345, 358
Near East 292, 325
Needham, Joseph 121–122, 431
Neo-evolutionism 65–71, 328, 338
Neo-Kantians 281–284
Neolithic 60–61
Nepal 292
Netherlands 250, 389
New Archaeology 251, 253
New Deal viii, 236, 248
New England 207–208
New Ethnography 179, 329–331
New Guinea 260, 293
New Mexico 228, 230
New School for Social Research 35
New Testament 131
New York 58, 209, 240
New York City 63, 240, 299–302
Newton, Isaac 41, 416
Nietsche, Friedrich 273, 276, 280, 319
Nimuendaju, Curt 292
Nisbet, Robert 9
Noble Redman 101, 104–105, 109, 218
Noble Savage
identified as American Indian 7, 84–85, 111, 193, 220, 258
identified as Polynesian 87
in anthropological thought 109
in literature 92–93, 102–106, 220
persona of 77, 79–80, 155
Nominalism 136
nomos 121, 122, 123, 126
Nordic peoples 104, 286, 389
normative personality 320–321, 420–421
Northern Plains Indians 245, 308
Northwest Coast Indians 299–300
Norwegian 389
novels 60, 95–97, 101–102, 111, 258, 371
see also fiction, literature

O

Oceania 93, 250, 257, 260, 371, 380
see also Melanesia, Polynesia
Ockham, Roger 137, 146
Ohio 229
Ojibwa Indians 223, 228
see also Chippewa Indians
Old Testament 80, 131
Omaha Indians 204
operas 95, 111
Opler, Morris 318, 326, 352–353
Oregon 228
organic model of society 48, 162
Oriental, Orientalism 275, 389
Orinoco River 90
Ortiz, Juan 215
Ottawa Indians 223
Oviedo, Gonzalo de 198
Owen, Robert 350
Oxford University 241, 369

P

Pacific Northwest 308
see also Northwest Coast
Pagden, Anthony vi, ix, 140, 143–144, 432
painters, paintings 111, 220–222
Paiute Indians 1, 231
Palacios Rubios, Juan 140
Paleolithic 60–81
paleontology 40, 50, 57
Pandian, Jacob 425
Papago Indians 237
papal authority 133, 139
paradigms 63, 244, 246–247, 251, 408

Park, Mungo 290
Park, Robert E. 352
Parsons, Elsie Clews 107
Particularism
in Boasian anthropology 298 310, 312
in Chinese anthropology 394
in German ethnography 287, 292, 296, 302, 381–382
in German Idealist philosophy 270, 276–281, 284
in Indianology 243, 258–259
in New Ethnography 330
in Scandinavian anthropology 389–390
in Soviet anthropology 385–386
Pascal, Blaise 18
Paternal Primitivism 77, 81, 85, 110
patrilineal kinship 53
Paulus, Roman jurist 129
Pausanias 81
Paz, Matías de 140
Peabody Museum 239–240, 243, 247, 295, 307
Pearce, Roy H. 98–99, 100, 207–208, 429–430, 434
peasants 142, 323–328
Pedro Martir 198
Peking University 393
Pennsylvania 208, 243
performance theory of language 381
Pericles 14, 123, 263
periodization 68
Péron, François 58
Persians 160
Perreiah, Alan xiii
personality 318–320
see also cultural personality
Peru, Peruvian 94–95, 98, 197, 257, 395
Peruvian anthropology 395
Philip, King of Spain 100
philosophy of history 10, 266–275, 278, 282–283, 286, 343
philosophy of mind 271
Philosophy of Values 282–283
Phoenicians 10
phonemics 329
phonetics 329
photographs 222
physical anthropology
and progressivist theory 49–50, 62, 368–369
at the Bureau of American Ethnology 232–233
role in American anthropology 249, 251, 309–310
role in British anthropology 372
role in French anthropology 373
role in Indian anthropology 392
personality 421, 422
physical laws 114–117, 119, 126
physics, physicists 114, 124, 402
physis 121, 122, 123, 124
Pike, Kenneth 329–330, 337
Pilling, John 231
Pima Indians 215
Pitt Rivers Museum 241
Plains Indians 221
Plato 15, 114, 119, 123–126, 187–188
Pliny 16, 144
Plutarch 82
Pocahontas 100, 221
poems, poetry
German Idealist 266, 286
Indianological 218, 258
Primitivist 78, 92, 97–98, 103–105
progressivist 14, 15, 38
political economy 40
political science 269, 316, 400
Pollard, Sidney 18, 40, 42, 46, 427
polyandry 53
Polybius 15
Polynesia, Polynesians 87, 256, 292, 371
see also Oceania
Ponca Indians 204
Pontiac, Chief 94, 100
popes 120, 139
Portugal 250

Positivism, positivists 42–46, 170–173, 186, 190, 340–342, 416
Postidealists 276
Postl, Karl 101
Postmodernism, postmodernists 331, 340, 415, 419
Powell, John Wesley 56, 58, 222, 227, 231–247, 294, 301
Powhatan Indians 215
Prague Linguistic Circle 357
prehistory, prehistoric
  American 164, 229–230, 254, 310–311, 316, 325
  conjectural 29–31
  Enlightenment ideas of 28, 29–31
  Germanic 286
  Greek ideas of 13–14, 29
  idea of 18, 29
  modern theories of 68
  see also archaeology, conjectural history
pre-Socratic 12–13, 71, 123, 171
Preuss, K. T. 292, 378
Priestley, Joseph 347
primate ethology 185–186, 191, 421
Primitivism, primitivists 75–112
  and German Idealism 272, 277
  and Marxism 346
  and natural law 116–117, 119–120, 153, 155, 187–188
  and Rationalism 339
  bibliography 428–430
  doctrine 75–78
  early modern 84–92
  historical contexts 78–80
  in anthropology 106–111, 332, 372, 375, 382, 384, 423
  in antiquity 80–82
  in Indianology 193, 210–211, 256, 258
  in literature 92–106, 219, 370–371
  in the Romantic Age 92–106
  medieval 82–84
  primitivist ethnography 85–88
  summary discussion 111–112
probabilistic theory 316
professionalism 244–245, 298, 300
Progressivism, progressivists 9–73
  and German Idealism 265, 268–270, 277–278
  and Indianology 225, 232, 256
  and natural law 116–120, 149, 153, 155, 160
  and Primitivism 75–76, 106, 111
  and Rationalism 336–338, 339–340
  bibliography 425–428
  in anthropology 49–73, 190–191, 332, 368–369, 372, 374–375
  in antiquity 12–16
  doctrines 9–12, 378–379
  Enlightenment 19–38
  medieval 16–18
  nineteenth century 39–63
  summary discussion 71–73
proletarian, proletariat 346, 412
Protagoras 13, 123
Protestant Reformation 146
Prussia 159
psychic unity of mankind 26, 291
psychoanalysis 358
psychology, psychologists 40, 255, 316, 318, 321, 358, 400, 406
Ptolemy 139, 142
Pueblo Indians 231–232, 344
puebloan ruins 230, 232
Pufendorf, Samuel 31, 33, 55, 152–155, 158
Puget Sound 204
Purchas, Francis Paul 206
Puritans, Puritanism 78, 203, 208
Putnam, Frederick Ward 239–240, 243–244, 300–301, 325
Putnam, Rufus 229
Pye, Henry J. 38

Q

Quakers 203
qualitative methodology 181, 316
quantitative methodology 316
Quebec 225

Quechua Indians 395
Quesnay, François 32
questionnaires 227–228, 236, 308

R

race, racism 49–50, 212, 232, 249, 278, 309
Radcliffe-Brown, A. R.
  functionalist doctrines 334, 338, 350–351, 360, 370, 374, 415–416
  influence on American anthropology 248, 317, 325–326, 334, 352–353
  influence on British anthropology 369–370, 372
Radicalism, radicals 347–351, 352
Radin, Paul 107, 180, 305, 307, 314, 316, 430
Rai, Binay Kumar 391
Raleigh, Walter 86
Ramusio, Gian Battista 206
Rasmussen, Knud 389
Rationalism, rationalists
  and natural law 15–16, 131, 145, 146, 162, 164
  and Utilitarianism 349
  in German Idealist philosophy 268–270, 277
  in the anthropology of Tylor 297
  opposition to 162–166, 190
  varieties of 335–340
  see also reason
Ratzel, Friedrich 285, 287, 289, 293–294, 299, 302, 314–315, 378
reason 118, 165, 270, 275, 336, 339, 348, 355, 375
  see also Rationalism, right reason
Redfield, Robert 279, 323–328, 352–353
reflexive anthropology 331, 415
Reformism, reform 167, 347–353
Reichard, Gladys 246, 305
Reill, Peter 267, 436
relaciones 199–200, 206
Relativism 161, 169, 277
  see also Cultural Relativism, Ethical Relativism, moral relativism
Remington, Frederic 221
Renaissance vi, 17, 57, 77, 80, 195–196, 258
research institutes 373, 392–394, 397, 410
revisionist ethnographies 258
revisionist histories 258
Richardson, William 94
Rickert, Heinrich 282–284
Rider Haggard, H. 217
Riesman, David 402
right reason 130, 147, 152, 154
  see also reason
Rights of Man 348
  see also universal rights
Ritter, Karl 285
Rivers, W. H. R. 56
Robertson, William 28, 33, 54, 60, 68
Robertson Smith, William 56
Rocky Mountains 226
Rogers, Robert 94
Rogers, Will 415
Romans, Roman
  anthropological ideas ix, 29
  law 133–135, 168
  natural law doctrines 119, 126–130, 180, 188
  Primitivism 80–82, 111
  Progressivism 15–16
Romanticism, romantic 85, 111, 162, 211, 217–220, 270, 273, 371
Romantic Movement 92–105
Romantic Primitivism 98
Rommen, Heinrich, 168, 170, 431
Roosevelt, Franklin 236
Rorschach tests 321
Rosenstiel, Annette 435
Rousseau, Jean-Jacques 32, 78, 88–95, 151–157
Royal Anthropological Institute 366, 368, 372
Royal Ethnographic Collection 295
Royal Museum for Ethnology 291
Rubruck, William of 197
Runge, Edith 429

Russell, Bertrand 93, 167, 271, 336, 438, 439
Russia, Russian 323, 366–367, 383–385
see also Soviet Union
Russian Geographical Society 383

S

Sahagún, Bernardo de 202
Sahlins, Marshall 67, 69, 109
Saint-Pierre, Abbé 19
Saint-Simon, Henri 19, 39–42, 61, 342
Salamanca School 141–144
salvage archaeology 237, 407
salvage ethnography 99, 107, 227, 237, 245–246, 308–309, 395–397, 405, 407
salvationism 84
Samoan 108
Sanderson, Stephen 428
Santo Tomás, Diego de 140
Sapir, Edward 107, 246, 305–309, 318, 320–321, 423
Sarana, Gopala 441
Sartre, Jean-Paul 358–359
Saussure, Ferdinand de 182, 354–357
Savigny, Friedrich von 168
scalping 216, 223
Scandinavia, Scandinavian 286, 389
see also Nordic
Scandinavian anthropology 389–390
Schebesta, Paul 292
Schelling, Friedrich von 274, 280
Schiller, Johann Friedrich 266, 304
Schlözer, August 286, 290
Schmidt, Dennis 115
Schmidt, Wilhelm 293, 380
Scholasticism, Scholastics 133–138, 148, 188
Schoolcraft, Henry Rowe 104, 227–228, 229, 236, 247, 259
Schopenhauer, Arthur 276
Schweinfurth, Georg 290
science, scientific
and anthropology 411, 415–417
and natural law 115–117, 150
and philosophy 2–5, 411, 415–419
and Positivism 341–342
and Progressivism 14–15, 17–18, 50, 63
and Rationalism 336
and Structuralism 354, 359
Science of Mind 281–284
Scotland, Scots, Scottish 22, 53, 91, 93, 157–158, 161, 278
Scott, Walter 99
Scripture, scriptural 116–117, 131, 134, 145–146, 151, 165–166, 189
Scythians 37, 79–82, 193
segregation 50, 120
Seler, Edouard 292
semiology 356
Seneca 79–80, 82–83, 127
Sepúlveda, Juan de 142–144, 217
Service, Elman 67
settlers 207–210, 214–215, 259
Seville 202
Seymour, Samuel 226
Shaftesbury, Lord 89, 347
Shakespeare, William 6, 31, 410
Shanin, Teodor 441
Shoshonean Indians 65
Siberia 383
Sigmund, Paul 123, 131, 135–136, 153, 163, 166, 431
Simmel, Georg 282–283
Simmons, William 104
Simms, William Gilmore 101
Simon, Y. R. M. 126
Sinha, Dharmi 441
Sinology 194, 196, 244, 258, 389
Sioux Indians 234, 236
see also Lakota Indians
Sitting Bull 223
Skinnerian psychology 65
slaves, slavery 138–140, 141, 280, 344, 414
Slavs, Slavic 264, 312
Slezkine, Yuri 384, 430
Smith, Adam 24, 27, 33, 55
Smith, Captain John 86, 199, 207, 215, 221
Smith, Sherry 210, 434
Smithsonian Institution 228, 230–231, 235, 238–239, 243, 307

Smollett, Tobias 218
social anthropology 397, 405
social contract 150–156, 159, 161, 167, 169, 189–190
Social Darwinism 64
Social Evolutionism
 see Evolutionism
Social Functionalism 316, 363
 see also Functionalism
social sciences 2–5, 47, 117, 166, 269, 316
social stratification 371
Socialism, socialists 46, 335, 347–351, 371
socialization 319
Sociocultural School of anthropology 249, 317, 324, 374
sociology, sociologists 40–49, 117, 170, 316, 391–392, 412–413
Socrates 263
Socratic 424
soldiers 210–212, 214, 259
 see also army officers
solidarity 2, 374
Solórzano, Juan de 34
Somme Valley 60
Sophists 123–124, 188
Sorokin, Pitirim 246
South America 96, 199, 202, 235, 242, 290, 292, 382, 396
 see also individual countries
South Carolina 209
Southall, Aidan 363
Southeast U.S. 213
Southeast Asia 250, 292, 325
Southerne, Thomas 96
Southey, Robert 98–99
Southwest U.S. 199, 213, 221, 230–232, 240, 246, 252, 322
Southwest Museum 241
Southwestern Indians 221
Soviet Union 358, 383–386, 388, 393, 396–397, 401
 see also Russia
Spadafora, David 427
Spain, Spanish 138, 140, 143–144, 189, 197, 217
Spanish conquests 257–258
Spanish debates 138–145
Spanish-Americans 322
Spencer, Herbert 25, 47–49, 51, 59, 173–174, 348, 374
Spengler, Oswald 276
Sperber, Dan 376
Spicer, Edward 109, 237, 326, 352–353
Spier, Leslie 107, 108, 246
Spinoza, Baruch 336
Spiro, Melford 320
Squier, Ephraim 230
Srinivas, M. N. 392
stage theory 31, 37, 45, 53–54, 61, 67, 278, 355, 374, 405
Stanley, John Mix 221
Statism, statist 280, 348
statistical methodology 181, 184, 316, 417
Steele, Richard 98
Stein, Peter 160, 432
Stevenson, Matilda Coxe 233
Steward, Julian 65–68, 179
Stewart, Dugald 28–29
Stocking, George 47, 61, 428, 430, 437–438, 440
Stoics 15, 82–83, 111, 125–126, 127, 131–133, 135, 147, 149, 151, 183, 188–189
Stone, John A. 100
Strabo 16, 80
Strange, Robert 101
structural anthropology 356–359
structural linguistics 182
Structural Marxism 356, 390
Structuralism, structuralists
 as natural law doctrine 175, 178, 182–183
 in American anthropology 360–361
 in British anthropology 360, 370, 372
 in Dutch anthropology 389
 in French anthropology 357–359, 375–376
 in Scandinavian anthropology 390
 historical development 355–361
 overview of 353–361
Sturm, Douglas 150

Sturm und Drang 21, 265, 273, 350
Suárez, Diego de 137–138
superorganic 312, 320
Sutton, Claud 275, 436
Swagerty, W. R. 433
Swanton, John 107
Swedish 389
Swift, Jonathan 85
Swimmer, Ross 236
Switzerland, Swiss 266, 295, 377
synderesis 135
synthesis 274–275, 344

T

tabula rasa 154
Tacitus 81
Tammany, Chief 103
Taoism 78
Tartars 107
Tax, Sol 317, 352–353
Taylor, Walter 65
technology 246, 265, 319
Tecumseh, Chief 100
Teggart, Frederick 44, 426
teleological approach to natural law 118–119
teleology, teleological
- and natural law 119, 124–125, 131, 135, 138, 172, 174
- and Rationalism 337
- and Structuralism 355
- in anthropology 177, 183, 187–190
- in German Idealist philosophy 272, 340
- opposition to 164, 166, 270

Tennessee Valley Authority 237
Tepoztlán 323, 327
Termination Policy 252–253
Tertullian 132
Thales 416
Thematic Apperception tests 321
themes
- *see* cultural themes

theology, theologians 115–117, 136, 138–139, 141, 145–146, 172, 189–190, 336
Thevet, André 206
Thirty Years' War 146, 267
Thomas, Cyrus 231
Thomasius, Christian 158–159, 168, 266
Thomism, Thomist 135–137, 146, 172
- *see also* Aquinas

Thompson, Laura 237, 320
Thomsen, Christian 60
Thoreau, Henry David 76, 79, 218
three-age theory 60
three-field conjunction 391–392, 396
three-stage theory 43
Thucydides 31
Thurnwald, Richard 292
Tierra del Fuego 382
Tindal, Matthew 89
Tishkov, Valery 388, 441
Tönnies, Ferdinand 279, 324
Torquemada, Juan de 198
totemism 59
Toynbee, Arnold 246
trade union movement 350
traders 213–214, 227, 259
trait distributions 308, 378
Transcendentalism 164, 268–270, 277
travelers 205–207, 214, 217, 254, 259
treaties 236, 253
Tree of Knowledge 83
Trojans 193
Tsars 383, 386
Tsimshian Indians 107
Tuck, Richard 432–433
Turgot, Jacques 20–21, 29, 32–33, 41, 68, 90, 361, 374, 376
Turkic peoples 384, 385
Turner, Victor 355, 363
Twain, Mark 218
Tylor, Edward B.
- as reformist 351, 414
- German influences on 287–288, 291, 296–298, 332, 362
- founder of British anthropology 351, 367
- mentalism 56, 297
- quoted 351
- Progressivism viii, 51, 56–57, 297, 367
- Rationalism 297, 339

U
U.S. Army 210
U.S. Geological Survey 231, 233
U.S. National Museum 238–239, 241
U.S. War Department 227–228
Ukraine, Ukrainians 384–385
Ulpian, Roman jurist 129
Uniformitarianism 44, 48, 59, 64, 67
unilinear evolution 67, 405
Universal Evolutionism 67
universal rights 122, 150, 180–181, 190–191
Universalism, universalist
  approaches to study of man 5–6
  in French anthropology 375, 377
  in German Idealist philosophy 374, 387
  in Marxism 347, 387
  in natural law theory 116, 161, 187
  in Structuralism 355–356, 375
universities 235, 243–247, 260, 292, 300, 302, 373, 389–397, 410
University of Berlin 299
University of California 240
University of Chicago 236, 248, 317, 325–326, 352, 362
University of Chile 396
University of Glasgow 24
University of Leiden 389
University of London 368
University of Pennsylvania 244, 260
University of San Marcos 395
University of Vienna 380
urban anthropology 412
Ussher-Lightfoot Chronology 30
Ute Indians 231
Utilitarianism, utilitarian
  doctrines 46, 166–168, 347–350
  forerunners 21
  influence on American
    anthropology 317, 352–353
  influence on British anthropology
    350–352, 371
  natural law doctrines 167–168, 171
Utopia, Utopianism 83, 90, 108, 111, 151, 169, 343–344, 347

V
Valladolid debates 143–145, 189
values
  see core values
Van Doren, Charles 10, 426
Van Valkenburgh, Richard 422
Vanishing Redman 99–100, 103, 107, 111, 247–248
Varen, Bernhardt 176
Vermeule, Hans 286
Vespucci, Amerigo 197
Vico, Giambattista 24, 35–36, 45, 46, 52
Victorian era viii, 12, 50, 52, 63, 72, 408
Vidyarthi, L. P. 391, 442
Vienna 289, 295, 380
Vienna School of anthropology 380
  see also Kulturkreis
Vietnam War 345
village studies 391–393
  see also peasants
Virchow, Rudolf 299, 302, 306
Virgil 80
Virginia 200, 207–208, 215, 225, 229
Vitoria, Francisco de 141–142, 143–145, 201
Vives, Juan Luis 31, 88
Voegelin, Carl 423
Volk, Völker 265, 273, 277–279, 280, 286, 324
Völkerkunde 286, 377
Volksgeist 265, 273, 276, 279–280, 283, 312–313, 323–324, 331, 333
  see also Geist
Voltaire, Henri-Marie 21–22
voluntarism 137, 346, 351–352
Von den Steinen, Karl 292

W
Wagar, W. Warren 427
Wagner, Richard 273, 286
Waitz, Theodor 287–289
Wallace, Anthony 363
Walsh, W. H. 272
Warner, W. Lloyd 317, 352
Washburn, Wilcomb xiii, 433, 434
Washington state 204, 245

Weatherford, Jack 412
Weber, Max 279, 339
Weltgeist 275
  see also world-view
Weltgeschichte 271, 275, 287
West Africa 380
Westermarck, Edward 362
western surveys of U.S. 230–231, 247, 259
Wheeler Survey 230–231
Whichcote, Benjamin 89
White, John 199
White, Leslie 300, 303, 312, 326–327, 344
Whiting, Henry 104
Whitman, Walt 218
Whitney, Lois 427, 429, 433
Wild West shows 219, 223–224
Wilken, Robert 431
will of God
  see divine will
William and Mary College 225
William of Ockham 136–137, 146
Williams, Roger 208
Windelband, Wilhelm 264, 281–284
Wissler, Clark 63, 107, 177, 179, 226, 242, 246, 305, 307
Withers, Carl 321
Wolf, Eric 328, 343
Wolff, Christian 158–159, 168, 266
Wood, William 208
Wordsworth, William 78, 98
World War I 73, 352
World War II
  effect on ethnographic fieldwork 243, 250, 322, 364, 393
  effect on French philosophic thought 358–359
  turning point in American anthropology 237, 250–251, 260, 325, 329, 364
  turning point in French anthropology 375
  turning point in Scandinavian anthropology 389–390
World's Columbian Exhibition 239, 241, 300
world-view 275, 324, 328, 422
Worsaae, J. J. A. 60
Wounded Knee 407
Wundt, Wilhelm 299

X

Xenophanes 13
Xinjiang 394

Y

Yahweh 152
Yakutia 304
Yang, Martin 393
Yankee City Studies 413
Yariko 95, 98
Yarrow, Henry C. 231
Yeats, William B. 106
Yucatán 323
Yunnan 394

Z

Zeitgeist 273, 276, 346–347, 400, 408, 417
zoology, zoologists 40, 57, 414
Zumárraga, Juan de 140
Zuni Indians 236, 318, 322
Zwernemann, Jürgen 437, 441